11–8 Part (1), cost of automobile, $9,358.52

11–9 Part (1), PV = $7,924.75

12–1 Part (4), investment in bonds, $547,570

12–2 Part (1), selling price of bonds, $917,766

12–3 Interest expense, 1984, $19,305

12–4 Selling price of bonds, $1,686,948

12–5 Part (1), loss on early retirement of debt, $21,000

12–6 Net long-term liabilities, 12/31/83, $99,200

12–7 EPS—if common stock issued, $3.84

12–8 Part (4), total interest expense, $104,000

12–9 Part (2), interest expense, 1984, $62,081

12–10 Part (3), loss on retirement of bonds, $47,592

13–1 Part (4), $4,633,000

13–2 Owners' equity, 6/30/82, $1,310,000

13–3 Owners' equity, 12/31/82, $430,890

13–4 EPS, net income, $5.16

13–6 Part (3), corrected net income, 1981, $53,000

13–7 Part (3), total dividends on preferred stock, $78,400

13–8 Unappropriated retained earnings, 12/31, $201,000

14–1 Part (3), gain on valuation of securities, $1,000

14–2 Part (4), unrealized loss on long-term securities, $6,000

14–3 Part (3), owners' equity, 12/31/82, $565,000

14–4 Part (2), unrealized loss on long-term securities, $5,000

14–6 Consolidated assets, 11/82, $5,000,000

14–7 Consolidated assets, 1/1/82, $820,000

14–8 Consolidated net income, 12/31/82, $60,000

14–9 Part (3), effect on income, short-term, decrease, $1,440

15–2 Increase in working capital, $29,000

15–3 Part (1), total sources of funds, $7,000

15–4 Total uses of funds, $92,000

15–5 Part (2), cash from operations, $10,000

15–6 Part (3), cash provided by operations, $177,000

15–7 Total sources of funds, $947,000

15–8 Part (2), total sources of cash, $685,200

16–2 Part (7), financial leverage, 2.5%

16–3 Part (3), 4 times

16–4 Ending inventory, $300

16–5 1982, net income, 8%

16–6 Part (6), 118 days

16–7 Part (2), quick ratio, 1.33 to 1

16–8 Rate of return, Plan C, 13%

16–9 Receivable turnover, 6.67 times

16–10 1982, 52 days to sell ending inventory

17–1 Part (2), 1981 income, $40,909

17–2 Total income recognized in 1982, $191,400

17–3 Part (2), net equipment, constant dollar, $392,991

17–4 Part (2), holding gain (net of inflation), $19,323

17–5 Purchasing power loss, $5,796

17–6 Part (2), holding loss (net of inflation), $11,460

17–7 Retained earnings (constant dollar), 12/31/78, $21,474

Introduction to
FINANCIAL
ACCOUNTING

Introduction to
FINANCIAL ACCOUNTING

PAUL HOOPER
University of New Orleans

JOHN PAGE
University of New Orleans

WEST PUBLISHING COMPANY
Saint Paul   New York   Los Angeles   San Francisco

Cover photo by photographer Paul Crosby
© Paul Crosby

DEDICATION
To Pamela, Lisa and Jody Hooper
and Bill and Jennifer Page

Copyright © 1982 By West Publishing Co.
                         50 West Kellogg Boulevard
                         P.O. Box 3526
                         St. Paul, Minnesota 55165

Printed in the United States of America

Library of Congress Cataloging in Publication Data

Hooper, H. Paul.
  Introduction to financial accounting.

  Includes index.
  1. Accounting. I. Title.
HF5635.H785   657   81-19812
ISBN 0-8299-0387-9   AACR2

Contents in Brief

Contents

4

**The Accounting
Cycle—End of
Period
Procedures   100**

5

**Classified Financial
Statements and
Corporate
Accounting   138**

Section II Merchandising Operations 177

6
Sales and Purchases 178

8

Cash and Receivables   250

9

Inventory and Cost of Goods Sold   288

**17
Accounting
Principles and
Changing
Prices   606**

Preface

Accounting has become a very popular field of study. The perception of accounting as a universally relevant discipline and the increased career orientation of university students explain much of the rise in accounting enrollment. Basic accounting courses are now attracting three types of diverse student groups in large numbers:

1. accounting majors, who have always been a fixture in introductory accounting

2. nonaccounting business majors, who have also traditionally been a part of introductory accounting

3. nonbusiness majors, who now routinely expect to take an accounting course as part of their general education

Because of these diverse student groups, introductory accounting texts must meet the needs of (1) a large number of students who will take no other accounting (perhaps even no other business-related) courses, and (2) students who will be accounting majors facing the demands of intermediate accounting and other courses. The challenge, then, is finding a basic accounting text designed to present the fundamental elements of financial accounting essential to all students. *Introduction to Financial Accounting* emphasizes those financial accounting topics necessary to a basic understanding of business. Financial statement preparation for external users is the focus of the book, and the perspectives of both the preparer and the user are taken throughout. The text is designed for a one–semester or two–quarter course.

Special Features of This Book

Introduction to Financial Accounting offers the following special features:

1. *Clarity of writing.* The flow and presentation of each chapter allow the student to read the material quickly, while grasping the important concepts and mechanics.

2. *Organization.* The book is organized into symmetrical sections, and each section presents a unified block of material, with logical breaking points

between sections. Chapters within each section relate to each other and focus on one major area of accounting activity. Each chapter is divided into four to six parts, which are approximately equal in content and length. This organized coverage provides students with a framework for their work in accounting.

3. *Illustrations.* All chapters are richly illustrated with diagrams, tables, and concept summaries of chapter content. The concept summaries, which appear after each major topic area in each chapter, synthesize important ideas into an easy-to-grasp brief format and provide an excellent study tool for students.

4. *Accounting and the real world.* These one-page excerpts from an accounting or business journal open each chapter and illustrate an interesting application of the chapter materials from the real business world.

5. *End-of-chapter material.* Each chapter concludes with a chapter summary which highlights the important points in the chapter, a list of the key terms introduced in the chapter, and a comprehensive review problem and solution which applies the chapter concepts in problem format.

6. *Problem material.* Class testing has demonstrated that students are able to comprehend the problem material after reading the chapter. The questions, exercises, and problems are graded in difficulty so that they integrate with the materials in the chapter and reinforce the important concepts.

7. *Appendixes.* A User Dictionary, giving definitions of all key terms introduced in the text, is presented at the end of the book. The dictionary is organized alphabetically for easy use, and terms are cross-referenced to the chapter in which they originally appear. This User Dictionary is a source book of the vocabulary of introductory accounting. Complete financial statements and accompanying notes for **IBM** Corporation are also included as an appendix to provide a real business application of the principles presented in the text.

8. *Balance.* The text provides a mix of concepts and procedures and thus is a mainstream introductory accounting textbook.

This book reflects fifteen years of classroom teaching of introductory accounting at the University of Virginia, the University of New Orleans, and Tulane University. Extensive classroom testing of the manuscript has contributed to the approach and pedagogy of the book.

Supplementary Materials

A complete learning package accompanies *Introduction to Financial Accounting.*

1. The study guide contains an outline of each chapter presented in a fill-in-the-blank format so the student can monitor his or her progress. Sample true/false and multiple choice questions with answers and short exercises

with complete solutions for each chapter provide practice and immediate feedback.

2. Working papers contain partially structured solutions to all problems, which provide students with needed structure and save unnecessary busy-work.

3. The practice case contains a detailed narrative and set of a month's transactions for a merchandising business. The practice case can be used after the first seven chapters of the book to illustrate the accounting cycle (including special journals and subsidiary ledgers), financial statements, and internal control.

4. A checklist of key figures contains an answer which students can use to check their progress in the solution of problems. This checklist appears on the inside of both the front and back covers of the text for ease of reference.

5. Transparencies contain all Concept Summaries from the text and solutions to problems in visual aid format for use by the instructor in the classroom.

6. The solutions manual contains complete solutions with explanatory comments to all questions, exercises, and problems presented in the text.

7. A test bank contains abundant true/false and multiple choice questions for each chapter, and a complete solution to the practice case.

Acknowledgments

This book is better because of the efforts of a number of people. Patty Harrison and Phyllis Cassidy of the University of New Orleans were major contributors to all phases of the development of the manuscript. Jeannie Welsh (University of New Orleans) and Laura Bell (University of Virginia) aided greatly in the development of problem material and Lydia Guydan and Lisa Farris of the University of New Orleans checked and double-checked each solution with great care and diligence. Joyce Fowlkes excellently typed all drafts of the manuscript in the best of good cheer.

We would also like to recognize the contribution of our colleagues who reviewed the manuscript at various stages and offered suggestions for improvements. The mark of each of the following people can be found somewhere in *Introduction to Financial Accounting*. They are: Edna M. Andrews, California State University-Long Beach; Lloyd Buckwell, Bowling Green University; Terry Campbell, University of Central Florida; J. F. Cook, University of Texas at Arlington; Nancy Desmond, University of Illinois at Urbana-Champaign; Michael A. Diamond, California State University-Los Angeles; John Gorman, Rider College; Joe Hoyle, University of Richmond; Celina Joszi, University of Southern Florida, Tampa Bay; Robert S. Linnell, The University of Tulsa; Lyle C. McIff, University of Arizona; James O'Connell, University of Massachusetts-Amherst; Russell J. Peterson, Arizona State University, Tempe; Joyce A. Rescho, Illinois

State University, Normal; John R. Simon, Northern Illinois University, DeKalb.

Special thanks go to the students of the University of Virginia for their patience in using this book in manuscript form and for their many positive comments.

Many capable people at West Publishing Company had a hand in bringing this project to completion. We would particularly like to recognize John Orr, our production editor, who helped the book (and the authors) through a difficult production schedule and contributed in a major way to the final product.

Paul Hooper
John Page

New Orleans, Louisiana

Introduction

What is accounting? Why should I study it? These questions are likely to be foremost in the mind of anyone entering this new field of study.

Purpose of Accounting

Accounting is often called "the language of business." Actually, accounting could more accurately be termed "the language of organizations." Accounting records and measures the financial activities of businesses, governments, political parties, churches, hospitals, and universities (as well as other organizations), and then presents a summary of these activities in a series of reports called financial statements. A responsible citizen should be able to read and interpret these financial statements and use the information they present to make effective decisions concerning the performance of an organization and its management.

Not-for-Profit versus Profit-Seeking Organizations

Although it is useful for all organizations, accounting makes a distinction between two types of organizations: those that are not-for-profit and those that are profit-seeking. Not-for-profit organizations include governments, political parties, churches, hospitals, and universities and other schools. Profit-seeking organizations are primarily businesses, but this category also includes some government agencies such as the Tennessee Valley Authority (TVA).

Accounting makes this fundamental distinction because, in profit-seeking organizations, there can be a measure of performance, called net profit, net earnings, or net income. This net income figure indicates how successful the business has been in its operations. Because this measure of performance is so important to business analysts and others, the recording and measurement of financial activities are somewhat different, and the related financial statements are wholly different for profit-seeking organizations as opposed to not-for-profit organizations.

This text focuses on accounting for business organizations. Once this fundamental type of accounting is mastered, accounting for other profit-seeking and not-for-profit organizations can be understood.

Capitalism versus Socialism

Accounting is fundamental to the effective functioning of capitalism and the free-enterprise system. Because all societies have only a limited amount of labor and capital, all societies have the problem of allocating scarce resources to potential industrial, merchandising, and service activities. This allocation of resources can be done either by individuals, as in the United States, or by government, as in the Soviet Union. The only reason individuals can allocate resources effectively is that there is a measure of performance, net income, that indicates which businesses are using current resources efficiently and productively. These businesses should attract additional resources. When the most effective entities receive any additional resources available in a society, the resources have been efficiently allocated. Success, then, as measured by accounting net income, becomes a magnet for attracting scarce resources in a free society.

In a socialist society, there is no accounting measure of success; therefore, resource allocation decisions are made by government. In this type of system, resources do not necessarily flow to the effective and productive segments of the society. The efficient flow of resources can occur only when an accounting measure of success exists and is widely accepted.

Uses of Accounting Information

Think for a moment about the institutions and individuals who might use accounting information as the basis of their decision making. A list of the regular users of accounting information would certainly include the following:

1. corporate stockholders and other business owners who must decide whether to invest, how much to invest, and when to invest;

2. business managers who make daily decisions about new factories, new products, and how to obtain money and spend it;

3. creditors of all types who must decide whether a loan should be made, the amount of the loan, the appropriate interest rate, and the repayment terms;

4. the Internal Revenue Service (IRS), which is charged with administering the federal tax laws and must determine whether an individual or business has paid the proper amount of income taxes;

5. state and local taxing authorities, which must determine and collect income, sales, and other taxes for their respective governments; and

6. government regulatory agencies that monitor the compliance of businesses and others with federal regulations.

Many other users of accounting information could be mentioned. In each instance, the primary (sometimes, the only) source of information for this decision making is accounting data. As a citizen in this society, it is almost a certainty that you will function in one or more of these roles.

Accounting versus Bookkeeping

The roles and tasks of accounting and bookkeeping are often confused. Bookkeeping is the mechanical task of processing financial information according to pre-established criteria within an accounting system. While important, bookkeeping is only one aspect of accounting.

Accounting is concerned with the design and implementation of systems for the processing of financial information and the criteria that should be used to process this information. Accounting is also concerned with determining which information should be processed and how this information should be communicated to individuals and groups outside the business.

Accounting involves choices and decisions about the recording, presentation, use, and interpretation of financial information. Those equipped by education, training, and experience to exercise this judgment are called accountants. Those who perform the mechanical processing of information are called bookkeepers.

Accounting and the Computer

Computers do not eliminate the need for accountants and will not ultimately replace them. Actually, increased use of computers expands the demand for accountants because, while computers can perform the mechanical tasks of bookkeeping extremely well, the judgments of the accountant are beyond their capacity. As more information becomes available and must be analyzed to be useful, accountants will be needed to perform this analysis.

The computer has had two primary effects on accounting: (1) the process of recording financial information has changed completely and (2) the computer's speed and vast memtory have made possible more timely and informative financial statements. Because of this second effect, computers are becoming ever more prevalent in accounting.

Whether or not a computer is used, the basic concepts of accounting remain the same. Thus, essentially everything in this text applies to both computerized and manual accounting. The practical effects of computers cannot be treated briefly and require an entire text of their own, with introductory accounting as the basis. For this reason, this text does not go into depth in this area.

Overview of the Text

Introduction to Financial Accounting explains the preparation and use of financial accounting information by dividing the material into seventeen chapters, which are grouped into four major sections.

Section I presents the basic accounting model; discusses and illustrates the output of the accounting process, called financial statements; and examines the process by which these statements are produced. The remainder of the book is an elaboration of the principles presented in Section I.

Sections II and III deal with the techniques used and the procedures followed in preparing financial accounting information. Understanding the source of this information and how it is developed will enable you to use it wisely in decision making.

Section IV focuses on how to use accounting information in your decisions. Thus, Section I is an overview, Sections II and III deal with development, and Section IV focuses on the application or use of accounting information.

Summary

This introduction began with two fundamental questions: What is accounting? Why should I study it? It is the purpose of this text to answer these questions more completely, but even at this early stage there are some preliminary answers.

Accounting is a means for measuring, recording, and reporting the financial activities of organizations of all types. Additionally, for profit-seeking organizations like businesses, accounting provides a measure of performance called net income by which the organization and its management can be judged.

You should study accounting because a knowledge of accounting will help you: (1) invest your money by buying ownership in business; (2) manage a business; (3) run your own business; (4) invest by lending money to goverments or businesses; (5) compute the amount of income tax you should pay (without overpaying); and (6) make more informed decisions about your local, state, and national governments.

Introduction to

FINANCIAL
ACCOUNTING

THE ACCOUNTING SYSTEM

CHAPTER 1

Introduction to Accounting

Chapter Outline

1.1 *Legal Forms of Business Organization.* Introduction to the environment of accounting; the important characteristics of the forms of business organization.

1.2 *Important Institutions in Accounting.* General discussion of the Securities and Exchange Commission, Internal Revenue Service, American Institute of Certified Public Accountants and Financial Accounting Standards Board; the work of accountants.

1.3 *Financial and Managerial Accounting.* The principal characteristics of each area of accounting study and the perspective of financial accounting.

1.4 *Basic Assumptions of Accounting.* The important assumptions on which financial accounting is based; introduction to financial statements.

1.5 *The Basic Accounting Equation and Business Transactions.* Types of accounting transactions; transaction analysis and the basic accounting equation; numerical illustration.

Accounting and the Real World

Have you ever wondered how large big business in the United States really is? Each year *Fortune* magazine publishes the Fortune 500, a list of the five hundred largest industrial companies in the United States. An industrial company is one that makes and sells a product as its primary business activity. This authoritative list ranks U.S. companies by the dollars of sales of products made during the previous year. Below are the top ten companies of the Fortune 500 for 1980 with some information on each company. Although the meanings of the terms used in this list may not be perfectly clear, a quick glance at the size of the numbers should give you an idea of the wealth and economic power of these businesses. Notice that the numbers for the largest businesses are stated in billions (ten hundred millions).

Rank '80	Rank '79	Company	Sales ($000)	Assets ($000)	Rank	Net Income ($000)	Rank
1	1	Exxon (New York)	103,142,834	56,576,558	1	5,650,090	1
2	3	Mobil (New York)	59,510,000	32,705,000	3	3,272,000	3
3	2	General Motors (Detroit)	57,728,500	34,581,000	2	(762,500)	490
4	5	Texaco (Harrison, N.Y.)	51,195,830	26,430,355	5	2,642,542	4
5	6	Standard Oil of California (San Francisco)	40,479,000	22,162,000	7	2,401,000	5
6	4	Ford Motor (Dearborn, Mich.)	37,085,500	24,347,600	6	(1,543,300)	491
7	7	Gulf Oil (Pittsburgh)	26,483,000	18,638,000	9	1,407,000	11
8	8	International Business Machines (Armonk, N.Y.)	26,213,000	26,703,000	4	3,562,000	2
9	10	Standard Oil (Ind.) (Chicago)	26,133,080	20,167,474	8	1,915,314	6
10	9	General Electric (Fairfield, Conn.)	24,959,000	18,511,000	10	1,514,000	10

As impressive as this list is, it does not include all very large companies. Missing from the Fortune 500 are companies not classified as "industrial" either because they are retail businesses (such as Sears and K-mart), or deal in a special service (such as transportation companies or banks), or are public utilities (such as American Telephone & Telegraph). Information on these companies is published in six Fortune 50 Largest Lists by industry. Incidentally, AT & T (the telephone company) is the largest company in the United States and in the world.

Reprinted from the 1981 *Fortune* Directory by permission.

Accounting is the servant of business. As a result, accounting is based upon the various types of businesses and their activities. As business has grown in size and sophistication, so accounting has developed to meet these new challenges.

An understanding of accounting depends upon an understanding of business—its types, its size, and its needs. A basic understanding of business is developed in this introductory chapter. In addition, this chapter defines accounting, tells what it does, and explains the purposes it serves.

1.1   Legal Forms of Business Organization

The activities of business, large and small, provide the environment in which accounting must function. Thus, an appreciation for the institution of business and for the size, wealth, and economic power of the organizations which it comprises is essential to the study of accounting. An important perspective on business activity can be gained by understanding the possible legal forms of business organization, the accounting implications of each type of organization, and how these legal forms affect those who come into contact with the business. Basically, all businesses assume one of three types of organization: sole proprietorship, partnership, or corporation.

Sole
Proprietorship

Sole proprietorships, or simply, proprietorships, are one-owner businesses. In the United States, there are approximately nine million proprietorships which produce a total of $220 billion in sales each year (an average sales per business of $25,000 per year). There are more proprietorships in the United States than all other legal forms combined. Proprietorships are usually very small as compared to other types of businesses and tend to have a higher failure rate than partnerships and corporations. This legal form of business is most often found in retail firms, service activities, and farming.

A proprietorship is a business where one person invests money and skill, and complete control of the business belongs to that person. The important accounting, legal, and taxation aspects of proprietorships are:

1. The business is very easy to form because of few legal restrictions or reporting requirements.

2. The legal life of the business is limited to that of the owner and terminates with his retirement or death.

3. The owner is liable personally for all debts of the business. Any personal assets of the owner (house, car, television set) may be claimed by business creditors for unpaid debts of the business.

4. Access to funds is generally limited to those of the owner because loans may be difficult to obtain. Funds are usually in short supply.

5. Accounting treats the proprietorship as a separate unit from the owner. Legally, the business and the owner are inseparable, however, and the owner is taxed directly for the income of the business. There is no direct income tax on proprietorships.

Partnership

Partnerships must have at least two owners (partners), but may have a very large number of partners. This is the least used major legal form in the United States with approximately one million partnerships producing total sales of $83 billion (average sales of $83,000 per partnership per year). Partnerships tend to be larger and somewhat more successful than proprietorships and are most often found in the professions of medicine, law, accounting, engineering, and architecture. For these professions, the advantages of multiple owners, such as pooling complementary skills, are important, but the corporate form may not be desirable. Most partnerships have only a few owners, although larger public accounting (CPA) firms may have as many as one thousand partners.

A partnership is a business where two or more persons invest money and/or skill and jointly form a business in which control belongs to the partners. Important aspects of partnerships are:

1. The partnership is slightly more complex to form than a proprietorship because of the need to balance the interests of the partners, and the existence of some legal and reporting requirements imposed by states.

2. The legal life of the partnership is limited to that of the owners and terminates with the retirement or death of a partner or the admission of a new partner.

3. The owners are liable personally for all debts of the business. Any personal assets of the partners (houses, cars, television sets) may be claimed by business creditors for unpaid debts of the business.

4. Access to funds is generally limited to those of the owners, but more than one owner makes the business a somewhat better risk for loans and for more owner funds.

5. Accounting treats the partnership as a separate unit from the partners. Legally the business and the partners are inseparable, however, and the partners are taxed directly for their respective shares of the business income. There is no direct income tax on partnerships.

Corporation

A corporation may have any number of owners. This type of organization is popular and accounts for most of the business activity in the United States and the world.

The economic dominance of corporations is astounding. There are approximately 1.5 million corporations which produce total sales of $1.5 trillion (an average sales per corporation per year of $1,000,000). All of the largest businesses in the world are corporations, proof of the success of this legal form. Corporations are found in all types of business activity.

A corporation is a business which any number of persons may form by obtaining an incorporation charter from a state's secretary of state. Ownership is evidenced by shares of stock. Stockholders elect a board of directors in whom control of the business is vested. The board selects corporate management which operates the business. All corporations have the following characteristics in common:

1. The corporation is complex to form because of many legal and reporting requirements imposed by the states and by the federal government if stock is sold to the general public.

2. The life of the corporation is generally assumed to be indefinite, so that the ability of the business to continue is not affected by any change in ownership.

3. The transfer of ownership interest is frequent and easy to accomplish for corporations listed on any stock exchange, but may be difficult for small or closely held corporations.

4. Stockholders enjoy limited liability and are not usually personally liable for the debts of the business. Personal assets of the owners are generally safe from seizure by corporate creditors. Thus, the maximum loss stockholders face is the price paid for their stock.

5. Corporations are better able to attract funds because of potentially widespread ownership, and their larger size makes loan funds generally more available.

6. Accounting treats the corporation as a separate unit from the stockholders, which is consistent with the legal view of corporations. Legally the corporation is a distinct unit from its owners and is taxed directly on its own income. Stockholders pay tax only on that portion of corporate income actually received.

Concept Summary

Important Characteristics of Business Organizations			
Type of Business	*Owners*	*Liability of Owners*	*Taxation*
Proprietorship	One owner only	Unlimited	No income tax on business, owner pays taxes on business income
Partnership	Any number of owners possible, but number is usually small	Unlimited	No income tax on business, owners pay taxes on their share of business income
Corporation	Any number of owners possible, and number is usually large	Limited to owner investment in business	Business pays tax on income, owners taxed only on amounts received from business

1.2 Important Institutions in Accounting

While business provides the general environment in which most accounting systems operate, other institutions also affect what accounting is and how it is practiced. This section discusses the four most important organizations that affect accounting: the Securities and Exchange Commission, the Internal Revenue Service, the American Institute of Certified Public Accountants, and the Financial Accounting Standards Board.

Securities and Exchange Commission

The Securities and Exchange Commission (SEC) is a federal agency created in 1934 to administer all federal securities laws. Federal securities laws govern the trading of investment securities—bonds and stocks, primarily—and define acceptable practice in the selling of these securities to the general public. The primary interest of the SEC is to assure disclosure of all relevant information about a security for use by investors. The SEC is important to the practice of accounting because it has the legal right to require that companies account for and report their activities in a certain way.

Internal Revenue Service

The Internal Revenue Service (IRS) is a federal agency empowered to administer the Internal Revenue Code and collect the appropriate amounts of income taxes from individuals and businesses. Income taxes are based on financial reports filed at least once each year with the IRS. The rules and procedures for these reports are derived from the Internal Revenue Code (a federal law), and therefore, proper accounting treatment of tax-related events is prescribed by law.

Because the practice of accounting may ultimately result in the generation of tax returns, accountants are necessarily concerned with the tax law. The IRS is important to the practice of accounting because it may define acceptable accounting treatment of events with income tax consequences.

The Accounting Profession

An important institution in the environment of accounting is the accounting profession itself. The profession is best represented by the **American Institute of Certified Public Accountants (AICPA),** which is the national professional organization of CPAs. The AICPA is the accountants' version of the American Medical Association (AMA) and the American Bar Association (ABA) in that it represents the interests of CPAs. About two-thirds of all CPAs in the United States belong to the AICPA (it has more than 100,000 members) and express their views about accounting through that organization.

The Big Eight Unlike any other profession, the public accounting profession is dominated by a few, very large firms. Although these firms are partnerships—in many ways not unlike the partnerships of other professions—they are the largest firms of this kind. These eight large partnerships are international in scope and operations, and are called collectively the Big Eight. These firms are a powerful force in the AICPA and in the ac-

FIGURE 1-1
An Audit of the Big
Eight (July 17, 1978)[1]

counting profession. Figure 1-1 presents an estimate of the worldwide and U.S. revenues, plus the number of Fortune 500 clients for the Big Eight as of the late 1970s. The figure also gives an insight into how the firms view themselves and how their competitors view them.

	Worldwide Revenues	U.S. Revenues	Fortune 500 Clients	How They See Themselves	How Competitors See Them
Peat, Marwick, Mitchell & Co.	$516	$365	67	Aggressive but not in an unprofessional way. We have the best people. Biggest weakness: too decentralized.	Trying to recover from past problems with SEC. Very aggressive. Price cutter. Expanding scope of practice.
Coopers & Lybrand	$490	$256	50	Tough. We work harder. We've got a winner's kind of feeling. Our real strength is in the management team.	Has changed a lot. Most aggressive of the eight in hustling business. Price cutter.
Price Waterhouse & Co.	$479	$245	99	The premier accounting firm. We are to accounting what sterling is to silver. Our clients are the cream.	Not very aggressive. Stuffy. Arrogant. Getting steamed up after losing some clients.
Arthur Andersen & Co.	$471	$351	72	Tough. Aggressive. We speak with one voice everywhere. Not well known outside the U.S.	Aggressive, likes publicity. First firm to emphasize growth. No room for individual thought.
Deloitte Haskins & Sells	$410	$220	53	Not as aggressive as most of the Big Eight. Technical leader in the profession. The auditor's auditor.	Not very aggressive. Narrow in scope of services. Getting their act together. Strong auditors.
Arthur Young & Company	$390	$210	52	Tend to be less aggressive than others. Heavy emphasis on client service. We do not want to be the biggest.	Not as aggressive as other Big Eight firms. Widely respected. Super professional.
Ernst & Whinney	$385	$285	61	A practical firm. Pragmatic. We put strong emphasis on quality service to our existing clients.	Sleepy. Not growing fast except in certain industries. Not on the competitive edge. Loosest organization overseas.
Touche Ross & Co.	$350	$185	24	We want to be the best. We're not as big as we want to be. We're not price cutters, but we are price competitors.	Very aggressive in hustling business. Enamoured of size. Price cutter. Weak overseas.

[1]The big accounting firms are private partnerships, and they have only recently begun releasing financial information about their own operations. Arthur Andersen was the first to issue an annual report, five years ago. Last year, Peat, Marwick, Mitchell and Price Waterhouse also published annual reports. Touche Ross has disclosed only its revenues. The other four firms released their revenue figures to FORTUNE—the first time they have let this information out. The Peat, Marwick figure for U.S. revenues is an estimate. The Touche Ross numbers do not reflect the firm's 1977 merger with J. K. Lasser.

[2]The data on FORTUNE 500 clients were prepared by Deloitte Haskins & Sells and Price Waterhouse.

The Financial Accounting Standards Board Until 1973, the accounting profession, through the AICPA, set the primary rules and procedures to govern the practice of accounting. Dissatisfaction with this within-the-profession approach to establishing the principles of accounting led to the creation of a new official rule-making body for accounting, called the **Financial Accounting Standards Board (FASB).** The FASB is independent of the AICPA and represents an attempt by the accounting profession to keep the original creation of accounting rules out of the hands of government agencies. However, because legal authority to establish these principles for many businesses rests with governmental agencies, the FASB must cooperate with and meet the needs of these institutions. Generally, the SEC and IRS have allowed the FASB to set accounting principles as long as these principles were consistent with the law and with the desires of these agencies.

The FASB is made up of members from public accounting, business, the investment profession, and the academic community. The members are appointed by an organization which is independent of the AICPA, and the FASB is funded independently of the AICPA.

In summary, original accounting principles, rules, and procedures are established by statements of the FASB. The FASB considers the opinions of the accounting profession through the AICPA, business, investment

Concept Summary

Important Institutions in Accounting		
Institution	Description	Impact
Securities and Exchange Commmission (SEC)	Federal agency administering securities laws designed to assure disclosure of relevant information to investors	Has the legal power to require companies to account for their activities in a given way.
Internal Revenue Service (IRS)	Federal agency that collects income taxes from individuals and businesses	May define acceptable accounting treatment for income tax purposes
American Institute of Certified Public Accountants (AICPA)	National association of accounting professionals	Represents the interest of accounting professionals before the SEC, IRS, FASB
Big Eight Accounting Firms	The eight largest accounting firms, all international in scope	Very strong influence on the AICPA
Financial Accounting Standards Board (FASB)	Rule-making body for accounting	In practice, defines acceptable accounting in most circumstances

professionals, and the government. The SEC and IRS may, however, ignore any accounting principles they feel are not consistent with the law and substitute their own. Although they have not done so frequently, it has happened from time to time.

The Work of
Accountants

Accountants find employment in all of these institutions, as well as in others. The work of accountants can be conveniently divided into three major areas: public accounting, industry accounting, and not-for-profit accounting.

Certified Public Accountants (CPAs) Certified Public Accountants (CPAs) are independent professionals who offer a variety of accounting services to the general public on a fee basis. CPAs are very much like physicians and attorneys in that they are granted a license to practice by a state. This license, called a CPA certificate, is issued only after educational requirements have been met, a rigorous two and one-half day exam has been passed, and a certain amount of practical experience in accounting has been obtained. A national uniform CPA examination is administered by the AICPA twice a year. Educational and experience requirements are determined individually by each state and, therefore, vary somewhat from state to state.

CPAs in public practice perform three types of services for clients. First, a CPA may express an independent opinion on the fairness of a business's financial reports. Bankers, investors, and others who use financial reports desire such independent assurance and, in some instances, law may require it. To issue an opinion on the fairness of financial reports, CPAs must examine the accounting system of the business and gather information about business activities; this process is called *auditing*. The auditor's opinion expresses the professional feeling of the CPA on the fairness and reliability of a business's financial reports.

Second, CPAs provide income tax services for clients, including tax planning and tax return preparation. Therefore, a thorough knowledge of tax laws and court decisions involving income tax cases is essential to the CPA. Third, CPAs are often called upon to use their training and experience in business procedures to give advice to management about the business. These management consulting activities are a growing part of the work of CPAs and are a natural extension of the CPA's familiarity with accounting and accounting systems.

Industrial Accountants Industry accounting involves employment with a private firm to carry out any number of possible accounting activities. Accountants determine costs of products, prepare budgets, prepare tax returns, and provide information for decision making by business management. In addition, these private accountants may design and develop new accounting systems or revise the existing systems of a business. A Certified Management Accountant (CMA) certificate, similar to the CPA, exists for industrial accountants. The chief accountant of a business is usually called the controller in recognition of the importance of accounting data in controlling business activities.

Not-for-Profit Accountants Accountants work for all types of not-for-profit organizations, such as hospitals, universities, and governments. Governmental accounting may mean employment in any of a number of federal or state agencies. Many governmental decisions are based on accounting data, and accountants are necessary to prepare and interpret these data for policy makers. The SEC and the IRS are the major employers of government accountants. Accounting data are the primary raw material of the operations of these agencies, and accountants are vital to their effectiveness.

Concept Summary

Opportunities in Accounting		
Types of Accountants	Employment	Duties
Certified Public Accountant (CPA)	Independent professionals contracted by individuals, business, and other organizations	Expressing an independent opinion on (auditing) financial statements of business
		Tax planning to reduce the amount of tax the client will pay and tax return preparation
		Management consulting to give advice about running the business
Industrial Accountant	Virtually every business employs accountants	Determining costs of products
		Preparing budgets
		Preparing tax returns
		Providing information for decision making
		Designing and developing accounting systems
Not-for-Profit Accountant	The government and virtually every not-for-profit organization employ accountants	All of the duties listed for industrial accountants
		Monitoring compliance with the securities laws
		Collecting taxes

1.3 Financial and Managerial Accounting

Accounting is a system for keeping track of the financial events in the life of any individual or organization in a manner that makes it possible for that individual or organization to report on its financial position and activities to anyone who may be interested. To apply this definition properly, it is necessary to be aware of the following three points about it:

1. Accounting is concerned with financial events only. This means that the accounting system does not provide all possible information about a business. Information that is not financial in nature, such as the personal qualities of management, is not reported by financial accounting and, therefore, must be secured from some other source.

2. The accounting system is applicable not only to businesses but also to individuals and organizations, such as governments, hospitals, churches, and universities, which are not businesses in a profit-making sense. Even though the approach to accounting is different in these not-for-profit organizations, accounting is, nonetheless, necessary.

3. During the life of even the smallest business, there are many individuals or groups that may desire some information on the position and activities of the business, including owners, creditors, certain governmental agencies (SEC, IRS), and management. The demands of company management are strongest on the accounting system, however, because this group must direct the progress of the business. Accounting systems, then, must provide information for the decision making, planning, and control of a business.

Although each business is likely to have only one accounting system, the tools, techniques, and output of accounting can be conveniently thought of as falling into one of two categories. These segments of accounting are called financial accounting and managerial accounting. It is useful to distinguish between these areas of accounting activity because they are usually studied separately, although in practice the systems and procedures are seldom completely separate.

Financial Accounting

Financial accounting supplies information about an organization to outside individuals and groups. For major corporations such as Exxon and IBM, there are many outside groups and individuals keenly interested in their financial activity. These outsiders might include the SEC, IRS, creditors such as banks, and the corporate owners (stockholders) themselves. In large corporations, the owners can be viewed as outsiders because they have no direct voice in the day-to-day activities of the business and do not directly participate in business decisions. Even in a small business, however, there is likely to be one external group, the IRS, demanding financial information. As a result, some financial accounting activity is carried on by all businesses.

Generally Accepted Accounting Principles (GAAP) The audiences served by financial accounting are generally outside the decision-making and control group of the business. These outside groups are consumers of financial information but do not prepare that information.

The information that results from financial accounting activity is prepared by the management group, the very group whose successes and failures may be documented in the financial accounting activity. However, outside groups want to be assured that the information they receive is objective (that is, fairly depicts what actually happened) and consistently presented. Guidelines, called **Generally Accepted Accounting Principles (GAAP),** are the "rules of the game" for producing and reporting financial information to external users. The certified public accountants (CPAs) are concerned with determining and certifying that these principles have been fairly and consistently applied in the financial activity of organizations.

A final important characteristic of financial accounting activity is its historical perspective. Financial accounting focuses on the immediate past activities of an organization and attempts to record and report to outsiders what has happened to that organization since the last financial information was presented to them. Financial accounting reports information on the past and leaves any prediction of the future to the users of this information.

Managerial Accounting

Managerial accounting represents a second important area of accounting activity for any organization. Managerial accounting is concerned with meeting the information needs of the decision-making and control group in an organization. Because managerial accounting activity must meet the needs of only one group, the reports that result from this process may be tailored specifically to the desires of management. In contrast, the reports resulting from financial accounting activity must be of a general nature because so many diverse groups use these reports for different purposes.

GAAP are less significant in managerial accounting activity because management prepares its own information on demand and, thus, externally imposed objectivity and consistency are not necessary.

Finally, the thrust of managerial accounting is future oriented. Management must be able to plan, make decisions, and then see to it that the decisions are carried out. All of these activities require information that helps to anticipate and predict future circumstances. Managerial accounting activity is concerned with reporting what has already happened only to the extent that this information is an aid to anticipating the future. Prediction is an important part of the managerial accounting process.

Together, financial and managerial accounting activity make up an organization's accounting system. The remainder of this book will be concerned with financial accounting activity only.

Concept Summary

Characteristics of Financial and Managerial Accounting		
Characteristics	*Financial Accounting*	*Managerial Accounting*
Users	Concerned with providing financial information to outside individuals and groups, such as governmental agencies, creditors, and corporate owners.	Concerned with providing information desired by management to aid in planning, decision making, and controlling the activities of an organization.
		(continued on next page)

**Concept
Summary**
(continued)

Characteristics	Financial Accounting	Managerial Accounting
Guidelines	Guidelines called Generally Accepted Accounting Principles are necessary so that objectivity and consistency can be assured in the financial information transmitted to outsiders.	GAAP are not an important consideration because the information consumers are also the preparers of the information. Cost versus benefits provide the most significant guidelines in the production of information.
Orientation	Orientation is toward reporting what has happened in the immediate past (since the last report) so that outsiders will know what has occurred and can use this information to assess the organization's activities and progress.	Orientation is toward anticipating and predicting the future so that management can effectively direct the activities of the organization using information on what is likely to occur in the immediate and distant future.

1.4   Basic Assumptions of Accounting

Financial accounting is based on certain assumptions about the nature of business, and a logical structure and process is developed using these basic assumptions. The assumptions cannot be proven to be true, but they have been found useful in developing a financial accounting system. These ideas should be studied carefully because they reveal something about the nature of financial accounting and provide broad guidelines to follow in understanding financial accounting activity.

Entity

Financial accounting assumes that all businesses are separate units (entities) for financial reporting purposes. As a result of this assumption, records of the activities of different entities should be maintained separately from one another, and the activities of all businesses should be kept separate from the personal activities of the owners. Where a particular business ends and another begins or where business activity ends and personal activity of owners begins often is a matter of judgment. For example, if one person owns a chain of restaurants at different locations, the business entity would likely be considered to be the entire chain. On the other hand, if that same person owns a restaurant and a plumbing shop, these would likely be considered separate business entities for financial accounting purposes. In both of these situations, any personal activities of the owner, such as the purchase of a family home or automobile, would be treated separately from business activities.

American Telephone & Telegraph (AT&T), the largest company in the world, owns Western Electric, the twenty-second largest industrial company in the United States. Mobil Oil, the second largest industrial company in the United States, owns Montgomery Ward, the ninth largest retailer in the United States. These four major corporations are all independent financial accounting entities in their own right in spite of this common ownership.

Once the boundaries of a business entity are determined, the entity assumption states that the affairs of that unit should not be mixed with those of other entities or those of the owners of that business.

Going Concern

In the absence of evidence to the contrary, financial accounting assumes that each business entity has an indefinite life and that there is no expectation that the business will terminate its activities in the foreseeable future. If a business is about to terminate its existence (voluntarily or otherwise), then this basic assumption is not applicable and financial activity must be interpreted differently. Normally, however, business activities are viewed as continuing indefinitely in the future. This long-term view of business life has a significant effect on financial accounting.

Accounting Period

Although businesses are assumed to have indefinite lives and their activities are interpreted accordingly, most outsiders would like to have financial information at short time intervals. For the purpose of providing information to outsiders, financial accounting assumes that the indefinite life of a business can be divided into intermediate time periods, called **accounting periods.** These accounting periods, then, become the basis for reporting on the activities of a business, and financial reports are prepared at the end of each period. In effect, the indefinite life of any business is viewed as consisting of a series of short, connected accounting periods.

Accounting periods have by custom, tradition, and, to some extent, law become one year for most U.S. businesses. The year may be calendar, January 1 to December 31, or it may be fiscal, beginning at any other date. Financial information prepared each accounting period must be interpreted carefully because the accounting period is short compared to the life of the business.

Monetary

In providing information, financial accounting must have some common denominator with which to express the many and varied activities of most businesses. The common unit of measure in financial accounting is the dollar, and all financial information provided to outsiders is expressed in dollar terms. Selection of the dollar as the common unit of measure seems reasonable and aids in the communication process because the dollar is objective, familiar, and fairly well understood.

The dollar as a measuring stick, however, does generate two potential problems for outside users of financial reports. First, comparisons must be made among activities that occur at different times, and these comparisons are made more useful by a constant or relatively constant unit of measure. Significant inflation means a changing measuring stick and makes any comparisons over time potentially misleading. Second, because everything is measured by the dollar, activities that are not susceptible to dollar valuation cannot be reported by financial accounting. Many important activities, such as the speed or quality of service, cannot be valued in dollar terms. As a result, a great deal of important information about a business is not disclosed by financial accounting.

Exchange

Using the dollar as a common denominator to measure all financial activity requires some assumption as to the proper amount of dollars to be assigned to each event. It would be possible to either (1) change the amount of dollars assigned as time passes or value changes, or (2) keep the amount constant once assigned. Actually, financial accounting has chosen a path somewhere between these two alternatives. All events, such as the cost of a building or a truck or the amount of money borrowed or repaid, have some exchange value at the moment they take place. This exchange value is called original, historical, or acquisition cost and is the amount of dollars used by financial accounting to measure all activity. Financial accounting, then, is concerned with the original exchange value of events and generally (although not always) ignores subsequent movements in value. This original (historical, acquisition) cost is objective, and reporting this amount avoids reflecting subjective opinions as to subsequent movements in "value" in the financial statements of a business.

Financial Statements

The goal of financial accounting is to provide meaningful financial information about an organization to individuals and groups outside the management group. Yet, the type and amount of information which could be provided about even a small business is almost endless. Some assumption must be made as to the types of information outsiders would like to have.

Financial accounting assumes that most external users would like to have at least two basic pieces of financial information, and thus, two financial reports (financial statements) are prepared to convey this information. First, it is desirable for outsiders to have a statement that depicts the financial position of a business at a point in time. This report lists the resources a business possesses and the obligations it faces as of a particular point in time (the end of an accounting period). This statement, which is similar to a still photograph capturing the business's financial position at a point, is called a **balance sheet.**

Second, outsiders want to know whether or not the business has been successful in its profit-seeking activities (that is, has shown a profit) since the last balance sheet at the end of the previous accounting period. The **income statement** summarizes the profit-seeking accomplishments of the business and the efforts expended; it compares accomplishment (revenues) and effort (expenses) to disclose whether or not the business is better off (net income) or worse off (net loss) because of these activities. These two financial statements, and two others that will be discussed in later chapters, are prepared at the end of each accounting period for each business entity and transmitted to outside individuals and groups interested in that business.

Concept Summary

Basic Accounting Assumptions	
Assumption	*Focus*
Entity	Each business is a separate reporting unit from other businesses and from owners.
Going Concern	Businesses enjoy an indefinite life and are accounted for accordingly.
Accounting Period	The indefinite life of business may be divided into shorter time periods (usually one year) for reporting purposes.
Monetary	The common denominator of measurement and reporting in accounting is the dollar.
Exchange	The basis of valuation in accounting is original, historical, or acquisition cost.
Financial Statements	The primary reports which result from the accounting process are the income statement and the balance sheet.

1.5 The Basic Accounting Equation and Business Transactions

At the most abstract level, there is no mystery to what businesses do or the role accounting systems play in the process of business. Every business, large or small, does essentially two major things. First, businesses acquire financial and productive resources from some source. Then, these resources are combined and used to create more resources. The basic idea of business activity is to make resources grow. To the extent resources grow, business activity has been, generally speaking, successful. If resources decline from business activity, efforts have been unsuccessful.

Assets

The resources businesses acquire and use are called assets. In the real world, every asset has a source; that is, it comes from some individual or organization. Sources of assets (places from which a business has acquired its resources) are called *equities*. Because every financial and productive resource in a business has either been acquired or created, the following applies to every business at all times

$$\text{Assets} = \text{Equities}$$

This simple equation is the basis for all of financial accounting. It is the foundation on which the entire accounting system is built. This equality is called the **basic accounting equation.**

Equities

Individuals or organizations that supply businesses with assets would like those assets or others of equal or greater value returned to them. Similarly, if a business has created new assets by its activities, the owners of that business would like ultimately to enjoy the benefits of those assets. This means that equities not only measure sources of assets, but also measure claims against the assets of the business. In effect, then, the basic accounting equation shows that all assets of a business have claims against them. These claims may have resulted because assets were supplied to the business or because the business has created its own assets and the owners have a right to participate in the business success by claiming these assets.

The Basic Accounting Equation

All financial accounting activity can be explained in terms of the basic accounting equation. The equation is simple, but the concepts underlying it are important. The essence of this equation is made clear by noting that the following three expressions are identical in meaning and represent different ways to view the same relationships:

$$\text{Assets} = \text{Equities}$$
$$\text{Assets} = \text{Sources of Assets}$$
$$\text{Assets} = \text{Claims Against Assets}$$

Assets Defined

Assets are financial and productive resources; however, not all resources are assets. To be an asset for a particular business, a resource must meet three criteria.

1. The resource must possess future value for that business.

2. The resource must be under the effective control of that business.

3. The resource must have a dollar value resulting from an identifiable event or events in the life of that business.

To be an asset, a resource must meet *all* of these criteria. If any one of the requirements is not met, the resource simply is not an asset in accounting terms, regardless of its physical existence.

Future Value Future value means the business must get some benefit in the future from holding the resource today. Resources exhibit future value either by exchange value or use value. *Exchange value* means the resource can be readily exchanged for other desired resources and is held for that exchange purpose. The clearest example of an exchange value resource is cash, which can be exchanged for any other resource. There are, however, other exchange value assets which may not be so obvious. For example, amounts of money owed to a business by its customers (called *accounts receivable*) represent a resource with exchange value. The receivable is collected (exchanged) in cash, which is exchangeable for anything. *Inventory*, which is the term used to indicate the goods held by a business for resale to its customers, is also an exchange value resource because the inventory is sold (exchanged) either for cash or for a receivable. Cash, accounts receivable, and inventory represent the primary exchange value resources.

Resources may exhibit a second type of future value called *use value*. For a resource to possess use value, it must be expected to contribute to a business by its physical use. Resources businesses use up, usually a little at a time, such as buildings, equipment, machines, trucks, and cars, fall into this category and represent the most common types of use value assets.

Control If a resource exhibits future value, it must then be determined whether the resource is under the effective control of the business. Effective control and legal ownership are not the same thing. Although it is possible for any business to possess ownership without control or vice versa, the usual circumstance is the existence of both characteristics at once or the existence of effective control without legal ownership.

This control criterion is an important factor in the determination of accounting assets. Air, sunshine, oceans, and highways are resources of great value, but are under the control of no particular business. These resources, therefore, could never be accounting assets to any business. On the other hand, a business may buy a truck or car on credit and have control over the vehicle while legal ownership rests with the financing bank or credit company. Such a vehicle would meet the control criterion for inclusion as an asset.

Dollar Valuation The standard unit of measure in financial accounting is the dollar; hence, resources must be valued in dollars to be accounting assets. Because objective valuation is preferable to subjective opinion, dollar valuation must result from an identifiable event (usually an exchange between independent parties) in the life of the business.

Certain valuable resources, such as a firm's favorable location or reputation for quality service and products, do not normally qualify as assets. Though valuable, these resources are very difficult to measure in dollars because they do not usually result from one event. Instead, they reflect the cumulative effect of many events and actions over long periods of time.

Concept Summary

Criteria for a Resource to be an Asset	
Criteria	*Description*
Future Value	Resource must provide some benefit in the future, either Exchange value—resource (1) can be readily exchanged for other desired resources and (2) is held for that exchange purpose or Use value—resource must contribute to the business by its physical use.
Control	Resource must be under the effective control of the business.
Dollar Valuation	Resource must have a dollar value, arising from an identifiable event.

Liabilities Defined

Equities measure sources of assets and, at the same time, claims against the assets of a business. A business may acquire assets from either its owners or nonowners. When persons or groups other than owners supply a business with assets, the claims against the business that result usually take the form of debt. That is, by accepting assets from "outsiders" (banks, suppliers, and others) the business assumes a legal obligation to return assets of equal or greater value to those outsiders. These sources of assets from nonowners are called **liabilities** in financial accounting. Liabilities represent the debts and legal obligations of a business which have resulted from the acquisition of assets from persons or groups other than the owners.

Owners' Equity Defined

A business may also secure assets from its owners. When the owners supply a business with assets, the resulting claim against those assets is called owners' equity (sometimes called stockholders' equity if the business is a corporation). As with liabilities, the business incurs an obligation by accepting assets from owners; however, owners' equity represents a different type of claim from that represented by liabilities.

Unlike liabilities, the business makes no specific promise to return these assets to its owners, and the extent to which these claims are ever satisfied depends upon the company's success. A certain amount of owner claims against the assets of any business are more or less permanent and will not be satisfied as long as the business continues to operate.

Figure 1-2 contrasts the characteristics of liabilities and owners' equity.

Expanded Basic Accounting Equation

Because equities can be subdivided into two major groups, liabilities and owners' equity, the basic accounting equation can be rewritten as follows

$$\text{Assets} = \text{Liabilities} + \text{Owners' Equity}$$

This expanded version of the basic accounting equation is the basis for the

FIGURE 1-2
Contrast of Liabilities with Owners' Equity

	Liabilities	Owners' Equity
Legal Status	Generally, nonowner claims are legal obligations of a business; if the obligations are not satisfied, the business risks its existence.	Generally, owners' claims are not legally enforceable; if the claims are not satisfied, the owners can only sell their ownership.
Amount Due	Amount is known with certainty or can be reasonably estimated.	Owners' claim is residual because the owners claim all assets not specifically claimed by nonowners; this may be a lot, a little, or nothing.
Date Due	Date at which the obligation must be satisfied is known with certainty.	Owners' claim is open-ended because there is no specific time in the future when the claim must be satisfied by the business.

balance sheet, one of the primary reports produced by financial accounting. The balance sheet is simply an elaboration of the Assets = Liabilities + Owners' Equity (often written $A = L + OE$) statement for a particular business.

Business Transactions

It is now possible to understand what financial accounting activity encompasses. An accounting **transaction** is a business event that affects one or more of the components of the basic accounting equation. Financial accounting records, classifies, summarizes, and communicates the effect of accounting transactions, so the raw material of financial accounting is the transaction.

Not all business events are transactions. An event may occur which does not affect the $A = L + OE$ equation and, if so, that event is ignored by the financial accounting process. For example, a new employee may be hired by a business. This event would not affect the basic accounting equation and would not be recorded.

Because the equation has only three components, only a limited number of basic accounting transaction types are possible. More important, each accounting transaction must have at least two separate effects on the accounting equation. If a transaction has an impact on only one component of the equation in only one way, equality is not maintained in the equation. Instead, each transaction affects the $A = L + OE$ equation in at least two different ways so that, after the effect of the transaction is recorded, the equation remains in balance.

Types of Transactions

Given the three major components of the basic accounting equation, only nine fundamental types of accounting transactions are possible. The first five of these nine transaction types depict the most common effects on the basic accounting equation, and the remaining discussion in this chapter will be limited to these. The last four types of transactions occur relatively rarely for most businesses and will be discussed in later chapters.

Increase in Assets and Decrease in Assets If a business purchases a building, truck, machine, inventory, or any other asset for cash, the effect is a simultaneous increase and decrease in assets by the same amount. Similarly, if a business collects an amount owed to it (accounts receivable), the result is an increase in assets (cash) and a decrease in assets (accounts receivable). After these transactions are recorded, the equation is in balance, as it always should be.

Increase in Assets and Increase in Liabilities Borrowing money from a bank would increase assets (cash) and liabilities (notes payable); purchasing any asset on credit, generally called "on account," would create a liability. Again, equality in the equation is constantly maintained because each transaction results in equal increases to both sides of the $A = L + OE$ expression.

Increase in Assets and Increase in Owners' Equity When an owner of a business invests money in the business, the result is an increase in assets (cash) and an increase in owners' equity. This activity is usually called *owner investment*, and in a corporation this investment takes the form of a purchase of stock from the business.

This same effect on the basic accounting equation may also result from the profit-seeking activities of a business. As a business sells products to its customers or performs services for its customers, assets (usually cash or accounts receivable) increase. The source of these assets is the profit-seeking activity of the business. This increase in assets represents accomplishment (revenues), and the fruits of this accomplishment belong to the owners; that is, the owners have a claim on these increases in assets and that fact is reflected by an increase in owners' equity. All revenue (accomplishment) transactions result in equal increases in assets and owners' equity.

Decrease in Assets and Decrease in Liabilities As a liability is paid, the result is a reduction of assets and liabilities. For example, if an amount owed by a business to its creditors is repaid, a liability is decreased (accounts payable or notes payable) and cash is decreased. Paying, often called *retiring*, a liability results in this effect on the equation.

Decrease in Assets and Decrease in Owners' Equity From time to time, owners may decide to withdraw some assets from the business for their own personal use. This withdrawal represents a satisfaction of some owner claims and is recorded as a decrease in assets, usually cash, and a decrease in owners' equity.

The same effect on the basic accounting equation results from the measurement of business effort in profit-seeking activities. As a business sells products to its customers or performs services for them, it may simultaneously use up some of its assets. For example, supplies may be consumed; tools, used; or cash, paid to employees for their services. In each of these instances, an asset has decreased in the process of producing revenue. These consumptions of assets in profit-seeking activity reduce owners' equity and represent effort on the part of a business. This effort, called expenses in financial accounting, must be netted against accomplishment (revenues) to determine the net benefit (net income) to the business from its profit-seeking activities. All expense (effort) transactions result in equal decreases in assets and owners' equity.

An accounting transaction is a business event that affects one or more components of the basic accounting equation. Analyzing a transaction simply means interpreting its effect on the $A = L + OE$ expression within the requirement that the equality of this expression must be maintained at all times.

Concept Summary

		Fundamental Types of Accounting Transactions			
	Assets =	Liabilities +	Owners' Equity		Example
1.	+, −				purchase building for cash
2.	+	+			borrow money
3.	+		+		owner investment
4.	−	−			pay off debt
5.	−		−		owner withdrawal
6.		+, −			*
7.		+	−		*
8.		−	+		*
9.			+, −		*

+ = increase in component
− = decrease in component
* = example deferred to later chapters

Transaction Analysis

To illustrate these transaction analysis ideas further, suppose that a business is engaged in the following events during its first month of operation:

August 1 Owner deposited $10,000 in a company bank account to begin the business.

6 Purchased inventory for $1,500 on credit.

12 Purchased a truck for $5,000 cash.

15 Sold products to customers for $2,000; $1,000 for cash and $1,000 on credit. It had cost the business $1,000 to purchase these products.

21 Collected $750 of the amount owed to the business by customers from the August 15 sale.

26 Paid the entire amount owed to suppliers from the August 6 purchase of inventory.

Figure 1-3 illustrates the effect of these accounting transactions on the basic accounting equation for this company. Notice that each transaction is analyzed from the duality viewpoint and that the equation is in balance after the effect of each event is recorded.

FIGURE 1-3

Transaction Analysis and the Basic Accounting Equation

	Cash	+	Accounts Receivable	+	Inventory	+	Truck	=	Accounts Payable	+	Owner Capital
			ASSETS					=	*LIABILITIES* +		*OWNERS' EQUITY*
August 1	+$10,000										+$10,000
August 6					+ 1,500				+ 1,500		
Balance August 12	$10,000 − 5,000				$1,500		+ 5,000	=	$1,500		$10,000
Balance August 15	$ 5,000 + 1,000		+ 1,000		$1,500 − 1,000		$5,000	=	$1,500		$10,000 + 2,000 − 1,000
Balance August 21	$ 6,000 + 750		$1,000 − 750		$ 500		$5,000	=	$1,500		$11,000
Balance August 26	$ 6,750 − 1,500		$ 250		$ 500		$5,000	=	$1,500 − 1,500		$11,000
Balance (end of month)	$ 5,250	+	$ 250	+	$ 500	+	$5,000	=	0	+	$11,000

Summary

The institution of business plays an important role in all aspects of society in the United States and the world. In order to operate, businesses must assume a legal form. The three legal forms of business organization are: (1) sole proprietorship, (2) partnership, and (3) corporation.

Several organizations in society have a direct impact on the practice of accounting. The Securities and Exchange Commission and Internal Revenue Service are governmental agencies with significant influence on business and accounting. In addition, private organizations, primarily the American Institute of Certified Public Accountants and the Financial Accounting Standards Board, affect the practice of accounting.

All organizations practice financial accounting, and most large businesses practice managerial accounting. Certified Public Accountants review the financial accounting practices of business and certify financial statements.

Financial accounting is based upon six fundamental assumptions which guide accounting activity. The application of these assumptions results in the preparation by businesses of financial statements called the income statement and balance sheet. At the heart of these financial statements is the basic accounting equation, Assets = Liabilities + Owners'

Equity. This equation reflects the results of business transactions.

Chapter 2 examines this basic accounting equation and the income statement and balance sheet which are derived from it.

Key Terms

Accounting period
American Institute of Certified
   Public Accountants (AICPA)
Asset
Balance sheet
Basic accounting equation
Certified Public Accountant (CPA)
Corporation
Entity
Financial accounting
Financial Accounting Standards
   Board (FASB)
Financial statements

Generally accepted accounting
   principles (GAAP)
Going concern
Income statement
Internal Revenue Service (IRS)
Liability
Managerial accounting
Owners' equity
Partnership
Securities and Exchange Commission
   (SEC)
Sole proprietorship
Transaction

Comprehensive Review Problem

The accounting data for Randall's Record Shop as of March 31, 1982 is given below (listed in alphabetical order).

Accounts payable	$ 5,000
Accounts receivable	3,000
Building	25,000
Cash	15,000
Inventory	10,000
Land	15,000
Notes payable	3,000
Owners' capital	60,000

Transactions

April 1 The $3,000 note was paid to the bank in full (interest is ignored).

   7 Collected $1,000 from customers for previous credit sales.

   8 Purchased inventory from suppliers on credit at a cost of $2,000.

   10 Mailed a check to suppliers for $5,000 to pay for March purchases.

   15 The city appraised the value of the building at $40,000.

   21 Sold records costing the business $2,000 to customers for $3,500. $2,000 of the sales were on credit and $1,500 were for cash.

   25 Owners withdrew $500 from the business for personal use.

Required:

1. Using a transactions analysis table like that presented in Figure 1-3, show that the accounting equation was in balance as of March 31, 1982.

2. Analyze the effect of each transaction on the equation and show that it is still in balance at April 30, 1982.

Solution to Comprehensive Review Problem

| | ASSETS | | | | | = | LIABILITIIES | | + | OWNERS' EQUITY |
	Cash +	Accounts Receivable +	Inventory +	Building +	Land =		Accounts Payable +	Notes Payable +		Owners' Capital
March 31	$15,000 +	$3,000 +	$10,000 +	$25,000 +	$15,000 =		$ 5,000 +	$3,000 +		$60,000
April 1	− 3,000							− 3,000		
Balance	$12,000	$3,000	$10,000	$25,000	$15,000 =		$ 5,000			$60,000
April 7	+ 1,000 −	1,000								
Balance	$13,000	$2,000	$10,000	$25,000	$15,000 =		$ 5,000			$60,000
April 8			+ 2,000				+ 2,000			
Balance	$13,000	$2,000	$12,000	$25,000	$15,000 =		$ 7,000			$60,000
April 10	− 5,000						− 5,000			
Balance	$ 8,000	$2,000	$12,000	$25,000	$15,000 =		$ 2,000			$60,000
April 15	(Event has no effect on accounting equation)									
April 21	+ 1,500 +	$2,000							+	3,500
			− 2,000						−	2,000
Balance	$ 9,500	$4,000	$10,000	$25,000	$15,000 =		$ 2,000			$61,500
April 25	− 500								−	500
Balance at April 30	$ 9,000 +	$4,000 +	$10,000 +	$25,000 +	$15,000 =		$ 2,000 +	0 +		$61,000

Questions

Q1-1. List three important characteristics of the corporate form of business.

Q1-2. Briefly discuss the structure and function of the FASB.

Q1-3. Describe the three types of services CPAs in public practice perform.

Q1-4. Distinguish between financial and managerial accounting.

Q1-5. List and briefly describe the basic assumptions of accounting.

Q1-6. What information is conveyed by the two major financial statements?

Q1-7. What criteria must a resource meet in order to be considered an accounting asset? What are the characteristics of liabilities and owners' equity?

Q1-8. Write out the basic accounting equation. Describe the five most common types of transactions which affect this equation and show the effect on the equation of each of these transaction types.

Exercises

E1-1. There are three major forms of business organization used in the United States. Indicate the important accounting, legal, and taxation aspects of each of these forms. Which is the least commonly used form? Which is the most commonly used form? Which accounts for most of the business activity in the United States?

E1-2. Identify the following organizations that have affected the development and practice of accounting.

    a. Agency whose primary interest is to assure disclosure of all relevant information about a security to potential investors for use in investment decisions

    ———————————————————————————————————

    b. Agency that has the authority to determine what is acceptable treatment of events with income tax consequences

    ———————————————————————————————————

    c. National professional organization of CPAs

    ———————————————————————————————————

    d. New, official rule-making body for accounting is composed of seven full-time members with four coming from public accounting and the remainder from business, investment professionals, and the academic community

    ———————————————————————————————————

E1-3. Give the three important characteristics of financial and managerial accounting. Would a company need two accounting systems in order to produce both of these types of information? Why or why not?

E1-4. On January 2, a business opens with $10,000 of assets, all of which were invested by the owner. On December 31, the owner determines total assets to be $11,000 but discovers that the firm owes $2,000 to ouside creditors. He complains that his basic accounting equation does not balance. Does it balance? What has he overlooked?

E1-5. There are six basic assumptions in financial accounting. Tell which assumptions are being used in each of the following situations:

    a. Judy Cochran is the owner of Cochran Marine Agency, a boat rental company, and Cochran, Inc. a real estate agency. Judy does a separate set of financial statements for each of these two businesses.

    b. Judy assumes in doing her statements that the businesses will not terminate their activities in the foreseeable future.

    c. In order to provide information to her banker, Judy prepares financial statements in dollar amounts covering the activities of each fiscal year.

    d. All of the ships owned by Cochran Marine were originally recorded at their acquisition price.

E1-6. Accounting financial statements are commonly used by at least the following groups: (a) management; (b) creditors, such as banks; (c) owners. For what specific purpose would each of these groups use financial statements? What kind of information from financial statements would be most important to each of these groups? Why?

E1-7. What is accounting? What are GAAP? How does an auditor use GAAP?

E1-8. Indicate whether the following resources found in Carl's Dry Cleaning Service exhibit exchange value or use value.

    a. Cash in the company's checking account

    b. A truck used to deliver cleaned clothing

28

c. A machine used in a special cleaning process
d. A supply of dry cleaning fluids
e. Amounts owed by customers of Carl
f. A patent for a special dry cleaning process

Problems

P1-1. *Requirement 1.* Which of the following are assets? For each item that is *not* an asset, explain why. For each asset, support your decision as to why it is an asset.

a. Copyright of a book
b. Highway next to the plant
c. A company's own capital stock not yet sold to stockholders
d. Amounts owed to the firm by customers
e. Amounts owed by the firm to suppliers
f. Amount paid to landlord for previous month's rent
g. Amount paid to landlord for next month's rent
h. Reputation of the firm based on years of quality service
i. Obsolete machine whose cost of removal would equal its proceeds

Requirement 2. Which of the following are liabilities? For each item that is *not* a liability, explain why. For each liability support your decision as to why it is a liability.

a. A bank overdraft
b. A customer's account that was overpaid
c. The estimated amount you will pay to your employees in salaries next year
d. A 90-day note signed when $1,000 was borrowed from the local bank in order to finance the purchase of machinery
e. Amounts owed by customers

P1-2. The following are balance sheet items found in the business operated by Harry Williams. Determine whether these items are assets, liabilities, or owners' equity. Substitute each in the basic accounting equation and prove its equality.

Supplies	$ 4,000	Income taxes payable	$ 5,000
Capital stock	161,000	Inventory	30,000
Cash	15,000	Building	60,000
Land	30,000	Office equipment	7,000
Sales taxes payable	2,000	Accounts payable	23,000
Accounts receivable	45,000		

P1-3. Across the top of a sheet of paper write the equation *Assets = Liabilities + Owners' Equity*. Indicate the effect of each of the transactions listed below on this equation. Verify after each transaction that the equation is still in balance.

a. Contributed $10,000 cash to the business and received stock worth $10,000.
b. Bought $400 of supplies to be used in the business.
c. Borrowed $3,000 from the bank; the proceeds are to be used in the business.
d. Paid the month's rent, $500.
e. Paid $3,200 cash for a used truck.

   f. Performed services for customers and billed them $2,400.

   g. $1,800 of these bills were paid by customers.

   h. Used up $200 of the supplies purchased in b in performing services for customers.

   i. Paid employees' salaries, $400.

   j. The first installment was due on the loan from the bank; paid $250 (ignore interest).

   k. Paid $500 to owners of the business for their personal use.

P1-4. Logan's Leather Products, a retail store, was organized ten years ago. Certain data are available for the current year. Total sales were $250,000. Of these sales, $200,000 were cash sales, and $50,000 were credit sales which are expected to be collected in the following year. The cost of the goods that were sold was $178,500. Salary expense for the year was $53,000. Other expenses included payroll taxes, $5,000; utilities, $3,000; rent expense, $12,000; advertising expense, $600; and miscellaneous expenses, $500. Was Logan's Leather Products better off or worse off as a result of these activities during the year? By what amount were they better or worse off?

P1-5. Bruno Brewing Corporation is preparing the annual financial report for its stockholders for the current year, 1982. The following information on cash flows is available for the year: cash inflow from operating revenues, $150,000; cash outflow for operating expenses, $85,000; sale of unissued Bruno Stock for cash, $69,000. During the year, $36,000 was paid to stockholders in cash dividends. A $28,000 cash payment was made on a note payable due during the year at Hibernia Bank. A used machine was sold for $2,000, and a new machine replaced it at a cost of $9,500. Cash was paid for the new machine.

Required:
Compute the net increase or decrease in cash during the year.

P1-6. Complete the following tabulation by entering the missing numbers. Consider each column independently.

	Column (1)	Column (2)	Column (3)
Assets 1/1	(1)	3,500	13,000
Assets 12/31	7,050	(4)	15,667
Liabilities 1/1	1,650	1,625	(7)
Liabilities 12/31	1,350	1,000	5,667
Owners' equity 1/1	3,000	(5)	9,000
Owners' equity 12/31	(2)	2,875	(8)
Revenues	10,600	(6)	6,500
Expenses	10,200	3,317	(9)
Additional investment by owners	(3)	167	1,000

P1-7. The GHF Tire Company was organized using the partnership form by Ray Goller, Andy Haynes, and Al Flowers. Each invested $10,000 cash to start the business. On December 31, 1982, the end of the first year of operations, the following information was obtained from the accounting records: cash on hand and in the bank, $25,000; amounts due from customers, $7,349; store equipment, $30,000; amounts owed to suppliers, $6,300; note payable at local bank, $3,000. The partners divided the year's profit of $44,049 equally among them. Each of the partners withdrew $7,000 in cash, and the remainder was left in the business to help provide for future growth. You are asked to prepare a balance sheet for GHF Tire Company on December 31, 1982.

P1-8. The Bissonet Truck Service opened for business April 1, 1982. The business specialized in hauling dirt and gravel for contractors building residential and commercial structures. The following transactions took place during April:

April 1 The corporate charter was received from the state, and the corporate books were opened with an investment of $16,000 by the two owners, Bob and Cathy Murray.

3 The corporation located a suitable office space and paid $1,200 for the first month's rent expense.

3 Paid $100 for a telephone deposit and $75 for the utility deposit, both of which will be returned after one year of satisfactory bill payment.

6 Paid $1,700 cash for office equipment.

6 Purchased office supplies on credit, $125.

7 Purchased two second-hand dump trucks. The total cost was $32,000. A $10,000 cash down payment was made, and a note was signed for the balance.

9 Paid $100 for advertisements in the local newspaper. This was charged to advertising expense.

15 Revenues from the truck service for the first half month were $3,600. $2,000 was paid in cash, and $1,600 is still owed by contractors.

15 Cost of gasoline, oil, and repairs to the trucks for the first half month was $800. Paid cash.

17 Paid $350 on the note payable for the trucks (ignore interest).

20–24 Collected $1,200 of the amount due from the contractors.

24 Paid the $125 owed for office supplies.

27 Paid utility bill, $60.

28 Collected $350 more of the amount owed by contractors.

30 Revenue for the second half of the month was $7,200. $5,000 was collected in cash, and $2,200 is still owed by contractors.

30 Cost of gasoline, oil, and repairs for the second half of the month was $2,000.

Required:

1. Set up the following accounting equation across the top of your paper:

$$\text{Cash} + \frac{\text{Accounts}}{\text{receivable}} + \frac{\text{Office}}{\text{supplies}} + \text{Deposits} + \frac{\text{Office}}{\text{equipment}} + \text{Trucks}$$

$$= \frac{\text{Notes}}{\text{payable}} + \frac{\text{Accounts}}{\text{payable}} + \frac{\text{Owners'}}{\text{equity}}$$

2. Record the effects of each of the above transactions on this equation.

Financial Statements

Chapter Outline

2.1 *The Balance Sheet—Assets and Liabilities.* Definition and valuation of assets and liabilities; illustration with two balance sheets.

2.2 *The Balance Sheet—Owners' Equity.* Definition, classification, and valuation of owners' equity; illustration with an unincorporated and corporate balance sheet.

2.3 *The Income Statement—Revenues and Expenses.* Concepts underlying the income statement; definition of revenues and expenses; illustration with two income statements.

2.4 *Statement of Retained Earnings/Owners' Capital.* Relationship of income statement and balance sheet; definition of dividends and withdrawals; illustration of retained earnings and owners' capital statements.

Accounting and the Real World

The Best and the Worst

As U.S. businesses report on their financial activities and position, it becomes clear which companies performed well and thus rewarded their owners and which performed poorly to the chagrin and financial loss of the owners. Each year, as a part of its Fortune 500 Directory, *Fortune* magazine cites the stars and laggards from the 500 list. The star performers are those companies with the highest percentage return earned by their owners, and the laggards are those companies with the lowest percentage return.

Below are the best and the worst for 1980. Notice that the best performer offered its owners a whopping 220 percent return in one year, while the owners of the poorest performer suffered a negative 63 percent return.

THE TEN HIGHEST

	Sales Rank	Rate of Return
Mitchell Energy & Development	496	220.26%
ConAgra	340	171.78
Wang Laboratories	457	156.78
LTV	42	153.13
Cameron Iron Works	385	145.39
NL Industries	177	125.14
Union Pacific	75	121.87
Shell Oil	12	120.08
Dean Foods	429	117.19
Litton Industries	88	117.17

THE FIVE LOWEST

	Sales Rank	Rate of Return
Commonwealth Oil Refining	258	−62.63%
Charter	84	−41.65
American Motors	155	−41.46
White Motor	350	−40.35
Monfort of Colorado	365	−40.28

Not to be ignored when discussing the worst performers of 1980 are the big money losers for that year. Below is a list of the largest dollar losses suffered by companies on the 500 list. By the way, the loss reported by Chrysler for 1980 was the largest ever reported by a U.S. company.

MONEY LOSERS

	Sales Rank	Loss
Chrylser	32	$1,709,700,000
Ford Motor	6	1,543,300,000
General Motors	3	762,500,000
International Harvester	49	397,328,000
GAF	268	233,476,000
American Motors	155	197,525,000
Firestone Tire & Rubber	73	105,900,000

Reprinted from the 1981 *Fortune* Directory by permission.

All business entities prepare a series of financial reports on their activities and position at the end of each accounting period. These financial reports assume that the business will enjoy an indefinite life and express the tentative results of operations for the current period and tentative financial position at the end of the period in dollar terms. These reports are called *financial statements*. Typically, four such statements result from financial accounting activity and are communicated to external parties. In this chapter the form and content of three of these statements will be discussed. The fourth, the *statement of changes in financial position*, is quite complex and thus will not be discussed until Section IV of the book.

2.1   The Balance Sheet—Assets and Liabilities

The foundation for the balance sheet is the basic accounting equation, which can be written

$$\text{Assets} = \text{Liabilities} + \text{Owners' Equity}$$

An appreciation for the balance sheet and an ability to prepare the statement requires a familiarity with the elements of the basic accounting equation. The definitions of assets, liabilities, and owners' equity; the classification (grouping) patterns used within each of these components; and the basis for assigning dollar values to each of the elements of the balance sheet must be understood. Simply stated, the key to the balance sheet lies in the definition, presentation, and valuation of assets, liabilities, and owners' equity.

In Chapter 1 conceptually sound and operational definitions of assets, liabilities, and owners' equity were presented. These definitions are important because they explain the nature of each of the major elements of the basic accounting equation, as well as how these elements fit together and interact with one another. The ideas behind valuation and financial statement presentation for assets, liabilities, and owners' equity are discussed in this chapter, and the income statement is introduced.

Figures 2-1 and 2-2 illustrate balance sheets for a small business and a large corporation, respectively. These balance sheets deserve your careful study as they will provide the basis for much of the discussion in this and the following section.

FIGURE 2-1
Balance Sheet of a
Small Business

P-J AUDIO COMPANY
Balance Sheet
February 1, 1982

ASSETS

Cash		$ 99,424
Accounts receivable	$149,693	
Allowance for bad debts	(6,449)	143,244
Inventory—appliances		95,000
Inventory—audio		90,000
Inventory—other		4,500
Supplies		1,200
Prepaid insurance		2,000
Prepaid advertising		2,500
Furniture and fixtures	30,000	
Less: Accumulated depreciation	(16,000)	14,000
Truck	10,000	
Less: Accumulated depreciation	(333)	9,667
Total assets		$461,535

LIABILITIES & OWNERS' EQUITY

Liabilities

Accounts payable	$ 12,762
Note payable	8,000
Interest payable	250
Loan payable	190,000
Total liabilities	211,012

Owners' equity

P-J, capital	250,523
Total liabilities & owners' equity	$461,535

Valuation of
Assets

The accounting problems associated with placing a dollar value on assets for balance sheet purposes will be discussed throughout most of this text. Presented here are only the basic principles underlying the valuation of assets. Because all assets result directly from a specific transaction or transactions, all assets have an **acquisition cost** at the moment they are acquired. It is this *original cost* (sometimes called **historical cost**) that is the basis for the valuation of assets in accounting. Assets are recorded at their original cost and then reported on subsequent balance sheets at the amount of that cost not yet used up by the business.

Generally speaking, balance sheets present the cost of assets not yet used up and do not disclose the current market value of assets or movements in that market value from one balance sheet to another. Some assets, specifically cash and receivables, do not have a cost as such and thus are valued somewhat differently. *Cash* can be assigned a dollar value by simply counting it, since the dollar is the basis for valuation of all other assets. *Receivables* present a particular problem because they represent a claim to the cash of another individual or entity. Ordinarily, receivables appear

FIGURE 2-2
Balance Sheet of a
Large Corporation

EXXON CORPORATION
Consolidated Statement of Financial Position

Assets	December 31, 1977	December 31, 1976
Current assets		
Cash, including time deposits of		
$1,127,529,000 and $972,148,000	$ 1,597,525,000	$ 1,278,578,000
Marketable securities, at cost, which		
approximates market	3,086,316,000	3,795,259,000
Notes and accounts receivable, less		
estimated doubtful amounts of $91,207,000		
and $95,810,000	5,708,177,000	5,354,462,000
Inventories		
Crude oil, products and merchandise	3,856,470,000	3,794,454,000
Materials and supplies	478,688,000	439,833,000
Prepaid taxes and other expenses	604,599,000	389,361,000
Total current assets	15,331,775,000	15,051,947,000
Investments and advances	1,575,212,000	1,563,211,000
Property, plant, and equipment, at cost, less		
accumulated depreciation and depletion		
of $11,973,840,000 and $10,830,579,000 .	20,537,873,000	18,671,208,000
Deferred charges and other assets	1,008,476,000	1,044,980,000
Total assets	38,453,336,000	36,331,346,000
Liabilities		
Current liabilities		
Notes and loans payable	1,385,175,000	1,859,844,000
Accounts payable and accrued liabilities	8,350,267,000	7,714,068,000
Income taxes payable	977,814,000	947,529,000
Total current liabilities	10,713,256,000	10,521,441,000
Long-term debt	3,869,960,000	3,696,798,000
Annuity and other reserves	807,135,000	646,668,000
Deferred income tax credits	2,655,607,000	2,149,931,000
Other deferred credits	69,187,000	71,630,000
Equity of minority shareholders in affiliated		
companies	825,272,000	774,526,000
Total liabilities	18,940,417,000	17,860,994,000
Shareholders' equity		
Capital	2,572,063,000	2,608,591,000
Earnings reinvested	16,940,856,000	15,861,761,000
Total shareholders' equity	$19,512,919,000	$18,470,352,000

Source: Exxon Corporation Annual Report for 1977.

on the balance sheet as the amount that is expected to be collected from the other party. This expected collectible amount is the total amount owed to the business minus any amounts that are not likely to be collected (often called bad debts or doubtful accounts).

The accounting basis which reports on balance sheets the unused original cost of assets held by a business is called the *historical cost basis* or *cost principle.*

| Valuation of Liabilities | The assignment of dollar values to liabilities is a fairly complex process; therefore, a detailed discussion will be deferred to later in the book. Generally, however, both current and long-term liabilities are accounted for and reported on balance sheets at the dollar amount that would be necessary to satisfy the obligation at the balance sheet date. For credit purchases of inventory or supplies, this means that a liability (accounts payable) is created for the cost of the asset acquired. When cash is borrowed, a liability (notes payable or bonds payable) is created for the amount of the cash received by the business. |

| Limitations of the Balance Sheet | All balance sheets have limitations. An understanding of the balance sheet and the information it contains requires an appreciation for the things this statement cannot do. |

Even with its limitations, however, the balance sheet is an important financial statement. It is the oldest and most basic of the four statements produced by the financial accounting process. If the fundamental purpose, characteristics, and limitations of the balance sheet are understood, this statement can provide useful information to external users.

Concept Summary

Limitations of the Balance Sheet	
Characteristics	*Description/Explanation*
Static statement	The balance sheet presents the assets and equities of a business as of a point in time. It is much like a still photograph in that it depicts financial position, but it does not explain how or why the financial position of a business has changed from an earlier point in time.
Not all resources are shown	Some valuable resources are not susceptible to objective dollar valuation and, therefore, are not shown on a balance sheet. Examples include the reputation of a company and the morale or skills of its employees, both of which are important but very difficult to assign a dollar value.
Market value is not shown	The basis of valuation for most assets is their original cost or unused original cost as of the balance sheet date. It can be misleading to read real "value" into the dollar figures for assets on present-day balance sheets.
Priority of claims on assets	There is a definite order or priority of claims on assets which is based mostly on law. Claims held by nonowners are assigned first priority; therefore, liabilities represent higher-order claims than do owner claims. Liabilities are primary claims, and owners' equity represents residual claims. The order in which equities appear on the balance sheet reflects this priority of claims.
Claims on assets are general	All equities represent general claims against the assets of the business rather than specific claims on individual assets. There is seldom a one-to-one relationship between an individual asset and a specific claim or source. Instead, financial accounting views the business as a collection of assets matched and balanced by a set of general claims which are assigned a priority reflected by the listing on the balance sheet.

2.2 The Balance Sheet—Owners' Equity

Owners' equity represents the total investment of dollars by owners in the business. Owners may supply a business with assets by turning over money to the business and receiving in return an ownership interest. As a result of this investment, the owners enjoy a claim on the assets of the business. Owners may also invest by not withdrawing assets which have been created by the successful profit-seeking activities of the business. A claim results from this type of investment as well.

Direct Investment of Owners

From time to time, the owners of all businesses may make an active, conscious decision to invest funds in a business. In a corporation, this investment decision takes the form of a purchase of shares of stock from a company by investors. The business gets cash (an asset), and the new owners get the shares of stock and a claim against the assets of the business (owners' equity). In an unincorporated business, such as a proprietorshp or partnership, an owner may increase his investment (or invest initially) by placing additional cash in the business bank account for business use.

The owners' equity which results when owners directly and voluntarily invest assets (usually cash) in a corporation is called **capital stock.** Capital stock is a category of owners' equity which reflects this direct, voluntary investment of all of the owners in a corporation. In an unincorporated business there is no stock to represent ownership interest, so the direct investment of owners appears on the balance sheet as a part of the owners' capital account.

Effect of Legal Form It is important at this point to note something about the legal forms of business organization introduced in Chapter 1 and the effect of these legal forms on the balance sheet. The balance sheet presentation of assets and liabilities is basically the same for proprietorships, partnerships, and corporations. The classification and presentation of assets and liabilities is independent of the business's legal form. The legal form of the business does, however, affect the balance sheet presentation of the owners' equity section. In fact, this section of the balance sheet directly reflects the proprietorship, partnership, or corporation status of a business.

Indirect Investment of Owners

The second type of owner investment in a business is somewhat more subtle. Successful profit-seeking activities result in the creation of assets. As a business operates successfully, assets tend to increase. These assets have no direct source in the sense that other assets do. Because they are not acquired from nonowners, liabilities are not created. Because they are not acquired directly from owners, new direct investment by the owners is not created. The assets that result from successful profit-seeking activities are created by the business rather than acquired. Nonetheless, these created assets must have a source on the equities side of the balance sheet in order for equality to be maintained. That source must be a part of owners' equity because the owners' claim is residual and they, therefore, claim all assets not directly claimed by another individual or entity.

As assets are created by successful operations, these assets accrue to the owners, increasing owners' equity. These created assets may be distributed to the owners; however, it is unusual for all created assets to be disbursed to the owners. Instead, most businesses retain some of the created assets in the business and use these assets to contribute to growth. To the extent that owners have not actually received all of the newly created assets to which they have a claim, they have reinvested assets in the business.

Created assets retained in the business represent a source of assets from owners. In a corporation, this source is called retained earnings (earnings reinvested) and is reported as a second basic category of owners' equity. In proprietorships and partnerships, this source is included with the direct, voluntary investment in the capital account of the owners.

Concept Summary

Classification and Valuation of Owners' Equity			
Type of Business	*Presentation on Balance Sheet*	*Nature of Claim*	*Basis of Valuation*
Proprietorship (X is the owner)	X, capital	Secondary and residual	The total of the direct and indirect investment of X in the business
Partnership (X, Y, and Z are the partners and owners)	X, capital Y, capital Z, capital	Secondary and residual	Each owner's capital account reflects the direct and indirect investment of that owner.
Corporation (the owners are any number of stockholders)	Capital stock	Secondary and residual	Direct investment of all stockholders in the business— amounts received by the business from the sale of stock to owners
	Retained earnings		Indirect investment of all stockholders in the business— assets generated by profit-seeking activities minus the amount of these assets withdrawn by stockholders (net income − dividends)

The area of presentation and valuation of owners' equity will be elaborated upon in the next section of this chapter and in later chapters. For now, refer to the balance sheets presented in Figures 2-1 and 2-2 and observe some concrete examples of the presentation and valuation ideas discussed so far.

Balance Sheet of a Small Business

From Figure 2-1, the balance sheet of a small business, you should be able to gather the following information:

1. The business has total assets as of February 1, 1982, of $461,535.

2. Of this total, $211,012 ($21,012 + $190,000) have been supplied by nonowners, and thus, nonowners have a *legal* claim on $211,012 of the total assets.

3. The business must be a sole proprietorship because owners' equity is presented in one figure and classified by the name of the owner.

4. The owner has provided $250,523 of the total assets of the business and, consequently, has a *residual* claim on that amount of assets.

5. It is not possible to determine the amount of assets supplied by the owner through direct investment and the amount of created assets retained in the business since its inception (indirect investment), because both are combined in a sole proprietorship balance sheet.

Balance Sheet of a Large Corporation

Now refer to the balance sheet of the large corporation presented in Figure 2-2. The basic information found in a corporate balance sheet is essentially the same as that presented in a proprietorship balance sheet except for the owners' equity section.

1. Exxon Corporation had total assets of approximately $38.5 billion at December 31, 1977.

2. Of the $38.5 billion, $18.9 billion were supplied by nonowners, and these nonowners had a *legal* claim of $18.9 billion on the assets of Exxon at December 31, 1977.

3. The business must be a corporation because owners' equity (shareholders' equity) is classified and reported as two different figures representing direct and indirect owner investment.

4. The stockholders of Exxon have provided $19.5 billion of the total assets and hold a *residual* claim on this amount of the assets.

5. Of the total of $19.5 billion in assets provided by the owners, $2.6 billion resulted from the direct, voluntary investment of owners in the business through the purchase of shares of stock from Exxon. However, most of the company's owner-derived assets are the result of indirect investment. Of the total assets of $38.5 billion held by Exxon, $16.9 billion have as their source the successful profit-seeking activities of the business. Over the life of the business, assets created from the profit-seeking activities of Exxon have exceeded assets disbursed to owners by $16.9 billion. Thus, $16.9 billion in assets created by successful operations have been retained in the business.

2.3 The Income Statement—Revenues and Expenses

The balance sheet presents the financial position, or status, of a business at certain points (the end of each accounting period) in the life of that business. By comparing several balance sheets of the same company, it is possible to observe that certain activities have taken place which have affected the financial position of the company. It is helpful to external parties to be able to focus on the activities and events that have brought about these observable changes. This is precisely what the remaining financial statements do.

Types of Business Activity

Businesses engage in only three types of activities between balance sheets. First, businesses perform activities designed to produce a profit, such as buying and selling products or performing services. These activities are called *profit-seeking* or *operating activities* and, if successful, produce an increase in assets. Second, businesses acquire assets directly from owners or nonowners by issuing stock or borrowing money, or return assets to owners or nonowners by repurchasing stock or repaying loans. These activities are called *financing activities* and they cause changes in assets but do not affect income. Third, a business may acquire some new assets by purchasing them for cash or may sell some old assets for cash. If any asset other than inventory (which is held specifically to be sold to customers) is purchased or sold, these activities are called *investing activities*. Every event engaged in by a business is an operating, financing, or investing activity. Together, these activities produce the observable changes in financial position disclosed in balance sheets. The *income statement* focuses on the operating activities that have taken place between balance sheets, and the *statement of changes in financial position* (discussed in Chapter 15) focuses on the financing and investing activities for that same period.

The Income Statement

The second primary statement produced by financial accounting is the income statement. This financial report is a dynamic statement in that it attempts to summarize the results of a business's operations (profit-seeking activities) for a period of time. The income statement shows the effect on the business of its profit-seeking activities for a specific accounting period. The "bottom line" of this statement, called **net income, net profit,** or **net earnings,** is the amount by which assets have increased as a result of successful operations. The income statement, therefore, is not independent of the balance sheet. The two statements formally interact through retained earnings for corporations or in the capital accounts for proprietorships and partnerships.

The Basic Accounting Equation and the Income Statement Examine closely the following progression of equations and observe the important relationship and interaction between the income statement and balance sheet. An appreciation of this relationship is critical to understanding the income statement and the information it conveys.

The basic accounting equation is

$$A = L + OE$$

where A = Assets
L = Liabilities
OE = Owners' Equity

But owners' equity can be divided into the direct and indirect investment of the owners, so the equation can be rewritten for corporations without changing its meaning as

$$A = L + CS + RE$$

where CS = Capital Stock
RE = Retained Earnings

Retained earnings The indirect investment of owners in the business represents assets created by operating activities over the life of the business minus the amount of those assets disbursed to owners during that time. The increase in assets resulting from successful operations is called net income, net earnings, or net profit. The amount of these assets disbursed to owners is called **dividends** in a corporation or **withdrawals** in a proprietorship and partnership. The same basic accounting equation can be expanded without changing its meaning by dividing retained earnings into its two parts as follows

$$A = L + CS + (NI - D) \text{ over the life of the business}$$

where NI = Net Income
D = Dividends

which can be rewritten

$$A = L + CS + \Sigma(NI - D)$$

where Σ is a summation sign indicating the cumulative, that is, net income minus dividends summed up for all years of the business's life.

Net income is, itself, the result of combining two important accounting measurements called revenue and expense, so the completely expanded version of the basic accounting equation becomes

$$A = L + CS + \Sigma[(R - E) - D]$$

where R = Revenues
E = Expenses

Owners' Equity and the Income Statement The expression within the parenthesis $(R - E)$ is equal to net income for an accounting period, while the expression within the brackets $[R - E - D]$ represents the increase in indirect investment by owners and, at the same time, the increase in claims against the assets of the business because of this indirect investment. Stated another way, $R - E - D$ measures the amount of assets generated by successful operations during an accounting period minus the amount of those assets distributed to the owners during that period.

If this increase in indirect investment for each accounting period is summed up over the business's life, the result is the balance sheet total for indirect investment by owners. If retained earnings (indirect investment) is added to capital stock (direct investment), the result is total owners' equity. This figure represents total owner claims on the assets of the business.

Concept Summary

Revenue, Expense, and Owners' Equity

$$A = L \quad + \quad OE$$

$$A = L + CS + \quad RE$$

$$A = L + CS + \Sigma(NI - D)$$

$$A = L + CS + \Sigma[(R - E) - D]$$

(1) Revenue minus Expense $\quad$ = Net Income
(2) Net Income minus Dividends = Change in Retained Earnings for the period
(3) Summation of Change in
$\quad$ Retained Earnings for $\quad$ = Retained Earnings Balance
$\quad$ all periods
(4) Capital Stock plus
$\quad$ Retained Earnings $\quad\quad\quad$ = Owners' Equity

Revenues and Expenses

Net income is the accounting system's measure of the success of a business. The determinants of net income are revenues and expenses. In the study of accounting, these two measurement ideas are among the most difficult to grasp for two reasons: (1) the concepts underlying them are complex, and (2) "layman notions" derived from general experience tend to get in the way of precision in this area.

Revenue Both revenue and expense are abstract measurement concepts. Both measure movements in assets and/or liabilities that are caused by profit-seeking activities within a given time period. Revenue measures increases in or inflows of assets resulting from the profit-seeking activities of a business during an accounting period. Note the following important aspects of this definition of revenue.

> **Revenue** is an abstraction which measures "real" movement in another component of the basic accounting equation. The actual movement takes place among the assets, and revenue is the expression used to measure the amount of that inflow of assets.

Assets may increase for many reasons, but revenue measures only those increases caused by profit-seeking activities, not those traceable to financing or investing events.

To elaborate further on the second point, consider the following example: a business may borrow money from a bank with the result being that assets increase. The act of borrowing money is a financing activity, rather than a profit-seeking activity, and thus no revenue is created. The profit seeking would occur when the business decided how to use the money it had borrowed. On the other hand, a business may sell some of its products to a customer, which would also cause assets to increase. This activity, however, is profit-seeking in nature and revenue would result. Both borrowing money and selling products cause assets to increase, but only the latter gives rise to revenue.

In accounting, the term revenue is used to distinguish between asset increases caused by profit-seeking events and all other increases in assets. In terms of the basic accounting equation, borrowing money causes assets to increase (cash) and liabilities to increase (notes payable) by the same amount, thus equality is maintained. Selling products causes assets to increase (cash or accounts receivable), but also causes revenue to increase. The progression of equations previously discussed indicates that, as revenue increases, so does retained earnings and, consequently, owners' equity. The result of the second event is quite different from the result of the first. The second event causes assets and owners' equity to increase by the same amount, and thus, equality is maintained.

Expense Expense is the direct opposite of revenue. Expense measures decreases in or outflows of assets, or increases in liabilities caused by the profit-seeking activities of a business. In other words, when a business consumes or uses up its assets or creates liabilities in the course of seeking a profit, expenses are created. The two important points about revenues made earlier also apply to expenses.

> **Expense** is an abstraction which measures "real" movement in another component of the basic accounting equation. The actual consumption takes place among the assets or the increase takes place among liabilities, and expense is the expression of these changes.

> Assets may decrease or liabilities increase for many reasons, but expense measures only those changes caused by profit-seeking activities, not those traceable to financing or investing events.

Suppose, for example, a business pays off a bank loan with a resulting decrease in assets. This act retires a legal obligation of the business; therefore, its effect on the basic accounting equation would be a reduction of assets and an equal reduction of liabilities. Similarly, a business that borrows money would show an increase in assets and liabilities by the same amount. In these events, either an asset decreases or a liability increases, but no expense is created.

Now consider the sale of products to a customer. The sale causes assets to increase, but at the same time an asset (inventory) is consumed as a result of the sale. This consumption is measured and separated from other asset consumptions by the creation of an expense (cost of goods sold). Again, the progression of equations indicates that, as expenses increase (a negative factor in the equation), retained earnings and owners' equity decrease. Assets have decreased and the balancing movement is a decrease in owners' equity.

Illustration

An example will help to make these ideas more concrete. Suppose a small business showed the following balance sheet at January 1.

SMALL BUSINESS
Balance Sheet
January 1

Assets		Liabilities		
Cash	$ 100	Accounts payable		$ 400
Accounts receivable	500			
Inventory	600	*Stockholders' Equity*		
		Capital stock	$600	
		Retained earnings	200	800
		Total liabilities and		
Total assets	$1,200	stockholders' equity		$1,200

Now, suppose that during the month only three events occurred in this small business.

1. $100 of accounts payable was paid with cash.

2. Inventory that cost the business $300 to purchase was sold for $450 on credit.

3. The business collected from its customers $200 of the amounts owed to it.

The balance sheet at the end of the month would be as follows. Each figure in this statement results from the combination of beginning balance sheet amounts and the transactions for the period.

SMALL BUSINESS
Balance Sheet
January 31

Assets		Liabilities		
Cash	$ 200	Accounts payable		$ 300
Accounts receivable	750			
Inventory	300	*Stockholders' Equity*		
		Capital stock	$600	
		Retained earnings	350	950
		Total liabilities and		
Total assets	$1,250	stockholders' equity		$1,250

The income statement for the month (the period between the two balance sheets) would look like this:

SMALL BUSINESS
Income Statement
For the Month of January

Revenue
Sales of product $450
Expense
Cost of inventory sold 300
Net Income $150

The "big picture" of financial statements should start to fit together. Events 1 and 3 are not profit-seeking activities. Although they do cause movements in assets, they generate neither revenue nor expense. Event 2 is a profit-seeking event and generates both revenue and expense. This event is interesting in that most profit-seeking events create either revenue or expense. However, each time inventory is sold, both are created. Event 2 increases assets (accounts receivable) by $450 and consumes assets (inventory) of $300. The net result is that assets increased by $150 from profit-seeking events for the period, and that increase is called net income. Because the owners withdrew none of these assets for their own use indirect investment (retained earnings) increased by that amount. Although simplified, these events represent the normal operating cycle for most businesses.

Income Statement for a Small Business

Figure 2-3 illustrates the income statement for P-J Audio Company whose balance sheet is given in Figure 2-1. Figure 2-4 presents the income statement for Exxon Corporation whose balance sheet is presented in Figure 2-2. Notice that Exxon presents comparative income statements for two periods.

From the income statement in Figure 2-3, the following information can be gathered:

1. Assets generated by operations for the year were $212,783. This increase in assets is called revenue in accounting. Assets for this company increased during the year because of (a) sales of products for cash ($91,815), (b) sales of products on credit creating accounts receivable ($122,430), (c) interest charged on amounts owed to the company ($788), and (d) a deduction because some sales of products were returned by customers and assets, probably cash were given back to these customers ($2,250).

2. Assets consumed by operations for the year were $162,112. These decreases in assets are called expenses in accounting. For example, it can be determined from the statement that inventory with a cost of $94,991 was sold during the year (cost of goods sold), and supplies with a cost of $425 were used. Each of these expenses measures a decrease in assets due to operating activities for the period.

FIGURE 2-3
Income Statement for
a Small Business

P-J AUDIO COMPANY		
Income Statement and Statement of Owner Capital		
For the Year Ending February 1, 1982		

Revenues
Sales revenue	$214,245	
Sales returns	(2,250)	
Net sales revenue	211,995	
Interest revenue	788	$212,783

Expenses
Cost of goods sold	94,911	
Bad debt expense	2,449	
Supplies expense	425	
Insurance expense	2,000	
Advertising expense	7,000	
Depreciation expense	933	
Salaries expense	16,535	
Commission expense	14,625	
Utilities expense	5,420	
Rent expense	15,000	
Interest expense	378	
Miscellaneous expense	2,356	162,112

Net income	$ 50,671
P-J, capital, February 1, 1981	199,852
P-J, capital, February 1, 1982	$250,523

3. Net income for the period was $50,671. This means that the net amount of assets (assets generated minus assets consumed) created by operating activities for the year was $50,671. P-J Audio Company is better off by this amount because of its profit-seeking activities for the period. The corresponding increase is in owners' equity, since none of these assets were withdrawn by the owner.

Income Statement for a Large Corporation

The information conveyed by Exxon's income statement in Figure 2-4 is similar to that just discussed. Notice, however, that the amount of detail presented in the statement is considerably less than that available from the small business income statement. Because of the large number of different types of revenues and expenses in large corporations, these companies tend to group revenues and expenses into major categories and to show only these categories on the income statement.

The basic format of the corporate income statement is almost identical to that of unincorporated businesses except for two areas. Corporate income statements show an additional expense, called income tax expense, and present an earnings per share figure along with net income. The income tax expense is necessary because corporations are taxed directly on their income while proprietorships and partnerships are not.

FIGURE 2-4
Income Statement for
a Large Corporation

Exxon Corporation Consolidated Statement of Income For the Year Ending December 31		
Revenue	*1977*	*1976*
Sales and other operating revenue (including excise taxes)	$57,529,219,000	$51,626,149,000
Dividends, interest and other revenue	929,186,000	958,672,000
	58,458,405,000	52,584,821,000
Costs and other deductions		
Crude oil and product purchases	29,274,010,000	26,776,289,000
Operating expenses	5,390,211,000	4,664,760,000
Selling, general and administrative expenses	2,954,671,000	2,718,677,000
Depreciation and depletion	1,558,326,000	1,448,369,000
Exploration expenses, including dry holes	596,642,000	423,625,000
Income, excise, and other taxes	15,578,609,000	13,507,802,000
Interest expense	398,902,000	396,094,000
Foreign exchange translation loss (gain)	186,581,000	105,411,000
Income applicable to minority interests	97,489,000	113,652,000
	56,035,441,000	49,943,857,000
Net income	$ 2,422,964,000	$2,640,964,000
Per share	$ 5.41	$5.90

Source: Exxon Corporation Annual Report for 1977.

Earnings per Share Corporations may have many owners, each of whom actually owns only a small percentage of the company. The information content of corporate income statements is improved if net income can be related to the number of shares of stock outstanding and a per share figure for income (earnings) presented. Earnings per share simply denotes the amount of the current period's income that each share of stock may claim. It is calculated as

$$\frac{\text{Net income}}{\text{Number of shares of stock outstanding}}$$

For an individual stockholder of Exxon, it may be difficult to identify with a net income of $2.4 billion, a very large figure. However, a per-share figure of $5.41 can be much more meaningful to an owner, particularly since the selling price of stock is stated on a per-share basis.

Accrual versus Cash Basis Accounting

One further point should be made before leaving the income statement. This point has to do with timing the recognition of revenue and expense. At what point in its profit-seeking activities should a business recognize accomplishment (revenue) and effort (expense)? The idea that a business should recognize accomplishment and the related effort when any asset (not just cash) is created or consumed is the basis for what is termed **accrual accounting.** The idea that revenue and expense should be recognized only when cash is affected is called **cash basis accounting.**

Most businesses use accrual accounting systems, while most individuals and some small businesses use cash basis accounting. In accrual systems, revenue is recognized when a product is sold or a service performed, even though cash may not be received at that point. Likewise, an expense can be recognized without requiring a payment of cash under accrual accounting. Accrual accounting divorces the recognitition of revenues and expenses from the inflow or outflow of cash. Throughout this book, the focus will be on accrual basis accounting for businesses.

Concept Summary

Guidelines for the Recognition of Revenue and Expense		
Accounting System	Revenue	Expense
Cash basis	Cash is received from profit-seeking activities.	Cash is paid for profit-seeking activities.
Accrual basis	Any asset is received from profit-seeking activites—usually when product is sold or services rendered.	Any asset is consumed or liability created from profit-seeking activities—usually matched to revenue.

2.4 Statement of Retained Earnings/Owners' Capital

Two primary statements produced by the financial accounting process and the major concepts underlying them have now been examined in detail. The balance sheet and income statement connect and interact at owners' equity. Net income minus the amount of assets withdrawn by the owners (dividends or withdrawals) represents the amount by which indirect investment has increased during a period. This interaction between the two major financial statements is so important that a third financial statement is created to emphasize and communicate the connection. This statement for a corporation is called a statement of retained earnings, and its purpose is to make explicit the effect of net income and dividends on the basic accounting equation. The general format of this statement is illustrated below for the small business whose income statement and balance sheets were presented earlier in this chapter.

SMALL BUSINESS
Statement of Retained Earnings
For the Month of January

Retained earnings, January 1 .... $200
Net income for the year 150
Dividends 0
Retained earnings, January 31 .... $350

Statement of Owners' Capital

Proprietorships and partnerships do not report a separate retained earnings figure. These unincorporated businesses report only one owners' equity figure per owner on the balance sheet, lumping together the direct and indirect investment of each owner. In this case, a statement of owners' capital would be prepared instead of a retained earnings statement. The basic format of this statement, however, is the same as that of a retained earnings statement.

SAMPLE PROPRIETORSHIP
Statement of Owners' Capital
For the Year Ending December 31, 1982

X capital, January 1, 1982		$XXX
Additional investment by X during 1982		XX
		XXX
Net income for 1982	$ XX	
Withdrawals by X during 1982	(XX)	XXX
X capital, December 31, 1982		$XXX

In a partnership, a separate statement of owners' capital would be prepared for each owner.

Retained Earnings Statement for a Large Corporation

Figure 2-5 presents a statement of retained earnings for Exxon Corporation. The earnings reinvested (retained earnings) statement for 1977 depicts several figures which together connect the income statement and balance sheet for Exxon. The balance at the beginning of the year ($15.8 billion) is the retained earnings figure which appears on the December 31, 1976, balance sheet given in Figure 2-2. Net income is taken from the income statement for 1977 given in Figure 2-4 ($2.4 billion), and dividends ($1.3 billion) are taken from the company records. The balance at the end of the year ($16.9 billion) appears as the retained earnings figure on the December 31, 1977, balance sheet in Figure 2-2.

This statement should make clear the connection between the income statement and balance sheet. The indirect investment of owners in a business is increased by net income and decreased by dividends. This fact can

FIGURE 2-5
Retained Earnings Statement for a Large Corporation

Exxon Corporation Consolidated Statement of Retained Earnings For the Year Ending December 31		
	1977	*1976*
Earnings reinvested		
Balance at beginning of year	$15,861,761,000	$14,440,931,000
Net income	2,422,964,000	2,640,964,000
Dividends ($3.00 per share in 1977 and $2.725 in 1976)	(1,343,869,000)	(1,220,134,000)
Balance at end of year	$16,940,856,000	$15,861,761,000

Source: Exxon Corporation Annual Report for 1977.

be confirmed by rechecking the expansion of the basic accounting equation presented earlier in this chapter. The difference between these two figures, approximately $1.1 billion for Exxon Corporation, is the net amount of assets generated by the profit-seeking activities of the current period that were retained in the business. In order for the basic accounting equation to balance, there must be a corresponding increase in owners' equity. That increase is reflected in retained earnings, and the retained earnings statement explains how the increase came about. The statement accounts for the change in retained earnings from one balance sheet to the next.

Refer to the P-J Audio Company income statement illustrated in Figure 2-3. The statement of owners' capital for this proprietorship is added to the bottom of the income statement. This treatment of a statement of owners' capital is not unusual and may be more convenient than preparing a separate owners' capital statement.

Concept Summary

Contrast of Statements of Retained Earnings and Owners' Capital		
	Retained Earnings	*Owners' Capital*
Number of statements each period	One statement which represents the indirect investment of all stockholders	One statement for each owner which represents the total investment of that owner
Inclusion of direct investment	Only indirect investment and the change resulting from current period's activities are reported	Direct investment and indirect investment for each owner and the change resulting from current period's activities are reported
Increases on statement	Net income	Owner contributions; net income
Decreases on statement	Dividends; net loss	Withdrawals; net loss

The important fundamental concepts underlying financial statements have now been examined. The discussions have necessarily been somewhat conceptual, but a strong grasp of fundamental principles will aid in handling the mechanics of the financial accounting process which follow.

Summary

The two primary financial statements produced by the financial accounting process are the income statement and balance sheet. The balance sheet is an elaboration of the basic accounting equation, $A = L + OE$. Preparing a balance sheet requires an understanding of the definition and valuation of assets, liabilities, and owners' equity.

The balance sheet is a static statement which presents assets, liabilitites, and owners' equity as of a specific point in time. Not all of the resources of a business will appear on its balance sheet, and those that are reported as assets are valued at their original or acquisition cost. Liabilities and owners' equity represent general claims against the assets of the business with liabilities measuring a primary, or prior, claim to that of owners' equity.

The income statement reports the results of operating (profit-seeking) activities for a period of time. It consists of revenues and expenses. Revenue is an abstraction which measures gross increases in assets traceable to profit-seeking activities. Expense is an abstraction which measures decreases in or consumption of assets traceable to profit-seeking activities. Revenue minus expense gives net income, which indicates the amount of new assets generated by the successful profit-seeking activities of the business.

The statement of retained earnings (or owners' capital) connects the income statement and balance sheet. Owners' equity is increased by net income for the period and decreased by the amount of these new assets withdrawn from the business by the owners for their personal use.

Thus, the income statement and balance sheet are related. The statements come together at owners' equity, and this connection is reflected in the statement of retained earnings (owners' capital).

The accounting process that produces these financial statements is examined in Chapters 3 and 4.

Key Terms

Accrual accounting	Expense
Acquisition cost	Historical cost
Capital stock	Indirect investment
Cash basis accounting	Net income
Direct investment	Retained earnings
Dividends	Revenue
Earnings per share	Withdrawals

Comprehensive Review Problem

Alice Adams opened Wonderful Bargains Fashions on January 1, 1982. The balance sheet on opening day was as follows:

WONDERFUL BARGAINS FASHIONS
Balance Sheet
January 1, 1982

ASSETS

Cash	$19,000
Inventory	8,000
Supplies	2,000
Prepaid advertising	3,000
Furniture and fixtures	12,000
Building	36,000
Total assets	$80,000

LIABILITIES & OWNERS' EQUITY

Liabilities

Accounts payable	$ 5,000
Notes payable	6,000
Loan payable	20,000
Total liabilities	31,000

Owners' equity

Alice Adams, capital	49,000
Total liabilities & owners' equity	$80,000

The following transactions occurred during the month:

1. An additional $12,000 of inventory was purchased on credit. Wonderful Bargains paid suppliers $6,000 during the month for previous credit purchases.

2. Monthly sales revenue was $20,000. Of these sales, $8,500 were for cash and $11,500 were on credit. The merchandise sold cost the business $12,500.

3. An examination of supplies on hand as of January 31 showed that $200 worth had been used up.

4. $1,000 of the prepaid advertising was used up during January.

5. Other expenses of the month were $300 for utilities, which had been paid, and $4,000 for salaries, which had not been paid.

6. $500 of defective furniture was returned to the manufacturer who agreed to reduce the amount owed by Wonderful by $500.

7. During the month, Alice Adams withdrew $150 worth of merchandise and $500 in cash for her personal use.

Required:

1. Prepare an income statement and statement of owner's capital for the month ended January 31, 1982.
2. Prepare a balance sheet as of January 31, 1982.

Solution to Comprehensive Review Problem

WONDERFUL BARGAINS FASHIONS
Income Statement
For the Month ended January 31, 1982

Sales revenue		$20,000
Expenses		
Cost of sales	$12,500	
Salaries	4,000	
Advertising	1,000	
Utilities	300	
Supplies	200	18,000
Net income		$ 2,000

WONDERFUL BARGAINS FASHIONS
Statement of Owners' Capital
For the Month ended January 31, 1982

Alice Adams, capital, January 1, 1982	$49,000
Net income	2,000
Withdrawals	(650)
Alice Adams, capital, January 31, 1982	$50,350

WONDERFUL BARGAINS FASHIONS
Balance Sheet
January 31, 1982

ASSETS

Cash[1]	$20,700
Accounts receivable	11,500
Inventory[2]	7,350
Supplies	1,800
Prepaid advertising	2,000
Furniture and fixtures	11,500
Building	36,000
Total assets	$90,850

LIABILITIES & OWNERS' EQUITY

Liabilities

Accounts payable[3]	$10,500
Notes payable	6,000
Salaries payable	4,000
Loan payable	20,000
Total liabilities	40,500

Owners' equity

Alice Adams, capital	50,350
Total liabilities & owners' equity	$90,850

[1]*Cash computation:*
$19,000 beginning balance
+ 8,500 cash sales for month
− 6,000 cash paid to suppliers
− 300 cash paid for utility bill
− 500 cash withdrawn by owner
$20,700 ending balance

[2]*Inventory computation:*
$ 8,000 beginning balance
+ 12,000 inventory purchased during month
− 12,500 cost of inventory sold during month
− 150 inventory withdrawn by owner
$ 7,350 ending balance

[3]*Accounts payable computation:*
$ 5,000 beginning balance
+ 12,000 purchases on credit
− 6,000 paid to suppliers on credit purchases
− 500 return of defective furniture to supplier
$10,500 ending accounts payable

Questions

Q2-1. How are assets usually valued for balance sheet purposes? How are cash and receivables valued for balance sheet purposes?

Q2-2. Summarize the major characteristics of owners' equity. How does corporate owners' equity differ from that of unincorporated businesses?

Q2-3. Are all the resources of value to a business listed on its balance sheet? Why or why not? If not, give three examples of resources which would not appear on a balance sheet.

Q2-4. Describe the three types of activities businesses engage in between balance sheets?

Q2-5. What do revenue and expense measure? What does net income measure?

Q2-6. Contrast accrual and cash-basis accounting.

Q2-7. What is the function of the statement of retained earnings? How does this statement differ from a statement of owners' capital?

Q2-8. All changes in owners' equity are recorded in revenue and expense accounts. Is this statement correct? If not, give two examples of changes in owners' equity that do not involve revenue or expense.

Exercises

E2-1. On which financial statement or statements would each of the following items appear?

a. Cash
b. Sales revenue
c. Notes payable
d. Net income
e. Capital stock
f. Rent expense
g. Dividends

E2-2. The Ward Tax Service Company increased its assets as the result of the following two transactions: (1) cash was borrowed from the bank; and (2) tax services were performed for a client and the related fee collected.

a. Which of these activities is a financing activity and which is an operating activity?
b. In which activity were assets "acquired" by the company? In which activity were assets "created" by the company? Why is this distinction important?

E2-3. As of January 1, 1982, Malcolm Holmes had voluntarily and directly invested $100,000 in the Malcolm Holmes Company. He is the only owner of the company. Undistributed earnings of the company at January 1 amounted to $135,000. Between January 1, 1982, and December 31, 1982, the company earned revenues of $315,000, incurred expenses of $252,000, and distributed $50,000 to Holmes.

a. Assume that the company is operating as a sole proprietorship. Prepare a statement of owners' capital for the year ended December 31, 1982.
b. Assume that the company is operating as a corporation and that the $50,000 distribution to Holmes is a dividend. Prepare a statement of retained earnings for the year ended December 31, 1982.

E2-4. During the month of October, the Carlton Consulting Firm engaged in the following operating activities:

a. On October 1, rent of $800 for the month of October was paid.
b. On October 5, fees in the amount of $15,000 were collected from a client for services rendered during September.
c. During the month of October, services were performed for clients the fees for which amounted to $16,800. These fees were billed on October 31 and would be collected in November.
d. On October 30, services of an appraiser were used on one of the jobs being performed in October. The appraiser charged $500 for his services, and it was agreed that the consulting firm would pay the appraiser. At October 31, the appraiser's fee had not been paid.

e. On October 31, the salaries of employees of the firm for October were paid. Total salaries amounted to $6,000.

Required:

1. Prepare a cash basis income statement for the Carlton Consulting Firm for the month of October.

2. Prepare an accrual basis income statement for the Carlton Consulting Firm for the month of October.

E2-5. *a.* On January 1, 1982, Bill opened his own business with an investment of $15,000 of cash. On December 31, 1982, Bill determined that the company has total assets of $18,000 and owed creditors $2,000. During the year, Bill made no additional contribution to the company and made no withdrawals.

(1) What is Bill's total equity in the company at December 31?
(2) Identify two types of investment in the company that Bill has made and the amount of each.

b. Assume the same facts above except that, on December 31, 1982, the company owed creditors $4,000 instead of $2,000.

(1) What is Bill's total equity in the company at December 31?
(2) Explain the difference between this amount and Bill's original investment in the company.

E2-6. Comparing a certain company's balance sheet at the beginning of the year with its balance sheet at the end of the year, it is determined that total assets have increased by $50,000, total liabilities have decreased by $10,000, and capital stock has remained unchanged. During the year, dividends of $5,000 were paid to stockholders. What was the net income of the company for the year? What would be the change in retained earnings between the beginning of the year and the end of the year?

E2-7. *a.* Indicate the dollar amount that would be assigned each of the following items on a balance sheet:

(1) Inventory that was purchased for $10,000, would cost $12,000 to replace, and can be sold to customers for $20,000.
(2) Land that was purchased for $50,000 five years ago and is currently appraised for $100,000.
(3) Accounts receivable arising from credit sales to customers in the amount of $8,000 of which $500 is uncollectible.
(4) Amounts due to suppliers for inventory in (1), assuming all the inventory was purchased on credit.
(5) Note due to the bank in amount of $5,000, the proceeds of which were used to purchase marketable securities currently worth $7,000.
(6) An employment contract with an employee who produces $200,000 per year in sales, three times as much as any other salesman employed by competitors.

b. Based on your answers in *a*, give two reasons the balance sheet rarely shows the true value of a business.

c. If this company were forced to go out of business, could the bank that had loaned the money described in (5) be assured of getting the money back from the proceeds of the sale of the securities? Why?

E2-8. On June 1, 1982, Max Latter embarked on a short-term business venture in which he hoped to make a profit on a real estate deal. Wishing to account for this separately from his personal affairs, he set up the Latter Company, a sole proprietorship, to handle the transactions. On June 1, Max put $25,000 of his personal funds into the newly formed company. On the same day, the company borrowed $75,000 from Max's father, David Latter. No interest was to be paid on this loan. On June 20, the company purchased a piece of land for $85,000. On September 15, the company sold the land for $100,000 in cash. On October 1, the assets of the company were distributed to the parties having claims to them, and the company was dissolved.

a. Prepare the balance sheet of the Latter Company as of the end of business June 1, 1982.
b. Prepare the income statement of the Latter Company for the period June 1 to September 30, 1982, and prepare the balance sheet of the company as of September 30, 1982.
c. On October 1, how much cash was distributed to each of the parties having claims against the assets of Latter Company?

Problems

P2-1. Below is a list of balance sheet items for the Rusty Piper Plumbing Company as of June 30, 1982.

Supplies	$ 560
Accounts payable	430
Cash	1,350
Tools and equipment (net of depreciation)	1,740
Notes payable	3,620
Piper, capital	?
Accounts receivable	1,500
Truck (net of depreciation)	4,080

During the next two days, the following transactions occurred:

a. Piper withdrew $800 in cash.
b. Payments of $210 were made on accounts payable.
c. Collections of $500 were made on accounts receivable.
d. A new piece of equipment was purchased for $600. A cash payment of $150 was made and a note for $450 was signed.
e. Additional supplies were purchased for $70 to be paid in 30 days.

Required:

1. Prepare a balance sheet for the Rusty Piper Plumbing Company as of June 30, 1982.

2. Prepare a balance sheet for the Rusty Piper Plumbing Company as of July 2, 1982, after all of the above transactions have been taken into account.

P2-2. Joe Lerop, the sole proprietor of Lerop Realty Company, needs financial statements for his company in order to apply for a loan from the bank. He began the company on April 1, 1982, and the company has been in operation for two months. He comes to you with the following information about the financial position of the company at May 31, 1982, and the results of its operations for the two months ended May 31, 1982.

Joe Lerop's investment in company on April 1	$4,000
Revenues for April and May	3,600
Cash on hand and in the bank	600
Cost of office furniture and equipment	3,200
Note payable on office equipment	2,400
Accounts receivable for appraisal work	400
Cost of supplies used during April and May	200
Salary paid to secretary for April and May	1,300
Rent expense for April and May	1,000
Prepaid rent	500
Accounts payable	300
Withdrawals by Lerop during April and May	3,000
Unused supplies at May 31	100

Additional information: The note payable is due in twenty-four equal monthly installments of $100. The first is due on June 15, 1982, and the last due May 15, 1984.

Required:

1. Prepare an income statement for the Lerop Realty Company for the two months ended May 31, 1982.

2. Prepare a statement of owners' capital for the two months ended May 31, 1982.

3. Prepare a balance sheet as of May 31, 1982.

P2-3. John Ferrero is the owner of Ferrero Cookie Company. Mr. Ferrero purchased the land adjacent to his plant site eight years ago for $50,000. This year the tax assessor appraised the land at $73,000, and last week someone offered him $82,000 for the property. For financial accounting purposes, what valuation should be used for this land? Why? How would the remaining two values be treated in the financial statements? What would be the effect on the basic accounting equation of a sale of the land for $82,000?

P2-4. The Bourbon Company has engaged in six transactions. The figures below give the effect of each transaction on the basic accounting equation.

	Cash	+	Accounts Receivable	+	Inventory	+	Equipment	=	Accounts Payable	+	Owners' Equity
	3,100	+	10,600	+	23,000	+	5,000	=	11,700	+	30,000
a.	600		(600)								
	3,700	+	10,000	+	23,000	+	5,000	=	11,700	+	30,000
b.			2,500								2,500
	3,700	+	12,500	+	23,000	+	5,000	=	11,700	+	32,500
c.					(2,000)						(2,000)
	3,700	+	12,500	+	21,000	+	5,000	=	11,700	+	30,500
d.							1,200		1,200		
	3,700	+	12,500	+	21,000	+	6,200	=	12,900	+	30,500
e.	(1,700)								(1,700)		
	2,000	+	12,500	+	21,000	+	6,200	=	11,200	+	30,500
f.					5,000				5,000		
	2,000	+	12,500	+	26,000	+	6,200	=	16,200	+	30,500

Required:

1. For each of the six transactions labeled a through f, give a description of the nature of the transaction.

2. Prepare a beginning balance sheet, an income statement, a statement of owners' capital, and an ending balance sheet.

P2-5. Information about the financial position of the Burton Company at December 31, 1982, is given below.

a. Owners of the company had invested $412,000 in the company through the purchase of capital stock.

b. Amounts due from customers and expected to be collected totaled $428,000.

c. The company had borrowed $200,000 from the bank and signed a note for this amount. The loan was to be repaid on February 15, 1983.

d. The company had temporary investments of $110,000 in U.S. Government bonds. These were expected to be sold in June of 1983.

e. The company owed its suppliers $422,000, all of which was to be paid in January of 1983.

f. The company had long-term investments in stocks and bonds of $175,000.

g. In recent years, the company had acquired $563,000 in cash from creditors by issuing a series of notes. The first repayments to noteholders were not due until 1985.

h. The company had cash in the bank of $227,000 and cash on hand of $14,000.

i. The company owned land that it had purchased for $100,000 and building and equipment that it had purchased for $1,276,000. The unused cost of the building and equipment was $569,000.

j. The company had an inventory of merchandise for resale of $647,000 and an inventory of supplies of $32,000.

k. On December 30, 1982, the company had paid an insurance premium of $24,000. The policy provided coverage from January 1, 1983 to December 31, 1984.

l. Retained earnings at December 31, 1982, were $729,000.

Required:
Prepare a balance sheet for the Burton Company as of December 31, 1982.

P2-6. The operating activities of Kennedy Electrical Service for the month of March are listed below.

a. Fees for jobs performed in March for which cash was collected
at the time the job was performed $15,000

b. Collection of accounts receivable 4,500

c. Fees for jobs performed in March to be collected later 7,000

d. Cash purchase of supplies 350

e. Payments to employees for salaries earned in February 2,000

f. Supplies used in March 600

g. Payments of March rents on office and trucks 2,500

h. Salaries earned by employees in March and paid in March ... 12,000

i. Salaries earned by employees in March to be paid in April ... 3,000

Required:
1. Prepare an accrual basis income statement for the month of March.

2. Prepare a cash-basis income statement for the month of March.

P2-7. The balance sheet for the Simon T. Stocker Company at August 31 is given below.

ASSETS

Cash	$ 6,000
Accounts receivable	17,100
Inventory	32,500
Equipment	9,400
Total assets	$65,000

LIABILITIES & OWNERS' EQUITY

Liabilities

Accounts payable	$15,300

Owners' Equity

Stocker, capital	49,700
Total liabilities & owners' equity	$65,000

During the first week in September, the following transactions took place.

a. Stocker withdrew $3,000 in cash from the company.

b. Collections on accounts receivable amounting to $6,200 were made.

c. Payments on accounts payable of $5,700 were made.

d. Cash sales for the week amounted to $800.

e. Credit sales for the week amounted to $1,400.

f. The cost of inventory sold during the week was $1,500.

g. Inventory costing $1,000 was purchased on account.

h. Equipment costing $2,700 was purchased for cash.

Required:

1. Prepare a transaction table like the one shown in problem 2-4. Begin the table with the balances shown on the balance sheet at August 31. Show the effects of each transaction listed above on the balance sheet amounts. Use a separate line for each transaction, and calculate new balance sheet amounts after each transaction.

2. Prepare an accrual basis income statement and a statement of owners' capital for the week ended September 7 and prepare a balance sheet at September 7.

P2-8. Below is the income statement and statement of owners' capital of the Harvey Couch Company for the month ended January 31, 1982.

HARVEY COUCH COMPANY
Income Statement and Statement of Owners' Capital
For the Month Ending January 31, 1982

Revenues		$26,000
Expenses		
Cost of goods sold	$17,000	
Rent expense	1,000	
Salaries expense	2,000	
Payroll tax expense	150	
Advertising expense	400	
Utilities expense	300	
Supplies expense	150	
Depreciation expense	200	21,200
Net income		$ 4,800
Couch, capital, December 31, 1981		49,600
Couch, capital, January 31, 1982		$54,400

The income statement was prepared on an accrual basis. Revenues were recognized when they were earned rather than when cash was received. Expenses were recognized when they were incurred rather than when cash was paid. Specific details about the nature and timing of operating activities of the company are listed below.

a. All revenues came from the sale of merchandise on hand at the beginning of the month. No inventory was purchased during the month. One half of sales were cash sales and one half were credit sales.

b. The rent for any given month is paid on the 15th of the preceding month.

c. Salaries for the month are paid on the 15th and 30th of that month.

d. Utility expenses are based on amounts billed for the month. Bills are received at the end of the month and paid at a later date.

e. All supplies used during the month were on hand at the beginning of the month. No purchases of supplies were made during the month.

f. Depreciation expense measures the use of office equipment owned by the company.

g. All other expenses are paid for in cash at the time the expense is incurred.

h. No payments were made on liabilities during the month.

i. An accurate balance sheet is prepared from the accounting records at the end of each month.

Required:

Based on the information provided above, answer the following questions:

1. What changes in asset accounts do revenues for January measure? Indicate the specific asset account or accounts affected, the amount by which they changed, and whether the change was an increase or a decrease.

2. What changes in assets and liabilities do expenses for January measure? For each expense item, indicate the specific asset or liability account affected, the amount by which it changed, and whether the change was an increase or a decrease.

3. What is the dollar amount of the net change (increases less decreases) in assets as a result of profit-seeking activities for January? Indicate whether this net change was an increase or a decrease. Show your calculation.

4. What is the dollar amount of the net change in liabilities as a result of profit-seeking activities for January? Indicate whether this net change was an increase or a decrease. Show your calculation.

5. What portion (dollar amount) of the net increase in assets from profit-seeking activities in January (calculated in part 3) is associated with an increase in creditors' claims?

6. What portion (dollar amount) of the net increase in assets from profit-seeking activities in January is associated with an increase in the owner's claims? What is this amount called?

CHAPTER 3

The Accounting Cycle—
Double-Entry Bookkeeping

Chapter Outline

3.1 *Double-Entry Bookkeeping.* Introduction to the mechanics of the accounting process and the basic ideas behind a manual recording system.

3.2 *Transaction Analysis.* Discussion of the duality idea in accounting, that is, that all transactions have at least two different effects on the basic accounting equation and that total debits equal total credits; illustration of transaction analysis for a service firm, sole proprietorship.

3.3 *General Journal.* Presentation of the form, role, and functioning of the general journal; illustration of service firm transactions in the general journal.

3.4 *General Ledger and Trial Balance.* Presentation of the form, role, and functioning of the general ledger; preparation of the trial balance at the end of the accounting period; illustration of posting of service firm transactions to the general ledger and the resulting trial balance.

Accounting and the Real World

Fra Luca Pacioli

Fra Luca Pacioli, an Italian mathematician who is considered to be the "Father of Accounting," lived from about 1445 to 1520 and was a close friend of Renaissance master Leonardo da Vinci. In 1494, Pacioli published *De Computis et Scripturis* ("Of Reckonings and Writings"), a supplement on double-entry record keeping for merchants. For the first time, he detailed the system of accounting that had been in wide use in the commercial center of Venice for many years.

Pacioli was born in Borgo San Sepolcro, a small town in central Italy, and was early apprenticed to a wealthy merchant family. When he was twenty, he went to Venice to tutor the sons of a rich merchant named Rompiasi. Later he studied at the great universities of his time. In the 1470s he joined the Franciscans and began to teach both mathematics and theology. While Pacioli was never in business himself, he assisted in the bookkeeping process and instructed the Rompiasi children who would someday be expected to assist with their father's business.

Pacioli wrote that Italian merchants kept track of their business activities by making two entries, a debit and a credit. Additionally, each transaction was viewed separately. Further, Pacioli arranged his assets in much the same order as they are listed in a modern balance sheet, with cash and near-cash items listed first, followed by others of a more fixed nature.

There is, however, a major difference between Pacioli's system and modern accounting. Profit was not measured then for a specified period, such as a year, but only for specific ventures, such as a ship voyage, or for the life of a business.

The system described by Pacioli was not original with him, but he was the first to bring many diverse elements together in a way that has proved to be the foundation of modern double-entry bookkeeping. Indeed, Pacioli would feel right at home with the debits and credits of today.

The Journal of Accountancy, December 1977, © 1977 by the American Institute of Certified Public Accountants, Inc.
The Woman CPA, January 1977.

The basic ideas underlying accounting and financial statements were discussed in the first two chapters. In those chapters it was stressed that the income statement, statement of owner's capital or retained earnings, and balance sheet represent the output of the accounting process. The accounting process itself is discussed in this chapter. The series of steps any business goes through to produce meaningful financial reports from all of the events that occur in its life is called the **accounting cycle.** This cycle is a seven-step process which has as its goal recording, classifying, summarizing, and communicating financial information.

The accounting cycle includes the following steps:

1. *Journalize* the accounting transactions.

2. *Post* the accounting transactions.

3. Prepare a *trial balance.*

4. Journalize and post *adjusting entries.*

5. Prepare an *adjusted trial balance.*

6. Prepare *financial statements.*

7. Journalize and post *closing entries.*

This orderly series of actions occurs for every business during each accounting period. The first three steps of this process are examined in this chapter, while the following four steps are the subject of Chapter 4.

3.1 Double-Entry Bookkeeping

Financial statements represent the end result of the accounting process, and they are typically prepared once each accounting period. Because a firm prepares financial statements infrequently, it needs a technique for keeping track of the accounting events that occur in the time between the preparation of these financial statements. This technique should keep track of these events in a way that makes financial statements reasonably easy to prepare. Such a technique exists in accounting, and it is called **double-entry bookkeeping.**

Double-entry bookkeeping is a mechanism for the recording and classification of events in the life of a business. As such, it consists of two primary instruments, called the journal and the ledger. The **journal** is a device which facilitates the recording of events as they occur in the life of a business. It is simply a place for recording transactions in an orderly manner. The **ledger** is used to classify these events according to their effect on the assets, liabilities, owner's equity, revenue, and expense of the business. Thus, double-entry bookkeeping systems consist of journals and ledgers, where events are first recorded and then classified.

Ledger

Although events are recorded before they are classified and, therefore, the use of the journal naturally precedes the use of the ledger, double-entry bookkeeping will be easier to understand if the ledger is presented first. A ledger in accounting consists of an **account** for each asset, liability, owner's equity, revenue, and expense used by a business. Each account represents a particular asset, liability, owner's equity, revenue, or expense and may take any one of a number of forms.

T Account A very common and useful form is called a T Account and is illustrated in Figure 3-1. There are four basic characteristics of this T Account that are generally true about all such symbols.

1. The account is a symbol which stands for a specific asset (cash, accounts receivable, inventory, etc.), liability (accounts payable, notes payable, etc.), owner's equity (common stock, retained earnings, etc.), revenue (sales revenue, service revenue, etc.), or expense (rent expense, salary expense, etc.). The title of the account tells you exactly what it represents, and as additional identification, each account is assigned a unique number.

2. The account is divided into two distinct sides. These could have been called the "left" side and the "right" side with perfect accuracy; however, the specialized terms in accounting for them are debit and credit, respectively. **Debit** means the left side of any account; there is no value judgment implied in the term. Debits sometimes represent increases and sometimes represent decreases, but they are *always* recorded on the left. The term debit must not be interpreted to mean any more than the left side of an account. By the same token, **credit** means the right side of any account and nothing more.

3. The act of writing a number on the debit side of any account (as illustrated by the XXXs in Figure 3-1) is called *debiting* the account or making a **debit entry.** Debit entries cause some accounts to increase and others to decrease. Also, writing a number on the credit side of any account (as illustrated by the XXXs in Figure 3-1) is called *crediting* the account or making a **credit entry.** Credits cause some accounts to increase and others to decrease.

FIGURE 3-1
Form of a T Account

	Title	#
	Debit Side	*Credit Side*
Debit Entries	$ XXX XXX XXX • •	$ XXX XXX • • •	Credit Entries
	$ XXX Debit Balance	*or*	$ XXX Credit Balance

4. Every account at any point during the accounting period has a balance. If the debits in an account are larger in total than the credits, the balance in the account will be a debit and will be equal to the difference between the total debits and total credits. If the debits total $500 and the credits total $200, the account will have a **debit balance** of $300. If the credits are larger, the sum of the debits should be subtracted from the sum of the credits and the resulting balance will be a credit. If the debits total $100 and the credits total $800, the account will have a **credit balance** of $700. Every account has a debit balance, a credit balance, or a zero balance.

Double-Entry Patterns

The ideas of the T Account and the basic accounting equation combine to form the fundamental principles of double-entry bookkeeping. A business ledger is a collection of one account for each asset, liability, owner's equity, revenue, and expense; therefore, it can be pictured as a loose-leaf notebook with an account on each page. No matter how many individual assets a business may have, the double-entry bookkeeping pattern is the same for every asset. Also, the patterns are alike for all liabilities, for all owner's equities, and so on.

In bookkeeping, because there are five types of accounts, there are five possible behavior patterns for accounts. These are illustrated in Figure 3-2.

Assets, Liabilities, and Owner's Equity Figure 3-2 indicates that *all* assets are increased by debits and decreased by credits. When numbers are written on the debit side of an account representing an asset, the balance of

FIGURE 3-2
Behavior Patterns for Accounts

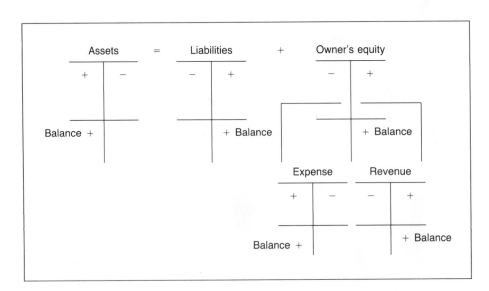

that account increases. Thus, a $200 debit to the cash account increases that account balance by $200. Similarly, numbers written on the credit side of any asset account cause that balance to decrease. Thus, a $100 credit to the cash account decreases that account balance by $100. At any time each asset must have a debit balance (or a zero balance if it has been used up) in a double-entry system. Liabilities and owner's equity accounts exhibit the opposite behavior pattern, with debits resulting in decreases and credits causing increases in balances. At any time, the balances in any liability or owner's equity account will be a credit or zero.

Revenue and Expense The double-entry pattern for revenue and expense is slightly more complex, primarily because the behavior of these account types is derived from that of owner's equity. The progression of equations in Chapter 2 demonstrated the conceptual relationship between owner's equity, revenue, and expense. For a sole proprietorship, the resulting equation would be

$$\text{Assets} = \text{Liabilities} + \text{Owner's Contributions}$$
$$+ \, \Sigma \, (\text{Revenue} - \text{Expense} - \text{Withdrawals by Owner})$$

For a corporation, the equation would be

$$\text{Assets} = \text{Liabilities} + \text{Capital Stock}$$
$$+ \, \Sigma \, (\text{Revenue} - \text{Expense} - \text{Dividends})$$

The double-entry bookkeeping rules for these accounts are simply mechanical reflections of these relationships. Expense is, in effect, a reduction of owner's equity. Thus, as expense increases, owner's equity decreases. The logical implementation of this connection in double-entry fashion is that debits cause expense to increase; but as expense increases, owner's equity decreases. A $100 debit to expense will cause expense to increase by $100, but will cause owner's equity to decrease by $100. Hence, the plus-minus pattern illustrated in Figure 3-2 is perfectly logical. By the same token, credits to expense (very rare, except for closing entries to be discussed in the next chapter) cause them to decrease.

The relationship between revenue and owner's equity is also demonstrated by the same equation set. As a business earns revenue, the ultimate effect on the basic accounting equation is an increase in owner's equity. Because this positive connection exists between revenue and owner's equity, the debit-credit rules should be the same for both of these types of accounts. In fact, the rules are exactly the same: Credits cause increases in revenue and owner's equity, and debits result in decreases. A $100 credit to revenue will increase revenue by $100 and increase owner's equity by $100.

The important tie-in between these income statement and balance sheet accounts was discussed in Chapter 2. These double-entry relationships are just a reflection of this tie-in. Thus, conceptual definitions of revenue and expense in Chapter 2 provide the logic behind the debit-credit rules for revenue and expense.

**Concept
Summary**

Debit and Credit Effects on Accounts		
Account	Debit Effect	Credit Effect
Assets	Increase	Decrease
Liabilities	Decrease	Increase
Owner's equity	Decrease	Increase
Revenues	Decrease	Increase
Expenses	Increase	Decrease
Account	Increased By	Decreased By
Assets	Debit	Credit
Liabilities	Credit	Debit
Owner's equity	Credit	Debit
Revenues	Credit	Debit
Expenses	Debit	Credit

3.2 Transaction Analysis

Double-entry bookkeeping is an internally logical system. There is no situation faced by a business which cannot be easily handled within its rules if the distinction made in accounting between events and transactions is clear, and the duality idea is understood.

**Events and
Transactions**

Accounting is not concerned with all of the events in which a business may engage. Business events that become a part of accounting are called **transactions** or **accounting events.** For an event to be considered by the accounting process (that is, recorded, classified, summarized, and communicated), the event must immediately affect one or more parts of the basic accounting equation. Transactions, then, are events that alter in some fashion the $A = L + OE$ equation (including the role of revenue and expense). Thus, transactions are the raw data of accounting.

Duality

Double-entry bookkeeping derives its name from its view of accounting transactions as two-sided events. All transactions have at least two different effects on the basic accounting equation (otherwise equality could not possibly be maintained). For *every* transaction, there is at least one debit effect and at least one credit effect, and the *total* debits *always* equal the *total* credits for each transaction. This is called the **duality** idea in accounting and is the basis for one of the self-checks built into the double-entry bookkeeping system. The process of determining the debit effects and the credit effects of an accounting event is called **transaction analysis.**

There is a second version of the basic accounting equation in bookkeeping terms. The following two statements are equivalent in accounting, except for the perspective taken. The first equation is the conceptually based basic accounting model of the firm, and the second is a mechanical bookkeeping oriented statement. Both are always true.

$$\text{Assets} = \text{Liabilities} + \text{Owner's Equity}$$
$$\text{Debits} = \text{Credits}$$

Concept Summary

Conceptual Model and Bookkeeping Orientations		
	Debit Balances	*Credit Balances*
Balance Sheet	Assets	Liabilities Owner's equity
Income Statement	Expense	Revenue

Sample Company

This chapter illustrates the first month of operation for the George S. Farnsworth Company. This firm is a sole proprietorship which provides real estate investment services and sells real estate on commission. This section discusses the activities of the month and the transaction analysis of those activities. Because accounting deals only with transactions, there may not be an accounting treatment for every activity. The remainder of this chapter shows how the accounting events are recorded, classified, and summarized for this firm. Before any transactions occur, the basic accounting equation is satisfied, because A, L, and OE are all zero $(0 = 0 + 0)$.

   A. *September 1, 1981. Mr. George S. Farnsworth opened a bank account for the George S. Farnsworth Company by depositing $15,000 of his own funds.* This bank deposit increased the assets of the firm by $15,000. At the same time, it created a claim by the owner in the amount of $15,000. Thus, the equality $A = L + OE$ was maintained, because both sides of the equation increased by $15,000.
   Increases in asset accounts are represented by debits, that is, entries on the left side of the account. Thus, the increase in cash by $15,000 would be represented by the following:

Cash	
A 15,000	

(Dollar signs are not normally used in ledger accounts.)
   Increases in owner's equity accounts are represented by credits, that is, entries on the right side of the account. Thus, the increase in the claim by the owner would be represented by the following:

Farnsworth, capital

	A 15,000

Therefore, the bookkeeping identity, debits = credits, is maintained, because both are equal to $15,000.

B. September 1, 1981. Mr. Farnsworth sent a check for $600 to LFR Enterprises as payment for September rent. Payment for a service of the current period increases expense by $600 and, thus, decreases owner's equity by $600. Cash, an asset, also decreased by $600. The basic accounting equation, therefore, stays in balance, because both sides of the equation decrease by $600.

Increases in expense are represented by debits. Thus, the increase in rent expense by $600 would be represented by the following:

Rent expense

B 600	

Decreases in assets are represented by credits. Thus, the decrease in cash would be represented by the following:

Cash

A 15,000	B 600

The bookkeeping identity is maintained, as both debits and credits for this transaction are equal to $600.

C. September 3, 1981. The company earned $100 in commission revenue from the sale of a small piece of rural property. The cash would be received next month. This occurrence creates one asset, while increasing owner's equity; therefore, it affects the basic accounting equation and is an accounting event. The asset created is a receivable, because the money will be sent later to the George S. Farnsworth Company. Revenue increased by the amount earned. Thus, the basic accounting equation remains in balance: Total assets increase by $100, while owner's equity also increases by $100.

Increases in assets are represented by debits. The creation of the receivable is represented by

Accounts receivable

C 100	

Increases in revenue are represented by credits, and the increase would be represented by

Commission revenue
	C 100

The bookkeeping identity is maintained because debits = $100 = credits.

D. September 4, 1981. The George S. Farnsworth Company received $8,000 as the real estate commission on the sale of a $150,000 house. Because cash is received, assets increase by $8,000. Similarly, a service has been performed and completed, so there is a commission revenue of $8,000. As revenue increases by $8,000, owner's equity increases by an equal amount. $A = L + OE$ remains true, as both sides of the equation increase by $8,000.

Increases in assets are represented by debits, so the receipt of cash would be represented by

Cash
A 15,000	B 600
D 8,000	

Increases in revenue (and, thus, in owner's equity) are represented by credits, so the recognition of revenue would be represented by

Commission revenue
	C 100
	D 8,000

The bookkeeping identity remains true, as both debits and credits are equal to $8,000.

E. September 7, 1981. Mr. Farnsworth met with a representative of Monogram Printing, Inc., and ordered $800 of office supplies, including company stationery. This occurrence is *not* an accounting event because it does not affect the basic accounting equation. No asset has been received or created because of this event. Similarly, no liability has been created, because it is still possible to cancel the order or to refuse the shipment.

F. September 10, 1981. Mr. Farnsworth negotiated a loan to the company of $2,100 from the Whitney National Bank. The loan was for sixty days at an annual interest rate of 12 percent. The bank loan increased cash and, hence, assets by $2,100. At the same time, the loan created a $2,100 claim by the bank against the assets of the company. This is a generalized claim against all assets of the company and is not tied specifically to particular assets.

Because the bank is a nonowner, this claim is a liability. Thus, assets go up by $2,100 and liabilities go up by $2,100, so the $A = L + OE$ equation is maintained. There is no liability yet for interest; that liability will be created as time goes by.

Increases in assets are represented by debits, so the receipt of $2,100 in cash would be represented by

Cash	
A 15,000	B 600
D 8,000	
F 2,100	

Increases in liabilities are represented by credits, so the creation of the $2,100 claim by the bank would be represented by

Note payable	
	F 2,100

The bookkeeping identity is, therefore, maintained; both the debit and the credit are for $2,100.

G. September 11, 1981. The company purchased a typewriter from IBM for cash. The total cost of the typewriter was $900. This transaction increased assets by $900, as the company obtained a $900 typewriter. On the other hand, the transaction decreased assets by $900, because the company paid out $900 in cash. Thus, the $A = L + OE$ equality is unchanged. One asset increased, but another decreased by the same amount, leaving no net change.

Asset increases are represented by debits, so the asset increase would be represented by

Equipment	
G 900	

The account *Equipment* is used rather than *Typewriter*, because most firms will have additional pieces of equipment besides the typewriter. Such pieces of equipment would include an intercom system, a postage meter, and the like. To avoid cluttering up the balance sheet, accountants generally collect all such assets under the account title *Equipment*.

Asset decreases are represented by credits, so the $900 payment would be represented by

Cash

A 15,000	B 600
D 8,000	G 900
F 2,100	

The debit and credit are both for $900.

H. September 15, 1981. Mr. Farnsworth paid Miss Manette Sartain for the first half of September for secretarial services. Miss Sartain is to receive a salary of $1,000 per month, paid on the fifteenth of every month. Because there has been only a half month's operation in September, she is only paid half of her regular salary. The cost of Miss Sartain's services is an expense to the company; because this payment is for half a month's services, the expense is $500. In effect, then, owner's equity will decrease by $500. Therefore, as a result of this transaction, (1) assets have decreased by $500 and (2) owner's equity has decreased by $500.

Increases in expenses are represented by debits, so the salary expense of $500 would be represented by

Salary expense

H 500	

Decreases in assets are represented by credits, so the payment to Miss Sartain would be represented by

Cash

A 15,000	B 600
D 8,000	G 900
F 2,100	H 500

The bookkeeping identity is maintained because debits and credits = $500.

I. September 18, 1981. The company paid $3,000 to the New Orleans **Times-Picayune** *for advertising in the first two weeks of the month.* The advertising has already appeared, so the $3,000 cost is an expense. (If the payment were for advertising that was to appear in the future, the cost would be recorded as an asset called *Prepaid advertising*). Expenses reduce owner's equity by that amount. At the same time, $3,000 was paid out of cash, so assets have been reduced by that amount. The $A = L + OE$ equation stays in balance because each side is reduced by $3,000.

Increases in expenses (and, thus, decreases in owner's equity) are represented by debits. This advertising expense would be represented by

Advertising expense

| I 3,000 |

Decreases in assets are represented by credits, and this reduction in cash would be represented by

Cash

A 15,000	B 600
D 8,000	G 900
F 2,100	H 500
	I 3,000

Debits and credits are both $3,000 in this transaction.

J. September 21, 1981. Monogram Printing delivered the office supplies ordered on September 7. An invoice requesting payment of $800 accompanied the shipment. Although the order of these supplies was not an accounting event, the delivery along with a request for payment is an event. Assets have increased by $800, and there is now a liability of $800 for the amount owed to Monogram. This maintains the $A = L + OE$ equality, because both assets and liabilities have increased by $800.

Increases in assets are represented by debits, so the increase of office supplies would be represented by

Supplies

| J 800 |

Increases in liabilities are represented by credits, so the increase in accounts payable would be represented by

Accounts payable

| J 800 |

Equality is maintained in the bookkeeping identity, because both debits and credits are equal to $800.

K. September 22, 1981. Stable Enterprises sent a check to the company for $1,500. This payment was for an appraisal the company was going to do of a small shopping center Stable is developing. Assets (in this instance, cash) increased by $1,500 as a result of this transaction. However, the company cannot recognize revenue in this amount because the service (an appraisal for Stable Enterprises) has not been performed. Instead, the company has incurred a liability of $1,500 because (1) it is now obligated to render the service to Stable, and (2) it must return the payment to Stable if the service is not performed. (When the service is subsequently performed, the liability will be extinguished and the revenue will be recognized.) Thus, the $A = L + OE$ equality is maintained, because both assets and liabilities increase by $1,500.

Asset increases are represented by debits, so the $1,500 receipt of cash would be represented by

Cash

A 15,000	B 600
D 8,000	G 900
F 2,100	H 500
K 1,500	I 3,000

Increases in liabilities are represented by credits, so the $1,500 liability would be represented by

Advances from customers

	K 1,500

Debits and credits are both $1,500.

L. September 24, 1981. The company paid $500 to Monogram Printing on account. The payment of $500 cash decreases assets by that amount. At the same time, the company reduces its liability to Monogram Printing by that same $500. The $A = L + OE$ equality is still valid, because both assets and liabilities have decreased by $500.

Liability decreases are represented by debits, so the decrease in the amount owed Monogram would be represented by

Accounts payable

L 500	J 800

Asset decreases are represented by credits, so the payment of $500 would be represented by

Cash

A 15,000	B 600
D 8,000	G 900
F 2,100	H 500
K 1,500	I 3,000
	L 500

Debits and credits are both equal to $500.

M. September 29, 1981. Mr. Farnsworth withdrew $2,500 from the busi-ness. The payment to Mr. Farnsworth of $2,500 reduced cash and, hence, assets by that amount. The same payment also reduced owner's equity by $2,500. Unlike the payment to the secretary (see H above), this payment is not an expense. Because the money is paid to the owner of a sole pro-prietorship, this payment is a withdrawal. The $A = L + OE$ equality is maintained, because assets and owner's equity decrease by an identical $2,500.

Decreases to owner's equity are represented by debits, so the with-drawal would be represented by

Farnsworth, withdrawals	
M 2,500	

Decreases of assets are represented by credits, so the $2,500 payment will be represented by

Cash			
A 15,000		B	600
D 8,000		G	900
F 2,100		H	500
K 1,500		I	3,000
		L	500
		M	2,500

Debits and credits are then both $2,500.

The discussion of these transactions has illustrated the two ways of viewing transactions:

1. How the transaction affects assets, liabilities, owner's equity, and the basic accounting equation.

2. How to translate the transaction into debit-credit terms and maintain the bookkeeping identity.

3.3 General Journal

The beginning of the accounting cycle is based almost entirely on trans-action analysis and the basic principles of double-entry bookkeeping. The first step in the cycle is to **journalize** the accounting transactions. This journalizing is usually done as the transactions take place or shortly af-terward. The journal should be thought of as the *book of original entry* because all transactions are first written down in the business journal.

Actually, most businesses use several different types of journals; however, this chapter will consider only one type, called the *general journal*. Several of the other most commonly used journals will be discussed in Chapter 7. Figure 3-3 is an example of a segment of a typical general journal.

FIGURE 3-3
General Journal

			GEORGE S. FARNSWORTH COMPANY General Journal			Page 1
Date			Transaction Accounts	PR	Debit Amount	Credit Amount
1981 Sept	1		Cash Farnsworth, capital Original capital contribution	1 90	15000	15000
	1		Rent expense Cash Payment of rent	15 1	600	600
	3		Accounts receivable Commission revenue Earn real estate commission	10 110	100	100
	4		Cash Commission revenue Receive real estate commission	1 110	8000	8000
	10		Cash Note payable Make loan from Whitney bank	1 55	2100	2100
	11		Equipment Cash Purchase typewriter from IBM	30 1	900	900
	15		Salary expense Cash Salary payment to M. Sartain	155 1	500	500
	18		Advertising expense Cash Payment to *Times-Picayune*	160 1	3000	3000
	21		Supplies Accounts payable Credit purchase from Monogram	20 50	800	800
	22		Cash Advances from customers Payment for appraisal by Stable	1 75	1500	1500
	24		Accounts payable Cash Payment to Monogram on account	50 1	500	500
	29		Farnsworth, withdrawals Cash Payment to owner	95 1	2500	2500

Characteristics of Journals

The primary task of journals, no matter what the type, is to accomplish the recording function of the accounting process. There must be a place where a business can record the accounting events as they occur. What is needed is a "diary" that gives a chronological history of the business. Additionally, these events must be recorded in a way that makes it easy to determine their effect on the assets, liabilities, owner's equity, revenue, and expense of the business. Hence, journals have a debit-credit orientation, so that all transactions can be recorded from that perspective. There are five important specific characteristics of journals.

Focus The focus of journals is on the accounting transaction. Each transaction is recorded in the journal separately from other transactions. Because transactions occur constantly in even the smallest of businesses, recording activity in journals tends to be daily and frequent.

Organization General journals are numbered by pages and are organized by dates, so that transactions are recorded when and in the order that they occur.

Recording Each transaction is analyzed and recorded in terms of its debit-credit effect. As discussed in the above section on transaction analysis, every transaction has a debit *and* a credit effect, which are equal. The specific account or accounts to be debited (increased or decreased) are written down first and against the margin. Then the accounts credited as a result of the transaction are entered indented from the left margin. The indentation must be sufficient to make it clear which accounts are debited and which are credited. A short explanation of the transaction is then given on the next line.

Posting The column headed **PR** is a **posting reference** column which tells where in the general ledger the amount has been posted, (that is, how it has been classified). To facilitate the use of this important information, each general ledger account is identified by a number as well as a name. As each amount is posted to (that is, classified in) the ledger, the account numbers are written in the PR column. Thus, the appearance of the number in the PR column indicates that the amount has been posted. By the same token, if the PR column is blank, that indicates that the amount has not been posted. This column will be dicussed in more depth in the next section of the chapter.

Amount Columns Finally, separate amount columns are provided for debit and credit amounts, with the debit amounts always written on the left as are the debit accounts.

Importance of Journal

The transactions journalized in Figure 3-3 are those presented earlier to illustrate transaction analysis. The recording of those transactions in the general journal in their debit-credit form follows directly from the transaction analysis. Because it is possible to determine the effects of a few simple transactions without the benefit of the general journal, the importance of these ideas may not be clear at this point. Analyzing and disclosing the effects of one hundred such transactions a day, every day for a year, however, would be difficult, if not impossible. For this reason, a precise instrument like a journal with a well-known and widely used format is necessary if a business is to record its accounting events properly.

Concept Summary

Conceptual and Bookkeeping Transaction Analysis		
George S. Farnsworth Company		
Transaction	*Debit Effect*	*Credit Effect*
A Owner contributed $15,000 cash	Asset + Cash 15000	Owner's equity + Capital 15000
B Paid $600 for rent	Expense + Rent expense 600	Asset − Cash 600
C Earned $100 as real estate commission	Asset + Receivable 100	Revenue + Commission revenue 100
D Received $8,000 for real estate commission	Asset + Cash 8000	Revenue + Commission revenue 8000
E Ordered $800 of office supplies	No effect	No effect
F Borrowed $2,100 from bank	Asset + Cash 2100	Liability + Note payable 2100
G Purchased typewriter for $900	Asset + Equipment 900	Asset − Cash 900
H Paid secretary $500	Expense + Salary expense 500	Asset − Cash 500
I Paid $3,000 for advertising	Expense + Advertising expense 3000	Asset − Cash 500
J Received supplies and invoice for them for $800	Asset + Supplies 800	Liability + Accounts payable 800
K Received $1,500 for work to be done later	Asset + Cash 1500	Liability + Advances 1500
L Paid $500 on account	Liability − Accounts payable 500	Asset − Cash 500
M Paid $2,500 to owner	Owner's equity − Withdrawals 2500	Asset − Cash 2500

3.4 General Ledger and Trial Balance

Recording the transactions of a business as they occur so that they are not forgotten or overlooked is critical to the accounting process, because the transactions are the raw data of the system. Recording, however, is only the beginning of the accounting cycle. To prepare useful reports about a business at the end of an accounting period, it is necessary to know the cumulative effect of all the transactions of a period on the accounts of the business. Determining this cumulative effect of all transactions on individual accounts is called *classification*. Classification involves the use of the second bookkeeping instrument, called the ledger.

Illustration of Posting

The second step in the accounting cycle is to **post** the transactions to the ledger. Figure 3-4 illustrates the posting of the first journal entry for the George S. Farnsworth Company. The general journal and both ledger accounts affected by this entry are included.

General Ledger Account This chapter has used a T account to represent each general ledger account. The T account has a number of advantages: it is clear, concise, and easy to use. However, because more information is needed, a more complex form of ledger account must be used in the accounting system of a real business. Figure 3-4 illustrates more realistic accounts for the George S. Farnsworth Company. To conserve space, the rest of the text will use abbreviated versions of these accounts.

Posting Order All components of the debit entry are posted first. Then all components of the credit entry are posted. In both instances, the first step is to put the amount in the proper ledger account. The second step is to transfer the date of the transaction from the journal to the ledger. The third step is to put the journal page number in the posting reference column of the general ledger account. The fourth and final step is to put the general ledger account number in the posting reference column of the journal. The explanation column is used to identify balances and is rarely used in the posting process.

Characteristics of Ledgers

The primary task of the ledger is to accomplish the classification function of the accounting process. The idea is to separate the debit and credit components of each transaction and then to group together all of the components that affect each individual asset, liability, owner's equity, revenue, and expense. Doing so will show the cumulative effect of all of the transactions on each account. There are five important specific characteristics of ledgers.

Focus The focus of the ledger is on the individual accounts of the business. Though fifty or one hundred or more transactions affecting cash may be spread throughout the journal, the ledger brings together all of these effects in the cash account so that the net change in cash from all of these events can be determined.

Timing of Posting Although it is important to know the net effect on all assets, liabilities, owner's equity, revenues, and expenses of a series of events, it is not necessary that the effect of each individual transaction be determined immediately as it occurs. The result is that posting to the ledger need not occur constantly. Posting usually takes place only after a number of transactions have occurred, perhaps every week or so.

FIGURE 3-4
Illustration of Posting
for the George S. Farnsworth Company

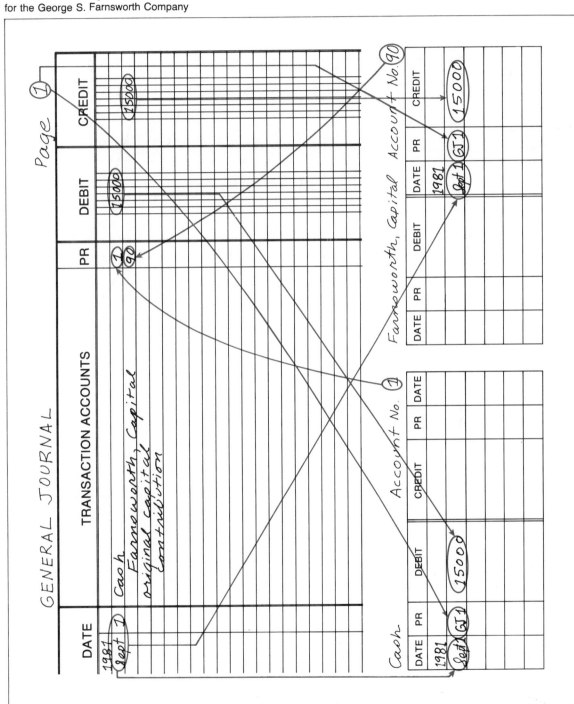

Posting Reference and Date Each posting is dated in the ledger with the date the transaction took place (and was entered in the journal), and a posting reference is included which indicates the journal and page from which the transaction was taken.

Cumulative Effect Posting to the ledger simply reproduces the information already recorded in the journal, but does so in a way that shows the cumulative effect of the transactions.

Order of General Ledger Finally, the accounts appear in the general ledger sequenced by account number. To further ease the use of the accounts in the general ledger, they are sequenced in the following overall order: (1) all assets appear first, in the order they appear on the balance sheet; (2) all liabilities appear next, in the order they appear on the balance sheet; (3) all owner's equity accounts appear next; (4) all revenues appear next, in the order they appear on the income statement; and (5) all expenses appear next in the order they appear on the income statement. A **chart of accounts** giving each account and its number for the George S. Farnsworth Company appears in Figure 3-5. The accounts are not numbered consecutively because other accounts may be added later and numbers will need to be assigned to them. These account numbers are used in the general journal of Figure 3-3.

Figure 3-6 gives the general ledger for the George S. Farnsworth Company after the transactions of September 1981 have been posted from the general journal in Figure 3-3.

Balances versus Transactions

Certain numbers in each account in Figure 3-6 exhibit checks (√) rather than journal and page information in the posting reference column. These numbers bring up the third step in the accounting cycle, called the **trial balance.** Numbers with checks in the PR column give the balance in the account at the date given in the date column. It is important to distinguish

FIGURE 3-5
Chart of Accounts

GEORGE S. FARNSWORTH COMPANY	
Chart of Accounts	
Account	*Number*
Cash	1
Accounts receivable	10
Supplies	20
Equipment	30
Accounts payable	50
Note payable	55
Advances from customers	75
Farnsworth, capital	90
Farnsworth, withdrawals	95
Commission revenue	110
Rent expense	150
Salary expense	155
Advertising expense	160

FIGURE 3-6 General Ledger

GEORGE S. FARNSWORTH COMPANY
General Ledger
ASSETS

Cash   #1

Date	PR	Debit	Date	PR	Credit
1981			1981		
9/1	GJ1	15000	9/1	GJ1	600
9/4	GJ1	8000	9/11	GJ1	900
9/10	GJ1	2100	9/15	GJ1	500
9/22	GJ1	1500	9/18	GJ1	3000
			9/24	GJ1	500
			9/29	GJ1	2500
9/30	√	18600			

Accounts receivable   #10

Date	PR	Debit	Date	PR	Credit
1981			1981		
9/3	GJ1	100			
9/30	√	100			

Supplies   #20

Date	PR	Debit	Date	PR	Credit
1981			1981		
9/21	GJ1	800			
9/30	√	800			

Equipment   #30

Date	PR	Debit	Date	PR	Credit
1981			1981		
9/11	GJ1	900			
9/30	√	900			

LIABILITIES

Accounts payable   #50

Date	PR	Debit	Date	PR	Credit
1981			1981		
9/24	GJ1	500	9/21	GJ1	800
			9/30	√	300

Note payable   #55

Date	PR	Debit	Date	PR	Credit
1981			1981		
			9/10	GJ1	2100
			9/30	√	2100

Advances from customers   #75

Date	PR	Debit	Date	PR	Credit
1981			1981		
			9/22	GJ1	1500
			9/30	√	1500

OWNERS' EQUITY

Farnsworth, capital   #90

Date	PR	Debit	Date	PR	Credit
1981			1981		
			9/1	GJ1	15000
			9/30	√	15000

Farnsworth, withdrawals   #95

Date	PR	Debit	Date	PR	Credit
1981					
9/29	GJ1	2500			
9/30	√	2500			

(continued on next page)

(Figure 3-6 continued)

REVENUE AND EXPENSE

Commission revenue   #110

Date	PR	Debit	Date	PR	Credit
1981			1981		
			9/3	GJ1	100
			9/4	GJ1	8000
			9/30	√	8100

Rent expense   #150

Date	PR	Debit	Date	PR	Credit
1981			1981		
9/1	GJ1	600			
9/30	√	600			

Salary expense   #155

Date	PR	Debit	Date	PR	Credit
1981			1981		
9/15	GJ1	500			
9/30	√	500			

Advertising expense   #160

Date	PR	Debit	Date	PR	Credit
1981			1981		
9/18	GJ1	3000			
9/30	√	3000			

between balances and transactions. A *balance* indicates the dollar value of an account at a specific point in time. A *transaction* is a change in an account as the result of an event that has taken place since the last balance.

Balances are arrived at by adding up the debits in the account and subtracting the credits, if the total debits are larger in amount than the total credits. If the credits in an account are larger than the debits, the process of determining a balance would be the opposite. For any account expected to show a credit balance in Figure 3-6 (that is, any liability, owner's equity, or revenue), the balance is arrived at by adding the credits and subtracting the debits.

For example, in Figure 3-6 accounts payable shows a zero balance at September 1 because there were no transactions involving accounts payable prior to September 1. During the month, two transactions occurred affecting accounts payable, one causing an increase of $800 and one causing a decrease of $500. Because this account is a liability and will usually have a credit balance, to determine the dollar value of accounts payable at September 30, add $800 + $0 and subtract $500. The number showing the cumulative effect of all transactions involving accounts payable prior to September 30 is $300; it is the balance in the account at that date.

Trial Balance

Any business needs to know the balance in each of its accounts at various times during its life, to be assured that the basic accounting equation ($A = L + OE$) is still intact and to help in the detection of errors. On the other hand, it is not necessary that balances in each account be determined after each posting. As a result, most businesses calculate balances showing the cumulative effect of all prior transactions at various points in their lives, but not as frequently as posting takes place.

Concept Summary

Comparison and Contrast of the Journal and the Ledger		
Characteristics	Journal	Ledger
Focus	Transaction	Account
Information Recorded	(1) Date (2) Accounts affected (3) Posting reference (4) Debit amount (5) Credit amount	(1) Date (2) Posting reference (3) Amount
When Updated	As transactions occur	Each accounting period
Dated	When transaction occurred	When transaction occurred
Posting Reference	Ledger account affected	Journal and page where recorded
Amount Recorded	Debit *and* credit effects of transaction	Debit *or* credit effect on individual account
Organization	In chronological order	In account number order

A somewhat informal, internal statement, called a **trial balance,** is usually created when these balances are determined. The trial balance is simply a list of all the accounts used by the business and the appropriate dollar values of each account at some date. It is used to summarize the effect of all transactions on the business. Periodically making such a statement can provide an overview of the accounts and amounts and can ensure that the debits = credits and $A = L + OE$ statements still hold for the business.

Figure 3-7 is an example of a trial balance for the George S. Farnsworth Company. As was true of the financial statements presented in the last chapter, the title of this report (1) starts with the name of the company, (2) continues with the name of the particular report, and (3) ends with the date or time period of the report. This general format is always followed in accounting reports.

It may appear that the financial statements can be prepared from the trial balance. After all, the trial balance contains the assets, liabilities, and owner's equities for the balance sheet and the revenues and expenses for the income statement. However, there are a number of accounting events that have not been incorporated in the trial balance. As one example, the George S. Farnsworth Company borrowed money from the bank during the month. As a result, at the end of the month the company owes interest on the borrowed money. This fact has not yet been reflected in the accounts. Transactions such as these will be discussed in the next chapter.

FIGURE 3-7
Trial Balance

GEORGE S. FARNSWORTH COMPANY Trial Balance September 30, 1981		
	Debit	*Credit*
Cash	$18,600	
Accounts receivable	100	
Supplies	800	
Equipment	900	
Accounts payable		$ 300
Advances from customers		1,500
Note payable		2,100
Farnsworth, capital		15,000
Farnsworth, withdrawals	2,500	
Commission revenue		8,100
Rent	600	
Salary expense	500	
Advertising expense	3,000	
	$27,000	$27,000

Summary

The accounting cycle is a seven-step process which results in the income statement, statement of retained earnings (owners' capital), and balance sheet. This cycle records, classifies, summarizes, and communicates financial information.

Double-entry bookkeeping is the method used in accounting to record and classify transactions engaged in by a business. This method is based upon the journal and the ledger. The journal is organized chronologically and focuses on the transaction. The ledger is organized by account and focuses on the cumulative effect of all transactions on each account.

All transactions enter the financial accounting system through the journal. No new information enters the system through the ledger. The ledger simply reorganizes the information in the journal by account.

Every transaction must affect the $A = L + OE$ equation in at least two ways in order for the equation to remain in balance. This double effect is called duality in accounting and is the reason the term double-entry bookkeeping is used. Double-entry bookkeeping expresses duality by assigning a debit effect and a credit effect to each transaction. This assignment is called transaction analysis, and both the journal and ledger reflect the results of transaction analysis. Periodically, the cumulative balance in each ledger account is determined and a trial balance is prepared.

This chapter has examined the first three steps in the accounting cycle. These steps occur during the accounting period. Chapter 4 completes the accounting cycle by examining those steps that occur only at the end of the accounting period.

Key Terms

Account	**Chart of accounts**
Accounting cycle	**Credit**

Credit balance
Credit entry
Debit
Debit balance
Debit entry
Double-entry bookkeeping
Duality
Journal

Journalize
Ledger
Post
Posting reference
T account
Transaction analysis
Trial balance

Comprehensive Review Problem

Climbing and Hiking sells camping equipment and leads wilderness trips. The trial balance of Climbing and Hiking at April 30, 1982, is as follows:

Acct. No.	Account Title	Debit	Credit
1	Cash	$ 7,650	
10	Accounts receivable	4,500	
20	Inventory	8,000	
25	Supplies	1,200	
27	Prepaid advertising		
30	Furniture and fixtures	4,200	
35	Truck	6,500	
37	Accumulated depreciation: Truck		$ 3,250
40	Accounts payable		1,700
45	Note payable		1,000
47	Salaries payable		
60	Advances from customers		2,100
65	Loan payable		10,000
70	Welsh, capital		14,000
71	Withdrawals		
75	Sales revenue		
77	Cost of goods sold		
80	Rent expense		
85	Salaries expense		
90	Utilities expense		
		$32,050	$32,050

The following transactions took place in May:

May 1 Paid rent for the month of May, $1,200.
      3 Paid suppliers $1,700 owed for equipment purchased on credit in April.
      5 Customer paid $3,250 owed for credit sales in April.
      7 Customers paid $1,500 as a deposit on a June 3 trip to Rabbit Ear Mountain. The balance owed for the trip ($1,500) is due June 2.
      7 Ordered $6,000 of camping supplies from Canoe and Paddles.
     17 Received $4,500 of the merchandise ordered from Canoe and Paddles.
     25 Paid $2,000 to the owner, Mary Jeanne Welsh.
     29 Sent a $25 check to University College newspaper for an advertsiement which will run from June 2 through June 8.
     31 Paid Central State Power $150 for utilities used in May.
     31 Sales of camping supplies for May were $11,500. Cash sales were $6,250, and credit sales were $5,250. The merchandise had cost the company $6,900.
     31 Employee salaries for the month of May were $1,800. Pay checks are issued June 5th.

Required:

1. Construct a general journal and journalize the above transactions.

2. Set up general ledger T accounts and enter beginning balances.

3. Post all transactions to T accounts.

4. Compute the balance in each account. Prepare a trial balance.

Solution to Comprehensive Review Problem

CLIMBING AND HIKING
General Journal   Page 1

Date		Transaction Accounts	PR	Debit Amount	Credit Amount
1982 May	1	Rent expense	80	1,200	
		Cash	1		1,200
		Payment of rent			
	3	Accounts payable	40	1,700	
		Cash	1		1,700
		Paid suppliers			
	5	Cash	1	3,250	
		Accounts receivable	10		3,250
		Customer payments for previous credit sales			
	7	Cash	1	1,500	
		Advances from customers	60		1,500
		Deposits received for June 3 trip			
	17	Inventory	20	4,500	
		Accounts payable	40		4,500
		Received merchandise ordered on credit			
	25	Withdrawals	71	2,000	
		Cash	1		2,000
		Paid cash to owner			
	29	Prepaid advertising	27	25	
		Cash	1		25
		Paid University College newspaper for June 2 through June 8 advertisement			
	31	Utilities expense	90	150	
		Cash	1		150
		Paid Central State Power utility bill			
	31	Cash	1	6,250	
		Accounts receivable	10	5,250	
		Sales revenue	75		11,500
		Monthly sales to customers			
	31	Cost of goods sold	79	6,900	
		Inventory	20		6,900
	31	Salaries expense	85	1,800	
		Salaries payable	47		1,800
		Employee salaries for the month of May			

CLIMBING AND HIKING
General Ledger

Cash #1

Date	PR	Debit	Date	PR	Credit
1982			1982		
4/30	√	7,650	5/1	GJ1	1,200
5/5	GJ1	3,250	5/3	GJ1	1,700
5/7	GJ1	1,500	5/25	GJ1	2,000
5/31	GJ1	6,250	5/29	GJ1	25
			5/31	GJ1	150
5/31	√	13,575			

Accounts receivable #10

Date	PR	Debit	Date	PR	Credit
1982			1982		
4/30	√	4,500	5/3	GJ1	3,250
5/31	GJ1	5,250			
5/31	√	6,500			

Inventory #20

Date	PR	Debit	Date	PR	Credit
1982			1982		
4/30	√	8,000	5/31	GJ1	6,900
5/17	GJ1	4,500			
5/31	√	5,600			

Supplies #25

Date	PR	Debit	Date	PR	Credit
1982			1982		
4/30	√	1,200			
5/31	√	1,200			

Prepaid advertising #27

Date	PR	Debit	Date	PR	Credit
1982			1982		
5/29	GJ1	25			
5/31	√	25			

Furniture and fixtures #30

Date	PR	Debit	Date	PR	Credit
1982			1982		
4/30	√	4,200			
5/31	√	4,200			

Truck #35

Date	PR	Debit	Date	PR	Credit
1982			1982		
4/30	√	6,500			
5/31	√	6,500			

Accumulated depreciation #37

Date	PR	Debit	Date	PR	Credit
1982			1982		
			4/30	√	3,250
			5/31	√	3,250

Accounts payable #40

Date	PR	Debit	Date	PR	Credit
1982			1982		
5/3	GJ1	1,700	4/30	√	1,700
			5/17	GJ1	4,500
			5/31	√	4,500

Note payable #45

Date	PR	Debit	Date	PR	Credit
1982			1982		
			4/30	√	1,000
			5/31	√	1,000

Salaries payable #47

Date	PR	Debit	Date	PR	Credit
1982			1982		
			5/31	GJ1	1,800
			5/31	√	1,800

Deferred revenue #60

Date	PR	Debit	Date	PR	Credit
1982			1982		
			4/30	√	2,100
			5/7	GJ1	1,500
			5/31	√	3,600

Loan payable #65

Date	PR	Debit	Date	PR	Credit
1982			1982		
			4/30	√	10,000
			5/31	√	10,000

Welsh, capital #70

Date	PR	Debit	Date	PR	Credit
1982			1982		
			4/30	√	14,000
			5/31	√	14,000

Sales revenue #75

Date	PR	Debit	Date	PR	Credit
1982			1982		
			5/31	GJ1	11,500
			5/31	√	11,500

Cost of goods sold #77

Date	PR	Debit	Date	PR	Credit
1982			1982		
5/31	GJ1	6,900			
5/31	√	6,900			

Rent expense #80

Date	PR	Debit	Date	PR	Credit
1982			1982		
5/1	GJ1	1,200			
5/31	√	1,200			

Salaries expense #85

Date	PR	Debit	Date	PR	Credit
1982			1982		
5/31	GJ1	1,800			
5/31	√	1,800			

Utilities expense #90

Date	PR	Debit	Date	PR	Credit
1982			1982		
5/31	GJ1	150			
5/31	√	150			

Withdrawals #100

Date	PR	Debit	Date	PR	Credit
1982					
5/25	GJ1	2,000			
5/31	√	2,000			

CLIMBING AND HIKING
Trial Balance
May 31, 1982

	Debit	Credit
Cash	$13,575	
Accounts receivable	6,500	
Inventory	5,600	
Supplies	1,200	
Prepaid advertising	25	
Furniture and fixtures	4,200	
Truck	6,500	
Accumulated depreciation: truck		$ 3,250
Accounts payable		4,500
Note payable		1,000
Salaries payable		1,800
Advances from customers		3,600
Loan payable		10,000
Welsh, capital		14,000
Withdrawals	2,000	
Sales revenue		11,500
Cost of goods sold	6,900	
Rent expense	1,200	
Salaries expense	1,800	
Utilities expense	150	
	$49,650	$49,650

Questions

Q3-1. List the seven steps of the accounting cycle.

Q3-2. Give the debit and credit behavior patterns of assets, liabilities, owners' equity, revenue, and expense.

Q3-3. What is a transaction? Give three examples of business events that are not transactions.

Q3-4. Define the duality idea in accounting. Why is it important?

Q3-5. Contrast the organization and orientation of the journal and the ledger.

Q3-6. What is the purpose of posting? What roles do the posting references play in this process?

Q3-7. Describe the difference between entries in an account and balances in that account. How is each derived?

Q3-8. Discuss the functions of the trial balance.

Exercises

E3-1. Explain the term *double-entry* as it is used in double-entry bookkeeping. Would a single-entry system be possible? If so, give an example of a single-entry record-keeping system.

E3-2. The functions of the bookkeeper are often confused with those of the accountant. Distinguish between the roles of the accountant and the bookkeeper and state which steps of the accounting cycle are likely to be performed by each.

E3-3. The general journal and the general ledger both contain the same information, but organized differently. Would you go to the general journal or to the general ledger to look up

a. all of the accounting transactions that occurred on a single day?
b. the balance of cash on hand?
c. how an event was originally recorded?
d. the book value of a particular asset?
e. the amounts owed to suppliers?
f. the specific date on which a particular transaction was recorded?

E3-4. The following accounts appeared in the ledger of Raintree Company at the end of August.

Rent income	$ 9,300
Accounts receivable	22,000
Salaries expense	6,000
Notes payable	3,000
Common stock	52,000
Service revenue	10,000
Store equipment	7,000

Tell whether each of these accounts is an asset, liability, owners' equity, revenue, or expense account. Indicate as well whether the account would be increased by a debit or a credit.

E3-5. Indicate whether the following events qualify as business transactions. Give the reason for your decision.

a. Supplies are ordered for delivery next week.
b. Inventory is purchased on account.
c. A potential new salesman is interviewed.
d. A customer buys merchandise on account.
e. The owner of the business brings home cash for his personal use.
f. The month's rent is paid.
g. Money is borrowed from the bank.

E3-6. Construct a general journal and record the following transactions.

Sept   2 Mr. Schreiber invested $8,000 cash in the business, a sole proprietorship.

   4 Mr. Schreiber borrowed $2,000 from the Pontchartrain State Bank for use in the business.

   7 Purchased supplies on account, $620.

  13 Paid $580 of the amount owed for supplies.

  15 Performed services and billed customers $10,000.

  15 Paid one month's rent, $900.

  25 Collected $7,500 from customers.

E3-7. Using the information in Exercise 3-6, set up the T accounts that would appear in the general ledger and post these transactions to the appropriate general ledger accounts. Prepare a trial balance to verify that the total debits equal total credits. Assume these were the only transactions for the month of September.

E3-8. The following T accounts appear in the general ledger of Haley Corporation. Give the journal entry, including a brief description, for each transaction involved.

Cash		Accounts receivable		Common stock	
A 20,000	B 8,000	C 4,000			A 20,000
C 3,000	D 1,000				
	E 600				

Equipment		Service revenue	
B 8,000			C 7,000

Salary expense		Rent expense	
E 600		D 1,000	

Problems

P3-1. Several of the accounts found in the general ledger of the Silverplatter Catering Company are entered in the tabulation below.

Account	Type of Account	Normal Balance—Debit or Credit
Rent payable		
Cash		
Short-term investments		
Salaries expense		
Salaries payable		
Notes payable		
Interest revenue		
Common stock		
Accounts receivable		
Utilities expense		
Supplies on hand		
Equipment		
Catering revenue		
Income tax expense		
Prepaid insurance		
Accounts payable		
Retained earnings		

Required:

1. Complete the tabulation by giving the type (asset, liability, owners' equity, revenue, expense) of each account and also indicate whether the account normally has a debit or credit balance.

2. Prepare a chart of accounts for Silverplatter Company similar to the one presented in Figure 3-5. You may omit account numbers.

P3-2. Below are the transactions for the Gravier Company, a sole proprietorship.

   a. C. Gravier invests $10,000 in the company.
   b. Supplies of $7,500 are purchased on credit from B-2 Corporation.
   c. A $15,000 loan is made from the Left Bank on a two-year note.
   d. Equipment is purchased for $5,000 on account from OK suppliers.
   e. Services of $5,200 are rendered to the following customers on credit:

Arthur $3,000
Alethea $2,200

f. $2,500 of accounts payable is paid.

g. $2,600 of accounts receivable is collected from Arthur.

h. Rent of $950 is paid.

i. $5,000 of services are rendered to the following customers:
Gwen $2,500 on credit
Kelly $2,500 for cash

j. Gravier withdraws $1,500 for personal use.

Required:
Journalize the above transactions in good general journal form.

P3-3. Below are transactions for the St. Louis Company, Inc.

a. The owners invested $55,000 in the company.

b. Purchased a building for $20,000 cash and $80,000 in notes.

c. Performed services of $10,000 on credit.

d. Purchased supplies for $17,000 on credit.

e. Made a loan from a bank for $50,000.

f. Collected $6,000 of accounts receivable.

g. Performed $24,000 of services for customers, 25 percent of which was for cash and 75 percent of which was on credit.

h. Paid rent of $2,800.

i. Paid dividends of $5,000.

j. Paid $8,000 on accounts payable.

Required:
Journalize the above transactions in good general journal form.

P3-4. Reproduced below is a chart of accounts for Superior Cleaners, Inc., which has been in business for several years. Following the chart of accounts is a list of transactions that took place during the current year. For each transaction, indicate the account(s) to be debited and credited by entering the relevant account number(s) on the right.

SUPERIOR CLEANERS, INC.
Chart of Accounts

Account	*Number*
Cash	1
Accounts receivable	10
Supplies	22
Prepaid insurance	24
Equipment	36
Patents	40
Notes payable	50
Accounts payable	55
Wages payable	60
Advances from customers	‹70
Capital stock	90
Retained earnings	95
Dividends	97
Service revenue	110
Wage expense	150
Rent expense	155

Transactions	Debit	Credit
a. *Example:* Owners invested cash to start the business and received stock in exchange.	1	90
b. Purchased new cleaning equipment. Paid three-fourths in cash and gave note payable for balance.		
c. Collected cash for services performed last period.		
d. Collected cash for services performed this period.		
e. Paid cash for a patent held by retiring competitor.		
f. Performed cleaning work this period on credit.		
g. Paid cash wages to employees.		
h. Paid current month's rent.		
i. Paid cash dividend to all shareholders.		
j. Bought supplies on credit.		
k. Paid amounts owed to creditors.		
l. Made payment on note in b above (ignore interest).		
m. Paid insurance premium for the coming year.		
n. Customer inadvertently overpaid an account.		

P3-5. A balance sheet depicts the financial position of a business at a point in time and expresses the equation $A = L + OE$. The balance sheet of the B. Saunders Company did not balance.

B. SAUNDERS
Simplified Balance Sheet
June 30

Cash	$ 3,210	
Accounts receivable	10,415	
Inventory	2,900	
Supplies on hand	250	
Accounts payable		$ 6,750
Notes payable		2,000
B. Saunders, capital		7,075
	$16,775	$15,825

A review of the accounting records revealed these errors:

a. Cash received from a customer in payment of an account was incorrectly recorded as $430 rather than $340 in both cash and accounts receivable.

b. When there was a cash sale of merchandise in the amount of $1,725, the asset cash was increased by $1,725 but owners' equity was only increased by $725.

c. When a payment was made to suppliers, cash was decreased by $200 and notes payable was decreased by $200 instead of accounts payable being decreased by $200.

d. When $25 was paid to a local newspaper for an advertisement, cash was decreased by $25 and owners' equity was increased by $25.

Required:
Prepare a corrected balance sheet as of June 30.

P3-6. Rusty Totora and Jimmy Martello decided to become business partners. Each of them had several years of experience in air conditioner repair work, and they decided now was the time to start a business of their own. The following entries were made in the general journal for the first two weeks:

April	*1*	Cash	10,000	
		R. Totora, capital		5,000
		J. Martello, capital		5,000
		Original capital investment		
	1	Trucks	10,000	
		Cash		4,000
		Notes payable		6,000
		Purchased a truck		
	2	Insurance expense	340	
		Cash		340
		Paid for insurance		
	3	Rent expense	450	
		Cash		450
		Paid rent		
	3	Deposit on utilities	115	
		Cash		115
		Paid utility deposit		
	4	Office equipment	1,100	
		Cash		1,100
		Purchased office equipment		
	4	Supplies	100	
		Cash		100
		Purchased supplies		
	5	Advertising expense	50	
		Cash		50
		Paid for advertising		
	7	Cash	500	
		Accounts receivable	700	
		Service revenue		1,200
		Performed services for customers		
	10	Salary expense	120	
		Cash		120
		Paid employee's salary		
	11	Cash	525	
		Accounts receivable		525
		Collected from customers		
	14	Cash	845	
		Accounts receivable	1,200	
		Service revenue		2,045
		Performed services for customers		

Required:
1. Post each of the above entries to the appropriate general ledger account, using the ledger form illustrated in Figure 3-4.
2. Prepare a trial balance as of April 14.

P3-7. After several years of dancing in Broadway productions, Laura Harrison decided to return to her native city and open a dancing school, Laura's Dance Academy. The following events took place during August 1982.

August 2 Laura contributed to the sole proprietorship $50,000 she had saved during her years of professional dancing. While home on vacation earlier in the year, she had discussed the type of facilities she would need for her school with her brother Bill, a real estate agent. He located a facility for sale by a retiring dancing teacher which suited Laura's needs exactly. The building and land were purchased for $50,000. Laura put down $10,000 cash and signed a mortgage for $40,000. The building was appraised at $35,000 and the land at $15,000.

4 Laura took out all the necessary insurance. A year's premium was $400.

10 While the studio was basically what Laura wanted, she felt that a new coat of paint on the inside would create an atmosphere more expressive of her personality. The painters charged her $150. She also had the floors refinished at a cost of $200.

11 Laura arranged to have utilities installed. She made deposits totaling $200, which are refundable after one year's satisfactory payment of bills.

12 Laura placed ads in several area newspapers giving information on types of instruction available, tuition, and registration dates. Cost of ads, $120.

14 Laura purchased miscellaneous supplies on credit at a cost of $75.

17 After a thunderstorm, the roof leaked. A roofer was called, and gave an estimate of $250 for roof repairs. Laura agreed to have the work done.

19 The roof was repaired, and Laura paid the $250.

20 Laura decided she would need several new leotards and dance shoes. She opened a business account at Dance Castle, a dance supply outlet. She purchased apparel worth $325 on account. The amount is due within 15 days.

24–31 Registration was held at the studio. Thirty-five prospective students registered. Each paid a $10 registration fee, which is not refundable, and a $20 tuition fee for the first month. Classes will start September 1.

Required:

1. Construct a general journal and journalize the above transactions.

2. Post to general ledger accounts. Assume the following chart of accounts:

1	Cash	15	Accounts payable
3	Supplies	16	Mortgage payable
5	Prepaid insurance	17	Tuition advances
7	Deposits on utilities	19	L. Harrison, capital
9	Dance apparel	21	Registration fee revenue
11	Land	23	Repairs expense
13	Building	25	Advertising expense

3. Prepare a trial balance.

4. Prepare an income statement for August and a balance sheet at August 31, 1982.

P3-8. The Chimney Sweep began operation as a sole proprietorship in January 1982. The owner, Charles Broome, offers chimney cleaning services to residents of a large metropolitan area. The following information is available for the first month of operations:

January   2   C. Broome invested $5,000 in the business. The money was deposited in a checking account.

      5   Broome wrote a check to Anna Schultz for $400. The check included $200 for a deposit and $200 for the first month's rent on a converted garage. Mrs. Schultz's husband had operated a business at this location before his retirement. The deposit is refundable if there are no damages when Broome moves out.

      5   Broome arranged to have utilities installed. He paid deposits of $175.

      6   Broome knew there was a large market for his services if residents were made aware of them. He paid $50 for an ad in the *Daily News* and also paid $100 to have handbills delivered in the neighborhood.

      7   Broome completed negotiations for a used truck needed for the business. The agreed purchase price was $3,300. He borrowed $1,500 from the bank, signing a one-year note, and took the remaining $1,800 from his checking account.

      7   Broome made arrangements immediately with his personal agent for insurance coverage on the truck. Cost of truck insurance was $400. At the same time, he obtained the business insurance required at a cost of $500. Both policies covered a one-year period.

      8   Broome went to City Hall and paid $60 to obtain the necessary licenses and permits to operate his business.

     12   Broome had realized earlier that he would need someone to take telephone messages and keep records for him. He would try to do no work on credit but would ask for cash at the completion of each job. Mrs. Schultz had done this type of work in her husband's business, and she and Broome entered into a verbal agreement that she would work five hours a day for $3.00 per hour.

     12   Broome purchased the required equipment for use in his business. The normal retail price of this equipment was $155, but he had a friend who got it for him at a wholesale price of $108. At the same time, he purchased supplies with a retail value of $60 for $42. He paid cash.

   13–16   Broome performed chimney cleaning services and was paid $280 by customers.

     16   Paid Mrs. Schultz her first week's salary of $60 as she had worked four days this week.

   19–23   Performed services and collected $625 from customers.

     23   Paid Mrs. Schultz's weekly salary of $75.

     26   One of the tires on the truck blew out. Cost of replacing the tire was $35.

     27   A check received last week from James Cleveland as payment for services in the amount of $72 was returned from the bank marked NSF. Broome knows Mr. Cleveland and is sure he can collect from him.

     28   Broome received the gas bill from George's Service Station

where he had been charging gasoline. The bill was for $95 and was due in ten days.

26–30 Collected $625 from customers. Included in this amount was a $55 check from Ray Gunther as payment in advance for a job Broome was to perform February 5.

30 Paid Mrs. Schultz's weekly salary.

30 Paid utilities, $48.

30 Paid $137 to the bank. This included $12 of interest.

30 Depreciation expense on equipment $4. (Debit depreciation expense and credit accumulated depreciation—equipment.)

30 The amount of insurance premium allocated to January is $75. (Debit insurance expense and credit prepaid insurance.)

30 License and permits used up, $12.

30 Broome had used all of the supplies purchased earlier, so he telephoned his friend and placed an order for $100 more of supplies.

30 Depreciation on truck, $83. (Debit depreciation expense and credit accumulated depreciation.)

30 Broome took $175 out of the business.

Required:

1. Construct a general journal and journalize the above transactions.

2. Assuming the following chart of accounts, set up the T accounts that would appear in the general ledger.

1	Cash	90	C. Broome, capital
10	Accounts receivable	95	C. Broome, withdrawals
12	Utility deposit	110	Service revenue
14	Supplies	150	Advertising expense
16	Licenses and permits	151	Depreciation expense
20	Prepaid insurance	152	Gasoline expense
22	Trucks	155	Insurance expense
23	Accumulated depreciation—truck	157	Interest expense
26	Equipment	160	Licenses and permits expense
27	Accumulated depreciation—equipment	162	Rent expense
30	Rent deposit	165	Repairs expense
50	Note payable	168	Salary expense
55	Accounts payable	170	Supplies expense
75	Advances from customers	175	Utilities expense

3. Post from the general journal to the general ledger.

4. Compute the balance in each account.

5. Prepare a trial balance.

6. Prepare an income statement and balance sheet.

CHAPTER 4

The Accounting Cycle—
End Of Period
Procedures

Chapter Outline

Accounting and the Real World

Advice
from Pacioli

Along with his ground-breaking description of the double-entry system, Pacioli freely dispensed a great deal of practical advice. Some of his comments hold true today:

1. Books should be closed each year, especially in partnership, because frequent accounting makes for long friendship.

2. Who does nothing makes no mistakes, who makes no mistakes learns nothing.

3. The law helps those that are awake—not those that sleep.

4. There are three things necessary to one who wishes to operate a business successfully. The most important is cash, or some equivalent economic power. The second is to be a good accountant and a ready mathematician. The third is that all the businessman's affairs be arranged in a systematic way so that he may get their particulars at a glance.

5. If each thing is not in its right place, great trouble and confusion will arise. As the saying goes, "Where there is no order, there is chaos."

6. A credit balance in the Profit and Loss account represents a profit, and a debit balance represents a loss, from which latter may God preserve every man.

7. The Profit and Loss Account will then be transferred into the Capital Account. It is consequently the receptacle of all other accounts.

8. If the grand total of debits and credits are equal, you may conclude that the Ledger was well kept and closed. However, if one grand total exceeds the other, it would indicate an error in the Ledger. This error must be searched out diligently.

9. The entire inventory is to be completed on the same day, otherwise there will be future difficulty in managing the business.

One of his comments, however, is inappropriate in the modern world:

10. The servants of the household can make the daily entries in the book of original entry, or they can also be made by the master's women if they know how to write.

The Journal of Accountancy, December 1977. © 1977 by the American Institute of Certified Public Accountants, Inc.
The Woman CPA, January 1977.

As part of its accounting cycle, every business (1) records accounting events in the journal, usually as they occur; (2) classifies the effects of these transactions on its accounts by posting to the ledger; and (3) determines the dollar amount of each account periodically and summarizes these balances in a trial balance. There are, in addition, a very important set of steps in the accounting cycle which occur only once each accounting period. These steps, beginning with Step 4, adjusting entries, are carried out only at the end of each accounting period and are called end-of-period procedures.

4.1 Adjusting Entries—Recognizing Expenses

To understand adjusting entries, it is necessary to make a distinction between the two basic types of events in which most businesses engage: external and internal.

External Events

External events, the usual kind of events, take place between a business and individuals or other businesses. These events are easy to identify because they occur at discrete points of time when a business interacts with its environment. Also, there are usually supporting documents (such as checks or invoices) created by one or both of the parties to the transaction indicating that a transaction has occurred. Examples of external events include selling goods, purchasing assets, borrowing money, issuing stock, repaying loans, and paying salaries.

External events are recorded, as they occur, in the first step of the accounting cycle because (1) they are discrete in nature and (2) certain legal relationships are created as a result of the event which require immediate recording. External events are the only transactions that require recording as they occur; therefore, Steps 1, 2, and 3 of the accounting cycle are concerned only with these sorts of events. In Step 1, external events are journalized. In Step 2, external events are posted. The trial balance of Step 3 depicts the effects of external events of the period.

Internal Events

There is a second major class of transactions which occur in the life of businesses. These internal events are more subtle and, consequently, are somewhat more difficult to grasp than external events. Essentially, internal transactions take place wholly within the firm; that is, no person or other business is directly involved in the transaction. In addition, these events tend to be continuous in nature, in that they occur constantly rather than at specific, identifiable points in time. Finally, there may be no source document supporting the transaction to alert the system to its occurrence.

Depreciation (that is, the consumption of the cost of assets) is an example of an internal event. The asset, such as a machine, is used by the firm and, thus, its consumption is an internal affair. In addition, the asset is consumed continuously over the month rather than at any specific point in time. Finally, there is no source document created by the use of an asset. Other internal events include interest expense and interest revenue.

Concept Summary

External Versus Internal Events		
	External	*Internal*
Who	Business and outsiders	Business only
When	Discrete occurrences identified by source documents	Constantly occurring; may be no source documents

Adjusting Entries

Because internal events usually do not concern "outsiders," the company need not record them as they happen. Because they are constantly taking place in any business, it would be cumbersome (as well as expensive) to record internal events in the same way as external events. As a result, internal events are handled quite differently from external events in the accounting cycle. Internal transactions occur during an accounting period, and then, at the end of the period, the *cumulative* effects of these continuous events are recorded by a series of entries called **adjusting entries.** To continue the above example, *one* adjusting entry will record the total depreciation of an asset for the *entire* month or accounting period.

Although an internal transaction need not be recorded as it happens, it is absolutely essential that all events, external and internal, be properly considered before financial statements are prepared. Adjusting entries are designed to bring the books of a business up to date for a group of events ignored during an accounting period. This process requires returning to the journal so that internal transactions can be recorded, then to the ledger so that they can be posted and classified.

Most businesses face only a few basic types of continuous internal transactions, so that there are only five fundamental types of adjusting entries. As discussed above, these basic types of adjustments are all recorded *only* at the end of the accounting period.

Type 1. Internal Expiration of Assets

As an accounting period goes by, businesses use up some of their assets (usually a little at a time) in the process of seeking a profit. This consumption of assets is wholly internal and goes on constantly. As the business engages in profit-seeking events, supplies and prepaid expenses are consumed; and buildings, machines, trucks, cars, tools, and other similar assets are used up. At the end of the period, a set of adjusting entries is made to reflect the expiration of these assets.

Supplies For example, suppose at the beginning of an accounting period, a business had supplies on hand of $300 and at the end of the period found only $200 of these supplies remaining. The firm must have used up $100 of supplies during the period. As these supplies were actually being used, the firm made no recognition of this usage in the accounts. However, the firm compensates for this by making an adjusting entry which (1) records all of the supplies used and (2) measures that usage by the creation of an expense. The entry would be

```
Supplies expense  .........  100
    Supplies  .....................  100
```

Prepaid Insurance Along the same vein, suppose a business purchased an insurance policy on January 1 for three months of insurance coverage at a total price of $450. When the $450 premium is paid by the business, an asset (namely, prepaid insurance) is created, while an asset (cash) of equal amount is consumed. Thus, no net increase or decrease of assets occurs. By the end of the month, however, one-third of the agreed-upon insurance coverage has been used up. The entry to record the expiration of this asset would be

```
Insurance expense  .........  150
    Prepaid insurance  ..............  150
```

Payment for the insurance policy is an external event to be recorded immediately, but the subsequent use of the services is an internal event to be recorded by an adjusting entry.

Depreciation When noncurrent assets (such as buildings and machines) are used up a little at a time in the course of profit seeking, the process is called depreciation. Because this expiration of assets is continuous and internal, recording depreciation is an adjusting entry of Type 1. Suppose, for example, a business purchased a truck for $3,000 which is expected to last five years or 60 months. Each month a certain portion ($3,000 ÷ 60 = $50) of the truck's services are used by the business. To record this, the entry would be

```
Depreciation expense  ........  50
    Accumulated depreciation  .........  50
```

There is an unusual credit in this entry. When noncurrent assets are consumed, a special account called a **contra-asset** is used to record the decrease. This special account, called **accumulated depreciation,** is credited instead of the asset itself, so that the original cost of the noncurrent asset will be kept intact in the business records until the asset is sold. The effect of using this contra-asset is exactly the same as if the asset were credited directly. Accumulated depreciation appears as a subtraction from the related asset on the business balance sheet and the asset is, in effect, decreased. Depreciation is recognized on all plant, property, and equipment assets except land. Land is presumed to have an unlimited life and, therefore, is not consumed.

Cost of Goods Sold The only other major Type 1 adjustment involves the determination of cost of goods sold for a merchandising firm. This expense would be determined by an adjusting entry. However, accounting for inventory and cost of goods sold involves some detailed procedures, the discussion of which will be deferred to Chapter 6.

These adjusting entries (called Type 1) are all of the same general format, only the specific account titles change. Type 1 adjustments *always* result in an increase in an expense and a decrease in an asset. Type 1 adjusting entries have the following form:

Expense XXX
    Asset XXX

The above are examples of the primary Type 1 adjustments, but there are certainly other adjustments of this type. The important task is to understand what a Type 1 adjustment is and how to recognize one. In all instances, there is an important distinction between the acquisition of an asset (which is an external event to be recorded as it occurs) and the use or consumption of that asset (which is an internal event and is recorded as an adjusting entry).

Type 2. Accruing an Expense

Accounting recognizes expenses when any asset has been consumed *or* any liability created as a result of profit-seeking events. This means that often an expense must be recognized even though no external transaction has actually occurred and no asset has been used up. Type 2 adjusting entries are concerned with liability-created events that take place internally during the accounting period. The process of recording these events is called "accruing an expense," and the resulting expense is called an **accrued expense.**

Salaries and Wages In the life of many businesses, an important example of Type 2 adjustments is salaries and wages. If payday for a business's employees does not fall on the day the accounting period ends, salaries and wages earned during the period, but not paid until the next period (when the payday occurs), must be accrued. Such salaries and wages should be expenses of the period in which the work was actually performed by employees. Also, as of the end of the current period, the business has incurred an obligation to the employees for these yet unpaid amounts. An adjusting entry of Type 2 recognizes both the existence of the liability and the creation of an expense for these earned, but not yet paid, salaries and wages.

Suppose, for example, a business pays its employees on the fifteenth of each month and that the total payroll is $800. Further, suppose the current accounting period ends on January 31. As of January 31, the employees have worked one-half month (January 16–31), but will not be paid for this until February 15. If no entry is made, both expenses and liabilities for the month will be understated. The Type 2 adjusting entry would be

```
Salaries and wages expense ............ 400
    Salaries and wages payable ................. 400
```

Paying employees is an external event. Accruing their wages, however, is an internal event.

Interest Expense This same reasoning would also apply to interest owed by a business on amounts borrowed. As time passes, interest accrues on loans; however, most interest is paid only at fixed points in time. If the accounting period ends between these interest payment dates, a Type 2 adjustment is necessary for expenses and liabilities to be properly stated.

Assume a business borrowed $1,000 at the beginning of a month at an annual rate of 12 percent to be repaid in three months. At the end of the month, a liability of $1,000 would exist from the external event of borrowing the money. Additionally, however, as time goes by, interest accrues on the amount borrowed. At the end of the month, an adjustment must be made to reflect the one month's interest owed but not yet paid. Because a 12 percent annual rate is 1 percent a month and $1,000 \times .01 = $10, the adjusting entry would be

```
Interest expense ............. 10
    Interest payable ................. 10
```

Borrowing the money and repaying the amount borrowed plus interest are both external events, but accruing the interest is an internal event.

The journal entry for a Type 2 adjustment always uses the following format:

```
Expense ................ XXX
    Liability ...................... XXX
```

4.2 Adjusting Entries—Recognizing Revenues

The first section of this chapter discussed two types of adjusting entries which recognize expenses. While each of these entries debits expense, one credits a liability and one credits an asset. The adjusting entries used to recognize revenue are similar to the entries discussed earlier in that they both credit revenue. One debits an asset, while one debits a liability.

Type 3. Accruing a Revenue

Accrual accounting requires that revenues be recognized and recorded as they are earned by a business, whether or not an external event occurs. If an asset has been generated as a result of the profit-seeking activities of a business, then revenue measures the amount of that increase in assets.

An internal event may take place which results in an increase in assets and, consequently, in revenue. If such an event occurs, recognition must be given to it in order for the accounts of the business to be properly stated. This process is called "accruing a revenue," and the resulting revenue is called an **accrued revenue.** It is the opposite of the Type 2 adjustment discussed above, and it always results in an increase in assets and in revenue.

Interest Revenue Suppose that a business had at the end of the month accounts receivable of $7,500, representing amounts owed to the business by its customers. Suppose this business adds a carrying charge of 1 percent as interest on unpaid amounts to all of its accounts receivable outstanding at the end of each month. In effect, the receivable is increased as a result of an internal event, and this increase is measured by revenue. The entry would be

```
Interest receivable  . . . . . . . . . . .  75
or Accounts receivable
    Interest revenue  . . . . . . . . . . . . . . . .  75
```

Because the interest has accrued on the unpaid amounts over the month, the process is continuous and internal, and assets and revenue would be understated if the adjusting entry were not recorded at the end of the period. The sale that created the accounts receivable (and sales revenue) was an external event and was recorded as it happened. When collections are made on the account, they, too, will be external events. A Type 3 adjusting entry always has the following format:

```
Asset  . . . . . . . . . . . . . . . . . .  XXX
(usually a receivable)
    Revenue  . . . . . . . . . . . . . . . . . . . . .  XXX
```

Type 4. Earning Revenue Received in Advance

Suppose a business received $500 from a customer before performing any service or delivering a product. In this instance, an external event has occurred, an asset has increased, and the increase in the asset will ultimately be the result of a profit-seeking activity. At the moment the event takes place, however, nothing has been done by the business to earn the revenue. To record such an external event, the following entry would be made at the time of occurrence:

```
Cash  . . . . . . . . . . . . . . . . . . . . .  500
    Advances from customers  . . . . . . . .  500
    or Deferred revenue
    or Unearned revenue
```

The account titles given as credits above are interchangeable and all represent a current liability for the business. In effect, this accounting treatment says that the business, by accepting cash from a customer, has obligated itself to deliver a service or product in the near future. Until the business does so, no revenue has been created. Assets have increased, but so have liabilities in the form of **deferred or unearned revenue.**

As the product or service is delivered to the customer, the obligation is satisfied and the asset (cash) is earned, resulting in the creation of revenue. Adjusting entry Type 4 involves the recognition of revenue previously received, but not yet earned. The receipt of cash and the creation of the resulting liability is an external event; however, the process of earning the revenue and extinguishing the liability is an internal adjustment.

Suppose a security firm received a check from a client for $200 on January 8 for guard services to be performed over the next month. On January 8 the following entry would be made:

$$\text{Cash} \quad \dots\dots\dots\dots\dots\dots \quad 200$$
$$\text{Advances from customers} \dots\dots\dots \quad 200$$

Now suppose that, as of January 31, three-fourths of the guard services have been performed for the customer. At January 31, there would then be a Type 4 adjusting entry to recognize and record the revenue earned and the liability satisfied:

$$\text{Advances from customers} \dots \quad 150$$
$$\text{Sales revenue} \quad \dots\dots\dots\dots\dots \quad 150$$

Thus, the basic format of this type of adjustment is

$$\text{Liability} \quad \dots\dots\dots\dots\dots \quad \text{XXX}$$
$$\text{Revenue} \quad \dots\dots\dots\dots\dots\dots \quad \text{XXX}$$

For most businesses this adjustment is rare; however, for businesses that traditionally collect in advance (such as magazine subscriptions, insurance companies, and landlords), this is a common and important entry.

4.3   Correcting the Accounts

There is an additional adjustment that is used if earlier entries in the accounting period turn out to be incorrect. In an above example, when the business purchased $300 of office supplies, the company debited an asset account, supplies, for that amount. When a physical count at the end of the month showed $200 of supplies on hand, an adjusting entry showing consumption of $100 was recorded.

Some companies, however, use a different approach. When they purchase assets like supplies, they assume that all will be used in the period. The journal entry then debits an expense account rather than an asset account. Thus, if the company purchased $300 of office supplies on credit, the journal entry would be

```
Supplies expense  . . . . . . . . .  300
    Accounts payable  . . . . . . . . . . . . . .  300
```

When $200 of supplies is found to be on hand at the end of the period, an adjusting entry of Type 5 is required to correct the expense entry. The entry would be

```
Supplies  . . . . . . . . . . . . . . . . .  200
    Supplies expense  . . . . . . . . . . . . . .  200
```

Thus, there are two possible approaches to recording the purchase of certain assets, which both net to the same result:

1. Debit an asset account when the goods are purchased. At the end of the period, a Type 1 adjusting entry measures the consumption of the asset.

2. Debit an expense account when the goods are purchased. At the end of the period, a Type 5 adjusting entry records the amount of the asset which has not been consumed.

A correcting adjustment similar to the entry discussed above involves revenue rather than expense. The discussion of Type 4 adjusting entries included an illustration of a security firm. The firm received $200 on January 8 for one month's guard services, and the illustration credited a liability. Using another approach, the journal entry when cash was received would be

```
Cash  . . . . . . . . . . . . . . . . . . . .  200
    Sales revenue  . . . . . . . . . . . . . . . .  200
```

At the end of the period, one-quarter of the services had not been performed. The Type 5 adjusting entry would be

```
Sales revenue  . . . . . . . . . . . . . .  50
    Advances from customers  . . . . . . . .  50
```

Thus, when cash is received before services are performed, there are two possible accounting approaches, which both net to the same result:

1. Credit a liability when the cash is received. At the end of the period, a Type 4 adjusting entry measures the amount of revenue earned in the period.

2. Credit a revenue when the cash is received. At the end of the period, a Type 5 adjusting entry records the amount of revenue which has not been earned.

Concept Summary

Basic Types of Adjusting Entries			
Type	Debit	Credit	Example
1. Internal expiration of assets	Expense	Asset	Consume supplies
2. Accruing an expense	Expense	Liability	Accrue interest payable
3. Accruing a revenue	Asset	Revenue	Accrue interest receivable
4. Earning revenue received in advance	Liability	Revenue	Earn subscription revenue by delivering magazine
5. Corrections	Asset	Expense	Do not use all supplies which were expensed
	Revenue	Liability	Do not perform all services required

Adjusted Trial Balance

Step 4 of the accounting cycle (adjusting entries) represents the first in a series of end-of-period procedures that every business must go through. Adjustments bring the accounts of a business up to date for those events that were not recorded as they happened; therefore, adjustments are a continuation of the basic summarization function of the accounting process. A second trial balance is then prepared after all adjusting entries have been made and posted. This internal statement, called an **adjusted trial balance,** is more complete than the trial balance prepared earlier by a business, because it includes *all* events (external and internal) in the life of the business. This adjusted trial balance concludes the summarization function.

Sample Company

Following are the adjusting entries for the George S. Farnsworth Company. Even in this small company, there are a number of adjusting entries of various types. Adjusting entries are not exotic or strange, but are fundamental to all businesses using accrual accounting, from the smallest to the largest.

Supplies The company purchased $800 of office supplies during the month. Thus, at the end of the month, the balance in the supplies account was $800. (The fact that the company did not fully pay for these supplies is here irrelevant.) However, a physical count at the end of the month showed that $600 of supplies were still on hand. To record this usage, the company must make the following entry:

```
Supplies expense .......... 200
     Supplies ..................... 200
```

Depreciation During the month, the company purchased a $900 typewriter, which is supposed to last five years. This means that the firm plans on using up a $900 asset over 60 months (5 years × 12 months/year), so the assumption is that $15 will be used up each month ($900 ÷ 60 = $15). Generally, businesses make no attempt either to depreciate assets for part of a month or to prorate depreciation over the days the company actually had the asset. Any adjusting entry will be for an entire month's depreciation. A common rule of thumb is that, if the asset is purchased in the first half of the month, it is depreciated for the month of purchase, and if the asset is purchased in the last half of the month, it is not depreciated for the month of purchase. Thus, the Type 1 entry for the George S. Farnsworth Company would be

```
Depreciation expense ........ 15
     Accumulated depreciation ......... 15
```

Salary The secretary gets paid on the fifteenth of the month. Thus, at the end of the month, she has earned one-half month's salary. If no entry is made, salary expense for September would only be $500 when, in fact, the company has obligated itself to pay her $1,000 for the month's work. There would then have to be a Type 2 adjusting entry as follows:

```
Salary expense ............ 500
     Salary payable ................. 500
```

When the secretary is paid on October 15, she will be paid $1,000. This salary payment will cover the time period from September 15 to October 15. The journal entry to record this payment would be

```
Salary expense .......... 500
Salary payable ............ 500
     Cash ........................ 1000
```

Only $500 of this payment is an expense in October; the other $500 was recognized as an expense in September.

Interest The company borrowed $2,100 on the tenth of September at an annual rate of 12 percent (which is equivalent to a monthly rate of 1 percent). If the company had the money for an entire month, the accrued interest would be $21 (that is, $2,100 × .01). However, because the company had the money for only two-thirds of the month, the Type 2 adjusting entry would be for $14, two-thirds of the $21 ($2,100 × .01 × 2/3 = 14)

```
Interest expense ............ 14
     Interest payable ................. 14
```

The calculation of interest expense concerns itself with the number of days the company has the money, whereas the calculation of depreciation does not. This difference arises because (1) interest is actually owed to the bank and the accounting records should reflect the amount owed as closely as possible, while (2) depreciation need not be so precise because it does not correspond to anything outside the business and is only based upon an estimate.

Earning Revenue The company received a check from a client for $1,500 on September 22 for an appraisal of the value of a piece of property. On September 30, Mr. Farnsworth estimated that one-half of the appraisal had been completed. The Type 4 adjusting entry (to recognize the revenue and to reduce the liability) would then be:

Advances from customers ... 750
    Appraisal revenue 750

There are then two revenue accounts, commission revenue and appraisal revenue. Strictly speaking, these are not both necessary: one revenue account would suffice. However, even in the smallest business, management would like to know the source of its revenue. In this instance, the two accounts will indicate to what extent revenue is generated from commissions and to what extent it is generated from appraisals.

Concept Summary

Transaction Analysis of Adjusting Entries		
George S. Farnsworth Company		
Transaction	*Debit Effect*	*Credit Effect*
A Company used $200 of supplies during the month	Expense + Supplies expense 200	Asset − Supplies 200
B Company used $15 of the cost of the typewriter during the month	Expense + Depreciation expense 15	Asset − Accumulated depreciation 15
C Secretary earned one-half of a month's salary, but was not paid	Expense + Salary expense 500	Liability + Salary payable 500
D Interest accrued on the money borrowed from the bank	Expense + Interest expense 14	Liability + Interest payable 14
E Company performed one-half of an appraisal	Liability − Advances from customers 750	Revenue + Appraisal revenue 750

FIGURE 4-1
Chart of Accounts

FIGURE 4-1
Chart of Accounts

GEORGE S. FARNSWORTH COMPANY	
Chart of Accounts	
Account	*Number*
Cash	1
Accounts receivable	10
Supplies	20
Equipment	30
Accumulated depreciation	31
Accounts payable	50
Salary payable	52
Interest payable	54
Note payable	55
Advances from customers	75
Farnsworth, capital	90
Farnsworth, withdrawals	95
Commission revenue	110
Appraisal revenue	120
Rent expense	150
Salary expense	155
Advertising expense	160
Supplies expense	165
Depreciation expense	170
Interest expense	175
Income summary	199

Chart of Accounts The chart of accounts used in Chapter 3 is no longer adequate for the company. The adjusting entries added seven new accounts: (1) supplies expense, (2) depreciation expense, (3) accumulated depreciation, (4) salary payable, (5) interest expense, (6) interest payable, and (7) appraisal revenue. These new accounts must be put in the chart of accounts. The new chart of accounts appears in Figure 4-1.

Adjusting Entries and Financial Statements Figure 4-2 gives the journal entries for these adjustments. A heading, adjusting entries, is placed in the general journal to set off these entries from the earlier ones.

There is an eighth account that must be added to the chart of accounts. This is number 199, income summary. Section 4.4, Closing Entries, includes a discussion of this account and its use.

The resulting adjusted trial balance for the George S. Farnsworth Company then appears in Figure 4-3 and the financial statements are given in Figure 4-4.

4.4 Closing Entries

Although financial statements are the end result and goal of the accounting process, they do not represent the final step in the accounting cycle. Once the communication function is fulfilled by preparation and dissemination of the income statement, statement of owners' capital (or retained earn-

FIGURE 4-2
General Journal

				Debit	Credit
		GEORGE S. FARNSWORTH COMPANY General Journal			
					Page 2
Date		Transaction Accounts	PR	Debit Amount	Credit Amount
		Adjusting Entries			
Sept	30	Supplies expense	165	200	
		Supplies	20		200
		Consumption of supplies			
	30	Depreciation expense	170	15	
		Accumulated depreciation	31		15
		Consumption of typewriter			
	30	Salary expense	155	500	
		Salary payable	52		500
		Accrue salaries owed			
	30	Interest expense	175	14	
		Interest payable	54		14
		Accrue interest owed			
	30	Advances from customers	75	750	
		Appraisal revenue	120		750
		Earn revenue as services performed			

FIGURE 4-3
Adjusted Trial Balance

GEORGE S. FARNSWORTH COMPANY
Adjusted Trial Balance
September 30, 1981

	Debit	Credit
Cash	$18,600	
Accounts receivable	100	
Supplies	600	
Equipment	900	
Accumulated depreciation		$ 15
Accounts payable		300
Salary payable		500
Interest payable		14
Note payable		2,100
Advances from customers		750
Farnsworth, capital		15,000
Farnsworth, withdrawals	2,500	
Commission revenue		8,100
Appraisal revenue		750
Rent expense	600	
Salary expense	1,000	
Advertising expense	3,000	
Supplies expense	200	
Depreciation expense	15	
Interest expense	14	
	$27,529	$27,529

FIGURE 4-4
Financial Statements

GEORGE S. FARNSWORTH COMPANY
Income Statement
For the Month Ending September 30, 1981

Revenues		
Commissions	$ 8,100	
Appraisals	750	
Total revenues		$ 8,850
Expenses		
Rent	600	
Salary	1,000	
Advertising	3,000	
Supplies	200	
Depreciation	15	
Interest	14	
Total expenses		4,829
Net income		$ 4,021

GEORGE S. FARNSWORTH COMPANY
Statement of Owners' Capital
For the Month Ending September 30, 1981

Farnsworth, capital, September 1	$ 0
Capital contributions	15,000
Net income for the month	4,021
Withdrawals	(2,500)
Farnsworth, capital, September 30	$16,521

GEORGE S. FARNSWORTH COMPANY
Balance Sheet
September 30, 1981

ASSETS

Cash		$18,600
Accounts receivable		100
Supplies		600
Equipment	$ 900	
Less: Accumulated depreciation	(15)	885
Total assets		$20,185

LIABILITIES & OWNERS' EQUITY

Liabilities		
Accounts payable		$ 300
Salary payable		500
Interest payable		14
Note payable		2,100
Advances from customers		750
Total liabilities		3,664
Owners' equity		
Farnsworth, capital		16,521
Total liabilities & owners' equity		$20,185

ings), and balance sheet, what remains at the end of the accounting period is a housekeeping step called closing the books. This last step in the cycle is designed to prepare the accounts of the business for the beginning of a new accounting period and a new accounting cycle. As was true of adjusting entries, a series of special entries must be recorded in the journal. After these entries have been posted to the ledger, the accounting cycle for a period is complete. Closing entries only affect revenue and expense accounts, plus the withdrawal and capital accounts. No other accounts are affected by this final step.

In effect, at the beginning of each period, revenue and expense accounts are created to keep track of the results of operations for that period. The amounts in these accounts then make up the income statement for the period, with owners' capital eventually increasing by the amount of net income and decreasing by withdrawals. Once this information has been collected and the statements prepared, these accounts are no longer useful for this period. In addition, when a new period starts, these revenue and expense accounts will have to start out at zero if that same information for the new period is to be collected.

Goals of Closing Entries

Each period must collect operating results, and the operating information from one period cannot be combined with that of the next or the statements will be useless. The closing process, then, is designed to

1. result in the zeroing-out of the balances in all revenue and expense accounts of the period just ended, so that the business can start fresh in measuring operations for the new period; and

2. transfer the difference between revenue and expense (net income or loss) to owners' capital and also transfer the balance in the withdrawals account to owners' capital.

Closing Process

To accomplish these goals, every business goes through the following four-step process as its books are closed:

1. A journal entry is recorded and posted which (a) causes all revenue accounts to have zero balances, and (b) transfers these amounts to a new account called **income summary.**

2. A journal entry is recorded and posted which (a) causes all expense accounts to have zero balances, and (b) transfers these amounts to income summary.

3. A journal entry is recorded and posted which transfers the balance in the income summary account to owners' capital, thus reducing the income summary balance to zero.

4. A journal entry is recorded and posted which transfers the balance in the withdrawals account to owners' capital, thus reducing the withdrawals account to zero.

Concept Summary

Closing Entries	
Goals of Closing Entries	1. Zero-out all revenue and expense accounts
	2. Transfer net income and withdrawals to owners' capital

Steps of Closing Process	1. Revenue accounts
	    Income summary
	      Transfer revenue amounts to income summary

	2. Income summary
	    Expense accounts
	      Transfer expense amounts to income summary

	3. Income summary
	    Owners' capital
	      Transfer net income to owners' capital

	4. Owners' capital
	    Withdrawals
	      Transfer withdrawals to owners' capital

The closing journal entries of the George S. Farnsworth Company appear in Figure 4-5. When these entries are posted to the ledger, the accounts will appear as shown in Figure 4-6. This posting will complete the accounting cycle for this firm.

FIGURE 4-5
Closing Entries

GEORGE S. FARNSWORTH COMPANY
General Journal
Page 3

Date		Transaction Accounts	PR	Debit Amount	Credit Amount
		Closing Entries			
Sept	30	Commission revenue	110	8100	
		Appraisal revenue	120	750	
		Income summary	199		8850
		Close revenues			
	30	Income summary	199	4829	
		Rent expense	150		600
		Salary expense	155		1000
		Advertising expense	160		3000
		Supplies expense	165		200
		Depreciation expense	170		15
		Interest expense	175		14
		Close expenses			
	30	Income summary	199	4021	
		Farnsworth, capital	90		4021
		Close income summary			
	30	Farnsworth, capital	90	2500	
		Farnsworth, withdrawals	95		2500
		Close withdrawal account			

The following points should be noted in the progression of entries given in Figure 4-5.

1. All revenues and expenses carry zero balances into the next period.

2. The income summary account is created to hold income statement information temporarily. It is then immediately closed out.

3. All revenues and expenses which appear in the income statement also flow through the income summary account.

4. Owners' capital increases by the amount of net income for the period and decreases by withdrawals for the period.

5. All figures that appear on the statements of owners' capital also flow through the owners' capital account.

6. The only balance sheet account affected by the closing process is owners' capital. Balance sheet accounts are *never* closed and, consequently, are termed **permanent** or **real** accounts.

7. Because only revenue, expense, and withdrawal accounts are *always* closed, they are called **temporary** or **nominal** accounts.

To check the accuracy of the closing entries, some firms prepare a **post-closing trial balance,** reflecting all closing entries. Most businesses, however, would not prepare such a trial balance.

FIGURE 4-6 General Ledger

GEORGE S. FARNSWORTH COMPANY
General Ledger

ASSETS

Cash   #1

Date	PR	Debit	Date	PR	Credit
1981			1981		
9/1	GJ1	15000	9/1	GJ1	600
9/4	GJ1	8000	9/11	GJ1	900
9/10	GJ1	2100	9/15	GJ1	500
9/22	GJ1	1500	9/18	GJ1	3000
			9/24	GJ1	500
			9/29	GJ1	2500
9/30	√	18600			

Accounts receivable   #10

Date	PR	Debit	Date	PR	Credit
1981			1981		
9/3	GJ1	100			
9/30	√	100			

Supplies   #20

Date	PR	Debit	Date	PR	Credit
1981			1981		
9/21	GJ1	800			
9/30	√	800	9/30	GJ2	200
9/30	√	600			

Equipment   #30

Date	PR	Debit	Date	PR	Credit
1981			1981		
9/11	GJ1	900			
9/30	√	900			

(continued on next page)

(Figure 4-6 continued)

Accumulated depreciation   #31

Date	PR	Debit	Date	PR	Credit
1981			1981		
			9/30	GJ2	15
			9/30	√	15

LIABILITIES

Accounts payable   #50

Date	PR	Debit	Date	PR	Credit
1981			1981		
9/24	GJ1	500	9/21	GJ1	800
			9/30	√	300

Salary payable   #52

Date	PR	Debit	Date	PR	Credit
1981			1981		
			9/30	GJ2	500
			9/30	√	500

Interest payable   #54

Date	PR	Debit	Date	PR	Credit
1981			1981		
			9/30	GJ2	14
			9/30	√	14

Note payable   #55

Date	PR	Debit	Date	PR	Credit
1981			1981		
			9/10	GJ1	2100
			9/30	√	2100

Advances from customers   #75

Date	PR	Debit	Date	PR	Credit
1981			1981		
			9/15	GJ1	1500
9/30	GJ2	750	9/30	√	1500
			9/30	√	750

OWNERS' EQUITY

Farnsworth, capital   #90

Date	PR	Debit	Date	PR	Credit
1981			1981	·	
			9/1	GJ1	15000
9/30	GJ3	2500	9/30	√	15000
			9/30	GJ3	4021
			9/30	√	16521

Farnsworth, withdrawals   #95

Date	PR	Debit	Date	PR	Credit
1981			1981		
9/29	GJ1	2500	9/30	GJ3	2500
9/30	√	0			

(continued on next page)

(Figure 4-6 continued)

Commission revenue #110

Date	PR	Debit	Date	PR	Credit
1981			1981		
			9/3	GJ1	100
			9/4	GJ1	8000
9/30	GJ3	8100	9/30	√	8100
			9/30	√	0

Appraisal revenue #120

Date	PR	Debit	Date	PR	Credit
1981			1981		
9/30	GJ3	750	9/30	GJ2	750
			9/30	√	0

Rent expense #150

Date	PR	Debit	Date	PR	Credit
1981			1981		
9/1	GJ1	600	9/30	GJ3	600
9/30	√	0			

Salary expense #155

Date	PR	Debit	Date	PR	Credit
1981			1981		
9/15	GJ1	500			
9/30	GJ2	500			
9/30	√	1000	9/30	GJ3	1000
9/30	√	0			

Advertising expense #160

Date	PR	Debit	Date	PR	Credit
1981			1981		
9/18	GJ1	3000	9/30	GJ3	3000
9/30	√	0			

Supplies expense #165

Date	PR	Debit	Date	PR	Credit
1981			1981		
9/30	GJ2	200	9/30	GJ3	200
9/30	√	0			

Depreciation expense #170

Date	PR	Debit	Date	PR	Credit
1981			1981		
9/30	GJ2	15	9/30	GJ3	15
9/30	√	0			

Interest expense #175

Date	PR	Debit	Date	PR	Credit
1981			1981		
9/30	GJ2	14	9/30	GJ3	14
9/30	√	0			

Income summary #199

Date	PR	Debit	Date	PR	Credit
1981			1981		
9/30	GJ4	4829	9/30	GJ3	8850
9/30	GJ3	4021			
			9/30	√	0

Summary

The last four steps of the accounting cycle are all performed once at the end of each accounting period.

Adjusting entries record the cumulative effect of internal events. Internal events occur continuously, and their effect is contained within the business. As with all journal entries, adjustments must be posted to the proper ledger accounts. External events, on the other hand, occur between the business and outsiders; and the effects of these events are recorded, classified, and summarized in the first three steps of the accounting cycle.

The adjusted trial balance then reflects the results of all events engaged in by the business, both external and internal. The income statement, statement of owners' capital, and balance sheet can be prepared directly from the adjusted trial balance.

Once financial statements are prepared, the final step in the accounting cycle is closing the books. Only accounts, such as revenues, expenses, and withdrawals, which are temporary extensions of owner's equity are closed. These accounts have collected information from the current accounting period. This information must be transferred to the permanent owners' equity accounts and temporary accounts given zero balances to start the new accounting period. Thus, the permanent balance sheet accounts reflect the cumulative effect of all transactions of all accounting periods.

Presentation of the accounting cycle and financial statements is completed in Chapter 5 with a discussion of classified financial statements and corporate accounting.

Key Terms

Accrued expense
Accrued revenue
Accumulated depreciation
Adjusted trial balance
Adjusting entries
Closing entries
Contra-asset
Deferred revenue (unearned revenue)
Depreciation
External events
Income summary

Internal events
Permanent accounts (real accounts)
Post-closing trial balance
Temporary accounts (nominal accounts)

Comprehensive Review Problem

Green Gardens Company provides gardening and landscaping services. The trial balance at December 31, 1982, follows:

GREEN GARDENS COMPANY
Trial Balance
December 31, 1982

Acct. No.	Account Title	Debit	Credit
1	Cash	$12,900	
5	Accounts receivable	2,900	
10	Unexpired insurance	2,000	
12	Prepaid rent	6,300	
15	Supplies	800	
20	Equipment	22,000	
21	Accumulated depreciation: Equipment		$ 2,200
25	Accounts payable		1,200
30	Note payable		5,000
33	Advances from customers		14,500
40	M. Many, capital		22,000
50	Withdrawals	1,000	
55	Services revenue		17,000
60	Salaries expense	11,500	
65	Utilities expense	1,500	
67	Supplies expense	1,000	
		$61,900	$61,900

Other accounts that appear in the general ledger with zero (—0—) balances are

35	Salaries payable
37	Interest payable
63	Rent expense
70	Depreciation expense
72	Insurance expense
78	Interest expense
80	Income summary

Additional information:

1. The balance in the prepaid rent account on January 1, 1982, was $2,100, representing rent for January to June paid in advance. On July 1, Green Gardens renewed the lease and paid the rent for one year in advance at $350 per month.

2. A count of supplies on December 31 reveals that $700 of supplies had been used up.

3. The useful life of the equipment has been estimated at ten years from the date of acquisition.

4. The yearly interest rate on the note payable is 12 percent. The money was borrowed on October 1, 1982, and interest is payable on the maturity date (September 30, 1983).

5. The company purchased a five-year, $2,000 insurance policy on January 1, 1982.

6. Gardening services worth $11,750 were provided for customers who had paid in advance.

7. At December 31, gardening services worth $725 had been provided for customers, but bills had not yet been sent.

8. Salaries earned but not yet paid amounted to $150 at December 31.

Required:

1. Set up a general ledger for Green Gardens Company using balances in the unadjusted trial balance. Journalize and post all necessary adjusting entries.

2. Prepare an adjusted trial balance.

3. Prepare an income statement and statement of owners' capital for the year ended December 31, 1982, and a balance sheet as of December 31, 1982.

4. Journalize and post all closing entries to be made on December 31, 1982.

Solution to Comprehensive Review Problem

GREEN GARDENS COMPANY
General Ledger

Cash   #1

Date	PR	Debit	Date	PR	Credit
1982					
12/31	√	12,900			

Accounts receivable   #5

Date	PR	Debit	Date	PR	Credit
1982					
12/31	√	2,900			
12/31	GJ2	725			
12/31	√	3,625			

Unexpired insurance   #10

Date	PR	Debit	Date	PR	Credit
1982			1982		
12/31	√	2,000	12/31	GJ2	400
12/31	√	1,600			

Prepaid rent   #12

Date	PR	Debit	Date	PR	Credit
1982					
12/31	√	6,300	12/31	GJ2	4,200
12/31	√	2,100			

Supplies   #15

Date	PR	Debit	Date	PR	Credit
1982					
12/31	√	800			
12/31	GJ2	300			
12/31	√	1,100			

Equipment   #20

Date	PR	Debit	Date	PR	Credit
1982					
12/31	√	22,000			

Accumulated depreciation: Equipment   #21

Date	PR	Debit	Date	PR	Credit
1982			1982		
			12/31	√	2,200
			12/31	GJ2	2,200
			12/31	√	4,400

Accounts payable   #25

Date	PR	Debit	Date	PR	Credit
			1982		
			12/31	√	1,200

Notes payable					#30
Date	PR	Debit	Date	PR	Credit
			1982		
			12/31	√	5,000

Advances from customers					#33
Date	PR	Debit	Date	PR	Credit
1982			1982		
12/31	GJ2	11,750	12/31	√	14,500
			12/31	√	2,750

Salaries payable					#35
Date	PR	Debit	Date	PR	Credit
			1982		
			12/31	GJ2	150
			12/31	√	150

Interest payable					#37
Date	PR	Debit	Date	PR	Credit
			1982		
			12/31	GJ2	150
			12/31	√	150

M. Many, capital					#40
Date	PR	Debit	Date	PR	Credit
1982			1982		
			12/31	√	22,000
12/31	GJ2	1,000	12/31	GJ2	8,675
			12/31	√	29,675

Withdrawals					#50
Date	PR	Debit	Date	PR	Credit
1982			1982		
12/31	√	1,000	12/31	GJ2	1,000
12/31	√	0			

Service revenue					#55
Date	PR	Debit	Date	PR	Credit
1982			1982		
			12/31	√	17,000
			12/31	GJ2	11,750
			12/31	GJ2	725
12/31	GJ2	29,475	12/31	√	29,475
			12/31	√	0

Salaries expense					#60
Date	PR	Debit	Date	PR	Credit
1982			1982		
12/31	√	11,500			
12/31	GJ2	150			
12/31	√	11,650	12/31	GJ2	11,650
12/31	√	0			

Rent expense #63

Date	PR	Debit	Date	PR	Credit
1982			1982		
12/31	GJ2	4,200	12/31	GJ2	4,200
12/31	√	0			

Utilities expense #65

Date	PR	Debit	Date	PR	Credit
1982			1982		
12/31	√	1,500	12/31	GJ2	1,500
12/31	√	0			

Supplies expense #67

Date	PR	Debit	Date	PR	Credit
1982			1982		
12/31	√	1,000	12/31	GJ2	300
12/31	√	700	12/31	GJ2	700
12/31	√	0			

Depreciation expense #70

Date	PR	Debit	Date	PR	Credit
1982			1982		
12/31	GJ2	2,200	12/31	GJ2	2,200
12/31	√	0			

Insurance expense #72

Date	PR	Debit	Date	PR	Credit
1982			1982		
12/31	GJ2	400	12/31	GJ2	400
12/31	√	0			

Interest expense #78

Date	PR	Debit	Date	PR	Credit
1982			1982		
12/31	GJ2	150	12/31	GJ2	150
12/31	√	0			

Income summary #90

Date	PR	Debit	Date	PR	Credit
1982			1982		
12/31	GJ2	22,535	12/31	GJ2	29,475
12/31	GJ2	6,940			
			12/31	√	0

GREEN GARDENS COMPANY
General Journal   Page 2

Date		Transaction Accounts	PR	Debit	Credit
		Adjusting Entries			
Dec.	31	Rent expense	63	4,200	
		Prepaid rent	12		4,200
		Prepaid rent used up Jan. 1, 1982, to Dec. 1, 1982			
	31	Supplies	67	300	
		Supplies expense	15		300
		Consumption of supplies			
	31	Depreciation expense	70	2,200	
		Accumulated depreciation: Equipment	21		2,200
		Depreciation on equipment for year ended Dec. 31, 1982			
	31	Interest expense	78	150	
		Interest payable	37		150
		Accrue three months interest on note payable ($5,000 $\times$ .12 $\times$ 3/12 = $150)			
	31	Insurance expense	72	400	
		Unexpired insurance	10		400
		Consumption of insurance			
	31	Advances from customers	33	11,750	
		Services revenue	55		11,750
		Earned revenue as services performed			
	31	Accounts receivable	5	725	
		Services revenue	55		725
		Accrue revenue for services performed			
	31	Salaries expense	60	150	
		Salaries payable	35		150
		Accrue salaries owed			
		Closing Entries			
Dec.	31	Services revenue	55	29,475	
		Income summary	90		29,475
		Close revenue accounts			
	31	Income summary	90	20,800	
		Salaries expense	60		11,650
		Utilities expense	65		1,500
		Rent expense	64		4,200
		Supplies expense	67		700
		Depreciation expense	70		2,200
		Interest expense	78		150
		Insurance expense	72		400
		Close expenses			
	31	Income summary	90	8,675	
		M. Many, capital	40		8,675
		Close income summary			
	31	M. Many, capital	40	1,000	
		Withdrawals	50		1,000
		Close withdrawals account			

GREEN GARDENS COMPANY
Adjusted Trial Balance
December 31, 1982

	Debit	Credit
Cash	$ 12,900	
Accounts receivable	3,625	
Unexpired insurance	1,600	
Prepaid rent	2,100	
Supplies	1,100	
Equipment	22,000	
Accumulated depreciation: Equipment		$ 4,400
Accounts payable		1,200
Notes payable		5,000
Advances from customers		2,750
Salaries payable		150
Interest payable		150
M. Many, capital		22,000
Withdrawals	1,000	
Services revenue		29,475
Salaries expense	11,650	
Rent expense	4,200	
Utilities expense	1,500	
Supplies expense	700	
Depreciation expense	2,200	
Insurance expense	400	
Interest expense	150	
	$ 65,125	$65,125

GREEN GARDENS COMPANY
Income Statement
For the Year Ended December 31, 1982

Services revenue		$29,475
Expenses		
Salaries	$ 11,650	
Utilities	1,500	
Rent	4,200	
Supplies	700	
Depreciation	2,200	
Interest	150	
Insurance	400	
Total expenses		20,800
Net income		$ 8,675

GREEN GARDENS COMPANY
Statement of Owners' Capital
For the Year Ended December 31, 1982

M. Many, capital, Dec. 31, 1981	$ 22,000
Net income	8,675
Withdrawals	(1,000)
M. Many, capital, Dec. 31, 1982	$ 29,675

GREEN GARDENS COMPANY
Balance Sheet
December 31, 1982

ASSETS

Cash		$12,900
Accounts receivable		3,625
Unexpired insurance		1,600
Prepaid rent		2,100
Supplies		1,100
Equipment	$ 22,000	
Less: Accumulated depreciation	(4,400)	17,600
Total assets		$38,925

LIABILITIES & OWNERS' EQUITY

Liabilities	
Accounts payable	$ 1,200
Notes payable	5,000
Advances from customers	2,750
Interest payable	150
Salaries payable	150
Total liabilities	9,250
Owners' equity	
M. Many, capital	29,675
Total liabilities & owners' equity	$38,925

Questions

Q4-1. What is the difference between external and internal events? When is each recorded?

Q4-2. List three types of adjusting entries affecting expenses and give two examples of each.

Q4-3. List three types of adjusting entries affecting revenues and give two examples of each.

Q4-4. Why do advances from customers create a liability? When is an adjusting entry needed for these advances?

Q4-5. Distinguish between a trial balance and an adjusted trial balance.

Q4-6. Which accounts are affected by closing entries? What is the purpose of the income summary account?

Q4-7. Financial statements should be prepared in a prescribed order. What is this order and why is it important?

Q4-8. In what order would the following steps be performed?
  a. Prepare income statement
  b. Journalize external events
  c. Post internal events
  d. Compute balance in each account
  e. Prepare balance sheet

f. Journalize and post closing entries

g. Post external events

h. Prepare statement of owners' capital

i. Journalize internal events

j. Compute adjusted balance in each account

Exercises

E4-1. The A-1 Guard Service Company uses accrual accounting and prepares monthly financial statements. Listed below are some of the external transactions to which the company was a party during March and April. Indicate which of these transactions would normally require an adjusting entry on March 31.

a. March 1, an automobile was purchased for cash.

b. March 8, additional shares of stock in the company were sold to owners.

c. March 13, fees for guard services to be provided customers for the period from March 15 through May 15 were collected.

d. April 25, interest was paid on a loan taken out from the bank on January 25.

e. April 25, the principal on the above loan was repaid.

E4-2. The following accounts were found in the general ledger of Anne Company. Prepare an adjusted trial balance.

Cash	$7,950	Service revenue	$10,500
Miscellaneous expense	50	Furniture	2,000
Accounts receivable	500	Notes payable	4,000
Utilities expense	400	Rent revenue	700
Prepaid insurance	300	Salaries expense	2,500
Anne, capital	3,000	Equipment	4,500
Supplies	150	Advertising expense	600
Accounts payable	750		

E4-3. Determine the effect of each of the following on the basic accounting equation, $A = L + OE$

a. Accrual of interest on accounts receivable

b. Repayment of bank loan including interest

c. Depreciation on equipment

d. Wages earned by employees which will be paid next accounting period

e. Decrease in supplies on hand since the beginning of the accounting period.

f. Advances from customers which were properly recorded and have now been earned

E4-4. On October 1, 1981, the Raw Company paid an annual insurance premium of $4800 for coverage from October 1, 1981 to September 30, 1982. Prepare the journal entry to record the payment and the adjusting entry to be made at December 31, 1981, under each of the following independent assumptions:

a. the company debited prepaid expenses when the payment was made; and

b. the company debited insurance expense when the payment was made.

E4-5. The Mutual Insurance Company pays its agents two times a month. On the twentieth of the month, agents are paid for the first fifteen days of the month.

Agents are paid for the second half of the month on the fifth of the following month. Assume that the agents earned $12,000 during the first half of May and $15,000 during the second half of May. The company prepares monthly financial statements at the end of each month.

    a. Prepare the journal entries that would be necessary on May 20, May 31, and June 5 with respect to agents' pay for May.

    b. Why is an adjusting entry necessary on May 31 when none is necessary on May 15?

E4-6. *a.* On August 15, a company prepays the rent of $600 for September. Prepare the journal entry to record this transaction and prepare any adjusting entries that would be necessary on August 31 and/or September 30. Be sure to date each entry.

    b. On March 1, a company makes a loan from the bank. The amount of the loan is $10,000, and the annual interest rate is 12 percent. The interest is due May 1. Prepare any adjusting entries that would be necessary on March 31 and/or April 30, and prepare the journal entry to record the interest payment on May 1. Be sure to date each entry.

E4-7. *a.* A piece of machinery is purchased for $8,000. Its estimated life is five years, at the end of which it is expected to be worthless. What is the annual depreciation expense? What is the monthly depreciation expense?

    b. A note has a face value of $20,000 and an annual interest rate of 12 percent. What is the annual interest expense if the note is outstanding for an entire year? What is the monthly interest expense if the note is outstanding for an entire month?

    c. The premium on an insurance policy that provides coverage for two years is $12,000. What is the annual insurance expense associated with this policy? What is the monthly expense?

    d. A company charges a finance charge of 18 percent per year on any overdue balances in accounts receivable. Assume that at January 31, total accounts receivable were $108,000 and that $30,000 of this amount was overdue. What is the interest revenue earned during January from finance charges?

E4-8. Below are the balances appearing in the accounts of the Lamarque Company at December 31, 1982, after all adjusting entries have been made and posted.

Advertising expense	$ 4,800
Equipment	11,000
Accounts payable	5,000
Salary expense	24,000
Cash	3,600
Lamarque, capital	8,400
Revenue	63,600
Notes payable	5,000
Interest expense	500
Accounts receivable	4,300
Rent expense	7,200
Accumulated depreciation	4,500
Prepaid expense	1,200
General expense	3,700
Lamarque, withdrawals	25,000
Depreciation expense	1,200

Prepare the closing entries for December 31, 1982. Assume all accounts have normal balances. Prepare a balance sheet for the Lamarque Company as of December 31, 1982.

Problems

P4-1. You have recently been engaged by the Landry Insurance Agency to perform certain accounting activities. The secretary of the company has recorded and posted all external transactions for the year and prepared an unadjusted trial balance. You are to perform all end-of-period activities. Below is the chart of accounts prepared by the accountant who previously served the company.

100	Cash	310	Landry, withdrawals
110	Due from clients	400	Commission revenue
120	Office supplies	410	Interest revenue
130	Prepaid rent	500	Salary expense
150	Furniture and fixtures	510	Advertising expense
151	Accumulated depreciation	520	Rent expense
200	Accounts payable	530	Utilities expense
210	Notes payable	540	Supplies expense
220	Salaries payable	550	Interest expense
230	Interest payable	560	Depreciation expense
240	Advances from clients	600	Income summary
300	Landry, capital		

Required:

Based on this chart of accounts, list seven specific adjusting entries that might be necessary at the end of the period. Your answer should consist of a brief explanation of each possible adjusting entry (similar to that which would appear in the journal) and an indication as to the account that would be debited and the account that would be credited in the entry.

P4-2. The Charles I. Allen Detective Agency is in the process of preparing its *annual* financial statements. The company does not prepare monthly financial statements and, hence, makes adjusting entries only at the end of the year.

a. The premium on an insurance policy that provides coverage for the period July 1, 1982 to June 30, 1984, was paid on June 15, 1982. The amount of the premium was $4,000. Prepaid insurance was debited when the premium was paid.

b. The company borrowed $9,000 from the bank on November 1, 1982. The annual interest rate charged by the bank for this loan is 12 percent, and the interest and principal are to be repaid to the bank on January 30, 1983.

c. The company has equipment that was purchased on January 1, 1981. The cost of the equipment was $24,000, and it is expected to last ten years. Depreciation expense was properly recognized at December 31, 1981.

d. On July 1, 1982, the company collected an advance payment of $2,000 from a customer for services to be provided by the company for one year ending June 30, 1983. The services are provided evenly over that year. The account, advances from customers, was credited when the payment was received.

e. The company charges a finance charge of 1 percent per month on all amounts due from customers that have been outstanding for the entire month. Total accounts receivable at December 31, 1982, amounted to $12,000. Of this total, $3,000 was subject to finance charges (assume all revenues from finance charges prior to December have already been recognized and recorded).

Required:

Prepare the adjusting entries that would be made at December 31, 1982, for each of the above items. Show all calculations.

P4-3. Below are the unadjusted trial balance and adjusted trial balance of the Kevin Kerney Company at October 31, 1982.

Account Title	Unadjusted Trial Balance Debit	Unadjusted Trial Balance Credit	Adjusted Trial Balance Debit	Adjusted Trial Balance Credit
Cash	6,300		6,300	
Accounts receivable	3,500		3,500	
Supplies	700		100	
Equipment	5,000		5,000	
Accumulated depreciation		2,000		3,000
Accounts payable		1,700		1,700
Notes payable		4,000		4,000
Advances from customers		1,900		1,500
Kerney, capital		6,100		6,100
Kerney, withdrawals	25,000		25,000	
Commission revenue		42,000		42,400
Rent expense	4,800		4,800	
Salary expense	6,900		7,200	
Advertising expense	5,500		5,500	
	57,700	57,700		
Supplies expense			600	
Depreciation expense			1,000	
Interest expense			200	
Interest payable				200
Salaries payable				300
			59,200	59,200

Required:

1. Prepare the adjusting entries that account for the differences between the unadjusted trial balance and the adjusted trial balance.

2. Prepare the closing entries to be made at October 31, 1982.

P4-4. The Bell Company makes adjusting entries once a year at December 31 in conjunction with the preparation of its annual financial statements. Two of the transactions to which the Bell Company was a party during 1982 are described below.

a. Rent for the twelve-month period from May 1, 1981 to April 30, 1982, was paid on April 15, 1981. The amount of the payment was $7200.

b. Cash of $1,200 was received from a customer on October 18, 1981. This was for services to be provided by the Bell Company evenly over the period from November 1, 1981 through April 30, 1982.

There are two ways in which each of these external transactions might have been journalized. Regardless of the choice of method, adjusting entries would be required on December 31, 1981, and on December 31, 1982.

Required:

1. Give one method of recording transaction a and the resulting adjusting entries that would be required.

2. Give a second method of recording transaction a and the resulting adjusting entries in that case.

3. Give one method of recording transaction b and the resulting adjusting entries that would be required.

4. Give a second method of recording transaction b and the resulting adjusting entries in that case.

P4-5. Below is selected information about certain activities of the Riggins-Rawlins Company for the period from March 31, 1982 to June 1, 1982. The company uses accrual accounting, prepares monthly financial statements, and enters adjusting entries in its formal accounting records each month.

   a. On March 31, the company paid rent for the months of April and May. The total amount of the payment was $1,000.

   b. On April 1, the company made a loan from the bank. The amount of the loan was $9,000, and the annual interest rate charged by the bank is 12 percent. The $9,000 plus interest for two months was paid back to the bank on June 1.

   c. The company pays its employees twice a month, on the tenth and on the twenty-fifth. The payment on the tenth is for work done during the last half of the previous month. The payment on the twenty-fifth is for work done during the first half of the current month. Below is a detail of wages earned by employees during April and May.

April 1–15	$2,300
April 15–30	$2,100
May 1–15	$1,900
May 15–31	$2,400

   d. On April 15, the company received an advance payment from a customer in the amount of $3,000. The payment was for services to be performed by the Riggins-Rawlings Company from April 15 through May 15. The services were performed evenly over that period.

   e. On May 1, the company purchased a delivery truck for $15,000. It was estimated that the truck would last five years, after which time it would be worthless.

Required:
Prepare all of the journal entries that would be made between March 31 and June 1 with respect to the above items. Be sure to record the external transaction as well as adjusting entries for each month and to date each entry. Treat each item separately, making all the journal entries for that item for the entire two-month period before going on to the next item. The salary payment made on April 10 may be omitted because information regarding its amount is not given.

P4-6. The unadjusted trial balance as of December 31, 1982, for the Merrick Architectural Firm is given below.

MERRICK ARCHITECTURAL FIRM
Unadjusted Trial Balance
December 31, 1982

Acct. No.	Account Title	Debit	Credit
1	Cash	$ 3,700	
10	Accounts receivable	5,000	
20	Supplies	600	
30	Furniture and equipment	9,600	
31	Accumulated depreciation		$ 3,000
50	Accounts payable		1,900
60	Notes payable		4,000
70	Advances from customers		2,700
90	Merrick, capital		6,000
95	Merrick, withdrawals	25,000	
100	Revenue		41,300
130	Rent expense	4,800	
140	Salary expense	7,000	
150	General expense	3,200	
		$58,900	$58,900

Additional information:
 a. Of the $600 of supplies, $500 worth have been used during the year.
 b. Depreciation expense for the year is $1,000.
 c. Unrecorded interest expense for the year is $200.
 d. All services for which clients made advance payments were performed by the end of the year.

Required:
 1. Set up a general ledger for the Merrick Architectural Firm, putting in the accounts the balance given above. Journalize and post all adjusting entries necessary at December 31, 1982. Add any accounts necessary to the general ledger.

 2. Prepare an adjusted trial balance at December 31, 1982.

 3. Journalize and post the closing entries to be made at December 31, 1982. Prepare the ledger for the next period with post-closing balances in all nominal accounts.

P4-7. A summary of the trial balance and adjusting entries for the Speedy Delivery Company for the month ended October 31, 1982, is presented below. The company adjusts and closes its accounts at the end of each month. The adjustments made at October 31 were based on the following information:

 a. A physical count shows the cost of supplies on hand at the end of the period to be $460.
 b. Unexpired insurance at the end of the month amounted to $5,000.
 c. Depreciation expense for the month was $980.
 d. During the month, interest that accrued on notes payable was $180.

e. Salaries earned by employees during the month but not paid were $1,100.

f. All services for which customers had paid in advance were performed by month's end.

g. Interest earned but uncollected during the month on notes receivable was $30.

SPEEDY DELIVERY COMPANY
Adjusting Entries
For the Month ended October 31, 1982

Account Title	Unadjusted Trial Balance		Adjusting Entries	
	Debit	Credit	Debit	Credit
Cash	6,600			
Notes receivable	2,400			
Accounts receivable	4,700			
Supplies	580			(a) 120
Prepaid insurance	6,000			(b) 1,000
Equipment	53,000			
Accumulated depreciation		16,000		(c) 980
Notes payable		18,000		
Accounts payable		2,200		
Advances from customers		750	(f) 750	
Fred Rogers, capital		32,500		
Fred Rogers, withdrawals	2,500			
Delivery revenue		12,860		(f) 750
Salaries expense	3,300		(e) 1,100	
Gasoline expense	1,800			
Rent expense	600			
Utilities expense	150			
Maintenance expense	230			
Advertising expense	450			
	82,310	82,310		
Supplies expense			(a) 120	
Insurance expense			(b) 1,000	
Depreciation expense			(c) 980	
Interest expense			(d) 180	
Interest payable				(d) 180
Salaries payable				(e) 1,100
Interest revenue				(g) 30
Interest receivable			(g) 30	
			4,160	4,160

Required:

Prepare an income statement and statement of owner's capital for the month ended October 31, 1982, and a balance sheet as of October 31, 1982.

P4-8. The unadjusted trial balance for the Pearl Maintenance Company as of December 31, 1982, is presented below.

PEARL MAINTENANCE COMPANY
Unadjusted Trial Balance
December 31, 1982

Acct. No.	Account Title	Debit	Credit
100	Cash	$12,600	
110	Accounts receivable	8,800	
120	Supplies	6,700	
130	Prepaid insurance	900	
150	Equipment	65,700	
151	Accumulated depreciation		$32,100
200	Accounts payable		2,200
210	Notes payable		10,000
250	Advances from customers		9,300
300	Maxi Pearl, capital		27,400
311	Maxi Pearl, withdrawals	3,000	
400	Revenues		91,800
500	Salaries expense	64,200	
510	Rent expense	6,000	
520	Utilities expense	1,800	
530	Interest expense	1,000	
540	Miscellaneous expense	2,100	
		$172,800	$172,800

Additional information:
a. A physical count shows the cost of supplies on hand at December 31 to be $1,300.
b. Unexpired insurance at December 31, is $200.
c. Depreciation expense for the year is $7,800.
d. Interest expense that has accrued during the year and not been recorded or paid is $200.
e. Two-thirds of the services for which customers made advance payments were performed during the year.
f. Salaries earned by employees during the year but unpaid at December 31 amounted to $1,100.

Required:

1. Set up a general ledger for the Pearl Maintenance Company using balances in the unadjusted trial balance. Journalize and post all adjusting entries.

2. Prepare an adjusted trial balance.

3. Prepare an income statement and statement of owner's capital for the year ended December 31, 1982, and a balance sheet as of December 31, 1982.

4. Journalize and post all closing entries to be made at December 31, 1982. Prepare the ledger for the new period with the post-closing balance in all nominal accounts.

CHAPTER 5

Classified Financial Statements and Corporate Accounting

Chapter Outline

5.1 *Classified Financial Statements.* Presentation of current and noncurrent asset and liability classifications and the specific types of assets and liabilities which comprise these classifications; illustration of classified financial statements for a large corporation.

5.2 *Corporation Accounting—Double-Entry Bookkeeping.* Introductory discussion of the differences between corporation and sole proprietorship accounting; illustration of the service firm transactions in the corporate context.

5.3 *Corporation Accounting—End-of-Period Procedures.* Comparison of end-of-period procedures for a sole proprietorship with those for a corporation; illustration of financial statements and closing entries for a corporate service firm.

5.4 *Worksheet.* Illustration of the worksheet which can be used to help prevent errors and when adjusting entries will not be entered into the accounting records.

Accounting and the Real World

Rich Is Better

Fashions change—in finance as well as in the length of skirts. Time was when no self-respecting treasurer would be caught with large cash balances; it was a sign that his company didn't know what to do with its money and constituted an open invitation to a takeover. But cash is coming back. At 15 percent interest, you can earn more with your cash than you can with many of your businesses.

Take Boeing Company, sitting with *$2.4 billion* in cash. Down the road, it will use that money to bring out the new generations of aircraft that will keep it competitive. Right now, it can earn $300 million a year just by investing that cash in U.S. Treasury Notes.

At the opposite extreme from the cash rich are the cash poor. When banks lend money at 7 percent, it almost pays to be cash poor; you can borrow what you need cheaply from the banks at an after-tax rate of only about 3.5 percent. But when the prime is at 15¾ percent, it's another matter, especially for companies that must borrow heavily for seasonal purposes.

"Cash is sterile," the bright young MBAs used to say. No more. Below are ten selected companies that are especially cash rich and ten others that are cash poor, ranked on the basis of cash as a percentage of current liabilities.

	The Rich						
		—Cash as Percent of—				Cash	
Company	Cash and Equivalents (mil)	Current Assets	Current Liabilities	Revenues (mil)	Latest 12-Months EPS	per Share 9/30/79	Recent Price
Cash Rich							
Walt Disney	$ 355.6	73.8%	295.1%	$ 796.8	$3.51	$11.01	37
Roadway Express	172.1	67.1	103.7	985.2	2.63	8.76	24¾
St. Regis	306.6	35.2	99.2	2,300.2	4.82	9.53	27½
Digital Equipment	389.2	25.6	96.6	1,804.1	4.37	9.58	63
National Gypsum	96.8	25.5	94.3	906.3	4.77	5.87	18⅜
Boeing	2,411.0	66.7	91.7	5,463.0	7.31	37.60	44⅝
American Home Products	401.2	27.1	84.2	3,062.6	2.44	2.58	27½
Congoleum	96.7	36.6	83.9	575.8	4.29	8.21	34½
American Broadcasting	200.5	26.5	83.0	1,784.0	5.71	7.26	39½
SmithKline	282.2	35.1	80.4	1,112.0	3.62	4.65	57½

The Poor						
Cash Poor						
Baxter Travenol Labs	8.4	1.2	2.8	1,004.2	3.30	0.25	46⅛
TRW	24.0	1.6	2.6	3,787.2	6.04	0.83	35⅜
Wickes	7.3	1.3	2.4	1,910.1	3.31	0.68	14⅜
Georgia-Pacific	18.0	1.6	2.3	4,403.0	3.18	0.18	24½
Di Giorgio	4.0	3.1	1.8	897.1	1.75	0.64	9⅞
Brunswick	2.7	0.5	1.6	1,126.4	2.25	0.14	11½
Wetterau	1.6	1.2	1.5	1,059.0	1.76	0.22	12
General Dynamics	9.2	0.9	1.2	3,205.2	6.51	0.34	46½
International Harvester	20.6	0.7	1.1	6,664.3	9.63	0.67*	37¾
Envirotech	0.2	0.1	0.1	551.4	1.23	0.04	12⅞

Forbes, December 10, 1979, Page 92.

Financial statements are the output of the financial accounting process. A full understanding of financial statements requires a grasp of the definition, valuation, and classification of each of the major components of the statements. The definition and valuation of financial statements were discussed in Chapters 1 and 2. Classification is discussed in the first section of this chapter. Other sections of this chapter consider the accounting cycle from a corporate viewpoint and explore the double-entry bookkeeping and end-of-period complexities specific to corporations.

5.1   Classified Financial Statements

An important part of the information conveyed by financial statements is the grouping of the components of the statements. This classification indicates that certain individual assets possess similar characteristics and that certain individual liabilities do also. Asset and liability classification, then, is an important part of financial statement preparation and use.

Classification of Assets

Assets are the resources of a business which possess future exchange or use value, are under the control of the business entity, and have a dollar value that results from a specific accounting transaction or transactions. Even the smallest business may have assets of several different types. If a financial report is to be prepared which presents these assets in a meaningful manner to outside parties, some guidelines for presentation are necessary. These guidelines should help determine the major types of assets a business may possess and how each type of asset should be presented on its balance sheet.

The asset classification pattern used most often in financial accounting recognizes two major categories of assets. The basis for classification of each individual asset into one of these two major groups is the liquidity (nearness to cash) and the expected life of the asset. The two categories are called current assets and noncurrent assets.

Current Assets Current assets are those that are expected to be converted to cash or used up within one accounting period or **operating cycle** (whichever is longer) from the balance sheet date. Notice several important aspects of this definition of current assets.

1. Classification of assets on a balance sheet requires consideration of the future and what is likely to happen to each asset in the upcoming accounting period. As a result, the intentions and expectations of company management are important to the classification process.

2. The basis of classification is time, and the point of reference is always the date of the balance sheet on which the classification is taking place.

3. Some current assets are converted directly into cash (collection of an account receivable), while others may be physically used up as time passes (consumption of supplies).

4. The operating cycle of a business is the time span between the purchase of goods for resale (inventory) and the receipt of cash from the sale of those goods to customers. For most businesses, this cycle requires less than one year; therefore, the basis for classification of current assets is the one-year period. Some businesses, however, may have operating cycles of more than one year and, thus, would classify assets based on the length of their operating cycles.

Noncurrent Assets Noncurrent assets are those assets whose future benefit to the business is expected to extend beyond the next accounting period. These are the assets of long-term benefit to the business, such as buildings, machines, cars, trucks, and land. Any asset not expected to be converted into cash or used up during the upcoming year (or operating cycle) would necessarily be classified as a noncurrent asset.

Classified Balance Sheets

Each of these two major groups of assets can be divided into several specific assets and presented on a balance sheet with current assets listed first and noncurrent assets listed next. Figure 5-1 presents the comparative balance sheets of a major corporation as of the end of two consecutive accounting periods. When two or more financial statements are presented together in this way, the statements are called comparative statements. Most large corporations present comparative financial statements in some form. In all classified balance sheets, the same basic classification scheme is used; however, some differences may be noted. These differences in classification and presentation result primarily because of the differences in size and scope of the businesses. Some of these differences, however, are traceable to matters of preference on the part of company management. Absolute agreement in matters of classification does not exist within accounting.

Figure 5-1 deserves careful study. Some discussion of the specific asset types illustrated in these statements will help develop a general understanding of all balance sheets. As these asset types are presented, keep in mind the definition of an asset discussed in Chapter 1 and apply it to each of these assets.

FIGURE 5-1
Classified Balance
Sheet

GENERAL MOTORS CORPORATION
Balance Sheet (dollars in millions)
December 31, 1979, and 1978

	1979	1978
ASSETS		
Current Assets		
Cash	$ 247.1	$ 177.3
United States Government and other marketable securities and time deposits—at cost, which approximates market:		
Held for payment of income taxes	373.0	791.3
Other	2,366.3	3,086.2
Accounts and notes receivable	5,030.4	5,638.7
Inventories	8,076.3	7,576.7
Prepaid expenses	463.4	729.3
Total current assets	16,556.5	17,999.5
Investments and miscellaneous assets	3,828.2	2,812.1
Common stock held for the incentive program	192.9	181.1
Property		
Real estate, plants, and equipment	24,879.4	22,052.0
Less accumulated depreciation	(14,298.2)	(13,438.8)
Net real estate, plants and equipment	10,581.2	8,613.2
Special tools—less amortization	1,057.0	992.4
Total property	11,638.2	9,605.6
Total assets	$ 32,215.8	$ 30,598.3
LIABILITIES & STOCKHOLDERS' EQUITY		
Current liabilities		
Accounts, drafts, and loans payable	$ 4,305.4	$ 4,612.4
United States, foreign, and other income taxes payable	478.6	944.8
Accrued liabilities	5,084.3	4,493.4
Total current liabilities	9,868.3	10,050.6
Long-term debt—less unamortized discount	880.0	978.9
Other liabilities	1,551.6	1,384.4
Deferred investment tax credits	651.7	519.9
Other deferred credits	84.9	94.6
Stockholders' equity		
Preferred stock ($5.00 series, $183.6; $3.75 series, $100.0)	283.6	283.6
Common stock	487.4	480.1
Capital surplus (principally additional paid-in capital)	1,034.6	792.0
Net income retained for use in the business	17,373.7	16,014.2
Total stockholders' equity	19,179.3	17,569.9
Total liabilities & stockholders' equity	$ 32,215.8	$ 30,598.3

Courtesy of General Motors

Types of Current Assets

Six basic types of current assets appear on most balance sheets. The corporate balance sheet in Figure 5-1 exhibits all six.

Cash Cash includes all amounts possessed by a business whether on hand in the business or in the bank. Cash is the most liquid asset (most readily usable for paying bills) and, thus, is always listed first on balance sheets of U.S. companies.

Marketable Securities Sometimes businesses may have excess cash on hand for a short time. When this happens, it is desirable to invest this cash in some type of short-term, temporary investment which will allow the business to earn more interest than that paid by a bank. When companies invest their cash in this way, usually in U.S. Government Bonds or similar securities, an asset very close to cash is created. This asset can be quickly converted to cash by selling the investment and is usually held for only short periods.

Receivables Receivables are amounts owed to a business by customers and others. The most common receivable, called **accounts receivable,** results from the sale of merchandise or performance of services on credit for customers. These amounts owed are expected to be collected within a short period of time. A second receivable, called **notes receivable,** also represents amounts owed to the business. The origin of these amounts may be from credit sales or services, or from a loan made by the business to employees, customers, suppliers, or others. With notes receivable, a formal, legal document exists between the business and the debtor, which is evidence of the debt. No such "note" exists for accounts receivable.

Inventory For businesses that sell a product, inventory is usually the largest current asset. **Inventory** on a balance sheet indicates the acquisition cost of the products being held by the business for resale to customers as of the balance sheet date. These goods held for resale are the stock-in-trade of the business. Only goods held for resale are called inventory.

Supplies Most businesses hold and use certain incidental assets, such as cleaning materials, paper, pens, pencils, and so on. These assets are purchased to be used up in the normal course of business operations. The cost of these items on hand at the balance sheet date is called **supplies.** Notice the basic difference between inventory, which is purchased to be resold to customers, and supplies, which are purchased to be physically used by the business.

Prepaid Items Businesses must pay for some services in advance. Once payment is made, a legal right to receive these services, such as insurance protection, advertising, or the use of a rented building, is created. This legal right is an asset to the business which has paid in advance. If a business has paid for such services and has not yet received them as of the balance sheet date, the assets are called, collectively, **prepaid items.** Generally, services paid for in advance are classified as current assets even though the actual service may not be received for several years. Because the amounts involved are usually very small, this exception is made to the general definition of current assets. The principle which allows very small amounts to be treated in the most convenient manner, even if the treatment is a departure from normal, is called the **materiality principle.** Immaterial (small) amounts may be treated in the most convenient manner.

The balance sheet in Figure 5-1 indicates that the presentation of current assets is essentially the same in large and small companies. Classification and presentation are more standardized for current assets than for noncurrent assets.

Types of Noncurrent Assets

Four fundamental types of noncurrent assets exist; however, the method of presentation of these asset types varies quite a bit. These variations are discussed in the examination of the four types of noncurrent assets.

Investments and Funds Investments and funds are the long-term counterpart of marketable securities. Sometimes businesses will invest in securities (stocks and bonds) of other companies for the purpose of gaining control of the other company or as a long-term income-producing investment, rather than as a temporary use of cash. When they do so, the investments are classified as noncurrent assets.

Property, Plant, and Equipment Property, plant, and equipment are the tangible assets used to operate the business and are the largest (in dollar terms) and most important of noncurrent assets. Included here are buildings, machines, tools, vehicles, fixtures, furniture, and land, as well as all natural resources used by the business in its operations. On the balance sheet of large businesses which possess great quantities of property, plant, and equipment, individual assets are generally combined and reported together in one figure on the balance sheet. In small businesses, these individual assets may be listed separately.

Intangibles An important characteristic of property, plant, and equipment is that these assets all have tangible, physical existence. Sometimes businesses possess productive or operating assets that have long-term benefit but are not characterized by tangible existence. Examples of this type of asset include patents, copyrights, trademarks and trade names, and goodwill. Intangible assets contribute to a business because they provide some special (usually legally based) right, or recognize some special advantages the business may have.

Both property, plant, and equipment and intangibles represent assets with use value. They contribute to a business by their ability to be used in business activity. In this sense, these assets are similar to the current asset, supplies, except that supplies are usually expected to be used up within one accounting period while long-term assets last several accounting periods. All use value assets are different from inventory, which is acquired specifically to be resold to customers and exhibits exchange value.

Deferred Charges and Other Assets Deferred charges and other assets is a catch-all category designed to accommodate those assets that do not fit into the other, more specific classifications. Deferred charges represent the long-term counterpart of prepaid items for those very long-term prepayments (perhaps, five years or more) in which a business may engage from time to time. An example would be the initial costs of starting a new business, often called organization costs, which are incurred and paid before the business is operating but benefit the business far into the future. Other assets could represent almost anything for a particular business; however, the most common assets found in this classification are long-term receivables (amounts owed to a business which will not be collected within the upcoming accounting period) and property, plant, and equipment that is no longer being used in the business and is held to be sold. Any unusual asset that cannot be otherwise classified would be reported in this category.

Concept Summary

Classification and Valuation of Assets		
Assets	*Type of Future Value*	*Basis of Valuation on Balance Sheet*
Current Assets		
Cash	Exchange	Amount on hand
Marketable securities	Exchange	Purchase cost
Receivables	Exchange	Amount expected to be collected
Inventory	Exchange	Purchase cost
Supplies	Use	Purchase cost
Prepaid items	Use	Purchase cost of services not yet used
Noncurrent Assets		
Investments	Exchange or Use	Purchase cost
Property, plant, and equipment	Use	Purchase cost minus amounts used up
Intangibles	Use	Purchase cost minus amounts used up
Deferred charges	Use	Purchase cost of services not yet used

Classification of Liabilities

The same principles of definition, classification, and valuation must be applied in the presentation of liabilities on balance sheets. Liabilities represent the obligations (usually legally based) of a business whose amounts and due dates are known with relative certainty.

The manner in which these debts are presented on a balance sheet should communicate something about the nature of the obligation and the immediacy and importance of the claim on the business. This is just what classification does. The classification of liabilities generally follows the same approach used in the classification of assets and, to some extent, depends upon how assets are classified. Liabilities are usually classified into two major categories called current liabilities and long-term liabilities. Classification into these groups depends upon when and how the obligation is expected to be satisfied.

Current Liabilities

Current liabilities include those obligations that are expected to be satisfied within one year or operating cycle, whichever is longer, from the balance sheet date by the use of current assets. Note the following important points about current liabilities.

1. They represent the most immediate debts facing the business and will be the first obligations satisfied in the upcoming accounting period.

2. They represent claims against the current assets of the business. If a debt is to be satisfied in the upcoming accounting period but will not be satisfied by the use of current assets, the debt is not a current liability and should be classified as long-term.

Any business may face a number of different types of short-term obligations. Two types of current liabilities, however, are most important at this stage of study. Several other specific current liabilities will be added in later chapters.

Accounts Payable Credit sales of goods to customers are an important activity of most businesses and give rise to accounts receivable. So also is the regular purchase of merchandise (inventory) and other current assets from suppliers. When such purchases take place using credit, a claim against the business results. These amounts owed by a business to its suppliers which are to be paid within the upcoming accounting period are called **accounts payable.** The phrase "purchase on account" is often used to indicate the acquisition of an asset on short-term credit.

Notes Payable From time to time a business may borrow money with the expectation of repaying the loan within the upcoming accounting period. Usually a formal, legal document called a note is created when this occurs, providing evidence of the amount owed by the business to the lender. When such a legal document exists, the claim against the business assets is called a **note payable.**

Long-Term Liabilities

Debts or obligations may exist that will not be satisfied in the next year or operating cycle, or will be satisfied by the use of other than current assets. These debts are reported as **long-term liabilities.** Two important types of long-term debts are found on many balance sheets.

Notes Payable If money is borrowed from a lender under an agreement which calls for repayment beyond the upcoming year (perhaps in two, three or more years from the balance sheet date), the resulting note payable would be classified and reported as a long-term liability. Thus, a note payable may be short-term or long-term depending upon when it is to be repaid.

Bonds Payable Sometimes a business may want to borrow very large amounts of money simultaneously from many lenders and repay the money over long periods of time. One way to accomplish this is for the business to create a series of formal IOUs and sell these to investors who are willing to lend money to the company. These IOUs are called bonds and represent a claim against business assets. They are obligations to be satisfied over several accounting periods.

Concept Summary

Classification and Valuation of Liabilities		
Liabilities	*Nature of Claim*	*Basis of Valuation on Balance Sheet*
Current Liabilities Accounts payable	Primary and legal	Amounts owed to suppliers of goods and services
Notes payable	Primary and legal	Amounts owed for which legal documents exist
Long-Term Liabilities Notes payable	Primary and legal	Amounts owed over several future periods for which legal documents exist
Bonds payable	Primary and legal	Amounts owed over several future periods to creditors holding bonds

5.2 Corporation Accounting—Double-Entry Bookkeeping

The three basic types of business organizations—sole proprietorships, partnerships, and corporations—were introduced in Chapter 1. That chapter also sketched out the legal differences between these types of business organizations. The different financial statements that these business organizations would prepare were examined in Chapter 2. The basic accounting cycle for unincorporated businesses was presented in Chapters 3 and 4. This section will show how accounting for individual transactions would differ if a business assumed the corporate form.

Specifically, the concern here is to show how the accounting for George Farnsworth's real estate firm (Chapters 3 and 4) would differ if it were organized as a corporation rather than as a sole proprietorship.

Proprietorship versus Corporation

From an accounting standpoint, the differences between a sole proprietorship and a corporation are in accounting for owner's equity. For a situation like the real estate firm of George Farnsworth, two specific differences are: (1) accounting for owner contributed capital and (2) accounting for payments to the owner.

Contribution of Capital A corporation is a legal entity separate from its owner(s). Thus, Mr. Farnsworth's original contribution of $15,000 will, in a corporation, be in exchange for shares of stock which will evidence his ownership. Assume, then, that Mr. Farnsworth created George S. Farnsworth, Incorporated. Mr. Farnsworth then contributed $15,000 to George

S. Farnsworth, Inc., and the company issued 150 shares of stock. The entry to record this capital contribution would be the following:

```
Sept  1     Cash  .............................................  15,000
                Capital stock  ............................................  15,000
            Issued 150 shares at $100 per share
```

This entry is very similar to the entry for a sole proprietorship. The corporation's chart of accounts could simply have capital stock as account #90 instead of Farnsworth, capital.

Payment to Owner The other area of difference is that of payments to the owner. For a corporation, this disbursement of assets (typically cash) is called a dividend. The entry would then be:

```
Sept 29     Dividends  ...........................................  2,500
                Cash  .................................................  2,500
            Pay dividends to owner
```

This journal entry is very similar to that for a sole proprietorship. The corporation would have dividends as account #95 instead of Farnsworth, withdrawals.

Concept Summary

Differences Between Sole Proprietorship and Corporation Accounting		
Area of Difference	Sole Proprietorship	Corporation
Owner contributes capital	Capital account	Capital stock
Payments to owner	Withdrawal account	Dividends

Figure 5-2 summarizes the differences in journal entries, depending upon whether the business is a sole proprietorship or a corporation.

Figures 5-3 and 5-4 then show the related effects on the general ledger accounts and the trial balance, respectively. The trial balance for the corporation is identical to the trial balance of the sole proprietorship, with two exceptions:

1. Capital stock has a credit balance of $15,000 in the corporation. In the sole proprietorship, the Farnsworth, capital account has a credit balance of $15,000.

2. Dividends has a balance of $2,500 in the corporation. In the sole proprietorship, the Farnsworth, withdrawals account has a debit balance of $2,500.

FIGURE 5-2
Journal Entries:
Different Forms of
Business Organization

Sole Proprietorship

Date			Transaction Accounts	PR	Debit Amount	Credit Amount
1981 Sept	1		Cash	1	15000	
			Farnsworth, capital	90		15000
			Original capital contribution			
	29		Farnsworth, withdrawals	95	2500	
			Cash	1		2500
			Payment to owner			

Corporation

Date			Transaction Accounts	PR	Debit Amount	Credit Amount
1981 Sept	1		Cash	1	15000	
			Capital stock	90		15000
			Original capital contribution			
	29		Dividends	95	2500	
			Cash	1		2500
			Pay dividend to owner			

FIGURE 5-3
Selected Ledger Accounts: Different Forms of Business Organization

Sole Proprietorship
Farnsworth, capital #90

Date	PR	Debit	Date	PR	Credit
1981			1981		
			9/1	GJ1	15000
			9/30	√	15000

Corporation
Capital stock #90

Date	PR	Debit	Date	PR	Credit
1981			1981		
			9/1	GJ1	15000
			9/30	√	15000

Farnsworth, withdrawals #95

Date	PR	Debit	Date	PR	Credit
1981 9/29	GJ2	2500	1981		
9/30	√	2500			

Dividends #95

Date	PR	Debit	Date	PR	Credit
1981 9/29	GJ2	2500	1981		
9/30	√	2500			

GEORGE S. FARNSWORTH, INC.
Trial Balance
September 30, 1981

	Debit	Credit
Cash	$18,600	
Accounts receivable	100	
Supplies	800	
Equipment	900	
Accounts payable		$ 300
Notes payable		2,100
Advances from customers		1,500
Capital stock		15,000
Dividends	2,500	
Commission revenue		8,100
Rent expense	600	
Salary expense	500	
Advertising expense	3,000	
	$27,000	$27,000

5.3   Corporation Accounting—End-of-Period Procedures

The section just completed dealt with some differences between accounting for a business as a sole proprietorship and accounting for a business
as a corporation. This section will go over how end-of-period procedures
are different in the corporate form.

**Corporate
Adjusting Entries**

The first end-of-period procedure is journalizing and posting adjusting
entries. All of the adjusting entries for the firm as a sole proprietorship
will also be adjusting entries for the firm as a corporation; however, there
will also be an additional adjusting entry for **income tax expense** on corporate income.

Income Taxes There is a major legal difference between the sole proprietorship and the corporation.

1. The owner of the sole proprietorship is taxed personally for the income
of the business. There is no direct income tax on proprietorships.

2. The corporation is legally distinct from its owners and is taxed directly
on its own income. Owners (stockholders) pay tax only on the money they
receive in dividends.

For this reason, a corporation must have one more adjusting entry (Type
2 accruing an expense) than a sole proprietorship. This additional adjusting entry will be to accrue federal income tax on the corporation's income.
The form of this entry would be

```
Income tax expense  . . . . . . . .  XXX
      Corporate income tax payable  . . . . .  XXX
```

Income Before Income Taxes The determination of net income in a corporation is, therefore, somewhat more complex than in a proprietorship because there is a new intermediate figure called income before income taxes. Income before income taxes is the difference between revenue and all expenses except the corporate income tax. At this point, the corporate income tax rate will be assumed to be 20 percent. Income tax expense is then 20 percent of income before income taxes. After this final expense is deducted, the result is net income.

Sample Company For George S. Farnsworth, Inc., revenue was $8,850, and the total of all expenses except the corporate income tax was $4,829. Income before income taxes is, thus, $4,021; and income tax expense is .20 × $4,021 = $804. Net income is, therefore, $4,021 − $804 = $3,217. The journal entry to accrue corporate income tax payable is

<pre>
Income tax expense 804
    Corporate income tax payable   804
</pre>

Corporate Financial Statements

The financial statements will be different in the corporate form. Figure 5-5 gives the income statement, the statement of retained earnings, and the balance sheet for George S. Farnsworth, Inc.

FIGURE 5-5
Company Organized as a Corporation: Financial Statements

GEORGE S. FARNSWORTH, INC.
Income Statement
For the Month Ending September 30, 1981

Revenues		
Commissions	$ 8,100	
Appraisals	750	
Total revenues		$ 8,850
Expenses		
Rent	600	
Salary	1,000	
Advertising	3,000	
Supplies	200	
Depreciation	15	
Interest	14	
Total expenses		4,829
Income before income tax		4,021
Income tax expense		804
Net income		$ 3,217

GEORGE S. FARNSWORTH, INC.
Statement of Retained Earnings
For the Month Ending September 30, 1981

Retained earnings, September 1, 1981	$ 0
Net income	3,217
Dividends	(2,500)
Retained earnings, September 30, 1981	$ 717

(continued on next page)

FIGURE 5-5
(continued)

GEORGE S. FARNSWORTH, INC.
Balance Sheet
September 30, 1981

ASSETS

Current assets

Cash	$ 18,600	
Accounts receivable	100	
Supplies	600	
Total current assets		$ 19,300
Noncurrent assets		
Equipment	900	
Less: Accumulated depreciation	(15)	
Total noncurrent assets		885
Total assets		$ 20,185

LIABILITIES & STOCKHOLDERS' EQUITY

Current liabilities

Accounts payable	$ 300	
Salary payable	500	
Interest payable	14	
Note payable	2,100	
Advances from customers	750	
Corporate income tax payable	804	
Total current liabilities		$ 4,468
Stockholders' equity		
Capital stock	15,000	
Retained earnings	717	
Total stockholders' equity		15,717
Total liabilities & stockholders' equity		$ 20,185

Corporate Closing Entries

The closing entries are the final difference between accounting for a sole proprietorship and a corporation.

Owner Capital For a sole proprietorship, there is one account (owner, capital) which records both direct and indirect investments by the owner. Thus, capital contributions are credited to this account and, as presented earlier in this chapter, income summary is closed to this account. Owner capital is, hence, credited in both cases.

Capital Stock and Retained Earnings The corporation, on the other hand, has two accounts for these two functions. Capital stock records direct investment by the owner, while retained earnings measures the indirect investment by the owner. Thus, capital contributions are credited to capital stock. Income summary, however, is closed to retained earnings. This procedure is the way the double-entry system performs the accounting task (discussed in Chapter 2) of providing a measure of the amount by which assets have increased as a result of profitable operations. The income summary account is then closed out in the following way:

Income summary .. 3,217
Retained earnings 3,217

Two accounts (capital stock and retained earnings) are used for a corporation, while only one (owner, capital) was used for a sole proprietorship. A separate account is needed for the corporation because, in many instances, state laws forbid paying dividends if they would reduce owner's equity below the amount of capital contributed by the owners. This situation is handled by creating a retained earnings account and allowing dividends only to the extent retained earnings is positive.

Owner Withdrawals In a sole proprietorship, a deduction to owner's equity is debited to an owner withdrawals account. The owner withdrawals account is then closed to owner capital.

Dividends In a corporation, on the other hand, deductions to owner's equity are debited to dividends. Retained earnings measure the amount by which assets have been created by profitable operations but have not been distributed to the owner. Thus, retained earnings increases by the amount of income (as discussed above), but then decreases by the amount of dividends. Dividends is, therefore, closed to retained earnings in the following way:

Retained earnings .. 2,500
Dividends 2,500

Concept Summary

Differences Between Sole Proprietorship and Corporate Accounting		
Area of Difference	*Sole Proprietorship*	*Corporation*
Owner-contributed capital	Asset (cash) Owner, capital	Asset (cash) Capital stock
Payments to owner	Withdrawals Asset (cash)	Dividends Asset (cash)
Income tax	No entry	Income tax expense Corporate income tax payable
Closing income to owner's equity	Income summary Owner, capital	Income summary Retained earnings
Closing deductions to owner's equity	Owner, capital Withdrawals	Retained earnings Dividends

Date		Transaction Accounts	PR	Debit Amount	Credit Amount
		Closing Entries			
Sept	30	Commission revenue	110	800	
		Appraisal revenue	120	750	
		Income summary	199		8750
		Close revenue			
	30	Income summary	199	5613	
		Rent expense	150		600
		Salary expense	155		1000
		Advertising expense	160		3000
		Supplies expense	165		200
		Depreciation expense	170		15
		Interest expense	175		14
		Income tax expense	180		784
		Close expenses			
	30	Income summary	199	3137	
		Retained earnings	92		3137
		Close income summary			
	30	Retained earnings	92	2500	
		Dividends	95		2500
		Close dividends			

Figure 5-6 provides the closing entries for George S. Farnsworth, Inc.

5.4 Worksheet

Financial statements represent the goal or culmination of all that is done in the financial accounting process. Everything is aimed at this step; that is, the communication of meaningful financial information about a business to anyone who may be interested. This communication takes the form of two primary statements (income statement and balance sheet) and one connecting statement (statement of owner's capital or retained earnings).

Uses of a Worksheet

The preparation of financial statements requires that the effects of adjusting entries be included; however, many firms prepare financial statements monthly, but do not want to record adjusting entries each month. It takes a great deal of time and effort to record the adjusting entries in the general journal and then to post them to the ledger accounts. Moreover, it is quite possible to make errors in the adjusting entries because there are so many of them and because they do not tie directly to a concrete transaction.

The **worksheet** is an informal document prepared by the accountant for his own use in developing the financial statements. A company can prepare a worksheet for monthly statements and then enter the necessary adjusting entries in the general journal only at the end of the year. Further, the financial statements can be prepared before the adjusting entries are made in the accounting records, thus providing a convenient check.

The worksheet is not part of the accounting records and it is possible to prepare the financial statements without it. These statements can be prepared easily from the adjusted trial balance. All of the information necessary for statement preparation is there, available, on the adjusted trial balance. Indeed, the financial statements for the George S. Farnsworth Company were prepared without using a worksheet.

Preparation of a Worksheet

A worksheet for the George S. Farnsworth Company is given in Figure 5-7. The seven steps in the preparation of the worksheet are discussed below.

Enter the Title and the Column Headings The title is centered, with the company name on the first line, then the identification as a worksheet, and on the third line the accounting period. The first column is for account titles. There are then six pairs of columns for (1) the unadjusted trial balance, (2) the adjusting entries, (3) the adjusted trial balance, (4) the income statement, (5) the statement of owner's capital or retained earnings, and (6) the balance sheet. Each pair consists of both a debit and a credit.

Enter the Unadjusted Trial Balance The account titles and the dollar amounts are recorded. Each balance must be entered in the proper debit or credit column. When the totals of both columns are equal, this step is complete. The procedure is essentially the same as that followed in developing the unadjusted trial balance. As a result, if a worksheet is prepared, a separate unadjusted trial balance can be omitted.

Enter the Adjusting Entries Generally speaking, the adjusting entries will require accounts that are not in the unadjusted trial balance. These accounts are added beneath the accounts for the unadjusted trial balance. As an illustration, the same five adjusting entries discussed earlier are entered on the worksheet in Figure 5-7. The first adjusting entry is a debit to supplies expense and a credit to supplies. Because supplies expense is not in the unadjusted trial balance, a line for supplies expense must be added at the bottom of the account title column. Supplies expense is debited for $200, so that amount is entered on the supplies expense line in the third column (that is, the DR column for adjusting entries). The corresponding credit is, then, put in the credit column on the line for supplies. Both the debit and the credit are labeled with a capital letter A to indicate all components of the first adjusting entry. A note at the bottom of the page labeled A then explains the purpose of this adjusting entry. Additional adjusting entries are then labeled B, C, D, and so on. After all adjusting entries have been made, both the debit and the credit columns are totaled to prove again the equality of debits and credits.

FIGURE 5-7

GEORGE S. FARNSWORTH COMPANY
Work Sheet
For the Month Ending September 30, 1981

LINE No.	Account Title	(1) Unadjusted Trial Balance DR	(2) CR	(3) Adjusting Entries DR	(4) CR
1	Cash	18600			
2	Accounts receivable	100			
3	Supplies	800			200 A
4	Equipment	900			
5	Accounts payable		300		
6	Note payable		2100		
7	Advances from customers		1500	E 750	
8	Farnsworth, capital, Sept 1		15000		
9	Farnsworth, withdrawals	2500			
10	Commission revenue		8100		
11	Rent expense	600			
12	Salary expense	500		C 500	
13	Advertising expense	3000			
14		27000	27000		
15					
16	Supplies expense			A 200	
17	Depreciation			B 15	
18	Accumulated depreciation				15 B
19	Salary payable				500 C
20	Interest expense			D 14	
21	Interest payable				14 D
22	Appraisal revenue				750 E
23				1479	1479
24					
25	Net income				
26					
27					
28	Farnsworth, capital, Sept 30				
29					
30					
31					
32	Explanation of adjusting entries				
33					
34	A consumption of supplies				
35	B consumption of typewriter				
36	C accrue salaries owed				
37	D accrue interest owed				
38	E earn revenue as service is performed				
39					
40					

| | 1 | 2 | 3 | 4 |

(5)	(6)	(7)	(8)	(9)	(10)	(11)	(12)
Adjusted Trial Balance		Income Statement		Statement of Owner's Equity		Balance Sheet	
DR	CR	DR	CR	DR	CR	DR	CR
18600						18600	
100						100	
600						600	
900						900	
	300						300
	2100						2100
	750						750
	15000				15000		
2500				2500			
	8100		8100				
600		600					
1000		1000					
3000		3000					
200		200					
15		15					
	15						15
	500						500
14		14					
	14						14
	750		750				
27529	27529	4829	8850				
		4021			4021		
		8850	8850	2500	19021		
				16521		16521	
				19021	19021	20200	20200

Develop the Adjusted Trial Balance This process involves adding or subtracting across the unadjusted trial balance and the adjusting entries. For example, cash is $18,600 in the unadjusted trial balance and was unaffected by any adjusting entries; hence, cash is again $18,600 in the adjusted trial balance. On the other hand, supplies has an $800 debit balance in the unadjusted trial balance, but has a $200 credit for an adjusting entry. Thus, the adjusted trial balance has a debit balance of $600 ($800 − $200). This process is then repeated for all the accounts.

When each account balance is put in the proper column for each account, the columns (both debit and credit) are totaled to again prove the equality of debits and credits. These columns contain the same information as the adjusted trial balance. If the worksheet is prepared, there is no need to prepare a separate adjusted trial balance.

Extend the Revenue and Expense Account Balances The revenues go in the credit column of the income statement column, while the expenses go into the debit column. Again, each of these columns must be footed; however, in this instance, the totals for the columns will, in general, not be equal. The difference between total revenues and total expenses is net income. (If expenses [i.e., debits] exceed revenues [i.e., credits], then the difference is called a net loss.) For convenience, net income is then added to the account title column, even though it is not an account. After the amount of net income is entered into the debit column, the totals for the two columns will then be equal. A net loss amount would be put in the credit column and again, the column totals would balance. The net income figure here is, in a sense, a plug figure: it is the amount that must be plugged in to make the two columns equal.

Extend the Owner's Equity Account Balances The statement of owner's capital columns will develop the information necessary for this statement. The owner capital account is extended to the credit column. Any withdrawals are extended to the debit column. Finally, net income is extended to the credit column. The columns are then totaled and, in general, will not be equal. The plug figure is the ending owner capital. The account is added at the bottom of the account title column. When the amount of ending owner capital is entered into the debit column, the totals of the two columns will be equal.

Extend the Asset, Liability, and Owner's Equity Account Balances Generally speaking, the assets will go in the debit column, while the liabilities and owner's equity accounts go in the credit column of the balance sheet columns; however, contra-asset accounts like accumulated depreciation will have a credit balance and go in the credit column. Again, the balance sheet columns must be totaled to prove equality of debits and credits.

The financial statements can then be prepared from the worksheet, and will be the same as those developed earlier.

Corporate
Worksheet

Figure 5-8 is the worksheet for the preparation of financial statements for George S. Farnsworth, Inc. The first four steps of the worksheet preparation—entering the title and column headings, entering the unadjusted trial balance, entering the adjusting entries (except for income tax expense), and developing the adjusted trial balance—are essentially the same steps with slightly different account titles. Income tax expense cannot be entered immediately, because income before income taxes has not been determined.

The next step is to extend the revenue and expense account balances into the income statement columns. For a corporation, the difference between debits and credits is income before income taxes, not net income. The actual amount of income before income taxes does not appear on the worksheet; however, that figure is used to compute income tax expense and, hence, to make the final adjusting entry. The adjusting entry is entered in the adjusting entries columns, the expense is extended to the income statement columns, and the payable is extended to the balance sheet columns. After the amount of net income is entered in the debit column of the income statement, the totals for the two columns will be equal. The statement of retained earnings columns and the balance sheet columns are then treated in essentially the same way as in the sole proprietorship.

Concept
Summary

Preparation of Worksheet		
Step	*Sole Proprietorship*	*Corporation*
Enter the title and column headings	Same in both instances	
Enter unadjusted trial balance	Same in both instances	
Enter the adjusting entries	Enter all adjusting entries.	Enter all adjusting entries except for income tax expense.
Develop the adjusted trial balance	Same in both instances	
Extend the revenue and expense account balances	Difference in column totals is net income.	Difference in column totals is income before income taxes; an additional adjusting entry for income tax expense is required.
		(continued on page 162)

FIGURE 5-8

GEORGE S. FARNSWORTH COMPANY
Work Sheet
For the Month Ending September 30, 1981

Line No.	Account title	(1) Unadjusted Trial Balance DR	(2) Unadjusted Trial Balance CR	(3) Adjusting Entries DR	(4) Adjusting Entries CR
1	Cash	18600			
2	Accounts receivable	100			
3	Supplies	800			200A
4	Equipment	900			
5	Accounts payable		300		
6	Note payable		2100		
7	Advances from customers		1500	E 750	
8	Capital stock		15000		
9	Retained earnings, Sept 1		-0-		
10	Dividends	2500			
11	Commission revenue		8100		
12	Rent expense	600			
13	Salary expense	500		C 500	
14	Advertising expense	3000			
15		27000	27000		
16					
17	Supplies expense			A 200	
18	Depreciation			B 15	
19	Accumulated depreciation				15B
20	Salary payable				500C
21	Interest expense			D 14	
22	Interest payable				14D
23	Appraisal revenue				750E
24				1479	1479
25					
26	Income tax expense			F 804	
27	Corporate income tax payable				804F
28	Net income				
29					
30					
31	Retained earnings, Sept 30				
32					
33	Explanation of adjusting entries				
34					
35	A consumption of supplies				
36	B consumption of typewriter				
37	C accrue salary owed				
38	D accrue interest owed				
39	E earn revenue as service is performed				
40	F income tax expense: 20% × ($8,850 − $4829) = $804				

	(5)	(6)	(7)	(8)	(9)	(10)	(11)	(12)
	Adjusted Trial Balance		Income Statement		Statement of Retained Earnings		Balance Sheet	
	DR	CR	DR	CR	DR	CR	DR	CR
	18600						18600	
	100						100	
	600						600	
	900						900	
		300						300
		2100						2100
		750						750
		15000						15000
		— 0 —				— 0 —		
	2500				2500			
		8100		8100				
	600		600					
	1000		1000					
	3000		3000					
	200		200					
	15		15					
		15						15
		500						500
	14		14					
		14						14
		750		750				
	27529	27529	4829	8850				
			804					
								804
			3217			3217		
			8850	8850	2500	3217		
					717			717
					3217	3217	20200	20200

(assuming a 20% corporate tax rate)

Concept Summary

(Continued from page 159)

Step	Sole Proprietorship	Corporation
Extend the owner's equity account balances	Use statement of owner's capital columns and accounts.	Use statement of retained earnings columns and accounts.
Extend the asset, liability, and owner's equity account balances	Extend ending owner's capital into balance sheet columns.	Extend corporate income tax payable and ending retained earnings into balance sheet columns.

Summary

Classification of financial statements is the process of grouping together assets, liabilities, and owners' equity with similar liquidity characteristics. For balance sheet presentation, assets may be classified as current or noncurrent. Current assets are those that are expected to be converted to cash or used up within one year or one operating cycle, whichever is longer, from the balance sheet date. Normally, cash, marketable securities, accounts and notes receivable, inventory, supplies, and prepaid items are considered current. Assets whose benefit to the reporting entity is expected to extend beyond the upcoming year or operating cycle are classified as noncurrent. Normally, investments and funds; property, plant, and equipment; intangibles; and deferred charges are considered as noncurrent.

Liabilities may also be classified as current or noncurrent (long-term). Current liabilities are obligations that are expected to be satisfied by the use of current assets within one year or one operating cycle, whichever is longer, from the balance sheet date. Accounts and notes payable are common current liabilities, although many others are possible. Long-term liabilities represent obligations that will not be satisfied during the upcoming year or operating cycle, or will be satisfied by the use of noncurrent assets. Notes and bonds payable are typical long-term liabilities.

Corporate accounting differs from the accounting for proprietorships and partnerships in three major areas. First, transactions directly involving owners' equity are recorded in accounts called capital stock and dividends rather than owner, capital and withdrawals. Second, corporations have a separate account, called retained earnings, which reflects all indirect investment by the owners. Indirect investment by owners of unincorporated businesses is reflected in the owner, capital account along with the direct investment. Third, because corporations are taxed directly on their income, an additional adjusting entry to record the income tax expense and liability is necessary. No such entry is necessary for proprietorships or partnerships.

An optional device, called a worksheet, can be useful in the preparation of financial statements when adjusting entries are not recorded until the year's end. Worksheets can also help prevent errors in the accounting records.

In section II, merchandising operations are discussed and some refinements are added to the basic accounting cycle. The accounting techniques for recording the sales and purchases of a merchandising business are presented in Chapter 6.

Key Terms

Accounts payable	Long-term liabilities
Accounts receivable	Marketable securities
Bonds payable	Materiality
Corporate income tax payable	Noncurrent assets
Current assets	Notes payable
Current liabilities	Notes receivable
Deferred charges	Operating cycle
Income tax expense	Prepaid items
Intangibles	Property, plant, and equipment
Inventory	Supplies
Investments	Worksheet

Comprehensive Review Problem

Following is an alphabetical list of the assets, liabilities, owners' equity, revenues, and expenses before closing entries of Eureka Enterprises, Inc., as of December 31, 1982:

Accrued liabilities	$ 8,400
Accumulated depreciation: Building	90,000
Accumulated depreciation: Equipment	20,000
Advances from customers	4,800
Advertising expense	12,000
Amounts owed by customers	62,000
Amounts owed to suppliers	38,000
Bonds payable	50,000
Building	300,000
Capital stock (10,000 shares outstanding)	?
Cash in bank	15,000
Cash on hand	5,000
Cost of products sold	424,000
Depreciation expense	40,000
Dividends	25,000
Equipment	50,000
Income tax expense	45,200
Income tax payable	11,000
Inventory	105,000
Investment in common stock of Small Stores, Inc.	75,000
Investment in government bonds (expect to be sold in the next 6 months)	24,000
Land	55,000
Note receivable	25,000

Note receivable from company vice-president due in 10 years	50,000
Notes payable (3 years)	47,000
Notes payable (6 months)	35,000
Patent	13,000
Prepaid insurance	9,000
Retained earnings	246,000
Salaries expense	186,000
Sales revenue	781,000
Supplies	5,000
Supplies used	6,000

Required:

1. Prepare an income statement and statement of retained earnings for 1982.

2. Prepare a classified balance sheet as of December 31, 1982.

3. List the items from the above financial statements that would not appear or would be titled differently if the business were not a corporation.

Solution to the Comprehensive Review Problem

1.

EUREKA ENTERPRISES, INC.
Income Statement
For the Year Ending December 31, 1982

Sales revenue		$ 781,000
Expenses		
Cost of products sold	$424,000	
Salaries expense	186,000	
Depreciation expense	40,000	
Advertising expense	12,000	
Supplies used	6,000	
Total expenses		668,000
Income before income taxes		113,000
Income tax expense		45,200
Net income		$ 67,800
Net income per share		$ 6.78

EUREKA ENTERPRISES, INC.
Statement of Retained Earnings
For the Year Ending December 31, 1982

Retained earnings, January 1, 1982	$ 246,000
Net income for the year	67,800
Dividends	(25,000)
Retained earnings, December 31, 1982	$ 288,800

2.

EUREKA ENTERPRISES, INC.
Balance Sheet
December 31, 1982

ASSETS

Current assets

Cash	$ 20,000	
Marketable securities	24,000	
Accounts receivable	62,000	
Note receivable	25,000	
Inventory	105,000	
Supplies	5,000	
Prepaid insurance	9,000	
Total current assets		$ 250,000

Noncurrent assets

Investment in Small Stores, Inc.		75,000	
Property, plant, and equipment			
Land	$ 55,000		
Building (net of accumulated depreciation, $90,000)	210,000		
Equipment (net of accumulated depreciation, $20,000)	30,000	295,000	
Patent		13,000	
Note receivable from officer		50,000	
Total noncurrent assets			433,000
Total assets			$ 683,000

LIABILITIES & STOCKHOLDERS' EQUITY

Current liabilities

Accounts payable	$ 38,000	
Accrued liabilities	8,400	
Advances from customers	4,800	
Income tax payable	11,000	
Short-term notes payable	35,000	
Total current liabilities		$ 97,200

Noncurrent liabilities

Notes payable	47,000	
Bonds payable	50,000	
Total noncurrent liabilities		97,000

Stockholders' equity

Capital stock	200,000	
Retained earnings	288,800	
Total stockholders' equity		488,800
Total liabilities & stockholders' equity		$ 683,000

3. Income before income taxes
   Income tax expense
   Net income per share
   Retained earnings would be a part of owner, capital
   Dividends would be titled withdrawals
   Income tax payable
   Capital stock would be a part of owner, capital
   Stockholders' equity would be owner's equity

Questions

Q5-1. State the difference between current and noncurrent assets. Give three examples of each.

Q5-2. State the difference between current and noncurrent liabilities. Give two examples of each.

Q5-3. Contrast the double-entry treatment of direct owner investment in a corporation and an unincorporated business.

Q5-4. Contrast the double-entry treatment of dividends and owner withdrawals.

Q5-5. Give an adjusting entry which would be necessary for a corporation but not for an unincorporated business. Why is this entry necessary?

Q5-6. Specify three areas of difference between the financial statements of a corporation and those of an unincorporated business.

Q5-7. Is a worksheet necessary for the accounting cycle? Why or why not?

Q5-8. What are the advantages of using a worksheet?

Exercises

E5-1. For each of the following items that are to appear on the balance sheet of the Castay Office Supply Company for October 31, 1982, indicate (1) the specific type of asset or liability, and (2) the classification of the item on a classified balance sheet.

    a. Cash kept in cash register to make change
    b. Ninety-day note due to the bank
    c. Securities purchased as temporary investments
    d. Rent payment for November 1982 (paid in October)
    e. Amount due in thirty days to suppliers for inventory items purchased on account
    f. Office supplies to be *used* by the Castay Office Supply Company in running its business
    g. Desks *used* by employees of the company
    h. Amounts due from customers within thirty days
    i. IBM stock purchased as a long-term investment
    j. Office supplies and furniture to be sold to customers
    k. Amounts due from owner that will be paid in July 1984
    l. Note due to the bank in two years

E5-2. The following items are to appear on the balance sheet of the Deitz Company dated December 31, 1982. Indicate for each item whether it would be classified as a (1) current asset, (2) noncurrent asset, (3) current liability or (4) long-term liability. Assume the Deitz Company has an operating cycle of less than one year.

    a. The purchase price of stock of the Carrington Company purchased November 1, 1982. The stock was purchased in hopes of eventually acquiring enough Carrington Company stock to gain control of the company.
    b. Amounts due on March 1, 1983, to retired employees of the company.

The amounts are paid out of a fund that is classified as a noncurrent asset.

    c. The purchase price of Republican Motor stock purchased in 1976. The stock is expected to be sold in June of 1983 to provide cash for expansion of Deitz's facilities.

    d. Amount of note due to the bank December 15, 1984.

    e. Amount of insurance premium paid on December 31, 1982. The premium provides coverage through December 31, 1984.

    f. Amount owed to a dealer for a piece of machinery purchased December 15, 1982. The payment is due January 15, 1983.

Which, if any, of the above items would be classified differently if the Deitz Company had an operating cycle of two years?

E5-3. Bill Johnson opened a wholesale tire company with an investment of $20,000. During the year, he withdrew $10,000 for his personal use. Prepare journal entries showing how these two events should be accounted for

    a. if Bill Johnson uses a proprietorship form of organization

    b. if Bill Johnson uses a corporate form of organization

E5-4. On January 1, 1982, the Taylor Company purchased a truck for $10,000. The truck is expected to last five years, after which time it will have no value. The company makes adjusting entries only once a year in conjunction with the preparation of its annual financial statements.

    a. Below is a portion of the Taylor Company worksheet for the year ended December 31, 1982. Complete this portion of the worksheet.

	Unadjusted Trial Balance		Adjusting Entries		Adjusted Trial Balance	
Account title	DR	CR	DR	CR	DR	CR
Equipment-truck Accumulated depreciation— truck						

    b. On what financial statement or statements would these two adjusted trial balance amounts appear? How would they be classified?

    c. What kind of account is accumulated depreciation?

E5-5. Below is a list of items that might be found in the account title column of a worksheet. For each of these items, indicate whether the amount associated with it would be extended to the income statement columns, statement of retained earnings, or balance sheet columns and whether the amount would be placed in the debit or credit column (assuming all accounts have normal balances).

    a. Accumulated depreciation

    b. Salary expense

    c. Interest payable

    d. Accounts receivable
    e. Revenue
    f. Dividends
    g. Prepaid expense
    h. Net income
    i. Depreciation expense
    j. Retained earnings, ending

E5-6. Record the following compound entries in general journal form.

    a. Kim Kuhne contributed $5,000 cash and a truck worth $4,000 in return for common stock of KK Corporation.

    b. Kim purchased equipment worth $5,500 by paying $3,000 as a down payment and signing a ninety-day note payable for $2,500.

    c. The corporation performed services for customers, of which $6,000 were paid for by check and $4,000 were billed to customers.

    d. Salaries were earned by employees for one week's work. The total salaries earned were $600, although only $300 was immediately paid to employees.

E5-7. The income statement of the Razel Consulting Firm, Inc., for the year ended December 31, 1982, is presented below.

RAZEL CONSULTING FIRM, INC.
Income Statement
For the Year Ended December 31, 1982

Revenue		$122,500
Expenses		
Salaries expense	$74,300	
Rent expense	9,600	
Supplies expense	3,400	
General expense	7,900	
Depreciation expense	2,700	97,900
Income before income taxes		24,600
Income tax expense		5,000
Net income		$ 19,600

The balance in retained earnings at Janaury 1, 1982, was $16,500. On the balance sheet as of December 31, 1982, retained earnings are reported as $25,000. Prepare the closing entries for the year.

E5-8. A. J. Mann runs his own small business. Below are the details of all activities affecting owner's equity for the year ended December 31, 1982.

Revenue	$28,000
Rent expense	3,600
General expense	4,700
Depreciation expense	2,000
Disbursement to owner	17,000

    a. Assuming the business is operated as a sole proprietorship, prepare all necessary closing entries at December 31, 1982.

    b. Assuming the business is operated as a corporation and $15,000 of the disbursements to Mann is treated as salary while $2,000 is treated as a dividend, prepare all necessary closing entries at December 31, 1982. (Ignore income taxes.)

Problems

P5-1. Comparative balance sheets at December 31, 1981, and 1982, for the Purple Midget Company, Inc., are presented below.

PURPLE MIDGET COMPANY, INC.
Balance Sheets
December 31

	1982	1981
ASSETS		
Current assets		
Cash	$ 72,000	$ 43,000
Marketable securities	47,000	76,000
Accounts receivable	63,000	70,000
Inventories	37,000	9,000
Supplies	3,000	2,000
Prepaid expenses	2,000	1,000
Total current assets	224,000	201,000
Investments	47,000	43,000
Property, plant, and equipment		
(less accumulated depreciation		
of $263,000 and $219,000)	523,000	421,000
Deferred charges and other assets	17,000	13,000
Total assets	$811,000	$678,000

LIABILITIES & OWNERS' EQUITY		
Current liabilities		
Notes payable	$ 4,000	$ 2,000
Accounts payable	51,000	52,000
Income taxes payable	15,000	31,000
Total current liabilities	70,000	85,000
Long-term debt	245,000	195,000
Total liabilities	315,000	280,000
Owners' Equity		
Capital stock	67,000	22,000
Retained earnings	429,000	376,000
Total owners' equity	496,000	398,000
Total liabilities & owners' equity	$811,000	$678,000

Required:

Based on the information provided in these balance sheets, answer the following questions:

1. Assuming the company has an operating cycle of less than one year, what portion of total liabilities at December 31, 1982, were expected to be paid within one year with current assets?

2. In 1982, how much did owners contribute to the company voluntarily, and through the company's retention of earnings?

3. If dividends of $31,000 were paid during 1982, what was the company's net income for 1982?

4. At December 31, 1981, what is the dollar amount of creditors' claims against total assets? What is the dollar amount of owners' claims? Had creditors or owners provided the company with more assets?

5. Calculate the increase in total assets, the increase in total liabilities, and the increase in total owners' equity between December 31, 1981, and December 31, 1982. Put these amounts into the basic accounting equation ($A = L + OE$). Does the equation balance if only the changes are used? Why or why not?

6. Short-term notes payable were $2,000 at December 31, 1981, and $4,000 at December 31, 1982. Does this necessarily mean that the company did not repay the $2,000 worth of notes due in 1981? Explain.

P5-2. Selected information from comparative balance sheets of the Astone Company at December 31, 1981, and December 31, 1982, are presented below.

ASTONE COMPANY, INC.
Balance Sheets
December 31

	1982	1981
ASSETS		
Current assets		
Cash	$ 53,000	$ 44,000
Receivables (less allowance for doubtful accounts of $2,000 and $1,500)	116,000	118,000
Inventories	(a)	170,000
Prepaid expense	8,000	(i)
Total current assets	(b)	339,000
Investments	19,000	16,000
Property, plant, and equipment		
(less accumulated depreciation of $210,000 and $285,000)	855,000	768,000
Deferred changes and other assets	21,000	(j)
Total assets	$ (c)	$1,145,000
LIABILITIES & OWNERS' EQUITY		
Current liabilities		
Notes payable	$ 60,000	$ (k)
Accounts payable	(d)	76,000
Total current liabilities	138,000	117,000
Long-term debt	(e)	529,000
Total liabilities	713,000	(l)
Owners' Equity		
Capital stock	337,000	(m)
Retained earnings	(f)	166,000
Total owners' equity	(g)	499,000
Total liabilities & owners' equity	$ (h)	$ (n)

Net income for the year ended December 31, 1982, was $77,000, and dividends of $25,000 were paid in 1982.

Required:
Provide the dollar amounts of items a through n that are missing on the balance sheets.

P5-3. Listed below in random order is information about the B.A. Dictor Chemical Company. Unless otherwise specified, the values are those at December 31, 1982.

Capital stock (50,000 shares outstanding)	$ 454,000
Accounts and notes receivable	195,000
Accounts payable	136,000
Marketable securities	47,000
Notes payable	215,000
Allowance for uncollectible accounts receivable	3,000
Prepaid expenses	8,000
Inventory	304,000
Bonds payable	564,000
Supplies	3,000
Cash	70,000
Revenue for year ended December 31, 1982	1,929,000
Property, plant, and equipment at cost	1,580,000
Accumulated depreciation representing used portion of property, plant, and equipment	522,000
Trade name and trademarks	12,000
Retained earnings at December 31, 1981	308,000

Total expenses for year ended December 31, 1982 broken down as follows:

Cost of sales	$1,425,000	
Selling, general, and administrative	165,000	
Depreciation expense	121,000	
Income tax expense	89,000	1,800,000
Deferred charges and other assets		28,000
Dividends paid during 1982		84,000

Additional information:

  a. The B.A. Dictor Chemical Company has an operating cycle of three months.
  b. All accounts and notes receivable are due by June 30, 1983.
  c. Of the marketable securities, $25,000 worth are expected to be held indefinitely while $22,000 are temporary investments that are expected to be sold within a few months.
  d. Notes payable of $90,000 are due March 15, 1983. The remainder of the notes payable are due October 15, 1984.
  e. Bonds payable are due as follows:

Face Value	*Maturity Date*
$226,000	February 15, 1986
$121,000	September 30, 1989
$217,000	March 1, 1998

Required:
Prepare a balance sheet for the B.A. Dictor Chemical Company as of December 31, 1982, and an income statement (including earnings per share) and statement of retained earnings for the year ended December 31, 1982.

P5-4. The trial balance of Blue Corporation on January 1, 1982, was as follows:

Acct. No.	Account Title	Debit	Credit
1	Cash	$ 7,320	
10	Accounts receivable	4,500	
25	Supplies	350	
30	Equipment	4,200	
51	Note payable		$ 4,000
53	Accounts payable		930
60	Federal income tax payable		720
65	Social security payable		240
68	State income tax payable		125
90	Capital stock		8,000
92	Retained earnings		2,355
95	Dividends		
115	Service revenue		
122	Advertising expense		
125	Salary expense		
130	Rent expense		
		$16,370	$16,370

The following transactions took place during January:

Jan. 2 Performed $12,000 of services for clients; $3,000 were for cash and $9,000 were on account.

   3 Collected $4,400 of amounts owed by clients for previous year's services.

   5 Paid the $930 owed on account.

   12 Purchased $200 more of supplies on account.

   13 Paid $400 due on the note payable (ignore interest).

   20 Paid employees' salaries of $800.

   25 The stockholders were paid $2,800 of dividends.

   28 Paid advertising expense of $250.

   31 Paid the month's rent of $1,200.

Required:

1. Construct a general journal and enter the above transactions in it. Begin with journal page 11.

2. Set up general ledger T accounts and enter beginning balances.

3. Post the transactions to the T accounts. Be sure to enter all posting references.

4. Compute the balance in each account.

5. Prepare a trial balance.

P5-5. Responses Inc., a telephone answering service, was organized in May 1982. The account titles and numbers used by the corporation are listed below.

Cash	1	Accounts payable	33
Accounts receivable	12	Mortgage payable	35
Supplies	18	Capital stock	50
Land	22	Retained earnings	52
Building	24	Dividends	54
Equipment	27	Service revenue	60
Office furniture	29	Salary expense	80

The following are the transactions for the first fifteen days of May:

May 5 Responses, Inc. was organized, and the corporate charter was granted by the state to Bob Parsons, the owner. Bob invested $100,000 cash and received 1,000 shares of stock.

7 The new corporation purchased land and a building from Gifts Galore, a specialty shop that was going out of business. The total purchase price was $60,000, of which $45,000 was attributable to the building and the remainder to the land. The terms of the purchase called for a cash payment of $12,000 and a mortgage of $48,000.

11 Specialized equipment was purchased at a cost of $30,000, paid in cash. A minimum amount of office furniture was purchased for 2,000 cash.

12 Purchased supplies of $3,000 on credit. According to terms, the total amount is due in fifteen days.

15 Billings to customers for the first half month were $5,000.

15 Salaries to employees for the first half month were $900.

15 Collections from customers during the first half month were $2,900.

15 Parsons withdrew $500 in dividends.

Required:

1. Prepare journal entries for the first half of May in a general journal you have constructed.

2. Set up ledger accounts and post to these accounts. Be sure to include posting references.

3. Compute the balance in each account.

4. Prepare a trial balance.

P5-6. The following are a few of the transactions posted into the ledger of Chatwell Interiors, Inc. For each of the transactions described below, indicate whether the transaction was correctly entered. If the transaction was incorrectly entered, tell whether the trial balance would have equal debits and credits. If the trial balance would have unequal debits and credits, give the dollar amount of the difference. Each instance is independent of the others.

a. An account payable of $2,000 was paid in full. The payment was recorded by a credit to cash of $2,000 and a credit to accounts payable of $2,000.

b. A $600 account receivable was collected in full. The collection was recorded by a debit to cash of $60 and a credit to accounts receivable of $60.

c. $200 was received in advance from a customer. This was recorded by debiting cash $200 and crediting service revenue $200.

d. Land was purchased for $12,000. This was recorded by debiting land $12,000 and crediting cash $12,000.

e. Office space was rented for $500 per month. This was recorded by a debit to buildings of $500 and a credit to cash of $500.

f. Supplies costing $290 were purchased on credit. The entry to record this included a debit to office supplies of $290 and a credit to accounts payable of $920.

g. George Stevens invested $5,000 in his corporation in return for capital stock. This was recorded by a debit to investments of $5,000 and a credit to G. Stevens, capital of $5,000.

h. Mel Farmer borrowed $1,000 from Tchefuncta State Bank. He recorded this by a debit to notes payable of $1,000 and a credit to cash of $1,000.

i. An adding machine was purchased from Computers, Inc., for $120. The purchase of the machine was not recorded at all.

P5-7. Mortimer B. Thorton is the sole owner of the Mortimer B. Thorton Company. Mortimer runs the company himself and employs no additional help. During the year 1982, the following transactions affecting owner's equity occurred.

   a. Mortimer invested $3,000 of his personal funds in the business.

   b. Mortimer withdrew from the company $21,000.

   c. After all end-of-period adjustments had been made, the results of operations of the company for the year were as follows:

Revenue	$30,000
Rent expense	2,400
Supplies expense	700
Depreciation expense	1,200
Utilities expense	950
Miscellaneous expense	630

Required:

1. Assuming that the business is operated as a sole proprietorship, prepare the journal entries to record items *a* and *b* and prepare all closing entries that would be made at December 31, 1982.

2. Assume that the business is operated as a corporation and that $15,000 of the $21,000 withdrawn by Mortimer is treated as a salary. The other $6,000 is treated as a dividend. Further assume that the corporation must pay income taxes of 25 percent of income before taxes. The income tax expense is accrued before closing entries are made. Prepare the journal entries to record items *a* and *b* and prepare all closing entries that would be made at December 31, 1982.

P5-8. Balances in the accounts of the Sullivan and Sullivan Company, Inc., at December 31, 1982, are given below. No adjusting entries have been made, and all accounts have normal balances.

Cash	$ 7,200
Accounts receivable	22,700
Prepaid expenses	4,800
Land, building, and equipment	133,000
Accumulated depreciation	50,400
Other assets	53,000
Notes payable	17,600
Accounts payable	19,400
Advances from customers	10,000
Long-term debt	45,800
Capital stock	20,000
Retained earnings	31,000
Dividends	4,000
Revenues	231,600
Salary expense	179,100
Advertising expense	10,600
General expense	11,400

Additional information:

   a. On July 1, 1982, an insurance premium of $4,800 was paid. The policy provides comprehensive coverage for the company from July 1, 1982 to June 30, 1983.

   b. The land, building, and equipment account is broken down as follows:

Land	$ 25,000
Building and equipment	108,000

There were no additions or reductions to the account during the year. Depreciable assets are being depreciated over twenty years with no salvage value.

c. Interest expense for the year amounts to $5,200. None of this has been recorded or paid.

d. On September 1, 1982, a major client made a prepayment of $10,000. This amount covered services to be performed by Sullivan and Sullivan during the period September 1, 1982 through January 31, 1983. The fee was based on a monthly rate of $2,000 per month. Sullivan and Sullivan has fulfilled its obligations to the client through December 31, 1982.

e. The company is subject to income taxes of 25 percent of its income before taxes.

Required:

Prepare a worksheet for the Sullivan and Sullivan Company, Inc. for the year ended December 31, 1982.

—

Merchandising Operations

CHAPTER 6

Sales and Purchases

Chapter Outline

6.1 *Types of Business and Business Activity.* Discussion of service, merchandising, and manufacturing businesses with emphasis on the effect of these different operating activities on assets, revenues, and expenses.

6.2 *Merchandising Operations.* The important characteristics of inventory, cost of goods sold, sales revenue, and sales returns, including determining the point of sale and purchase for merchandisers.

6.3 *Accounting for Merchandising—Periodic Approach.* Presentation of the rationale, procedures, and mechanics of periodic inventory systems and illustration of the approach with sample transactions.

6.4 *Accounting for Merchandising—Perpetual Approach.* Presentation of the rationale, procedures, and mechanics of perpetual inventory systems and illustration of the approach with sample transactions.

Accounting and the Real World

K Mart's Fast Track

Sears, Roebuck and Company has been the nation's largest retailer for so long, in both merchandising volume and profits, that it's hard to break the habit of calling it number one. But some key Wall Street analysts believe Sears could be surpassed in at least one key area—merchandising profits—by the end of 1980.

Savvy observers like Suzanne R. Holmes of Loeb Rhoades, Hornblower and Terence McEvoy of Oppenheimer think that fast-growing K Mart Corporation, riding its growing discount chain, has a good chance of passing Sears in retailing profits in the next two years or so—despite smaller revenues of under $12 billion.

Why do McEvoy and Holmes like K Mart's prospects more, even though its yield currently is about half of Sears' and it, too, would be hurt by an economic slowdown?

"A key factor," says Holmes, "is the way K Mart structured itself differently right from the start. It's still paying off today. Sears and J. C. Penny Company typically go into regional shopping malls, with all their high costs and services. That doesn't enable them to be as price-competitive. K Mart is outside the malls and isn't part of that higher-price syndrome. It draws because of price. That becomes increasingly important in today's inflationary environment."

"Too," she says, "K Mart has much less exposure to hard goods than Sears. They won't be hurt at all by insurance the way Sears will be in 1979 and 1980. So I look for about a 10 percent earnings gain for K Mart this year and 13 percent over the next three to five years."

K Mart can easily increase its dividend because, alone among the major mass merchandisers today, it is a generator of excess cash. It has lots of higher-margined older stores maturing and has been opening roughly 170 new ones each year. Says Suzanne Holmes: "I predicted a few years ago they would have an excess-cash problem and it will only grow. They're so big now that all but a big acquisition would be meaningless and I don't expect one." Thus, even K Mart is beginning to mature—but at a higher

179

growth level than Sears'. So increasing the dividend may be more than an option, there may not be much choice.

Is K Mart soon to be the new retailing earnings champion?

Forbes, April 30, 1979, page 97.

Part One of this book was concerned with understanding the "big picture" of what accounting is and how it actually works. To accomplish this, the accounting cycle was described in Chapters 3 and 4 for a simple, straightforward kind of business called a service firm. Although this business engaged in a limited set of transactions, the process and procedures illustrated are universally applicable to all business. In this chapter more complex kinds of business activity are introduced and integrated into the basic accounting process. Accounting procedures for these new activities are illustrated and expanded to include merchandising firms.

6.1 Types of Business and Business Activity

There are only a few basic types of activities any business can engage in to produce income. A business may perform for a fee some service desired by customers, or it may sell to customers some kind of product. If a product is sold, that product may be purchased from some other business or manufactured (created). Classified by type of operating (profit-seeking) activity, then, there are three fundamental kinds of businesses. Firms that sell a service instead of a tangible, physical product are called **service businesses.** Firms that purchase a product and, in turn, sell that product to customers are called **merchandising businesses.** Finally, firms that purchase certain raw materials, then turn those materials into a finished product and sell that product are called **manufacturing businesses.**

Although any business may engage in all of these types of profit-seeking activities, all businesses can be classified as primarily service, merchandising, or manufacturing. For example, AT&T is primarily a service business, while Sears is a merchandiser and Exxon is primarily a manufacturer.

Classifying Business Activity

There are two distinct ways to classify business activity, and these classification schemes should not be confused. From a legal organization point of view, a business may be a sole proprietorship, a partnership, or a corporation. Based on what it does to earn a profit, a business may be service, merchandising, or manufacturing. Any combination of these two classifications is possible and can be found in the world.

Service Businesses

For accounting purposes, the easiest business to understand is a service business. Here, revenue is generated by the sale of a service to customers.

The service sold is usually some particular talent, knowledge, or expertise, or, at a minimum, a willingness to do some task. None of these characteristics is an accounting asset, however, because they tend to be difficult to value objectively in dollar terms.

Accounting Characteristics of Service Businesses The sale of a service instead of a physical product means that

1. there is no inventory among the assets on the balance sheet;

2. there is no cost of products sold among the expenses on the income statement, because no asset has been sold;

3. revenue is called service revenue or fees revenue; and

4. returns of sales do not appear on the income statement, because it is more difficult to return a service than a product.

Because the significant accounting problems associated with each of the above items is avoided in a service business, accounting for service businesses is considerably less complex than accounting for businesses that sell a product. There are many different kinds of service businesses in many different industries. Most professionals (doctors, lawyers, accountants, architects, and engineers) form service firms, as do many nonprofessionals, such as plumbers and hairdressers. In each of these instances, some knowledge or talent is being sold rather than a product.

Merchandising Businesses

Most businesses deal in some sort of product, offering it for sale to customers and earning revenue from these sales. One kind of business that deals in a product is a merchandising firm. There are probably more merchandising companies in the United States than any other type of business. Also, most people deal more with merchandisers than with service businesses or manufacturers and, therefore, are more familiar with this type of business.

The outstanding characteristic of all merchandising businesses is that they sell a product which has been purchased from some other supplier. The product sold is physically the same as the product purchased except that the price has been increased. What functions do merchandising firms perform which allow them to increase the price of a product even though the physical form of the product has not been changed? All merchandisers provide

1. convenient locations and/or attractive facilities;

2. a wide variety of choice and purchase quantity; and

3. readily available credit.

Without changing the nature of a product, merchandising firms can exist because they are important in the distribution of the product and because they facilitate consumer credit.

There are two types of merchandising businesses in the United States, typically called retailers and wholesalers. *Retailers* purchase products in large quantities from wholesalers and then sell in any quantity to ultimate consumers. *Wholesalers* purchase in very large quantities from manufacturers and typically sell in large quantities to retailers. The distribution chain for most products is from manufacturer to wholesaler to retailer to ultimate consumer. Some companies, however, are able to act in more than one of these capacities. For example, Exxon Corporation is clearly a manufacturing firm, but it also sells products (particularly gasoline) directly to consumers through service stations owned by the company and is, thus, also a wholesaler and a retailer. Sears is a retailer, but also acts as its own wholesaler.

Accounting Characteristics of Merchandising Businesses The sale to consumers of a product that has been purchased from a supplier generally means the following:

1. There is an asset called inventory among the current assets on the balance sheet, which represents the purchase cost of products on hand held for resale.

2. There is an expense called cost of goods sold (or, perhaps, cost of sales) among the expenses on the income statement, which represents the purchase cost of products sold to customers during the accounting period.

3. Revenue is called sales revenue or, simply, sales on the income statement and represents the selling price of all products sold to customers during the accounting period.

4. Returns of sales, representing the selling price of all products originally sold to customers and then returned by them, appear on the income statement or are netted against sales revenue to produce a figure called net sales revenue.

5. Sales discounts, representing reductions in the selling price of goods sold because customers pay early according to a predetermined schedule, will appear on the income statement or will be netted against sales revenue to produce net sales revenue.

Accounting for merchandising firms, then, typically means keeping track of the purchase cost of inventory as it is acquired so that this purchase cost will become an expense as the products are sold. Also, the selling price of products must be available for the determination of sales revenue, sales returns, and sales discounts. Much of this chapter and a later chapter are devoted to the accounting procedures necessary to account for the inventories of merchandisers.

Manufacturing Businesses

The most complex type of business in terms of operating activities is manufacturing. Although accounting for manufacturing firms will not be discussed in depth in this book, it will help to get an overview of this type of business now. Manufacturers sell a product to customers (usually wholesalers) and, in that sense, have many of the same inventory problems merchandisers have; however, the large difference between merchandisers and manufacturers lies in the manner of acquisition of products to be sold. Products sold by manufacturers are essentially created by them. Manufacturers purchase one type of product, usually called *raw materials*, and then change the basic nature of the raw materials by creating something called *finished goods*. It is these finished goods that are sold to customers. Unique to manufacturing is the transformation of one type of inventory (raw materials) into another type of inventory (finished goods). This transformation is complex, and the inventory accounting process must reflect the transformation.

Accounting Characteristics of Manufacturing Businesses The sale of a product that has been manufactured from other products which are, in turn, purchased from some supplier means the following:

1. There are several different kinds of inventory among the assets on the balance sheets of a manufacturer representing (a) the purchase cost of materials on hand (raw materials), (b) the manufactured cost of products ready for sale to customers (finished goods), and (c) the manufactured cost of products only partly finished (goods in process).

2. There is an expense called cost of goods sold (or cost of sales) among the expenses on the income statement, which represents the manufactured cost of products sold to customers during the accounting period.

3. Revenue is called sales revenue or, simply, sales on the income statement and represents the selling price of all products sold to customers during the accounting period.

4. Returns of sales and sales discounts appear on the income statement or are netted against sales revenue to produce a figure called net sales revenue.

Concept Summary

Important Characteristics of Service, Merchandising, and Manufacturing Businesses				
Type of Business	*Assets*	*Revenues*	*Returns*	*Expenses*
Service	No inventory.	Fee basis for the performance of service.	None, although adjustments in the fee for the service could be made.	No cost of goods sold.
				(continued on next page)

Concept Summary *(continued)*

Type of Business	Assets	Revenues	Returns	Expenses
Merchandising	One inventory whose value is based on the purchase cost of products still on hand at the balance sheet date.	Selling price of all products sold during the period.	Selling price of all products returned during the period.	Cost of goods sold whose value is the purchase cost of all products sold during the period.
Manufacturing	Three inventories: raw materials, goods in process, finished goods.	Same as for merchandising.	Same as for merchandising.	Cost of goods sold whose value is the manufactured cost of all products sold during the period.

Notice that the basic differences among service, merchandising, and manufacturing businesses centers on an asset called inventory and an expense called cost of goods sold. Figure 6-1 presents the income statement of a merchandising firm to illustrate these differences.

Gross Profit

Examine the merchandising income statement in Figure 6-1 in greater depth. The revenue is titled sales, and from that figure the cost of sales is

FIGURE 6-1
Merchandising Income
Statement

SAFEWAY STORES, INCORPORATED AND SUBSIDIARIES		
Income Statement		
For the 52 Weeks Ended December 30, 1978, and December 31, 1977.		
	1978	*1977*
Sales	$ 12,550,569,000	$ 11,249,398,000
Cost of sales	9,829,071,000	8,916,719,000
Gross profit	2,721,498,000	2,332,679,000
Operating and administrative expenses	2,371,949,000	2,082,246,000
Operating profit	349,549,000	250,433,000
Interest expense	74,110,000	70,104,000
Loss on translation of foreign currencies	7,856,000	3,253,000
Other (income), net	(9,135,000)	(7,171,000)
Income before provision for income taxes	276,718,000	184,247,000
Provision for income taxes	130,600,000	81,942,000
Net income (per share: $5.60 and $3.93)	$ 146,118,000	$ 102,305,000

Courtesy of Safeway Stores

deducted. The difference between sales and cost of sales (cost of goods sold) for a merchandising firm is called the **gross profit** or gross margin of the business. This figure gives the difference between the selling price of all goods sold and the purchase cost of these same goods; that is, the physical quantity of goods used to calculate sales revenue and cost of goods sold is the same (units sold during the period). The figure for gross profit simply gives the absolute difference between selling price and purchase cost for this quantity of goods.

Markup Gross profit can be expressed as a percentage of either cost of goods sold or of sales revenue in the following manner:

$$\frac{\text{Gross profit}}{\text{Cost of goods sold}}$$

$$\frac{\text{Gross profit}}{\text{Sales revenue}}$$

The first calculation is called *markup on cost,* and the second is termed *markup on sales.* These figures give in percentage terms the difference between sales revenue and cost of goods sold and can tell the financial statement reader how much, on the average, the merchandiser adds to the purchase cost of products to determine selling price. Although gross profit in absolute or percentage terms may not be shown on a merchandising income statement, as long as sales and cost of goods sold appear, these important figures can be determined.

Merchandising Income Statement

All merchandising businesses have expenses other than the cost of products sold, such as selling expenses, administrative expenses, interest expense on borrowed funds, and income taxes. *Selling expenses* include those costs incurred to sell the product (such as salesmen's salaries, delivery costs, and advertising), while *administrative expenses* are costs necessary to operate the business that are not directly associated with the product (such as secretaries' salaries and the cost of the accounting and legal departments). Together, these expenses are called the *operating expenses* of the business.

Merchandising income statements may be prepared in a single-step format or a multiple-step format. The single-step format emphasizes the two major categories of revenues and expenses, and provides net income as the only difference. The multiple-step format presents several categories, with resulting sub-totals and differences, and net income as the final figure. Figure 6-2 illustrates the single-step and multiple-step formats using the same set of income statement data.

Figure 6-2 illustrates the two extremes of income statement presentation. Most published statements have more categories than a single-step statement, but fewer categories than a complete multiple-step statement. Figure 6-1, presented earlier, gives the income statement for Safeway Stores. This statement shows gross profit, operating profit, and income before income taxes in addition to net income, and is typical of published corporate income statements.

FIGURE 6-2
Single-Step versus Multiple-Step Income Statements

Single-Step			Multiple-Step		
Net sales revenue		$1,985,000	Sales revenue		$2,000,000
Expenses			Sales returns		(15,000)
Cost of goods sold ..	$1,145,000		Net sales revenue		1,985,000
Selling expenses	300,000		Cost of goods sold		1,145,000
Administrative			Gross profit		840,000
expenses	125,000		Operating expenses		
Interest expense	20,000		Selling expenses	$300,000	
Income tax expense ..	190,000	1,780,000	Administrative		
Net income		$ 205,000	expenses	125,000	425,000
			Operating income		415,000
Per Share (20,000 shares)		$ 10.25	Interest expense		20,000
			Income before taxes		395,000
			Income tax expense		190,000
			Net income		$ 205,000
			Per share (20,000 shares)		$ 10.25

6.2 Merchandising Operations

To apply the accounting cycle to merchandising operations, it is necessary to understand how to deal with the following four questions, which are not a part of the accounting process for service businesses:

1. What is the cost of inventory, that is, which types of expenditures should be considered a part of the purchase cost of inventory?

2. At what point do purchases and sales actually occur (how is point of sale recognized) when buyer and seller are not face-to-face?

3. What are the accounting procedures for sales and sales returns of products?

4. What are the accounting procedures for recording inventory and determining cost of goods sold?

The first two of these questions will be answered in this part of the chapter, while the second two will be answered in the last two sections of the chapter.

Determining the
Cost of Inventory

As inventory is acquired by a merchandising firm, a number of expenditures may take place. An important question arises as to which of these expenditures to include as a part of the purchase cost of the inventory. Generally, all expenditures necessary to acquire and transport products to the buyer's location should be considered a part of the purchase cost of the inventory. On the face of it, this seems quite straightforward; however, some complications may arise.

Purchase Discounts Consider first the amount actually charged the merchandiser by the seller for the products purchased. This amount is ordinarily called the **invoice cost** of the products, where the invoice is simply the bill from the seller (supplier) to the buyer (merchandising firm). Frequently when goods are purchased by merchandisers, a discount from the invoice cost of the products is offered for early payment of the bill. If the merchandiser pays for the goods within a specified period of time, the amount actually paid is the invoice cost minus the discount. The amount of the discount and period within which payments must be made are called the terms of the purchase. Terms are usually stated in abbreviated fashion such as

2/10, n/30 (read as "2, 10, net 30")

which indicates that a 2 percent discount is available if the purchase is paid for within ten days of the invoice date, but that the entire invoice amount is due within thirty days of the invoice date. Any combination of discount percentage and period of payment is possible, depending upon negotiations between the purchaser and supplier.

Cash Equivalent Cost The invoice cost of a purchase of products minus the discount is called the net cost or cash equivalent cost of the goods. The discount is called a **purchase discount** from the buyer's point of view and a **sales discount** from the seller's.

Theoretically, the proper purchase cost for inventory is the cash equivalent cost. If, for some reason, the discount is not taken and the total invoice cost is paid, the difference between the total invoice cost and the cash equivalent cost should be treated as an interest expense rather than as a part of the cost of inventory. Because most purchase discounts are quite generous (for example, saving 2 percent by paying twenty days early is roughly equivalent to 36 percent interest per year), merchandisers typically pay within the specified period and take advantage of the discount. If a company chooses to do otherwise, it is simply financing the purchase over a longer time period with the extra payment, and the extra amount paid is interest. The first element in the acquisition cost of inventory, then, is the cash equivalent cost of the goods.

Transportation The second major component of inventory cost is the cost of transporting the goods from the seller to the buyer. This cost, usually called *freight in* or *transportation in*, is included in the purchase cost of products only if it is paid by the purchaser. The cost of inventory acquired is the cash equivalent cost of the goods plus freight paid by the buyer to get the goods to the buyer's place of business. Note that this freight cost may be paid directly to a transportation company, such as a trucker, or it may be reimbursed to the supplier if paid for in advance and added to the invoice cost of the goods.

Purchase Returns Finally, the cost of inventory may be affected by the return to suppliers of some purchased goods. Merchandising firms, like consumers, may, from time to time, return goods that are damaged or are unsatisfactory for some other reason. These returned goods are called **purchase returns.** They lower the cost of inventory because the goods are no longer on hand and will not be paid for. The payment of freight on returned goods is usually a matter of negotiation between buyer and seller or is based on a prior agreement between the two.

To summarize, the cost of purchased inventory (called **net purchases**) for an accounting period is equal to

> the cash equivalent cost of the goods purchased
> + freight in on the purchased goods paid by the buyer
> − the cost of goods returned to the supplier
> = the cost of net purchases.

Recognizing Point of Sale

The discussion of accrual accounting in Chapter 2 emphasized that revenue should be recognized when the earning process is complete even though no cash has been received by the business. For most firms, the earning process is complete when the agreed upon service has been performed or the product sold. In a service business, determining the point at which the agreed upon service has been performed usually presents no problem, because both parties to the transaction come together at that point. For some merchandising businesses, it is also easy to determine the point of sale of the product. For example, a sale across the counter to a customer in a department store or a customer check-out at a supermarket represent easily fixed points of sale.

Consider, however, the circumstance where a merchandiser and customer (a sale) or merchandiser and supplier (a purchase) are not face-to-face or even in reasonable proximity to each other. It is possible for buyer and seller in a product transaction to be in different cities, states, or even different countries, hundreds or thousands of miles apart. In these instances, the goods must be transported long distances, and a significant amount of time may pass between release of the goods by the seller and their receipt by the buyer. Here, the **point of sale** of the product is not as easy to determine because goods are not transferred directly from seller to buyer. Is the point of sale when the seller turns the goods over to the shipper? Does it occur sometime during transport? Or is it when the goods are received by the buyer? Because each of these is a possibility, some guidelines are needed to determine the point of sale when buyer and seller are not face-to-face.

Free on Board (f.o.b.) Financial accounting appeals to the rules of law to help solve this point of sale dilemma. The point of sale should occur when ownership of the goods passes from seller to buyer. Ownership passes with the transfer of legal title, and this transfer may take place either when the goods are released by the seller or received by the buyer, depending upon the agreement between the parties. The phrase used to reflect this agreement and indicate when the transfer of legal title actually takes place is **free on board** (f.o.b.).

The designation *f.o.b. shipping point* indicates that title to the goods passes to the buyer at the shipping point and, therefore, that the goods belong to the buyer when they are delivered to the shipper by the seller. In other words, while in transport, the goods are the buyer's property. The designation *f.o.b. destination* denotes that ownership of the goods remains with the seller until they are actually physically received by the buyer. In transport, the goods are the seller's property. The f.o.b. designation reflects the negotiated arrangement between the parties and, thus, can be used to determine the point of sale of the goods.

Concept Summary

Point of Sale Distinctions for Buyer and Seller		
Party	*f.o.b. Shipping Point*	*f.o.b. Destination*
Seller	1. Title passes when goods are delivered to shipper. 2. Goods in transit belong to buyer (inventory of buyer). 3. Revenue is recognized when goods are delivered to shipper (released by seller).	1. Title passes when goods are received by buyer. 2. Goods in transit belong to seller (inventory of seller). 3. Revenue is recognized when goods are received by buyer.
Buyer	1. Title passes when goods are delivered to shipper. 2. Goods in transit belong to buyer (inventory of buyer). 3. Purchase of inventory is recognized when goods are delivered to shipper (released by seller).	1. Title passes when goods are received by buyer. 2. Goods in transit belong to seller (inventory of seller). 3. Purchase of inventory is recognized when goods are received by buyer.

Consignment It is important to remember that physical receipt by the buyer or physical transfer from the seller to the buyer is not necessary for a point of sale to be recognized. If legal title and ownership have passed, then the point of sale has occurred. Sometimes, however, a physical transfer of goods will take place without point of sale recognition. A merchandising firm may temporarily accept goods from a supplier and attempt to sell them on behalf of the supplier for a commission. Title and ownership of the goods remain with the supplier until they are sold, and if they are not sold, the goods are returned to the supplier. This type of arrangement is called consignment, and the goods are termed goods on consignment. On a consignment, the merchandiser has physical control of the goods, but does not take title or ownership. Revenue equal to the commission on the goods rather than the selling price is, thus, recognized; and there is no cost of goods sold for the merchandiser of these goods.

6.3 Accounting for Merchandising—Periodic Approach

The basic difference between service and merchandising businesses centers on the effect of selling a product on the assets, revenues, and expenses of the business. Applying the steps in the accounting cycle to merchandisers means understanding a new set of procedures for handling inventory, cost of goods sold, sales revenue, and returns. The fundamental approaches to accounting for the special problems of inventory and its related effect on the income statement are called **basic inventory systems.** Two basic inventory systems are widely used by merchandising firms: periodic and perpetual. Periodic and perpetual systems are approaches to accounting for inventory. Every merchandising business uses one or both of these approaches in accounting for its inventory, cost of goods sold, sales revenue, and returns.

The periodic approach to inventory is designed to be an inexpensive, minimum record-keeping system. A firm's inventory may consist of products that are individually low cost and sell at a very high volume. High-volume, low-value inventory, such as grocery items in a supermarket or most items in a department store, pose a particular problem for merchandisers. The purchases and sales of these goods must be accounted for; however, the system for doing so must be simple because of the large volume of goods. Also, the system should not be expensive to operate because each item of inventory has a low value. **Periodic inventory systems** are designed to accommodate this sort of merchandising situation.

The major characteristics of the periodic approach to accounting for inventory are discussed in the sections that follow.

Beginning
Inventory

In the general ledger, an account called inventory is used to maintain a record of the purchase cost of inventory on hand at the end of the previous accounting period and, therefore, at the beginning of the current period. This account reflects no inventory activity during the period.

Purchases of
Inventory

As purchases of inventory take place during the period, the cost of the purchase is debited to a separate general ledger account called **purchases** as follows:

Purchases
Cash *or* Accounts Payable

The purchases account is an **adjunct account** to inventory. Adjunct accounts are special valuation accounts whose balances are added to the balance in the general ledger account to which they pertain.

The Net Method of Recording Purchases When the cash equivalent cost of purchased inventory (invoice cost minus purchase discount) is debited to the purchases account, the **net method** of recording purchases is being used. The net method is most preferred because it reflects the idea that the true cost of the goods is the cash equivalent cost and treats any additional costs of purchase as a financing charge. Under the net method, purchase discounts not taken because payment is made after the discount period are treated as an interest expense to the buyer.

The Gross Method of Recording Purchases Although conceptually superior, the net method is not as widely used as the gross method of recording inventory purchases. The gross method records inventory purchases at the invoice cost of the goods. When goods are paid for within the discount period (the usual case), a special contra account called purchase discounts is created. The balance in this account is then deducted from the balance in the purchases account to determine the cash equivalent cost of purchases. The purchase discount account is unique to the gross method because, with the net method, all purchases are recorded net of discounts.

Net and Gross Compared Both methods for recording inventory purchases result in the same figures for ending inventory and cost of goods sold when all purchase discounts for a period are taken. The difference in methods is one of emphasis. The net method assumes that all purchase discounts will be taken, records the cash equivalent cost of purchases, and highlights as an expense any discounts not taken. The gross method records purchases as though discounts will not be taken and then creates a special account for discounts as they are realized. The gross method is less complex to implement for most businesses and, thus, is widely used.

Three events are affected by the net or gross choice: inventory purchases on credit, payment within the discount period, and payment after the discount period has elapsed. The journal entries and/or amounts are different in each instance.

Concept Summary

Net and Gross Methods of Recording Purchases and Payments		
Accounting Event	*Net Method*[1]	*Gross Method*[2]

Purchase of Inventory	Purchases
	    Accounts payable
		Purchases
		    Accounts payable

Payment within Discount Period	Accounts payable
	    Cash
		Accounts payable
		    Cash
		    Purchase discounts

Payment after Discount Period	Accounts payable
	Interest expense
	    Cash
		Accounts payable
		    Cash

[1]The normal sequence is assumed to be purchase at cash equivalent cost and payment within the discount period. Method assumes that all discounts will be taken and creates a special account (interest expense) to highlight the amount of lost discounts.

[2]Records purchases at invoice cost and creates a special contra account (purchase discounts) to record discounts as they are taken. Discounts not taken become a part of purchases and cost of goods sold.

Freight In

If the merchandising firm pays freight charges on its purchases of inventory, these charges are debited to a separate adjunct account called freight in or transportation in as follows:

Freight in
Cash

By creating these special accounts, it is possible to keep freight charges separate from the cost of the products and to keep purchases of the period separate from the inventory on hand at the beginning of the period.

Purchase Returns

If goods are returned to suppliers, the cost of the returned goods is credited to a special contra account called purchase returns.

Cash *or* Accounts payable
Purchase returns

In this way, the amount of purchase returns for the period can be highlighted in the records as an aid to future purchase decision making.

Sales Revenue

As sales of inventory occur during the accounting period, the selling price of the units multiplied by the number of units sold is credited to sales revenue. The debit may be to cash or accounts receivable, depending on whether the sale was for cash or on credit. The *cost* of the sale is not recorded when the sale takes place; only the sale is recorded.

Cash *or* Accounts receivable
Sales revenue

Sales Returns

If goods are returned by customers, the selling price of the goods multiplied by the units returned is debited to a special contra revenue account called sales returns.

Sales returns
Cash *or* Accounts receivable

A contra account is used so that returns for the period can be highlighted in the ledger for management information and analysis.

Cost of Goods Sold

Although revenue has been recorded as sales occurred, the cost of goods sold for the period has not yet been recorded. The periodic approach to inventory records the cost of goods sold for all sales of the period at the end of the period as an adjusting entry. The basis for this adjusting entry is an important calculation called the **basic inventory formula.** This formula determines the cost of goods sold for the period.

The basic inventory formula is as follows:

Inventory on hand at the beginning of the period
+ purchases for the period (net or gross depending on method)
− purchase discounts if the gross method of recording purchases is used
+ freight in for the period
− purchase returns for the period

$=$ cost of goods available for sale for the period
$-$ inventory on hand at the end of the period
$=$ cost of goods sold for the period.

All of the information needed for the basic inventory formula is found in the financial accounting records except the cost of inventory on hand at the end of the period. To obtain this figure, a physical count of the inventory items on hand at the end of the period must be made and the cost of these items determined. (Determination of these costs is the subject of Chapter 9).

Year-End Adjusting Entry The adjusting journal entry used by periodic inventory systems to record cost of goods sold for the accounting period is of the following format

> Inventory (ending amount)
> Purchase returns
> Cost of goods sold
>   Inventory (beginning amount)
>   Purchases
>   Freight in

The credit to the inventory account removes the cost of inventory on hand at the beginning of the period from the records (the balance in this account has not been affected by purchases and sales for the period), while the debit to inventory establishes the cost of inventory on hand at the end of the period in the records.

The debit to purchase returns and the credits to purchases and freight in remove from these accounts the amounts that represent purchase activity for the period and establish their balance at zero. If the gross method had been used, an additional debit to purchase discounts would be necessary for the amount of discounts taken during the period. The amount necessary to make the journal entry debits equal journal entry credits will be the amount for cost of goods sold for the period. This adjusting entry is simply the basic inventory formula in double-entry journal form.

Although there are other journal entry techniques for reflecting cost of goods sold in periodic inventory systems, the approach described above is clearest because it closely reflects the inventory formula on which all cost of goods sold calculations are based. Also, a cost of goods sold account in the general ledger is created, reflecting the expense amount for the period. Like all expenses, cost of goods sold would be closed to income summary during the closing process.

The Periodic Approach Illustrated

The mechanics of a periodic inventory system can now be illustrated with a numerical example. Suppose during an accounting period (one month in this instance) a merchandising business engaged in the purchase and sale transactions given in Figure 6-3. The general journal entries (including adjusting and closing entries) to record these inventory-related transactions in a periodic system are given in Figures 6-4 and 6-5. The net method of recording purchases has been assumed in this illustration. Operating

FIGURE 6-3

Sample Inventory-
Related Transactions

September	1	Inventory on hand at this date (250 units) had a cost of $490.
	4	Purchased $1,000 of inventory (500 units) from a supplier in another city on credit terms of 2/10, n/30. Freight of $50 was paid to the shipper when the goods arrived.
	7	Purchased $800 of inventory (400 units) on credit terms of 2/10, n/20. Freight of $25 on the shipment was paid by the supplier.
	12	Returned to supplier $100 of inventory (50 units) with a cash equivalent cost of $98 from the September 4 purchase. Paid the remaining amount due from the September 4 purchase.
	15	Sold 500 units of product to customers on credit at $4 per unit. Cost of the goods sold was $1,004.
	20	Customers returned 10 units from the sales on September 15 because the products were of the wrong type. Cost of the returned goods was $20.
	25	Paid the amount due from the September 7 purchase.
	30	A physical count of inventory disclosed that 610 units were on hand. The cost of these goods was determined to be $1,222.

expenses, interest, and income taxes have been omitted so that the problem may focus on the treatment of inventory-related transactions. These figures illustrate the use of adjunct and contra accounts by the periodic approach and the important role of the basic inventory formula as it is reflected in the adjusting entry to determine cost of goods sold.

FIGURE 6-4

Journal Entries for a
Periodic System

	General Journal		
Date	Transaction Accounts	Debit	Credit
Sept 4	Purchases	980	
	Freight in	50	
	Accounts payable		980
	Cash		50
	(1,000 × .98 cash equivalent cost)		
7	Purchases	784	
	Accounts payable		784
	(800 × .98 cash equivalent cost)		
12	Accounts payable	98	
	Purchase returns		98
	(Given in transaction)		
12	Accounts payable	882	
	Cash		882
	(980 − 98)		
15	Accounts receivable	2,000	
	Sales revenue		2,000
	(500 × $4)		
20	Sales returns	40	
	Accounts receivable		40
	(10 × $4)		
25	Accounts payable	784	
	Interest expense	16	
	Cash		800
	(Purchase discount $16 is lost)		

FIGURE 6-5
Adjusting and Closing Entries for a Periodic System

General Journal				
Date	Transaction Accounts		Debit	Credit
	*Adjusting Entry**			
Sept 30	Inventory		1,222	
	Purchase returns		98	
	Cost of goods sold		984	
	Inventory			490
	Purchases			1,764
	Freight in			50
	Closing Entries			
30	Sales revenue		2,000	
	Income summary			2,000
	Income summary		1,040	
	Sales returns			40
	Interest expense			16
	Cost of goods sold			984
30	Income summary		960	
	Retained earnings			960

*Beginning inventory		490	
Purchases	1,764		
Freight in	50		
Purchase returns	(98)	1,716	
Goods available for sale		2,206	
Ending inventory		(1,222)	
Cost of goods sold		984	

6.4 Accounting for Merchandising—Perpetual Approach

The perpetual approach to inventory is designed for those situations where close control of inventory within the accounting records is important. Where inventory consists of relatively high-value but low-volume items, such as new cars or major appliances, a somewhat more expensive and complex inventory system can be justified. Here, the high value of individual inventory items makes it important that purchases and sales be carefully accounted for as they occur. **Perpetual inventory systems** do just this.

The major characteristics of the perpetual approach to accounting for inventory are described in the sections that follow. These characteristics will be demonstrated with the transactions that were used to illustrate the periodic approach earlier in this chapter. In this way, comparison of the periodic and perpetual approaches will be possible.

Beginning Inventory

In the general ledger, the inventory account reflects the purchase cost of inventory on hand at the end of the previous accounting period and, therefore, at the beginning of the current period. Unlike the periodic approach, however, this account will reflect all inventory activity for the period.

Purchases of Inventory

An important characteristic of perpetual systems is the absence of inventory-related adjunct and contra accounts. As purchases of inventory take place during the period, the cash equivalent cost of the purchase is debited directly to inventory in the following manner:

> Inventory
>   Cash *or* Accounts payable

Purchase discounts are credited directly to the inventory account if the gross method is used.

Freight In If freight is paid on purchases, these charges are also debited directly to the inventory account.

> Inventory
>   Cash

Notice that, in the perpetual approach, all purchase activity is recorded in the inventory account.

Purchase Returns

If goods are returned by a merchandiser to its supplier, the cost of the returned goods is credited directly to the inventory account as follows:

> Cash *or* Accounts payable
>   Inventory

The inventory account becomes a complete running balance of the dollar amount of inventory on hand.

Sales Revenue

As sales of inventory occur during the accounting period, the selling price of the goods multiplied by the number of units sold is credited to sales revenue. The debit may be to cash or accounts receivable. The most important difference between the periodic and perpetual approach appears here, at the point of sale. Perpetual systems record both the sale of products and the cost of sales simultaneously as sales occur. It is this feature that makes perpetual systems somewhat complex and expensive to operate.

Recording sales requires knowing the selling price of each product (something that must be known anyway for customer purposes); however, to record the cost of the sale, the cost of individual products must be immediately available from the system. An inventory system that can produce a product cost on demand with each sale must be carefully designed. This is what perpetual systems do.

> Cash *or* Accounts receivable
>   Sales revenue

and

> Cost of goods sold
>   Inventory

Sales Returns	If goods are returned by customers, the selling price of the goods multiplied by the units returned is debited to a special contra revenue account called sales returns. Because, in a perpetual system, the inventory account represents a running balance of inventory on hand, it is necessary to reflect the return of goods immediately in inventory. This can be done by debiting inventory and crediting cost of goods sold for the cost of goods returned. The perpetual approach requires that both the sale and the cost of the sale be reversed when goods are returned by customers.

Sales returns
    Cash *or* Accounts receivable

and

Inventory
    Cost of goods sold

Cost of Goods Sold	The perpetual inventory system keeps all accounts up-to-date so that no adjusting entry is necessary at the end of the period to determine cost of goods sold. Financial statements can be prepared directly from the records.

A physical count of inventory is still an important part of inventory procedures; however, the count can be accomplished at any time and compared to inventory balances shown in the records at that time. Sometimes the count may show an amount of inventory on hand that is different from the amount shown by the accounting records. This discrepancy may be the result of "unrecorded" inventory transactions, such as thefts or spoiled goods. In these instances, an entry must be made to reconcile the accounting records with physical reality. This entry would debit an appropriate expense account and credit inventory directly.

The perpetual approach may actually seem simpler in a textbook or classroom context with only a few transactions; however, the information needed in a real situation to make perpetual systems function is much more extensive than that required for periodic systems.

Concept Summary

Different Approaches to Inventory Accounting		
Characteristics	*Periodic*	*Perpetual*
Applicable Situations	Low-cost inventory items that move at high volume.	High-cost inventory items that move at low volume.
Complexity and Cost	Minimum paperwork; simple and inexpensive system.	Sophisticated records; complex and expensive system.
Physical Count of Inventory on Hand	Required each accounting period to determine cost of goods sold and inventory on the balance sheet.	Not required to determine cost of goods sold or inventory, but may be used to check the accuracy of records.

(continued on next page)

Concept Summary *(continued)*

Characteristics	Periodic	Perpetual
Determination of Cost of Goods Sold	End-of-period adjusting entry is necessary; accounting records do not reflect cost of goods sold or inventory on hand until the adjustment is made.	Cost of goods sold and inventory on hand are determined directly from accounting records; no adjusting entry is necessary.
Control over Inventory	Minimum contol over inventory is achieved by the system; control is accomplished outside the formal accounting records.	Close control is achieved directly in the accounting records.

The Perpetual Approach Illustrated

The general journal entries to record in a perpetual inventory system the inventory related transactions given in Figure 6-3 are presented in Figures 6-6 and 6-7. Again, the net method of recording purchases has been assumed.

The recording of these events in a perpetual system should be compared to the recording of the same events under the periodic approach. These two approaches to accounting for merchandising inventory represent different systems for different types of products. The nature of a merchandiser's inventory and the willingness to incur high costs in accounting for inventory determine the type of system that will be used. For most large companies, both inventory systems would likely be found for different kinds of products. For example, an auto dealership would probably use a perpetual system for new cars and a periodic system for parts and supplies; while a major retailer would apply the perpetual approach to large appliances and the periodic approach for toys and hardware items. In this way, the inventory system fits the product.

Summary

Businesses may be classified according to the type of profit-seeking activity they perform. Using this classification system, a business may be thought of as primarily service, merchandising, or manufacturing. Service businesses earn revenue by performing a service or by selling expertise; consequently, they have no inventory. Merchandising businesses sell a product that has been purchased intact from a supplier. As a result, inventory is an important current asset, and cost of goods sold is an important expense for this type of business. Manufacturing businesses sell a product that has been created from raw materials.

Because merchandising businesses acquire the product they sell from suppliers, accounting for the purchase cost of inventory is the most important consideration. The purchase cost of goods includes the invoice cost

FIGURE 6-6
Journal Entries for a
Perpetual System

General Journal			
Date	Transaction Accounts	Debit	Credit
Sept 4	Inventory	1,030	
	Accounts payable		980
	Cash		50
	(1,000 × .98) + 50		
7	Inventory	784	
	Accounts payable		784
	(800 × .98)		
12	Accounts payable	98	
	Inventory		98
	(Given in transaction)		
12	Accounts payable	882	
	Cash		882
	(980 − 98)		
15	Accounts receivable	2,000	
	Sales revenue		2,000
	(500 × $4)		
15	Cost of goods sold	1,004	
	Inventory		1,004
	(Given in transaction)		
20	Sales returns	40	
	Accounts receivable		40
	(10 × $4)		
20	Inventory	20	
	Cost of goods sold		20
	(Given in transaction)		
25	Accounts payable	784	
	Interest expense	16	
	Cash		800
	(Purchase discount of $16 is lost)		

FIGURE 6-7
Adjusting and Closing
Entries for a Perpetual
System

General Journal			
Date	Transaction Accounts	Debit	Credit
	Adjusting Entry		
	No adjusting entry for cost of goods sold will be necessary in a perpetual system unless a physical count of inventory shows the actual amount of inventory on hand at the end of the period to be different from the running balance of the inventory account.		
	Closing Entries		
Sept 30	Sales revenue	2,000	
	Income summary		2,000
30	Income summary	1,040	
	Sales returns		40
	Interest expense		16
	Cost of goods sold		984
30	Income summary	960	
	Retained earnings		960

if the gross method is used or the cash equivalent cost if the net method is used. In either event, transportation costs are included in the purchase cost of goods.

Two approaches are available and generally used to account for the purchases and sales of merchandising inventory. The periodic approach is used where inventory consists of items that are individually low cost, but sell at a high volume. This approach uses adjunct and contra accounts to record the acquisitions and returns of inventory and treats the determination of cost of goods sold as an adjusting entry at the end of the accounting period. The perpetual approach is used where inventory consists of items that are individually high cost, but sell at a low volume. This approach records all purchases and cost of sales directly in the inventory account. Thus, the general ledger account for inventory reflects all movements in inventory as they occur. The inventory account, therefore, provides a running balance of inventory on hand.

Some double-entry bookkeeping refinements which a merchandising business may use in recording and classifying its transactions and some control techniques which ensure that the accounting system can protect itself from accidental and deliberate errors are examined in Chapter 7.

Key Terms

Adjunct account	**Merchandising business**
Basic inventory formula	**Net method**
Basic inventory system	**Net purchases**
Cash equivalent cost	**Periodic inventory system**
Cost of goods sold	**Perpetual inventory system**
F.o.b. (shipping point or destination)	**Point of sale**
Freight (transportation)	**Purchase discount**
Gross method	**Purchase return**
Gross profit	**Purchases**
Invoice cost	**Sales discount**
Manufacturing business	**Sales return**
Markup	**Service business**

Comprehensive Review Problem

The following events relate to Charlie's Cheese Store, Galveston, Texas, for the month of August. Charlie's Cheeses uses the net method for recording inventory purchases. All amounts given are stated in terms of invoice cost.

August *1* Inventory on hand cost $5,400.

5 Purchased $4,750 of inventory from Chunky Cheese, Inc. (located in Dallas, Texas). The goods were shipped f.o.b. Dallas on credit terms of 2/10, n/30. Freight charge of $45 was paid to the shipper at the time of delivery.

6 $600 of spoiled cheese was returned to Chunky Cheese and a credit given for the return.

9 $1,200 of New York Cheddar was purchased from Blue Clover Dairy

Products on credit. Terms were 2/10, n/20, and Blue Clover paid the freight charge.

14 Chunky Cheese was paid for the August 5 purchase.

15 Merchandise was sold to customers on credit for $8,000. The markup to determine the selling price is 25 percent of the cost of the merchandise.

17 Customers returned $200 of American because it had been substituted on an order for Swiss. Credit of $200 was given.

29 Received notice from Contented Cows Cheese Foods that $700 of cheese balls had been shipped f.o.b. Galveston with terms of 2/10, n/30.

31 Paid Blue Clover Dairies full amount owed for August 9 purchase.

31 A physical inventory showed $4,448 of goods remaining on hand.

Required:

Prepare journal entries including any necessary adjusting and closing entries for these transactions assuming that

1. Charlie uses the periodic inventory approach.

2. Charlie uses the perpetual inventory approach.

Solution to Comprehensive Review Problem

1.

CHARLIE'S CHEESES
Journal Entries for a Periodic System

General Journal

Date	Transaction Accounts	Debit	Credit
Aug. 5	Purchases	4,655	
	Freight in	45	
	Accounts payable		4,655
	Cash		45
	Purchased cheese from Chunky Cheese, Inc.		
	($4,750 × .98 = $4,655)		
6	Accounts payable	588	
	Purchase returns		588
	Returned spoiled cheese to Chunky		
	Cheese for credit ($600 × .98 = $588)		
9	Purchases	1,176	
	Accounts payable		1,176
	Purchased $1,200 of New York Cheddar from Blue Clover		
	Dairies. Terms 2/10, n/20 ($1,200 × .98 = $1,176)		
14	Accounts payable	4,067	
	Cash		4,067
	Paid Chunky Cheese the balance due on Aug. 5 purchase		
	($4,655 − $588 = $4,067)		
15	Accounts receivable	8,000	
	Sales		8,000
	Sold goods to customers		
17	Sales returns	200	
	Accounts receivable		200
	Cheese returned by customers		

[Aug. 29 purchase is not recorded until goods are received because they were sent f.o.b. destination.]

31	Accounts payable	1,176	
	Interest expense	24	
	Cash		1,200

Paid Blue Clover Dairies for August 9 purchase plus lost discount

Adjusting Entry

31	Inventory	4,448	
	Purchase returns	588	
	Cost of goods sold	6,240	
	Inventory		5,400
	Purchases		5,831
	Freight in		45

To adjust for cost of goods sold:

Beginning inventory		$ 5,400	
Purchases	$5,831		
Freight in	45		
Purchase returns	(588)	5,288	
Goods available for sale		10,688	
Ending inventory		(4,448)	
Cost of goods sold		$ 6,240	

Closing Entries

31	Sales	8,000	
	Income summary		8,000

Close gross revenues to income summary

31	Income summary	6,464	
	Sales returns		200
	Interest expense		24
	Cost of goods sold		6,240

Close deductions to income summary

31	Income summary	1,536	
	Charlie, capital		1,536

Close income summary to owner capital

2.

CHARLIE'S CHEESES
Journal Entries for a Perpetual System

General Journal

Date	Transaction Accounts	Debit	Credit
Aug. 5	Inventory	4,700	
	Accounts payable		4,655
	Cash		45
	Purchased cheese from Chunky Cheese, Inc.		
	($4,750 × .98) + $45 freight = 4,655 + 45 = 4,700		
6	Accounts payable	588	
	Inventory		588
	Returned spoiled cheese to Chunky Cheese		
	($600 × .98 = $588)		
9	Inventory	1,176	
	Accounts payable		1,176
	Purchased $1,200 of New York Cheddar from Blue Clover Dairy		
	($1,200 × .98 = $1,176)		

14	Accounts payable	4,067	
	Cash		4,067

Paid Chunky Cheese the balance due on Aug. 5 purchase ($4,655 − $588 = $4,067)

15	Accounts receivable	8,000	
	Sales		8,000

Sold goods to customers

15	Cost of goods sold	6,400	
	Inventory		6,400

Sold goods to customers (cost = $8,000/1.25 = $6,400)

17	Sales returns	200	
	Accounts receivable		200

Cheese returns of $200 by customer

17	Inventory	160	
	Cost of goods sold		160

Cheese returned by customers
(cost = $200/1.25 = $160)

[Aug. 29 purchase is not recorded until goods are received because they were sent f.o.b. destination.]

31	Accounts payable	1,176	
	Interest expense	24	
	Cash		1,200

Paid Blue Clover Dairies for August 9 purchase plus lost discount.

[No adjusting entry needed for cost of goods sold.]

Closing Entries

31	Sales	8,000	
	Income summary	8,000	

Close gross revenues to income summary

31	Income summary	6,464	
	Sales returns		200
	Interest expense		24
	Cost of goods sold		6,240

Close deductions to income summary

31	Income summary	1,536	
	Charlie, capital		1,536

Close income summary to owner capital

Questions

Q6-1. How would the income statement and balance sheet of a service business differ from those of a merchandising business?

Q6-2. What is the major difference between merchandisers and manufacturers?

Q6-3. Explain the term *free on board*. What is its significance?

Q6-4. Distinguish the periodic approach to accounting for inventory from the perpetual approach.

Q6-5. To which kinds of inventories is the periodic approach usually applied? What are the primary advantages and disadvantages of this approach?

Q6-6. To which kinds of inventories is the perpetual approach usually applied? What are the primary advantages and disadvantages of this approach?

Q6-7. Contrast the gross method of recording inventory purchases with the net method. Which is preferable? Why?

Q6-8. Would the gross method and net method always result in the same figures for inventory and cost of goods sold for a given accounting period? If not, describe the circumstances in which the amounts would differ.

Exercises

E6-1. Match the following terms:

1. invoice cost
2. freight in
3. f.o.b. shipping point
4. cash equivalent cost
5. raw materials inventory
6. discount
7. perpetual system
8. cost of goods available for sale

    a. cost of goods sold plus ending inventory
    b. goods belong to buyer when delivered to shipper
    c. goods in transit belong to the seller
    d. amount deducted from invoice cost if payment is made within a specified time period
    e. invoice cost minus the discount
    f. the amount actually paid or promised to be paid for the products purchased
    g. cost of transporting goods from seller to buyer
    h. a system for high-value, low-volume items
    i. a system for low-value, high-volume items
    j. an inventory item in a manufacturing firm

E6-2. Inventory on hand at the beginning of the period was $19,000. Inventory of $74,000, subject to terms of 2/10, n/30, was purchased during the period. Freight in was $500. Of these purchases, $1,300 was returned to suppliers. Inventory on hand at the end of the period was $30,000. Compute the cost of goods available and cost of goods sold for the period using the net method of recording purchases.

E6-3. Determine the amount of beginning inventory from the following information:

Sales	$49,400
Sales returns	650
Purchases	18,000
Freight in	800
Purchase returns	1,000
Ending inventory	1,800
Cost of goods sold	18,200

E6-4. Prepare an income statement for Anthony Company, Inc., given the following data for the calendar year 1982:

Beginning inventory	$125,000
Purchases	150,000

Transportation in on purchases	1,000
Operating expenses other than taxes	19,500
Ending inventory per physical count	137,500
Sales	200,000
Sales returns	12,000
Income tax rate	40%

E6-5. Using the information in Exercise 6-4, journalize the adjusting entries to establish cost of goods sold and income tax expense and also the closing entries relating to this data.

E6-6. Determine the correct amount of ending inventory to report for Abbacus Company using the following information:

 a. Items counted in store by inventory crew $45,000

 b. Invoice on hand for goods ordered from Maxwell Inc. and shipped f.o.b. shipping point 600

 c. Items shipped today f.o.b. destination; invoice has been mailed to customer, Gingham Enterprises 400

 d. Items in shipping department not included in Item a; invoices have not been mailed to customers 210

 e. Items shipped today f.o.b. shipping point. 450

 f. Items in receiving department returned by customer 150

 g. Items included in Item a held on consignment 325

E6-7. Give any required journal entry for each of the following events:

 a. Lemac Corporation, which uses the perpetual inventory system and the net method, purchases goods from Wegman Inc., on account for $13,000 with terms 2/20, n/30. Lemac had a beginning inventory of $6,300.

 b. Freight in of $175 is paid in cash.

 c. $1,500 of the goods are unsatisfactory and are returned to the supplier.

 d. Goods costing $2,500 are sold for $3,850 on credit.

 e. Paid Wegman the amount owed within the discount period.

 f. Wegman has a new experimental item on the market, and Lemac accepts $8,000 of merchandise on consignment.

 g. Goods costing $14,000 are sold on credit for $21,560.

 h. Customers were dissatisfied with $1,155 of the goods and returned them. Cost of these goods to Lemac was $750.

 i. Collected $20,000 on account from customers.

E6-8. Lafayette Trading Company uses a periodic inventory system. Ending inventory from the previous period was $18,970. Purchases, on credit, for the period were $62,000. Terms were 2/10, n/30. $50,000 of this amount was paid during the discount period. Another $9,000 was paid after the discount period but before the end of the accounting period. $500 of purchases were returned to the supplier. Total freight in, paid in cash, on purchases was $1,275. Sales, all on credit, were $115,000, and sales returns were $8,350. Assume that ending inventory is $25,150 and that the net method is used. Journalize the above data and also make any required adjusting and closing entries.

E6-9. Assume the same data as in Exercise 6-8 except that Lafayette uses a perpetual inventory system and the net method. Cost of all goods sold for the period was $59,699, and the cost of the sales returns was $4,334. Journalize the basic data and make any required adjusting and closing entries.

E6-10. Arrowhead Company had the following income statement for 1982:

ARROWHEAD COMPANY
Income Statement
For the Year Ended December 31, 1982

Sales revenue			$800,000
Cost of goods sold			
Beginning inventory	$ 50,000		
Purchases	425,000		
Goods available for sale	475,000		
Ending inventory	125,000		
Cost of goods sold		$350,000	
Operating expenses		300,000	
Total expenses			650,000
Net income (pretax)			$150,000

The following errors were not discovered until after the above income statement had been completed:

a. Accrued expenses of $30,000 had not been recognized.

b. Included in the sales revenue figure were $20,000 of advances from customers.

c. $50,000 of goods were held on consignment from Avergno Company. No purchase had been recorded for these goods; however, they were included in the ending inventory.

d. Goods costing $15,000 had been ordered by Arrowhead, which uses the net method, from Iiams Company and had been shipped f.o.b. shipping point. These goods had not yet been received and were not included in the ending inventory. No purchase had yet been recorded. Terms of the purchase were 2/10, n/30.

Prepare a corrected income statement for Arrowhead Company.

Problems

P6-1. Given below are various errors which affect the five financial statement amounts listed.

Error	Accounts Receivable	Inventory	Accounts Payable	Sales	Cost of Goods Sold
a. Goods were shipped to customer f.o.b. shipping point. They were not counted in ending inventory, and a sale was not recorded.					
b. Goods held on consignment were counted in ending inventory and were recorded as a credit purchase.					

Error	Accounts Receivable	Inventory	Accounts Payable	Sales	Cost of Goods Sold
c. Goods purchased f.o.b. destination were recorded as a purchase but excluded from ending inventory.					
d. Goods sold and shipped f.o.b. shipping point were included in ending inventory and were not recorded as a sale.					

Required:

Complete the above tabulation. Enter *O* if the amount would be overstated, *U* if the amount would be understated, and *NE* if there would be no effect on the amount.

P6-2. The following information appeared on the financial statements of the Kelley Fitzpatrick Company for 1982:

Earnings per share	$ 4.50
Common stock outstanding during the year	22,500 shares
Net earnings for the year	101,250
Net sales	450,000
Cost of goods sold	270,000
Beginning inventory	31,500
Ending inventory	40,500
Retained earnings 12/31/82	675,000
Assets	1,350,000
Stockholders' equity	900,000

Required:

After the financial statements were prepared, it was discovered that there had been an error in computing ending inventory. Goods being held on consignment valued at $3,000 had been incorrectly included in the count. Given this information, indicate any corrections that should be made to the figures above.

P6-3. The following information appeared in the trial balance of Impala Corporation at December 31:

Cash	$ 10,000
Accounts receivable	20,000
Merchandise inventory	22,000
Accounts payable	30,000
Sales revenue	494,000
Sales returns	4,000
Purchases of merchandise	180,000
Purchase returns	6,000
Transportation on purchases	8,000
Purchase discounts lost	2,000

Required:

Prepare the adjusting and closing entries relating to the data, assuming that a physical count revealed ending inventory to be $18,000.

P6-4.　Carl Company, Inc., which uses a perpetual inventory system and the net method of recording purchases, had the following transactions during the month of June:

June 1 Inventory on hand, 450 units at $100 each.

　2 Purchased 90 units for cash, $9,000.

　3 Purchased 200 units on credit from Smith Wholesale Company, $20,000, terms 2/10, n/30. Also paid freight bill, $175.

　4 Sold 500 units of merchandise on credit, $62,500. Cost of these units was $50,000.

　5 Returned 10 of the units purchased June 3 from Smith because they were unsatisfactory. Paid the balance owed Smith.

　7 Purchased 400 additional units from Smith. Total cost of the units was $42,041, subject to credit terms of 2/10, n/30. Paid cash of $300 for freight.

　10 Customers returned 8 units from the sales on June 4. Customers were given credit for the $1,000 of sales returns.

　15 Paid expenses of $2,500.

　18 Sold 550 units for cash, $68,750. Cost of these units was $55,965.

　20 Purchased 450 additional units on credit from Haywood Corporation. Total cost was $48,711, subject to terms 3/10, n/30. Also paid freight of $335.

　21 Collected $58,000 of accounts receivable.

　22 Paid Smith amount owed for the June 7 purchase.

　25 Paid operating expenses, $5,000.

　30 Sold 200 units on credit, $25,000. Cost of these units was $20,973.

Required:

1. Journalize the above events.

2. Post to T accounts.

3. Prepare an income statement for June.

4. Journalize the closing entries.

P6-5.　Reproduced below are comparative income statements for Greenleaf Corporation for the years 1979 through 1982.

	1979	1980	1981	1982
Sales	$35,000	$37,000	$43,000	$44,000
Cost of goods sold	15,000	15,500	18,700	19,400
Operating expenses	6,000	6,700	7,000	6,800
Pretax income	$14,000	$14,800	$17,300	$17,800

Required:

It has recently been discovered that the 1980 ending inventory was overstated by $4,000. The ending inventory for 1981 was understated by $1,500. Recast the income statements, taking these errors into consideration.

P6-6.　The following data are available for the B & P Partnership for the three years ended December 31, 1982. The firm sells its merchandise at 25 percent above cost.

	Sales	Beginning Inventory	Ending Inventory	Operating Expense
1980	$ 93,600	$20,000	$24,000	$ 4,000
1981	124,800	24,000	34,000	16,000
1982	158,000	34,000	28,000	6,000

Required:
Determine the amount of purchases and net income for each of the three years.

P6-7. E. R. Rore Company was organized January 2, 1980, and is being audited in February of 1982. Reported income was $35,100 in 1980 and $40,200 in 1981. The auditor detects the following errors during the examination of the records:

a. Merchandise costing $4,500 was being held on consignment late in December 1980. The merchandise was incorrectly included in the ending inventory.

b. In counting the December 1980 ending inventory, one batch, costing $1,900, was counted twice.

c. Merchandise purchased from a supplier for $5,200 was shipped f.o.b. shipping point on December 29, 1980. Because it did not arrive until January 5, 1981, it was not included in the ending inventory count December 31, 1980. The purchase was not recorded until the goods were received.

d. In taking the inventory December 31, 1981, an amount of $2,400 was mistakenly added into the inventory count as $4,200.

e. Merchandise with a retail value of $1,235 and a cost of $950 was shipped December 31, 1981, f.o.b. destination. A sale was not recorded and the merchandise was not included in ending inventory because the goods had already been shipped.

Required:
1. Determine the correct net income before taxes for each year.

2. Were any amounts on the balance sheet in error each year? If so, which accounts and by what amount was each in error?

P6-8. Presented below is the balance sheet for Mary Company, which uses a periodic inventory system.

MARY COMPANY
Balance Sheet
October 31, 1982

ASSETS

Cash	$ 12,000
Accounts receivable	60,000
Inventory	30,000
Office equipment (net)	2,000
Trucks (net)	8,000
Total assets	$112,000

LIABILITIES & OWNERS' EQUITY

Notes payable	$ 7,000
Accounts payable	31,000
Total liabilities	38,000
Mary, capital	74,000
Total liabilities & owners' equity	$112,000

The following are the transactions that took place during November:

Nov. 2 Collected $57,000 on account from customers.

3 Paid $25,000 net to creditors on account within the discount period.

5 Sold merchandise for $15,000 on account.

6 Purchased merchandise on credit from Heather Company for $25,000, terms 2/20, n/30. Paid freight $145.

10 Paid salary expenses of $2,100.

13 Gave customers credit for $200 of goods returned.

17 Purchased merchandise for $18,000 on account from Pike Company, terms 2/10, n/30. Paid $90 freight.

19 Paid creditors $6,125, which included $125 of purchase discounts lost.

20 Paid Heather Company the amount owed it.

23 Sold merchandise to customers for $60,000 on account.

25 Returned $650 of goods purchased November 17 from Pike Company.

26 Paid salary expenses of $900.

30 Collected $50,000 from customers on account and accepted $400 of returns from credit customers.

30 Paid Pike Company the amount owed it.

30 Depreciation on office equipment and trucks was $60 and $130, respectively.

30 Interest to accrue on the note is $50.

30 A physical count revealed inventory on hand to be $14,500.

Required:

1. Set up T accounts and enter the beginning balances.

2. Journalize the above transactions, including the adjusting entries.

3. Post to the T accounts.

4. Take a trial balance.

5. Prepare an income statement and a balance sheet.

6. Journalize the closing entries, and post these to the T accounts.

P6-9. Presented below is the balance sheet for Zoe Company, which uses a perpetual inventory system.

ZOE COMPANY
Balance Sheet
December 31, 1981

ASSETS

Cash	$ 66,000
Accounts receivable	120,000
Inventory	95,000
Office equipment (net)	25,000
Trucks (net)	24,000
Total assets	$330,000

LIABILITIES & OWNERS' EQUITY

Notes payable	$ 20,000
Accounts payable	110,000
Total liabilities	130,000
Zoe, capital	200,000
Total liabilities & owners' equity	$330,000

The following transactions took place during January 1982:

Jan. 2 Collected $105,000 owed by customers.

5 Sold merchandise on account for $45,000. Cost of these goods was $34,600.

8 Purchased merchandise on credit from David Company for $50,000, terms 2/10, n/30. Paid freight, $265.

12 Paid salary expenses of $5,000.

13 Gave customers credit for $500 of goods returned. Cost of these items was $385.

14 Paid creditors $100,000 within the discount period.

15 Purchased merchandise on account for $40,000 from Elmwood Company, terms 2/10, n/30. Paid $180 freight.

16 Paid David Company for the purchase of January 8.

19 Sold merchandise for cash, $85,000. Cost of the merchandise was $65,500.

21 Returned $1,000 of goods to Elmwood from the January 15 purchase.

23 Paid salary expenses of $3,500.

24 Paid half the amount owed Elmwood Company.

27 Collected $40,000 from customers on account.

29 Paid Elmwood the remaining amount owed.

30 Accepted returns from customers and gave them credit for $1,400. Cost of these goods was $1,075.

31 Paid salary expenses of $3,700.

31 Depreciation on the office equipment was $100 and on the trucks, $300.

31 Interest to accrue on the note is $150.

Required:

1. Set up T accounts and enter the beginning balances.

2. Journalize the above transactions.

3. Post to the T accounts.

4. Take a trial balance.

5. Prepare an income statement and a balance sheet.

6. Journalize the closing entries, and post these to the T accounts.

P6-10. The selling expenses of Craig, Inc., were 10 percent of sales. The general expenses were 15 percent of sales and also were equal to 25 percent of the cost of goods sold. A physical count of inventory at the end of the year revealed inventory of $140,400. Ending inventory was 30 percent greater than beginning inventory. Income for the year, before taxes, was $180,000. The tax rate was 40 percent. Prepare an income statement for Craig, Inc., for the year ended December 31, 1982.

CHAPTER 7

Accounting Transactions and Internal Control

Chapter Outline

7.1 *Subsidiary Ledgers and Special Journals.* Concept and use of subsidiary ledgers in an accounting system; subsidiary ledgers and their relationship to the general ledger; purpose of special journals.

7.2 *Special Journals Illustrated:* Discussion and illustration of the sales, purchases, cash receipts, and cash disbursements journals.

7.3 *Basic Concepts of Internal Control.* Introduction to the ideas that the accounting system must protect assets and the accuracy of data from accidental and deliberate errors.

7.4 *Internal Control of Cash and Inventory.* Methods of stealing cash and covering the theft in the acounting records; techniques and procedures to eliminate or help prevent thefts; basic tasks involving internal control of inventory including purchasing, custody, and record keeping.

7.5 *Basic Elements of Internal Control.* Fundamental concepts of internal control to be adapted to particular situations, because no one set of procedures applies in every situation.

Accounting and the Real World

PEKING: A 58-year-old woman led a ring of embezzlers who milked nearly $400,000 from a company in northeast China, according to the *People's Daily*.

She was a cashier who took control of the company during the Cultural Revolution 12 years ago when the manager and company secretary were purged as "capitalist roaders" and sent to work in the countryside.

The amount the gang had stolen since 1972 totaled twice the amount of the company's fixed assets, the paper said. They kept falsified records of coal sales and drew wages for nonexistent casual workers.

The woman used much of the money to bribe more than 200 officials in 90 other departments and enterprises.

She kept some of the money hidden, but also spent lavishly on television sets, phonographs, and other electrical appliances, eiderdown quilts, fur coats, furniture, wine, cigarettes, and expensive canned food.

LONDON: The chairman and two directors of a bank who masterminded a £40m fraud (almost $100,000,000) were jailed yesterday at the Old Bailey, within a stone's throw of their office.

Investors' money had gone into dishonest hands, and the liquidator discovered that £30m in unsecured loans had been advanced to four small companies in Liechtenstein, in which the chairman had interests. The chairman himself obtained a £1 million interest-free overdraft without any security from his bank.

NEW ORLEANS: More than $49,000 in cafeteria funds were stolen from Delgado College. Sources say the funds were siphoned off over an 11-month period from July 1978 through May 1979.

The missing funds were uncovered late in May when the Delgado business manager noticed conflicts in financial reports submitted by a clerk in the school's fiscal office and the school's cafeteria manager. According to one person, the clerk was allegedly able to skim funds from the cafeteria account because "nobody checked his figures . . . nobody."

The cafeteria manager routinely turned over revenues to the clerk and was issued receipts, all of which he saved. The clerk then prepared the funds for deposit with an armored car agency. He allegedly pocketed some of the funds and filled out deposit slips incorrectly, according to one source.

New Orleans *Times-Picayune.*
London *Daily Telegraph.*

The accounting cycle discussed in Chapters 3 and 4 represents a complete view of the concepts underlying accounting systems for businesses; however, taking this cycle from the textbook to the real world requires certain additional mechanical recording and classifying devices and control techniques. These refinements of the basic accounting cycle allow the efficient and accurate processing of repetitive events.

In this chapter, special devices for the mass processing of transactions and techniques for their control are introduced. When this material is understood, it is possible to appreciate how basic accounting systems work.

7.1   Subsidiary Ledgers and Special Journals

The term accounts receivable is used to represent amounts owed to a business by its customers and others, and accounts payable indicates amounts owed by a business to its suppliers and others. In Chapter 3, T accounts were created in a general ledger to represent these amounts—that is, one account for all amounts owed to the business and one account for all amounts owed by the business. For balance sheet purposes, this approach is adequate because all that is needed is the total asset (receivable) and total liability (payable) existing at the balance sheet date.

However, the management of a business, its customers, and its suppliers require much more information about receivables and payables. Specifically, management must (1) know the exact amount owed to the business by each individual customer; (2) know when a specific customer has reached his limit of credit; (3) be able to give specific customers credit for payments received; and (4) for control purposes, have a general history of the purchase and payment patterns of each customer. In addition, any business would want to know exact amounts owed to individual suppliers so that purchases could be controlled and payments made on time.

Subsidiary Ledgers

It is not possible to get this type of detailed information from one account depicting total receivables and another showing total payables. Even a business with only a few customers and suppliers needs some supplementary breakdown of aggregate amounts owed to and owed by the business. This breakdown should be by individual customer and supplier. As a business gets larger, say 100 or 100,000 customers and 15 or 1,500 suppliers, a mechanical technique for keeping track of exact individual amounts owed to and owed by it becomes absolutely necessary. The technique used by accounting systems for this purpose is the subsidiary ledger.

Subsidiary ledgers provide a detailed breakdown of the information that appears in certain general ledger accounts. The subsidiary ledger idea can be applied to any general ledger account; however, the need for this kind of detailed information is most critical in the area of receivables and payables.

Accounts Receivable Subsidiary Ledger Figure 7-1 illustrates the general-subsidiary ledger relationship for accounts receivable and a **schedule of accounts receivable** using sample data. Notice that the sum of the amounts in the subsidiary ledger equals the total given in the general ledger account. Both the general ledger and the subsidiary ledger present the same ac-

FIGURE 7-1
Accounts Receivable
Subsidiary Ledger

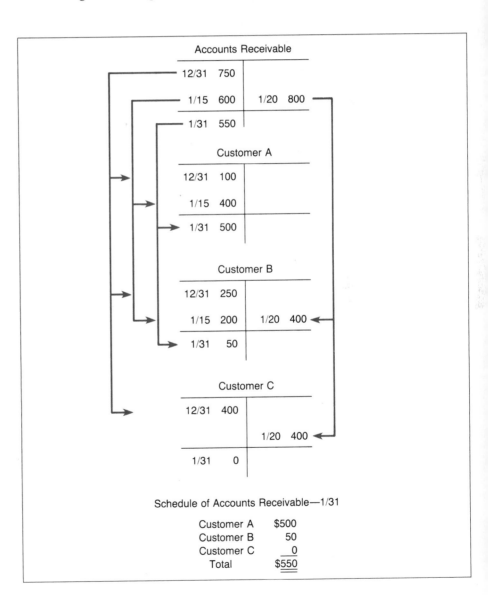

Accounts Receivable

12/31	750		
1/15	600	1/20	800
1/31	550		

Customer A

12/31	100
1/15	400
1/31	500

Customer B

12/31	250		
1/15	200	1/20	400
1/31	50		

Customer C

12/31	400		
		1/20	400
1/31	0		

Schedule of Accounts Receivable—1/31

Customer A	$500
Customer B	50
Customer C	0
Total	$550

counts receivable information, but from a different point of view. The total of all amounts owed to a business (shown in the accounts receivable general ledger account) is necessary for balance sheet purposes, and a detailed breakdown of this total by customer (A, B, and C) is necessary for collection and control purposes.

The information in the subsidiary ledgers is simply a breakdown of the amounts in the general ledger account and is based on the same transactions as the general ledger account. General ledger accounts for which additional, detailed information is kept in a subsidiary ledger are called **control accounts.** Accounts receivable and accounts payable are always control accounts for any business. Often, a schedule of accounts receivable and a schedule of accounts payable is prepared to reflect amounts owed to a business and by a business. These statements are prepared at various times during an accounting period for internal management use.

Accounts Payable Subsidiary Ledger Figure 7-2 presents the general-subsidiary ledger relationship for accounts payable. Individual supplier balances have been assumed for illustrative purposes. Also, a **schedule of accounts payable** is illustrated.

The same process could be used if management decided that additional information on inventory, plant and equipment, or any other asset, lia-

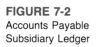

FIGURE 7-2
Accounts Payable
Subsidiary Ledger

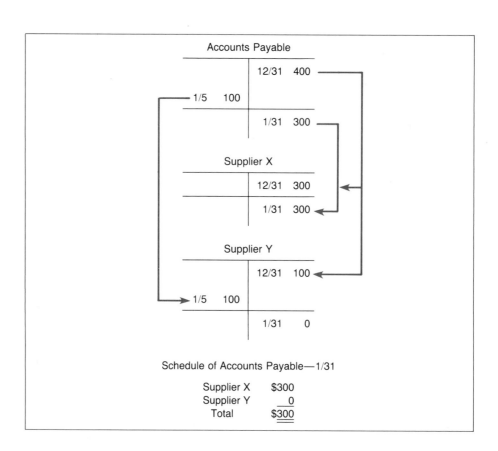

bility, owners' equity, revenue, or expense would be useful for decision-making or control purposes. The basis for these subsidiary ledgers might be type of inventory, category of plant and equipment, or any other breakdown that could provide management with needed information. The subsidiary ledgers presented in Figures 7-1 and 7-2 are in T account form for illustrative purposes. In most accounting systems, these subsidiary ledgers would appear on a file card or a notebook sheet (or be computerized) and would contain more detailed information about a customer or supplier. The basic function of the subsidiary ledger is the same irrespective of the specific form used.

Concept Summary

Typical General Ledger Control Accounts					
	Accounts Receivable	Accounts Payable	Inventory	Furniture and Fixtures	Capital Stock
Information in Control Account	Total amounts owed to the business	Total amounts owed by the business	Total cost of inventory on hand	Total cost of furniture and fixtures on hand	Total direct investment by stockholders
Basis of Organization of Subsidiary Ledger	Customer	Supplier	Type of inventory item	Type of furniture and fixture	Stockholder
Information in Subsidiary Ledger	Amount owed by each individual customer	Amount owed to each individual supplier	Cost of each type of inventory item on hand	Cost of each type of furniture and fixture on hand individual stockholder	Direct investment by each individual stockholder

Special Journals   The discussions of the accounting cycle in Chapters 3 and 4 indicated that all accounting transactions are first journalized as a way of recording the event before it is forgotten or its documents lost. At that time, the general journal was presented and its form illustrated. For the purpose of understanding the basic flow of data in an accounting system, the general journal is both necessary and sufficient. It is, however, not the only journal used in an accounting system and may actually be the least used recording device in terms of transactions recorded.

Most businesses would probably use a number of supplementary journals, called special journals. It would be typical to find four such specialized journals in an accounting system for a merchandising business—sales journal, purchases journal, cash receipts journal, and cash disbursements journal—in addition to the general journal.

To understand why these special devices are necessary, consider the recording problems of a business. Although the individual events occurring each day might be quite numerous, most of them are actually the same kinds of transactions happening over and over again. The possible types of transactions in which most businesses may engage are almost limitless, but, in fact, only a few actually occur with great frequency. The basic recording problem that an accounting system must solve, then, is how to process repetitive transactions efficiently in a manner that allows classification and financial statement preparation. This is exactly what special journals do.

Basic Business Transactions Merchandising businesses engage in four major kinds of transactions constantly.

1. *Sell goods to customers.* Sales may be made for cash or on credit; this type of transaction is usually the most frequent for any business.

2. *Purchase goods from suppliers.* Purchases may also be made for cash or on credit; however, most businesses purchase in larger quantities (and consequently less often) than they sell.

3. *Receive cash.* Cash inflows usually result from cash sales or collections of receivables, although other types of events may give rise to the receipt of cash.

4. *Disburse cash.* Cash outflows for the purchase of goods, payment of accounts payable, and payroll are most frequent, although other types of payments can occur.

Businesses can and do engage in other types of transactions; however, the purchase-sell-collect-pay sequence (the operating cycle) accounts for most business activity. In recognition of this fact, accounting systems use one specialized recording instrument for each constantly recurring type of transaction. Each of these special journals is designed to record one type of event as efficiently as possible, thus making possible quicker and more accurate processing of that transaction than can be accomplished by means of the general journal. That is the idea behind the use of special journals.

7.2 Special Journals Illustrated

Although the design of the general journal is sufficiently broad to handle all types of transactions, its format is somewhat cumbersome. As a result, most systems use the general journal to record only those transactions that do not fit into one of the special journals. It is helpful to think of the general journal as the "journal of last resort." If a transaction is of the type covered by one of the special journals, it should be recorded there. Otherwise, it should be recorded in the general journal. Each event is journalized only once, and no event should ever be divided between journals.

The exact format and makeup of special journals depends on the particular accounts affected by the purchase-sell-collect-pay transactions of a business; therefore, the design of special journals differs somewhat from business to business. Nonetheless, the common ingredients and functioning of special journals can be illustrated and discussed.

Sales Journal

Figure 7-3 is an example of a typical sales journal. Because every credit sale results in an equal debit to accounts receivable and credit to sales revenue, it is necessary for the sales journal (which records only this type of transaction) to have only one amount column. Whenever posting takes place, the total of the amount column is posted as a debit to the accounts receivable control account and as a credit to the sales revenue account. Individual sales amounts are posted directly to the accounts receivable subsidiary ledger for each customer. The check (√) in the PR column indicates that individual amounts were posted to a subsidiary ledger account, while the account numbers (3 for accounts receivable and 21 for sales revenue) show that total credit sales were posted to the general ledger. The sum of the subsidiary ledger postings equals the receivable total.

These posting references would be filled in as the amounts are posted to the ledger, not when the events are originally journalized. This provides an effective cross-check, that everything has been properly posted and leaves a trail through the system from the original transaction to the financial statements.

As in all journals, the sales journal is organized by date of transaction, and each sales event is recorded by the specific customer to whom the sale was made. A special column is provided for the number of the source document that results from the sale and is the basis for the journal entry. This information is particularly important for control purposes so that all transactions can be traced back to the original documents created when the event occurred. Also, information from these documents can be traced forward to the financial statements. The source document may be an invoice, sales slip, or some other document.

FIGURE 7-3
Sales Journal

Date		Source Document #	Customer Account		PR	Amount
1982 January	2	201	Customer	A	√	50
	2	202		B	√	200
	4	203		C	√	600
	8	204		D	√	150
	15	205		C	√	75
	30	206		A	√	750
						1825
						(3/21)

The sales journal is simply a convenient listing of all credit sale transactions for a period. This listing makes the recording and classifying of this repetitive event much easier because the format of the journal is specifically designed to record credit sales. Posting is also facilitated because all credit sale information appears in one place.

Purchases Journal

Figure 7-4 is an example of a typical purchases journal. The design of this journal is sufficiently broad so that all acquisitions on credit—inventory, supplies, or any other asset—may be easily and properly recorded. Because the journal illustrated here can record all invoices (bills) in one place, it is often called an invoice register. Other, more restrictive journal formats which record only inventory and supplies purchases are possible.

Most credit purchases by a business result in an increase in total accounts payable (general ledger) and also result in the creation of a specific liability to a particular supplier. Posting takes place from the purchases journal to the control accounts payable account, while the specific amount owed each individual supplier is posted to the appropriate accounts payable subsidiary ledger. The check ($\checkmark$) in the PR column indicates an amount posted to a subsidiary ledger account, and the account number (98) at the bottom of the column shows that the total was posted to accounts payable control. The sum of the subsidiary ledger postings equals the accounts payable total. These posting reference numbers or symbols are filled in as posting takes place, so that it is possible to know when posting is complete. Also, cross-references are established throughout the accounting system.

The purchases journal, like all journals, is organized by date of transaction. Each purchase is recorded by the specific supplier from whom the purchase was made.

Because this journal is designed to handle all credit purchases of assets on account, several different debits may result from the events to be recorded. Most often, however, the debits will involve accounts related to inventory or supplies because these are the most frequent purchase activities of most businesses. To facilitate recording these repetitive events, special debit columns have been provided which require writing only the amounts involved in each transaction. Then, only the total amounts for

FIGURE 7-4
Purchases Journal

Date		Supplier Account	PR	Credit Accounts Payable	Debits			Other Accounts		
					Purchases	Freight-In	Supplies	Account	PR	Amount
1982										
January	6	Supplier X	$\checkmark$	1,050	1,000	50				
	15	Supplier Y	$\checkmark$	600			600			
	20	Supplier X	$\checkmark$	900	900					
	21	Equipment								
		Supplier W	$\checkmark$	2,000				Equipment	54	2,000
				4,550	1,900	50	600	—	—	2,000
				(98)	(26)	(27)	(31)			

a period need be posted to the general ledger for each of these account numbers.

In addition to the inventory and supplies transactions that make up most of the activity in a purchases journal, a business will, from time to time, purchase other assets on account. The other assets that may be purchased are extremely varied, and these other purchases tend to be relatively infrequent. Thus, no special columns are provided for these acquisitions. Instead, three generalized columns appear in the journal so that the particular asset account affected, its account number for posting reference purposes, and the amount of the transaction can be recorded.

Many different accounts may appear in these generalized columns, so posting must be done individually by each specific account. It would not be meaningful to post this amount column in total, because the individual accounts affected are all different. Thus, no posting reference is provided in that column. A total is needed for this column, however, so that the equality of total debits and credits for the journal can be checked.

Cash Receipts and Cash Disbursements Journals

The most important and most repetitive transactions a business engages in are those involving the inflow (receipt) and outflow (disbursement) of cash. The frequency with which cash transactions occur coupled with the nature of cash itself makes this asset difficult for a business to control. The recording and classifying procedures involving cash must be the most carefully designed and monitored in the accounting system. The devices used for this purpose are the cash receipts journal and the cash disbursements journal.

Cash Receipts Journal The orderly recording of all cash inflows in one place is the major goal of the cash receipts journal. The format illustrated in Figure 7-5 allows for the efficient mass processing of this frequent event

FIGURE 7-5
Cash Receipts Journal

Date		Explanation	Debit	Credits			Other Accounts			
			Cash	Sales	PR	Amount	Account	PR	Debit	Credit
1982										
January	4	Owner investment	10,000				Cap. stock	100		10,000
	5	Customer A	500		√	500				
	6	Cash sales Week 1	750	750						
	13	Cash sales Week 2	1,000	1,000						
	16	Bank loan	2,000				Notes pay	99		2,000
	19	Customer B	800		√	800				
	20	Cash sales Week 3	1,200	1,200						
	25	Customer C	100		√	200	Sales			
							return	22	100	
	27	Cash sales Week 4	1,100	1,100						
			17,450	4,050	—	1,500	—	—	100	12,000
			(1)	(21)		(3)				

in a manner that makes classification (posting) easy to perform and, at the same time, contributes to the control of cash.

Cash Disbursements Journal Inflows of cash, although probably the most important event in the life of most businesses, represent only one side of the cash-related activity. Cash outflows (disbursements) are almost as constantly recurring as inflows and are at least as important for the total control of cash. The cash disbursements journal is specifically designed to record all disbursements of cash in one place. By coupling this journal with the cash receipts journal, a business can effectively monitor its cash assets. A typical cash disbursements journal appears in Figure 7-6.

Important Features of the Cash Receipts and Cash Disbursements Journals

All receipts of cash and disbursements of cash, no matter what the reason, should be recorded in the cash receipts and cash disbursements journals. These journals are designed so that all transactions involving the inflow or outflow of cash can be recorded in one place.

Although cash may be increased for a number of different reasons, most businesses find that cash inflows occur primarily because of sales of merchandise for cash and collections of accounts receivable. Because a cash receipt can probably be traced to one of these two recurring events, the cash receipts journal establishes special columns for cash sales and accounts receivable.

Although cash may be paid out for many reasons, most businesses find that cash expenditures occur primarily because of cash purchases of mer-

FIGURE 7-6
Cash Disbursements Journal

Date		Check #	Explanation	Credit Cash	Debits Accts. Pay. PR	Debits Accts. Pay. Amount	Wage Expense	Purchases	Credit Purchase Discounts	Other Accounts Account	Other Accounts PR	Other Accounts Debit	Other Accounts Credit
1982 January	5	98	Supplier X	980	√	1,000			20				
	10	99	Purchase inv.	500				500					
	15	100	Paid rent	300						Rent exp.	143	300	
	20	101	Supplier Y	150	√	150							
	25	102	Purchased truck	1,000						Truck	55	5,000	
										Note pay.	99		4,000
	30	103	Pd. advert.	100						Prepaid advertising	51	100	
	31	104– 106	Payroll	2,000			2,000						
				5,030 (1)		1,150 (98)	2,000 (140)	500 (26)	20 (29)	—		5,400	4,000

chandise, payment of accounts payable, and payments to employees for salaries and wages. Because many cash outflows are traceable to one of these three recurring events, the cash disbursements journal establishes special columns for purchases, accounts payable, and salary and wage expense debits. If the gross method of recording purchases is used, a special credit column for the contra-account purchase discounts can also be created.

To allow for the recording of all transactions that result in a cash increase or decrease, an "other accounts" group of columns is provided in both journals in which any account title and amount may be written. Note that provision is made for a debit or credit, because a cash inflow or outflow could result from events that include other debit or credit effects in addition to cash.

If a transaction increases or decreases cash at all, even though it may affect many other accounts also, it should be recorded in the cash receipts or cash disbursements journal. This is true without regard to whether the cash effect is major or minor in light of the total transaction.

These journals are organized chronologically and an explanation column is provided so that brief elaborations or necessary additional information about a transaction may be supplied.

Concept Summary

Journals and Their Use					
	Sales	*Purchases*	*Cash Receipts*	*Cash Disbursements*	*General*
Transactions Recorded	All credit sales	All credit purchases	All receipts of cash	All disbursements of cash	All events not recorded in special journals
Specific Account Columns	Customer account, Amount	Purchases, Supplies, Accounts payable	Cash, Accounts receivable, Sales	Accounts payable, Wage expense, Purchases, Cash	No
Other Accounts Columns	No	Yes	Yes	Yes	No
Organization	Date of transaction	Date of transaction	Date of transaction	Date of transaction	Date of transaction

Using Special Journals and Subsidiary Ledgers

It may appear at first glance that special journals and subsidiary ledgers needlessly complicate a simple recording process. In the context of a textbook or classroom where only a few illustrative transactions are presented, the use of only a general journal may seem sufficient and subsidiary ledgers, unnecessary. Consider, however, the problems of recording 50 to 100 transactions a day, every day, in the general journal, and then individually posting each of these transactions to the ledger. What about keeping track of amounts owed to a business by, say, 250 customers and amounts that a business owes to another 25 suppliers?

Without special journals that are streamlined to record the most repetitive transactions efficiently and aid in classification by reducing the posting burden, accounting systems could simply collapse under their own weight. Likewise, without some form of organized, detailed information on specific amounts owed to and owed by a business, efficient and accurate collection and payment would be impossible. These refinements of the basic accounting system are necessary for the system to work in actual business situations.

7.3 Basic Concepts of Internal Control

Earlier discussion centered on fundamental accounting concepts and the related techniques needed to use these concepts effectively in practice. Attention focused on how to accomplish the necessary accounting tasks in the most efficient manner possible. This section turns to another side of accounting systems, namely accidental and deliberate errors in the processing of transactions and how to prevent these errors.

Accounting Controls versus Administrative Controls

Basically, all accounting system protection procedures have two major aims:

1. To protect assets (especially cash and inventory) from being lost or stolen.

2. To ensure that the accounting records are accurate and complete.

It is not sufficient for a system to be simple, efficient, and provide management with the information it requires. The system must also accomplish the two aims given above.

These aims are so important that the techniques, methods, and procedures which help accomplish them are given a special name: **internal control.** Internal control is, then, all of the means employed to accomplish the objectives stated above. The word "internal" serves to emphasize that these techniques are contained *within* the system.

The accounting records are separate from the actual assets and operations of the business, but they should accurately reflect what is going on in the real world of assets and operations. The accounting records may not accurately reflect what happens to the business because of errors. Errors, both accidental and deliberate, will inevitably occur; and unless control is applied, the system will just as inevitably go "out of control" and no longer reflect accurately the facts of asset operations. In addition, there is a federal law, the Foreign Corrupt Practices Act, which requires an adequate system of internal controls.

In recent years, internal control has taken on an expanded meaning as a result of the increase in scope of many business activities. Large companies, such as General Motors, have hundreds of thousands of employees located all over the world. The chairman of the board of Textron was able to claim at his confirmation hearing as head of the Federal Reserve System that he was a small businessman: his company had sales totaling less than the profit of IBM, and his company "only" had 65,000 employees.

The problem is that, with such a vast number of employees, top management cannot supervise (in any direct sense) all of the workers. As a result, controls must be developed to ensure that top management's policies and directives are carried out. Thus, in addition to the two objectives listed above, internal control has the following further objectives:

3. To promote efficient operations by reducing waste and duplication of effort.

4. To encourage compliance with company policies and procedures.

The first two objectives of internal control are generally distinguished from the last two. The first two are the area of **accounting controls;** whereas, the last two are the area of **administrative controls.**

Detecting
Accidental Errors

Accidental improper processings of transactions are simply mistakes. People will always make some errors, and no system can possibly prevent them all. However, the system should point out the existence of an error as soon as possible. Typical accounting systems contain a number of features designed to detect errors.

Double-Entry Method The most important error-detecting feature is the double-entry method itself. The constant requirement that debits equal credits will point out numerous mistakes. Balancing the special journals prior to posting, preparing the trial balance, and preparing the adjusted trial balance are all examples of attempts to catch errors as soon as possible. If an accounting record (such as a journal, trial balance, or ledger) does not have equal debits and credits, it is said to be out of balance, to not balance, or to not be in balance.

The trial balance is a particularly important means of identifying errors when debits do not equal credits. Aside from arithmetic errors, such as adding improperly, there are six common errors that cause the trial balance not to balance:

1. Copying improperly from the general ledger to the trial balance.

2. Posting improperly a debit as a credit or vice versa.

3. Failing to post from the journal to the ledger.

4. Transposing (reversing) digits while posting.

5. Misplacing decimals while posting.

6. Recording improperly when the original entry is made in the journal.

Audit Trail The second most important error-detecting feature is the audit trail. The figures in the financial statements come from ledger balances. The ledger accounts indicate by their posting reference the journal source of all the debits and credits. Thus, it is possible to check the journals to see the original entries and, hence, find the supporting documents. Similarly, it is possible to go from the source documents forward through the ledger to their appearance on the financial statements by using the posting reference in each journal.

When an error is discovered in an accounting number, it is necessary to go back to see where the number came from to determine the source of the mistake. Even if an error is small in amount, it may be a symptom of a larger problem, the start of a growing problem, or the result of major (but offsetting) errors; therefore, it must always be possible to get to the root of a problem. Thus, the audit trail is absolutely essential.

Subsidiary Ledgers The control accounts in the general ledger for accounts receivable and accounts payable should always equal the total of the individual accounts in the respective subsidiary ledgers. If the control does not agree with (or in accounting terminology, balance to) the total of the subsidiary ledger accounts, there is an error somewhere.

It is quite possible for these totals not to agree. If a cash receipt on accounts receivable is entered properly in the cash receipts journal but is not posted to the individual account in the subsidiary ledger, the accounts receivable ledger will be correct while the subsidiary ledger will be incorrect. Also, if a sales return is recorded in the general journal, it may be that only one of the two necessary postings (that is, to the control account and to the subsidiary ledger) will be made.

Customer Statements An additional error-detecting feature is the use of billing statements for credit customers. It is certainly possible that a cash receipt on account or a credit sale could be posted to the wrong individual account. Both the control total and the total of the subsidiary ledger will be correct. The individual accounts will be incorrect: one account will be overstated by some amount, while another will be understated by the same amount. Because these two errors cancel each other out when the subsidiary ledger is totaled, balancing is not effective in detecting this error. It is extremely likely, however, that if statements of account are sent to the customers, they will identify any incorrect entries.

Communication with Vendors Vendors do not receive statements as do customers; nevertheless, the vendors will complain if they are not paid enough. Suppose, for example, a firm paid one of its vendors, Fireplaces Unlimited, but debited the account of Fireworks Unlimited. The total of the subsidiary ledger would be correct: one balance would be understated, but another would be overstated by an equivalent amount. Fireworks would then not be paid because it would appear that they had already received payment; however, they would probably complain. And if Fireplaces were paid again, it is at least possible that they would notice that they had been overpaid and would send a refund check. Thus, communication with vendors helps to clear up mistakes.

Concept Summary

Basic Error-Detecting Features of a Manual Accounting System ·	
Double-entry Method	Points up errors, because rarely will an error in one half of an entry be exactly offset by an equivalent error in the other half.
Audit Trail	Allows the accountant to track backwards through the accounting records to the cause of an error.
Subsidiary Ledgers	Provides cross-checks of the general ledger control account with the subsidiary ledger.
Customer Statements of Account	Provides independent check of accounts receivable subsidiary ledger account balances.
Communication with Vendors	Provides an independent check of accounts payable subsidiary ledger account balances.

7.4 Internal Control of Cash and Inventory

Defalcations of Cash Disbursements

Cash disbursements is the area of greatest dollar loss from **embezzlement,** so this subject should have particular emphasis. **Defalcation** has the same meaning as embezzlement and is the term commonly used in accounting.

Checks Payable to Other Firms A bookkeeper might prepare checks payable to other firms, so that the checks appear to be normal payments on account. After the checks are signed, he can divert the funds to himself by either: (1) forging the endorsement of the check and then cashing it or (2) depositing the checks to a bank account which he has created. The problem then becomes one of getting an authorized signature on the checks. Techniques for doing so would depend upon whether the bookkeeper created the payee firm or used an existing and real firm. If he created the firm, he would also need to create false invoices from it, as well as any supporting documents that might be required for signature. If he used a real vendor, he could simply resubmit invoices that had already been paid.

Checks Payable to Employees Padding the payroll is another method of issuing checks to others and then appropriating them. In this method, an employee might either: (1) continue paying checks for people after they have quit or been fired, or (2) add fake employees to the payroll. Padding can be accomplished by a number of people besides the bookkeeper. If the foreman distributes paychecks, he might "forget" to inform the office that an employee has quit and appropriate the check. Similarly, the person who adds employees might add a brother-in-law or cousin to the payroll.

Checks Payable to Himself Another possibility is for the embezzler to prepare checks to himself using either a check that was not prenumbered or a prenumbered check from the back of the checkbook. He can get the check signed either by forging an authorized signature or by using checks that have been signed in blank (that is, with the date, payee, and amount not yet filled in).

Such a check cannot be recorded in the cash disbursements journal. As a result, the general ledger cash balance would not reflect all cash outflows. The general ledger cash balance can be reduced by overfooting the cash column of the cash disbursements journal. (*Footing* is the adding of the numbers in a column to get the total. *Underfooting* is the misadding of a column to get too small a total, while *overfooting* is the opposite.) However, credits will then exceed debits in the journal. He must then either decrease credits by underfooting purchase discounts or increase debits by overfooting expenses.

Defalcations of Cash Receipts

Even though the largest dollar amounts lost from embezzlement involve cash disbursements, the majority of individual incidents involve cash receipts.

Cash Sales If the embezzler takes cash from cash sales, he can keep the books in balance by not recording the transaction or by recording an amount smaller than the actual sale. If a cash register or sales slip is part of the system, either can be used improperly. For example, in a bar the cash register need not be used at all because the customer does not expect a receipt.

In a movie theater where tickets are serially prenumbered, the cashier can sell the same ticket twice and pocket the amount received for the second sale. The cashier can get used tickets back from the ticket taker. If the taker must tear the tickets and return half to each customer, he can take one of a couple's two tickets, tear it, and give the two halves back to the couple. A complete ticket is then available for reuse. Some conspiracy is necessary to make this scheme work, and the cashier must usually split the proceeds with the ticket taker.

Collections of Accounts Receivable A major technique for stealing collections on accounts receivable is called **lapping.** Lapping consists essentially of stealing Paul's payment, but then paying Paul's account by using the next receipt, say that of Peter. Peter's account is then paid by the next receipt, and the process continues indefinitely. Many embezzlers view this process as a form of "borrowing" rather than theft: they feel that, at some point, they will put the money back and everything will be covered.

Another possibility is to bill for a sale at the total amount due, while recording the sale at some lower amount. The embezzler can then appropriate the difference when the customer pays his bill.

A bolder method involves taking the cash, but then recording the collection as usual in the cash receipts journal. This shortage can be covered by underfooting the cash column and overfooting the sales discount column in the cash receipts journal, thus keeping debits equal to credits.

If a payment from a customer does not take a discount because the discount period has expired, the embezzler can still record the receipt incorporating the discount and take the discount himself.

Finally, the embezzler may not record the cash receipt at all. Because the customer might complain about an incorrect bill, the embezzler must then intercept the statement of account and any letters requesting or demanding payment that might follow. The debit balance simply continues on the books and, to reduce the balance, a credit must be obtained. The embezzler can get this desired credit by creating a credit memo.

Concept Summary

Defalcations of Cash		
Area of Defalcation	How to Obtain Cash	How to Cover in Accounting Records
Cash Disbursements	Issue checks to others and appropriate the checks.	1. Create false invoices. 2. Use invoices twice for support. 3. "Pad" the payroll.
	Issue checks to himself.	1. Incorrectly foot the cash disbursements journal. 2. Increase recorded amount of another check.
Cash Receipts	Take cash from cash sales.	1. Record no amount. 2. Record less than was received.
	Take cash collections of accounts receivable.	1. Lapping. 2. Bill for full amount, but record sale at lower amount. 3. Record cash receipt but incorrectly use the journal. 4. Do not record cash receipt but intercept statements of account. 5. Do not record cash receipt but create credit memo or write off the amount.

Techniques Designed to Prevent or Detect Errors

Some companies will try to justify poor internal control by saying the company is too small to prevent or detect mistakes or that such mistakes do not occur; however, effective error detection and prevention is possible and desirable in all businesses. At least, the system should consist of the elements listed in Figure 7-7.

Internal Control of Inventory

Many small businesses, such as real estate firms and doctor's offices, are basically service oriented and, thus, do not have significant amounts of inventory. But firms, such as retail stores and wholesalers, that have significant amounts of inventory must have procedures to protect these valuable assets.

Purchasing Purchasing is the important task of buying the inventory the company needs at the best price possible. This area should be centralized under a responsible official, usually called the purchasing agent. Because inventory purchasing is usually one of the primary areas of operations, proper support for checks and the cancellation of the support after pay-

FIGURE 7-7
General Control Techniques

Techniques	Reasons for Techniques
Use only prenumbered checks for disbursements.	To ensure that all checks are accounted for.
Alter but keep voided checks.	To ensure that "voided" checks are not used and that all checks are accounted for.
Reconcile bank statements monthly.	To ensure that all checks are authorized and recorded and that receipts are deposited.
Use a cash register and check register daily.	To ensure that all cash receipts are recorded.
Deposit cash receipts intact.	To ensure that all cash receipts are deposited.
Have checks signed by management officials with no access to records.	To ensure that accounting records accurately reflect checks written.
Have proper support for checks.	To ensure that only properly authorized and justified expenditures are paid.
Cancel supporting documents when paid.	To ensure that payment is made only once, even for proper expenditures.
Mail check directly to payee.	To ensure that payee and only payee receives disbursement.
Use prenumbered invoices.	To ensure that all invoices are accounted for.
List mail collections and compare them with journal entries.	To ensure that all mail collections are retained by firm.
Review monthly comparative financial statements.	To check any unusual revenue, expense, asset, or liability amounts.
Approve all entries to general journal.	To ensure that only authorized and proper journal entries are made.

ment become even more important (see Items 7 and 8 in Figure 7-7). Purchase returns then become a major item and must be supervised to ensure that proper credit is obtained for the returned merchandise. Finally, if an operating department requests that inventory be purchased, the department should fill out a requisition form and have it approved to ensure that all purchases are properly authorized.

Because inventory purchases involve large dollar amounts, there is a great potential for fraud. The primary problem is that the purchasing agent can collude with the supplier. The purchasing agent may then act in the supplier's best interest rather than in the purchasing firm's best interest. The purchasing agent could (1) buy more goods than are actually needed or (2) pay a higher price than is actually required. The supplier may then make payments to the purchasing agent to reward this behavior. Such payments are usually called "kickbacks."

Custody Custody of the inventory involves receiving, storing, and eventually transferring the merchandise. Purchasing and receiving should be performed by different employees, so that each can provide a check upon the other. Similarly, receiving and storekeeping should be independent operations to provide additional checks. Finally, there should be a **physical inventory** count taken on a regular basis by employees who are not in charge of the inventory. It is essential that the firm periodically check its inventory to make sure that the amount is reasonable given the levels of purchases and sales.

Finally, there should be physical control of the inventory. The value of the inventory should dictate the amount of physical control: unset one-karat diamonds require more control than two-penny nails. Locks, keys, guards, and authorization for withdrawal should be used as appropriate.

Record Keeping Record keeping is the act of keeping track of the amount in inventory. The person in charge of inventory should not also keep the related accounting records. If the same person does both, then a loss of merchandise can be covered in the accounting records. When merchandise is moved from the storeroom to the sales department, a document should be prepared to assign responsibility, and the sales clerk should sign it to indicate receipt of the goods. All documents should be prenumbered to ensure their physical control.

If practicable, a perpetual inventory system should be used. A perpetual system involves constantly keeping track of the receipts and withdrawals of each item of inventory as they occur. Thus, if the system is operated properly, the accounting records will always be up-to-date and should agree with the physical realities of inventory.

Voucher System

When paying for needed inventory, any business wants to make sure that (1) the purchase was properly authorized, (2) the goods were received, and (3) the payment is made only from an original invoice. A standard method for doing so is the **voucher system.** The voucher system uses a voucher register and check register which replace the purchases journal, the cash

Concept Summary

Inventory Control Techniques	
Purchasing	1. Centralize under a responsible official. 2. Attach purchase invoices to checks for payment. 3. Cancel support when check is paid. 4. Supervise all returned purchases. 5. Use requisitions to initiate purchases.
Custody	1. Separate purchasing from receiving. 2. Separate receiving from storekeeping. 3. Take physical inventory regularly. 4. Use independent employee for physical inventory. 5. Physically control access to inventory.
Record Keeping	1. Separate record keeping from custody. 2. Use vouchers on merchandise moved to sales area. 3. Require all documents to be prenumbered. 4. Use a perpetual system, if possible. 5. Compare results of physical inventory with records.

disbursements journal, and accounts payable subsidiary ledger. The system is built around the *voucher*, a document that must be filled out and approved before any cash disbursement can be made.

Use of Vouchers Vouchers are prenumbered to ensure that all are accounted for. When an amount is owed a creditor or supplier, the next consecutive voucher is filled out. After the voucher has been approved, it is recorded in the voucher register. The approved voucher is then filed in the unpaid vouchers file by due date, so that it is immediately clear which bills are due and in what order. When the voucher is approved for payment, a check is drawn and recorded in the check register. Because the check ties to a specific voucher, an entry is then made in the voucher register's payment columns to indicate that the voucher has been paid. After the payment has been made, this fact is noted on the voucher and the voucher is then filed in the paid vouchers file by voucher number.

A detailed breakdown of the amounts due suppliers is then given by a schedule of all unpaid vouchers, which are simply those with blank payment columns in the voucher register. The following three amounts must be in agreement: (1) the total of the schedule of unpaid vouchers, (2) the balance of the vouchers payable account, and (3) the total of the vouchers in the unpaid file.

It is important to realize, however, that the voucher system may not communicate directly the total amount owed particular suppliers. Because different purchases could have different due dates, a company might very well have more than one voucher for the same supplier. The total owed that supplier would then not be available directly.

Even though the voucher system is used, the financial statements remain the same, because it is customary to use the title accounts payable instead of vouchers payable in published financial statements.

7.5 Basic Elements of Internal Control

It is impossible to memorize enough lists of internal control procedures and techniques to handle every situation. It is possible, however, to keep the general concepts in mind and then be able to apply these concepts in particular situations. The following six elements of internal control should be part of any system. To the extent any of these six elements is missing, the system is deficient in internal control.

Honest and
Capable
Employees

Any system is critically dependent on the people who use it. If the people are dishonest or incompetent, even the finest system cannot perform properly. In contrast, honest and capable employees can function even in a situation where the other five elements of internal control are lacking. Even with honest and able employees, however, the system must have effective internal control. Embezzlers are often basically honest, but the temptation can become too strong to resist.

Clear Delegation
and Separation of
Duties

For a system to work properly, the employees must know what they are to do and what others are to do. This can be partly accomplished by an organization chart, but that is not always sufficient. Job descriptions may be necessary for proper delegation.

Even more important is the clear separation of duties. Custody of assets must be separated from the record keeping for those assets. For example, if someone is in charge of inventory and keeps the inventory records, he may cover the stealing of inventory by manipulation of the accounting records. He may cover stealing even if he is not the one stealing because he does not want to point out his failure to protect the assets.

Authorizing transactions must be separated from recording the transaction in the journals, and both must be separated from posting the transactions to the ledgers. The discussion earlier about cash defalcations gives a number of potential abuses if this rule is not followed.

Finally, for inventory it is important to separate the purchasing function from the receiving function. This was discussed at greater length earlier.

Proper
Procedures for the
Processing of
Transactions

Proper procedures must start with proper authorization. Although a corporation's board of directors has ultimate authority, the day-to-day operating authority is delegated to top management with specific guidelines to follow (for example, the maximum amount to be borrowed without authorization by the directors). In turn, top management might allow others to give the authorization for credit sales to customers as long as a credit limit is not exceeded. This delegation of authority is necessary; but it must be suitable under the circumstances, and there should be checks that the guidelines are followed. Other specific procedures have been discussed, but some of the most important are: to ensure proper support before signing any checks; to approve all general journal entries and credit memos; and to cancel supporting documents once they have been used.

Suitable
Documents and
Accounting
Records

Documents should be (1) as simple and easy to use as possible to help cut down on error; (2) prenumbered to make it easier to keep physical control over them; (3) as few in number as possible to minimize confusion and form cost; and (4) designed to ensure that they will be properly filled out, by providing, for example, blocks for necessary approval signatures.

Among documents that are always useful are the following:

1. *Comparative financial statements.* As discussed earlier in the chapter, these statements provide a basis of comparison for the current period's accounting results.

2. *Chart of accounts.* The chart of accounts should contain a list of the account numbers and names for all asset, liability, owners' equity, revenue, and expense accounts. In addition, it should contain a description of each account and guidance on when each should be used.

3. *Procedures manual.* The chart of accounts and the procedures to be followed should be documented in a procedures manual. This manual is necessary to train new employees in the operation of the system and to ensure that the same types of transactions will always be handled in the same way.

Adequate Physical
Control Over
Assets and
Records

The specific assets and accounting records involved will dictate what represents adequate physical control. Inventory should be kept in a stockroom, under the custody of one person to allow the assignment of responsibility. Additionally, critical paper, such as cash, marketable securities, accounting journals, and accounting ledgers, should be stored in fireproof safes.

It is always necessary to consider the cost and time of reconstructing documents or accounting records. If the risk of their loss is great enough, copies may be justified. A related problem is, then, the need for reasonable record retention and storage. The needs of the firm, the volume of the records to store, and the relevant state and federal rules on records all must be considered.

Independent
Verification of
Performances

No one is able to verify or evaluate his own performance very effectively. Thus, the verification must be done by someone independent of the subject and the system. A subordinate can never be independent because of the natural fear of reprisal.

As time passes, procedures become sloppy and people get careless. In addition, there is always the potential for both accidental and deliberate errors. Thus, independent verification of performance is periodically necessary to help ensure that the system works properly.

Important means of independent verification were discussed earlier. Some examples include: (1) the bank reconciliation if done by a person other than the one who controls cash or the related accounting records; (2) a list of cash receipts made when the mail is opened; (3) the physical counting of inventory to compare with perpetual inventory records; and (4) an **audit** by an outside CPA firm at periodic intervals.

In the final analysis, the ultimate success of accounting systems requires that the basic concepts and elements of internal control be applied creatively to particular business situations.

Concept Summary

Elements of Internal Control	
Honest and Capable Employees	1. Hire qualified people with good references. 2. Require annual vacations. 3. Bond employees in positions of trust. 4. State conflict of interest policy.
Clear Delegation and Separation of Duties	1. Develop organization chart. 2. Separate record keeping from custody of assets. 3. Separate authorization from record keeping. 4. Separate purchasing from receiving.
Proper Procedures for Processing Transactions	1. Ensure proper authorization of transactions. 2. Sign checks only with proper support. 3. Approve all general journal entries and credit memos. 4. Cancel all supporting documents once they have been used.
Suitable Documents and Accounting Records	1. Prenumber important documents. 2. Develop comparative financial statements. 3. Describe accounting methods in manuals. 4. Prepare budget of anticipated results.
Adequate Physical Control over Assets and Records	1. Limit access to inventory. 2. Safeguard all important records. 3. Deposit cash receipts intact daily. 4. Keep all voided checks.
Independent Verification of Performance	1. Reconcile bank statement independently. 2. Prelist cash receipts. 3. Take complete inventory regularly. 4. Have an annual audit by a CPA firm.

Summary

Certain refinements to the journalizing and posting steps of the accounting cycle are useful in the mass processing of transactions. These refinements are called special journals and subsidiary ledgers.

Four special journals are commonly used. The sales journal records only credit sales. The purchases journal records all acquisition of assets on credit. The cash receipts journal records all receipts of cash, while the cash disbursements journal records all payments of cash. These journals supplement but do not replace the need for the general journal.

A single amount representing the balance in a general ledger account is all that is needed for financial statement purposes; however, for management and control of a business, detailed breakdowns of some general ledger balances are necessary. These detailed breakdowns are kept in subsidiary ledgers. Two general ledger accounts for which subsidiary ledgers are necessary are accounts receivable and accounts payable.

Even if an accounting system can process transactions efficiently, it may not do so because the system must be operated by people. Because of this dependence on people, the accounting system must be designed to prevent both the accidental and deliberate errors that can occur in the processing of transactions. Internal control is the collection of techniques and procedures used by a business to protect itself from these potential problems.

Accidental errors (i.e., mistakes) may occur in the analysis of transactions, recording and posting of transactions, and computation of account balances. Deliberate errors such as embezzlement and fraud most often affect cash and inventory.

Most accidental and deliberate errors can be prevented by: (1) separating the task of record keeping from physical custody of assets, (2) using sequentially numbered documents, (3) voiding and storing all documents that have been processed, (4) depositing all cash receipts in the bank intact, (5) requiring proper document support for all cash disbursements, (6) limiting access to inventory, and (7) requiring proper support for all general journal entries.

Chapter 8 deals in depth with the assets of cash, accounts receivable, and notes receivable.

Key Terms

Accounting controls	Internal control
Administrative controls	Lapping
Audit	Padding
Audit trail	Physical inventory
Authorization	Purchases journal
Cash disbursements journal	Sales journal
Cash receipts journal	Schedule of accounts payable
Control account	Schedule of accounts receivable
Customer statements	Special journal
Defalcation	Subsidiary ledger
Embezzlement	Voucher system

Comprehensive Review Problem

The following are descriptions of systems of internal control for three companies:

A. When Mr. Clark orders goods for his wholesale business, he sends a duplicate purchase order to the receiving department. When inventory is delivered, Mr. Smith, the receiving clerk, records the receipt of the shipment on this purchase order. Mr. Smith sends the purchase order to the accounting department where it is used to record inventory purchased and accounts payable. The inventory is transported to the storage area, and the purchased quantities are entered on storage records.

B. Every day hundreds of employees clock in using time cards at Abbott Corporation. The timekeepers collect these cards once a week and deliver them to the payroll department. There the time cards are used in the preparation of the payroll checks. The treasurer, Mrs. Webber, signs the checks, and returns the payroll checks to Mr. Strode, the supervisor of the payroll department. The payroll checks are distributed to the employees by Mr. Strode.

C. The smallest branch of Connor Cosmetics in South Bend employs Mary Cooper, the branch manager, and her sales assistant, Janet Hendrix. The branch uses a bank account in South Bend to pay expenses. The account is kept in the name of "Connor Cosmetics—Special Account." To pay expenses, checks must be signed by Mary Cooper or by the treasurer of Connor Cosmetics, John Winters. Ms. Cooper receives the canceled checks and bank statements. She reconciles the branch account herself and files canceled checks and bank statements in her records. She also periodically prepares reports of disbursements and sends them to the home office.

Required:

1. List the weaknesses in internal control for each of the situations described above.

2. For each weakness, state the type of error(s) that is (are) likely to result. Be as specific as possible.

3. Describe how you would improve each of the three systems.

Solution to Comprehensive Review Problem

Requirement 1

A. Supplying the receiving department with the purchase order is a weakness because department members may be less careful in checking goods than they would be if they were working without a record of the quantities that should be received. The failure to have the storekeeper sign for the inventory when it is sent to him from the receiving department or to tie the items placed in stores to the purchase constitutes a weakness in control because responsibility for shortages cannot be definitely placed on either receiving or stores. The receiving department might, in collusion with a vendor, report receipts of inventory that never arrived. Also, either the receiving department or the stores department might take inventory. Because of the lack of a record of responsibility, the company would be unable to determine which department was guilty.

B. The payroll checks should not be returned to the supervisor, but should be distributed by persons independent of those having a part in making up the payroll data. There is a lack of internal certification of the hours, rates, payroll amounts, and existence of employees.

C. The bank statement and canceled checks should not be reconciled by the manager. They should be sent by the bank directly to the home office where the reconciliations against the manager's report of disbursements should be made.

Requirement 2

A. This weakness increases the possibility of theft of shipments larger than the amount ordered. The failure to isolate responsibility for shortages also increases the likelihood of obsolescence because employees are likely to be less concerned when they are not held accountable. Because the company cannot isolate responsibility, it might also encourage either the receiving or storage department to take goods.

B. The payroll could be padded with fictitious names and the checks taken when they are returned after they have been signed. There may be errors in hours, rates, and payroll amounts, and nonworking employees may be paid.

C. The manager may draw checks to herself or others for personal purposes and either omit them from her list of disbursements or inflate other reported disbursement amounts.

Requirement 3
The respective companies should:

A. use a copy of the purchase order without amounts on it or a separate receiving report without a copy of the purchase order.
use perpetual inventory records to hold the storekeeper accountable. The storekeeper should also initial the receiving report or purchase order when he receives the goods.

B. have the checks handed out by an independent person and not returned to Strode.
have internal confirmation of that information by Webber or someone else.

C. have all bank statements sent directly to the home office and have Cooper report to the home office a list of expenditures and all supporting documentation.

Questions

Q7-1. Give four general ledger accounts for which subsidiary ledger information would be useful. How would each of these four subsidiary ledgers be organized?

Q7-2. What information can be obtained from the accounts receivable subsidiary ledger that cannot be obtained from the accounts receivable control account? What about accounts payable?

Q7-3. List the four most common types of business transactions and give the special journal used to record each.

Q7-4. Why do businesses use special journals even though the general journal is designed to handle all types of transactions?

Q7-5. What are the four major goals of a system of internal control? Distinguish between accounting and administrative controls.

Q7-6. The double-entry system and subsidiary ledgers are two important characteristics of accounting systems that help detect errors. Describe how they accomplish this purpose.

Q7-7. Discuss two techniques for the embezzlement of cash receipts and two techniques for the embezzlement of cash disbursements and specify how these embezzlements could be prevented.

Q7-8. How can the use of prenumbered documents improve internal control? If checks are not prenumbered, what might happen?

Q7-9. Why is the separation of record keeping from physical custody of assets an important internal control feature? Give three examples of areas where separation would be essential.

Q7-10. Explain why access to the general journal should be limited and all general journal entries properly authorized.

Exercises

E7-1. Distinguish the relationship of a special journal to a general journal from the relationship of a subsidiary ledger to a general ledger. What functions do special journals and subsidiary ledgers serve in accounting systems? Are the devices absolutely necessary?

E7-2. A company uses general, sales, purchases, cash receipts, and cash disbursements journals like those illustrated in the text. Indicate the journal in which each of the following transactions would be recorded:

a. Collection of an amount due from a customer
b. Payment of a cash dividend
c. Purchase of supplies on credit
d. Purchase of land by paying $2,500 in cash and signing a note payable for $7,500
e. Payment of a bill for freight on shipment of inventory
f. Accrual of interest on a note payable
g. Sale of merchandise on credit
h. Sale of capital stock to owner
i. Payment of salaries to employees
j. Sale of merchandise for cash

E7-3. Figure 7-4 in the text is an example of a purchases journal for a company using a periodic inventory system. Show the column headings that would be used in the purchases journal of a company with a perpetual inventory system.

E7-4. For each of the following types of businesses, name the journals that would be used in recording accounting events:

a. Doctor's office where patients pay upon leaving
b. Department store
c. Hot dog vendor
d. Doctor's office with customer billing
e. Gift shop with cash and major credit card sales only

E7-5. Indicate whether each of the following would be an accounting control or an administrative control.

a. Each new employee must pass a physical examination.
b. All checks are prenumbered.
c. Each salesman is required to make at least five calls per day.
d. There are two quality control checks before product A leaves the packing department.
e. All supporting documents are canceled when a voucher is paid.
f. The bank statement is reconciled monthly.
g. Each new employee is given a basic training session explaining company organization and policies.

E7-6. On April 3, the bookkeeper of the Brady-Masow Company makes the following two journal entries:

April	3	Advertising expense	....	600	
		Cash	....		600
	3	Cash	....	1,320	
		Revenue	....		1,320

She realizes after making these entries that they are in error. The $600 cash expenditure was a payment on an account payable. Also the revenues for the day were $1,230, not $1,320. She corrects these errors on April 3. Assuming no other entries were made on April 3, show all of the journal entries for April 3 as they would appear in the general journal.

E7-7. The sales clerk at Rumney Company correctly prepared a sales invoice for $9,300, but the invoice was entered as $3,900 in the sales journal and was posted as $3,900 to the general ledger and accounts receivable subsidiary ledger. The customer remitted only $3,900, the amount of the statement. What would you recommend as an effective procedure for preventing this type of error?

E7-8. For each of the following defalcations involving cash, indicate how the embezzler would cover the situation:

a. A bookkeeper resubmits invoices that have already been paid to an actual vendor of the company and has a second check drawn. He forges the endorsement and cashes the check himself.

b. A bookkeeper prepares a check to himself by using a check that has been signed in blank.

c. A bookkeeper intercepts a customer's cash receipt and does not record the receipt at all.

E7-9. There are three basic areas of concern in the control of inventory: purchasing, custody, and record keeping. Listed below are several inventory control techniques. Indicate in which of the three areas each of these controls is providing protection.

a. A purchasing agent should authorize all purchases of inventory.

b. When merchandise is moved from the storeroom, vouchers should be prepared to assign responsibility and should be signed by the recipient of the goods.

c. A physical inventory should be taken regularly.

d. Locks, keys, and guards should be used as appropriate.

e. All supporting documents should be canceled when payment is made.

f. All documents should be prenumbered.

g. Receiving should be separated from storekeeping.

h. Purchasing should be separated from receiving.

i. A perpetual inventory system should be used if possible.

E7-10. The Galliano Company, a client of your firm, has come to you with the following problem.* It has three clerical employees who must perform the following functions:

a. Maintain general ledger.

b. Maintain accounts payable ledger.

---

*Adapted from the AICPA examination.

c. Maintain accounts receivable ledger.
d. Prepare checks for signature.
e. Maintain cash disbursements journal.
f. Issue credit memos on sales returns.
g. Reconcile the bank account.
h. Handle and deposit cash receipts.

Assuming that there is no problem as to the ability of any of the employees, the company requests that you assign the above functions to the three employees in such a manner as to achieve the highest degree of internal control. It may be assumed that these employees will perform no other accounting functions other than the ones listed and that any accounting functions not listed will be performed by persons other than these three employees.

Required:
1. State how you would distribute the above functions among the three employees. Assume that, with the exception of the nominal jobs of the bank reconciliation and the issuance of credit memos on sales returns, all functions require an equal amount of time.

2. List four possible unsatisfactory combinations of the above listed functions.

Problems

P7-1. The accounting system of the Brunett Company includes a general journal (J), a sales journal (S), a purchases journal (P), a cash receipts journal (CR), and a cash disbursements journal (CD). The company maintains a general ledger, an accounts receivable subsidiary ledger, and an accounts payable subsidiary ledger. The accounts payable subsidiary ledger consists of the accounts shown below. Balances at September 30 and all postings made to the accounts during October are shown. The abbreviations given above are used to indicate the journal from which the amounts were posted.

A-1 COMPANY, INC.

Date		Explanation	PR	Debit	Credit	Balance
1982						
Sept.	30	Balance				2,680
Oct.	2		J5	210		2,470
	15		CD10	2,470		0
	28		P10		1,720	1,720

D. MIX, INC.

Date		Explanation	PR	Debit	Credit	Balance
1982						
Sept.	30	Balance				560
Oct.	10		CD10	560		0
	19		P10		230	230
	26		P10		750	980

H. SELLS AND SONS

Date		Explanation	PR	Debit	Credit	Balance
1982 Oct.	5		P10		550	550
	20		P10		130	680
	22		J5	130		550

Z. Z. Z. SUPPLIERS, INC.

Date		Explanation	PR	Debit	Credit	Balance
1982 Sept.	30	Balance				1,170
Oct.	7		P10		830	2,000
	20		CD10	1,170		830

Required:

1. Set up the general ledger accounts payable account. Put in the balance at September 30, and post the entries made to the account during October. Assume that one page in each special journal is used to record transactions for one month. Postings to subsidiary ledgers are made daily and postings to general ledger accounts are made at the end of each month. Be sure to include dates and posting references in the accounts payable control account.

2. Give an explanation for each of the entries in the accounts payable control account.

P7-2. The accounting system of the Sutherland Company includes a general journal (J), a sales journal (S), a purchases journal (P), a cash receipts journal (CR), and a cash disbursements journal (CD). The company maintains a general ledger, an accounts receivable subsidiary ledger, and an accounts payable subsidiary ledger. The accounts receivable subsidiary ledger consists of the accounts shown below. Balances at June 30 and all posting made to the accounts during July are shown. The abbreviations given above are used to indicate the journal from which the amounts were posted.

T. BAXTER

Date		Explanation	PR	Debit	Credit	Balance
1982 June	30	Balance				360
July	8		S7	210		570
	17		S7	180		750
	28		CR7		360	390

L. GRANT

Date		Explanation	PR	Debit	Credit	Balance
1982						
July	2		S7	760		760
	6		J4		520	240
	6		S7	480		720

M. MOORE

Date		Explanation	PR	Debit	Credit	Balance
1982						
June	30	Balance				1,630
July	12		S7	1,060		2,690
	15		CR7		1,630	1,060
	21		S7	500		1,560

B. WHITE

Date		Explanation	PR	Debit	Credit	Balance
1982						
June	30	Balance				800
July	31		J4	12		812

Required:

1. Set up the general ledger accounts receivable account. Put in the balance at June 30, and post the entries made to the account during July. Assume that one page in each special journal is used to record transactions for one month. Postings to subsidiary ledgers are made daily and postings to general ledger accounts are made at the end of the month. Be sure to include dates and posting references in the accounts receivable control account.

2. Give an explanation for each of the entries in the accounts receivable control account.

P7-3. Buzz Electrical Repair Company is a sole proprietorship owned and operated by Buzz Watts. Buzz requires cash payment from customers at the time the work is completed. All cash receipts of the business are deposited in the company checking account. All cash disbursements of the business are made by check, and supplies are paid for at the time of purchase. The business uses cash basis accounting. Transactions for the month of February as recorded in the checkbook are as follows:

DEPOSITS

Date	Source	Amount
Feb. 1	Bank loan	$1,000
7	Customers	100

14		Customers	200
20		Buzz Watts, investment	250
21		Customers	300
28		Customers	1,300

CHECKS WRITTEN

Date	Check #	Explanation	Amount
Feb. 1	110	Truck rental	$ 300
5	111	Supplies	20
7	112	Gasoline for truck	25
8	113	Watts, withdrawal	500
13	114	Supplies	30
15	115	Watts, withdrawal	400
18	116	Gasoline for truck	25
20	117	License	100
22	118	Supplies	150
28	119	Watts, withdrawal	500

The design of the cash receipts journal and cash disbursements journal used in the business are as follows:

Cash Receipts Journal

		Debit	Credit	Other Accounts			
Date	Explanation	Cash	Revenue	Account	PR	Debit	Credit

Cash Disbursements Journal

			Credit	Debits						
							Other Accounts			
	Ck			Supplies	Gasoline	Owner				
Date	#	Explanation	Cash	Expense	Expense	Withdrawals	Account	PR	Debit	Credit

Required:

1. Journalize the above transactions in the cash receipts journal or the cash disbursements journal.
2. If the cash balance for the business was $100 at January 31, what was it at February 28? Show calculations.
3. What was the total change in cash for the month? What was cash basis income for the month? Reconcile the two figures by starting with cash basis income and adding other sources of cash and deducting other uses of cash to arrive at the change in cash.

P7-4. Below are the transactions for the Conti Company (a sole proprietorship):

a. Carl Conti invests $10,000 in the company.
b. Inventory of $7,500 is purchased on credit from A-1 Corporation.
c. A $15,000 loan is made from the Left Bank on a two-year note.
d. Equipment is purchased for $5,000 on account from P-U Suppliers.
e. Sales of $5,200 are made to the following customers on credit: Leroy, $3,000; Mervin, $2,200.
f. $2,500 of accounts payable is paid to A-1.
g. $2,600 of accounts receivable is collected from Leroy.
h. Salaries of $950 are paid to employees, Rob and Roy.

     i. $5,000 of sales were made to the following customers: Ralph, $2,500 on credit; Miguel, $2,500 for cash.

     j. Carl withdraws $1,500 for personal use.

Required:

1. Journalize the above transactions in good form using the sales journal, purchases journal, cash receipts journal, cash disbursements journal, and general journal.

2. Post these transactions to the appropriate general and subsidiary ledger accounts.

P7-5. The cashier of the Easy Company intercepted customer A's check payable to the company in the amount of $500 and deposited it in a bank account which was part of the company petty cash fund, of which he was custodian. He then drew a $500 check on the petty cash fund bank account payable to himself, signed it, and cashed it. At the end of the month, while processing the monthly statements to customers, he was able to change the statement to customer A so as to show that A had received credit for the $500 check that had been intercepted. Ten days later, he made an entry in the cash received book which purported to record receipt of a remittance of $500 from customer A, thus restoring A's account to its proper balance, but overstating cash in bank. He covered the overstatement by omitting from the list of outstanding checks in the bank reconcilement, two checks, the aggregate amount of which was $500.*

Required:

Discuss briefly what you regard as the more important deficiencies in the system of internal control; in addition, include what you consider to be a proper remedy for each deficiency.

P7-6. Henry Brown is a large independent contractor. All employees are paid in cash because Brown believes this arrangement reduces clerical expenses and is preferred by his employees. You find in the petty cash fund approximately $200, of which $185 is stated to be unclaimed wages. Further investigation reveals that Brown has installed the procedure of putting any unclaimed wages in the petty cash fund so that the cash can be used for disbursements. When the claimant to the wages appears, he is paid from the petty cash fund. Brown contends that this procedure reduces the number of checks drawn to replenish the fund and centers the responsibility for all cash on hand in one person inasmuch as the petty cash custodian distributes the pay envelopes.*

Required:

1. Does Brown's system provide proper internal control of unclaimed wages? Explain fully.

2. Because Brown insists in paying wages in cash, what procedures would you recommend to provide better internal control over unclaimed wages?

P7-7. Internal control is so important that accounting systems often contain methods, procedures, or a division of duties that appear wasteful to an outsider, such as:

---

*Adapted from the AICPA examination.

    a. Having two financial officers, a treasurer and a controller.

    b. Budgeting expenses and capital expenditures.

    c. Requiring that every customer be given a cash register tape of his purchase.

    d. Requiring that cash disbursements be made by check when cash receipts for the day could be used.

    e. Not allowing the bank to cash checks payable to the company, even when the company needs cash on hand.

    f. Keeping voided checks even though they cannot be used and they take up space.

    g. Reconciling the bank statement, even though the bank almost never makes a mistake.

    h. Making a separate list of mail collections, even though the bank deposit slip will contain a breakdown of the cash received and deposited.

    i. Approving all general journal entries, even though they are almost always routine.

    j. Requiring prenumbered checks and sales invoices rather than simply stacks of available forms.

Required:

For each of the above, explain why it is an important internal control technique.

P7-8. You have been recently engaged by the Alaska Branch of Far Distributing Company. This branch has substantial annual sales which are billed and collected locally. As a part of your review, you find that the procedures for handling cash receipts are as follows:*

    a. Cash collections on over-the-counter sales and COD sales are received from the customer or delivery service by the cashier. Upon receipt of cash, the cashier stamps the sales ticket "paid" and files a copy for future reference. The only record of COD sales is a copy of the sales ticket, which is given to the cashier to hold until the cash is received from the delivery service.

    b. Mail is opened by the credit manager's secretary, and remittances are given to the credit manager for his review. The credit manager then places the remittances in a tray on the cashier's desk. At the daily deposit cutoff time, the cashier delivers the checks and cash on hand to the assistant credit manager who prepares remittance lists and makes up the bank deposit which he also takes to the bank. The assistant credit manager also posts remittances to the accounts receivable ledger cards and verifies the cash discount allowable.

    c. You also ascertain that the credit manager obtains approval from the executive office of Far Distributing Company, located in Chicago, to write off uncollectible accounts, and that he has retained in his custody as of the end of the fiscal year some remittances that were received on various days during last month.

Required:

  1. Describe the irregularities that might occur under the procedures now in effect for handling cash collections and remittances.

---

*Adapted from the AICPA examination.

2. Give procedures that you would recommend to strengthen internal control over cash collections and remittances.

P7-9. The Generous Loan Company has one hundred branch loan offices. Each office has a manager and four or five subordinates who are employed by the manager. Branch managers prepare the weekly payroll, including their own salaries, and pay employees from cash on hand. The employee signs the payroll sheet signifying receipt of his salary. Hours worked by hourly personnel are inserted in the payroll sheet from timecards prepared by the employees and approved by the manager. The weekly payroll sheets are sent to the home office along with other accounting statements and reports. The home office compiles employee earning records and prepares all federal and state salary reports from the weekly payroll sheets. Salaries are established by home office job-evaluation schedules. Salary adjustments, promotions, and transfers of full-time employees are approved by a home office salary committee based upon the recommendations of branch managers and area supervisors. Branch managers advise the salary committee of new full-time employees and terminations. Part-time and temporary employees are hired without referral to the salary committee.*

Required:
Based upon your review of the payroll system, explain how funds for payroll might be diverted.

*Adapted from the AICPA examination.

Cash and Receivables

Chapter Outline

8.1 *Cash.* Different types of cash; the bank reconciliation statement and its relationship to the journals; necessity of special procedures in the control of cash, including imprest petty cash system.

8.2 *Accounts Receivable and the Income Statement Approach.* Relationship of sales and uncollectible accounts expense, because not all credit sales will actually be collected; recovery of accounts written off.

8.3 *Accounts Receivable and the Balance Sheet Approach.* Estimating bad debts from ending accounts receivable; aging the accounts receivable to determine if the allowance account is properly stated.

8.4 *Notes Receivable.* Distinguishing notes receivable from accounts receivable; accounting for issuing and collecting notes receivable; accounting for default on payment of the note; notes receivable discounted.

Accounting and the Real World

Credit for Deadbeats

W. T. Grant lost control of its accounts receivable and collapsed into bankruptcy in October 1975. "We gave credit to every deadbeat that breathed," growls a former finance executive. Each store had orders to sell on credit and were given quotas to meet.

Prior to 1974, Grant had 1,200 credit offices, with each store keeping all credit information and receiving all payments. This led to abuses, such as military personnel buying goods just before being transferred. When they moved to their new base, they simply stopped paying and the store that extended credit could not track them down. The receivable remained on the books, however.

In addition, Grant permitted thirty-six months to pay, with a $1 minimum monthly payment. (The standard payment schedule in the retail business is a $10 minimum with twenty-four months to pay.) As a result of this loose credit policy, accounts receivable in January 1974 were up to $602 million, compared to $556 million in 1973 and $324 million in 1969. This was an 86 percent increase in five years.

Grant sunk into bankruptcy after being in what appeared to be a solid position as the nation's seventeenth largest retail company in 1972. Its 1,200 stores reported sales of $1.6 billion, with profits of $38 million. In 1974, however, Grant had a loss of $177 million, including the writing-off of $92 million of uncollectible accounts receivable. In 1975 there were additional losses of $111 million until the October bankruptcy.

The effects of Grant's collapse are widespread, perhaps more than any U.S. corporate bankruptcy. The company's bankers wrote off $234 million in loans to it. The company's suppliers wrote off an additional $110 million in receivables owed them by Grant. Over 1000 stores were closed and 80,000 people lost their jobs.

A complete account of the W. T. Grant bankruptcy appears in *Business Week,* July 19, 1976.

Previous chapters of this text have presented the basic concepts underlying accounting and the entire accounting cycle for both service and merchandising firms. Only the most basic topics could be discussed in such a survey. Topics that were but briefly introduced will now be discussed in more detail. This chapter concentrates on some of the most liquid assets, namely cash, accounts receivable, and notes receivable. All three are critically important assets for almost every merchandising firm.

8.1   Cash

Everyone has an intuitive notion of what cash is. Certainly, currency and coins are cash. Additionally, the amount in a bank checking account is cash. For a proprietorship or partnership, a bank savings account could also be cash. It is against banking regulations, however, for a corporation to have a savings account. Thus, corporate funds can only be deposited in non-interest-bearing checking accounts rather than in interest-bearing savings accounts.

To get around this restriction, most corporations invest any excess cash in certificates of deposit, which are essentially short-term interest-bearing notes issued by the bank. The certificate of deposit is very flexible, in that it can be for as short a time as three months. The difficulty is that, if the certificate of deposit is converted to cash before it matures, then the bank will pay no interest or pay interest only at a reduced rate. This policy places a premium on careful cash planning to ensure that all cash necessary for business operations is available, but that any excess cash is invested wisely.

The accounting information about cash necessary for financial statements is distinct from the information necessary for internal purposes. For financial statements, cash on hand in currency and coins, cash in the bank, and cash in certificates of deposit are all reported as one cash figure on the balance sheet. For internal purposes, however, there should be a separate account for certificates of deposit, a separate account for each bank account, and another account for cash on hand, called petty cash (discussed later in the chapter). The financial statement amount would then be the sum of all these accounts.

The Bank
Reconciliation

As discussed in the last chapter, cash assets are the most difficult for any business to control and safeguard. Cash is the medium of exchange for all other assets, it is small in size, and it is cumbersome to specifically identify. Thus, control procedures, such as those presented in the preceding chapter, must be carefully designed and rigorously implemented. Although internal control procedures for all assets were described in Chapter 7, a discussion of the additional technique of bank reconciliation will be helpful here.

The cash receipts and cash disbursements journals represent a first step in keeping close control of cash; they bring together *all* transactions affecting cash in special journals specifically designed to handle these events. What these journals cannot provide, however, is an independent, externally verified record of cash receipts and expenditures. Such a record is extremely valuable in the control of cash; and for most businesses, one is available. It is called the **bank statement.**

Business transactions involving cash (except those from a small petty cash fund) eventually pass through a bank account called a checking account. As a business receives cash or checks from customers, they are deposited in the company bank account. Similarly, as a business pays its bills, checks are written which will ultimately be paid by the company's bank and returned to the business.

Banks then send monthly statements to the business which provide the bank's records of the deposit and check-paying activity of the month. These bank statements show (1) the amount of cash in the account as of the last statement, (2) each deposit of funds and the date of the deposit, (3) each check written by the business which has been paid by the bank, (4) all miscellaneous deductions from the account made by the bank, such as bank service charges, and (5) the amount of cash in the account as of the date of the statement. A typical bank statement is illustrated in Figure 8-1. Although the exact format of the statement depends upon the particular bank, all statements contain the same sort of information about an account.

The cash receipts and cash disbursements journals should contain basically the same information as the bank statement (an independent record kept externally from the business) except for timing differences and miscellaneous deductions.

Timing Differences As checks are written, recorded, and posted, they immediately reduce the general ledger cash account. However, it may be days or even weeks before these checks are paid by the bank and deducted from the company's bank account. The checks must be mailed to the suppliers, deposited in the suppliers' bank accounts, and finally, sent from those banks back to the company's bank for payment. Checks that have been written but have not yet been paid by the bank are called **outstanding checks.** Because most businesses are almost constantly engaging in cash disbursements, when the bank statement is prepared, there will probably be outstanding checks. Outstanding checks are one reason the company's general ledger cash account may not be the same as its bank balance as reported in the bank statement.

These same timing differences also apply to deposits that have been recorded immediately by the company and then mailed to the bank. Such deposits are called **deposits in transit.** As a deposit is recorded and posted, it immediately increases the general ledger cash account; however, the bank will not increase the company's bank balance until the deposit is received and processed. It is typical for deposits made at the end of a month (say, July) to be recorded in July by the company but not be credited to the company account by the bank until the beginning of August.

No journal entries are required to account for timing differences.

Miscellaneous Deductions The bank sometimes imposes a monthly service charge on an account or makes deductions for other services performed. Usually the amount of these deductions is not known by the business until

FIGURE 8-1
Bank Statement

STATEMENT OF ACCOUNT WITH
CENTRAL
NATIONAL BANK OF NEW ORLEANS

SAMPLE COMPANY
1215 PINE ST.
NEW ORLEANS, LA. 70118

ACCOUNT NUMBER	PAGE
42 014 980	1
STATEMENT DATE	
DECEMBER 31, 1981	

13

DEBITS		DATE		BALANCE
	CREDITS			
	BALANCE FORWARD	NOV	20	10,968.93
50 00		NOV	21	10,918.93
135 00	1 618 91	NOV	27	12,402.84
50 00 54 75		NOV	29	12,298.09
311 67		NOV	30	11,986.42
226 88		DEC	01	11,759.54
50 00		DEC	06	11,709.54
35 00		DEC	07	11,874.54
	2 193 74	DEC	12	13,868.28
530 00 265 00		DEC	13	13,073.28
1 108 00		DEC	15	11,965.28
50 15		DEC	18	11,915.13
172 65		DEC	19	11,742.48

SUMMARY OF ACTIVITY

BALANCE FORWARD	DEBITS		CREDITS		BALANCE AS OF STATEMENT DATE
	NUMBER	AMOUNT	NUMBER	AMOUNT	
10 968 93	13	3 039 10	2	3 812 65	11 742 48

CODE
CC   CERTIFIED CHECK
CM   CREDIT MEMO
DM   DEBIT MEMO
EC   ERROR CORRECTION
LS   LIST OF CHECKS

PLEASE EXAMINE AT ONCE
IF NO ERRORS ARE REPORTED WITHIN TEN DAYS,
THE ACCOUNT WILL BE CONSIDERED CORRECT
KINDLY REPORT ALL EXCEPTIONS TO AUDITING DEPT.
RECONCILEMENT FORM ON REVERSE SIDE

CODE
MS   MISCELLANEOUS
OD   OVERDRAWN
RE   REVERSING ENTRY
RT   RETURNED CHECK
SC   SERVICE CHARGE

the bank statement arrives, although these amounts may have been deducted from the bank balance. A typical example of these sorts of deductions would be the cost of printing new checks.

Another important deduction is for checks that were previously deposited but not paid by the bank of the person who wrote the checks. These checks are called NSF (for Not Sufficient Funds) checks. If checks deposited by the business are returned NSF, the bank deducts the unpaid check from the bank balance and returns the check to the company for possible collection. Because this check had previously been recorded (erroneously) as a cash receipt, the general ledger cash balance must now be reduced.

In each of these instances, journal entries are necessary to correct the general ledger cash account.

Unexplained Differences Any discrepancies between the company records and bank balance for cash must be explained in terms of the above differences. The process of doing so is called reconciling (explaining) the bank balance. Thus, upon receipt of each bank statement, a **bank reconciliation** should be prepared and retained in company files. If this reconciliation is done each time a bank statement is received, any unexplained differences will be immediately apparent and steps can be taken to discover the reason for the differences.

The reason for an unexplained difference can be an error by the company in processing transactions, such as recording a check or deposit in the wrong account. If such an error is discovered, a journal entry must be made to correct the records. There could also be an error by the bank. Even today, banks make mistakes and the bank statement cannot be taken as necessarily correct. This bank reconciliation statement is an absolutely critical step in the control of cash and in the discovery of errors in cash transactions.

Sample Reconciliation Consider the following example. On November 4, 1981, the St. Ann Company received a bank statement giving a balance in the bank account of $2,354 as of October 31, 1981. A check of the general ledger showed a balance in the cash account of $3,790 on October 31. Further investigation revealed that there was $150 in the cash register on October 31. Also, on that same day, a deposit of $1,200 was mailed to the bank. In addition, the bank statement revealed that a service charge of $5 was deducted, a check for $362 from Ralph Flax was returned NSF, the bank charged the company $24 for checks, and the bank made an automatic monthly payment of $200 (of which $20 was interest) on a company car. Finally, the company mailed three checks on October 31 in payment of company bills. These checks were #136 for $30, #137 for $25, and #138 for $450.

Figure 8-2 is an example of a bank reconciliation statement. The following characteristics of this form of reconciliation are important:

1. The basic idea of the statement is to reconcile both the bank cash balance and the general ledger cash balance to the correct cash balance as of the date of the bank reconciliation statement. Regardless of whether there are timing or other differences between the bank account and company records, there is only one correct cash figure.

2. Neither the bank nor the book balance for cash as of that date is likely to be correct because timing or other differences can affect both balances.

3. The amount of cash reported by the bank on the bank statement is likely to be different from correct cash because of outstanding checks and deposits in transit; nonetheless, these are legitimate cash transactions that have occurred, and therefore, correct cash must reflect them.

4. The amount of cash reported by the bank can also be different from correct cash balance because of bank errors. The most common bank errors

FIGURE 8-2
Bank Reconciliation
and Journal Entries

THE ST. ANN COMPANY		
Bank Reconciliation Statement		
October 31, 1981		

Balance on bank statement, October 31		$2,354
Less:		
Outstanding checks		
#136	$ 30	
#137	25	
#138	450	(505)
Add:		
Deposit in transit		1,200
Cash in cash register		150
Correct cash balance, October 31		$3,199

Balance from company records, October 31		$3,790
Less:		
Bank service charge	$ 5	
NSF check	362	
Charge for checks	24	
Payment by bank	200	(591)
Correct cash balance, October 31		$3,199

Journal Entries		
October 31 Miscellaneous expense	29	
Cash		29
To reflect bank charges		
31 Accounts receivable, Ralph Flax	362	
Cash		362
To reinstate receivable		
31 Note payable	180	
Interest expense	20	
Cash		200
To reflect payment on note		

are charging the wrong account for a check or deposit and posting the wrong amount for a check.

5. Company records may not show the correct cash figure because of miscellaneous deductions from the company's account made by the bank. The business records cannot reflect these charges until the amount is learned when the bank statement arrives.

6. Company records also may not show the correct cash figure because of errors (accidental or intentional) made in the journalizing or posting of cash receipts or disbursements.

7. Because either Reason 5 or Reason 6 may result in an overstatement or understatement of cash in company records, appropriate adjustments must be made both on the bank reconciliation statement and on the books of the business. Any adjustment to the cash balance from company records that is necessary in the reconciliation statement must be accompanied by an appropriate journal entry to adjust the books.

Concept Summary

Form of a Bank Reconciliation

SAMPLE COMPANY
Bank Reconciliation Statement
December 31, 1981

Balance on bank statement, December 31		$X,XXX	Balance from company records, December 31		$X,XXX
Less:			*Less:*		
Outstanding checks:			Bank service charge	$ X	
			NSF checks:		
	$ XXX				
	XXX			$ XX	
	XX	$XXX		XXX	XXX
Any bank errors causing cash to be too high	XX	(XXX)	Any company errors causing cash to be too high	XX	(XXX)
Add:			*Add:*		
Deposits in transit:			Any company errors causing cash to be too low		XX
	XXX				
	XX	XXX			
Any bank errors causing cash to be too low	XX	XXX			
Correct cash balance, December 31		$X,XXX	Correct cash balance, December 31		$X,XXX

Petty Cash

Though disbursements should generally be made by check, almost all companies require cash to pay for items like postage due. For this reason, most firms have a small amount of cash on hand. This amount is called **petty cash.** Generally speaking, defalcations involving petty cash are particularly easy, because they simply involve taking cash from the petty cash. There can be little effective detection.

Because of this risk, many firms use an **imprest petty cash system.** In such a system, a certain amount (such as $100) is set as the amount for petty cash. The petty cash fund begins with a $100 check drawn to petty cash. The journal entry would be

Petty cash 100
    Cash   100

Petty cash is thus set up as an asset account; after the check is cashed, the petty cash fund is established.

To obtain cash from the fund, a voucher is prepared which states the reason for and the amount of the cash needed. (The voucher discussed in the last chapter is quite similar to the voucher here.) After approval by a responsible official, the voucher is placed with the petty cash fund, and the cash is withdrawn. Thus, the sum of all of the vouchers plus the cash still on hand should always equal $100.

When the cash in the fund becomes too low or the end of an accounting period is reached, another check is drawn to petty cash in the amount of the total of all of the vouchers. The vouchers are then removed from the petty cash fund and the cash added; the cash should again total $100. The journal entry should then debit the expense (or possibly asset) accounts affected by the cash payments supported by the vouchers.

8.2   Accounts Receivable and the Income Statement Approach

The concept of credit sales was introduced in Chapter 6. Business today is very heavily based upon sales on credit. Most companies sell on credit because they feel that sales, and hence net income, will increase once purchasing is made easier for the customer.

There are three steps to the process of credit sales: (1) the customer charges a purchase, (2) a bill is sent to the customer, and (3) the customer pays the bill. This seemingly simple process is an important area of management concern and involvement. The internal control problems connected with credit sales and the subsequent cash collections were discussed in the last chapter. Two additional major problems are credit policy and cash collections.

Credit Policy

Not everyone who buys on credit is able or willing to pay for his purchases, but it is impossible to tell exactly which customers will pay and which will not. In this context, the term "liberal credit policy" is used where credit is easily granted. The tradeoff is that the more liberal the credit policy is, the more sales there will be, but the higher the losses from accounts that cannot be collected. On the other hand, if credit is restricted to only those who are sure to pay, then many sales will be lost.

As an example, three leading furniture stores in the same town have widely varying credit policies. Twenty-five percent of the credit sales of Store R, 10 percent of the credit sales of Store K, and 1 percent of the credit sales of Store H are uncollectible. All three stores are well run and very profitable. The different stores have different clienteles and different credit policies, which are intimately related to quality of merchandise and pricing. Store R's customers have low incomes and are generally poor credit risks; the quality of merchandise is correspondingly low; and the markup is correspondingly high. If Store R tried to reduce uncollectible accounts to the level of Store H, virtually all its sales would be lost. Store H has low uncollectible accounts because it sells high quality merchandise to high income customers.

Cash Collections

Credit customers sometimes do not pay promptly. Trade accounts receivable between companies (such as between a wholesaler and a retailer) do not charge interest on the amount owed. Given the high interest rates of borrowing, it is in the customer's best interest to delay payment as much as possible. As mentioned in Chapter 6, companies give discounts to encourage prompt payment. Beyond this, a firm but polite insistence on payment is necessary to receive payment within a reasonable period.

This book will not go into the details of credit management and how to make credit and collection decisions; however, it is important to realize that accounting information can be an excellent check on how well these decisions have been made. A company will want accounting reports concerning how many accounts are uncollectible. Additionally, looking at the total amount of accounts receivable in relation to total credit sales will indicate how long it is taking to collect accounts receivable from customers. Chapter 16 discusses these topics in greater depth.

When some of a company's customers are unable or unwilling to pay for merchandise purchased, accounting procedures must correct the books for these uncollectible accounts. There are two basic methods of accounting for uncollectible accounts: the direct write-off method and the allowance method.

Direct Write-Off Method

Many firms make primarily cash sales, with credit sales consisting of only a small percentage of total sales. In such instances the company and its accountants can decide to use the direct write-off method of accounting for uncollectible accounts. If this method is used, an **uncollectible accounts expense** is recognized when the individual account is determined to be uncollectible. Thus, the journal entry to recognize Kathy Hebert's account of $500 as uncollectible would be

```
Uncollectible accounts expense ..............................  500
    Accounts receivable, K. Hebert ...........................          500
    (posted to both control and subsidiary)
```

With this method, accounts receivable are stated at a somewhat greater amount than will actually be collected. This misstatement, however, may be so small as to make no practical difference.

If the customer whose account has been written off later pays, that indicates the write-off was a mistake and a correcting entry is needed. The entries if Kathy Hebert later paid the amount would be

```
Accounts receivable, K. Hebert .............................  500
    Uncollectible accounts expense ..........................          500
    To reverse the incorrect entry

Cash ......................................................  500
    Accounts receivable, K. Hebert ..........................          500
    To record the receipt of cash
```

Allowance Method   To understand the purposes of the allowance method of accounting for uncollectible accounts, consider the effect on a business's accounts of selling products on credit but then not collecting the amounts owed. Accrual accounting principles require that revenue be recognized at the point of sale of the product. When a credit sale is made, accounts receivable (both control and individual subsidiary ledger) is increased and sales revenue is increased. If the receivable is never converted to cash by collection, then the individual account receivable is worthless and, as a result, receivables are overstated. Similarly, sales revenue for the period is also overstated because some goods were actually given away (that is, no real assets were received in exchange). It is the task of the allowance method to adjust accounts receivable and sales revenue at the end of a period for credit sales made during the period that will likely never be collected.

A business does not know at the point of sale exactly which specific customers will not ultimately pay (or the sale would never be made), and it may be a year or more before these individuals are known with certainty. The basic problem of the allowance method can now be appreciated. A business makes credit sales during a period, and while doing so, the business knows that some of the receivables resulting from the sales will never be collected. It does not, however, know which particular accounts are no good and cannot wait until specific individuals are identified because assets and revenue would be constantly overstated during the waiting period.

The allowance method solution to this problem is to estimate at the end of each period the percentage of that period's credit sales which are unlikely to be collected in future periods. This percentage is then used to determine the amount by which assets and revenue are likely to be overstated. Suppose credit sales were $210,000 and 1 percent were estimated to uncollectible. Then, as an adjusting entry of Type 1 (similar to depreciation), these accounts are corrected in the general journal as follows:

Uncollectible accounts expense	2100	
Allowance for uncollectible accounts		2100

Important characteristics of the allowance method are discussed in the paragraphs that follow.

Expense Related to Revenue   An expense is created which offsets the overstatement of revenue. The expense is placed in the same accounting period as the revenue overstatement so that income for the period can be measured reasonably accurately.

Contra Account   Since the company does not know what particular accounts are worthless, it is impossible to credit accounts receivable because a related subsidiary ledger account cannot be credited. As a result, a contra account, **allowance for uncollectible accounts,** is credited instead. Like all contra accounts, allowance for uncollectible accounts is used to decrease the balance in another account indirectly. The balance sheet would report receivables among current assets as follows:

Cash		$ 17,600
Accounts receivable	$40,100	
Less: Allowance for uncollectible accounts	(2,100)	38,000
Inventory		120,100
Supplies		600
Prepaid insurance		2,000
Total current assets		$178,300

Write-Off Finally, as specific individual accounts receivable are identified as worthless because they will never be collected, the contra account can be lowered and accounts receivable (control and subsidiary) can be reduced to the amount that represents the remaining collectible claims on customers. This process is called "writing off" specific accounts and may take place anytime a business feels a certain receivable is no good. The general journal entry for a write-off of a $500 account of Kathy Hebert would be

Allowance for uncollectible accounts 500	
Accounts receivable, K. Hebert	500
(Posted to both control and subsidiary)	

Effect of Write-Off When an account is written off as uncollectible, there is no change in the net amount of accounts receivable shown on the balance sheet. The decrease in the accounts receivable account is exactly offset by the decrease in the allowance for uncollectible accounts. Thus, no asset is consumed when an account is written off and, hence, no expense is recognized. The expense was recognized at the time of the adjusting entry which added to the allowance account. After the $500 account was written off, the current asset section would read as follows:

Cash		$ 17,600
Accounts receivable	$39,600	
Less: Allowance for uncollectible accounts	(1,600)	38,000
Inventory		120,100
Supplies		600
Prepaid insurance		2,000
Total current assets		$178,300

In both instances, the net amount of accounts receivable is $38,000.

It sometimes happens that an account which has been written off will actually be collected. The entry here is a correcting entry because the write-off turned out to be in error. As a result, when an account previously written off is collected, there are two entries:

Accounts receivable, K. Hebert 500	
Allowance for uncollectible accounts	500
To reverse the incorrect entry	

Cash 500	
Accounts receivable, K. Hebert	500
To record the receipt of cash	

The first entry is to reverse the entry in which the account was incorrectly written off. The second entry then records the receipt of the cash. Both entries to accounts receivable are posted to both the control account and the subsidiary account, so that all transactions with that customer are recorded in the subsidiary ledger together.

Concept Summary

Basic Entries in Uncollectibles Accounting		
	Direct Write-off Method	*Allowance Method*
Sale is Made	Accounts receivable Sales	Accounts receivable Sales
End of Period Adjusting Entry	None	Uncollectible accounts expense Allowance for uncollectible accounts
Account Is Written off	Uncollectible accounts expense Accounts receivable	Allowance for uncollectible accounts Accounts receivable
Account Is Later Collected	Accounts receivable Uncollectible accounts expense Cash Accounts receivable	Accounts receivable Allowance for uncollectible accounts Cash Accounts receivable

Note: Every entry to accounts receivable applies to a particular customer and is posted to both the general ledger and the accounts receivable subsidiary ledger.

8.3 Accounts Receivable and the Balance Sheet Approach

The above discussion contrasted the direct write-off and the allowance methods of accounting. There are, however, two different possible approaches to the allowance method. The approach discussed earlier is called the **income statement approach** because the adjusting entry for uncollectible accounts expense is based upon the company's sales. In this method, the emphasis is on the proper statement of income for the period. The balance sheet figure for allowance is, then, a residual.

On the other hand, some firms use a **balance sheet approach** to determine uncollectible accounts expense. The argument is that no account which has already been collected can become uncollectible. Thus, the balance sheet approach estimates uncollectible accounts as a percentage of ending accounts receivable. Because those are the accounts that have not yet been collected, they are the only accounts that can become uncollectible. Emphasis is on the proper statement of accounts receivable on the balance sheet. The income statement figure for uncollectible accounts expense is, then, a residual figure.

Assume that a company had a balance of $50,000 in accounts receivable at the beginning of an accounting period and that the balance in the allowance account was $1,500. During the period, credit sales of $100,000 were made, $70,000 were collected from customers, and $400 of accounts were written off. Ending accounts receivable is therefore $50,000 + $100,000 − $70,000 = $80,000, and the ending balance of the allowance account is $1,500 − $400 = $1,100.

If the company determines uncollectible accounts expense based upon credit sales and estimates uncollectible accounts to be 2 percent of credit sales for the period, the adjusting entry would be

Uncollectible accounts expense   2,000
    Allowance for uncollectible accounts   2,000

because $100,000 sales × 2 percent uncollectible accounts = $2,000 uncollectible accounts.

On the other hand, assume the company determines uncollectible accounts expense based upon ending accounts receivable and estimates uncollectible accounts to be 3 percent of ending accounts receivable. The estimated amount of uncollectible accounts at the end of the period is then

$$\begin{array}{rl} \$80{,}000 & \text{ending accounts receivable} \\ \times \quad 3\% & \text{estimated uncollectible accounts} \\ \hline \$\ 2{,}400 & \text{estimated uncollectible accounts} \end{array}$$

This $2,400 is the estimated amount that will never be collected and is, thus, what the ending allowance for uncollectible accounts should be. But the allowance account has a balance of $1,100. The adjusting journal entry necessary to bring the balance in the allowance account up to $2,400 would be

Uncollectible accounts expense   1,300
    Allowance for uncollectible accounts   1,300

Aging Accounts Receivable

The estimation of uncollectible accounts can be more sophisticated than applying a single percentage to the total ending balance of accounts receivable. The longer an account receivable remains uncollected, the more likely it is to become uncollectible. Thus, different percentage estimations of uncollectible accounts should be applied to different ages of accounts receivable. This technique is called **aging the accounts receivable.** An example appears in Figure 8-3. The basic steps of this technique are:

1. Analyze each customer's account balance to determine how old it is, that is, how long the bill has been unpaid. For example, if a purchase of June 1 is unpaid as of July 15, the balance is considered forty-five days old.

FIGURE 8-3
Aging Accounts
Receivable

AGING OF ACCOUNTS RECEIVABLE

Number	Customer Name	Total	Current	Over 30	Over 60	Over 90
1001	H. Wolbrette	750	750			
1002	K. Wood	1,200	1,000	200		
1003	R. Pfister	400	400			
1004	R. Dozier	200		100	100	
1005	R. Flax	350				350
.	.	.	.	.	.	.
.	.	.	.	.	.	.
.	.	.	.	.	.	.
1162	L. Friedmann	650	300	250	100	
1163	C. Wells	150	150			
		80,000	65,000	10,000	1,500	3,500

ESTIMATION OF ALLOWANCE ACCOUNT

	Percent of Total	Amount	Estimated Percent Uncollectible	Allowance for Uncollectible Accounts
Current	81.2%	65,000	1%	650
Over 30 days	12.5	10,000	5	500
Over 60 days	1.9	1,500	15	225
Over 90 days	4.4	3,500	45	1,575
Total	100.0	80,000		2,950

ADJUSTING JOURNAL ENTRY

Uncollectible accounts expense 1,850

   Allowance for uncollectible accounts 1,850

To bring the allowance account up to the total determined above

This amount is calculated as follows:

   Amount allowance account should total .... $ 2,950

   Current balance in allowance account .... (1,100)

   Amount of adjusting entry .... $ 1,850

2. Group the account balances into monthly age groups. Every balance less than thirty days old is usually considered current. There will be another group for balances over thirty but less than sixty days, and so on.

3. Develop a total for each age group. This task is eased by using the spread sheet approach illustrated in Figure 8-3. The sum of the age group totals should equal the overall total.

4. Apply the percentage of uncollectible accounts appropriate for each age group. The older an account balance becomes, the less likely it is that it will ever be collected; therefore, the percentage of uncollectible accounts will be higher for older age groups.

5. Determine the total allowance for uncollectible accounts. This will be the sum of the allowances for each of the age groups. In Figure 8-3 the total allowance for uncollectible accounts comes to $2,950.

6. Make an adjusting entry to bring the current balance in the allowance account up to what it should be, as determined in Step 5 above. Assuming a current balance of $1,100, the $1,850 adjusting entry is given in Figure 8-3.

Even when the income statement approach to accounting for uncollectible accounts is used, it is a good idea to age the accounts receivable periodically to ensure that the allowance account is properly stated. Because the basis of the allowance account is an estimate, it can become misstated when events do not happen as planned. Also, to obtain financial statements that look more favorable, management may deliberately underestimate expense. If uncollectible accounts expense is understated, both net income and assets are overstated.

The process of writing off uncollectible accounts is based on judgment. As illustrated, it is possible to write off an account that is subsequently collected. A more common problem, however, is the failure to write off accounts that will never be collected because writing them off will make management look bad.

Extended
Example

An extended example will clarify these concepts. Following are the April transactions for Robert Nelms & Associates, which prepares financial statements monthly. On April 1, the balance of accounts receivable was $226,900 and the balance in the allowance for uncollectible accounts was $3,760. During the month, there were credit sales of $190,100 (of which 1.5 percent were estimated as uncollectible) and collections on accounts receivable of $182,000. Mary Matlick's account of $1,540 was written off as uncollectible; however, Linda Zaleski paid her account of $680 in full despite the fact that it had been written off as uncollectible. On April 30, there were $25,000 of overdue accounts, 15 percent of which were estimated to be uncollectible. Only 1 percent of the current receivables were estimated to be uncollectible.

The entries for the credit sales and cash collections would be the same regardless of which method was used to deal with uncollectible accounts. The remaining entries would depend upon the method of accounting for uncollectible accounts used.

Direct Write-off Method The entry to write off Mary Matlick's account would be

Uncollectible accounts expense	1,540	
Accounts receivable, M. Matlick		1,540

The entry to reinstate Linda Zaleski's account would be

```
Accounts receivable, L. Zaleski .............................   680
    Uncollectible accounts expense ...........................          680
```

The entry to record the collection of the account would be

```
Cash .......................................................   680
    Accounts receivable, L. Zaleski ...........................          680
```

With the direct write-off method there would be no end-of-period adjusting entry.

Allowance Method The entry to write off Mary Matlick's account would be

```
Allowance for uncollectible accounts  ......................  1,540
    Accounts receivable, M. Matlick .........................          1,540
```

The entry to reinstate Linda Zaleski's account would be

```
Accounts receivable, L. Zaleski .............................   680
    Allowance for uncollectible accounts  .......................          680
```

The entry to record the collection of the account would be

```
Cash .......................................................   680
    Accounts receivable, L. Zaleski ...........................          680
```

The *income statement approach* would estimate uncollectible accounts expense as 1.5 percent of credit sales or $190,100 \times 1.5\% = \$2,851.50$. The end-of-period adjusting entry would then be

```
Uncollectible accounts expense ........................  2,851.50
    Allowance for uncollectible accounts  ...............          2,851.50
```

The *balance sheet approach* would estimate uncollectible accounts expense based upon ending accounts receivable. On April 30, the balance in accounts receivable was $235,000 ($226,900 beginning + $190,100 credit sales − $182,000 collections). The allowance for uncollectible accounts should then be

$$
\begin{array}{lll}
\$210,000 & \text{current} \times \;\; 1\% = & \$2,100 \\
\underline{25,000} & \text{overdue} \times 15\% = & \underline{3,750} \\
\$235,000 & & \$5,850
\end{array}
$$

However, the balance in the allowance account was $2,900 ($2,760 beginning + $680 reinstatement − $1,540 account written off). The end-of-period adjusting entry to state the allowance account properly would be

```
Uncollectible accounts expense ...........................  2,950
    Allowance for uncollectible accounts  ....................          2,950
```

The $2,900 balance plus this $2,950 entry would then total $5,850, the amount the allowance account should equal.

Concept Summary

Contrast of the Income Statement and Balance Sheet Approaches			
	Description	*Directly Calculated Amount*	*Residual Amount*
Income Statement Approach	Focuses on the determination of net income through a proper statement of the relationship between net sales revenue and uncollectible accounts expense	Uncollectible accounts expense as a percentage of net sales revenue	Allowance for uncollectible accounts
Balance Sheet Approach	Focuses on the determination of the net realizable value of accounts receivable through a proper statement of the relationship between accounts receivable and allowance for uncollectible accounts	Allowance for uncollectible accounts as a percentage of ending accounts receivable	Uncollectible accounts expense

8.4 Notes Receivable

As discussed earlier, sales between business firms are generally made on credit and are treated as accounts receivable. In general, this method for credit purchase and subsequent collection works quite well, because it does not require onerous paperwork or special legal forms or documents.

Uses of Notes Receivable

There are three basic types of situations, however, where accounts receivable are not adequate and have to be replaced by a more formal document, a note receivable (illustrated in Figure 8-4).

Customer Is Unable to Pay Promptly Generally speaking, accounts receivable cannot accrue interest. Thus, if a customer cannot pay when he is supposed to, the creditor will often extend the time for payment. (After all, receiving money later is better than receiving no money at all.) However, the creditor will often insist that the customer sign a note receivable. The note receivable will call for payment of not only the principal amount, but also interest on that principal.

Amount of Interest Is Large In some instances, the interest amount foregone by having an account receivable is so great that the selling firm must

FIGURE 8-4
Form of a Note
Receivable

_____ 19 ____

_____ After Date _____ Promise to Pay to

the Order of _____

_____ Dollars

For Value Received with Interest at _____ per annum

Payable at _____

$2,000.00   New Orleans, Louisiana   December 1   19 81

Sixty days   After Date   We   Promise to Pay to

the Order of   Dozier's Wholesale Hardware

Two thousand and 00/100 —————   Dollars

For Value Received with Interest at   12%   per annum

Payable at   Whitney National Bank, New Orleans

Wolbrette's Retail Hardware

Henri Wolbrette, III

charge interest. Two such instances are when the purchase is for a large amount or when the payment is over an extended period. In these instances, a note receivable will be signed by the purchaser at the point of sale.

Selling Firm Needs Cash Before Payment Companies may have their customers sign notes receivable, enabling them to sell their receivables more easily to a bank for cash. Accounts receivable is classified as a current asset; however, receivables cannot be used for many important tasks, such as meeting the weekly payroll. Thus, companies sometimes need to "turn receivables into cash." Accounts receivable are difficult to use for this purpose because there is no written promise to pay made by the customer. Under certain circumstances, it is possible to sell accounts receivable; doing so is called *factoring* the accounts receivable. Factoring is extremely expensive for the selling firm, so it is only used as a last resort.

Advantages of Notes Receivable The note receivable has two major advantages over the account receivable: (1) interest can be charged for the time the principal is uncollected and (2) the note is a written promise to pay, so that it can be sold more easily to a bank for cash, if necessary.

Form of Note Receivable

The note receivable has a standard form and terminology, given in Figure 8-4. It promises "to pay to the order of" a particular firm or individual; this firm or individual is called the **payee.** In the example given, the payee is Dozier's Wholesale Hardware. The individual or firm that promises to pay is called the **maker.** In Figure 8-4, the maker is Wolbrette's Retail Hardware. The note is dated when it is signed, but payment is due at some future date. This date when payment is due is called the **maturity date.** As in similar situations, the amount on the face of the note (in this instance, $2,000) is called the **face amount,** the **principal amount,** or simply the **principal.** The total amount due at the maturity date (that is, principal plus interest) is called the **maturity value.**

The note has specific characteristics which qualify it as a negotiable instrument with certain legal privileges and make it easier to sell.

Unconditional Promise to Pay It is an unconditional promise to pay. There are no clauses to the effect that payment will be forthcoming only if certain conditions are met. Any such conditions would make the bank reluctant or unwilling to buy the note.

Pay to the Order of It is a promise to pay to the order of the payee but *not* to the payee only. As a result, the payee can sell the note and order that payment be made to its purchaser. If the note did not promise to pay to the order of the payee, the note would be more difficult to sell because of certain legal technicalities.

Certain Dollar Amount It has a certain dollar amount, namely the principal amount plus the interest accrued at the stated rate. If the note did not have a certain dollar amount (for example, if the note were based on the amount realized from the sale of goods), the bank would be reluctant or unwilling to buy the note.

Determinable Future Date The note is payable at a determinable future date. The note is dated, and it is payable a fixed number of days after that date. It is possible to determine the exact future maturity date. Again, if the note were due only when some indeterminable future event occurred, the note would be difficult to sell.

Also, because the note receivable is a physical document, all notes can be filed together by maturity date. This file will be, in effect, a subsidiary ledger for the notes receivable control account.

Payment The note is payable at a particular place, usually the payee's bank. This requirement for payment is a convenience for the payee, because it means the money will be put in his account without the necessity of a deposit. Payment could be made by the maker by arriving at the bank and paying the note in person. In most instances, however, doing so is inconvenient, especially if the maker and the payee are in different cities. In these instances, the maker simply pays his bank, which forwards the money to the bank of the payee.

Journal Entries for the Acceptance of Notes Receivable

There are three basic occasions when a note receivable is accepted; however, these basic occasions result in only two types of journal entries. A note receivable is often made when the customer cannot pay on time. In this instance, there is an exchange of a note receivable for an account receivable. The accounting entry would then be

```
Notes receivable .......................................    2,000
    Account receivable, Wolbrette ..........................          2,000
Record exchange of note for account receivable
```

When the amount of interest is large or the selling firm needs cash, the purchaser signs a note at the point of sale. In this instance, firms prefer to concentrate all transactions for a particular customer in that customer's accounts receivable subsidiary ledger. For this reason, the accounting entries should be

```
Accounts receivable, Wolbrette ..........................    2,000
    Sales .................................................          2,000
Record sales of goods
```

and then

```
Notes receivable .......................................    2,000
    Accounts receivable, Wolbrette .........................          2,000
Record acceptance of note
```

Basic Computations

There are two basic computations connected with notes receivable, computing the maturity date and computing the interest due on that date.

Compute the Maturity Date When Payment Is Due The determination of the maturity date involves counting the days of the note, including the last day, but not including the day the note is made. The general principle is that each transaction is assumed to occur at the end of each business day. The calculation for the example note is:

Number of days in December	31
Less date of note (12/1 *not* counted)	1
	30
Days required in January (1/30 is counted)	30
Days of the note	60

Because thirty days are thus required in January to add up to sixty and because the last day is counted, the maturity date is January 30, 1982.

Compute Interest Due at the Maturity Date The computation of interest is given by the following formula:

$$\text{Interest due} = \text{principal} \times \text{annual rate of interest} \times \frac{\text{days of note}}{360}$$

This formula prorates the annual interest over the number of days of the note. The number 360 is used instead of 365 for the days in a year primarily for historical and convenience reasons. For the example, in Figure 8-4, the calculation is

$$\text{Interest due} = \$2,000 \times 12\% \times \frac{60}{360} = \$40$$

The maturity value (that is, the amount due at the maturity date) is, then, the principal plus interest, which, in this example, is $2,040 ($2,000 + $40).

It is sometimes possible to save time in computing interest by using the *sixty-day 6 percent method.* This method states that, for a sixty-day time period and a 6 percent interest rate, the amount of interest can be calculated by moving the decimal point of the principal amount two places to the left. For example, the interest for sixty days at 6 percent interest of $2,000.00 is $20.00. The reason for this is the following:

$$\text{Interest} = \text{principal} \times 6\% \times \frac{60}{360}$$
$$= \text{principal} \times 1\%$$

and multiplying by 1 percent is the equivalent of moving the decimal point two places to the left.

This method can be extended to handle situations other than just sixty days and 6 percent interest. For example, sixty days at 12 percent interest is twice sixty days at 6 percent interest, while thirty days at 6 percent interest is one-half of that amount. Thus, the interest on $2,000 for sixty days at 12 percent interest can be computed in two steps:

1. Move the decimal point two places to the left for the $2,000 principal to get $20.

2. Multiply the $20 by two to get $40 (as obtained above), because 12 percent interest is twice 6 percent.

This method can also be used for other interest rates, such as 9 percent, by the following technique:

Interest on $2,000 for 60 days at 6% interest $20
Interest on $2,000 for 60 days at 3% interest <u>10</u> (½ × $20)
Interest on $2,000 for 60 days at 9% interest $<u><u>30</u></u>

Finally, this method can also be used for different time periods by prorating the interest for sixty days. As an example, twenty days is one-third of sixty days. Thus, interest on $2,000 for twenty days at 9 percent interest is ⅓ × $30 or $10. Using the same approach, interest on $2,000 for thirty days at 6 percent interest would be:

$$\frac{30 \text{ days}}{60 \text{ days}} \times \text{interest on \$2,000 for 60 days at 6\% interest}$$
$$= \frac{1}{2} \times \$20$$
$$= \$10.$$

Adjusting Entry

Because the note receivable earns interest, an adjusting entry is required if an accounting period ends before the maturity date. As discussed in Chapter 4, there must be a Type 3 adjusting entry to accrue interest receivable and interest revenue.

For example, assume the Dozier Wholesale Hardware Company will prepare financial statements for the year ending December 31, 1981. At that point, the note has accrued interest for thirty days (the first day is not counted, but the last day is). The calculation of interest earned would be

$$\text{Interest earned} = \$2,000 \times 12\% \times \frac{30}{360} = \$20$$

and the journal entry would be

Interest receivable	20	
Interest revenue		20

The normal event is for the maker to pay in full the amount due on the maturity date. Assuming collection of the note, the journal entry on January 30, 1982, would be

Cash	2,040	
Note receivable		2,000
Interest receivable		20
Interest revenue		20

An additional $20 of interest has been earned in the thirty days of January.

Dishonor a Note

Unfortunately, however, the maker of a note sometimes does not pay the note when it is due. In this instance, the note is said to be **dishonored.** When the note is dishonored, the payee then must make an entry eliminating the note receivable and creating an account receivable for the total amount due, including both principal and interest. The interest is accrued because, after the maturity date, the maker is liable for the total maturity value, not just the principal. For the example note, the entry upon dishonor of the note on January 30, 1982, would be

Accounts receivable, Wolbrette	2,040	
Note receivable		2,000
Interest receivable		20
Interest revenue		20

In such an instance, the maker should be aggressively pursued for payment because he is still liable for the note.

Exchange of Notes	A less common transaction involving notes receivable is the exchange of one note for another. Such a transaction occurs when the maker is given additional time in which to make payment. To help ensure that the process will not be continued indefinitely, the payee usually insists on payment of at least the interest due and perhaps some of the principal. For example, assume for the note in Figure 8-4 that, at maturity, payment of the interest plus $1,000 of the principal was made and another note was issued for the balance of the principal due. The journal entry on January 30, 1982, would be:

```
Cash  ...................................................  1,040
Notes receivable  ......................................  1,000
    Notes receivable  .....................................              2,000
    Interest receivable  ...................................                 20
    Interest revenue  .....................................                 20
```

Concept Summary

Basic Entries for Notes Receivable		
Date of Note	*Adjusting Entry*	*Maturity Date*

Notes receivable
  Accounts receivable, Maker
Record exchange of note for
  account receivable
 	
When the customer is unable
  to pay, the debt is made
  more formal by acceptance
  of note, and interest begins
  to accrue.
		Cash
		  Notes receivable
		  Interest receivable
		  Interest revenue
		Note is collected from maker

Accounts receivable, Maker
  Sales
Record sale of goods
 	
Notes receivable
  Accounts receivable, Maker
Record issue of note
 	
When the amount of interest is
  large or the selling firm
  needs cash; a note
  receivable may be used.
  Entries concentrate all
  transactions in the
  customer's subsidiary ledger
  account.
	Interest receivable
	  Interest revenue
	Accrue interest
		Accounts receivable, Maker
		  Notes receivable
		  Interest receivable
		  Interest revenue
		Note is dishonored by maker
		
		Cash
		Notes receivable
		  Notes receivable
		  Interest receivable
		  Interest revenue
		Note is exchanged for another

Notes Receivable Discounted	One of the advantages of the formality of a note receivable is that the note can be sold to the bank for cash, if necessary. Selling a note to a bank is called **discounting a note;** a note that has been sold is called a discounted note. The bank will buy the note and pay cash for it, with the intention

of collecting the principal plus interest at the maturity date; however, the bank will not pay the full maturity value. In effect, the bank charges interest by paying less than the maturity value and then collecting the full amount later.

Example Note

For example, assume the bank charges 15 percent annual interest. The amount the bank will pay for the example note (Figure 8-4) on December 11, 1981, is computed as follows:

Principal	$2,000.00
Interest due at maturity	40.00
Maturity value	2,040.00
Bank interest charge $\left(2{,}040 \times 15\% \times \dfrac{50}{360}\right)$	42.50
Proceeds from bank	$1,997.50

The annual interest is, thus, prorated over the fifty days the bank must wait to collect the note. Again, the first day is not counted and the last is, so the bank will hold the note twenty days in December (December 11 is not counted) and thirty days in January. The journal entry for the sale on December 11 would then be

Cash	1,997.50	
Interest expense	2.50	
Notes receivable		2,000.00

The difference between the cash received and the amount of the note is treated as an interest expense because it is the cost of obtaining the money early and not waiting until the maturity date.

Contingent Liabilities

When a firm discounts a note receivable, that firm may have to pay off the note to the bank at maturity, if it is dishonored. The amount of this potential liability is known with certainty. What is not known is whether or not there will be a liability. A prospective creditor or investor of a firm would want to know of such potential liabilities, so they are important and cannot be ignored. In accounting, such liabilities are called **contingent liabilities.** Contingent liabilities are generally disclosed by a footnote to the financial statements which gives the nature and amount of such potential liabilities.

Summary

Cash and receivables represent the majority of liquid assets of most businesses. Accounting for cash presents no major conceptual difficulties; however, there are significant internal control problems associated with cash because it is physically small, difficult to trace, and readily exchangeable.

    The bank reconciliation is an important technique in any company's internal control system. It provides an independent verification of cash receipts and disbursements. In reconciling the cash balance in the general ledger to the cash balance in the bank statement, there are two types of adjustments. Timing differences in recording cash transactions, such as deposits in transit and outstanding checks, are normal and do not require journal entries. Differences that require journal entries include bank service charges and errors in the recording or classifying of cash transactions on the company's books.

The primary accounting problem associated with accounts receivable is uncollectible accounts. There are two basic methods of accounting for uncollectible accounts, the direct write-off and the allowance method. If the direct write-off method is used, uncollectible accounts expense is recognized when an individual account is judged uncollectible. If the allowance method is used, uncollectible accounts expense is estimated in the period of the sale by an adjusting entry. This adjusting entry can be based on either net credit sales or the ending balance in accounts receivable.

Notes receivable represent amounts owed to a company which are evidenced by a written formal document. Journal entries for notes receivable are necessary when the note is created, for the accrual of interest at the end of the accounting period, and when the note matures. Sometimes a note is sold prior to its maturity. This process, called discounting the note, requires a journal entry at the discount date of the note and at the maturity date.

Accounting procedures for inventory and the determination of cost of goods sold are discussed in Chapter 9.

Key Terms

Aging accounts receivable	Imprest petty cash system
Allowance for uncollectible accounts	Income statement approach
Allowance method	Maker
Balance sheet approach	Maturity date
Bank reconciliation	Maturity value
Bank statement	Outstanding checks
Contingent liability	Payee
Deposits in transit	Petty cash
Direct write-off method	Timing differences
Discount a note	Uncollectible accounts expense
Dishonor a note	Write-off
Face amount (principal amount)	

Comprehensive Review Problem

Rare Teas and Spices sells to retailers through its wholesale warehouse and to the general public at its own retail store. Selected transactions relating to the company's receivables are given below. The company uses the allowance method in accounting for uncollectible accounts, and the balance in accounts receivable on January 1 was $15,900. The balance at that time in the allowance for uncollectible accounts was $795.

January   5   Sold $5,000 of herbs to Otwell's Spot-of-Tea on credit.
          7   Wrote off $250 account receivable from P. Burke.

> 15 Received a sixty-day note from Tran's Oriental Restaurant in settlement of a $1,200 open account. The interest rate on the note is 6 percent.
>
> February 10 P. Burke unexpectedly paid the $250 account receivable, which previously had been written off.
>
> 24 Sales to Easy Credit Card holders amounted to $7,800. Easy Credit charges a 3 percent fee.
>
> 28 The bank statement showed that P. Burke's check had been returned NSF. Rare Teas and Spices decided to try to collect on the account one more time.
>
> March 16 Tran's Oriental Restaurant paid the sixty-day note with interest.
>
> 30 Received full payment from Easy Credit Card for February 24 sale.
>
> April 1 Received a ninety-day $5,000 note from Otwell's Spot-of-Tea in settlement of his open account balance. The interest rate on the note was 8 percent per annum.
>
> 22 Collected $5,300 on accounts receivable from J. Charlton.
>
> May 1 Discounted Otwell's $5,000 note to the bank at 9 percent discount rate.
>
> 15 Credit sales of $18,500 were made to Wholesome Groceries.
>
> 30 Tom Lee's account receivable of $825 was written off as uncollectible.
>
> 31 Accepted a sixty-day note receivable for $600 from M. Allen in settlement of an open account. The interest rate on the note is 8 percent.
>
> June 30 Aging of accounts receivable indicates that the balance in the allowance for uncollectible accounts should be $950.

Required:

Journalize the above transactions. Assume the company closes its books on June 30 and include any adjusting entries relating to receivables. Use T accounts to show the effect of these transactions on the balance in accounts receivable and the allowance account.

Solution to Comprehensive Review Problem

RARE TEAS AND SPICES

General Journal

Date		Transaction Accounts	Debit	Credit
Jan.	5	Accounts receivable, Otwell's Spot-of-Tea	5,000	
		Sales		5,000
		Sale of merchandise		
	7	Allowance for uncollectible accounts	250	
		Accounts receivable, P. Burke		250
		Wrote off uncollectible account		
	15	Notes receivable	1,200	
		Accounts receivable, Tran's Oriental Restaurant		1,200
		Issued 60-day note at 6% in settlement of $1,200 open account		
Feb.	10	Accounts receivable, P. Burke	250	
		Allowance for uncollectible accounts		250
		To reverse previous write-off of account		
	10	Cash	250	
		Accounts receivable, P. Burke		250
		Payment on account		

	24	Accounts receivable, Easy Credit Card	7,566	
		Interest expense	234	
		Sales		7,800
		Sale of goods on credit cards		
		(Interest 3% × $7,800 = $234)		
	28	Accounts receivable, P. Burke	250	
		Cash		250
		Check returned NSF		
Mar.	16	Cash	1,212	
		Note receivable		1,200
		Interest revenue		12
		Collected 60-day note plus interest from Tran's Oriental		
		Restaurant		
		(Interest = 6% × 60/360 × $1,200 = $12)		
	30	Cash	7,566	
		Accounts receivable, Easy Credit Card		7,566
		Payment received from Easy Credit Card		
Apr.	1	Notes receivable	5,000	
		Accounts receivable, Otwell's Spot-of-Tea		5,000
		Received a 90-day note at 8% interest in settlement of		
		account		
	22	Cash	5,300	
		Accounts receivable, J. Charlton		5,300
		Collected on accounts		
May	1	Cash	5,023.50	
		Interest revenue		23.50
		Notes receivable		5,000
		Discounted note, proceeds computed as follows:		
		Principal .... $ 5,000.00		
		Interest at maturity 100.00		
		Maturity value 5,100.00		
		Bank interest ($5,100 × .09 × 60/360) . (76.50)		
		Proceeds from bank .... $ 5,023.50		
	15	Accounts receivable, Wholesome Grocers	18,500	
		Sales		18,500
		Credit sales		
	30	Allowance for uncollectible accounts	825	
		Accounts receivable, T. Lee		825
		Wrote off uncollectible account		
	31	Notes receivable	600	
		Accounts receivable, M. Allen		600
		Received 60 day 8% note in settlement of an account		

Adjusting Entries

June	30	Uncollectible accounts expense	980	
		Allowance for uncollectible accounts		980
		To provide for uncollectibles:		
		Required balance $950		
		Present balance, debit 30		
		Required increase $980		
	30	Interest receivable	4	
		Interest revenue		4
		Accrue interest on May 31 note of M. Allen		
		(30/360 × .08 × $600 = $4)		

Accounts Receivable			
Bal. 1/1	15,900		
1/5	5,000	1/7	250
2/10	250	2/15	1,200
2/24	7,566	2/10	250
2/28	250	3/30	7,566
5/15	18,500	4/1	5,000
		4/22	5,300
		5/30	825
		5/31	600
Bal. 6/30	26,475		

Allowance for Uncollectible Accounts			
		Bal. 1/1	795
1/7	250	2/10	250
5/30	825	6/30	980
		Bal. 6/30	950

Questions

Q8-1. Give three reasons the general ledger account for cash could show an amount different from that shown on the bank statement.

Q8-2. For what type of differences in cash between bank and books would journal entries be necessary? Give two examples.

Q8-3. What is petty cash? Describe an imprest petty cash system. Why is it useful?

Q8-4. Contrast the direct write-off and the allowance methods of accounting for uncollectible accounts.

Q8-5. Contrast the income statement and balance sheet approaches to the allowance method of accounting for uncollectible accounts.

Q8-6. Why is it a good idea to age accounts receivable periodically even if the income statement approach to accounting for uncollectible accounts is used?

Q8-7. When the allowance method is used, what is the journal entry to write off an uncollectible account? What is the effect on the income statement and balance sheet of this write-off?

Q8-8. List four specific characteristics of a note receivable.

Q8-9. Define the following terms: maker, payee, face amount, maturity value, and maturity date.

Q8-10. Explain what is meant by the phrase "discount a note." How does this process result in a contingent liability?

Exercises

E8-1. On January 1, the Merrill Company established a petty cash fund by writing and cashing a check for $100. On January 31, the petty cash box contained $15 in coins and currency and vouchers which were summarized as follows: postage expense, $25; supplies, $20; freight in on purchases, $35; and miscellaneous expenses, $5. Give the journal entries to record the establishment of the petty cash fund on January 1 and to record the replenishment of the fund on January 31, assuming the company uses a imprest petty cash system.

E8-2. Give the journal entries to record each of the following credit sales:

a. A $200 sale charged on a bank credit card. The bank card charges vendors 3 percent for its services.

b. A $500 sale charged on a nonbank credit card. The credit card company charges vendors 5 percent for its services.

E8-3. The Kimble Clothing Company, Inc., had one of its credit customers sign the note presented below in conjunction with a credit sale.

$4,000	New York, New York	December 4	19 82

Sixty days _____ After Date _____ We _____ Promise to Pay to

the Order of _____ Kimble Clothing Company, Inc. _____

_____ Four thousand and 00/100——————— _____ Dollars

For Value Received with Interest at _____ 12% _____ per annum

Payable at _____ Chase Manhattan Bank, New York _____ .

Fashion Five, Inc.

Joyce Hill, Pres.

1. Who is the maker of the note?

2. Who is the payee of the note?

3. What is the face value of the note?

4. What is the maturity date of the note?

5. What is the maturity value of the note?

E8-4. Give the maturity date and the total interest revenue for each of the following notes receivable. Show all calculations.

1. A 60-day note with a face value of $10,000 and an annual interest rate of 15 percent signed on August 1, 1982.

2. A 90-day note with a face value of $8,000 and an annual interest rate of 12 percent signed on September 16, 1982.

3. A 120-day note with a face value of $12,000 and an annual interest rate of 16 percent signed on March 5, 1982.

E8-5. The Rapp Company makes an adjusting entry at the end of each month to record uncollectible accounts expense. The following information was taken from the records of the company before adjusting entries were made at May 31, 1982.

a. Credit sales for May, $13,000.
b. Accounts receivable at May 31, $21,000.
c. Allowance for uncollectible accounts at May 31, $900.

Give the entry to record the uncollectible accounts expense for the Rapp Company for May under each of the following assumptions:

1. The company uses the income statement approach to accounting for uncollectible accounts and has found that approximately 1 percent of all credit sales will be uncollectible.

2. The company uses the balance sheet approach to accounting for uncollectible accounts and has found that approximately 5 percent of accounts receivable at any point in time will be uncollectible.

3. The company uses the direct write-off method of accounting for uncollectible accounts, and accounts determined to be uncollectible at May 31 amounted to $200.

E8-6. On July 1, 1982, Freret Distributors, Inc., had one of its credit customers, Daisy Drug Stores, Inc., sign a sixty-day, 12 percent note for $3,000, the balance in its open account. On August 30, 1982, the Daisy Drug Store paid the interest due on the note and $1,500 of the principal. A new sixty-day note was signed by them for the balance of the principal due. Give the journal entries to record these transactions, including the adjusting entry that would be made by Freret Distributors on July 31.

E8-7. On the December 31, 1981 balance sheet of the Lynch Company, cash was reported at $1,230 (the balance in its sole cash account). On January 1, 1982, the company established an imprest petty cash system by writing and cashing a check for $50. Disbursements from the petty cash fund from January 1 to February 15 are shown below:

Voucher #	Date	Account to be Charged	Amount
1	1/6	Postage expense	$ 1.10
2	1/11	Office supplies	10.60
3	1/15	Miscellaneous expense	2.70
4	1/17	Postage expense	2.40
5	1/21	Freight in	12.50
6	1/19	Miscellaneous expense	3.30
7	2/3	Postage expense	3.80
8	2/7	Office supplies	5.30
9	2/15	Miscellaneous expense	2.60

1. Give the journal entry to record the establishment of the petty cash fund on January 1.

2. If debits to the cash account during January totaled $5,280 and credits to the account during January totaled $4,920, what amount would be reported for cash on a January 31 balance sheet?

3. Give the journal entry to record the replenishment of the petty cash fund on February 15, if currency in the fund amounted to $4.70.

4. Assume that the company increased the amount of the petty cash fund by $25 on February 16. Give the journal entry to record this transaction.

E8-8. The Krantz Company uses the income statement approach to accounting for uncollectible accounts and makes an adjusting entry at the end of each month to record uncollectible accounts expense. Give the journal entries (in general journal form) to record the following external transactions and give the adjusting entry that would be made at August 31 to record the uncollectible accounts expense for the month. Experience has shown that approximately 2 percent of all credit sales will be uncollectible.

1. Sales for August amounted to $30,000, 60 percent of which were credit sales.

2. Collections on accounts receivable during August amounted to $9,000. Of this amount, $300 was collected from P. Whalen, whose account had previously been written off.

3. The account of F. Hank with a balance of $500 was written off on August 31.

E8-9. On May 1, 1982, the J. Curtin Company had one of its credit customers, B. Murphy, sign a note for the $4,000 due on his account. The note was due in sixty days and carried an annual interest rate of 12 percent. On May 31, the J. Curtin Company discounted the note to the JBT Bank. The bank charged 15 percent annual interest. On June 30, B. Murphy dishonored the note, and the J. Curtin Company was forced to pay the bank the maturity value of the note plus a protest fee of $10. On August 2, the Curtin Company collected the total amount due from B. Murphy. Assuming that J. Curtin Company uses a footnote to disclose its contingent liability with respect to discounted notes, give the journal entries that would be made to record all of the transactions with respect to the note.

E8-10. The Kimble Company uses the balance sheet approach to accounting for uncollectible accounts and makes adjusting entries at the end of each month to record uncollectible accounts expense. The unadjusted trial balance at December 31 shows accounts receivable at $54,000 and allowance for uncollectible accounts at $810. The following information is taken from the aging of accounts receivable.

	Amount	Percent Uncollectible
Current	$42,000	1
Over 30 days	9,000	5
Over 60 days	1,000	20
Over 90 days	2,000	50

1. Give the adjusting entry that would be made at December 31 with respect to uncollectible accounts.

2. Show how accounts receivable would be reported on the balance sheet at December 31.

Problems

P8-1. The Tubit Gift Shop makes a large number of credit sales on Pony Express Card and on the Fusa Card. The shop also has its own store accounts for credit sales. On November 8, the following credit sales were made:

a. Sale of $50, charged on a Fusa Card by M. Snow, sales slip No. 116.
b. Sale of $100, charged on a Pony Express card by E. Wilson, sales slip No. 117.
c. Sale of $25 charged on store account by C. Blanchard, sales slip No. 118.

Required:
1. Design a sales journal and a cash receipts journal for the Tubit Gift Shop that will facilitate the recording of all credit sales.

2. Assuming that both Pony Express and Fusa charge 5 percent for their services, enter the above transactions in the appropriate special journal.

P8-2. On April 30, the general ledger cash accounts of Interiors, Inc., showed a balance of $4,635. A bank statement dated April 30 was received from the First National Bank. The following information was determined by comparing the bank statement with company records:

   a. The cash balance on the bank statement as of April 30 was $5,720.

   b. The checks outstanding as of April 30 were as follows:

#731	Utility Company	$ 125
#733	J. Wort Company	1,300
#734	Thoms Advertising Agency	875

   c. The bank service charge for April was $5.

   d. The deposits mailed on April 29 and 30 for $580 and $720, respectively, did not appear on the bank statement.

   e. Check No. 711 for $230 had been erroneously recorded in the cash disbursement journal as $320. The check had been written to AA Supply Company for office supplies.

Required:

1. Prepare a bank reconciliation as of April 30.

2. Prepare the journal entries necessary to correct the cash balance at April 30.

P8-3. On March 1, the Wiltz Company accepted a 120-day, 15 percent note for $1,800 from one of its customers whose account receivable was overdue. On April 1, the Wiltz Company discounted the note at 18 percent. On June 29, the customer paid the note.

Required:

1. Give the journal entries to record the above transactions. (Show calculations. Round to nearest dollar.)

2. Give the journal entries that would be made had the customer defaulted on the note and the Wiltz Company been forced to pay the holder the maturity value of the note plus a $15 protest fee.

P8-4. The Mayo Company uses the income statement approach to accounting for uncollectible accounts. Uncollectible accounts expense is estimated at 1 percent of credit sales. The company makes adjusting entries at the end of each month. Below is a summary of the transactions of the company for the month of June that affect accounts receivable.

   a. Credit sales, $8,600.

   b. Collection of receivables, $9,120.

   c. Account written off, $125.

   d. Collection of account previously written off, $95.

Required:

1. Prepare journal entries in general journal form to record each of the above external transactions.

2. Prepare the adjusting entry to record uncollectible accounts expense for the month of June.

3. Set up a T account for accounts receivable with a May 31 balance of $12,730 and a T account for allowance for uncollectible accounts with a May 31 balance of $365. Post to these from the journal entries made in 1 and 2 above.

4. Show how accounts receivable would be reported on a balance sheet at June 30.

P8-5. Because of a cash flow problem, the Pailet Paint Company instituted a policy of obtaining promissory notes from customers whenever possible. These notes were then discounted by the Pailet Paint Company at its bank to speed up the cash inflow. The following transactions took place with respect to one such note.

March 6 Sold merchandise to B. Mack for $1,500. Mack signed a sixty-day, 12 percent note for the amount of the purchase.

April 6 Discounted the Mack note at the bank. The bank discount rate was 15 percent.

May 5 Received notice from the bank that Mack dishonored his note due that day. Made payment to the bank for the maturity value of the note plus a protest fee of $10.

July 5 Collected the full amount due from Mack plus interest of 12 percent on the maturity value of the note from May 5.

Required:
1. Prepare in general journal form the entries necessary to record the transactions of April 6, May 5, and July 5.

2. Explain how the contingent liability with respect to the Mack note would be disclosed in the April 30 financial statements of the Pailet Paint Company.

P8-6. The Lattum Company sells to retailers on open account. Any customer who fails to pay invoices within sixty days is required to sign a promissory note for the overdue amount. There are no finance charges for amounts paid within sixty days, and no cash discounts are offered. The following transactions took place with respect to the account of the Terry Company.

August 15 Sold merchandise to the Terry Company on account for $48,000.

October 16 Received a 12 percent, thirty-day note from the Terry Company dated today in settlement of its account of $48,000.

November 15 The Terry Company paid $30,000 plus interest on the note and signed a new 12 percent, thirty-day note for the balance of $18,000.

December 14 The Terry Company defaulted on its note.

21 Amount due from the Terry Company was collected.

Required:
1. Prepare in general journal form the entries necessary to record the above transactions, assuming that the Lattum Company prepares financial statements and makes adjusting entries only on December 31.

2. Prepare in general journal form the entries necessary on October 31 and November 15, assuming that the Lattum Company prepares financial statements and makes adjusting entries at the end of its fiscal year on October 31.

P8-7. The following information pertains to the credit sales and accounts receivable of the Worth Company.

a. Accounts receivable balance at December 31, 1982, $64,780.

b. Allowance for uncollectible accounts balance at December 31, 1982, $950.

c. Credit sales during 1982, $542,000.

d. Accounts written off during 1982: T. Brent, $350; F. Faye, $175; B. Mort, $635.

f. Collection in 1982 of account written off in 1981: B. Will, $360.

f. Summary of aging of accounts receivable at December 31, 1982:

	Amount	Percent Uncollectible
Current	$51,520	1
Over 30 days	9,350	5
Over 60 days	2,160	20
Over 90 days	1,750	40

Required:

1. Assume the company uses the income statement approach to accounting for uncollectible accounts and estimates uncollectible accounts expense as ½ percent of credit sales. Prepare the journal entries to record the write-off of accounts, collection of accounts written off, and uncollectible accounts expense for 1982.

2. Assume the company uses the balance sheet approach to accounting for uncollectible accounts and estimates uncollectible accounts expense based on the aging of accounts receivable. Prepare the journal entries to record the write-off of accounts and the collection of accounts written off. Assuming the balance given in b above for the allowance account reflects these entries, record uncollectible accounts expense for 1982.

3. Assume the company uses the direct write-off method of accounting for uncollectible accounts. Prepare the journal entries to record the write-off of accounts, the uncollectible accounts expense for 1982 and the collection of accounts written off.

P8-8. The information necessary for preparing a bank reconciliation for the McDermiad Company at November 30, 1982, is given below.

a. The general ledger account, Cash-Hibernia Bank, showed a balance at November 30 of $3,231.00.

b. The Hibernia Bank statement dated November 30 showed a balance in the McDermiad account of $3,580.13.

c. Comparison of paid checks returned by the bank with company records showed that three checks issued in November had not been paid by the bank as of November 30. These were No. 515 for $28.15, No. 520 for $167.50, and No. 521 for $590.00.

d. Enclosed with the bank statement was a debit memorandum for $4.35 for service charges for November.

e. Also included with the bank statement was a debit memorandum for $315.37 for an insurance premium paid directly by the bank. The deduction did not apply to the McDermiad Company, and the bank was notified of its error.

f. A third debit memorandum included with the statement was attached to a check drawn by Max Delp, a customer of McDermiad. The check, marked NSF, was for $256.00.

g. A credit memorandum enclosed with the November bank statement indicated that a note receivable from Barry Robin, left with the bank for collection, had been collected. The proceeds of $1,020 were credited to the McDermiad account. Of the proceeds, $1,000 was principal and $20 was interest. One-half of the interest had been accrued by McDermiad on October 31.

h. A deposit of $916.80 made by the company on November 30 was not shown on the statement.

i. It was discovered that a check from Bob Jordy, a McDermiad customer, for $162 in payment of his account had been erroneously entered in the cash receipts journal as $126 on November 15.

Required:

1. Prepare a bank reconciliation as of November 30.

2. Prepare the journal entries necessary to correct the cash balance at November 30, assuming that an entry is made to record the NSF check.

P8-9. For purposes of monthly financial statements, the Wholesale Appliance Company uses the income statement approach to accounting for uncollectible accounts and records estimated uncollectible accounts expense at the end of each month. For purposes of its annual financial statement, the balance sheet approach is used. An aging of accounts receivable as of December 31 is prepared, and from this the appropriate balance for the allowance for uncollectible accounts is calculated. The balance in allowance for uncollectible accounts resulting from monthly entries under the income statement approach is then adjusted to the balance determined under the balance sheet approach. The company uses ½ percent of credit sales as an estimate of uncollectible accounts expense monthly. At year end, 1 percent of current accounts, 5 percent of accounts over thirty days, 30 percent of accounts over sixty days, and 60 percent of accounts over ninety days are estimated to be uncollectible. Below is the pertinent information about the accounts receivable of the company.

a. Accounts receivable balance at December 31, 1981, $29,700.

b. Allowance for uncollectible accounts balance at December 31, 1981, $1,120.

c. Credit sales during 1982, $287,000.

d. Collection of receivables during 1982, $282,680.

e. Accounts written off during 1982, Burns Company $1,500.

f. Collection of account previously written off, AA Appliance, $810.

g. Accounts receivable subsidiary ledger at December 31, 1982 (only portion related to current balances shown).

AIMES APPLIANCES, INC.   #3

Date			PR	Debit	Credit	Balance
1982		Balance				0
Dec.	18	Sale	S87	2,820		2,820

GAINES, INC.   #5

Date			PR	Debit	Credit	Balance
1982		Balance				4,190
Oct.	8	Sale	S85	1,680		5,870
	10	Payment	CR92		4,190	1,680
Nov.	12	Sale	S86	2,910		4,590
Dec.	2	Sale	S87	1,550		6,140

MOTCO, INC.   #6

Date			PR	Debit	Credit	Balance
1982		Balance				10,610
Dec.	8	Payment	CR95		10,610	
	10	Sale	S87	12,730		12,730

REED FURNITURE CO.   #7

Date			PR	Debit	Credit	Balance
1982		Balance				0
Apr.	21	Sale	S81	920		920

WILL'S APPLIANCES   #8

Date			PR	Debit	Credit	Balance
1982		Balance				3,720
Nov.	10	Sale	S86	4,710		8,430
	15	Payment	CR98		3,720	4,710
Dec.	2	Sale	S87	5,200		9,910

Required:

1. Prepare journal entries in general form to record credit sales, collection of receivables, accounts written off, and collection of accounts written off for 1982.

2. Prepare the adjusting entry to record the uncollectible accounts expense as it was estimated monthly. (One entry should be made that summarizes the monthly entries.)

3. Set up T accounts with December 31, 1981, general ledger balances for accounts receivable and allowance for uncollectible accounts. Post from the journal entries in 1 and 2 above to these two general ledger accounts.

4. Prepare an aging of accounts receivable similar to that shown in Figure 8-3 as of December 31, 1982. Include a calculation of allowance for uncollectible accounts based on the aging of accounts receivable.

5. Prepare the journal entry to adjust allowance for uncollectible accounts at December 31, 1982, to agree with amount based on the aging of accounts receivable.

6. Show how accounts receivable would be reported on the balance sheet at December 31, 1982.

7. What would be the amount of uncollectible accounts expense reported on the income statement for the year ended December 31, 1982?

CHAPTER 9

Inventory
and Cost
of Goods Sold

Chapter Outline

9.1 *The Inventory Costing Problem.* Review of the periodic and perpetual approaches to accounting for inventory; introduction of the need for inventory costing methods in financial accounting.

9.2 *Specific Identification and Weighted Average.* Discussion of the rationale for and significant characteristics of these inventory costing methods; illustration of the mechanics of applying each to an inventory problem.

9.3 *First-in, First-out and Last-in, First-out.* Discussion of the rationale for and significant characteristics of these inventory costing methods; illustration of the mechanics of applying each to an inventory problem.

9.4 *Special Inventory Considerations.* Examination of the types of inventory errors and their effect on financial statements; the lower of cost or market rule and its relationship to historical cost valuation.

9.5 *Inventory Estimating Techniques.* Discussion of the characteristics and uses of the gross profit and retail methods of estimating inventories; illustration of the mechanics of applying each to an inventory problem.

Accounting and the Real World

How LIFO Tarnished An Earnings Report

Last-in, first-out accounting makes sound business sense in a time of inflation because it more accurately reflects current earnings, minimizing income taxes. At the same time, however, it distorts reported asset values. Consolidated Refining Company, which employs LIFO, illustrates this phenomenon. Consolidated is a fabricator of products—made from gold, silver, and other precious metals—that are sold to jewelry manufacturers and electronics concerns. The company's main raw material is gold, which it buys at free market prices, passing along any fluctuations to customers.

Lately, the company has prospered, with steadily increasing revenues, earnings, and dividends. And Consolidated's stock, a beneficiary of the enthusiasm for gold, doubled between last November and early February, when it hit 21¾.

As the price of gold fell from its high, Consolidated's stock eased off, too. But on February 15 it dropped 3 points to 16. The previous day Consolidated had reported a 21 percent drop in fourth-quarter earnings per share to 26¢. This overshadowed the rest of the announcement that earnings rose 36 percent to $1.54 for all of 1979.

In fact, Consolidated could have reported a 60 percent profit increase to 53¢ a share in the fourth quarter had it not been for LIFO accounting. But in the last three months of 1979, Consolidated stockpiled gold in excess of its sales. Because of a complicated provision of LIFO, the company recorded the inventory at prices dating from the beginning of 1979, when gold prices were half what they were in the fourth quarter, when the gold was actually bought. The difference between purchase price and recorded price amounted to 27¢ a share, and it reduced Consolidated's fourth-quarter earnings by that amount.

Meanwhile, the stockpiled gold and the other inventory have greatly appreciated in value as precious metals prices have soared. "The paradox is that because of the gold purchases the company reported lower earnings and stated book value, but the actual asset value increased," says one shareholder. He estimates that the inventory, before fourth-quarter additions, is worth at least $30 million, yet as of September 30, 1979, it was carried on the books at $1.9 million.

A spokesman for Consolidated says he does not expect further inventory additions in 1980. Thus, the company could report a huge increase in fourth-quarter earnings in 1980.

The particular accounting problems of merchandising firms, with emphasis on inventories and cost of goods sold, were discussed in Chapter 6. Every merchandiser accounts for inventory using one of two basic inventory systems. These systems are called periodic and perpetual, and the choice between them represents the first inventory-related decision all merchandising firms must make. Once a basic inventory system is chosen, a second inventory-related decision must be made. This second decision, called an inventory costing choice, is discussed in this chapter and related to the two inventory approaches presented in Chapter 6. In addition, several other techniques that aid in accounting for inventory and cost of goods sold are introduced.

9.1 The Inventory Costing Problem

Before the problem of costing inventory is presented, the periodic and perpetual approaches to inventory should be reviewed.

Periodic Inventory Systems

Periodic systems record the revenue effect of sales of inventory as the sales occur, but do not immediately reflect the cost of sales in the accounting records. Instead, these systems record the cost of sales for an entire accounting period as an adjusting entry at the end of the period. The basis for this adjusting entry is the basic inventory formula which brings together all inventory amounts from the general ledger and a physical count of inventory at the end of the period to determine cost of goods sold.

The purpose of the basic inventory formula is the determination of the cost of sales for a period as follows:

Beginning inventory (from the inventory account in general ledger)

+ purchases (from the purchases account in general ledger)

+ freight in (from the freight or transportation account in general ledger)

− purchase returns (from the purchase returns account in general ledger)

− purchase discounts (from the purchase discounts account in general ledger, if gross method used)

= cost of goods available for sale for the period

− **ending inventory** (a physical count of inventory on hand at the end of the period multiplied by the cost of those items)

= cost of goods sold for the period

The important figure necessary in a periodic system which cannot be taken from the general ledger is ending inventory. It must be determined by a physical count of units remaining on hand at the end of the accounting period.

Perpetual Inventory Systems

Perpetual systems record both the revenue and the cost of each sale as it occurs. In these systems, each sale of merchandise is recognized as immediately affecting revenue, expense, and assets (inventory). At each sale, the selling price and cost of the products sold must be known, and cost of goods sold is determined by multiplying the cost of items by the number of units sold. At the same time, inventory is reduced by this same amount so that all inventory-related accounts are up-to-date.

The important figure to determine directly in perpetual systems is cost of goods sold for each sale. The cost of sales must be calculated directly, and the amount of inventory on hand results from the deduction of costs of sales from the inventory account in the general ledger.

The distinction between approaches is important to understanding the inventory costing problem. Both periodic and perpetual systems produce an amount for inventory on hand for the balance sheet and cost of goods sold for the income statement. The periodic approach values ending inventory directly by a physical count, and cost of goods sold results from the basic inventory formula. The perpetual approach values cost of goods sold directly with each sale, and ending inventory results from the deduction of these amounts from the inventory account.

The Need for an Inventory Costing Method

The inventory costing problem can now be placed in perspective. To illustrate the problem, suppose a merchandising firm engages in the inventory-related events for a single product depicted in Figure 9-1 for a one-month period. The products, themselves, are physically identical; but because they were purchased at different times, their purchase costs are different. This situation is not unusual for most merchandising businesses, although the differences in purchase costs in Figure 9-1 have been exaggerated to demonstrate the problem and its effect. Over an accounting

FIGURE 9-1
Inventory Transactions for a Month

Date	Event	Units	Cost or Revenue per Unit	Total Cost	Sales Revenue
March 1	Beginning inventory	1	$1	$ 1	
5	Purchase	2	1	2	
10	Purchase	3	2	6	
15	Sale	5	5		$25
20	Purchase	4	3	12	
25	Sale	3	5		15
31	Ending inventory*	2	*		

*The amount to be reported as ending inventory on the balance sheet and cost of goods sold on the income statement will depend upon the basic inventory system and the inventory costing method used.

period, many factors, such as inflation and the volume of purchases, may result in identical products being purchased at different costs.

Attaching Costs to Products The inventory problem in periodic and perpetual systems should become apparent. Assume that the merchandiser in Figure 9-1 uses the periodic approach. A physical count of inventory at the end of the month reveals that two units remain on hand; but, because the units are identical, the question is which two units at what cost. Do these two units represent beginning inventory, early purchases, purchases from the middle of the month, or month-end purchases? The particular purchase costs assigned to ending inventory will affect cost of goods sold and, thus, both major financial statements. A decision on which costs to assign to the units on hand must be made before the adjusting entry to record cost of goods sold can be recorded and the income statement and balance sheet prepared.

If the same firm used a perpetual system, with each sale a decision on which purchase costs to assign to the units sold would be necessary. The inventory costing problem is present in both periodic and perpetual systems as long as physically identical units of products are purchased at different costs over an accounting period.

Inventory Costing Methods

Two techniques are available to determine ending inventory and cost of goods sold in these situations. These techniques are based on either specific identification or on a series of assumptions and may be described as follows:

1. A merchandising firm may somehow differentiate otherwise identical products and keep track of each product's individual cost so that specific products can be recognized as they are sold or are counted as a part of year-end inventory. This technique is called **specific identification.**

2. A merchandising firm may make an assumption about how purchase costs are to be transferred to the income statement during an accounting period and treat costs as though products were actually sold in this manner. Such assumptions are called **cost flow assumptions,** and three are generally accepted in financial accounting. They are **weighted average, first-in, first-out (FIFO),** and **last-in, first-out (LIFO).**

All merchandisers, then, approach the inventory costing problem using one of the following four **inventory costing methods:**

1. specific identification

2. weighted average

3. first-in, first-out

4. last-in, first-out

The first of these costing methods represents an exact depiction of the **physical flow** of products, while the latter three methods are based on assumptions about the flow of purchase costs and, thus, may or may not reflect the actual physical flow of products. Nonetheless, all four are acceptable for financial accounting and income tax purposes. The rationales for and mechanics of each of these inventory costing methods are explained in the next two sections of this chapter using the sample transactions presented in Figure 9-1.

9.2 Specific Identification and Weighted Average

Determining the value of ending inventory for balance sheet purposes requires two steps. First, the quantity of goods on hand must be counted. Then, these goods must be assigned a cost. Determining the quantity of goods remaining on hand is called *taking the inventory*, and assigning a cost to these goods is called *costing the inventory*. Most people are familiar only with the first step because inventory costing is primarily an accounting function.

Specific Identification

Specific identification is a method of assigning costs to physical units of product. This method requires that each item in inventory be physically differentiated and that the specific cost of each item be attached to it in the accounting records. Then, when a unit is sold, its specific cost can be transferred to cost of goods sold and matched against the specific sales revenue produced by that unit.

Characteristics of the Specific Identification Method The advantages of the specific identification method are as follows:

1. The flow of inventory purchase costs through a merchandising firm reflects exactly the physical flow of products through the firm.

2. The matching concept so important to accrual accounting is implemented completely, because each individual item's specific purchase cost is matched against the item's revenue as sales take place.

There is, however, a major drawback to the specific identification approach. This drawback concerns the practicalities of actually carrying out the method. Where inventory consists of many identical items with low costs which sell at a high volume, it may be impossible (or, at best, very expensive) to implement specific identification. Specific identification may be practical only where inventory is made up of high-cost items in relatively small quantities which sell at a low volume. For example, car dealerships and jewelry stores with highly differentiated products would likely use specific identification, while supermarkets and department stores would not.

Specific Identification Illustrated

Once an accounting system is able to keep track of the specific purchase costs of individual products, actually implementing specific identification is fairly easy.

Periodic Suppose that the two items in ending inventory from the example in Figure 9-1 come from the March 5 purchase (one unit) and the March 20 purchase (one unit). Ending inventory would be valued as follows if the firm used a periodic inventory system and specific identification costing.

March 31 Ending inventory	$4
(1 unit at $1 from March 5	
1 unit at $3 from March 20)	

Cost of goods sold can be calculated using the basic inventory formula and the appropriate adjusting entry made.

Beginning inventory	$ 1
Purchases	
2 units at $1	
3 units at $2	
4 units at $3	20
Cost of goods available for sale	21
Ending inventory	4
Cost of goods sold	$17

March 31 Inventory (ending)	4	
Cost of goods sold	17	
Purchases		20
Inventory (beginning)		1

Perpetual If the firm used a perpetual system with the specific identification method, the numerical results for ending inventory and cost of goods sold would be exactly the same. The approach, however, would be different, because with each sale, an entry would be made to record the cost of the sale as follows:

March 15 Cost of goods sold	8	
Inventory		8
(1 unit at $1 from March 1		
1 unit at $1 from March 5		
3 units at $2 from March 10)		
March 25 Cost of goods sold	9	
Inventory		9
(3 units at $3 from March 20)		
March 31 Ending inventory	$4	
(1 unit at $1 from March 5		
1 unit at $3 from March 20)		

An entry to record the sales revenue from the sale would also be made at each of the above dates. If the above entries were posted to the general ledger, the results for inventory and cost of goods sold would be identical to those under a periodic system. Because each unit is specifically identified, the numerical results for ending inventory and cost of goods sold are not affected by the inventory system used.

Weighted Average

Sometimes it may not be possible or even desirable to specifically identify each unit of inventory. In these situations, some assumption must be made about the flow of costs through the business so that ending inventory and cost of goods sold may be determined. One such assumption is called weighted average.

Where a merchandising inventory consists of products that are physically mixed, such as gallons of gasoline, pounds of chemicals, or bushels of grain, it may be impossible to distinguish between different purchases of inventory. In effect, as new units of inventory are added, they become inextricably mixed with inventory already on hand so that, as products are sold, particular units from individual purchases cannot be identified. Because the products, themselves, are mixed, it is logical to apply a cost flow assumption that mixes the purchase costs of the goods. This is exactly what the weighted average assumption does.

Weighted Average Illustrated

With weighted average costing, each unit of ending inventory and each unit sold are assigned a cost equal to the average of the purchase costs of all units of inventory acquired. Each unit is valued at a mixture (average) of all costs.

Periodic Return to the company presented in Figure 9-1, and now assume that weighted average costing is to be used with the periodic approach. In this instance, ending inventory and cost of goods sold would be valued as follows:

Cost of goods available for sale ($1 + $2 + $6 + $12)	$21.00
Units available for sale (1 + 2 + 3 + 4)	10
Average cost of units available ($21 ÷ 10)	$ 2.10
Cost of goods sold (8 units × $2.10)	$16.80
March 31 Ending inventory (2 units × $2.10)	$ 4.20

Notice that, in weighted average costing under the periodic approach, each unit of inventory and each unit sold carry the same average cost for the period. One weighted average cost is computed each accounting period. The following adjusting entry would be made at the end of the period.

March 31 Inventory (ending)	4.20	
Cost of goods sold	16.80	
Purchases		21
Inventory (beginning)		1

Perpetual The weighted average costing assumption is generally easy to apply in periodic inventory systems and reflects reality quite well for those situations where products are, themselves, mixed. When the average approach is applied in perpetual systems, however, the calculations can become complex if purchases and sales are frequent. Because perpetual systems require an entry for cost of goods sold with each sale, an average reflecting all acquisitions of inventory to the date of each sale must be computed. This average is called a **moving average** because each new purchase (unless it happened to be at exactly the previously computed average cost) will cause the average cost to "move" or change somewhat. An illustration of the moving average calculation used by the perpetual approach is given below, together with the required journal entries.

March 15 Cost of goods sold	7.50	
Inventory		7.50
(5 units at $1.50)		

To make this entry, a weighted average of all purchase costs of inventory on hand as of this date must be calculated by dividing the cost of units on hand by the number of units on hand.

Cost of units on hand as of March 15	
($1 + $2 + $6)	$9
Units on hand as of March 15 (1 + 2 + 3)	6
Weighted average cost	$1.50
Units sold	5

March 25 Cost of goods sold	8.10	
Inventory		8.10
(3 units at $2.70)		

Again, because sales have occurred, it is necessary to have a weighted average cost ready. However, a purchase has taken place since the last sale, and that new purchase will cause the average cost to move. The new average cost of products available for sale must be calculated.

Cost of units on hand:	
1 unit at March 15 average cost	$ 1.50
4 units at $3 from March 20	12.00
Total cost of units on hand	$13.50

Units on hand:	
Remaining after March 15 sale	1
Purchase of March 20	4
Total units on hand	5

Weighted average cost ($13.50 ÷ 5)	$ 2.70
Units sold	3
Units on hand	2

March 31 Ending inventory (2 units × $2.70)	$ 5.40

After each average, the units sold as well as those remaining are assigned the average cost. Goods on hand always enter the next average calculation at the amount of the previous weighted average cost. With each new average, the previous average cost is replaced by the new amount. If, for example, a sale of one unit had taken place on March 26 from the two units remaining on hand at March 25, the cost of goods sold for the sale would be $2.70.

Characteristics of Weighted Average Weighted average periodic costing requires only one average calculation for each accounting period, while in weighted average perpetual costing, a new average must be calculated each time products are sold. As a result, the figures for ending inventory and cost of goods sold are likely to be different using average costing under the two basic inventory systems even though the underlying transactions are identical. For the sample company, the periodic approach resulted in different figures for ending inventory and cost of goods sold from those realized using the perpetual approach.

The weighted average cost flow assumption is most appropriate for merchandising situations where inventory units are physically mixed. In these situations, an "average" product sold for an average cost implements the matching concept reasonably well. Weighted average is a cost flow assumption, however, and therefore may be applied to inventory situations where goods are not physically mixed and still be acceptable for financial accounting and income tax purposes.

The only significant disadvantage to weighted average costing can come when the method is applied in a perpetual system with frequent purchases and sales. The calculations become complex, and computer assistance may be required to implement inventory accounting.

Concept Summary

Comparison of Specific Identification and Weighted Average Inventory Costing Methods		
	Specific Identification	*Weighted Average*
Periodic Inventory System	This combination is not likely to be found. If a product can be specifically identified, then it is likely to be accounted for perpetually.	Only one average calculation is necessary for each accounting period.
		Ending inventory and cost of goods sold will be different from perpetual system because of different calculation.
		Simple calculations make this combination easy to implement.
Perpetual Inventory System	Theoretically sound; flow of inventory purchase costs reflects the physical flow of products exactly.	Calculates a new average each time products are sold (called a moving average).
	Very difficult to implement; useful only where there are high-cost items in small quantities which sell at low volume.	Ending inventory and cost of goods sold will be different from periodic system because of different calculation.
		Complex calculations make this combination difficult; computer assistance is necessary.

9.3 First-in, First-out and Last-in, First-out

The two most widely used inventory costing assumptions are first-in, first-out (FIFO) and last-in, first-out (LIFO). These assumptions are available to companies that cannot specifically identify products or do not wish to calculate averages.

First-in, First-out

The costing method called first-in, first-out (FIFO) is based on the assumption that the first purchase costs of product into the firm chronologically (by purchase) will be the first costs out (by sale) and transferred to cost of goods sold. Under FIFO, as sales of inventory occur, the purchase costs of the oldest units still on hand become attachable to the units sold, from the oldest to most recent. In this way, all purchase costs of inventory are ultimately passed through the business in an orderly, predictable manner.

The general result of applying FIFO is that ending inventory on the balance sheet will be valued at the cost of the most recent purchases made by the merchandiser during the year. Cost of goods sold will then be valued at the cost of goods on hand at the beginning of the period and the cost of earlier purchases of the period.

FIFO Illustrated

Using the transactions given in Figure 9-1, note how FIFO works in a periodic inventory system. Ending inventory and cost of goods sold would be valued as follows:

March 31 Ending inventory .... $ 6
    (2 units at $3 from March 20)

The basic inventory formula can be used to compute cost of goods sold for the period.

Beginning inventory	$ 1
Purchases	20
Cost of goods available for sale	21
Ending inventory	6
Cost of goods sold	$15

The $15 figure for cost of goods sold could also have been computed directly as follows by adding the purchase costs of the first eight inventory acquisitions of the period:

1 unit at $1 from beginning inventory	$ 1
2 units at $1 from March 5	2
3 units at $2 from March 10	6
2 units at $3 from March 20	6
Cost of goods sold	$15

The adjusting entry at March 31 would be

March 31 Inventory (ending)	6	
Cost of goods sold	15	
Purchases		20
Inventory (beginning)		1

Perpetual Using FIFO with perpetual systems is slightly more involved. The basic idea that the cost of the earliest purchases should become cost of goods sold first still holds, but first-in, first-out must be applied to each sale individually under the perpetual approach. Below are the journal entries that would result from FIFO costing in a perpetual system for our sample company.

March 15	Cost of goods sold	7	
	Inventory		7
	(1 unit at $1 from beginning inventory		
	2 units at $1 from March 5		
	2 units at $2 from March 10)		
March 25	Cost of goods sold	8	
	Inventory		8
	(1 unit at $2 from March 10		
	2 units at $3 from March 20)		
March 31	Ending inventory		$6
	(2 units at $3 from March 20)		

Characteristics of FIFO The particular inventory system used by a merchandising firm does not affect the valuation of ending inventory and cost of goods sold with FIFO costing. Because the earliest purchases become expenses first under FIFO, the balance sheet and income statement reflect the same values under both periodic and perpetual systems. Of course, the procedures for each of the systems are quite different. Remember that FIFO is a *cost* flow assumption and, therefore, may be used by any merchandiser to value inventory and cost of goods sold even if the *physical* flow of goods is different. It is not necessary to show that goods are actually sold in the order assumed by the costing method.

Advantages of FIFO Over the years, FIFO has been the single most popular inventory costing method. Its popularity has slipped recently in favor of LIFO for reasons that will be clear from the discussion of LIFO which follows. Nonetheless, FIFO still has significant advantages that account for its continued widespread use.

Most merchandisers actually attempt to sell their oldest goods first and hold in inventory the most recently purchased products. This is particularly true where perishable goods are involved; however, it is also generally true for all types of products. Because FIFO assumes that costs are flowing through the business this way, the method very closely reflects what is happening for most merchandising firms. The inventory records accurately depict the actual physical movement of goods through the business.

FIFO is quite simple to implement in either periodic or perpetual systems, and a given set of transactions always produces the same numerical valuation for ending inventory and cost of goods sold. The balance sheet and income statement are not affected by the inventory system chosen.

Where prices are consistently rising (a likely state of affairs for some time to come), FIFO always transfers to cost of goods sold the oldest, and therefore the least expensive, purchase costs of inventory. With rising prices, goods purchased later in an accounting period will have higher purchase costs than those acquired earlier. As a result, FIFO values cost of goods sold at the lowest possible dollar amount for a given set of inventory transactions and values ending inventory at the cost of the most recent purchases. Cost of goods sold is not "understated" in the sense of an error, but is simply stated at the lowest possible costs for any particular inventory situation. Net income, an important figure in financial accounting, is then stated as high as it can be within generally accepted accounting procedures for inventory. A high net income figure may have significant advantages for some businesses.

This last "advantage" of FIFO does have a cost, however. A low cost of sales figure means that income subject to taxes will be higher than it might be if another costing method had been used and, thus, income taxes will also be higher. The higher net income figure resulting from the use of FIFO costing is acquired at the price of higher income taxes for the business.

Last-in, First-out (LIFO)

The polar extreme from FIFO is the costing method last-in, first-out (LIFO). LIFO is based on the assumption that the last costs into the firm chronologically (by purchase) will be the first costs out (by sale) and transferred to cost of goods sold. Under LIFO, the purchase cost of the newest units on hand become attachable to the units sold first, and costs are transferred out to cost of goods sold from the most recent purchases to the oldest. Costs flow through the business in an orderly, systematic manner, but in the direction opposite from that observed with FIFO.

LIFO Illustrated

LIFO results in ending inventory being valued at older purchase costs. The goods in inventory may be new, but the costs attached to them under LIFO can be the costs of goods purchased many years earlier and never transferred to cost of goods sold. Cost of goods sold is then valued at the cost of the purchases of the current period.

Periodic Applying LIFO costing in a periodic system to the sample company in Figure 9-1 would result in ending inventory and cost of goods sold being valued as follows:

March 31 Ending inventory	$2
(1 unit at $1 from beginning inventory	
1 unit at $1 from March 5)	

Using the basic inventory formula, it is possible to compute cost of goods sold for the period.

Beginning inventory	$ 1
Purchases	20
Cost of goods available for sale	21
Ending inventory	2
Cost of goods sold	$19

The $19 figure for cost of goods sold could also be calculated directly by summing the purchase costs of the last eight inventory acquisitions of the period.

4 units at $3 from March 20	$12
3 units at $2 from March 10	6
1 unit at $1 from March 5	1
Cost of goods sold	$19

The adjusting entry at March 31 would be

March 31 Inventory (ending)	2	
Cost of goods sold	19	
Purchases		20
Inventory (beginning)		1

Perpetual With a perpetual inventory system, the last-in, first-out idea must be applied each time a sale is made. To record the cost of sales as they occur, the purchase costs of the most recent purchases to the date of the sale are transferred to cost of goods sold first. LIFO-perpetual works backwards from the date of each sale rather than from the end of the accounting period. Below are the journal entries that would result from LIFO costing in a perpetual system for the sample company.

March 15 Cost of goods sold	8	
Inventory		8
(3 units at $2 from March 10		
2 units at $1 from March 5)		
March 25 Cost of goods sold	9	
Inventory		9
(3 units at $3 from March 20)		
March 31 Ending inventory		$4
(1 unit at $3 from March 20		
1 unit at $1 from beginning inventory)		

Characteristics of LIFO The valuation for ending inventory and cost of goods sold is different between periodic and perpetual systems under LIFO costing. The reason for this discrepancy is that last-in, first-out is applied only once at the end of the accounting period in the periodic approach, but is applied each time a sale is made in perpetual systems. Like all costing methods, LIFO may be applied to any merchandising situation even though the physical flow of goods is known to be different from the assumed flow of costs. Cost flow assumptions may or may not approximate the actual movement of products through the business.

It is interesting to note that FIFO and LIFO represent two ends of a spectrum of possible cost flow assumptions. These assumptions could not be further apart, yet either may be chosen under generally accepted accounting principles. This fact reveals something about GAAP that may not have been apparent from earlier chapters. Generally accepted accounting principles are not precise guidelines with one prescribed procedure for each accounting circumstance. Instead, they represent an umbrella of alternative procedures from which a business may pick and choose the accounting treatment that seems most appropriate for its events and transactions.

Advantages of LIFO LIFO has grown in popularity as an inventory costing method primarily because of the advantages it offers.

LIFO transfers to cost of goods sold the purchase costs of the most recent acquisitions of inventory and works backward from there. In times of rising prices, the most recent purchases are also the most expensive purchase costs. As a result, cost of goods sold is valued at the highest possible dollar amount for a given set of circumstances, and net income is as low as possible when LIFO is used. Low net income may not seem to be much of an advantage, but consider that, with a high cost of goods sold, income subject to taxes is low. This means that, with LIFO costing, income taxes are as low as can be achieved. LIFO will result in lower income taxes than other inventory cost flow assumptions as long as prices are increasing. This factor alone accounts for most of LIFO's popularity.

LIFO transfers to cost of goods sold recent purchase costs which tend to approximate the costs to replace the goods being sold. For a going concern, inventory sold must be constantly replaced by new purchases. Some businessmen and accountants feel that the matching concept is best carried out if an approximation of the cost of replacing the goods sold is matched against the revenue produced. Ultimately, this current period revenue must be used to purchase new inventory to be sold in future periods. There is some theoretical support for this idea of using **replacement cost** in accounting, and LIFO comes closest of all costing methods to approximating it. To those who believe in replacement cost, its use constitutes an advantage. In fact, the Securities and Exchange Commission in 1976 instituted a requirement that many of the largest companies in the United States disclose the replacement cost of their inventories on hand at the balance sheet date and show what cost of goods sold would be on a replacement cost basis. These replacement cost figures are required as supplementary information to financial statements.

Disadvantages of LIFO There are some significant drawbacks to the use of LIFO which should be considered and balanced against its advantages.

Accompanying lower income taxes is lower reported net income than would appear under other costing methods. To the extent that owners and other investors react negatively (or perhaps less positively) to a lower net income figure, the use of LIFO can be a disadvantage. There is some disagreement as to whether investors actually do react to reported lower net income which results from a choice among accounting procedures (rather than from underlying facts), however.

To some extent, business management can, under LIFO, manipulate the valuation of cost of goods sold and net income by the timing of purchases of inventory at year's end. Particularly in periodic systems, management can accelerate purchases at the end of an accounting period and transfer the costs of these products immediately to cost of goods sold. If prices are rising, the result would be to increase cost of sales and decrease net income. On the other hand, a decision could be made to defer purchases to the beginning of the next accounting period and transfer older, less expensive costs to cost of goods sold. No other costing method offers this degree of possible manipulation.

Last-in, first-out contradicts the likely physical flow of goods in most merchandising firms. Few businesses actually sell their newest products first and hold their oldest products in inventory. This lack of reflection of physical movement by the accounting records does not prevent the use of LIFO, but does cause some concern.

If a business uses LIFO for many years and consistently transfers to cost of goods sold the costs of the most recent purchases, the costs of the oldest purchases will remain attached to the units on hand in inventory. As a result, inventory on the balance sheet may be valued at the purchase costs of many years ago. This could make the balance sheet figure for inventory misleading to external users. Because inventory is one of the largest assets on the balance sheet, the total asset figure for a merchandising firm may not give a useful picture of resources. Under LIFO, the valuation for inventory will be lower than would be true with other costing methods as long as prices are rising.

Inventory Costing Methods Compared

Figure 9-2 brings together all of the various valuations of ending inventory and cost of goods sold which could result from the transactions of the sample company given in Figure 9-1. To focus on the differences that can result, it has been assumed that no operating expenses exist. The following important points about inventory systems and costing methods are illustrated by Figure 9-2.

1. All of the different results for inventory and cost of goods sold were derived from the same sample company with the same set of events. It is possible for a given set of facts to be reported quite differently within the umbrella of generally accepted accounting principles. By choosing one

FIGURE 9-2
Summary of Results Under Various Combinations of Basic Systems and Costing Methods

	Financial Statement Item	Specific Identification	Weighted Average	FIFO	LIFO
Periodic	Sales revenue	$40.00	$40.00	$40.00	$40.00
	Cost of goods sold	17.00	16.80	15.00	19.00
	Income before taxes	23.00	23.20	25.00	21.00
	Income taxes (assume 50%)	11.50	11.60	12.50	10.50
	Net income	$11.50	$11.60	$12.50	$10.50
	Ending inventory	$ 4.00	$ 4.20	$ 6.00	$ 2.00
Perpetual	Sales revenue	$40.00	$40.00	$40.00	$40.00
	Cost of goods sold	17.00	15.60	15.00	17.00
	Income before taxes	23.00	24.40	25.00	23.00
	Income taxes (assume 50%)	11.50	12.20	12.50	11.50
	Net income	$11.50	$12.20	$12.50	$11.50
	Ending inventory	$ 4.00	$ 5.40	$ 6.00	$ 4.00

inventory costing method over another, a company can alter (sometimes significantly) its reported financial statement results. The principle of consistency in accounting, however, dictates that, once a costing method is chosen, it should be applied consistently each reporting period. Because inventory costing methods are not the only area in which this kind of choice is possible, it should be clear that there is no one concept of "cost," nor is there one true accounting net income.

2. The dollars assigned to ending inventory and cost of goods sold under specific identification costing are not affected by the basic inventory system chosen. Periodic and perpetual systems yield identical results. The same is true under FIFO costing. However, the choice of inventory system does affect the valuation of ending inventory and cost of goods sold (and therefore, the balance sheet and income statement) when weighted average and LIFO costing methods are applied.

3. When prices are rising, as was true in the sample company, FIFO and LIFO provide the extremes of possible inventory and cost of goods sold valuation. FIFO results in the highest income taxes, net income, and ending

Concept Summary

Comparison of FIFO and LIFO		
	FIFO	*LIFO*
Matches Physical Flow of Goods	Approximately because oldest goods are usually sold first.	Only in unusual circumstances; normally, opposite of physical flow.
Use of Periodic or Perpetual System	Numerical results for cost of goods sold and ending inventory are not affected by the basic inventory system used.	Numerical results for cost of goods sold and ending inventory will be different under periodic and perpetual.
Cost of Goods Sold When Prices are Increasing	Low because oldest and least expensive costs are charged to expense first.	High because most recent and most expensive costs are charged to expense first.
Income Taxes When Prices are Increasing	High because of low cost of goods sold.	Low because of high cost of goods sold.
Net Income When Prices are Increasing	Same as income taxes.	Same as income taxes.
Inventory Value on Balance Sheet When Prices are Increasing	High because most recent and most expensive costs remain in inventory at year's end.	Low because oldest and least expensive costs remain in inventory at year's end.

inventory, while LIFO produces the lowest income taxes, net income, and ending inventory. All other costing methods produce results equal to or between these extremes. The high income characteristic of FIFO and the low income taxes characteristic of LIFO account for the widespread use of these costing methods.

9.4 Special Inventory Considerations

The processing of inventory-related transactions affects both primary financial statements. Inventory is one of the largest assets on merchandising balance sheets, and cost of goods sold is the largest expense on the income statement. Inventory transactions are numerous and can be complex to process completely and correctly. Matters of point of sale, legal title, freight, returns, discounts, and physical counts of inventory all enter into the recording of inventory events and their reflection in financial statements.

From time to time, even the most sophisticated inventory systems or the people that operate them make errors. It is important to understand the types of inventory processing errors that can occur and the effects of these errors on the financial statements of merchandising businesses.

Types of Inventory Errors and Their Effect

Basically, three types of inventory errors may occur.

1. Errors may occur in the previous accounting period with the counting of inventory at the end of that period. When such an error goes undetected, the current period beginning inventory figure is not correct. This error will have an effect on current period figures for cost of goods sold, net income, and owners' equity.

2. Errors may occur in the current period as purchases, discounts, freight, and returns are recorded. These errors affect current period figures for inventory, cost of goods sold, net income, and owners' equity.

3. Errors may occur in the ending inventory figure for the current period with a resulting incorrect inventory figure on the balance sheet and errors in cost of goods sold, net income, and owners' equity for the current period. Also, because this ending inventory figure becomes the beginning inventory for the next period, cost of goods sold and net income for that period will be incorrect.

Any error that affects cost of goods sold (an expense) also affects net income (revenue minus expense). If net income is incorrect, then owners' equity must also be incorrect. An error in inventory at the end of a period affects the asset figure on the balance sheet.

Causes of Inventory Errors Errors in beginning or ending inventory could occur because of a miscount of units or because units were incorrectly costed (the inventory costing method was improperly applied). Also, goods purchased may have mistakenly not been included in the inventory count (goods purchased but not yet received by the business) or goods that should not be a part of inventory (consignment products) may have mistakenly been counted. Errors in purchases could have their origin in the incorrect treatment of discounts, freight, or returns, or in the failure to record a purchase transaction.

Three important points about inventory errors should be kept in mind.

1. The potential effect of an inventory error is widespread, but the most important effect is on the income statement.

2. Errors in ending inventory are clearly the most significant because they both affect financial statements in the year of the error and cause a misstatement in the income statement of the following period.

3. All inventory errors, if not discovered and corrected, reverse themselves in two accounting periods. The misstatements in the following period's statements offset those in the period of the error and subsequent financial statements are correct. Inventory errors are very difficult to discover after this offsetting has occurred.

Concept Summary

Inventory Errors and Their Effect on Financial Statements					
		INCOME STATEMENT		BALANCE SHEET	
Location of Error	Type of Error*	Cost of Goods Sold	Net Income	Inventory	Owners' Equity
Previous Period Ending Inventory, which is the same as Current Period Beginning Inventory	↑	↑	↓	No effect	No effect
	↓	↓	↑	No effect	No effect
Current Period Purchases	↑	↑	↓	No effect	↓
	↓	↓	↑	No effect	↑
Current Period Ending Inventory	↑	↓	↑	↑	↑
	↓	↑	↓	↓	↓

Errors in previous period beginning inventory and previous period purchases "wash out" and have no effect on the current period financial statements.

*↑ overstated   ↓ understated

Lower of Cost or Market

A second area of special consideration has to do with the valuation of inventories at their historical (acquisition) cost. The general rule that assets are valued at historical cost certainly applies to inventories as well. There is, however, one exception to this rule that may, in unusual circumstances, be applied to inventory. The exception is called **lower of cost or market** valuation. The lower of cost or market idea had its origin in the striving for conservatism by the accounting profession. The principle of **conservatism** implied that all valuations used in financial accounting should guard against overstatement of assets and income. Lower of cost or market valuation is an application of this principle to inventories.

Because of deterioration, obsolescence, or declining selling prices for a product, the cost to a merchandiser of replacing certain products already in inventory may be less than the original historical cost of those products. For lower of cost or market purposes, the cost of replacing an item already in inventory is called market. Market means the merchandiser's purchase market. The lower of cost or market rule, then, should really be stated as, "lower of original historical cost or replacement cost." In the early days of accounting when the balance sheet was the primary (perhaps the only) financial statement and creditors were the principal users of financial accounting, the feeling of conservatism dictated that inventory not be valued on the balance sheet at more than it could be replaced for in the current period. This principle is expressed in the lower of cost or market rule.

Mechanics of Lower of Cost or Market If a situation occurs where goods could actually be replaced for less than they originally cost, the lower of cost or market rule requires a write-down of inventory to its replacement cost and the creation of a special loss in the period in which the decline in value occurred. The rule may be applied to individual items of inventory, to groups of items, or to the entire inventory as a whole, at a company's discretion. Figure 9-3 illustrates the application of the lower of cost or market rule to inventory valuation.

Over the years, as the income statement increased in importance and other external users of financial accounting appeared, the lower of cost or market rule has been modified and limited. The result of these modifications has been to restrict the use of lower of cost or market valuation severely. It is unlikely that any company's entire inventory would have a replacement cost below its original historical cost so that, practically speaking, this exception to the cost basis of valuation is not a significant force in financial accounting. Nonetheless, lower of historical cost or re-

FIGURE 9-3
Applying the Lower of Cost or Market Rule

Item	Quantity On Hand	Original Cost	Market	Lower of Cost or Market By Item
X	50	$ 750	$ 650	$ 650
Y	60	300	320	300
Z	90	900	950	900
		$1,950	$1,920	$1,850

Possible inventory valuations under lower of cost or market are as follows:
1. If the rule is applied to individual items of inventory, the valuation would be $1,850.
2. If the rule is applied to the inventory as a whole, the valuation would be $1,920.
3. If the market valuation, either by item or for the inventory as a whole (the likely circumstance except for extremely unusual cases), were greater than the original historical cost, the valuation would be $1,950.

placement cost still exists as a part of generally accepted accounting principles and must be used where applicable.

9.5 Inventory Estimating Techniques

One of the important characteristics of the perpetual approach to inventory is that the accounting records are up-to-date and accurately reflect the actual state of affairs in inventory. With a perpetual system, financial statements can be prepared anytime without a physical count of inventory. This is not true with a periodic system. Here, the accounting records are not kept up-to-date, and a physical inventory count and inventory costing must take place before an income statement and balance sheet can be prepared. Most merchandising businesses prefer to (or may be required to) produce financial statements more often than once a year; however, taking a physical inventory can be a costly and time-consuming process. If a firm desires monthly or quarterly statements, a technique for estimating inventories on hand at the end of each month or quarter is necessary. Two such **inventory estimating techniques** are widely used by merchandising firms. The techniques are called the gross profit method and the retail method.

The Gross Profit Method

The gross profit method is based on the assumption that merchandisers experience a relatively stable average gross profit percentage and that this percentage can be used to estimate cost of goods sold and inventory. To implement this estimating technique, four steps are necessary.

1. The historical **gross profit percentage** for a business is multiplied by net sales for the period (month or quarter) to determine estimated gross profit for the period.

2. Estimated gross profit is then subtracted from net sales to determine estimated cost of goods sold for the period.

3. Beginning inventory and net purchases are taken from the records and added to determine cost of goods available for sale for the period.

4. Estimated cost of goods sold (Step 2) is then subtracted from the cost of goods available for sale (Step 3) to determine estimated ending inventory for the period. Notice that this is just the opposite of the procedure normally followed at year's end when a physical count of inventory takes place. At year's end, ending inventory is subtracted from cost of goods available for sale to get cost of goods sold.

Figure 9-4 illustrates the application of the gross profit method with a numerical example.

Usefulness of the Gross Profit Method In addition to providing inventory and cost of goods sold data for interim (monthly or quarterly) financial statements, the gross profit method has two other important uses. The

FIGURE 9-4
Gross Profit Method

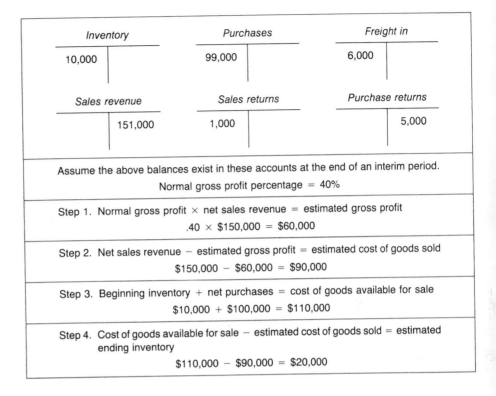

Inventory	Purchases	Freight in
10,000	99,000	6,000

Sales revenue	Sales returns	Purchase returns
151,000	1,000	5,000

Assume the above balances exist in these accounts at the end of an interim period.
Normal gross profit percentage = 40%

Step 1. Normal gross profit × net sales revenue = estimated gross profit
.40 × $150,000 = $60,000

Step 2. Net sales revenue − estimated gross profit = estimated cost of goods sold
$150,000 − $60,000 = $90,000

Step 3. Beginning inventory + net purchases = cost of goods available for sale
$10,000 + $100,000 = $110,000

Step 4. Cost of goods available for sale − estimated cost of goods sold = estimated
ending inventory
$110,000 − $90,000 = $20,000

method may be used to verify the reasonableness of inventory and cost of goods sold amounts determined at year's end by comparing these figures to the average results of previous periods. Also, the method can help determine the approximate inventory on hand if a fire or some other disaster destroys a firm's physical inventory, but not its accounting records.

The Retail Method   The second inventory estimating technique, called the retail method, is particularly useful in department stores and other merchandising situations where a wide variety of different types of products are sold at a high volume. In these situations, it is more convenient for inventory to be counted and valued at selling prices rather than at cost, because selling prices are already marked on the products. Instead of applying one of the costing methods discussed earlier in this chapter, it is possible to convert the figure for inventory at selling price (retail) to inventory at cost by using the current period **cost-to-selling-price percentage.** Inventory at cost, the figure needed for balance sheet purposes, can be determined without the use of an inventory costing method.

The retail method of estimating inventories can be used without a physical count of inventory if a business keeps its accounting records for beginning inventory and net purchases at both purchase cost and selling price. Beginning inventory and net purchases at selling prices would be supplemental to the normal ledger balances for these accounts.

The retail method can be implemented in four steps.

1. Determine from the accounting records the goods available for sale at purchase cost (from the general ledger) and at selling price (from supplementary records).

2. Compute the cost-to-selling-price (retail) percentage from the two figures given in Step 1. This percentage represents the relationship that exists between purchase cost and selling price for the current period.

3. Subtract net sales revenue from the goods available for sale at selling price given in Step 1. This figure gives the approximate ending inventory at selling price (retail).

4. Multiply the cost-to-selling-price percentage (Step 2) by the ending inventory at selling price (Step 3), and the result will be an estimate of ending inventory at purchase cost.

The retail method at work is illustrated in Figure 9-5 with a numerical example.

Usefulness of the Retail Method In practice, the retail method can become quite complex to apply because the selling prices of products fluctuate up and down during even a short interim period. The proper cost-to-selling-

FIGURE 9-5
Retail Method

Inventory	Purchases	Freight in
5,000	27,000	2,000

Sales revenue	Sales returns	Purchase returns
42,543	500	1,000

Assume the above balances exist in these accounts at the end of an interim period.

From supplementary records:
Inventory at selling price	$ 7,500
Net purchases at selling price	$39,643

Step 1. Beginning inventory + net purchases = goods available for sale
at cost: $5,000 + $28,000 = $33,000
at selling price: $7,500 + $39,643 = $47,143

Step 2. Goods available for sale at cost ÷ goods available for sale at selling price
= cost to selling price percentage
$33,000 ÷ $47,143 = 70%

Step 3. Goods available for sale at selling price − net sales revenue = ending inventory at selling price
$47,143 − $42,043 = $5,100

Step 4. Cost-to-selling-price percentage × ending inventory at selling price = ending inventory at cost
.70 × $5,100 = $3,570

price relationship can become difficult to determine. These changes in selling prices, known as additional markups and markdowns, must be added into the calculation of the retail method, making the technique more difficult to carry out.

The gross profit and retail methods are actually very similar in many ways. Both can be used to estimate inventory and cost of goods sold for interim financial statements, and both can be used to verify results derived from other methods of calculating these amounts. Also, like the gross profit method, the retail method can be used to estimate the purchase cost of inventories on hand at some point if the goods themselves are destroyed. This latter feature may be very important for insurance and tax purposes.

The primary difference between these techniques lies in the origin of the cost to selling price relationship which is at the heart of both methods. The gross profit method uses a gross profit percentage which is the result of the experience of previous years, while the retail method uses the cost to selling price percentage which exists in the current period. Although the basic purpose and use of these estimating techniques is the same, the retail method is more widely used by large merchandisers for financial statement purposes.

Concept Summary

Inventory Accounting Considerations
1. Purchase cost of inventory includes (Chapter 6) cash equivalent cost of product (invoice cost − purchase discounts) + freight-in cost on products paid by purchaser − cost of products returned by purchaser
2. Purchases may be accounted for by (Chapter 6) net method, which assumes that all purchase discounts will be taken and records purchases at cash equivalent cost, with discounts lost treated as interest expense gross method, which assumes that purchase discounts will not be taken and records purchases at invoice cost, with discounts taken treated in a contra account as reductions of the purchase cost of inventory
3. Basic inventory systems are (Chapter 6) periodic, which is a low-cost system for inventory items that are low value but high volume perpetual, which is a more sophisticated system for inventory items that are high value but low volume
4. Inventory costing methods are (Chapter 9) specific identification weighted average FIFO LIFO
5. Inventory estimating techniques are (Chapter 9) gross profit method retail method

Summary

All merchandising businesses must make two decisions in accounting for inventory. First, a basic inventory system must be chosen. Then, an inventory costing method must be selected. The selection of an inventory costing method is necessary whether a periodic or a perpetual inventory system is used.

Four inventory costing methods are generally accepted. The specific identification method requires that each unit of inventory be uniquely identified and its particular cost be recorded. As this unit is sold, its specific cost is transferred to cost of goods sold. Although specific identification is the most conceptually sound inventory costing method, the practical difficulties of using it limit its application to high-value, low-volume items.

The weighted average costing method is based on the assumption that the purchase costs of certain inventory items should be mixed and that each item should carry a cost equal to the average cost of all items purchased. This cost flow assumption is most applicable where inventory units are, themselves, physically mixed and, therefore, not distinguishable.

The FIFO costing method is based on the assumption that the purchase costs of the oldest units still on hand should be transferred to cost of goods sold first. Inventory at the end of the period is then valued at the cost of the most recent purchases. In times of rising prices, FIFO results in a cost of goods sold figure that is as low as it can be for a given set of inventory transactions and a net income figure that is as high as possible.

The LIFO costing method is based on the assumption that the cost of the most recent purchases of the period should be transferred to cost of goods sold first. Ending inventory is then valued at the oldest purchase costs not yet transferred to cost of goods sold. In times of rising prices, LIFO results in a cost of goods sold figure that is as high as it can be for a given set of inventory transactions and net income and income taxes figures that are as low as possible.

Weighted average, FIFO, and LIFO are based on cost flow assumptions that can be used regardless of the actual physical flow of products through the business.

Two inventory estimating techniques, the gross profit method and the retail method, can be used to determine ending inventory and cost of goods sold if detailed records are not available and a physical count is not possible.

Section III is concerned with the most important assets and equities on business balance sheets. Accounting procedures for property, plant, and equipment and the determination of related expenses are discussed in Chapter 10.

Key Terms

Beginning inventory	Ending inventory
Conservatism	First-in, first-out (FIFO)
Cost flow assumption	Gross profit method
Cost-to-selling-price percentage	Gross profit percentage

Inventory costing method
Inventory errors
Inventory estimating technique
Last-in, first-out (LIFO)
Lower of cost or market
Moving average

Physical flow
Replacement cost
Retail method
Specific identification
Weighted average

Comprehensive Review Problem

The following information relates to purchases and sales by Elephants, Inc., during the month of September:

		Purchases				Sales	
Date		Units	Price/Unit	Total Cost		Date	Units Sold
Sept. 1	Inventory on hand	300	$5	$ 1,500		Sept. 6	100
10	Purchase	500	6	3,000		11	300
15	Purchase	200	7	1,400		17	200
26	Purchase	400	8	3,200		23	300
30	Purchase	100	9	900		28	200
	Total	1,500		$10,000			1,100

Required:
Determine the amount of ending inventory and cost of goods sold under each of the following inventory systems and cost flow assumptions:

1. Weighted average periodic

2. FIFO periodic

3. FIFO perpetual

4. LIFO periodic

5. LIFO perpetual

Solution to Comprehensive Review Problem

1. *Weighted average periodic*

Cost of goods available for sale $10,000
Units available for sale 1,500
Cost/unit = cost ÷ number of units ($10,000 ÷ 1,500) .... $ 6.66
Cost of goods sold (1,100 × $6.66) .... $ 7,333
Ending inventory (400 × $6.66) .... $ 2,667

2. *FIFO periodic*

Ending inventory

Sept. 30 purchase	100 units @ $9	$ 900
Sept. 26 purchase	300 units @ $8	2,400
Ending inventory	400 units	$3,300

Cost of goods sold

Cost of goods available for sale	$10,000
Ending inventory	(3,300)
Cost of goods sold	$ 6,700

3. *FIFO perpetual* Under FIFO, inventory and cost of goods sold will be the same for both the periodic and perpetual inventory systems.

Ending inventory

Sept. 30 purchase	100 units @ $9	$ 900
Sept. 26 purchase	300 units @ $8	2,400
Ending inventory	400 units	$3,300

Cost of goods sold

Sept. 6 sale	100 units @ $5	$ 500
Sept. 11 sale	200 units @ $5	1,000
	100 units @ $6	600
Sept. 17 sale	200 units @ $6	1,200
Sept. 23 sale	200 units @ $6	1,200
	100 units @ $7	700
Sept. 28 sale	100 units @ $7	700
	100 units @ $8	800
Cost of goods sold	1,100 units	$6,700

4. *LIFO periodic*

Ending inventory

Sept. 1 beginning inventory	300 units @ $5	$1,500
Sept. 10 purchase	100 units @ $6	600
Ending inventory	400 units	$2,100

Cost of goods sold

Cost of goods available for sale	$10,000
Ending inventory	(2,100)
Cost of goods sold	$ 7,900

5. *LIFO perpetual*

Ending Inventory

Sept. 30 purchase	100 units @ $9	$ 900
Sept. 26 purchase	200 units @ $8	1,600
Sept. 1 purchase	100 units @ $5	500
Ending Inventory	400 units	$3,000

Cost of goods sold

Sept. 6 sale	100 units @ $5	$ 500
Sept. 11 sale	300 units @ $6	1,800
Sept. 17 sale	200 units @ $7	1,400
Sept. 23 sale	200 units @ $6	1,200
	100 units @ $5	500
Sept. 28 sale	200 units @ $8	1,600
Cost of goods sold	1,100 units	$7,000

Summary

Costing Method	Cost of Goods Sold	Ending Inventory
Weighted Average	$7,333	$2,667
FIFO Periodic	6,700	3,300
FIFO Perpetual	6,700	3,300
LIFO Periodic	7,900	2,100
LIFO Perpetual	7,000	3,000

Questions

Q9-1. Give the basic inventory formula. With which type of inventory system is it used?

Q9-2. Under what product cost conditions is it necessary for a business to choose an inventory costing method? Under what conditions do all inventory costing methods give the same results?

Q9-3. Describe the specific identification method of inventory costing. Name an advantage and a disadvantage of this method.

Q9-4. Describe the weighted average cost flow assumption. Under what circumstances is this cost flow assumption most appropriate?

Q9-5. Describe the FIFO cost flow assumption. Why might this cost flow assumption be popular in a period of rising prices? Why might it be unpopular?

Q9-6. Describe the LIFO cost flow assumption. Why might this cost flow assumption be popular in a period of rising prices? Why might it be unpopular?

Q9-7. List three types of inventory errors and give their effect on current period cost of goods sold and ending inventory.

Q9-8. What is the lower of cost or market rule?

Q9-9. Contrast the gross profit and retail methods of estimating inventory.

Q9-10. Give three circumstances in which an inventory estimating technique would be necessary or very useful.

Exercises

E9-1. Indicate whether each of the following statements describes a periodic or a perpetual inventory system.

    a. This system requires an adjusting (or closing) entry for ending inventory.

    b. This system provides more control features.

    c. Merchandise inventory is debited when a purchase is made.

    d. Cost of goods sold is computed as a residual.

    e. Cost of goods sold is computed directly.

    f. Ending inventory is computed as a residual.

    g. A sale requires two entries.

    h. Freight on inventory purchases is entered in a separate account.

    i. An income statement may be prepared without taking a physical inventory.

    j. A department store is more likely to use this type of system.

    k. An automobile dealer is more likely to use this type of system for new cars.

E9-2. Indicate whether each of the following statements best describes a LIFO, FIFO, specific identification, or weighted average costing method.

    a. In a period of rising prices, this method tends to give the highest reported net income.

    b. In this inventory costing method, the oldest costs incurred rarely have an effect on the ending inventory valuation.

    c. The book value of ending inventory of an item whose acquisition cost changes frequently will be the same if perpetual records are kept as it would be under a periodic inventory method, if this costing method for ending inventory is used.

    d. This method requires that each item in inventory be physically differentiated.

    e. Under this method, each unit sold carries a cost equal to the average of all units of inventory acquired.

    f. This method generally results in ending inventory being valued at very old purchase costs.

    g. This method is most appropriate for merchandising situations where inventory units are physically mixed.

    h. In this method, the flow of costs through the firm reflects exactly the physical flow of products.

    i. Under this method, the valuation for cost of goods sold is usually different between perpetual and periodic systems.

    j. With this method, the matching concept is implemented completely.

E9-3. Triangle Corporation closes its books monthly. The beginning inventory and purchases and sales for May are given below:

Date	Event	Units	Dollars/Unit
May 1	Beginning inventory	2,500	$3.50
6	Sales	1,000	5.00
9	Sales	500	5.00
14	Purchase	3,700	4.00

21	Sales	2,500	5.00
29	Purchase	1,300	4.50
31	Sales	2,000	5.25

Required:

Compute ending inventory May 31 under (a) FIFO periodic costing procedures and (b) FIFO perpetual costing procedures.

E9-4. Refer to the data in Exercise 9-3. Compute ending inventory May 31 assuming (a) LIFO periodic and (b) LIFO perpetual costing procedures.

E9-5. Refer to the data in Exercise 9-3. Compute ending inventory May 31 assuming (a) weighted average periodic and (b) weighted average perpetual costing procedures.

E9-6. Wheeler Imports, Inc., is an automobile dealership. At the beginning of February, the following inventory was on hand:

Stock Number		Cost
1132		$10,950
1147		13,653
1149		8,763
1151		14,865

Purchases for the period included:

1152		$11,459
1153		11,500
1154		12,960
1155		14,672
1156		14,850
1157		13,920
1158		15,840
1159		9,594
1160		10,420
1161		13,860

Sales for the period included items 1132, 1147, 1149, 1152, 1154, 1156, 1157, 1158, 1160, and 1161.

Required:

Determine the ending inventory and cost of goods sold for the period assuming Wheeler uses specific identification and a perpetual inventory system. By how much would ending inventory differ if Wheeler used a periodic rather than a perpetual system?

E9-7. The income statement for Transam Corporation for the current year included the amounts shown on the first line of the tabulation presented below. Four errors subsequently discovered are also listed on the tabulation. Determine the correct amount for each item by adding, subtracting, or entering a zero in each block to recognize the effect of the described error. The firm uses a periodic inventory system.

Income Statement Item Reported Amounts	Revenues $42,000	Cost of Goods Sold $18,000	Net Income $6,000
a. Beginning inventory was understated by $360.			
b. A $600 credit purchase during the year was not recorded and was not included in ending inventory.			
c. A $2,400 credit sale was not recorded. The goods costing $2,100 were not included in ending inventory.			
d. Ending inventory was overstated by $1,200.			
Corrected amounts			

E9-8. Indicate the effect of each of the following errors on the cost of goods sold of a merchandising business that uses a periodic inventory system.

   a. 150 units of Item 56, valued at $2.00 per unit, were incorrectly included in the ending inventory. The purchase was recorded.

   b. 75 units of Item 92, valued at $1.50 per unit, were correctly included in ending inventory but their purchase was not recorded.

   c. 130 units of Item 10, valued at $1.00 per unit, were incorrectly excluded from ending inventory. The purchase was not recorded.

   d. 50 units of Item 13, valued at $.75 per unit, were incorrectly excluded from the beginning inventory. A purchase was recorded for these items during the current period.

   e. 60 units of Item 23, valued at $3.00, were purchased during the current period. The purchase was recorded at $810 rather than $180.

   f. 165 units of Item 15, valued at $2.25 per unit, were incorrectly excluded from the ending inventory. The purchase was recorded.

   g. 112 units of Item 11, valued at $1.50 per unit, were incorrectly included in the beginning inventory.

E9-9. The general ledger of Brennan Company contained the following information on October 17, 1982.

Inventory, January 1, 1982	$ 55,000
Purchases	575,000
Purchase returns	25,000
Sales, January 1 to October 17	600,000
Sales returns	60,000

A flood destroyed the inventory on October 17. Compute the amount of flood loss assuming gross profit is 25 percent of sales.

E9-10. The general ledger of Topex Company contained the following account balances at the end of an interim period:

Inventory, beginning	$ 36,000
Purchases	194,400
Freight in	14,400
Sales revenue	306,310

Sales returns	....	3,600
Purchase returns	....	7,200

From supplementary records it was determined that beginning inventory at selling price was $54,000 and net purchases at selling price were $285,430. Using the retail method, estimate inventory and cost of goods sold for the interim financial statements.

Problems

P9-1. The Lois Corporation sells product T. Answer each of the following questions using the information presented in the table below.

Product T

	Units			Unit Price	Dollars		
Date	Received	Issued	Balance		Received	Issued	Balance
Feb. 1			20	$1.50			$30
3	60			1.55	$93		
5		16					
9		28					
12	30			1.60	48		
16		26					
20		22					
25	30			1.70	51		
28		28					

Required:

1. What would be the value of ending inventory if a FIFO cost flow and a perpetual system were assumed?

2. What would be the value of ending inventory if a LIFO cost flow and a perpetual system were assumed?

3. What would be the value of ending inventory if a weighted average perpetual basis were used?

4. What would be the value of ending inventory if a FIFO cost flow and a periodic system were assumed?

5. What would be the value of ending inventory if a LIFO cost flow and a periodic system were used?

6. What would be the value of ending inventory if a weighted average periodic basis were used?

P9-2. The Kelly Company reported the following amounts for net income and inventories for its first three years of operations:

	Year 1	Year 2	Year 3
Net income using FIFO	$ 78,000	$136,500	$175,500
Ending inventory, FIFO basis	234,000	359,000	351,000
Ending inventory, LIFO basis	175,500	292,500	249,600

Required:
Compute the net income for each of these first three years assuming the LIFO rather than FIFO costing method.

P9-3. The auditor for Apollo Corporation found four errors while auditing the company's records. The uncorrected records before the audit indicated the following amounts:

Net purchases	$60,000
Accounts payable	8,000
Ending inventory	12,000
Net income	4,000

The four errors discovered were:

a. Goods costing $400 were in transit f.o.b. shipping point at the end of the period. The invoice had been received, and the purchase had been recorded. The goods were not included in the count of ending inventory.

b. Items that arrived in damaged condition were being held for return to the vendor. These items were incorrectly counted in ending inventory. A purchase of $1,200 had been recorded for these goods.

c. Goods in transit f.o.b. shipping point costing $400 were not counted in ending inventory. A purchase was not recorded.

d. Goods costing $10,000 were purchased from Duffy Corporation. The purchase was correctly recorded, but in the ending inventory count these goods were incorrectly valued at $12,000.

Required:

1. Indicate the effect of each error on purchases, net income, accounts payable, and ending inventory.

2. Compute the correct balance at year end for each of these items.

P9-4. The Mildred Company has the following items in its inventory:

	Quantity	Unit Cost	Market
Class A			
Item 100	9,200	$ 1.25	$ 1.35
Item 101	13,800	1.05	.85
Class B			
Item 200	4,600	4.05	3.65
Item 201	4,140	5.25	5.45
Class C			
Item 300	8,050	7.90	7.40
Item 301	6,440	10.15	11.10

Required:

Compute the value of the company's inventory using cost or market, whichever is lower, applied to:

1. Individual inventory items.

2. Inventory classes.

3. Inventory as a whole.

P9-5. The Robillard Company's income statements for the years 1979, 1980, 1981, and 1982 contained the following information:

	1979	1980	1981	1982
Sales	$108,000	$126,000	$144,000	$117,000
Cost of goods sold	64,800	68,940	90,180	70,200
Gross profit	43,200	57,060	53,820	46,800
Expenses	27,000	30,060	34,380	28,440
Pretax income	$ 16,200	$ 27,000	$ 19,440	$ 18,360

After the above statements were prepared, it was discovered that the physical inventory taken by the company's employees on December 31, 1980, was overstated by $4,000 and that the physical inventory on December 31, 1981, was overstated by $6,000.

Required:

1. Redo the above income statements for the four years, making any changes required by the discovery of the inventory errors.

2. Determine the total pretax income over the four-year period using the original statements. Compare this with the total pretax income for the four years on the corrected statements. If there is a difference between the two amounts, explain what caused the difference. If there is no difference between the two amounts, explain why they are the same.

P9-6. Lapsley Company uses a periodic inventory system. The following information is available for 1982. Beginning inventory was 7,840 units with a cost of $13 each; purchases during 1982 consisted of 29,400 units at a cost of $16 each; expenses other than income taxes totaled $253,820; a physical count at the end of the period revealed that 8,820 units were on hand. Sales price was $30 per unit, and the applicable tax rate is 25 percent.

Required:

1. Complete the tabulation below.

		INVENTORY COSTING METHOD		
Income Statement	Units	FIFO	LIFO	Average
Sales revenue	_____	$_____	$_____	$_____
Cost of goods sold				
Beginning inventory	_____	_____	_____	_____
Purchases	_____	_____	_____	_____
Goods available for sale	_____	_____	_____	_____
Ending inventory	_____	_____	_____	_____
Cost of goods sold	_____	_____	_____	_____
Gross profit		_____	_____	_____
Expenses		_____	_____	_____
Pretax income		_____	_____	_____
Income taxes		_____	_____	_____
Net income		_____	_____	_____

2. Which method is preferable in terms of cash flow given this situation of rising prices?

P9-7. Truett Company's fiscal year ends on September 30, 1981. The company uses a periodic inventory system. The unaudited financial statements prepared by the company contained the following amounts: ending inventory, $660,000; accounts receivable, $660,000; accounts payable, $220,000; sales, $4,400,000; purchases, $1,760,000; and pretax income, $330,000. The following items were discovered by the auditor when he performed his examination:

a. Merchandise that cost $66,000 was not counted in ending inventory and was not recorded as a sale for $82,500 on September 27, 1981. The goods had been specifically segregated. According to the terms of the sale contract, ownership did not pass until actual delivery.

b. Merchandise costing $77,000 was in transit September 30, 1981. The goods had been shipped f.o.b. shipping point by the vendor. The goods were excluded from the inventory count. The purchase was recorded on September 28, 1981, when the invoice was received.

c. Merchandise that cost $110,000 and was sold on September 29, 1981, for $154,000 on credit was included in the ending inventory. The sale was recorded. The goods were in transit, shipped f.o.b. destination.

d. Merchandise that cost $198,000 was excluded from inventory, and the related sale for $235,000 was recorded. The goods were in transit September 30, 1981, and had been shipped f.o.b. destination.

e. Merchandise that cost $113,000 was in transit having been shipped f.o.b. shipping point by the vendor. The goods were not included in ending inventory, and a purchase was not recorded.

Required:

Determine the correct amount that should be reported for ending inventory, purchases, accounts receivable, accounts payable, sales, and pretax income.

P9-8. Raymond Company uses a periodic inventory system. The trial balance of the company at June 30, the end of the fiscal year, is given below:

Cash	$ 1,000	
Accounts receivable	13,500	
Notes receivable	35,000	
Merchandise inventory	14,000	
Supplies	2,500	
Unexpired insurance	500	
Buildings	37,500	
Accumulated depreciation, buildings		$ 1,500
Accounts payable		4,000
Capital stock		31,000
Retained earnings		47,900
Sales revenue		56,400
Sales returns	400	
Interest revenue		500
Purchases	30,000	
Freight in	600	
Purchase returns		200
Selling expenses	4,300	
General and administrative expenses	2,200	
	$141,500	$141,500

A physical inventory was in progress June 30 when the entire warehouse was destroyed by a fire.

Required:

1. Assuming that a normal gross profit percentage for Raymond Company has been 30 percent, use the gross profit method to estimate ending inventory. Prepare an income statement for Raymond for the current year.

2. Given the above trial balance and the additional information that beginning inventory at selling price was $18,740 and net purchases at selling price were $44,824, use the retail method to estimate ending inventory.

P9-9. Bama Corportion sells three products: jams, yams, and rams. Information about the three products for the month of November is as follows:

BEGINNING INVENTORY

Product	Number of Units	Date of Purchase	Unit Cost
Jams	100	10-27-82	$3.00
Yams	200	10-25-82	.75
	92	10-23-82	.70
Rams	325	10-29-82	5.00

PURCHASES DURING NOVEMBER

Date	Product	Number of Units	Unit Cost
11-01-82	Jams	50	$3.10
11-01-82	Yams	50	.75
11-01-82	Rams	75	5.05
11-03-82	Yams	80	.80
11-05-82	Jams	200	3.15
11-06-82	Yams	25	.78
11-13-82	Jams	40	3.05
11-17-82	Rams	30	5.10
11-20-82	Jams	90	3.20
11-21-82	Yams	120	.85
11-23-82	Jams	56	3.25
11-25-82	Yams	65	.87
11-28-82	Jams	30	3.30
11-30-82	Rams	15	5.20

NOVEMBER SALES

Date	Product	Number of Units	Selling Price
11-01-82	Jams	75	$4.00
11-02-82	Yams	265	1.30
11-03-82	Rams	250	7.00
11-05-82	Yams	65	1.30
11-07-82	Jams	190	4.00
11-10-82	Rams	125	7.00
11-14-82	Jams	82	4.00
11-14-82	Yams	65	1.30
11-21-82	Jams	110	4.00
11-22-82	Yams	140	1.30
11-27-82	Jams	40	4.00

Required:

Assuming Bama uses a periodic inventory system, compute the gross profit for each of the three products and the total gross profit for the company under (1) a FIFO system, (2) a LIFO system, and (3) a weighted average cost system. Round all totals to the nearest dollar.

ASSETS AND EQUITIES

CHAPTER 10

Property, Plant, and Equipment

Chapter Outline

10.1 *Acquisition of Property, Plant, and Equipment.* Definition and measurement of the acquisition cost of assets; capital and revenue expenditures; recording the acquisition of property, plant, and equipment assets.

10.2 *Consumption—Straight-line Method.* Depreciation, amortization, and depletion defined; straight-line method illustrated.

10.3 *Consumption—Other Methods.* Sum-of-the-years'-digits, double-declining-balance, and units-of-output methods illustrated; discussion of the primary types of intangibles and the amortization process; discussion of natural resources and the depletion process.

10.4 *Subsequent Expenditures.* Categories of subsequent expenditures and their treatment; recording subsequent expenditures.

10.5 *Disposal of Property, Plant, and Equipment.* Discussion and illustration of techniques for recording the scrapping, sale, and trading in of property, plant, and equipment assets.

Accounting and the Real World

The Business of
Sports

Though a professional sports team may be a loser in the won-loss column, it can be a winner to its owners. Most professional sports franchises are held as partnerships by owners who have many other profitable business interests. The practical effect of this form of ownership is that losses which result from the operations of the sports team are used by the owners to offset income from other sources, thus lowering their overall tax bill.

The interesting twist at work here has to do with the costs of player contracts and bonuses paid to players. Often player contracts call for "deferred payments"; that is, payments which will be made to players over many future years. These can be distinguished from player salaries, which are paid only during an athlete's playing years. A sports team, then, may incur two types of player costs: deferred payments and salaries. The salaries are deductible for tax purposes as they are paid. On the other hand, the deferred payments are viewed as an investment in an asset (the player contracts) which can be deducted (amortized) over the expected playing life of the athletes.

The business of sports should now begin to make sense. Player contracts represent the largest and most important asset for any sports team. The cost of these contracts can be deducted for income tax purposes long before they are actually paid out in cash. The result is a business which can consistently show accrual accounting losses that are offset against other income to lower taxes, while at the same time producing positive cash flows for the owners.

Consider the following example:

CITY SLICKERS FOOTBALL TEAM
for the year 1982

	Income Statement	Cash Flow
Revenues (ticket sales, radio and television, other)	$1,100,000	$1,100,000
Expenses (salaries, travel, administration, other)	1,000,000	1,000,000
Profit before amortization	100,000	100,000
Amortization of player contracts and bonuses	200,000	0
Net profit (loss)	$ (100,000)	+$ 100,000

The owners enjoy a deductible loss of $100,000 and an increase in cash of $100,000, a very nice combination. The deductible loss of $100,000 will lead to an income tax savings of $50,000—money the owner can keep and not send to the government. The hallmark of most tax shelters is the creation of tax deductions in advance of the actual cash expenditures.

Do you begin to see the score?

The Journal of Taxation, November 1973.

Property, plant, and equipment, sometimes called fixed assets, represent the largest category of assets in dollar terms on most balance sheets. These assets are long-lived and indicate the productive or operating capacity of the business in that they are acquired to be used in business operations rather than to be resold.

The life cycle of property, plant, and equipment assets can be thought of as consisting of three stages: acquisition, consumption, and disposal. Accounting for these assets closely follows these three phases. Figure 10-1 presents the important accounting questions that must be answered at each phase. Acquisition, consumption, and disposal of fixed assets and the accounting principles and procedures used in each phase are discussed in this chapter.

10.1   Acquisition of Property, Plant, and Equipment

Long-term operating assets represent a bundle of future services that will ultimately be consumed by the business. A company acquires the bundle of services all at one time by purchasing the asset, then uses up the services a little at a time over the life of the asset. When all services inherent in the asset have been consumed or when a business no longer desires the remaining future services, the asset can be disposed of.

The similarity between property, plant, and equipment and supplies should be kept in mind throughout this chapter. Both asset types exhibit use value and, therefore, are purchased to be used rather than resold. The differences between these assets can be traced to the time frame over

FIGURE 10-1
Life Cycle of Property, Plant, and Equipment

Stage of Life	Important Accounting Questions
Acquisition	1. What should be included in acquisition cost? 2. How is cost measured? 3. How are acquisitions recorded?
Consumption	1. How is consumption measured? 2. How is consumption recorded? 3. What are subsequent expenditures? 4. How are subsequent expenditures recorded?
Disposal	1. What is recorded when assets are damaged or scrapped? 2. How are sales of assets recorded? 3. How are trade-ins of assets recorded?

which the asset will be used. Supplies are used over a short time period, usually within one accounting period, while property, plant, and equipment assets have lives of many years and are used up gradually.

Equally important to understand is the basic difference between property, plant, and equipment and inventory. Inventory is purchased and held specifically to be sold to customers. Often, an asset (such as a truck or car) that is normally considered to be noncurrent could be inventory to a certain type of business. To an automobile dealership, cars and trucks are inventory even though these assets would be property, plant, and equipment to most other businesses.

Care should be taken in classifying long-lived productive assets as property, plant, and equipment. Assets, such as land or buildings, that are held as investments or to be sold should be classified as investments or other assets. Classification as property, plant, and equipment requires that the long-lived productive asset be currently in use in the operating activities of the business, rather than held as an asset for resale.

Acquisition Cost

The acquisition cost of property, plant, and equipment assets includes all expenditures that are necessary and reasonable to purchase the asset and ready it for its intended use in business operations, except for interest charges incurred to purchase the asset. Acquisition cost should be the cash equivalent cost of the asset. Interest or other charges related to purchasing the asset on credit should become interest expense. Expenditure means a cash payment or the incurring of a liability that will result in a cash payment in the future.

The terms necessary and reasonable can best be illustrated by an example. Suppose a company in New Orleans agrees to purchase a machine from a vendor in New York. The list price of the machine is $10,000, and payment terms of 1/30, n/60 are offered. Sales tax of 5 percent is applicable to the purchase, and freight charges of $900 must be paid by the purchaser. On route from New York to New Orleans, chains holding the machine on the truck break, and the machine falls from the truck, causing $750 in damage that must be paid by the purchaser. When the machine arrives, installation costs of $500 and testing costs of $300 are paid by the purchaser. The acquisition cost for this asset would be determined as follows:

List price	$10,000	
Discount available (1% × $10,000)	(100)	
Cash equivalent cost		$ 9,900
Sales tax (5% × $9,900)		495
Freight		900
Installation		500
Testing		300
Acquisition cost of machine		$12,095

All of the expenditures included in the acquisition cost of the machine are incurred to purchase (cash equivalent cost and sales tax), transport (freight), or ready for use (installation and testing). The amount of the discount, if not taken, represents interest and should not become a part of the asset's cost. The repair cost resulting from damage in transit is "unreasonable" in that most businesses would not expect to incur such a cost each time a machine is transported. Because this repair cost is unusual, it should be debited to a special expense of the period in which it is incurred.

Recording Acquisition for Cash The acquisition of the machine would be recorded in the books in the following manner:

Machine	12,095	
Cash		12,095

This presumes that all expenditures necessary to acquire the machine are paid immediately.

Machine repair expense	750	
Cash		750

This expense would appear on the income statement of the current period.

Recording Acquisition on Credit Assume now that the company purchasing the machine decided to pay the purchase price of the asset only after the allowed sixty days had elapsed. All other expenditures connected with the acquisition are paid in cash. The following entries would result:

Machine	12,095	
Cash		2,195
Accounts payable		9,900
Machine repair expense	750	
Cash		750

After sixty days, when the machine is paid for, this entry would be made

Accounts payable	9,900	
Interest expense	100	
Cash		10,000

Notice that the cash equivalent cost of the asset is not affected by the manner of payment chosen by the acquiring company. Any time-payment charges will be expensed as they are incurred and, therefore, cannot affect the cost of the asset. Expenditures that do affect the acquisition cost of the asset are those necessary and reasonable to purchasing, transporting, or readying the asset for its intended use. All other expenditures are expensed immediately.

Capital and Revenue Expenditures Expenditures that are debited to an asset account and become a part of the asset's cost are called **capital expenditures.** These expenditures are expected to benefit several future accounting periods, and the creation of an asset recognizes this fact. On the other hand, expenditures that produce no future benefit beyond the current accounting period are called **revenue expenditures.** The term revenue expenditures indicates that these amounts will be matched against revenue of the current period and will not affect future income statements. Revenue expenditures become expenses as they are incurred in the current accounting period, while capital expenditures become assets and are charged to expenses in future periods as the benefits of the asset are consumed. All expenditures made upon the acquisition of an asset must be classified as either capital or revenue expenditures.

Lump Sum Purchases Often a business will acquire several different property, plant, and equipment assets with one lump sum purchase. This is particularly true in the purchase of a building which will necessarily include the land on which the building is located. Because land is not subject to depreciation while buildings are, the cost of these lump sum purchases must be allocated to the individual assets acquired. The basis for this allocation of purchase cost is usually an independent appraisal of the values of the individual assets acquired; however, the sum of the appraisal values of the individual assets may not equal the purchase cost of those assets as a package. Suppose, for example, a company acquired a building together with land for a price of $50,000. Appraisals indicate the land has a value of $18,000 and the building, $42,000. The allocation of the purchase cost of $50,000 would be as follows:

	Appraisal	% of Total	Allocation of Cost
Land	$18,000	30% × 50,000 =	$15,000
Building	42,000	70% × 50,000 =	35,000
	$60,000	100%	$50,000

Separate ledger accounts would be established for land and building at the allocated amounts stated above. In this way, the $35,000 cost of the building could be subject to depreciation over the life of the building.

Similarly, land may be acquired on which some improvements, such as fences, parking lots, and driveways, have been made. These improvements have a limited life and are subject to depreciation. Thus, their cost must be separated from the cost of the land, which is not subject to depreciation. A separate ledger account, called **land improvements,** is often created for the cost of these assets.

Sometimes a lump sum purchase of land and a building occurs, but the intention of the purchasing company is to acquire only the land, and the existence of the building is incidental. In these instances, the acquiring company does not intend to use the building, so only one asset, land, is actually being purchased. The entire purchase cost, including any costs of removing the unwanted building, should be debited to the land account. If any cash receipts or receivables result from the sale of materials from the old building, these amounts would reduce the cost of the acquired land.

Constructed Assets Instead of purchasing a property, plant, and equipment asset, a business may construct it. In these instances, the cost of all materials and labor used in the construction plus any indirect costs associated with the construction should become the cost of the asset. Outside expenditures, such as architectural or survey fees, would also be included in the asset's cost. These outside expenditures include interest incurred while the asset is under construction. Interest incurred after the asset is ready for use should be expensed. Constructed assets, then, are generally valued at the cost of construction even though the same asset could have been purchased at a different cost.

Concept Summary

Acquiring Property, Plant, and Equipment Assets

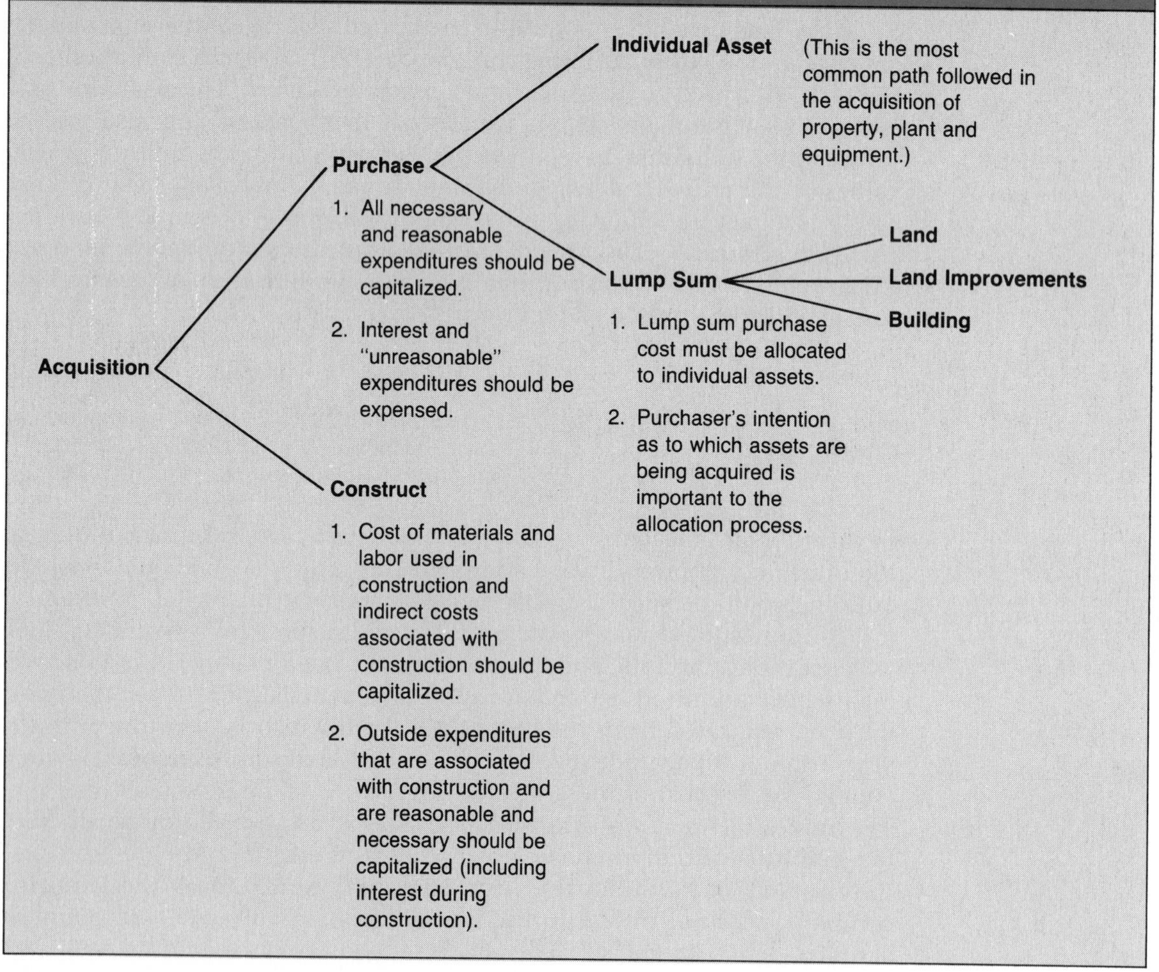
Acquisition
Purchase
1. All necessary and reasonable expenditures should be capitalized.
2. Interest and "unreasonable" expenditures should be expensed.
Construct
1. Cost of materials and labor used in construction and indirect costs associated with construction should be capitalized.
2. Outside expenditures that are associated with construction and are reasonable and necessary should be capitalized (including interest during construction).
Individual Asset
(This is the most common path followed in the acquisition of property, plant and equipment.)
Lump Sum
1. Lump sum purchase cost must be allocated to individual assets.
2. Purchaser's intention as to which assets are being acquired is important to the allocation process.
Land
Land Improvements
Building

10.2 Consumption—Straight-Line Method

An important characteristic of property, plant, and equipment assets is that they represent a bundle of future services to be used by a business over a number of accounting periods. Except for land, however, all of these assets have a limited life. That is, they will be of benefit for only a defined number of future periods. Land is viewed by accounting as having an unlimited life and, therefore, as being of benefit indefinitely into the future or until sold.

Consumption Defined

Businesses incur expenditures to acquire operating assets and then consume the services represented by the asset over several years. This consumption is recorded in financial accounting by allocating the cost of property, plant, and equipment assets to the periods that benefit from the use of the asset. Allocation of an asset's cost results in the creation of an expense each accounting period which represents an approximation of the cost of the asset's services used up in that period. In this way, as services are consumed, an expense is created for inclusion on the income statement.

Types of Consumption

The process of measuring and recording the consumption of property, plant, and equipment assets is called by one of three terms: depreciation, amortization, or depletion.

- **Depreciation** is the process of allocating the cost of tangible operating assets to the periods that benefit from the use of the assets.

- **Amortization** is the process of allocating the cost of intangible assets to the periods that benefit from the use of the assets.

- **Depletion** is the process of allocating the cost of natural resources to the periods that benefit from the use of the assets.

Notice that the basic meaning and process of consumption is the same in all three instances. This process is called by three different titles, however, with each specific title describing the consumption of a different major category of property, plant, and equipment assets.

Consumption as an Allocation Process An important aspect of consumption (depreciation, amortization, and depletion) is that it is an allocation process. The acquisition cost of an asset is allocated to future periods by the consumption process. Depreciation, amortization, and depletion do not represent attempts to record the changing "value" of an asset. In fact, recording the consumption of asset services is necessary to implement the matching concept even if the value of an asset is increasing.

Measuring Consumption

The remaining discussions in this section focus on depreciation, although the points made throughout apply to amortization and depletion as well. Measuring depreciation, amortization, and depletion requires that three variables about each asset be specified. Each of these variables is, to some extent, an estimate; therefore, the measurement of the consumption of property, plant, and equipment assets is necessarily an estimate also.

1. **Depreciation base** is the amount of dollars to be allocated to expense over the life of an asset. The debits to expense over the life of an asset will equal that asset's depreciation base. It is calculated as acquisition cost minus salvage value. Acquisition cost is determined in the first stage of an asset's life as it is acquired. **Salvage value** (sometimes called **residual value**) is an estimate of what the asset is likely to be sold for at the end of its life. The cost of each asset minus the amount expected to be realized upon its sale (salvage or residual value) is the amount of dollars to be debited to expense over the asset's life. Because salvage or residual value is an estimate of the worth of an asset in the very distant future, it is not unusual to find a salvage value of zero assigned to an asset. This is because it may be difficult to estimate any other value with the uncertainties of wear and tear and obsolescence. If salvage value is zero, depreciation base then equals acquisition cost.

2. **Useful life** is the period of expected benefit to the business from the asset. Useful life will be equal to physical life for some assets, such as buildings. These assets tend to be of benefit and contribute to a business until complete physical deterioration occurs. For other assets, the period of benefit may be much shorter than expected physical life because of technological obsolescence. In these instances, useful life will be equal to the economic life of the asset. A computer is a good example of an asset with a useful life that is shorter than its physical life.

3. **Depreciation method** is the calculation technique used to spread the depreciation base over the useful life for each asset. The depreciation method determines the rate at which an asset will be depreciated and the amount of depreciation expense for each accounting period.

Depreciation Methods

Several calculation techniques for measuring consumption are generally accepted and widely used. A business may choose the depreciation method it feels is most suited for each of its assets and is free to use different methods for different assets. In addition, a business may use different depreciation methods on the same asset for financial statement and income tax purposes. The most widely used depreciation, amortization, and depletion methods are the straight-line, sum-of-the-years'-digits, double-declining-balance, and units-of-output methods.

Straight-Line Method

The straight-line method is the simplest and most widely used depreciation method and was applied in earlier chapters when depreciation was encountered. It results in an equal amount of depreciation being allocated to each year of the asset's life and, therefore, is most appropriate for assets whose services are expected to be uniformly consumed. The formula for the calculation of annual depreciation under the straight-line method is:

$$\frac{\text{depreciation base}}{\text{useful life in years}} = \text{annual depreciation expense}$$

The above calculation is necessary only once for each asset to which straight-line depreciation is applied. Then, at the end of each accounting period, an adjusting entry would be made to record annual depreciation expense as follows:

```
Depreciation expense ........................................... XX
    Accumulated depreciation ..................................        XX
```

Depreciation expense should be reported on the income statement for the current period. **Accumulated depreciation** is a contra-asset account and should appear on the balance sheet as a deduction from the asset. Accumulated depreciation reflects the total depreciation taken on an asset since acquisition. Over an asset's life, the total of all depreciation expense taken (accumulated depreciation) will be equal to the depreciation base of the asset.

Property, plant, and equipment assets are reported on balance sheets at the amount of acquisition cost not yet allocated to expense. This amount is calculated as acquisition cost minus accumulated depreciation and is called the **book value** of the asset. The financial accounting measurement book value does not reflect the market value of the asset because depreciation is not a valuation process. At this point, it is important to note the difference between book value (cost minus accumulated depreciation) and depreciation base (cost minus salvage value).

Figure 10-2 gives complete data on a depreciable asset which will be used to illustrate the straight-line method and other depreciation methods throughout the remainder of this section. The same example will be used so that the four depreciation methods can be compared in terms of their income statement and balance sheet effects.

Calculation of Straight-Line Depreciation Straight-line depreciation is calculated as follows:

```
Depreciation base (10,500 − 500) .......................       $10,000
Useful life in years .......................................             5
Annual depreciation expense (10,000 ÷ 5) ................       $ 2,000
```

FIGURE 10-2
Asset Data for
Calculating
Depreciation

```
Acquisition cost of asset ............................................       $10,500
Estimated salvage value  ...........................................       $   500
Useful life in years .................................................             5
Useful life in units of output ......................................       100,000
    Year 1 ...............................................    15,000
    Year 2 ...............................................    30,000
    Year 3 ...............................................    20,000
    Year 4 ...............................................    15,000
    Year 5 ...............................................    20,000
Date of acquisition ..................................................        1/1/82
Accounting period ................................................... calendar year
                                                                          (1/1 – 12/31)
```

The depreciation entry for year 1 of the asset's life, as well as each of the remaining years, would be as follows:

```
Depreciation expense ................................... 2,000
    Accumulated depreciation ............................       2,000
```

The balance sheet at the end of year 1 would include the following:

```
Property, plant and equipment ........................... $10,500
Less: Accumulated depreciation .........................   (2,000)   $8,500
```

The complete depreciation schedule for the asset's life using the straight-line method would be

Year	Computation	Depreciation Expense	Accumulated Depreciation	Book Value
				$10,500
1	⅕ × 10,000	$2,000	$ 2,000	8,500
2	"	2,000	4,000	6,500
3	"	2,000	6,000	4,500
4	"	2,000	8,000	2,500
5	"	2,000	10,000	500

A five-year life converts to an annual rate of 20 percent (100% ÷ 5) on a straight-line basis or, stated differently, one-fifth of the total each year.

Partial Year's Depreciation The above illustration has assumed that the depreciable years for the asset exactly coincide with the accounting periods for the business. This means that a full year's depreciation is recorded each accounting period. For this to occur, each depreciable asset would have to be purchased on the first day of the accounting period. Obviously, businesses acquire property, plant, and equipment assets at various times during an accounting period. When this happens, a partial year's depreciation must be recorded in the first and last year of the asset's life. For example, suppose the asset depicted in Figure 10-2 is acquired on April 1 by a business using an accounting period of a calendar year. At December 31, the following entry for a partial first year's depreciation would be recorded:

```
Depreciation expense ................................... 1,500
    Accumulated depreciation ............................       1,500
(⅕ × 10,000 × ¾ of a year)
```

The following accounting period would reflect a full year's depreciation of $2,000.

Use of Straight-Line Depreciation Straight-line depreciation is most often applied to assets whose services are uniformly consumed over their life. These assets, such as buildings, exhibit no impairment in function as they grow old, and the recording of consumption should generally reflect this pattern of services. Also, amortization of intangibles is recorded on a straight-line basis for the same reason.

Concept Summary

Estimating Consumption		
Variable	*Description*	*Example*
Depreciation Base (Amortization or Depletion Base)	Amount of dollars to be expensed over the asset's useful life; the depreciation base is the acquisition cost less the salvage value.	Acquisition cost of $18,000 and an estimated salvage value of $3,000 gives a depreciation base of $15,000.
Useful Life	The period of expected benefit from the asset; equal to the physical life for some assets, such as buildings, or the economic life for other assets, such as computers.	The useful life is ten years.
Depreciation Method (Amortization or Depletion Method)	The calculation technique used to spread the depreciation base over the useful life for each asset.	Straight-line depreciation would result in expense of $\frac{\$15,000}{10} = \$1,500$ for each of ten years.

10.3 Consumption—Other Methods

There are two widely used accelerated depreciation methods available under generally accepted accounting principles: the sum-of-the-years'-digits method and the double-declining-balance method. **Accelerated depreciation** means that larger than proportionate amounts of depreciation are taken in the early years of an asset's life and proportionately less in the later years. Some assets, because of their nature, contribute more and better services during the early years of their life, and this contribution decreases as the asset grows old. Accelerated depreciation reflects this different contribution by matching large amounts of depreciation expense against revenue during those periods when contribution is great. Similarly, when the contribution is lower, a smaller amount of depreciation expense is matched to revenue.

Sum-of-the-Years'-Digits Method

The sum-of-the-years'-digits method accomplishes the calculation of accelerated depreciation by multiplying a decreasing depreciation rate by the depreciation base of the asset. This decreasing rate is calculated as follows:

$$\frac{\text{years of useful life remaining at beginning of year}}{\text{sum of the years of useful life}} = \text{depreciation rate}$$

Because the remaining years of useful life will decrease each year, the depreciation rate will also decrease. Thus, a smaller amount of depreciation expense will result.

Consider the asset data provided in Figure 10-2, which will now be used as the basis for sum-of-the-years'-digits depreciation calculation.

Sum-of-the-years'-digits depreciation (first year):

Depreciation base	$10,000
Depreciation rate	⁵⁄₁₅ or ⅓
Remaining years of useful life	
at beginning of 1st year	5
Sum of years of useful life	
(5 + 4 + 3 + 2 + 1)	15
Depreciation expense (first year)	$ 3,333

The depreciation entry for year 1 of the asset's life would be as shown below; however, each year the amounts of depreciation taken would decrease resulting in different annual entries.

Depreciation expense	3,333	
Accumulated depreciation		3,333

The balance sheet at the end of year 1 would include the following:

Property, plant, and equipment	$10,500	
Less: Accumulated depreciation	(3,333)	$7,167

The complete depreciation schedule for this asset using sum-of-the-years'-digits depreciation is given below:

Year	Computation	Depreciation Expense	Accumulated Depreciation	Book Value
				$10,500
1	⁵⁄₁₅ × 10,000	$3,333	$ 3,333	7,167
2	⁴⁄₁₅ × 10,000	2,667	6,000	4,500
3	³⁄₁₅ × 10,000	2,000	8,000	2,500
4	²⁄₁₅ × 10,000	1,333	9,333	1,167
5	¹⁄₁₅ × 10,000	667	10,000	500

At the end of the asset's useful life of five years, book value is equal to the expected salvage or residual value of the asset. In this manner, the amount at which the asset is carried on the books is equal to the amount expected to be received when the asset is disposed of at the end of its useful life. The balance sheet at the end of year 5 would include the following:

Property, plant, and equipment	$ 10,500	
Less: Accumulated depreciation	(10,000)	$500

Partial Year's Depreciation If this asset had been acquired on April 1, a partial year's depreciation would be taken in the first accounting period. The first depreciation entry for this asset would be

Depreciation expense	2,499	
Accumulated depreciation		2,499
($\frac{5}{15}$ × 10,000 × $\frac{3}{4}$ of a year)		

Depreciation expense for the second year would be $2,834 ($\frac{5}{15}$ × 10,000 × $\frac{1}{4}$) + ($\frac{4}{15}$ × 10,000 × $\frac{3}{4}$).

Double-Declining-Balance Method

The double-declining-balance method is the most widely used and most "rapid" of the generally accepted accelerated methods of depreciation. This method gives the largest depreciation expense earliest in an asset's life and, therefore, provides the business with the lowest taxable income and lowest income taxes for a given asset situation.

Calculation of Double-Declining-Balance Depreciation Double-declining-balance depreciation is actually calculated by multiplying a constant depreciation rate by the book value (not the depreciation base) of the asset. The constant depreciation rate is equal to twice the straight-line rate which would apply to the asset. For example, an asset with an expected life of ten years would have a straight-line rate of 10 percent, or one-tenth. The double-declining rate would then be 20 percent, or one-fifth.

The double-declining method is the only generally accepted depreciation calculation that does not use depreciation base. Instead, the depreciation rate is applied to the asset's book value, which decreases each year. Thus, the amount of depreciation expense decreases also. If an asset does have a salvage or residual value, however, double-declining depreciation must end when the book value of the asset equals this salvage value. In this way, salvage value is indirectly a factor in the double-declining-balance method.

Consider the asset data provided in Figure 10-2, which will now be used as the basis for double-declining depreciation calculation.

Double-declining depreciation (first year):

Book value (equals cost in first year of useful life, because no depreciation has yet been taken)	$10,500
Depreciation rate (straight-line rate = .20 or $\frac{1}{5}$)	.40 or $\frac{2}{5}$
Depreciation expense (first year)	$ 4,200

The same depreciation entry illustrated earlier would be made at the end of year 1, except that the amount of depreciation expense would be $4,200. Also, the book value of the asset presented on the end of year 1 balance sheet would be $6,300 ($10,500 − $4,200). The complete depreciation schedule for this asset using the double-declining-balance method is given below:

Year	Computation	Depreciation Expense	Accumulated Depreciation	Book Value
				$10,500
1	⅖ × 10,500	$4,200	$ 4,200	6,300
2	⅖ × 6,300	2,520	6,720	3,780
3	⅖ × 3,780	1,512	8,232	2,268
4	⅖ × 2,268	907	9,139	1,361
5	—	861	10,000	500

Under the double-declining-balance method, no computation is necessary in the last year of the asset's useful life. Instead, depreciation expense becomes the amount necessary to reduce the book value of the asset to its expected salvage value, in this instance, $861. In this way, the asset is not depreciated below the amount of its expected salvage or residual value.

Partial Year's Depreciation Again, depreciation for the first year of asset use would have to be apportioned if the purchase took place during the accounting period. An April 1 acquisition of this asset would have resulted in the following first year depreciation entry:

```
Depreciation expense  .......................................  3,150
    Accumulated depreciation  ..............................        3,150
    (⅖ × 10,500 × ¾ of a year)
```

Depreciation expense for the second year would be $2,940 (⅖ × 10,500 × ¼) + (⅖ × 6,300 × ¾).

Reasons for Use of Accelerated Depreciation

Two arguments are most often offered in support of accelerated depreciation. First, some types of assets contribute more to a business when they are new, and this contribution may decrease dramatically as the asset grows old. Assets subject to rapid technological change are most likely to exhibit this pattern. Depreciation of these assets should generally reflect this pattern of consumption of asset services; that is, it should be greater in earlier years than in later years. Second, as assets age, they are likely to require additional repair and maintenance to continue to perform at a satisfactory level. With increasing repair and maintenance expenditures, a decreasing depreciation charge results in a more uniform total annual charge for the asset's services over its life. In fact, however, the most significant argument for accelerated depreciation may be that it results in the reduction of income taxes (because of large depreciation expense) in the earliest years after the acquisition of a property, plant, and equipment asset.

Units-of-Output Method

The three depreciation methods discussed so far have all measured depreciation as a function of time. Straight-line, sum-of-the-years'-digits, and double-declining-balance all view an asset's useful life in terms of years and relate consumption to the passage of time. This is logical because the consumption of the services of many assets is directly related to time, and it is probably easiest to think of useful life in years. For some assets, however, services are consumed only by physical use, and the passage of time plays no part in the reduction of future benefits inherent in the asset. In these instances, a depreciation method that ties the measurement of consumption to the physical use of the asset is needed. The units-of-output method does just that. Calculating units-of-output depreciation begins with the formula given below:

$$\frac{\text{depreciation base}}{\text{useful life in physical activity}} = \text{depreciation per unit of physical activity}$$

Physical activity might be units produced by a machine, miles driven by a truck, barrels of oil produced by a well, or cubic feet of gas from a gas well. In each of these instances, the activity measure that best reflects the use of the asset is selected. Then, the expected useful life of the asset is expressed in terms of this activity measure so that depreciation per unit of physical activity can be calculated. Depreciation expense for each accounting period is determined as follows:

$$\begin{matrix} \text{depreciation per unit of} \\ \text{physical activity} \end{matrix} \times \begin{matrix} \text{physical activity for} \\ \text{the period} \end{matrix} = \begin{matrix} \text{annual depreciation} \\ \text{expense} \end{matrix}$$

Calculation of Units-of-Output Depreciation Once again, the asset data from Figure 10-2 will be used to illustrate the calculation of depreciation. This time the units-of-output method will be used.

Units-of-output depreciation (first year):

Depreciation base	$ 10,000
Useful life in units of output	100,000
Depreciation rate per unit of output	.10
Units of output in year 1	15,000
Depreciation expense (first year)	$ 1,500

Depreciation expense of $1,500 would be reflected in the year-end adjusting entry for depreciation. The book value of the asset reported on the balance sheet at the end of year 1 would be $9,000 ($10,500 − $1,500). The complete depreciation schedule for this asset using the units-of-output method is given below:

Year	Computation	Depreciation Expense	Accumulated Depreciation	Book Value
				$10,500
1	.10 × 15,000	$1,500	$ 1,500	9,000
2	.10 × 30,000	3,000	4,500	6,000
3	.10 × 20,000	2,000	6,500	4,000
4	.10 × 15,000	1,500	8,000	2,500
5	.10 × 20,000	2,000	10,000	500

No Partial Year's Depreciation Calculation Although depreciation is recorded annually at the end of each accounting period, the amount of depreciation expense depends upon physical activity for the period. Unlike other depreciation methods, the units-of-output method records no depreciation if there is no activity. This means that the time of asset acquisition during the year is not a factor in the depreciation calculation, only the activity level for the year. As long as the depreciation rate per unit of physical activity is multiplied by the actual activity for the period, no partial year calculations are necessary. Under the units-of-output method, depreciation is not a function of time.

The actual consumption of the services of many assets is probably best measured by the units-of-output approach; however, estimating useful life in terms of physical activity and then monitoring the amount of that activity for each asset can be very difficult. As a result, the units-of-output method is most often used with natural resources. Estimates of activity and output are somewhat easier to make with natural resources and, at any rate, are usually made anyway independent of consumption in order to evaluate the asset.

Figure 10-3 contrasts the effects on depreciation expense of using each of the depreciation methods with the sample asset data.

Intangible Assets and Natural Resources

A business may possess long-term operating assets that do not have physical substance in the manner of a machine or a building. These assets are called intangibles, and they exhibit many of the same characteristics as property, plant, and equipment assets. Intangibles possess use value and tend to be used up gradually over a long life.

As with assets, other than land, the cost of intangibles must be charged to expense over their useful life. Accounting principles require that the useful life of intangibles not be estimated at more than a maximum of forty years, but may be much shorter. Intangible assets are charged to expense by a process called **amortization.** Amortization resembles depreciation, except that the asset account itself is credited rather than a contra account. Amortization is typically calculated on a straight-line basis.

The acquisition of natural resources, such as oil wells, gas wells, gold mines, coal mines, and many others, is recorded in the same way as other long-term operating assets. Because natural resources are use value assets, their cost is also written off over their useful lives.

The process of writing off the cost of a natural resource asset is called **depletion.** Like amortization, depletion is recorded by a debit to expense

FIGURE 10-3

Comparison of the Effects of Different Depreciation Methods on the Amount of Depreciation Expense

Period	Straight-Line	Sum-of-the-Years'-Digits	Double-Declining Balance	Units-of-Output*
Year 1	$2,000	$3,333	**$4,200**	$1,500
Year 2	2,000	2,667	2,520	3,000
Year 3	2,000	2,000	1,512	2,000
Year 4	2,000	1,333	907	1,500
Year 5	2,000	667	861	2,000

*These amounts depend upon the level of use (activity) of the asset rather than on the passage of time and could be different over this same time period.

and a credit to the asset being depleted. No contra account is used. Depletion, however, is most often computed on a units-of-output basis, because most natural resources are accounted for on the basis of output.

Figure 10-4 illustrates the basic issues involved with intangibles and natural resources.

FIGURE 10-4

Basic Issues for Intangibles and Natural Resources

Type of Asset	Primary Examples	Consumption of Asset	Examples of Journal Entries
Intangibles	Patents—exclusive right to use a unique machine, device, or process granted by the U.S. government for seventeen years; asset cost would include the cost of any patent infringement lawsuits.	Amortization resembles depreciation except that the asset account itself is credited rather than a contra account. Amortization is typically calculated on a straight-line basis.	Acquisition of patent with remaining legal life of ten years for $20,000 cash Patent .... 20,000 Cash ...... 20,000 If the patent's useful life is the same as the remaining legal life, the following entry would be made each year for the next ten years Amortization expense .... 2,000 Patent 2,000
	Copyrights—similar to patents, but they apply to books and musical compositions; the exclusive right lasts for the life of the author plus another fifty years.		
	Trademarks—similar to patents, but they apply to a special symbol or brand name, such as "Coca-Cola," and the specific shape of the letters in advertisements.		
	Organization costs—costs incurred with the formation of a corporation, such as attorney's fees, incorporation fees, and payments to promoters; income tax regulations allow amortization over a period of not less than five years.		
Natural Resources	Oil wells, gas wells, gold mines, and coal mines.	Depletion resembles depreciation, except that the asset account itself is credited rather than a contra account. Depletion is typically calculated on a units-of-output basis.	Acquisition of oil well for $500,000 cash, where $100,000 is for drilling and other equipment. The well is expected to produce 1,000,000 barrels of oil over the next five years. Oil well ..... 400,000 Equipment .. 100,000 Cash .... 500,000 Production of 300,000 barrels of oil in the first year: Depletion expense .... 120,000 Oil well ... 120,000 (300,000 × $.40 depletion/barrel)

**Consumption
Summarized**

Some important points about depreciation, amortization, and depletion can now be made. These points should be carefully considered because they express the nature and limitations of the consumption process.

1. The consumption process is based on the historical or acquisition cost of assets. The various depreciation, amortization, and depletion methods simply allocate this acquisition cost differently over the life of the asset. In every instance, the upper limit on recorded consumption is the acquisition cost of the asset.

2. Some movement away from reporting only strict historical cost-based consumption can now be observed in financial accounting. In 1976, the Securities and Exchange Commission (SEC) began to require large corporations to disclose the estimated replacement cost of property, plant, and equipment assets and to estimate and report depreciation on a replacement cost basis. This replacement cost basis information is intended to supplement, not substitute for, traditional historical cost information. Replacement cost disclosure is made by footnote to the financial statements contained in a special report (Form 10K) filed with the SEC.

3. Depreciation, amortization, and depletion are unlike other expenses in that they result essentially from an estimation process. It is possible for one or more of these estimates to change over the life of an asset, resulting in a change in the amount of consumption to be recorded on the asset. When estimates of salvage value or useful life change, revisions of depreciation, amortization, or depletion must be made. Revisions of depreciation are quite simple to record. The new undepreciated cost of the asset (after revision of estimate) is spread over the new remaining useful life (after revision of estimate) by whatever depreciation method is being used. In this way, revised depreciation expense is measured and recorded.

4. A second difference between consumption and other expenses is the cash effect of the expense. Depreciation, amortization, and depletion expenses require no cash outlay at the time the expense is recorded. A cash outlay generally occurs when the asset is acquired, and the subsequent recognition of depreciation expense has an effect on net income and income taxes but not on cash outflow.

5. An important characteristic of accelerated depreciation methods is that they result in lower income taxes in the years immediately following the purchase of a property, plant, and equipment asset. This is a very desirable circumstance for most businesses and accounts for much of the popularity of the double-declining-balance method. Remember that any business may use different depreciation methods on different assets and different depreciation methods on the same asset for income tax and financial statement purposes.

Concept Summary

Property, Plant, and Equipment Categories and Consumption		
Asset Category	*Consumption*	*Method*

Tangible Operating Assets
  Buildings
  Machines
  Equipment
  Vehicles
	Depreciation	Straight-line
		Sum-of-the-years'-digits
		Double-declining-balance
		Units-of-output

Intangibles
  Patent
  Copyright
  Trademark
  Organization costs
	Amortization	Straight-line

Natural Resources
  Oil well
  Gas well
  Mines
  Timber
	Depletion	Units-of-output

10.4   Subsequent Expenditures

In the discussion of the acquisition of property, plant, and equipment assets presented earlier, the importance of classifying expenditures as capital or revenue was emphasized. This distinction is important because capital expenditures become a part of the cost of an asset and affect income over the life of the asset, while revenue expenditures affect income immediately in the current period. Expenditures incurred in the purchase of property, plant, and equipment assets that are reasonable and necessary to the acquisition are capital expenditures. All other expenditures of acquisition are revenue expenditures.

Subsequent Expenditures Defined

An important characteristic of all acquisition expenditures is that they take place prior to placing the asset into service. Once an asset is in service and functioning, additional expenditures may be necessary from time to time to keep the asset performing at an acceptable level. Also, expenditures may occur to improve or add to an asset. Expenditures that occur after a property, plant, and equipment asset is in use and functioning are called **subsequent expenditures.** These subsequent expenditures, like acquisition expenditures, must be recorded as capital or revenue expenditures. Subsequent expenditures may be classified into four types: small expenditures, significant expenditures that are normal and recurring, additions and betterments, and extraordinary repairs.

Small expenditures Small expenditures should be treated in the most expedient manner. The principle at work here is materiality, which states that all small amounts, no matter what their nature, may be recorded in the most straightforward manner. Small subsequent expenditures should be recorded as revenue expenditures. This is accomplished by debiting an appropriate expense and crediting cash or a liability as the expenditure occurs.

Significant expenditures that are normal and recurring Normal repairs and regular maintenance are examples of significant expenditures that are normal and recurring. These expenditures may not be small in amount, but are expected by a business and are necessary to keep property, plant, and equipment assets performing at an acceptable level. Normal and recurring expenditures are treated as revenue expenditures by debiting repair and maintenance expense (or some similar expense account) and crediting an appropriate asset or liability.

Additions and betterments These expenditures are not typically normal and recurring, and do involve significant amounts. An example of an addition would be a new room or wing on a building. A significant new component is added to the asset. A betterment, such as replacing an old gasoline tank on a truck with a significantly larger one, improves the asset's capacity to perform as intended. In both of these instances, the asset has been significantly altered, and the alterations will benefit future periods.

The proper treatment for additions and betterments is to record them as capital expenditures by debiting the appropriate asset account. If a new wing were added to an existing building, the cost of the new wing would be debited to the building account and depreciated over the remaining life of the building. Likewise, the cost of a large gasoline tank would be debited to the truck account and depreciated accordingly. The most important characteristic of additions and betterments is that they improve an asset's capacity to perform in its intended use or create new uses for the asset. With either result, future accounting periods will benefit.

Extraordinary repairs Some repairs are to be expected over the life of most long-term assets; however, sometimes it becomes necessary for a business to incur unusual and nonrecurring repair expenditures to keep an asset functioning properly. These extraordinary repairs may occur only once in the life of most assets. When they do occur, the result is usually an extension of the useful life of the asset because some critical component has been reconditioned or replaced. Examples of extraordinary repairs include a new engine for a truck, motor for a machine, or roof for a building. In each of these instances, some future benefit has been created and, therefore, a capital expenditure is necessary.

Because the future benefit is in the form of an increase in useful life rather than in the creation of a new or significantly better asset, this type of capital expenditure is recorded differently. Subsequent expenditures that increase the useful life of an asset are recorded by debiting the cost of the repairs to the accumulated depreciation account of the asset. This lowers the balance in accumulated depreciation and increases the book value of the asset but does not alter acquisition cost. The new book value is then depreciated over the remaining useful life of the asset.

A simple example will help illustrate this treatment. Suppose a machine is purchased on January 1, 1982, for $5,000 and is expected to last for five years. Salvage value is zero, and straight-line depreciation of $1,000 is taken each year for four years. At the end of the fourth year, a rebuilt motor is installed on the machine at a cost of $1,400. The new motor is expected to extend the life of the machine three years beyond the original useful life; the new useful life being four years from the extraordinary repair. The journal entry and relevant ledger accounts to illustrate the treatment of the above situation are given below:

```
12/31/85   Accumulated depreciation: Machine  . . . . . . . . . . . . .   1,400
             Cash   . . . . . . . . . . . . . . . . . . . . . . . . . . . . . . . . . . .          1,400
```

The new annual depreciation amount would be $600 calculated as follows:

$$(\$1,000 + \$1,400) \div (\text{new useful life of 4 years})$$

The T accounts reflecting this situation are shown below.

Machine		Accumulated depreciation: machine		
1/1/82 5,000		12/31/85 1,400	12/31/82	1,000
			12/31/83	1,000
			12/31/84	1,000
			12/31/85	1,000
			12/31/86	600
			12/31/87	600
			12/31/88	600
			12/31/89	600

The cash and depreciation expense accounts that would be affected by these entries have been omitted. Notice that the 12/31/85 extraordinary repair of $1,400 decreases accumulated depreciation and increases book value. The new useful life is reflected in lower depreciation expense for the remaining life of the asset. Book value of the asset at the end of its useful life (12/31/89) is zero, as it should be.

Concept Summary

Subsequent Expenditures and Their Treatment	
Subsequent Event Classification	*Proper Treatment*

Small amounts (immaterial)
  Window on building
  Door on building
  Battery on vehicle
  Tire on vehicle
	Expense
	Cash or Liability

	(continued on next page)

Concept Summary
continued

Subsequent Event Classification	Proper treatment
Normal and recurring Painting trim on building Roof shingles on building 6,000 mile check-up for vehicle Paint job for vehicle	Expense Cash or Liability
Additions and betterments New wing on building Air conditioning system for building Trailer for vehicle Larger gasoline tank for vehicle	Asset Cash or Liability
Extraordinary repairs New roof for building New foundation for building New engine for vehicle New axle for vehicle	Accumulated depreciation Cash or Liability

10.5 Disposal of Property, Plant, and Equipment

When a business has consumed all of the services inherent in a long-term asset or the asset has worn out or become obsolete, it must be disposed of in some manner. Property, plant, and equipment assets may be disposed of by scrapping the asset, selling the asset, or trading the old asset in on a new asset.

Updating Depreciation

Most asset disposals take place during an accounting period rather than at the end of the period. Yet, depreciation on property, plant, and equipment assets is normally recorded at the end of each period as an adjusting entry. When an asset is disposed of at other than year's end, an entry that brings the expense and accumulated depreciation accounts up-to-date for depreciation since the previous year's end must be made prior to the disposal. This depreciation entry is important because the asset has been used during the period of its disposal, and a portion of its cost must be allocated accordingly. Also, the entry that records depreciation for the fraction of the year ending on the date of disposal affects the book value of the asset, and book value is an important factor in recording asset disposal.

Disposing of a property, plant, and equipment asset, then, is a two-step procedure: (1) bring depreciation records up-to-date, and (2) record scrapping, selling, or trading in the asset.

Methods of Disposal

Figure 10-5 presents representative data for a property, plant, and equipment asset that is being disposed of under several different assumptions.

FIGURE 10-5
Asset Data for
Recording Disposal of
Property, Plant, and
Equipment

Cost of equipment $20,000
Salvage value 0
Date of purchase 1/1/81
Useful life .... 10 years
Method of depreciation .... Straight-line

Assume:
1. The equipment is scrapped at the end of its useful life on 12/31/90.
2. The equipment is scrapped on 12/31/89.
3. The equipment is sold for $2,500 on 12/31/89.
4. The equipment is sold for $1,750 on 12/31/89.
5. The equipment is traded in for a new machine with a list price of $25,000 on 12/31/89. A trade-in allowance of $3,000 is given on the old equipment.
6. The equipment is traded in for a new machine with a list price of $25,000 on 12/31/89. A trade-in allowance of $500 is given on the old equipment.

This basic data will be used to illustrate the various ways in which disposals of long-term assets occur.

Asset Scrapped—No Gain or Loss In this instance an asset is scrapped at the end of its useful life. The asset is fully depreciated with no salvage value and, thus, has a book value of zero at the point of its disposal. Whenever a property, plant, and equipment asset is disposed of, the cost of the asset must be removed from the books by a credit to the asset account, and the related accumulated depreciation, removed by a debit. The net of these two amounts is book value, and the difference between book value and the amount received for the asset represents a **gain or loss** on the disposal. When an asset with zero book value is scrapped, no gain or loss results. The transaction would be recorded as follows:

Accumulated depreciation: Equipment	20,000	
Equipment		20,000

Nothing has been received for the asset, and the book value of zero is removed from the books. Total assets and net income are not affected by this transaction.

Asset Scrapped—Loss Is Recognized Here, the asset is scrapped at the end of the ninth year of its useful life. Book value is $2,000 (cost = $20,000; accumulated depreciation = $18,000), and nothing is received for the asset. The result of this disposal is a reduction in total assets of $2,000 and a special expense-type account called a loss is created to recognize this total asset decrease. The entry appears below.

Loss on equipment disposal	2,000	
Accumulated depreciation: Equipment	18,000	
Equipment		20,000

The loss would be reported as a deduction on the income statement and would result in lower net income and owners' equity. Thus, the ultimate effect of this transaction is an equal decrease in assets and owners' equity.

Asset Sold—Gain Is Recognized One year before the end of its useful life, the asset with a book value of $2,000 is sold for $2,500. Assets increase for the business by a net of $500 and a special revenue-type account called a gain is created to recognize this total asset increase. The entry for this transaction is as follows:

```
Cash  ..............................................   2,500
Accumulated depreciation: Equipment  ...................  18,000
    Equipment  ........................................          20,000
    Gain on equipment disposal  .........................             500
```

The gain increases net income and, correspondingly, owners' equity is increased. Thus, the ultimate result of this asset sale is an equal increase in assets and owners' equity.

Asset Sold—Loss Is Recognized The amount received from the sale of the asset under this assumption is less than book value. Assets will decrease, and a loss recognized as follows:

```
Loss on equipment disposal  ...........................     250
Cash  ...............................................   1,750
Accumulated depreciation: Equipment  ...................  18,000
    Equipment  ........................................          20,000
```

Assets and owners' equity decrease, and the loss is reflected on the income statement for the period.

Asset Traded In—No Gain Recognized Trade-ins of similar assets occur frequently, particularly with machines, equipment, and vehicles. Two figures not encountered when assets are scrapped or sold are important to the trade-in process. These are the list price of the new asset and the trade-in allowance on the old asset. Typically, a business will give up its old asset plus some cash and receive in exchange a new, similar asset. The list price of the new asset minus the trade-in allowance on the old asset determines the amount of cash to be paid in the transaction. The trade-in allowance may exceed the book value of the old asset, creating what seems to be the possibility of a gain on the exchange; however, list prices are often unrealistically high and may not approximate the cash price of the asset. This high list price makes possible a higher trade-in allowance on old assets. Because these amounts may not be realistic indicators of the true worth of either the new or the old asset, gains are not recognized on the trade-in of assets. Instead, the new asset is recorded on the books at an amount equal to the cash given up plus the book value of the old asset. In this way, no gain is created. The entry to accomplish this exchange is

```
Equipment (new) .......................................    24,000
Accumulated depreciation: Equipment (old) .............    18,000
    Equipment (old) ......................................            20,000
    Cash ..............................................            22,000
```

Cost of new equipment:
```
    Book value of old equipment ................    $ 2,000
    Cash given up (list price = $25,000
        minus trade-in allowance = $3,000) ........    22,000
                                                       $24,000
```

This exchange results in no change in total assets and no effect on net income. Notice that the list price and trade-in allowance are not recorded on the books. They are used only to determine the amount of cash that must be paid in the transaction.

Asset Traded In—Loss on Financial Accounting Records; No Loss for Tax Purposes Because the trade-in allowance may be lower than book value when an asset is traded in, the possibility of a loss on an exchange of similar assets exists. Significant (material) losses on trade-ins should be recognized in the financial accounting records. No losses on trade-ins of similar assets are permitted for tax purposes, however. This situation is one of those circumstances where financial accounting rules and income tax regulations do not agree, and each does not recognize the treatment of the other. Exchanges involving significant losses, then, must be recorded in two different ways, one for financial accounting and one for income tax purposes. The two entries necessary are given below:

Financial accounting—loss recognized

```
Loss on equipment disposal ...........................    1,500
Equipment (new) .......................................    25,000
Accumulated depreciation: Equipment (old) .............    18,000
    Equipment (old) ......................................            20,000
    Cash .............................................            24,500
```

Loss on equipment disposal is equal to book value ($2,000) minus trade-in allowance ($500). The asset is recorded at list price.

Income tax—no loss recognized

```
Equipment (new) .......................................    26,500
Accumulated depreciation: Equipment (old) .............    18,000
    Equipment (old) ......................................            20,000
    Cash .............................................            24,500
```

Here, the new asset is recorded as the cash given up ($24,500) plus the book value of the old asset ($2,000) in a manner similar to that discussed for an asset traded in with no gain recognized.

Exchanges that result in small losses are usually recorded in only one way, the income tax approach. Only significant losses on exchanges must be recorded in the financial accounting books.

Updating Depreciation Illustrated To illustrate the process of bringing depreciation up-to-date before disposing of a property, plant, and equipment asset, suppose the asset presented in Figure 10-5 is disposed of on April 1, 1989. An entry would be necessary prior to the disposal for the fractional period of use in 1989 as follows:

Depreciation expense	500	
Accumulated depreciation: Equipment		500
(20,000 × 1/10 × 1/4)		

Then, the appropriate entry to record the disposal of the equipment can be made.

Concept Summary

Disposal of Property, Plant, and Equipment		
Method of Disposal	*Gain or Loss*	*Effect on Financial Statements*
Scrap Asset	No gain or loss	No effect on total assets or net income
	Loss recognized	Total assets and net income decreased
Sell Asset*	Gain recognized	Total assets and net income increased
	Loss recognized	Total assets and net income decreased
Trade In Asset	No gain recognized	No effect on total assets or net income
	No loss recognized (income taxes only)	———
	Loss recognized (financial accounting)	Total assets and net income decreased

*It would be rare, but an asset could be sold at exactly its book value, resulting in neither a gain nor a loss.

Summary

The life cycle of property, plant, and equipment assets consists of three stages: acquisition, consumption, and disposal.

In the acquisition stage the purchase cost of a property, plant, and equipment asset is measured and recorded. All expenditures that are reasonable and necessary to acquire, transport, and ready for use should be included in the asset's cost. Interest, which is a cost of financing, is not normally capitalized, but is treated as an expense of the period.

The consumption of the services of a property, plant, and equipment asset is called depreciation, amortization, or depletion. In estimating consumption, the depreciation base, useful life, and depreciation method must be determined for each asset.

Expenditures made on an asset after it is performing in its intended capacity are called subsequent expenditures. These expenditures may be treated as revenue expenditures if they are small or are normal and recurring. Subsequent expenditures that increase the capacity of an asset to perform or increase its useful life should be capitalized.

Property, plant, and equipment assets are disposed of by scrapping, selling, or trading in. Scrapping an asset may result in a loss, while selling may create a gain or a loss. Only losses are recognized on trade-ins of similar assets.

Intangible assets include patents, copyrights, trademarks, organization costs, and goodwill. These assets are amortized over their useful life. Natural resources include oil wells, gas wells, gold mines, and coal mines. These assets are depleted over their useful life.

The detailed principles and procedures necessary to account for the most important equities of a business are presented in the next three chapters. Chapter 11 deals with current liabilities.

Key Terms

Accelerated depreciation	Extraordinary repairs
Accumulated depreciation	Gain or loss
Acquisition	Intangible assets
Additions and betterments	Land improvements
Amortization	Lump sum purchase
Book value	Natural resources
Capital expenditure	Revenue expenditure
Consumption	Salvage (residual value)
Depletion	Straight-line
Depreciation	Subsequent expenditure
Depreciation base	Sum-of-the-years'-digits
Disposal	Units-of-output
Double-declining-balance	Useful life

Comprehensive Review Problem

The following events apply to Mechanized Organic Farming Commune during the year 1982:

On January 2, the commune borrowed $25,000 from the bank at a 10 percent yearly interest rate and signed a five-year note. Part of the proceeds were used to buy an incubator for $22,000, terms 2/30, n/60. There was a 5 percent sales tax, and freight charges incurred were $800. The farm owners installed the incubator themselves; but while installing it, they knocked down a gate. The gate repairs cost $35, and the labor cost of installing the machine was $115. The incubator is estimated to have a ten-year life with a salvage value of $2,500. Straight-line depreciation will be used.

On March 22, the commune purchased a small neighboring lot and barn for $2,000. The land was appraised at $2,500, and the commune spent $75 removing the building.

On July 1, the commune traded in its old tractor for a new fuel-efficient model. The old tractor had been purchased for $17,000 on Janaury 1, 1980, and was being depreciated by the double-declining-balance method over a ten-year estimated life. The new tractor was a bargain. The list price was $14,000, and the trade-in allowance on the old tractor was $10,000. Commune members estimate that the new tractor will last five years with a salvage value of $800. Sum-of-the-years'-digits depreciation will be used.

The commune has a copyright on its book, *Mechanized Organic Vegetable Farming*, which it is amortizing over a twenty-year period. The original value of the copyright was $500.

Required:

1. Prepare journal entries to record the transactions described.

2. Make the necessary adjusting entries required on December 31, 1982, when the commune prepares its financial statements.

Solution to Comprehensive Review Problem

MECHANIZED ORGANIC FARMING COMMUNE

General Journal

Date		Transaction Accounts	Debit	Credit
1982				
Jan	2	Cash	25,000	
		Note payable		25,000
		Issued a 5-year note, 10% interest		
	2	Machinery: Incubator	23,438	
		Cash		23,438
		Purchased an incubator for $22,000, terms		
		2/30, n/60. Cost of the machine determined		
		as follows:		
		Machine price .... $22,000 × .98 = $21,560		
		Sales tax .... 5% × $21,560 = 1,078		
		Freight 800		
		Total cost $23,438		
	2	Machinery: Incubator	115	
		Salaries payable		115
		Capitalize labor costs of incubator installation		
	2	Repair expense	35	
		Cash		35
		Repaired gate		
Mar	22	Land	2,075	
		Cash		2,075
		Purchased land. Cost = purchase price + cost of removing		
		building: $2,000 + $75 = $2,075		

July	1	Depreciation expense	1,088	
		Accumulated depreciation: Tractor		1,088
		Record six months' depreciation on tractor prior to sale:		
		Yr. 1 20% × $17,000 = $3,400 (1979 depr.)		
		Yr. 2 20% × ($17,000 − $3,400) = $2,720		
		(1980 depreciation)		
		Yr. 3 6/12 × 20% × ($17,000 − $6,120) = $1,088		
		(1981 depreciation)		
	1	Tractor, new	13,792	
		Accumulated depreciation: Tractor	7,208	
		Tractor, old		17,000
		Cash		4,000
		To record purchase of new tractor and trade-in of old tractor:		
		List price $14,000		
		Less: trade-in 10,000		
		Cash paid .... $ 4,000		

Adjusting Entries

Dec	31	Interest expense	2,500	
		Interest payable		2,500
		Accrue interest on note payable		
		(10% × $25,000)		
	31	Depreciation expense	2,105	
		Accumulated depreciation: Incubator		2,105
		Record depreciation on incubator		

$$\left(\frac{\$23,553 - \$2,500}{10} = \$2,105\right)$$

	31	Depreciation expense	2,165	
		Accumulated depreciation: Tractor		2,165
		Record depreciation on tractor		
		($13,792 − $800) × 5/15 × 6/12 = $2,165		
	31	Amortization expense	25	
		Copyright		25
		To record yearly amortization on copyright		
		($500 ÷ 20 yrs = $25)		

Questions

Q10-1. Define acquisition cost as it relates to property, plant, and equipment assets.

Q10-2. What is the difference between the treatment of capital expenditures and the treatment of revenue expenditures? Is this distinction important only in the acquisition of property, plant, and equipment assets?

Q10-3. Describe how the acquisition cost of individual assets is determined when a lump sum purchase occurs.

Q10-4. Which depreciation method does not use depreciation base in its calculations? Is salvage or residual value a factor in applying this method?

Q10-5. Give the formula for the units-of-output method of depreciation. How is annual depreciation expense determined with this method?

Q10-6. List four types of subsequent expenditures and give an example of each.

Q10-7. How is the acquisition cost of a new asset determined if it is obtained by the trade-in of an old asset and the payment of cash?

Q10-8. Can a gain or loss be recorded on the scrapping of an asset? The sale of an asset? The trade-in of an asset?

Q10-9. Give three examples of common intangible assets. What method is usually used to calculate the consumption of these assets? Why?

Q10-10. Give three examples of natural resources. What method is usually used to calculate the consumption of these assets? Why?

Exercises

E10-1. In the blanks provided, write the letter of the item most closely associated with each statement. Some items may be used more than once, and some may not be used at all.

a. fixed assets	*h.* natural resources
b. investments	*i.* capital expenditures
c. patents	*j.* revenue expenditures
d. copyrights	*k.* appraisal values
e. trademarks	*l.* land improvements
f. depletion	*m.* depreciation
g. depreciation base	*n.* amortization

1. ___ These assets have tangible substance and long but limited lives and include gold mines and oil wells.

2. ___ Fences, parking lots, and driveways would be included in this category.

3. ___ These assets, which represent the largest category of assets in dollar terms on most balance sheets, are long lived and are acquired to be used rather than resold.

4. ___ These expenditures are debited to an asset and become part of its cost.

5. ___ This is the process of allocating the cost of natural resources to the periods that benefit from their use.

6. ___ This is the process of allocating the cost of intangible operating assets to the periods that benefit from their use.

7. ___ This asset represents rights granted by the federal government to use and control inventions.

8. ___ This is the process of allocating the cost of tangible operating assets to the periods that benefit from their use.

9. ___ These expenditures contain no future benefit beyond the current accounting period.

10. ___ This amount is calculated by subtracting salvage value from acquisition cost.

E10-2. Carol Company acquired new office furniture for its executive offices. The furniture had a list price of $12,000, but was subject to credit terms of 3/10, n/30. Sales tax of 6% was charged on the net price. Carol paid the invoice within the discount period. Transportation costs of $325 were paid by Carol. An interior decorator was paid $500 for overseeing the unloading and placement of the furniture in the executive offices. Compute the cost of the new furniture that should be debited to the office furniture account.

E10-3. The Mittens Corporation acquired land, building, and equipment from the Irwin Company for $125,000. Before this sale, an appraisal had indicated the following values:

Land	$93,000
Building	46,500
Equipment	15,500

If Mittens Corporation made a down payment of $50,000 and assumed a mortgage for the balance due, give the journal entry required to record the acquisition of assets from Irwin Company.

E10-4. Give the required journal entry for each of the following situations involving the acquisition of assets:

1. X Company paid $65,000 for a parcel of land on which a warehouse will be located. The land at time of purchase was vacant, but it was surrounded by a twelve-foot chain link fence. The value of the fence was $6,000.

2. $115,000 was paid for land and building by Y Company. The building was valued at $20,000 and the land, at $95,000. The company bought the property because of the location of the land. The building was unsuitable for the company's purposes and was torn down. Wreckers charged $4,000 to remove the building. Receipts from the sale of scrap material from the building amounted to $1,200.

3. Z Company has owned an undeveloped piece of land for several years. This year, the company decided to construct a new building on this land after receiving a bid from an outside firm of $200,000 on the building. Z Company incurred materials costs of $95,000 and labor costs of $60,000 in constructing the building. Building permits were $200 and survey fees were $300.

E10-5. Turner Corporation purchased a machine January 2, 1981, for a total cost of $24,000. The asset has an economic life of three years and an estimated salvage value of $1,500. The machine is estimated to produce 20,000 units of output in 1981, 18,000 units in 1982, and 12,000 units in 1983. Prepare a depreciation schedule to cover the life of the asset under each of the following methods:

1. Straight-line

2. Sum-of-the-years'-digits

3. Double-declining-balance

4. Units-of-output

E10-6. The following information is available concerning the King Lee Company:

a. The building that houses Lee's business was acquired January 2, 1977, at a cost of $52,000. The estimated life is twenty years, and estimated salvage value is $2,000. Lee has used straight-line depreciation on this building.

b. Lee acquired a patent early in 1978 to cover a process used in his operations. He paid $15,000 for the patent which, at that time, had twelve years of life remaining.

c. Lee purchased special equipment in 1981 for $12,000. The equipment has a useful life of five years, a $700 salvage value, and is being depreciated by the double-declining-balance method.

d. Lee acquired mining rights on certain property in May 1982 at a cost of $75,000. It is estimated that 60,000 tons of ore are available at the site. In 1982, 15,000 tons of ore were mined.

Required:

1. Prepare the required journal entries for the above transactions for the year ended December 31, 1982.

2. Prepare a partial balance sheet as of December 31, 1982, and show how each of the above would be presented.

E10-7. Consider each of the items below independently. Indicate the account or accounts to be *debited* when recording each transaction using the preferred accounting treatment by placing the proper letter in the blank space provided.

a. Building	f. Land
b. Equipment	g. Land improvements
c. Intangible assets	h. Depletion
d. Expense	i. Amortization
e. Accumulated depreciation: Building	j. Accumulated depreciation: Equipment

1. ___ Equipment was installed at a cost of $60.

2. ___ The cost of extensive plumbing repairs on a building just purchased was $3,000.

3. ___ New windows were installed in the building at a cost of $120.

4. ___ A parking lot was added to the land adjacent to the building at a cost of $4,000.

5. ___ A new motor was installed on a piece of equipment for $500.

6. ___ A new roof was placed on the building at a cost of $3,000.

7. ___ Paid $100 for a land survey upon purchase of the land.

8. ___ Acquired a copyright at a cost of $700.

9. ___ Installed a new safety lock on the front door of the building at a cost of $35.

10. ___ Replaced belts on four pieces of equipment at a cost of $100.

E10-8. Juliette Company acquired a machine on September 1, 1980, which had a selling price of $42,000 but was subject to terms of 2/10, n/30. Juliette did not pay within the discount period and, thus, paid the full amount for the machine. Transportation charges of $250 were paid by Juliette, and an additional $890 was paid to have the machine installed and made ready for use. The machine had an estimated life of five years and an estimated salvage value of $2,500. Juliette elected to use the sum-of-the-years'-digits method of depreciation. On September 1, 1982, Juliette discontinued the product line manufactured by this machine and disposed of the machine. Give the entry to record the disposal under each of the three following assumptions:

1. The machine was sold for $25,000.

2. The machine was sold for $15,000.

3. The machine was sold for $18,420.

E10-9. Record in journal entry form the trade-in of the assets described below. Each instance is independent of the other.

Truck A was acquired January 1, 1980, at a cost of $7,200. It was estimated to have a useful life of three years and a salvage value of $500. The double-declining-balance method of depreciation has been used. On June 30, 1982, Truck A was traded in for a similar truck with a list price of $10,000. A trade-in of $1,500 was allowed on the truck, and $8,500 was paid in cash. If there had been no trade-in, the cash purchase price would have been $9,500.

Truck B was acquired January 1, 1981, at a cost of $6,600. It had an estimated life of three years and an estimated salvage value of $600. The sum-of-the-years'-digits method of depreciation has been used. On April 1, 1982, Truck B is traded in on a new truck with a list price of $8,000. A $1,000 trade-in was allowed on Truck B, and $7,000 was paid in cash. If there had been no trade-in, the cash price would have been $8,000.

E10-10. Prepare a partial balance sheet at December 31, 1982, for Gregory Corporation whose accounts reveal the following information:

Item	Description	Cost
a. Copyright	Acquired January 1, 1977; estimated economic life, twenty years.	$ 15,000
b. Organization costs	Incurred January 1, 1976; being written off over ten years.	$ 6,000
c. Equipment	Purchased July 1, 1978; ten-year life; no salvage; straight-line depreciation.	$ 50,000
d. Oil well rights	Acquired March 15, 1982; estimated reserves, 100,000 barrels; output in 1981, 30,000 barrels.	$250,000
e. Patent	Acquired September 1, 1978; estimated economic life, eight years.	$ 72,000
f. Land	Purchased January 2, 1976.	$ 60,000
g. Land improvement	Acquired April 1, 1976; no salvage value; estimated life, fifteen years; straight-line depreciation.	$ 20,000
h. Building	Purchased January 2, 1976; estimated salvage value, $15,000; estimated life, twenty years; straight-line depreciation.	$ 80,000

Problems

P10-1. What is the objective of the accounting concept of depreciation? Does systematic depreciation provide the cash to replace an asset at the end of its useful life? Distinguish among depreciation, amortization, and depletion.

P10-2. Determine the cost to be used in recording the acquisition of each of the following assets and prepare the required general journal entry in each case.

1. Machine M was acquired at a list price of $10,000 with terms 3/10, n/30. The invoice was not paid within the discount period. Transportation costs were $410. Installation costs were $225. Normal maintenance and repairs for the first month were $60.

2. In May, Company C made an offer of $30,000 for land on which it desired to build a factory. The offer was rejected. In August, the land was acquired in exchange for 300 shares of the company's stock. The stock was selling at $125 a share at that time. The company's president felt sure the land was worth at least $40,000.

3. Truck D was acquired under an installment contract. The terms of the contract called for thirty-six payments of $175 each plus a down payment of $1,500. The cash price of the truck was $6,500. Sales tax on the truck was $390. Tags and fees amounted to $30; both were paid in cash.

4. Equipment with an original cost of $27,000 and a book value of $18,000 was exchanged for similar equipment with a list price of $27,600. Besides trading in the old equipment, $10,200 was paid in cash. What is the cost of the new equipment for financial accounting purposes? For income tax purposes?

P10-3. Toby Corporation acquired office equipment May 1, 1980. The equipment had a list price of $8,000 and was subject to terms of 2/10, n/30. Transportation costs on the equipment were $90. The equipment is estimated to have an economic life of five years and a salvage value of $300. The equipment is estimated to have a total output of 60,000 units. 10,000 units were produced in 1980; 15,000 units, in 1981; and 17,000 units, in 1982.

Required:
Prepare a schedule showing depreciation expense for 1980, 1981, and 1982 assuming depreciation is computed under each of the following methods:

1. Straight-line

2. Sum-of-the-years'-digits

3. Double-declining-balance

4. Units-of-output

P10-4. Dyer Company is on a calendar year basis. The straight-line method of depreciation is used on all of its plant and equipment. On January 2, 1978, equipment was purchased with a cash price of $230,000. A $50,000 down payment was made, and Dyer agreed to make forty-eight monthly payments of $4,740. Transportation costs on the equipment were $330. Installation costs were $375, and the costs of a trial run were $95. Useful life was estimated to be ten years, and residual value was estimated at $5,000.

On December 31, 1981, before an adjusting entry for depreciation was made, the company concluded that the estimate of useful life should be revised. There had been many technological changes in this type of equipment in recent years, and it was now estimated that useful life would be six rather than ten years, and salvage value would only be $3,000.

On April 30, 1982, Dyer Company sold the equipment for $60,000.

Required:

Prepare general journal entries to record the acquisition of the equipment, the depreciation expense at the end of each of the four years, and the disposal of the equipment.

P10-5. Compute the answer to each of the following questions:

1. A machine with an estimated life of eight years and a residual value of $1,400 was acquired at a cost of $13,000. Depreciation for the third year of use, determined by using the double-declining-balance method, is _____ .

2. Equipment purchased for $20,000 at the beginning of the year has an estimated life of six years and a residual value of $2,400. Depreciation for the second year of use, determined by using the sum-of-the-years'-digits depreciation method, is _____ .

3. A truck with a cost of $7,500 and accumulated depreciation of $1,500 and $5,000 in cash are given in exchange for a similar truck with a cash price of $8,500. The gain or loss on the disposal for accounting purposes is _____ .

4. Refer to the data in Part 3 of this problem. The gain or loss on disposal that would be recognized for income tax purposes is _____ .

5. An item of office furniture with a cost of $12,000, estimated life of five years, and a residual value of $1,500 is depreciated using the straight-line method. This asset is sold for $7,000 at the end of the fourth year of use. The amount of gain or loss to recognize on disposal is _____ .

6. An old machine with a book value of $4,000 was traded in on a new machine. The new machine, which had a list price of $45,000, was acquired for $34,000 cash plus the old machine. For accounting purposes, the cost of the new machine would be _____ .

7. Property that included land, a building, and equipment was purchased for $175,000. Just prior to the purchase, the land was appraised at $85,000, the building was appraised at $75,000, and the equipment was appraised at $20,000. For accounting purposes, the land should be recorded at a cost of _____ .

8. There were eight trucks in the company's fleet. During December, $150 was spent on tune-ups, $200 for brake relinings, and $115 for radiator repairs. An old gasoline tank on one truck was replaced by a new one with a larger capacity at a cost of $250. The amounts and accounts in which these expenses should be entered are _____ .

9. A building was acquired five years ago at a cost of $64,000. The estimated life was twenty years, and salvage value was estimated to be $4,000. At the end of the fifth year, $3,000 was spent on a new roof, which was expected to increase estimated life five years. The estimate of salvage value was not changed. The amount of depreciation expense to record at the end of the fifth year is _____ .

10. A fixed asset has a cost of $10,000 and a salvage value of $1,000. The asset has a three-year life. If depreciation expense in the third year was $1,500, the depreciation method used was _____ .

P10-6. In reviewing the books of Crowley Corporation on December 31, 1982, before the accounts have been closed for the year, you discover the following account:

Delivery trucks

1/2/80	Truck A	7,500	4/1/82	Proceeds from sale	
7/1/80	Truck B	6,000		of Truck B	4,300
1/1/81	Truck C	6,900			

You discover that, although each truck had zero salvage value and an estimated life of three years, no depreciation had ever been recorded. Truck B was sold because the company implemented a new policy regarding deliveries, and the volume no longer justified keeping this truck. At the time of sale, cash was debited $4,300, and the proceeds were simply credited to the delivery trucks account. Truck A is to be scrapped December 31, 1982.

Required:

Give the correcting and adjusting entries required December 31, 1982, assuming straight-line depreciation is appropriate.

P10-7. Five transactions involving intangibles are described below. For each transaction, prepare the journal entry to record the acquisition of the intangible and also prepare the journal entry to record the amortization of the intangible at the end of the first year.

1. The Alana Corporation purchased a patent for $37,800 on January 2 of the current year. On the date of purchase, the patent had a remaining legal life of thirteen years; but because of rapid technological advances in this area, it was estimated that the remaining economic life of the patent would be only six years. On July 1 of the current year, $5,000 was paid in legal fees to settle an infringement suit involving this patent.

2. Olivier Corporation purchased the assets of Snyder Company for $115,000 on January 2. The fair value of the assets of Snyder at the time of purchase was only $90,000; therefore, $25,000 of goodwill is recognized. Olivier amortizes goodwill over forty years.

3. At the beginning of the current year, Pommard Corporation acquired leasehold rights from Kenner Company for $75,000. The leasehold rights cover a period of five years.

4. On January 2, Kibby Company acquired a franchise to open an outlet of Aunt Sally's Pancake House. These breakfast restaurants had gained a reputation in the South, and the management of Aunt Sally's was eager to spread west. Kibby acquired the franchise for a price of $70,000. Kibby management paid $20,000 in cash and signed a note payable for $50,000 at 8 percent interest. Principal payment at the end of the first year was $10,000.

5. Beethe Company acquired a copyright from a young musician for a song he composed at a price of $50,000 cash in January of the current year.

P10-8. For each of the four situations described below, give the journal entries required in the accounts to record the exchange of similar assets. Also, in each situation, indicate what the cost basis of the asset would be for income tax purposes.

Part A. Gandolphi Company had an old truck that originally cost $8,000 and had depreciation to date of $6,500. The old truck was exchanged for a new truck that had a firm cash price of $7,000. Two independent situations are assumed:

Situation 1 There was a direct exchange. No cash difference was paid or received.

Situation 2 Gandolphi Company exchanged the old truck for the new truck and paid a cash difference of $4,300.

Part B. Brown Corporation had old equipment that had originally cost $38,400 and has accumulated depreciation to date of $25,600. The old equipment was exchanged for similar new equipment that had a firm cash price of $11,520. Two independent situations are assumed:

Situation 3 There was a direct exchange. No cash difference was paid or received.

Situation 4 Brown Corporation exchanged the old machine for the new machine and paid a cash difference of $1,600.

P10-9. Black Corporation, a manufacturer of offshore oil drilling equipment, was organized January 2, 1979. The partial depreciation and amortization schedules presented below for 1981 and 1982 have been prepared by the accounting department of Black Corporation. All of the figures entered in the schedule are correct.

  a. Land A and Building A were acquired together at a cost of $120,000. Just prior to the purchase, the land had been appraised at $23,750 and the building, at $95,000.
  b. May 1, 1980, Land B was purchased for $72,000. At the time of purchase, it was also necessary to pay attorney's fees of $250 and a survey fee of $40. Immediately after acquiring the land, Black spent $2,000 to have the land cleared and graded. A fence costing $4,000 was erected around the land. Driveways were installed at a cost of $3,500.
  c. Equipment B was acquired January 2, 1980, through a trade-in of Equipment A, which had been acquired at a cost of $15,000. Accumulated depreciation on Equipment A at the date of trade-in was $6,200. Besides trading in Equipment A, Black paid cash of $8,000. Equipment B had a list price of $18,000.
  d. Truck B was acquired October 1, 1981. Truck A, which had a book value of $4,500, was traded in on Truck B. Black also paid $5,000 in cash. The cash price of Truck B if there had been no trade-in was $8,000.
  e. Patent A was acquired April 1, 1980, at a cost of $8,400 from a competitor who was liquidating his business. Black Company's president was certain the patent was worth at least $20,000. When purchased the patent had a remaining legal life of ten years. Black Company's president estimates the patent will have an economic life of five years.
  f. Organization costs of $11,000 were incurred January 2, 1979. Black Company has chosen to amortize these over five years.
  g. Goodwill of $33,600 was acquired through the purchase of a subsidiary company June 1, 1981.

Required:
Complete the schedules using the above additional information obtained from company records.

				BLACK COMPANY Depreciation Schedule For Years Ended December 31, 1981, and 1982				
Asset	Acquisition Date	Cost	Salvage Value	Depreciation Method	Est. Life	Depreciation Expense		
						1981	1982	
Land A	January 2, 1979	(1)	——	——	——	——	——
Building A	January 2, 1979	(2)	$6,000	Straight-line	(3)	$3,600	(4)
Land B	May 1, 1981	(5)	——	——	——	——	——
Land Improvements	May 1, 1981	(6)	0	Straight-line	(7)	$500	(8)
Equipment B	January 2, 1980	(9)	$1,800	(10)	5 years	(11)	$3,000
Truck B	October 1, 1981	(12)	$1,000	Double-declining-balance	4 years	(13)	(14)

				BLACK COMPANY Amortization Schedule For Years Ended December 31, 1981, and 1982			
Asset	Acquisition Date	Cost	Amortization Method	Est. Life	Amortization Expense		
					1981	1982	
Patent A	April 1, 1980	(15)	Straight-line	(16)	(17)	(18)
Organization Costs	January 2, 1979	(19)	Straight-line	(20)	(21)	(22)
Goodwill	June 1, 1981	(23)	Straight-line	(24)	$490	(25)

CHAPTER 11

Current Liabilities and Valuation Concepts

Chapter Outline

Accounting and the Real World

Were the Indians Wrong?

Indians sold Manhattan Island to Peter Minuit of the West India Company in 1626 for $24. If the $24 had been invested at 8 percent interest, it would be worth over $16 trillion by 1982. The following table shows the growth of the investment.

Date	Significance	Approximate Value
1626	Sale of Manhattan	$24
1776	Declaration of Independence	$2,000,000
1865	End of Civil War	$2,000,000,000
1982	Present Day	$16,000,000,000,000

Do you suppose Manhattan is worth $16 trillion today? If not, did the Indians enjoy the greater profit from the sale? One of the most important differences between an amateur investor and a seasoned pro concerns the amateur's way of calculating the profit on an investment. Consider the following example.

On February 17, 1978, Larry bought 300 shares ot Itek Corporation at $26 per share. The total cost, including commissions, was $7,712. "I think I'll get a good bounce out of it," he said at the same time. On February 1, 1980, he sold the 300 shares at $30, which brought him $8,950. "It's topping out," he said. "It looks to me like it's gone as far as it's going to go."

How well did Larry do? In his own estimation, the answer is "very." What was his reason for that judgment? "Well," he said, "I spent about $7,700. And I got back $8,950. That's a $1,250 gain on a $7,700 investment. Not bad."

Is he right? Suppose he had invested the $7,700 in a one-year bank certificate that earned him 10 percent per annum, the interest to be paid in a lump sum at maturity. Ignoring tax considerations for a moment, suppose he then repeated the process. Investing the $7,700 + $770 = $8,470 at 10 percent would have brought him $847. At the second maturity date, Larry would have had $9,317.

He held his Itek stock for approximately two years. Even taking into consideration the more favorable tax treatment accorded capital gains on stock than interest earned, he in fact did no better than he'd have done had his $7,700 remained in a bank certificate.

Larry's view of stock market profits is entirely typical. What he omits from his calculations, the majority of investors also overlook: namely, the time value of money. A dollar you owe today differs from the one you owed yesterday, and a dollar you receive tomorrow is not the same as the one you receive today. There is a date attached to every investment you make, and the longer your money is invested, the more it has to earn just for you to break even.

Forbes, March 3, 1980, page 114–115.

Liabilities are debts (1) whose existence is known with certainty and (2) where the amount owed is known or estimable. Accounts payable is a perfect example of a debt with both of these characteristics. Only liabilities that have these characteristics are reflected in the financial statements.

Even within the relatively short period of one year or the operating cycle, the time value of money can be important. The time value of money is the concept that money *now* can be invested and earn interest and hence, is, preferable to money in the future. The basic accounting implications of this concept are discussed in the final two sections of this chapter. The time value of money is even more important in relation to long-term liabilities and will be used extensively in the next chapter.

11.1   Notes Payable

Figure 8-4 illustrates a note signed by Henri Wolbrette of Wolbrette's Retail Hardware promising to pay Dozier's Wholesale Hardware $2,000 sixty days after December 1, 1981, plus interest at 12 percent per annum. As discussed in Chapter 8, this is a note receivable (an asset) for the payee which, in this instance, is Dozier's Wholesale Hardware. Viewed from the other direction, however, this is a note payable (a liability) for the maker, Wolbrette's Retail Hardware. Accounting for the note as a receivable was presented in Chapter 8; accounting for the note as a payable is discussed in this chapter.

There are three basic events in the cycle of a note payable: making the note, adjusting interest expense, and paying the note.

Making the Note

On the date the note is made, the maker must record the associated liability. For the sample note, the journal entry for Wolbrette's Retail Hardware would be:

```
Accounts payable, Dozier ...............................  2,000
   Notes payable  .........................................          2,000
```

The specific account payable is identified so that Wolbrette's accounts payable subsidiary ledger account for Dozier will be updated.

Adjusting Interest Expense

At the end of every accounting period prior to the maturity date of the note, it is necessary for the maker to record interest expense and accrue interest payable. (This is a Type 2 adjusting entry as discussed in Chapter 4.) For the sample note, the required adjusting entry on December 31, 1981, would be:

Interest expense	20	
Interest payable		20

The interest amount is calculated in exactly the same way as the interest amount for the payee to accrue as a receivable and as a revenue. Chapter 8 has a complete discussion of this calculation.

Paying the Note

When the maturity date occurs, the maker must (1) accrue any remaining interest and (2) pay the face value plus all accrued interest. The journal entry for the sample note would be:

Notes payable	2,000	
Interest payable	20	
Interest expense	20	
Cash		2,040

A more common form of note payable, however, is the note payable to a bank. The form is similar to that of the note given in Chapter 8, but the name of the bank is printed on the note. There are two basic types of bank notes: notes with explicit interest and notes with implicit interest.

Notes with Explicit Interest

Notes with **explicit interest** have an interest rate stated on the face of the note. Figure 11-1a is a note with explicit interest. By this note on July 1, 1981, Mr. Keith Wood has obligated Wood Lumber, Inc., to pay the Whitney National Bank, after one year, $1,000 plus 10 percent interest. The interest rate of 10 percent per annum is stated explicitly on the note.

The related journal entries will be very similar to the entries for the note payable discussed earlier. The journal entry when the note is made and the money borrowed would be

Cash	1,000	
Notes payable		1,000

At the end of the year, Wood Lumber, Inc., must make an adjusting journal entry to reflect the related interest expense and interest payable:

Interest expense	50	
Interest payable		50

(The amount of interest accrual is calculated as $1,000 \times 10\% \times \frac{1}{2} = \$50$.) When the note is due, the company must accrue the remaining interest and pay the amount due. The journal entry on July 1, 1982, would then be

FIGURE 11-1
Form of a Note

a. Explicit Interest

$1,000.00 _____ New Orleans, LA _____ July 1 _____ 19 81 _____

_____ One Year _____ After Date _____ We _____ Promise to Pay to

the Order of _____ the Whitney National Bank _____

_____ One thousand and 00/100————— _____ Dollars

For Value Received with Interest at _____ 10% _____ per annum

Wood Lumber, Inc.
Keith Wood, Pres.

b. Implicit Interest

$1,000.00 _____ New Orleans, LA _____ July 1 _____ 19 81 _____

_____ One Year _____ After Date _____ We _____ Promise to Pay to

the Order of _____ the Whitney National Bank _____

_____ One thousand and 00/100————— _____ Dollars

Wood Lumber, Inc.
Keith Wood, Pres.

Notes payable	1,000	
Interest expense	50	
Interest payable	50	
Cash		1,100

The amount paid out, $1,100, is equal to the amount received, $1,000, plus 10 percent interest ($1,100 = $1,000 + 10\% \times $1,000 = $1,000 + $100).

Notes with Implicit Interest

Notes with **implicit interest** do not have an interest rate stated on the face. For this reason, these notes are often called "non-interest-bearing." This term is misleading, however, because money is never lent without interest being charged. Figure 11-1b is an example of a note with implicit interest. In this instance, Wood Lumber promises to pay $1,000 in one year to the Whitney National Bank, but the bank did not give Wood Lumber the full $1,000. Interest was, in effect, charged by not giving the maker the face value of the note. The difference between the face value and the cash proceeds actually received is called the **discount on notes payable.** Under this arrangement, the face value of the note equals the maturity value. The cash proceeds are somewhat less; this difference is the discount. In both instances, the interest owed is growing continuously, but the interest expense is only recorded twice, once at the end of the accounting period and once at the maturity date of the note.

Assume that Wood Lumber receives $900 from making this note. The journal entry to record this transaction would be:

```
Cash .................................................   900
Discount on notes payable ..............................   100
    Notes payable .........................................        1,000
```

This procedure is followed because, as in the earlier instance, the notes payable account should reflect the face value of the notes. The account, discount on notes payable, is a contra-liability account. As such, it has a debit balance. This discount account is credited by adjusting entries when interest expense is recorded. In this example, the total interest expense will be $100, the difference between the amount paid to the bank and the amount received from the bank.

The journal entry at the end of the year would be

```
Interest expense .............................................   50
    Discount on notes payable ...................................        50
```

At the maturity date of the note, there would be two journal entries, one to record the remaining interest expense and eliminate the discount amount and another to record payment. The journal entry to record remaining interest would be

Concept Summary

Accounting Treatment of Explicit versus Implicit Interest		
	Explicit Interest	*Implicit Interest*

July 1, 1981 Borrow with a one-year note having a face value of $1,000 at 10% interest	Cash 1,000
	    Notes payable 1,000
	Amount borrowed is the face value.
	Effective rate = stated rate = 10%
		Cash 900
		Discount on notes
		    payable 100
		    Notes payable 1,000
		Amount borrowed is face value less interest.
		Effective rate = $\frac{100}{900}$ = 11.1%

December 31, 1981 Accrue interest at the end of the accounting period	Interest expense 50
	    Interest payable 50
	Amount of interest is face value × interest rate.
		Interest expense 50
		Discount on notes
		    payable 50
		Amount of interest is face value × interest rate.

July 1, 1982 Accrue remaining interest and pay off note	Notes payable 1,000
	Interest expense 50
	Interest payable 50
	    Cash 1,100
	Amount repaid is the maturity value (face value + interest).
		Interest expense 50
		Discount on notes
		    payable 50
		Notes payable 1,000
		    Cash 1,000
		Amount repaid is the face value.

Interest expense 50
    Discount on notes payable 50

The journal entry to record payment would be

Notes payable 1,000
    Cash 1,000

11.2 Payroll and Related Liabilities

Payroll expenditures are extremely important in almost every business and, hence, must be subject to careful control. Complicating the matter further are a number of government regulations and requirements that must be met by even the smallest firms. Basically, however, payroll accounting procedures arise from the problems of withholdings and fringe benefits.

Withholdings

The salaries and wages earned by employees will always be more than the amounts actually received by those employees. The reason for this discrepancy is that entities (organizations and government agencies) other than the employee have a claim on the employee's earnings. Usually, the business paying the salaries and wages acts as a collecting agent for these external entities and withholds amounts due others from the earnings of employees. From the paying company's point of view, this means that salary and wage expense will be larger than the cash paid out to employees, since some amounts earned and included in salary and wage expense will ultimately be paid out to other organizations and entities.

The most important deductions are those for **federal income taxes withheld** and **state income taxes withheld** and for the employee's required share of social security taxes. Social security taxes are authorized by the **Federal Insurance Contributions Act (FICA)** and, hence, are often called FICA taxes. Also included might be a wide range of more or less optional deductions authorized by the employees, such as life and hospitalization insurance, pension plans, savings bonds, and union dues. In all of these instances, the employer simply holds out from the employee's earnings the amounts necessary to cover these deductions and then pays the employee what is left. These various withholdings do not belong to the employer, however, and are eventually paid out to the proper entities.

Fringe Benefits

The total cost of maintaining a labor force is always more than the employees earn in salaries and wages. The reason for this is that employees actually earn more (and, therefore, cost more) than their salary or wage. These extra costs always associated with labor are called collectively, **fringe benefits.** Some fringe benefits are required by law, while others result from mutual agreement between business and labor, or are granted voluntarily by business.

In the fringe benefit category would be the employer's share of social security for each employee; unemployment taxes for each employee, which must be paid by the employer; plus various insurance and pension plans funded by the employer. The fringe benefits required by law are usually called payroll taxes (an expense), and the others may be classified under a number of different expense categories.

Basic Payroll Example

As an example, assume that a business employs three people who are paid at the end of January a total of $2,000 in salary. The FICA tax rate will be assumed to be 7 percent. Of the $2,000, $300 is withheld for federal income tax, $110 for state income tax, and $140 (7% × $2,000) is withheld for FICA. Further, $140 (7% × $2,000) is the company's matching share of FICA tax. The entire earnings of $2,000 become an expense as the wages are paid, but the employees actually receive only $1,450 to take home. The difference represents three separate liabilities of the employer which must be satisfied with cash later. The journal entry would be:

Salary expense	2,000	
FICA payable		140
Federal income tax withheld		300
State income tax withheld		110
Cash		1,450

In addition, the business is required by law to match the social security contribution of its employees, as well as to contribute a certain portion of wages earned by its employees to an unemployment fund (2.7 percent to the state and 0.7 percent to the federal government). To record these payroll taxes, a general journal entry would be made as follows on January 31:

Payroll tax expense	208	
FICA payable		140
State unemployment tax payable		54
Federal unemployment tax payable		14

When the amounts are actually remitted to the various organizations and agencies, the entry would then be a cash disbursement.

The above discussion covers the basic concepts of payroll. There are, however, a number of complexities that must be dealt with in actually applying these concepts.

Independent Contractors versus Employees

Not everyone who performs services for a business is an employee of that business. An example is an independent CPA who prepares the company's tax return: the CPA is not an employee of the company for which he provides services. Thus, the law makes a distinction between an independent contractor and an employee. With an independent contractor, the company states the overall task to be done, but does not tell him exactly how to accomplish the task. Since the independent contractor is not an employee, withholdings are not necessary. Examples of independent contractors would include lawyers retained for a particular lawsuit, painters contracted to paint a building, and real estate agents. In these instances, the lawyer is directed to handle the lawsuit, the painter is directed to paint the building, and the real estate agent is directed to sell the house, but their day-to-day activities are not specified. With employees, on the other hand, the company can directly supervise their activities.

Withholding Authorization

The amount of federal and state income tax for an employee is based, in part, upon the individual's marital status and number of dependents (such as children). For the employer to withhold the proper amount, the employee must furnish this information. The employee fills out an IRS form when he is hired and must sign and date it, thus authorizing that level of withholdings. This authorization protects the employer in case the withholding amount turns out to be incorrect by a large amount. It is not uncommon for employees to claim an excessive number of dependents so that less money will be withheld.

FICA Tax

As discussed above, there is a fixed percentage tax for all employees. For example, the tax rate in 1981 was 6.65 percent. However, the tax only applies up to some maximum amount, and in 1981 the maximum amount was $29,700. Thus, all earnings equal to or under $29,700 have a FICA tax of 6.65 percent. All earnings over $29,700 have no FICA tax.

Unemployment Tax

The basic concept that applies to FICA also applies to unemployment tax, that is, a tax rate and a maximum amount. The tax rate for the **state unemployment tax** is 2.7 percent, while the tax rate for the **federal unemployment tax** is 0.7 percent. In both instances, the maximum is $6,000: additional earnings for an employee are not taxed. As a result, for one employee making $24,000 a year, a company will pay one-fourth of the unemployment tax it would pay for four employees each making $6,000 a year. The effect is to place a greater unemployment tax burden on companies with many, lower-paid employees than that on companies with fewer, better-paid employees.

State Unemployment Tax Rate

As discussed above, the basic state unemployment tax rate is 2.7 percent, but it is sometimes possible to have a lower rate. Each state takes its unemployment tax receipts and places the money in a trust fund. These funds are then used to make unemployment compensation payments to employees who have been laid off or fired without adequate cause.

Some companies rarely lay off employees, and thus, their unemployment tax payments to the state can greatly exceed the amount paid out by the state as unemployment compensation to their employees. In these instances, the state may reduce the tax rate as a reward to that firm and as an incentive for other firms. In any event, the federal unemployment tax rate remains 0.7 percent.

Income Tax Withholdings	The direct calculation of these withholdings is complex, because they depend on the employee's marital status, the number of dependents, and the amount of income. To ease this problem, both the federal and state authorities provide withholding tables in which the exact amounts to be withheld under various conditions are listed.
Determination of Payroll	The **payroll register** provides an organized means of developing each employee's gross salary (or wages) and then taking the proper deductions to arrive at net pay. It also provides the information necessary to make the related payroll journal entry.

One line in the payroll register is devoted to each employee. The payroll amounts are based upon the employee's total gross pay. From the total gross (regular gross plus overtime, if any), the appropriate deductions are computed. The net pay for each employee is then calculated. To check this

Concept Summary

Basic Entries for Payroll

Recording Entry	Adjusting Entry	Retirement Entry

Salary and wage expense
  FICA payable
  Federal income tax withheld
  State income tax withheld
  Other deductions* payable
  Accrued payroll payable
Record payroll
	Salary and wage expense
	Payroll tax expense
	  FICA payable
	  State unemployment tax
	    payable
	  Federal unemployment tax
	    payable
	  Accrued payroll payable
	Accrue payroll and payroll tax
		Accrued payroll payable
		  Cash
		Pay employees

		FICA payable Federal income tax withheld Cash Pay federal taxes
		State income tax withheld Cash Pay state withholding

Payroll tax expense
  FICA payable
  State unemployment tax payable
  Federal unemployment tax payable
Record payroll tax
		State unemployment tax
		    payable
		  Cash
		Pay state unemployment

		Federal unemployment tax
		    payable
		  Cash
		Pay federal unemployment

		Other deductions* payable Cash Make other payments

*Additional deductions might be made for insurance premiums, union dues, payroll savings plan, United Way contributions, and the like.

work, each column of earnings or deduction information is totaled. Subtracting the totals of each deduction from the total gross of all employees should give the total of net pay for all employees. The number of the check paid to each employee is entered on the appropriate line to control the sequence of the prenumbered checks.

Individual
Employee
Records

A company will compute the payroll each pay period and record the information in the payroll register. The accumulated payroll registers provide access to earnings information by payroll period. However, it is also necessary to maintain earnings information by employee. For this reason, companies also keep an individual earnings record for each employee. This record is essentially a separate sheet for each employee. There will be a separate line for each paycheck. The information on each line will be the same as the corresponding line on the payroll register. Thus, the same pay information is kept by pay period in the payroll register and by employee in the individual earnings record.

11.3 Income Taxes and Related Liabilities

The adjusting entry corporations must make for income taxes was discussed in Chapter 5. The corporation must determine income before income taxes and then apply the statutory tax rate to determine the amount of income taxes. Assuming a 50 percent corporate income tax rate and $1,000,000 of income before income taxes, part of the income statement would appear as follows:

Income before income taxes	$1,000,000
Income taxes	(500,000)
Net income	$ 500,000

Chapter 5 assumed a 20 percent income tax rate, which is appropriate for the smallest corporations; however, the corporate income tax is graduated, and approximately 50 percent is more appropriate for large corporations. The tax laws change frequently, and the exact rate will vary from year to year. For ease in computation, a tax rate of 50 percent will be assumed in the remainder of this section.

Taxable Income

The amount of income tax immediately payable to the government is computed by applying the statutory tax rate to a figure called taxable income, rather than to income before income taxes. Taxable income is determined by applying the rules detailed in the Internal Revenue Code. The methods used to determine income for tax purposes are not necessarily the same as those used in accounting for financial statement purposes.

For most small businesses, taxable income is identical to the accounting figure of income before income taxes. In large businesses, on the other hand, these figures can be quite different. The primary reason for this difference is that there are often alternative methods of accounting for the same event, one chosen for financial statement purposes and one for tax purposes. Depreciation is the most important example of an event to which two distinct accounting methods are often applied.

Alternative Methods of Depreciation

For example, suppose the Appearance Corporation purchased an $800,000 machine on January 1, 1981 which had a four-year life. As discussed in Chapter 10, the company has a choice of depreciation methods. Typically, the company would use the straight-line method for financial statement purposes and the sum-of-the-years'-digits or double-declining-balance method for tax purposes.

To illustrate the effects of these different choices, Figure 11-2 gives the relevant facts for the Appearance Corporation. The amounts are given in thousands to make them easier to deal with. For each of four years, the company had sales revenues of $2,000,000 for both financial statement purposes and tax purposes. In addition, the company had expenses other than depreciation of $800,000 each year.

For financial statement purposes, the company will depreciate the $800,000 machine over four years using the straight-line method; therefore, depreciation will be $200,000 each year ($800,000 ÷ 4 = $200,000). Thus, the income statement will be the same in all four years. Sales are $2,000,000; expenses are $1,000,000; and income before income taxes is

FIGURE 11-2
Deferred Income
Taxes

APPEARANCE CORPORATION			
Deferred Income Taxes			
Purchase $800,000 machine in first year			
	1981	1982	1983	1984
---	---	---	---	---
Financial Statement Purposes				
Sales	$2,000	$2,000	$2,000	$2,000
Expenses				
Other expenses	800	800	800	800
Depreciation	200	200	200	200
Total expenses	1,000	1,000	1,000	1,000
Income before income taxes	1,000	1,000	1,000	1,000
Income taxes	500	500	500	500
Net income	$ 500	$ 500	$ 500	$ 500
Tax Purposes				
Sales	$2,000	$2,000	$2,000	$2,000
Expenses				
Other expenses	800	800	800	800
Depreciation	320	240	160	80
Total expenses	1,120	1,040	960	880
Taxable income	$ 880	$ 960	$1,040	$1,120
Corporate income taxes payable	$ 440	$ 480	$ 520	$ 560
Deferred income taxes				
Beginning balance	$ –0–	$ 60	$ 80	$ 60
Increase during year	60	20	(20)	(60)
Ending balance	$ 60	$ 80	$ 60	$ –0–

$1,000,000. Applying the 50 percent tax rate gives income taxes of $500,000 each year.

For tax purposes, the company will depreciate the $800,000 machine over four years using the sum-of-the-years'-digits method. Therefore, depreciation will be different each year. In 1981, depreciation will be:

$$\$800,000 \times \frac{4}{10} = \$320,000$$

As is characteristic of this method, depreciation will decrease in subsequent periods.

Deferred Income Taxes

Taxable income will be $880,000 in 1981. Applying the 50 percent tax rate gives corporate income taxes payable of $440,000. The company thus owes $440,000 to the government. But, as given above, the company will have an expense of $500,000 for income taxes. The $60,000 difference ($500,000 − $440,000) represents the amount the firm owes the government as tax on the income of the period, but which is not immediately due. Thus a long-term liability of $60,000 is created. This long-term liability is called **deferred income taxes.** The journal entry to reflect income taxes must then be

Income taxes	500,000	
Corporate income taxes payable		440,000
Deferred income taxes		60,000

A similar situation will result in 1982. Corporate income taxes payable will be $480,000, and the journal entry will be

Income taxes	500,000	
Corporate income taxes payable		480,000
Deferred income taxes		20,000

At the end of 1982, deferred income taxes will, therefore, have a balance of $80,000.

In 1983, however, deferred income taxes will decrease because straight-line depreciation will exceed sum-of-the-years'-digits depreciation. Corporate income taxes payable will be $520,000, while the expense will remain $500,000. The journal entry will be

Income taxes	500,000	
Deferred income taxes	20,000	
Corporate income taxes payable		520,000

The income tax journal entry in 1984 will reduce deferred income taxes to 0. The journal entry will be

Income taxes	500,000	
Deferred income taxes	60,000	
Corporate income taxes payable		560,000

Deferred income taxes result from the different depreciation treatment of a particular asset for financial statement and tax purposes. As a result, when the asset is fully depreciated, there will no longer be any deferred income taxes relating to that asset.

Reasons for Different Depreciation Methods

The company uses different depreciation methods for financial statement and tax purposes because there is a different audience in each instance.

Financial Statement Audience For financial statement purposes, the users are prospective investors and creditors. Thus, the company wants to report income as high as possible by making depreciation as low as possible. The higher net income is, the better and more profitable the company appears. Straight-line depreciation will exceed sum-of-the-years'-digits depreciation eventually, but for the short term, straight-line depreciation will give the highest net income.

Tax Return Audience For tax purposes, the user is the Internal Revenue Service. Thus, the company wants to make income as low as possible by making depreciation as high as possible. The lower taxable income is, the less the company must pay to the IRS. Sum-of-the-years'-digits depreciation will be less than straight-line depreciation eventually; but for the short term, sum-of-the-years'-digits depreciation will give the lowest taxable income.

Long-Run Equality of Accounting and Taxable Income

Over the complete life of the firm, income before income taxes will equal taxable income in total. For example, the total for the four years of Appearance Corporation is $4,000,000 in both instances. As a result, income tax expense is based upon the income reported on the financial statements. Any differences between the expense and the necessary cash flows for tax payments to the government are then accrued like any other expense.

Deferred Income Taxes May Never Decrease

In the example of the Appearance Corporation given in Figure 11-2, deferred income taxes began at zero, increased somewhat, and then declined back to zero. In actual practice, however, for most companies deferred income taxes increases. The reason for this is that the company may continue to buy new machines or other assets every year.

Not only do most companies buy additional machinery each year, but the amount spent on machinery increases each year. This increase is the result of inflation. If a company continues to buy machinery each year, deferred income taxes will *never* decrease. The depreciation for tax purposes will *never* be less than the depreciation for financial statement purposes. Only if the company goes out of business or stops buying new machinery will deferred income taxes decrease.

Concept Summary

Deferred Income Taxes			
Condition	*Example*	*Result*	*Entry*

Expenses deducted on income tax form exceed expenses deducted on income statement.	Accelerated depreciation on tax form and straight-line depreciation on income statement in early years of asset life.	Income tax expense (based on the income statement) is greater than income tax payable (based on the tax form).	Income taxes
			  Corporate income
			    taxes payable
			  Deferred income
			    taxes

Expenses deducted on income statement exceed expenses deducted on income tax form.	Same as above, but in the later years of asset life where accelerated depreciation is less than straight-line depreciation.	Income tax expense (based on the income statement) is less than income tax payable (based on the tax form).	Income taxes
			Deferred income taxes
			  Corporate income
			    taxes payable

Other Liability Considerations

Contingent Liabilities Contingent liabilities have that title because they are contingent upon some future event that may or may not occur. An example was discussed in Chapter 8: discounted notes receivable. The company that discounts the note must pay the bank if the maker does not pay. But it is impossible to predict this future event. Another contingent liability is a lawsuit the company may or may not lose. Because of this contingency, these liabilities are not reflected in the financial statements.

Estimated Liabilities To be a liability, an obligation must not only be known with certainty and known or estimable in amount, but also be traceable to events that have already occurred. For example, suppose a company signs a union contract that obligates the company to pay certain wages. No liabilities is created because the future payments to the workers are wholly traceable to future events.

On the other hand, suppose a company has a product warranty, where the company agrees to repair products if they break within a certain time from the date of sale. In this instance, the future payments to repair products are wholly traceable to an event that has occurred: the sale.

All of the sales revenue is recognized in the period of sale. To record expenses in the same period, the company must also recognize the related warranty expense. Because products do break, warranty costs in the future are a certainty. Further, companies can often predict the future costs associated with warranties. Thus, this situation meets the requirements for an accrual.

Assume that Seller Corporation had sales of $1,500,000 during an accounting period and that past experience indicated that 1 percent of sales would be needed to pay warranty claims. The necessary adjusting entry at the end of the accounting period would be:

Warranty expense 15,000
    Accrued warranty liability   15,000

As money is spent on warranty claims, the debit is to the liability account rather than to an expense account. A $400 claim payment would be recorded as follows:

Accrued warranty liability 400
    Cash   400

11.4 Valuation of Liabilities

There are several reasons a dollar now is worth more than a dollar in the future. Accounting numbers reflect only one of these reasons, namely the time value of money. The time value of money means that a dollar now can be invested and can be earning interest until some future date.

It is important to understand exactly what the time value of money means and what it does *not* mean. There are three basic reasons a dollar now is preferable to a dollar some years in the future: greater utility, inflation, and the interest earning power of money. The first two of these reasons are irrelevant to the time value of money.

Greater Utility

The dollar now has greater utility than the dollar in the future because the dollar now can be spent now and its results, enjoyed. The dollar in the future, on the other hand, cannot be spent until the future date arrives. This difference in utility has nothing to do with the time value of money.

Inflation

The dollar now is worth more because inflation will reduce the value of the dollar by the time the future date arrives. This, too, is irrelevant to the time value of money. Inflation does have an important impact because the higher the rate of inflation the higher the rate of interest will be; but there will be a time value of money even in times of decreasing prices as long as there is a non-zero interest rate. Chapter 17 is largely devoted to discussing possible accounting responses to the effects of inflation. Here, inflation will be ignored as a separate factor.

Time Value of Money

The dollar now can be invested now and can earn interest. This is the **time value of money** concept, and it is the only factor accounting uses to reflect payments in the future.

Future Value of Lump Sum

Suppose $1 is put in a bank on January 1, 1981, where it earns 10 percent interest. After one year, that $1 will grow to $1.10:

Original amount invested on 1/1/81 .... $1.00
Interest earned during 1981 (10% on $1) 10
Investment, 12/31/81 .... $1.10

After two years, the $1 will grow to $1.21:

Investment, 1/1/82 .... $1.10
Interest earned during 1982 (10% × $1.10) .... .11
Investment, 12/31/82 .... $1.21

These calculations are saying that $1 available immediately is equivalent to $1.10 after one year at 10 percent interest. Another way of saying this is that $1 after one year at 10 percent interest has a **future value** of $1.10. Also, $1 after two years at 10 percent interest has a future value of $1.21.

Figure 11-3 is a table of future values. The row gives the number of years the **lump sum** is invested, and the column gives the rate of interest. For example, the row for one year in the 10 percent interest rate column gives the future value of $1.10. The row for two years in the 10 percent interest rate column gives the future value of $1.21. Both amounts check with the numbers determined above. (Numbers in Figure 11-3 have been stated to four decimal places for more accurate results in more complicated computations.)

Suppose $1 was invested for thirty years. If the interest rate was 5 percent, the investment would be worth $4.32; however, if the interest rate was 10 percent, the investment would be worth $17.45. Thus, a doubling of the interest rate causes the investment to increase more than fourfold. This example illustrates the effect of **compound interest.** The interest earned by the investment is compounded in future years because interest is earned on the interest.

Future Value of an Annuity

An **annuity** is a series of equal payments equally spaced. Suppose, then, that a company is to receive a three-year annuity of $1 on January 1, 1981. This means the company will receive $1 on January 1, 1982; $1 on January 1, 1983; and $1 on January 1, 1984. The future value of the annuity is the total amount the three receipts will be worth on January 1, 1984.

FIGURE 11-3
Future Value of $1

NUMBER OF PERIODS	RATE OF INTEREST						
	1%	3%	4%	5%	6%	8%	10%
1	1.0100	1.0300	1.0400	1.0500	1.0600	1.0800	1.1000
2	1.0201	1.0609	1.0816	1.1025	1.1236	1.1664	1.2100
3	1.0303	1.0927	1.1249	1.1576	1.1910	1.2597	1.3310
4	1.0406	1.1255	1.1699	1.2155	1.2625	1.3605	1.4641
5	1.0510	1.1593	1.2167	1.2763	1.3382	1.4693	1.6105
6	1.0615	1.1941	1.2653	1.3401	1.4185	1.5869	1.7716
7	1.0721	1.2299	1.3159	1.4071	1.5036	1.7138	1.9487
8	1.0829	1.2668	1.3686	1.4775	1.5938	1.8509	2.1436
9	1.0937	1.3048	1.4233	1.5513	1.6895	1.9990	2.3579
10	1.1046	1.3439	1.4802	1.6289	1.7908	2.1589	2.5937
15	1.1610	1.5580	1.8009	2.0789	2.3966	3.1722	4.1772
20	1.2202	1.8061	2.1911	2.6533	3.2071	4.6610	6.7275
25	1.2824	2.0938	2.6658	3.3864	4.2919	6.8485	10.8347
30	1.3478	2.4273	3.2434	4.3219	5.7435	10.0627	17.4494

FIGURE 11-4

Future Value of an Annuity of $1

NUMBER OF PERIODS	RATE OF INTEREST						
	1%	3%	4%	5%	6%	8%	10%
1	1.0000	1.0000	1.0000	1.0000	1.0000	1.0000	1.0000
2	2.0100	2.0300	2.0400	2.0500	2.0600	2.0800	2.1000
3	3.0301	3.0909	3.1216	3.1525	3.1836	3.2464	3.3100
4	4.0604	4.1836	4.2465	4.3101	4.3746	4.5061	4.6410
5	5.1010	5.3091	5.4163	5.5256	5.6371	5.8666	6.1051
6	6.1520	5.4684	6.6330	6.8019	6.9753	7.3359	7.7156
7	7.2135	7.6625	7.8983	8.1420	8.3938	8.9228	9.4872
8	8.2857	8.8923	9.2142	9.5491	9.8975	10.6366	11.4359
9	9.3685	10.1591	10.5828	11.0266	11.4913	12.4876	13.5795
10	10.4622	11.4639	12.0061	12.5779	13.1808	14.4866	15.9374
15	16.0969	18.5989	20.0236	21.5786	23.2760	27.1521	31.7725
20	22.0190	26.8704	29.7781	33.0660	36.7856	45.7620	57.2750
25	28.2432	36.4593	41.6459	47.7271	54.8645	73.1059	98.3471
30	34.7849	47.5754	56.0849	66.4388	79.0582	113.2832	164.4940

The future value of the annuity is dependent on the interest rate, and the assumption will be that the interest rate is 10 percent. The 1982 receipt will grow to $1.21 by 1984, and the 1983 receipt will grow to $1.10 by 1984. The future value of the annuity will then be

Receipt	Value on January 1, 1984
$1 on 1/1/82	$1.21
$1 on 1/1/83	$1.10
$1 on 1/1/84	$1.00
	$3.31

Thus, the future value of a three-year annuity at 10 percent interest is $3.31. Figure 11-4 provides a table for the future value of annuities which is similar in concept to Figure 11-3. The row gives the number of years of the annuity, while the column gives the interest rate. The row for three years in the 10 percent interest column gives the future value of $3.31, which checks with the number computed above.

To summarize, then, an individual or business would prefer to have a dollar now rather than a dollar some time in the future, even if the future dollar is certain to be received. Similarly, any individual or business would prefer to pay out a dollar some time in the future rather than to pay it out immediately. This preference is based upon the knowledge that, if money is available now, it can be invested and can earn interest until the future date.

Present Value of a Lump Sum

The sum of $1,000 invested now at 8 percent will be worth $1,080 in one year. The calculation is as follows:

$1,000   value now
$+$ <u>80</u> + <u>interest earned</u> (8% × $1,000)
$1,080   value in one year

Assume that a company purchased a piece of equipment with a note promising the payment of $1,000 in one year. The *form* of the journal entry would be:

Equipment XX
    Note payable   XX

An accounting problem then arises: at what dollar value should the asset and liability be recorded? Both have to be given the same value, but that value cannot be $1,000 because the payment of $1,000 in one year is not equivalent to the payment of $1,000 immediately.

The solution to this problem involves reconsidering the earlier example of investing $1,000 at 8 percent interest for one year. In such situations, the amount invested is called the **present value,** while the amount the investment is worth after one year is called the **future value.** Using this terminology, the future value calculation is:

$1,000   present value
$+$ <u>80</u> + <u>interest earned</u> (= interest rate × present value)
$1,080   future value

In general, then, the basic equation is:

Future value = present value + (interest rate × present value),

which can be rewritten

Future value = present value × (1 + interest rate)

Checking this formula with the above example gives

$$\text{Future value} = \$1,000 \times (1 + 0.08)$$
$$= \$1,000 \times 1.08$$
$$= \$1,080$$

which is the correct answer. Thus, $1,000 now is equivalent to $1,080 one year from now at 8 percent interest.

However, in this example, the present value is given and the future value calculated, while in the equipment example, the future value ($1,000) is given, and the present value is to be calculated. This can be accomplished by rewriting the above equation.

$$\text{Present value} = \frac{1}{(1 + \text{interest rate})} \times \text{future value}$$

Thus, in the equipment example, the present value of $1,000 one year from now at 8 percent is

$$\text{Present value} = \frac{1}{1.08} \times \$1,000 = \$925.90$$

The journal entry would then be

Equipment	925.90	
Note payable		925.90

This is saying that the $925.90 now is equivalent to $1,000 one year from now at 8% interest.

Use of Tables The basic equation should then be looked at in the following way

$$\text{Present value} = \text{factor} \times \text{future value}$$

where the **factor** depends upon the interest rate and the number of time periods. To make the calculations easier, tables of these factors are given in Figures 11-5 and 11-6. The rows give the number of periods, and the columns give the interest rate. In the equipment example, the number of periods is one and the rate of interest 8 percent, so the proper factor is in the first row, sixth column. The term is 0.9259, and the present value can be calculated.

$$\text{Present value} = \text{factor} \times \text{future value}$$
$$= 0.9259 \times \$1,000$$
$$= \$925.90$$

Suppose the note called for payment in five years rather than one, but the interest rate was still 8 percent. The proper factor would be in the fifth row, sixth column, and the calculation would be

$$\text{Present value} = \text{factor (5 periods, 8\%)} \times \text{future value}$$
$$= 0.6806 \times \$1,000$$
$$= \$680.60$$

FIGURE 11-5
Present Value of $1

NUMBER OF PERIODS	RATE OF INTEREST						
	1%	3%	4%	5%	6%	8%	10%
1	0.9901	0.9709	0.9615	0.9524	0.9434	0.9259	0.9091
2	0.9803	0.9426	0.9246	0.9070	0.8900	0.8573	0.8264
3	0.9706	0.9151	0.8890	0.8638	0.8396	0.7938	0.7513
4	0.9610	0.8885	0.8548	0.8227	0.7921	0.7350	0.6830
5	0.9515	0.8626	0.8219	0.7835	0.7473	0.6806	0.6209
6	0.9420	0.8375	0.7903	0.7462	0.7050	0.6302	0.5645
7	0.9327	0.8131	0.7599	0.7107	0.6651	0.5835	0.5132
8	0.9235	0.7894	0.7307	0.6768	0.6274	0.5403	0.4665
9	0.9143	0.7664	0.7026	0.6446	0.5919	0.5002	0.4241
10	0.9053	0.7441	0.6756	0.6139	0.5584	0.4632	0.3855
15	0.8613	0.6419	0.5653	0.4810	0.4173	0.3152	0.2394
20	0.8195	0.5537	0.4564	0.3769	0.3118	0.2145	0.1486
25	0.7798	0.4776	0.3751	0.2953	0.2330	0.1460	0.0923
30	0.7419	0.4120	0.3083	0.2314	0.1741	0.0994	0.0573

FIGURE 11-6

Present Value of an Annuity of $1

NUMBER OF PERIODS	RATE OF INTEREST						
	1%	3%	4%	5%	6%	8%	10%
1	0.9901	0.9709	0.9615	0.9524	0.9434	0.9259	0.9091
2	1.9704	1.9135	1.8861	1.8594	1.8334	1.7833	1.7355
3	2.9410	2.8286	2.7751	2.7232	2.6730	2.5771	2.4869
4	3.9020	3.7171	3.6299	3.5460	3.4651	3.3121	3.1699
5	4.8534	4.5797	4.4518	4.3295	4.2124	3.9927	3.7908
6	5.7955	5.4172	5.2421	5.0757	4.9173	4.6229	4.3553
7	6.7282	6.2303	6.0021	5.7864	5.5824	5.2064	4.8684
8	7.6517	7.0197	6.7327	6.4632	6.2098	5.7466	5.3349
9	8.5660	7.7861	7.4353	7.1078	6.8017	6.2469	5.7590
10	9.4713	8.5302	8.1109	7.7217	7.3601	6.7101	6.1446
15	13.8651	11.9379	11.1184	10.3797	9.7122	8.5595	7.6061
20	18.0456	14.8775	13.5903	12.4622	11.4699	9.8181	8.5136
25	22.0232	17.4132	15.6221	14.0939	12.7834	10.6748	9.0770
30	25.8077	19.6004	17.2920	15.3725	13.7648	11.2578	9.4269

The journal entry would then be

```
Equipment  .........................................  680.60
    Note payable  ......................................          680.60
```

Finally, suppose the note called for payment of $1,000 in ten years, and the interest rate was 10 percent. The proper factor would be in the tenth row and the 10 percent column. The calculation would then be

$$\text{Present value} = \text{factor (10 periods, 10\%)} \times \text{future value}$$
$$= 0.3855 \times \$1,000$$
$$= \$385.50$$

Present Value of an Annuity

Suppose the equipment is purchased with a note calling for payment of $1,000 at the end of each of the next five years at 8 percent interest. In essence, then, there are five separate present value calculations for this note—for one year at 8 percent, for two years at 8 percent, and so on. These calculations can be summarized as follows:

```
Payment in 1 year   = factor (1 period, 8%) × $1,000 = $  925.90
Payment in 2 years  = factor (2 periods, 8%) × $1,000 =    857.30
Payment in 3 years  = factor (3 periods, 8%) × $1,000 =    793.80
Payment in 4 years  = factor (4 periods, 8%) × $1,000 =    735.00
Payment in 5 years  = factor (5 periods, 8%) × $1,000 =    680.60
Total present value
    of payments  ....................................  $3,992.60
```

The journal entry for this purchase would be:

```
Equipment  .......................................  3,992.60
    Note payable  ...................................          3,992.60
```

The above calculation, while correct, was long and tedious. Further, it would become even more difficult if the payments extended for fifteen, twenty, or more years. Fortunately, the table in Figure 11-6 is available to assist in calculations of this type.

As mentioned earlier, a payment of a constant amount at the end of a series of equally spaced intervals is called an annuity. Thus, in the above example, the equipment was purchased in return for a promise to pay an annuity of $1,000 for five years at 8 percent interest. The present value of an annuity can then be found using the table given in Figure 11-6 and the following formula:

$$\text{Present value} = \text{annuity factor (number of periods, interest rate)} \times \text{constant payment}$$

Using Figure 11-6 for the above examples gives

$$\begin{aligned}\text{Present value} &= \text{annuity factor (5 periods, 8\%)} \times \$1,000 \\ &= 3.9927 \times \$1,000 \\ &= \$3,992.70\end{aligned}$$

Notice that this result is essentially the same as calculated earlier. The difference of 10¢ ($3,992.70 as opposed to $3,992.60) is caused by rounding errors, because numbers in Figure 11-6 are given to only four decimal places.

Concept Summary

Present Value and Future Value Illustrations							
Illustration	*Explanation*	*Now*	1	2	3	4	5
Dollar now is equivalent to $1.61 in five years assuming 10 percent interest.	Future value table (Figure 11-3) in the 10 percent column and 5 period row $1 × 1.6105	$1					$1.61
$0.62 now is equal to dollar in five years assuming 10 percent interest.	Present value table (Figure 11-5) in the 10 percent column and 5 period row $1 × .6209	$0.62					$1
$2.49 now is equal to a three-year annuity of $1 assuming 10 percent interest.	Annuity table (Figure 11-6) in the 10 percent column and 3 period row $1 × 2.4869	$2.49	$1	$1	$1		
$2.06 now is equal to a three-year annuity of $1 beginning in year 3 assuming 10 percent interest.	Annuity table (Figure 11-6) in the 10 percent column, the difference between the 5-year factor and the 2-year factor (3.7908 − 1.7355 = 2.0553)	$2.06			$1	$1	$1

11.5 Further Present Value Analysis

The tables in Figures 11-5 and 11-6 are extremely valuable tools, but they can be misused if the assumptions behind them are not satisfied. There are five basic assumptions underlying these tables.

Basic Assumptions

1. The interest rate and the periods are stated in the same time units. If the interest rate is stated as 6 percent per year, the number of periods must be in years. If, on the other hand, the interest rate is 1 percent per month, the number of periods must be in months. For example, if a note called for payment of $5,000 in 6 months at an annual interest rate of 12 percent, the tables could not be used directly.

2. The interest rate is given in the table. In Figures 11-5 and 11-6, the interest rate must be 1, 3, 4, 5, 6, 8, or 10 percent. If a situation arises where a different interest rate is applicable, these tables cannot be used directly.

3. For annuities, payments are equal amounts. If there is a $2,500 payment the first period, then there must be a $2,500 payment for each successive period of the annuity. If the amount of payment goes up or down during the payment period, the table cannot be used directly.

4. For annuities, payments begin at the end of the first period. If the first payment occurs immediately or if the first payment is not for several periods, the tables are not directly applicable.

5. For annuities, payments are made every period. If, for example, there are ten periods, the payments must begin in period one and continue to period ten without interruption. No payment can be skipped in the middle and added on to the end, or the tables cannot be used directly.

Even though the tables cannot be used *directly* if the above assumptions are violated, the problems can still be solved. In each instance, however, the problem must be restated so that the assumptions are satisfied.

Annual Interest, Monthly Periods

Assume a company purchases a truck with a note calling for payment of $5,000 in six months at an annual interest rate of 12 percent. Assumption 1 of the tables is violated because the time period is given in months, while the interest rate is on an annual basis. However, 12 percent on an annual basis will be 6 percent for six months. Thus, the situation can be stated: the note calls for $5,000 in one six-month period at an interest rate of 6 percent for that six-month period. The term is then in the one-period row and the six percent column, and the present value is

$$\text{Present value} = \text{factor (1 period, 6\%)} \times \$5,000$$
$$= 0.9434 \times \$5,000$$
$$= \$4,717$$

Compounding Semiannually

A related problem occurs with annuities. Most annuities have one payment each year. Nonetheless, it is common to find payments every six months, that is, two payments every year. In such instances, the interest rate is still stated on an annual basis, but it is said to be compounded semiannually. This means that interest is calculated twice a year.

As calculated earlier, $1,000 invested at 8 percent interest on January 1 will be worth $1,080 on December 31 if compounded *annually*. If the $1,000 were invested at 8 percent compounded *semiannually*, the situation would be slightly different:

$1,000.00 Value at January 1
+   40.00 Interest earned in first 6 months (4% × $1,000)
$1,040.00 Value at July 1
+   41.60 Interest earned in last 6 months (4% × $1,040)
$1,081.60 Value at December 31

The second interest calculation (for the second six months) builds upon the interest earned in the first six months.

Example Suppose, then, that a company purchased a piece of land at 6 percent interest, where there were to be ten years of semiannual payments of $1,000. This arrangement is an annuity of twenty periods with an interest rate of 3 percent per period. The present value of these payments is

Present value = annuity factor (20 periods, 3%) × $1,000
= 14.8775 × $1,000
= $14,877.50

and the journal entry would be

Land 14,877.50
Note payable 14,877.50

Interpolation

Assume a company buys a typewriter on March 1, 1981, and promises to pay $1,000 on March 1, 1982, where the interest rate is 9 percent. The tables have factors for 8 percent and 10 percent but not for 9 percent, therefore, it is necessary to use interpolation. The factor for 9 percent is halfway between the factors for 8 percent and 10 percent. In symbols, then the formula is:

$$\text{Factor (1 period, 9\%)} = \frac{\text{factor (1 period, 8\%)} + \text{factor (1 period, 10\%)}}{2}$$
$$= \frac{0.9259 + 0.9091}{2}$$
$$= 0.9175$$

The present value of the payment of $1,000 in one year at 9 percent interest is $1,000 × 0.9175 = $917.50.

Assume the same facts as above for the typewriter purchase, but the payment is due September 1, 1981, rather than March 1, 1982. In this instance, there are six months of interest at an annual rate of 9 percent. Thus, there will be 4.5 percent interest for the six-month period. Again, the tables do not have factors for 4.5 percent interest, so it is necessary to interpolate between the factors for 4 percent and 5 percent interest. In symbols

$$\text{Factor (1 period, 4.5\%)} = \frac{\text{factor (1 period, 4\%)} + \text{factor (1 period, 5\%)}}{2}$$

$$= \frac{0.9615 + 0.9524}{2}$$

$$= 0.9570$$

The present value is then 100×0.9570 or $957.00.

Increasing Payments

Assume a company buys a building with a note calling for payment of $100,000 at the end of the first year, $200,000 at the end of the second year, and $300,000 at the end of the third year, with an annual interest rate of 10 percent. Assumption 3 for annuities is violated because the amount increases every year. Thus, the present value amount must be calculated from each individual payment:

$$
\begin{aligned}
\text{Present value} &= \text{factor (1 period, 10\%)} \times \$100,000 \\
&+ \text{factor (2 periods, 10\%)} \times \$200,000 \\
&+ \text{factor (3 periods, 10\%)} \times \$300,000 \\
&= (0.9091 \times \$100,000) + (0.8264 \times \$200,000) \\
&+ (0.7513 \times \$300,000) \\
&= \$90,910 + \$165,280 + \$225,390 \\
&= \$481,580
\end{aligned}
$$

This purchase could also be viewed as an annuity of $100,000 for three periods, plus an additional $100,000 after two periods and an additional $200,000 after three periods. The calculation would be

$$
\begin{aligned}
\text{Present value} &= \text{annuity factor (3 periods, 10\%)} \times \$100,000 \\
&+ \text{factor (2 periods, 10\%)} \times \$100,000 \\
&+ \text{factor (3 periods, 10\%)} \times \$200,000 \\
&= (2.4869 \times \$100,000) + (0.8264 \times \$100,000) \\
&+ (0.7513 \times \$200,000) \\
&= \$248,690 + \$82,640 + \$150,260 \\
&= \$481,590
\end{aligned}
$$

which is the same as calculated above, except for a rounding error.

Deferred Annuity

Assume a company purchases a piece of land for eight annual payments of $10,000 with an interest rate of 6 percent annually; the purchase is on February 1, 1981, and the first payment is not due until January 31, 1984. The purchase arrangement is pictured below.

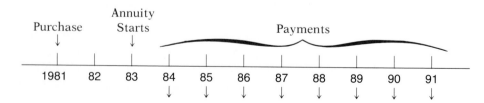

Assumption 4 is violated, because the first payment is not one year from the purchase date. It is, therefore, advisable to use the difference of factors. In this instance, the difference will be between the factor for a ten-year annuity and the factor for a two-year annuity:

$$
\begin{aligned}
\text{Factor} &= \text{annuity factor (10 periods, 6\%)} - \text{annuity factor (2 periods, 6\%)} \\
&= 7.3601 - 1.8334 \\
&= 5.5267
\end{aligned}
$$

The present value of these payments is then $10,000 × 5.5267 or $55,267.

There is, however, another way of looking at this problem. From February 1, 1983, there is an annuity of eight payments of $10,000 at 6 percent interest. The present value at February 1, 1983, is then

$$
\begin{aligned}
\text{Present value (2/1/83)} &= \text{annuity factor (8 periods, 6\%)} × \$10,000 \\
&= 6.2098 × \$10,000 \\
&= \$62,098
\end{aligned}
$$

February 1, 1983, is two years from the purchase date. The present value at the purchase date is then

$$
\begin{aligned}
\text{Present value (2/1/81)} &= \text{factor (2 periods, 6\%)} × \$62,098 \\
&= 0.8900 × \$62,098 \\
&= \$55,267
\end{aligned}
$$

The journal entry recording the purchase would be:

Land	55,267	
Note payable		55,267

Omitted Payments Assume a company purchases a building on May 1, 1981, with a note calling for six equal payments of $20,000 at 8 percent interest on April 30 of 1982, 1983, 1984, 1986, 1987, and 1988. This violates Assumption 5 because 1985 is omitted and 1988 is added to the years for payment. The purchase arrangement is pictured below.

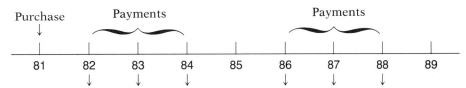

This payment stream can be considered as two three-year annuities, one beginning at the date of purchase and other beginning four years later. The calculation would be:

$$
\begin{aligned}
\text{Present value} &= \text{annuity factor (3 periods, 8\%)} × \$20,000 \\
&\quad + (\text{annuity factor (7 periods, 8\%)} - \text{annuity factor} \\
&\quad\quad \text{(4 periods, 8\%)}) × \$20,000 \\
&= 2.5771 × \$20,000 + (5.2064 - 3.3121) × \$20,000 \\
&= \$51,542 + 1.8943 × \$20,000 \\
&= \$51,542 + \$37,886 \\
&= \$89,428
\end{aligned}
$$

There is another approach, however. The present value can be calculated by calculating the value of a seven-year annuity and then subtracting the value of the omitted payment. This solution procedure is, in essence, to put in the 1985 payment to get the value of an annuity and then to take it out to get the value of the actual payments. Thus,

Present value of building payments
$$= \text{present value of 7-year annuity of } \$20,000 \text{ at } 8\%$$
$$- \text{present value of } \$20,000 \text{ in 4 years}$$

or

$$
\begin{aligned}
\text{Present value} &= \text{annuity factor (7 periods, 8\%)} \times \$20,000 \\
&\quad - \text{factor (4 periods, 8\%)} \times \$20,000 \\
&= 5.2064 \times \$20,000 - 0.7350 \times \$20,000 \\
&= \$104,128 - \$14,700 \\
&= \$89,428
\end{aligned}
$$

which is the same as the amount calculated above.

Concept Summary

Basic Assumptions Behind Present Value Tables		
Assumption	*Common Violation*	*Basic Solution*
1. Interest rate and periods have the same time units.	Interest rate is annual; periods are in months.	Restate interest rate and periods to common units.
2. All useful interest rates are in the table.	Needed interest rate is not in table.	Interpolate between factors given in tables.
3. For annuities, the payments are all the same amount.	Payments become larger in future years.	Add up present value of each individual payment.
4. For annuities, the payments begin at the end of the first period.	Payments begin several periods in the future.	Subtract factors to reflect omitted payments.
5. For annuities, the payments are made every period.	Payments are interrupted.	Add present values of separate, individual annuities.

Summary

Current liabilities are obligations that are expected to be satisfied by the use of current assets during the upcoming accounting period or operating cycle, whichever is longer.

Notes payable represent liabilities evidenced by a formal, written document. Notes with an interest rate stated on their face are called explicit interest-bearing notes. Notes without such an interest rate are called implicit interest-bearing notes. In an explicit interest-bearing note, the amount borrowed is equal to the face value of the note, and the amount repaid is the maturity value. Interest is the difference between the face value and the maturity value. In an implicit interest-bearing note, the amount borrowed is less than the face amount, and the amount repaid is the face amount. The difference between the amount borrowed and the face amount represents interest and is called discount on notes payable.

Payroll liabilities reflect obligations to employees, governmental agencies, and other outside entities. Payroll accounting is based on two important facts. First, employees always receive less than the amounts earned by them because of certain required and optional withholdings from employee earnings. Second, the total cost to a business of its employees is always more than the amounts earned by them because of certain required and optional fringe benefits.

Income taxes payable is applicable to corporations only and indicates the obligation for income taxes expected to be paid within the upcoming accounting period. Deferred income taxes indicate the corporate obligation for income taxes from current and past income which is expected to be paid in future accounting periods beyond the upcoming period. Deferred income taxes are, therefore, a long-term liability.

The time value of money is applicable in the valuation of some liabilities. The time value of money reflects the fact that money has interest-earning power and, thus, can be invested to earn a return. Money in hand today can be invested to earn interest, and thus, money grows over time. This time value of money can be expressed as future value or as present value. Thus, it is possible to calculate the (1) future value of a lump sum, (2) future value of an annuity, (3) present value of a lump sum, and (4) present value of an annuity.

In Chapter 12, bonds payable, the most important long-term liability, is discussed, and these present value ideas are applied to their valuation.

Key Terms

Annuity
Compound interest
Deferred income taxes
Discount on notes payable
Explicit interest
Factor
Federal income taxes withheld
Federal Insurance Contributions Act (FICA)
Federal unemployment tax
Fringe benefits

Future value
Implicit interest
Interpolation
Lump sum
Payroll register
Present value
State income taxes withheld
State unemployment tax
Time value of money
Withholdings

Comprehensive Review Problem

The balance sheet of Firmin's Furriers on December 31, 1981, included the following current liabilities section:

Current liabilities

Accounts payable		$ 5,100
Notes payable (12%, 1 year)	$10,000	
Less: Discount on notes payable	(900)	9,100
Income taxes payable		4,750
Federal income tax withheld		4,000
State income tax withheld		500
FICA payable		2,400
State unemployment tax payable		600
Federal unemployment tax payable		200
Total current liabilities		$26,650

The following selected transactions occurred during 1982:

January   5 Paid accounts payable within the discount period.

23 All liabilities relating to payroll were retired by appropriate payments.

March   15 Paid income taxes due for 1981.

April   28 Purchased $17,000 of furs on open credit of 2/10, n/30. The net method was used to record the purchase in a periodic inventory system.

May   31 $10,000 cash was paid on accounts payable.

August   1 Borrowed $15,000 from Blue Ridge Bank and Trust and signed a one-year, 12 percent note payable.

October   1 This is the maturity date of the discount note payable. The note was paid.

December 31 The payroll for December is summarized below:

Salaries and wages earned	$22,000
Federal income tax withheld	4,200
State income tax withheld	600
FICA withheld	1,320
State unemployment tax	700
Federal unemployment tax	250

The take-home pay was paid in cash. None of the taxes had been paid as of the year's end.

31 After the preparation of all adjusting entries, the income statement for Firmin's Furriers showed income tax expense of $9,500, while the income tax return indicated that $8,300 was currently payable.

Required:

1. Prepare journal entries for the above transactions including any necessary adjusting entries.

2. Prepare the current liabilities section of the balance sheet as of December 31, 1982. Explain the disposition of any liability omitted from the current liabilities section.

Solution to Comprehensive Review Problem

1.

FIRMIN'S FURRIERS
General Journal

Date	Transaction Accounts	Debit	Credit
1982			
Jan 5	Accounts payable	5,100	
	Cash		5,100
	Paid suppliers within discount period		

	23	Federal income tax withheld	4,000	
		State income tax withheld	500	
		FICA payable	2,400	
		State unemployment tax payable	600	
		Federal unemployment tax payable	200	
		Cash		7,700
		Paid payroll-related liabilities		
Mar	15	Income taxes payable	4,750	
		Cash		4,750
		Paid income taxes due		
Apr	8	Purchases	16,660	
		Accounts payable		16,660
		Purchased inventory ($17,000 × .98 = $16,660)		
May	31	Accounts payable	9,800	
		Interest expense	200	
		Cash		10,000
		Paid for inventory, but lost $200 discount		
Aug	1	Cash	15,000	
		Note payable		15,000
		Made one-year, 12% note		
Oct	1	Notes payable	10,000	
		Interest expense	900	
		Cash		10,000
		Discount on notes payable		900
		Paid discount note at maturity		
Dec	31	Salaries and wages expense	22,000	
		Federal income tax withheld		4,200
		State income tax withheld		600
		FICA payable		1,320
		Cash		15,880
		Paid employees for December		
	31	Payroll tax expense	2,270	
		State unemployment tax payable		700
		Federal unemployment tax payable		250
		FICA payable		1,320
		Accrue payroll taxes		
	31	Interest expense	750	
		Interest payable		750
		To accrue interest on explicit interest-bearing note		
		($\frac{5}{12}$ × 12% × $15,000 = $750)		
	31	Income tax expense	9,500	
		Income taxes payable		8,300
		Deferred income taxes		1,200
		Record income tax expense		

2. *Current liabilities*

Accounts payable	$ 6,860
Notes payable	15,000
Interest payable	750
Income taxes payable	8,300
Federal income tax withheld	4,200
State income tax withheld	600
FICA payable	2,640
State unemployment tax payable	700
Federal unemployment tax payable	250
Total current liabilities	$39,300

Deferred income taxes of $1,200 represent taxes traceable to income recognized in 1982 which will be payable beyond 1983. Thus, they are classified as a long-term liability.

Questions

Q11-1. Contrast the accounting treatment of liabilities whose existence is known with certainty to the treatment of liabilities whose existence is uncertain as of the balance sheet date. Give two examples of each type of liability.

Q11-2. Distinguish explicit and implicit interest-bearing notes.

Q11-3. Give the relationship between amount borrowed (cash proceeds), face value, and maturity value for both explicit and implicit interest-bearing notes.

Q11-4. What are the primary reasons for the difference between the amounts earned by employees and take-home pay? What are the primary factors that cause the total cost of a work force to be more than the amounts earned by employees?

Q11-5. Explain the difference between income taxes payable and deferred income taxes.

Q11-6. Explain why accelerated depreciation for income tax purposes coupled with straight-line depreciation for financial statement purposes gives rise to deferred income taxes.

Q11-7. Give three reasons a dollar today is preferable to a dollar received some time in the future. Which of these reasons is at the heart of the time value of money theory?

Q11-8. Define an annuity. How is the present value of an annuity calculated?

Q11-9. List five assumptions made in applying present value tables.

Exercises

E11-1. Albert's Coiffures signed a note payable on November 1, 1981, to Antoine's Suppliers in settlement of $1,800 owed on account to Antoine's. The terms of the note called for the payment of $1,800 plus interest at 11 percent per annum ninety days after November 1, 1981. Prepare the journal entries at November 1, 1981, to record the note; at December 31, 1981, to accrue interest; and at January 30, 1982, to pay off the note.

E11-2. Tara, Inc., borrowed $15,000 for a period of one year by signing a note payable at the local bank on October 1, 1981. The interest rate of 12 percent was explicitly stated on the note. Prepare the required journal entries for Tara, Inc., at October 1, 1981, to record the note; at December 31, 1981, to accrue interest; and at September 30, 1982, to pay off the note.

On March 1, 1981, Butler Company signed a note at the Second National Bank in which Butler promised to pay Second National Bank $25,000 at the end of one year. Butler received proceeds of $22,250 from making this note. Prepare the required journal entries for Butler on March 1, 1981, to record the note; on December 31, 1981, to record interest expense; and on February 28, 1982, to pay off the note.

E11-3. The Lafer Corporation uses straight-line depreciation for financial accounting purposes, and sum-of-the-years'-digits depreciation for tax purposes. This is the only difference between the company's accounting income before income taxes and its taxable income. The differences over a three year period are summarized as follows:

Year Ended December 31	Income Before Income Taxes	Taxable Income
1980	$100,000	$ 80,000
1981	80,000	80,000
1982	120,000	140,000

Assuming a tax rate of 50 percent, give the journal entries to record the income tax expense and related income tax liabilities at December 31, 1980, 1981, and 1982, for the Lafer Corporation.

E11-4. Match the following by entering the appropriate letter to the left of the statement.

a. federal withholding taxes
b. state withholding taxes
c. social security taxes
d. fringe benefits
e. state unemployment taxes
f. federal unemployment taxes
g. payroll tax expense
h. overtime pay

1. ___ This amount includes fringe benefits that are required by law, such as the employer's share of social security and unemployment taxes.

2. ___ These taxes are authorized by the Federal Insurance Contributions Act (FICA) and are paid by both employer and employee.

3. ___ The amount withheld from the employee's salary for income taxes due to the state.

4. ___ These taxes are computed at a rate of 0.7 percent applied to a maximum of $6,000 of wages earned.

5. ___ The amount withheld from the employee's salary for income taxes due to the federal government.

6. ___ Included in this category are the employer's share of social security and unemployment taxes plus various insurance and pension plans funded completely by the employer.

7. ___ Any hours worked over 40 in one week and compensation on a time-and-one-half basis.

8. ___ These taxes are computed at a basic rate of 2.7 percent on the first $6,000 of earnings, although it is sometimes possible to use a lower rate.

E11-5. Hamilton, Inc., incurred $2,600 of salary expense for the week ended February 14. Federal income tax withholdings were 18 percent of the total payroll, and state income tax withholdings were 4 percent of the total payroll. The only other deductions were 7 percent for FICA taxes and $40 for union dues. Give the entries that must be made on the books of Hamilton, Inc., to record the payroll and the tax accruals to be recognized by the employer assuming unemployment taxes of 2.7 percent (state) and .7 percent (federal).

E11-6. Dilcey, Inc., sells major appliances that come with a one-year warranty on parts and service. During 1981, sales of these appliances totaled

$1,620,000. In preparing adjusting entries at December 31, 1981, it was estimated that 2 percent of the sales would require warranty work in 1982. Prepare the adjusting entry required December 31, 1981, and also prepare the entry for $1,200 of warranty work done February 12, 1982.

E11-7. Using tables in the text, compute the present values of the following sums due at the end of the designated periods:

1. $4,800 due in ten years with interest compounded at 6 percent per annum.

2. $6,200 due in fifteen years with interest compounded at 10 percent per annum.

3. $15,000 due in five years with interest compounded at 8 percent per annum.

4. $8,000 due in five years with interest at 12 percent per annum compounded quarterly.

5. $12,000 due in ten years with interest compounded at 4 percent for the four periods nearest to now and at 6 percent for the six periods nearest to the due date.

E11-8. Using the appropriate interest table, compute the present values of the following periodic amounts due at the end of the designated periods:

1. $7,500 receivable at the end of each period for seven periods compounded at 8 percent.

2. $3,000 payments to be made at the end of each period for fifteen periods compounded at 5 percent.

3. $6,000 to be received at the end of each of twenty periods compounded at 6 percent.

4. $12,000 payable at the end of the seventh, eighth, ninth, and tenth periods at 10 percent.

E11-9. Wade Corporation bought equipment with a note calling for payment of $20,000 at the end of the first year, $15,000 at the end of the second year, $10,000 at the end of the third year, and $5,000 at the end of the fourth year with an annual interest rate of 8 percent. Compute the present value of the note using two different methods. Prepare a suitable journal entry to record the purchase of the equipment.

E11-10. Mary Maloney was named beneficiary on an insurance policy that provided she could choose any one of the following four options:

1. $25,000 immediate cash.

2. $2,000 every six months payable at the end of each six months for ten years.

3. $18,000 immediately and $500 every three months for five years payable at the end of each three-month period.

4. $2,000 every three months for two years and $500 each quarter for the following twenty-two quarters with all payments payable at the end of each quarter.

If the value of money is assumed to be 12 percent per annum, which option would you recommend that Mary accept?

Problems

P11-1. Indicate how each of the following items should be reported on the balance sheet:

a. The currently maturing portion of a long-term note amounts to $5,000.

b. The amount owed for the credit purchase of merchandise inventory is $7,200.

c. Customers' accounts having credit balances of $2,200 (overpayments).

d. $15,000 of cash dividends on the company stock, payable in thirty days.

e. A note payable for $12,000 due in three years.

f. Estimated payments to workers under a two-year union contract for $150,000.

g. Estimated income taxes payable of $43,000.

h. A discount on notes payable of $2,500. The note is due in five years.

i. $225 of interest accrued on a one-year note payable of $10,000.

j. $468 of social security tax withheld from employees.

k. The corporation is being sued for $3,000,000 by a customer who was injured while shopping in one of the company's stores. The suit is presently being litigated, and company attorneys are optimistic concerning the outcome of the suit.

l. The company estimates that $14,000 will be spent in the next year to satisfy warranty claims arising from this year's sales.

m. $1,650 was withheld from employees' salaries for union dues.

P11-2. The Beta Corporation pays federal income taxes at a rate of 50 percent of taxable income. The only difference between accounting income before income taxes and taxable income is depreciation expense. Beta uses straight-line depreciation for financial accounting purposes and double-declining-balance depreciation for income tax purposes. Information necessary to calculate Beta's income tax expense and related income tax liabilities for the year 1982 is as follows:

Sales revenue (all taxable)	$350,000
Expenses other than depreciation (all tax-deductible)	200,000
Depreciation, straight-line basis	100,000
Depreciation, double-declining-balance method	125,000

Required:

1. Calculate the Beta Corporation's income tax expense for the year 1982.

2. Calculate the Beta Corporation's corporate income taxes payable for the year 1982.

3. Give the journal entry to record Beta's income tax expense and income tax liabilities for the year 1982.

P11-3. The following information relates to the payroll of Zeringue Company for the month of October 1982. The total payroll was $840,000. Of this amount, $480,000 represented payments in excess of $29,700 to certain employees. The amount paid to employees in excess of $6,000 was $720,000. Federal income taxes in the amount of $96,000 and state income taxes of $25,200 were withheld from the employee's salaries. Union dues of $3,500 were also withheld. The state unemployment tax rate is 2.7 percent and the federal rate is .7 percent. Assume the current FICA tax is 7 percent for employees.

Required:
Prepare the necessary journal entries assuming salaries and employer payroll taxes are recorded separately, and also prepare the journal entries to record the payment of the salaries due employees and the subsequent remittance of the withholdings and payroll taxes.

P11-4. Oustalet Company operates on a fiscal year ending June 30. On March 1, 1981, Oustalet signed a $16,350, one-year, non-interest-bearing note payable and, in return, received $15,000 cash.

Required:

1. What was the imputed rate of interest?

2. Give the entry required March 1, 1981, in the accounts of Oustalet Company.

3. Give the adjusting entry required June 30, 1981, on Outstalet's books.

4. Give the entry required February 28, 1982, the due date of the note.

P11-5. Indicate the proper accounting treatment for each of the contingencies described below and give an explanation as to why this is the preferable treatment:

a. An aging of accounts receivable at the end of the current year indicates a need for an allowance account of $5,300 to cover possible failure to collect accounts currently outstanding.

b. Knightlinger Corporation manufactures automatic washing machines. Sales for 1982 amount to $3,275,000. Each machine has a one-year warranty on all parts and service. Knightlinger Corporation knows from past experience that approximately 1½ percent of sales will be needed to pay warranty claims.

c. Varnau Corporation manufactures power saws. During the current year, a blade on one of the saws slipped off and caused serious injury to a user. The customer has retained legal counsel and is suing Varnau for $5,000,000. The suit is still unsettled at the end of the year. The company's defense lawyers are of the opinion that the court will award damages, but they cannot estimate what the amount of the award will be.

d. Delmar Groceries, Inc., operates a local chain of ten grocery stores. This year, a display counter in Store Number 8 collapsed and caused injury to a customer standing near the display. Delmar paid medical expenses; however, the customer is suing for an additional $500,000 for pain and suffering. The suit is unsettled at the end of the year, but the company's defense lawyers agree the court will rule in favor of the customer and they agree the award will be about $100,000.

e. Taylor Company is unionized and has just signed a three-year contract with the union providing hourly increases for workers of $.75. It is estimated that this pay increase will cost Taylor an additional $500,000 a year in wages for each of the next three years.

f. Kezar Corporation guaranteed $6,500,000 of notes payable of its subsidiary Cordelia, Inc., on December 30, 1982. Cordelia, Inc., is in good financial position at the end of 1982.

P11-6. Alice LaBonne is planning to take a trip to Europe with her friend Odessa Shuster three years from now and estimates that, at that time, she will need $9,000. Alice desires to place her money in a savings account today so that it can earn interest at an annual rate of 10 percent until the time of the trip.

Required:
1. Compute the amount Alice should invest assuming the investment earns simple interest for three years (no compounding occurs).

2. Compute the amount Alice should invest assuming the investment earns interest compounded annually for three years.

3. Compute the amount Alice should invest assuming the investment earns interest compounded semiannually for three years; but, in this instance, assume that the appropriate rate of interest is 9 percent.

4. Prove the answers arrived at in Parts 1 through 3.

P11-7. Using the appropriate interest table, answer each of the following questions. Each case is independent of the others.

1. Milling Company plans to deposit $30,000 today in a savings account. If the appropriate interest rate is 8 percent and interest is compounded annually, how much money will be in the account at the end of fifteen years?

2. Dodds Company holds a note receivable which states that it is entitled to receive $54,000 from Seymour Company at the end of three years. Dodds needs cash immediately and is willing to accept a 9 percent discount rate to obtain it. Under these conditions, how much cash would Dodds receive?

3. Ronald Zoller is planning to retire at the end of the current year. He estimates that he will need $18,000 a year for the next fifteen years to meet his needs. Assuming the appropriate interest rate is 10 percent, how much should Zoller deposit December 31 of the current year in order to be able to withdraw $18,000 at the end of each of the next fifteen years?

4. L. Ballay deposited $15,000 in a savings account in which interest was compounded annually. At the end of three years, the balance in the savings account was $17,865. Determine the interest rate that was used for compounding.

5. Gullo Company needs special purpose equipment which Bennett Company has manufactured for it. Because Gullo is short of cash and has been a good customer of Bennett in the past, Bennett has agreed to a nominal down payment of $1,000 and credit terms of $5,000 payable at the end of each of the next four years. Bennett requires an 8 percent rate of return on its money. Determine the cost of the equipment to Gullo for accounting purposes.

P11-8. Answer each of the following questions. Each case is independent of the others.

1. John Shulling acquired an automobile to use in his business by paying $2,000 down and signing a note that called for the payment of $7,800 in six months at an annual interest rate of 12 percent per annum. Determine the cost of the automobile to Shulling for accounting purposes.

2. Duckett Corporation purchased equipment to use in the business by signing a note that required fifteen years of semiannual payments of $2,500 with a relevant interest rate of 10 percent per annum. Determine the present value of Duckett's note.

3. Grofenhurst Corporation acquired special purpose machinery with a note calling for payment of $60,000 at the end of the first year, $120,000 at the end of the second year, and $180,000 at the end of the third year. At what amount should Grofenhurst record the machinery assuming 5½ percent per annum is an appropriate interest rate?

4. Nickerson & Associates acquired a piece of land May 1, 1982, in exchange for a note requiring six annual payments of $15,000 at an interest rate of 8 percent annually with the first payment due April 30, 1984. Compute the present value of the note on May 1, 1982.

5. Foley, Inc., purchased land with a factory on it by signing a note in which it agreed to pay eight equal payments of $125,000 at 10 percent interest on August 31 of 1982, 1983, 1984, 1985, 1987, 1988, 1989, and 1990. Compute the present value of the note.

P11-9. On January 2, 1982, Berdou Corporation acquired new machinery to use in its plant by signing a note calling for payment of $2,500 at the end of each of the next four years, where an appropriate interest rate is 10 percent.

Required:

1. Compute the purchase price of the machinery for Berdou Corporation.

2. Prepare a table to compute the principal and interest components of each payment.

3. Prepare all of the required journal entries for the four years of the note.

4. What would be the liability for notes payable on the balance sheet December 31, 1984?

CHAPTER 12

Long-Term Liabilities—Bonds

Chapter Outline

12.1 *Characteristics of Bonds.* Discussion of the roles of borrower and lender; the concepts of face amount, bond rate of interest, effective date, interest payment dates, and maturity date.

12.2 *Determining the Selling Price of Bonds.* Presentation of the market rate of interest, and the relationship of market rate and bond rate; journal entries by issuer and investor for a bond issued at face amount.

12.3 *The Life Cycle of Bonds Sold at a Discount.* The relationship of market rate and bond rate to the selling price of discount bonds; journal entries by issuer and investor for bonds issued at a discount; the balance sheet presentation of discount bonds.

12.4 *The Life Cycle of Bonds Sold at a Premium.* The relationship of market rate and bond rate to the selling price of premium bonds; journal entries by issuer and investor for bonds issued at a permium; the balance sheet presentation of premium bonds.

12.5 *Special Considerations with Bonds.* The concepts and mechanics of accrued interest, interest adjusting entries, callable bonds, and convertible bonds; discussion of sinking fund, the role of underwriters, and financial leverage; effective interest amortization.

Accounting and the Real World

From Blue to Red

Of all blue-chip stocks and bonds, few radiate so pure as IBM's. Thus, when the mammoth computer corporation decided to raise $1 billion, half of it in twenty-five-year bonds, some Wall Street underwriters anticipated a field day. To be sure, interest rates were expected to go up another notch in late October, but by moving up the launching date two weeks, IBM and its principal underwriters, Salomon Brothers and Merrill Lynch, were confident that the timing was right. It was hideously wrong. The bond issue turned out to be perhaps the greatest underwriting fiasco in Wall Street history.

In all, 228 underwriters—including the Abu Dhabi Investment Company—were involved in the syndicate selling the issue, and their losses may run as high as $25 million. The main reason was that the Federal Reserve Board jumped the gun in pushing up the interest rate to banks to a record 12 percent.

Historically, bonds have been difficult to sell at a time of rapidly rising interest rates. The IBM paper carried a yield of 9.41 percent, whereas even the new Treasury notes and government bonds returned fractionally higher interest. Also, over the Columbus Day weekend, rumors began to circulate that IBM's third-quarter earnings were down. In fact, as announced late in the week, they fell 18 percent. The unsold bonds, possibly $300 million worth, were dumped on the open market, where they fared badly. IBM's timing ignored an old Wall Street axiom: "Never commit yourself to a major issue before a long weekend. Who knows, we may be at war by Tuesday." There was no war, but the underwriters were routed, nonetheless.

If a company acquires long-lived assets, such as machines or buildings, or needs large amounts of cash for operating purposes, long-term liabilities are often used as a source of assets. By acquiring assets under long-term debt arrangements, businesses are able to use the income and cash flow generated by the assets to retire the obligations created to purchase them. Long-term liabilities, then, are important to the acquisition of expensive assets, whose use will be spread over many accounting periods, because they make it possible for the debt resulting from this acquisition to be retired over the productive life of the asset. Businesses need these large sources of nonowner funds, particularly as expansion and growth occur.

12.1   Characteristics of Bonds

Long-term debt most often takes the form of notes payable or bonds payable. That is, businesses may secure assets by signing a note payable to a bank or other lending institution, or by selling to investors a series of bonds payable. Generally, when cash or other assets are acquired by the use of notes payable, the business deals with only one (or a very few) creditors. The typical example of this type of transaction would be a company borrowing a large sum of money from a bank (or a few banks) and agreeing to repay the loan over several years. The relationship between borrower and lender is close so that the note payable is usually the result of negotiation between the two and reflects the desires of both parties.

A business may want to borrow more money than it can secure from lending institutions or it may want to repay the loan over a very long period of time. In these instances, a special borrowing vehicle, called a bond, may be used. A bond makes possible the simultaneous borrowing of money in varying amounts from many different lenders. It is convenient to think of bonds as formal IOUs which a company may create and sell to investors for some amount of money. Then, the borrowing company pays these IOUs according to an agreed upon schedule.

With bonds, the relationship between the borrower and lenders is not close and, thus, the terms of the bonds are not subject to negotiation. Instead, the borrowing company deals simultaneously with large numbers of investors and attempts to get as much as possible for its bonds as they are sold. As the bonds are sold, the business receives cash from the purchasers. Later, cash decreases when the bonds are paid off and the obligation satisfied.

Important Bond Features

When a business desires to borrow funds from many lenders simultaneously, negotiation with each lender individually is not possible. Instead, the borrower creates a series of identical debt securities and attempts to sell these securities to lenders. These debt securities are called bonds and represent an obligation of the borrower to pay specified future amounts to the lender. Figure 12-1 illustrates the appearance of a typical bond. All bonds have the following important features in common: a borrower, a lender or lenders, a specified face amount, an interest rate, an effective date, interest payment dates, and a maturity date.

FIGURE 12-1
Sample Bond Certificate
Reprinted with the permission of Exxon Corporation

Borrower The borrower is often called the seller or issuer of the bonds. The borrower may be a corporation or other business; a city, state, or federal governmental agency; or a nonprofit organization, such as a hospital or university. When a state, county, or local governmental agency or nonprofit organization issues bonds, the interest paid to lenders on those bonds is exempt from federal taxation. This tax-exempt feature may make these bonds particularly attractive to investors.

Lender The lender is often called the investor or purchaser of the bonds. Purchasers of bonds become investors because they give up cash now in exchange for a return of greater amounts of cash in the future. Bonds that contain the name of the lender on the bond certificate are called **registered bonds.** With registered bonds, the borrower or a representative of the borrower must keep records that identify uniquely each bond and its owner. As registered bonds are sold from one owner to another, the records of the borrower must be changed to reflect the new ownership. Sometimes bonds that do not contain the identification of the lender are sold. These bonds are called **bearer or coupon bonds,** and no elaborate records are necessary for the borrower; however, the bonds are subject to theft because there is no independent registration of ownership. Most bonds issued in recent years have been registered to investors.

Face Amount The face amount is often called the maturity amount of the bonds. This is the amount of dollars that will be repaid to the purchasers of the bonds at the bond's termination. Typically, bonds are sold with face amounts of $1,000, although much larger face amounts are often found. Bonds with face amounts below $1,000 are unusual. The selling prices of bonds are quoted as percents of face amount, such as 98 or 103. These quotations indicate a selling price of $980 or $1,030, respectively, for a $1,000 bond.

Interest Rate The interest rate is often called the **bond rate, coupon rate,** or **stated rate of interest.** This is the interest rate the borrower agrees to pay the lender as long as the lender's money is being used by the borrower. The dollar amount of interest each purchaser of a bond will receive is determined by multiplying the bond rate of interest by the face amount of the bond. The borrower, then, is obligated to pay this amount of interest to the lender each year.

Effective Date The effective date is the first date on which the bonds may be sold. All interest payments are counted from this date, and thus, bonds may be sold on their effective date or any time thereafter. The date on which bonds are originally sold is called the *issue date.*

Interest Payment Dates The interest payment dates are the dates on which the promised amount of interest (bond rate × face amount) will be paid to investors (lenders). Although the bond rate of interest is always an annual rate, interest on bonds may be paid annually or semiannually.

Maturity Date The maturity date is the due date or the termination date of the bond. It is the date on which the face amount will be paid to the holder of the bond. The bond liability will be satisfied on this date, and the relationship of borrower and lender, terminated.

Concept Summary

Important Bond Characteristics	
Borrower	The borrower is called the issuer or seller of the bonds and may be a business; federal, state, county, or local governmental agency; or nonprofit organization.
Lender	The lender is called the investor or purchaser of the bonds and may be an individual, business, or any other organization.
Face Amount	This is the amount to be paid by the issuer of the bonds to the investor at the end of the bond's life (maturity date). Face amounts are usually $1,000.
Bond Rate of Interest	The bond rate is called the coupon or stated rate, and this rate multiplied by the face amount gives the annual amount of interest to be paid by the issuer of the bonds to the investor.
Effective Date	This is the earliest date on which the bonds may be sold, and all interest payments are counted from this date. Bonds may be sold on or after this date.
Interest Payment Dates	These are the dates on which interest will be paid by the bond issuer to investors. Interest may be paid annually or semiannually.
Maturity Date	This is the date on which the face amount of the bonds will be paid by the issuer to investors. The time period from the effective date to the maturity date is the life of the bonds.

12.2 Determining the Selling Prices of Bonds

A bond represents an exchange of cash over time between a borrower and many lenders. Every bond contains two future promises by the borrower to make fixed payments to lenders. All bonds promise to pay (1) the face amount of the bond at the maturity date and (2) the bond rate of interest multiplied by the face amount in interest each year until the maturity date. These future payments are printed on the bond certificate and cannot be changed. Each potential investor knows *exactly* the future amounts that will be received from the bond. The important question in bond transactions is: What are these future amounts worth today or what should the lender give up today to receive these future amounts?

The Market Rate of Interest

The amount that should be given up today to purchase the bond depends upon how much the lender desires to earn from his investment in the bonds. The more investors desire to earn, the less they will be willing to give up today to receive the fixed amounts promised by the bond in the future. This **rate of return** desired by investors is called the **market**, or **effective**, rate of interest.

Risk and the Market Rate Each bond carries some risk for the investor; that is, there is some chance that the promised future amounts may not be paid by the borrower. The rate of interest desired to be earned by lenders is a function of the risk perceived in the bond. Bonds with more inherent risk that future payments may not be honored are expected to offer more return to investors. Because bonds with a wide range of potential risk may be offered for sale, a range of market rates of interest exists, each reflecting the return desired by investors at these different risk levels.

Rating Bonds for Risk The amount of risk offered in a particular bond may be related to the financial strength and profitability of the borrower, the borrower's past history with bonds, and the current amount of debt owed by the borrower, as well as to many other factors. As an aid in determining and communicating risk, bonds are often rated by independent financial services such as Standard and Poors. A typical rating scale is given below. Note that a range of market rates of interest would be applicable to each risk class of bonds. Further, as economic conditions (such as the prime rate of interest and inflation) change, this scale of market rates may change also.

Risk Rating	Desired Market Rate
AAA	9–10%
AA	10–11%
A	11–12%
BBB	13–15%
•	
•	
•	
D (stands for defaulted, meaning some promised payments have been missed by borrower)	?

Bond Selling Price and Present Value

The selling price of any bond should be the present equivalent of the promised fixed future amounts of the bond. For every bond, there are two important interest rates to consider: the bond rate and the market rate. The bond rate is used only in the determination of the amount of interest to be paid each year. The market rate is used in finding the present equivalent of the future amounts promised by the bond. The selling price of a bond depends upon the relationship of these two interest rates in the following manner:

1. If the market rate equals the bond rate, the bond should sell at its face amount.

2. If the market rate is greater than the bond rate, the bond should sell at a price below its face amount.

3. If the market rate is less than the bond rate, the bond should sell at a price above its face amount.

The remainder of this section and the next two sections are devoted to an explanation of why these three statements are true and the accounting implications of the three circumstances.

Figure 12-2 presents an example that will be used throughout these sections to illustrate the nature of bonds, the determination of bond prices, and the accounting entries necessary for bonds over their life.

Calculation of Bond Selling Price The future amounts promised by the bond depicted in Figure 12-2 and the present equivalent of these flows are presented in Figure 12-3. The borrower promises to pay the purchaser of this bond the face amount of $1,000 at the end of ten years plus $100 (bond rate × face amount) each year until the maturity date. The expected selling price of the bond is the total of the present value of the lump sum face amount plus the present value of the interest annuity. This means that, if the investor pays $1,000 today for the bond and then collects the amounts from the bond as promised, the desired market rate of 10 percent per year will be earned.

Issuer's Journal Entries for Bonds Sold at Face Amount

The accounting implications of this bond issued are reflected in the journal entries made over the life of the bond. On the date this bond is sold, the following entry is recorded by the borrower:

```
12/31/80  Cash  ................................   1,000
             Bonds payable  ......................          1,000
```

FIGURE 12-2
Data for Sample Bond

A company decides to issue one bond with the following features:
Face amount $1,000
Bond rate of interest .... 10 percent
Effective date .... December 31, 1980
Interest payment dates .... Annual, starting December 31, 1981
Maturity date (the bonds have a life of ten years.) .... December 31, 1990
Suppose the bond is issued on its effective date (December 31, 1980) and on that date the applicable market rate of interest is 10 percent.

FIGURE 12-3
Bond Flows and
Present Value

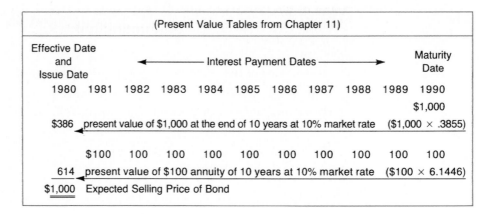

At December 31 in each of the next ten years (the interest payment dates), an entry to record the annual interest expense and the payment of cash to bondholders is made.

```
12/31/81  Interest expense .........................    100
through 12/31/90    Cash  .................................          100
```

Then, at the maturity date of the bond, an entry to retire the bond obligation by paying the face amount to bondholders is made.

```
12/31/90  Bonds payable .........................  1,000
          Cash  .................................          1,000
```

These three entries (issue, interest, and retirement) form the basis of the accounting for bond liabilities from the borrower's point of view. Other entries may be required from time to time for a particular bond issue; however, the issue-interest-retirement sequence is applicable to all bonds.

Investor's Journal
Entries for Bonds
Purchased at
Face Amount

Whether the investor is an individual or another business, accounting for the bond can be viewed from the lender's perspective. From this point of view, the accounting entries become the mirror image of those made by borrower. The following entries would be made by the investor for the bond depicted in Figure 12-2:

```
12/31/80  Investment in bonds ......................  1,000
          Cash  ................................          1,000

12/31/81  Cash  .................................    100
through 12/31/90    Interest revenue  .......................          100

12/31/90  Cash  .................................  1,000
          Investment in bonds ...................          1,000
```

The account, investment in bonds, would be reported as an asset by the investor, and interest revenue would appear on the investor's income statement each year.

Concept Summary

Journal Entries for Bonds Issued at Face Amount		
	Issuer	*Investor*

Issue	Cash
	    Bonds payable
		Investment in bonds
		    Cash

Annual Interest	Interest expense
	    Cash
		Cash
		    Interest revenue

Retirement	Bonds payable
	    Cash
		Cash
		    Investment in bonds

12.3 The Life Cycle of Bonds Sold at a Discount

The relationship between the rate of interest desired by investors who purchase a bond (the market rate) and the fixed rate of interest promised by that bond (the bond rate) determines the selling price of the bond. The market rate is determined by investors in the bond market and is a function of the risk perceived in the bond, as well as the general interest rate and inflation levels in the economy. The bond rate is determined by the borrower and is subsequently printed on the bond and fixed for the life of the bond.

The time lag between when a borrower establishes the relevant variables of a bond issue, including the bond rate of interest, and the actual sale of the bonds may be substantial. As a result, the desired market rate of interest for the level of risk offered by a particular bond may change. Consequently, when a bond issue is sold, the market rate may differ from the bond rate.

The Concept of Bond Discount

When bonds are sold, the rate of return desired by investors may be greater than that promised by the bonds. Thus, the market rate will be greater than the bond rate of interest. Refer to Figure 12-2 where the date for a sample bond issue is given. Now suppose that the bond rate of interest for this sample bond is 9 percent. The 10 percent market rate of interest indicates that, for the risk inherent in this bond, investors demand this return. The bond promises a fixed return of only 9 percent and, thus, would hold no attraction for investors unless the price of the bond is less than that of other bonds. Because the future payments promised by the bond are fixed, the rate earned on the bond by investors increases as the price of the bond decreases.

Calculation of Bond Selling Price for a Discount Bond Figure 12-4 presents the flows promised by the sample bond with a bond rate of 9 percent, together with the present equivalent of these flows in a 10 percent market. The borrower promises to pay the purchaser of this bond the face amount

FIGURE 12-4
Discount Bond Flows
and Present Value

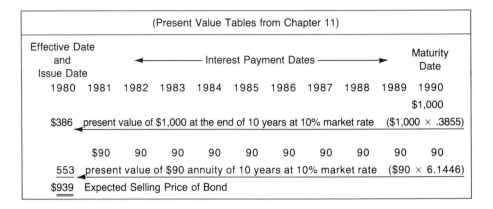

of $1,000 at the end of ten years plus $90 (bond rate × face amount) each year until the maturity date. The expected selling price of the bond is the total of the present value of the lump sum face amount plus the present value of the interest annuity. The interest annuity is always calculated as the bond rate of interest multiplied by the face amount of the bond ($1,000 × .09). The bond rate is always used to determine the amount of interest and has no other relevance. The present value of the promised bond flows is always found at the prevailing market rate of interest.

Interpreting the Bond Discount If an investor pays $940 (rounded from $939 for ease of calculation) for the bond and then collects the promised amounts from the bond, the desired market rate of 10 percent per year will be earned. This bond is called a **discount bond** because its selling price is below its face amount. The discount is the face amount ($1,000) minus the selling price ($940). This discount ($60) represents interest the investor will earn from the borrower over the life of the bond in addition to the annual interest of $90 per year.

Issuer's Journal Entries for a Bond Sold at a Discount

The accounting procedures for a discount bond reflect the three primary transactions between borrower and lender: issue of the bond, payment of interest, and retirement of the bond. On the date the bonds are sold, the following entry would be made for this discount bond:

```
12/31/80 Cash  ...................................   940
         Discount on bonds  .....................    60
              Bonds payable  .....................          1,000
```

Discount on bonds is a contra-liability account and would be shown as a deduction from bonds payable in the long-term liabilities section of the balance sheet in the following manner:

```
Long-term liabilities:
    Bonds payable  ........................  $1,000
    Discount on bonds  ....................    (60)   $  940
```

In this way, the **net bond liability** (carrying value) is valued and reported at the present equivalent of the payments that will be made to satisfy the liability. Because the investor gives up $940 and receives $1,000 at the maturity date of the bond, the $60 difference (the discount) is additional interest the borrower pays over the life of the bond issue. Thus, the total cost of borrowing is the annual interest payments plus the amount of the discount. This additional cost of borrowing is reflected in the amount of interest expense recorded by the borrower.

Amortizing a Discount The accounting technique that reflects this additional interest is called **discount amortization.** The discount is written off to interest expense over the bond's life. Two techniques, **straight-line amortization** and **effective interest amortization,** may be used to write off bond discounts to interest expense. Under either technique, the annual interest entry affects the same general ledger accounts; only the dollar amounts for interest expense and discount amortization are different. The straight-line method will be used here, and the effective interest approach will be summarized later in the chapter.

Under straight-line amortization, the annual discount write-off would be $6 ($60 discount ÷ 10 year life of bonds). On each interest payment date, an entry to record annual interest expense, the amortization of the discount, and the payment of cash to bondholders is made:

12/31/81	Interest expense	96	
through 12/31/90	Discount on bonds		6
	Cash		90

This entry reflects an annual cost of borrowing of $96, of which $90 is paid to investors each year as promised by the bond agreement. The remaining $6 will be paid at the maturity date as part of the face amount. Each year, the borrower accrues an amount of interest expense (the amount of the discount amortized), which is to be paid only at the end of the life of the bonds. The net bond liability, then, increases each year to reflect this additional amount owed. This bond would be shown on the balance sheet at 12/31/81 as follows:

Long-term liabilities:
Bonds payable $1,000
Discount on bonds .... (54) $ 946

at 12/31/85

Long-term liabilities:
Bonds payable $1,000
Discount on bonds .... (30) $ 970

and, at 12/31/90

Long-term liabilities:
Bonds payable $1,000
Discount on bonds .... (0) $1,000

The T account for discount on bonds is shown in Figure 12-5. The bond liability increases each year as the discount is amortized and equals the

FIGURE 12-5
Discount Account for
Sample Bond

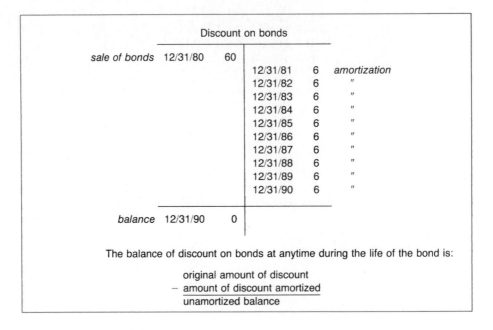

Discount on bonds

sale of bonds 12/31/80 60		
	12/31/81 6	*amortization*
	12/31/82 6	"
	12/31/83 6	"
	12/31/84 6	"
	12/31/85 6	"
	12/31/86 6	"
	12/31/87 6	"
	12/31/88 6	"
	12/31/89 6	"
	12/31/90 6	"
balance 12/31/90 0		

The balance of discount on bonds at anytime during the life of the bond is:

original amount of discount
− amount of discount amortized
---
unamortized balance

face amount when the discount is completely amortized at the bond maturity date. Then, at the maturity date, an entry to retire the bond obligation by paying the face amount to bondholders is made.

12/31/90 Bonds payable 1,000
        Cash   1,000

**Total Cost of a
Discount Bond
Issue**

The total cost of borrowing to the issuer of the bonds can be calculated as follows:

Total cash payments over the life of the bond:
  Face amount $1,000
  Total interest ($90 × 10 years) 900 $1,900
Cash received upon sale of bonds   940
Total cost of borrowing .... $ 960
Annual cost of borrowing ($960 ÷ 10 years) .... $ 96

The accounting entries made by the borrower reflect this annual cost of borrowing since interest expense is debited with this amount annually. Because of the discount, interest expense is greater than cash actually paid to bondholders each year.

**Investor's Journal
Entries for a Bond
Purchased at a
Discount**

From the investor's perspective, the entries reflect the accounting implications of purchasing a discount bond. The journal entries for the sample bond presented in Figure 12-2 and modified to a 9 percent bond rate are as follows:

12/31/80 Investment in bonds	940	
Cash		940

Notice that the transaction is recorded at the amount paid by the lender and that there is no separate discount on bonds account.

12/31/81 Cash	90	
through 12/31/90 Investment in bonds	6	
Interest revenue		96

With each interest payment by the borrower, the investor receives $90 in cash (the promised amount of interest); however, a portion of the bond discount is earned by the investor, but not received, so the lender's investment in the bonds is increased by this amount. At the end of the life of the bonds, the investment will be equal to the face amount of the bonds. The following entry is made by the investor to record the receipt of that face amount:

12/31/90 Cash	1,000	
Investment in bonds		1,000

Concept Summary

Journal Entries for a Bond Issued at a Discount		
	Issuer	*Investor*
Issue	Cash Discount on bonds Bonds payable	Investment in bonds Cash
Annual Interest	Interest expense Discount on bonds Cash	Cash Investment in bonds Interest revenue
Retirement	Bonds payable Cash	Cash Investment in bonds

12.4 The Life Cycle of Bonds Sold at a Premium

A bond issue may be sold at a time when the return desired by investors for assuming the risk inherent in the bonds is less than the rate of interest promised. In this instance, the market rate of interest would be less than the bond rate.

The Concept of Bond Premium

Refer to the sample bond data presented in Figure 12-2 and assume now that the bond rate of interest is 11 percent. This bond offers no additional risk to investors but does offer a higher bond rate of interest than other bonds. Because lenders can invest elsewhere and earn only 10 percent, this bond would attract significant attention among investors. Borrowers, realizing the favorable situation, would likely bid this bond price beyond that of other bonds. With fixed future payments, the rate of return earned on the bond by investors decreases as the price of the bond increases.

Calculation of Selling Price for a Premium Bond Figure 12-6 presents the flows promised by the sample bond with a bond rate of 11 percent, together with the present equivalent of these flows in a 10 percent market. The borrower promises to pay the purchaser of this bond the face amount of $1,000 at the end of ten years plus $110 (bond rate × face amount) each year until the maturity date. The expected selling price of the bond is the total of the present value of the lump sum face amount plus the present value of the interest annuity. The interest annuity is calculated as the bond rate of interest multiplied by the face amount of the bond.

Interpreting the Bond Premium If an investor pays $1,060 (rounded from $1,062 for ease of calculation) for the bond and then collects the promised amounts from the bond, the desired market rate of 10 percent per year will be earned. This bond is called a **premium bond** because its selling price is above its face amount. The premium is the selling price ($1,060) minus the face amount ($1,000). The premium represents a reduction in the amount of interest the investor will earn from the borrower over the life of the bond.

Issuer's Journal Entries for a Bond Sold at a Premium

The accounting entries for a premium bond follow the same pattern of issue, interest payment, and retirement over the life of the bond. On the date the bonds are sold, the following entry is made for the sample premium bond:

```
12/31/80  Cash .....................................  1,060
              Premium on bonds .....................           60
              Bonds payable ........................        1,000
```

FIGURE 12-6
Premium Bond Flows and Present Value

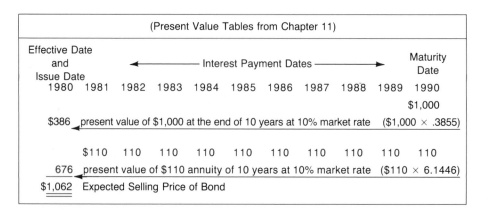

Premium on bonds is an adjunct liability account and would be shown as an addition to bonds payable in the long-term liabilities section of the balance sheet in the following manner:

```
Long-term liabilities:
    Bonds payable  ......................  $1,000
    Premium on bonds  ...................      60    $1,060
```

The bond liability is valued and reported at the present equivalent of the payments that will be made to satisfy the liability. The investor has given up $1,060 and receives $1,000 at the bond maturity date; the $60 difference (the premium) reduces the total amount of interest earned by the bond-holder. This means the total cost of borrowing is the annual interest paid minus the amount of the premium. The reduction in the cost of borrowing is reflected in the amount of interest expense recorded by the borrower.

Amortizing a Premium The accounting technique that reflects this interest reduction is called **premium amortization.** The premium is written off against interest expense over the bond's life. The straight-line amortization method will be demonstrated here, and the effective interest approach will be summarized later in the chapter.

Using straight-line amortization, the annual premium write-off would be $6 ($60 premium ÷ 10-year life of bonds). On each interest payment date, an entry to record annual interest expense, the amortization of the premium, and the payment of cash to bondholders is made.

```
12/31/81    Interest expense  .......................    104
through 12/31/90  Premium on bonds  ......................      6
            Cash  ................................              110
```

This entry reflects an annual cost of borrowing of $104, although $110 is actually paid to bondholders as promised by the bond agreement. The difference of $6 represents a portion of the total premium paid in by the bondholder which is being returned as a part of each interest payment. Each year the borrower records an amount of interest expense which is the true cost of borrowing. The bond liability decreases each year because some of the amounts owed to the investor are being returned as a part of each interest payment. This bond would be shown on the balance sheet at 12/31/81 as follows:

```
Long-term liabilities:
    Bonds payable .........................................  $1,000
    Premium on bonds ...................................        54    $1,054
```

at 12/31/85

```
Long-term liabilities:
    Bonds payable .........................................  $1,000
    Premium on bonds ...................................        30    $1,030
```

and, at 12/31/90

```
Long-term liabilities:
    Bonds payable .........................................  $1,000
    Premium on bonds ...................................         0    $1,000
```

The T account for premium on bonds is shown in Figure 12-7. The bond liability decreases each year as the premium is amortized reflecting the decreasing amount owed and equals the face amount when the premium is completely amortized at the maturity date. The entry to retire the bond obligation by the payment of face amount to the bondholders is then made as follows:

12/31/90 Bonds payable	1,000	
Cash		1,000

Total Cost of a Premium Bond Issue

The total cost of borrowing can be calculated for this premium bond in the same way it was for the discount bond discussed earlier.

Total cash payments over the life of the bond:		
Face amount	$1,000	
Total interest ($110 × 10 years)	1,100	$2,100
Cash received upon sale of bonds		1,060
Total cost of borrowing		$1,040
Annual cost of borrowing ($1,040 ÷ 10 years)		$ 104

The accounting entries made by the borrower reflect this annual cost of borrowing since interest expense is debited with this amount annually. Because of the premium, interest expense is less than cash actually paid to bondholders each year.

FIGURE 12-7
Premium Account for Sample Bond

```
                        Premium on bonds

                                    12/31/80   60  sale of bonds
        amortization  12/31/81   6
             "        12/31/82   6
             "        12/31/83   6
             "        12/31/84   6
             "        12/31/85   6
             "        12/31/86   6
             "        12/31/87   6
             "        12/31/88   6
             "        12/31/89   6
             "        12/31/90   6


                                    12/31/90    0  balance
```

The balance of Premium on bonds at anytime during the life of the bonds is

original amount of premium
− amount of premium amortized
unamortized balance

| Investor's Journal Entries for a Bond Purchased at a Premium | The investor's journal entries for the sample bond modified to an 11 percent bond rate are as follows: |

```
12/31/80  Investment in bonds .....................  1,060
              Cash ................................         1,060
```

The investor records the transaction at the amount actually paid for the bond without the use of a separate premium account.

```
          12/31/81  Cash ................................  110
through 12/31/90      Investment in bonds ...................          6
                      Interest revenue ......................        104
```

With each interest payment by the borrower, the investor receives $110 in cash (the promised amount of interest). Some of this payment, however, represents a return of investment, and thus, the investment in the bond is decreased by this amount. At the end of the life of the bonds, the lender's investment will be equal to the face amount of the bonds. The following entry is made by the investor to record the receipt of that face amount:

```
12/31/90  Cash ................................  1,000
              Investment in bonds ...................         1,000
```

Concept Summary

Journal Entries for a Bond Issued at a Premium		
	Issuer	*Investor*
Issue	Cash 　　Premium on bonds 　　Bonds payable	Investment in bonds 　　Cash
Annual Interest	Interest expense Premium on bonds 　　Cash	Cash 　　Investment in bonds 　　Interest revenue
Retirement	Bonds payable 　　Cash	Cash 　　Investment in bonds

12.5 Special Considerations with Bonds

The sample bond example presented in the preceding sections assumed the most straightforward circumstances. Additional accounting problems may arise in more complicated situations.

| Bonds Issued Between Interest Dates | Because interest is paid semiannually on most bonds, there is a chance that bonds will be sold to investors between interest payment dates. Thus, the issuer will be incurring interest expense only from the date the bonds |

are actually sold, which may be only a portion of the total interest period; however, interest actually paid to investors on the next interest date will be for the full interest period. The mechanism that allows full interest payments to be made even though bonds may not have been held by investors for a full interest period is called accrued interest.

Accrued Interest When a bond is sold between interest payments, the investor pays the market price of the bond plus the interest accrued on the bond from the last interest payment to the day the bond is issued. The issuer can then pay full interest payments to all bonds outstanding having already collected from investors amounts of interest not earned by them.

To illustrate, return to the sample bond in Figure 12-2 and assume this bond is sold at a price of $950 with a bond rate of 9 percent. Suppose the bond is sold on July 1, 1981, rather than December 31, 1980 (the effective date of the bonds). Although a full interest check ($90) will be forwarded to the bondholder on December 31, 1981, the investor will actually be receiving unearned interest for six months (January 1–July 1). This interest is called accrued interest and is added to the price of the bond. The bond is then sold for market price plus accrued interest. The entry to record issuing this bond would be

7/01/81	Cash	995	
	Discount on bonds	50	
	Bonds payable		1,000
	Interest expense		45

On December 31, 1981, the interest payment date, a full year's interest will be paid to the investor no matter when the bond is purchased. The normal interest entry would be made as follows:

12/31/81	Interest expense	92.64	
	Discount on bonds		2.64
	Cash		90.00

Because the bond is sold six months after its effective date (on July 1, 1981), the remaining life of the bond is only nine and one-half years at the time of sale. The discount that results from the sale should be amortized over remaining life of the bond from the point of sale, in this instance, nine and one-half years. The amortization for 1981, then, is $2.64 calculated as follows:

Total discount	$50
Life of bond (9½ years)	114 months
Discount amortization per month ($50 ÷ 114)	$ .44
Amortization for 1981 (6 × $.44)	$ 2.64

The discount amortization for 1982 and each year thereafter to the maturity date of the bond will be $5.28 (12 × $.44). Discounts or premiums are always amortized over the life of the bond remaining as of the date of sale. The interest expense account at December 31, 1981, will reflect an interest expense for the year of $47.64 as the amount paid when the accrued interest is offset against the full interest expense.

	Interest expense		
12/31/81	92.64	7/1/81	45
Balance 12/31/81	47.64		

The bond issuer has collected interest in advance that will be paid to the bondholder but is not earned. The investor receives a $90 interest check at year's end which includes $45 paid in at the purchase of the bond. In this way, full interest payments can be made regardless of when bonds are sold.

Interest Payment Dates During Accounting Period

If interest payment dates occur during the accounting period rather than at the end of the period, an adjusting entry must be made for interest expense. This entry should record interest expense and discount or premium amortization from the last interest date to the end of the accounting period. Also, the liability for interest payable is recorded as a part of this entry.

Suppose the sample bond of $1,000 in Figure 12-2 is originally sold on September 1, 1981, at a discount of $60 with a bond rate of 9 percent. If the interest payment date on this bond is September 1, the following adjusting entry for four months interest and discount amortization would be made at the end of each year over the life of the bond:

12/31/81	Interest expense	32	
through 12/31/90	Discount on bonds		2
	Interest payable		30

Then, at each interest payment date following 1981, interest payments to bondholders would be recorded as follows with interest expense and discount amortization for eight months:

09/01/82	Interest expense	64	
through 09/01/90	Interest payable	30	
	Discount on bonds		4
	Cash		90

The interest payable liability is created in the adjusting entry each year and retired on the interest payment date when interest is paid to bondholders. Also, interest expense for the year is $96 ($32 + $64), and discount amortized is $6 ($2 + $4), both correct amounts. If the bond had been originally sold at a premium, the premium would be amortized as a part of any necessary adjusting entry at year's end. Such an adjusting entry is necessary whenever interest payments do not coincide with the end of the accounting period.

Special Bond Features

The seven characteristics described in the first section of this chapter are common to all bonds. All bond issues have a borrower, lenders, a face amount, a bond rate of interest, an effective date, interest payment dates, and a maturity date. Some bond issues may, at the option of the issuer, contain certain special features in addition to these characteristics. These special features include the callable feature, the convertible feature, and the establishment of a bond sinking fund.

The Callable Feature The callable feature allows the issuer to repurchase the bonds from investors at a predetermined price during predetermined periods of time in the bond's life. The price at which the bonds may be repurchased is referred to as the *call price*, and the time period over which the bond may be repurchased is the *call period*. The call price and call period, as well as the order in which the bonds may be called, are specified in the bond agreement.

Callable bonds give the issuer an option to repurchase the bonds directly from investors without having to go through the mechanism of the bond market. This option can be exercised by the issuer even though the investor may not want to sell the bond. It is important, then, that investors be aware of the existence of the particulars of a call feature on bond issues. If a bond is callable, the call price is stated as a percent of face amount, such as 103.

Suppose that the sample bond in Figure 12-2 was originally sold at a discount of $60 and is called on January 1, 1986. At the time this bond is called, its carrying value is $970 (original selling price of $940 plus discount amortization of $6 per year for five years) and it is retired for $1,030, resulting in a loss of $60 ($1,030 − $970) to the borrower. If this bond had been retired at a price below its carrying value, a gain would have resulted. These gains or losses on retirement of bonds should be reported as extraordinary items on the issuer's income statement.

Most bond issues contain a call provision so that an issuer may repurchase the bonds if funds are no longer needed by the business, or if these funds can be acquired at a lower cost because of declining interest rates.

The Convertible Feature The convertible feature gives the bondholder an option to exchange the bond investment for shares of common stock in the same company. The price at which shares of common stock will be exchanged for convertible bonds is called the *conversion price* and the time period over which the bondholder may exercise this option is called the *conversion period*. Both conversion price and period are specified in the bond agreement.

The conversion price is usually set above the price at which the common stock is selling at the time the bonds are originally sold. The number of common stock shares a bondholder will receive in exchange for a bond can be determined by dividing the face amount of bonds being converted by the conversion price of the common shares. If a $1,000 bond has a conversion price of $25 per share, the bond can be exchanged for forty shares of common stock. As the selling price of the stock rises above $25, the conversion feature becomes attractive to bondholders.

No gain or loss for the borrower results from the conversion of bonds because the carrying value of the bonds is transferred to the common stock account. Unlike the calling of bonds, which decreases cash, assets are not affected by the conversion of bonds.

The convertible feature is used less often than the callable feature; however, **convertible bonds** are popular with investors. They present the opportunity for bondholders to benefit from increases in the price of a profitable company's stock through the conversion process. At the same time, the bondholder is given the option of maintaining the favorable status of creditor if business activities do not result in stock price increases. Because the convertible feature is popular with investors, bonds that carry this provision can usually be sold at lower interest rates than comparable nonconvertible bonds with approximately the same risk.

Bond Sinking Fund To increase investor confidence in a particular bond issue, borrowers sometimes establish an independent fund during the life of the bonds and make periodic payments to this fund. These periodic (usually annual) payments are made to a trustee. They are placed in a fund called a **sinking fund** and are invested by the trustee. The periodic payments by the issuer plus the earnings on the fund accumulate to an amount sufficient to retire the bonds at maturity, thus, the retirement of the bonds is assured. Any cash remaining in the sinking fund after bonds are retired is returned to the issuer.

A bond sinking fund should be classified on the balance sheet of the borrowing company as an investment among the noncurrent assets. Because use of the fund is restricted to the retirement of bonds, it cannot be reported as a current asset.

The Role of Underwriters

Borrowers prefer to sell an entire bond issue and receive all funds at once. Individual investors, on the other hand, prefer to purchase small or medium quantities of any particular bond. A middleman is usually needed so that issuer and investor preferences can be met and the smooth transfer of bonds, ensured. This middleman is called an **underwriter.** Underwriters (there may be many on any bond issue) purchase bonds directly from the issuing company in large or medium quantities and sell to investors in any quantity they desire. The underwriters' profit is the difference between the price paid to the issuer for the bonds and the price at which they are sold to investors.

Bonds as a Source of Long-Term Funds

Bond interest expense is deductible in arriving at income subject to income taxes, while dividends on stock are not. Thus, the true cost of acquiring funds through debt is the amount of interest on the debt minus the taxes saved by deducting this interest in arriving at taxable income. This is called the **after-tax interest cost** of the debt. High income tax rates make this deductibility particularly significant for bond issuers.

Assume that a company wishing to expand its operations is considering acquiring $1,000,000 in new funds. These funds can be obtained by the issue of 30,000 shares of common stock or by the sale of $1,000,000 of 10 percent bonds. Earnings before interest and income taxes are deducted are expected to be $300,000 per year. Figure 12-8 illustrates this situation.

After-Tax Interest Cost of Bonds   The true cost of the bonds is the $100,000 of interest paid minus the $40,000 income taxes saved by deducting this bond interest in determining corporate income taxes. The actual interest cost of the bonds is 6 percent (10 percent interest paid on the bonds minus the 40 percent income tax rate). Current owners would benefit from financing this expansion by the use of bonds: earnings per share will be $4.00 if bonds are sold, as opposed to $3.00 if common stock is issued.

Financial Leverage   The use of low-cost borrowed funds (debt) to improve the return to owners is called **leverage** or **trading on the equity** and is a common practice among large businesses. The more debt a business carries, however, the greater the fixed payments and thus the greater the risk that some of these payments may not be met as they come due. Businesses risk their existence when they use excessive debt to obtain funds. The concept of financial leverage is covered more extensively in Chapter 16.

Effective Interest Amortization

The discounts or premiums that result from the sale of bonds may be amortized by either the straight-line or effective interest method. The straight-line method results in a uniform interest expense for the borrower and, thus, is easier to apply. The effective interest approach, however, is more conceptually sound in that it closely reflects the actual annual cost of borrowing, as well as movements in the net bond liability.

The accounts affected under effective interest amortization are the same as those affected by the straight-line approach. Only the amounts for annual interest expense and discount or premium amortization are different using effective interest. The amounts for interest expense with effective interest discount amortization and interest expense with effective interest premium amortization for the sample bond are presented in Figure 12-9.

FIGURE 12-8
Financing Through
Bonds versus Stock

	Issue 30,000 New Shares of Common Stock	Sell $1,000,000 of 10% Bonds
Income before interest and income tax	$300,000	$300,000
Bond interest expense	0	100,000
Income subject to income tax	300,000	200,000
Income taxes (assume 40%)	120,000	80,000
Net income	$180,000	$120,000
Number of shares of common stock outstanding	60,000	30,000
Earnings per share	$3.00	$4.00

Concept Summary

Special Bond Situations			
	Description	*Effect on Borrower*	*Effect on Lender*
Callable Feature	Allows borrower to repurchase bonds from lenders during the bond's life at a fixed price.	Can repurchase bonds directly, without going through the bond markets; a gain or loss on retirement of bonds may result.	May lose large interest payments when interest rates decline.
Convertible Feature	Allows lender to exchange the bond investment for common stock at a fixed conversion ratio.	Bonds can be sold at a lower interest rate; no gain or loss on conversion results.	Can benefit from increases in the stock price of a profitable company.
Bond Sinking Fund	Independent fund administered by a trustee; borrower makes annual payments into fund.	Should classify fund as an investment among noncurrent assets.	Assures bonds will be retired at maturity because cash has been set aside.
Underwriters	Firms that purchase bonds directly from the issuing company and then sell them to investors.	Can sell entire bond issue and receive all funds at once.	Can purchase small or medium quantities of any particular bond.
Financial Leverage	Interest payments are tax deductible, thus reducing the true cost of the bonds.	Can increase return to owners by financing expansion with bonds rather than stock.	Can increase risk if firm incurs excessive debt.

Discount Amortization with Effective Interest The journal entries for the sample discount bond for the first and second interest period would be as follows:

```
12/31/81  Interest expense ........................  94.00
              Discount on bonds ....................            4.00
              Cash .................................           90.00
12/31/82  Interest expense ........................  94.40
              Discount on bonds ....................            4.40
              Cash .................................           90.00
```

The journal entry amounts for the remaining years may be taken from the amortization table given in Figure 12-9a. Under effective interest amortization, interest expense in each year is equal to the market rate of interest

FIGURE 12-9
Effective Interest
Amortization

Face amount	$1,000
Effective date	December 31, 1980
Interest payment dates	Annual, Starting December 31, 1981
Maturity date	December 31, 1990
Sold on December 31, 1980	10 percent market rate

a. AMORTIZATION TABLE FOR SAMPLE DISCOUNT BOND
Bond Rate of Interest of 9%

Interest Period	A Interest Paid (9% × 1,000)	B Interest Expense (10% × E)	C Discount Amortization (B − A)	D Unamortized Discount	E Net Bond Liability (1,000 − D)
				$60.00	$ 940.00
1	$90	$94.00	$4.00	56.00	944.00
2	90	94.40	4.40	51.60	948.40
3	90	94.84	4.84	46.76	953.24
4	90	95.32	5.32	41.44	958.56
5	90	95.86	5.86	35.58	964.42
6	90	96.44	6.44	29.14	970.86
7	90	97.09	7.09	22.05	977.95
8	90	97.80	7.80	14.25	985.75
9	90	98.58	8.58	5.67	994.33
10	90	95.61*	5.61	0.00	1,000.00

b. AMORTIZATION TABLE FOR SAMPLE PREMIUM BOND
Bond Rate of Interest of 11%

Interest Period	A Interest Paid (11% × 1,000)	B Interest Expense (10% × E)	C Premium Amortization (A − B)	D Unamortized Premium	E Net Bond Liability (1,000 + D)
				$60.00	$1,060.00
1	$110	$106.00	$4.00	56.00	1,056.00
2	110	105.60	4.40	51.60	1,051.60
3	110	105.16	4.84	46.76	1,046.76
4	110	104.68	5.32	41.44	1,041.44
5	110	104.14	5.86	35.58	1,035.58
6	110	103.56	6.44	29.14	1,029.14
7	110	102.91	7.09	22.05	1,022.05
8	110	102.21	7.79	14.26	1,014.26
9	110	101.43	8.57	5.69	1,005.69
10	110	104.31*	5.69	0.00	1,000.00

*Because of rounding, interest expense in the last period is equal to interest paid to bondholders minus the remaining belance in unamortized premium or plus the unamortized discount.

(10 percent) multiplied by the net bond liability (carrying value) at the end of the previous year. This amount is the true interest cost for the period. The discount amortization is the difference between the true interest cost of the period and the amount actually paid to investors (bond rate × face amount).

Because only a portion of the annual interest cost is paid each period, the unpaid amount is added to the net bond liability. As this liability increases, the interest cost of the subsequent period increases because more of the investor's money is being used by the borrower. This increasing annual interest cost continues until the maturity of the bond.

Effective interest amortization results in a constant relationship between interest expense and the net bond liability over the life of the bond. Interest expense is always the market rate of interest multiplied by the net bond liability for the period.

Premium Amortization with Effective Interest The journal entries for the sample premium bond for the first and second interest period would be as follows:

12/31/81	Interest expense	106	
	Premium on bonds	4	
	Cash		110
12/31/82	Interest expense	105.60	
	Premium on bonds	4.40	
	Cash		110

The journal entry amounts for the remaining years can be taken from the amortization table given in Figure 12-9b. Under effective interest amortization, interest expense is equal to the market rate of interest (10 percent) multiplied by the net bond liability (carrying value) at the end of the previous year. As is characteristic under effective interest amortization, this is the true interest cost for the period. The premium amortization is, then, the difference between the amount actually paid to investors (bond rate × face amount) and the true interest cost of the period.

Because the amount paid to investors represents both interest and return of original investment, the return of original investment is deducted from the net bond liability. As this liability decreases, the interest cost of the subsequent period decreases because less of the investor's money is being used by the borrower. This decreasing annual interest cost continues until maturity of the bond.

The constant relationship of interest expense and net bond liability expressed at the market rate of interest is reflected in the journal entries.

Summary

When a company desires to borrow more money than can be obtained from a single lender or a small number of lenders, bonds are a useful borrowing instrument. Bonds allow a company to borrow simultaneously from a large number of lenders under fixed terms.

Two rates of interest are important in the sale or purchase of bonds. The bond rate of interest when multiplied by the face amount of the bond gives the annual interest annuity to be paid on the bond. The market rate of interest, which reflects the desired rate of return by investors for the risk inherent in the bond, is used to determine the present value of bond payments.

When the bond rate of interest equals the market rate, the return promised on the bond equals the return desired by investors and the bond will sell at its face amount. When the market rate is greater than the bond rate, investors desire a higher return than promised on the bond, and the bond will only sell at a discount. When the market rate of interest is less than the bond rate, the bond promises to pay more interest than investors require for the risk inherent in the bond, and the bond will sell at a premium.

Whether purchased at a discount or a premium, bonds held to maturity will return to the investor (and will cost the issuing company) the market rate of interest that prevailed when the bonds were sold.

Two special features often attachable to bonds are the callable and convertible provisions. The callable feature allows the bond issuer to retire bonds prior to their maturity date at a fixed price. The convertible provision allows bondholders to exchange their bonds for shares of stock at a fixed ratio, if they desire.

The legal characteristics of corporations and the accounting principles applicable to corporate owners' equity are discussed in Chapter 13.

Key Terms

Accrued interest

After-tax interest cost

Bearer bond (coupon bond)

Bond rate of interest (coupon rate, stated rate)

Borrower (issuer)

Callable bond

Convertible bond

Discount

Discount amortization

Effective date

Effective interest amortization

Interest payment date

Lender (investor)

Leverage

Market rate of interest (effective rate)

Net bond liability

Premium

Premium amortization

Rate of return

Registered bond

Risk rating

Sinking fund

Straight-line amortization

Underwriter

Comprehensive Review Problem

In the midst of rapid expansion, Scott's Stores of the Stars, Inc., is raising large amounts of funds through the bond market. On January 1, 1981, Scott's issued $800,000 of 9 percent, five-year callable bonds. Interest is paid annually on December 31 of each year. The market rate of interest for these bonds at the time of their issue was 10 percent. On April 1, 1981, $500,000 of 10 percent, ten-year convertible bonds were issued at 102 plus accrued interest. Interest is paid semi-annually on July 1 and December 31 of each year. The $800,000 bond issue was called at 101 on December 31, 1984, and the $500,000 bond issue was converted to common stock on July 1, 1985. Each $1,000 bond is convertible into twenty-five shares of common stock. The stock sold for $45 a share on the date of conversion.

Required:

1. Calculate the selling price of the $800,000 bond issue.

2. Give all necessary journal entries for both bond issues for 1981. Give the journal entries to call the $800,000 bond issue on December 31, 1984, and to convert the $500,000 bond issue on July 1, 1985.

3. Prepare an effective interest amortization table for the $800,000 bond issue assuming the issue remains to its maturity date.

Solution to Comprehensive Review Problem

1. Calculation of selling price of $800,000 bond issue:

Present value of $800,000 at the end of five years at 10% ($800,000 × 0.6209)	$496,720
Interest annuity = $72,000 ($800,000 × 9%)	
Present value of $72,000 for five years at 10% ($72,000 × 3.7908)	272,938
Selling price of $800,000 bond issue	$769,658

2.

Date	Transaction Accounts	Debit	Credit
1981 Jan 1	Cash	769,658	
	Discount on bonds	30,342	
	Bonds payable		800,000
	Issue 9% bonds at discount		
Apr 1	Cash	522,500	
	Bonds payable		500,000
	Premium on bonds		10,000
	Interest expense		12,500
	Issue 10% bonds at premium: premium = 2% × $500,000 = $10,000 interest expense = 3/6 × 1/2 × 10% × $500,000 = $12,500		
July 1	Interest expense	24,745	
	Premium on bonds	255	
	Cash		25,000
	Semiannual interest payment and amortization of premium on $500,000 bonds: cash paid = 1/2 × 10% × $500,000 = $25,000 premium amortization = $\dfrac{\$10,000}{(10 \text{ yrs.} \times 12) - 3 \text{ mos}}$ = $\dfrac{\$10,000}{117 \text{ mos}}$ = $85/mo. The entry is for 3 months.		
Dec 31	Interest expense	78,068	
	Discount on bonds		6,068
	Cash		72,000
	Annual interest payment and amortization of discount on $800,000 bonds: $\dfrac{\$30,342 \text{ discount}}{5 \text{ years}}$ = $6,068/yr.		
31	Interest expense	24,490	
	Premium on bonds	510	
	Cash		25,000
	Semiannual interest payment and amortization of premium of $500,000 bond issue: cash paid = 1/2 × 10% × $500,000 = $25,000 premium amortization = $85/mo. × 6 mos. = $510		

1984
Dec 31   Bonds payable 800,000
              Loss on bond retirement 14,070
                  Discount on bonds   6,070
                  Cash   808,000
              Call bonds at 101: original discount = $30,342 amortized for 4
                  of 5 years; unamortized discount = $30,342 − (4 ×
                  $6,068) = $6,070 (difference due to rounding)

1985
July 1   Bonds payable 500,000
              Premium on bonds 5,665
                  Capital stock   505,665
              Convert bonds to stock (500 × 25 = 12,500 shares):
              original premium = $10,000 amortized for 51 of 117 periods;
                  unamortized premium = $10,000 − (51 × $85) =
                  $5,665 (difference due to rounding)

3.

Interest Period	A Interest Paid (9% × $800,000)	B Interest Expense (10% × Col. E)	C Discount Amortization (B − A)	D Unamortized Discount	E Net Bond Liability ($800,000 − D)
				$30,342	$769,658
1	$72,000	$76,966	$4,966	25,376	774,624
2	72,000	77,462	5,462	19.914	780,086
3	72,000	78,009	6,009	13,905	786,095
4	72,000	78,610	6,610	7,295	792,705
5	72,000	79,295*	7,295	−0−	800,000

*Because of rounding, interest expense in the last period is equal to interest paid to bondholders plus the remaining balance in unamortized discount.

Questions

Q12-1. Distinguish between borrowing situations in which notes would be used and those in which bonds would be used.

Q12-2. How is the bond rate of interest used in the determination of the selling price of a bond? How is the market rate used?

Q12-3. Describe the three possible relationships between the bond rate of interest and the market rate of interest and give the likely effect of each of these relationships on the selling price of a bond.

Q12-4. What does a discount on bonds represent to the borrower? To the lender? What is the effect of amortizing a discount on the borrower? On the lender?

Q12-5. What does a premium on bonds represent to the borrower? To the lender? What is the effect of amortizing a premium on the borrower? On the lender?

Q12-6. Describe the role of underwriters in marketing a bond issue.

Q12-7. Why must investors pay market price plus accrued interest for bonds purchased between interest payment dates?

Q12-8. Define the callable feature on bonds. Who benefits from this feature? Why?

Q12-9. Define the convertible feature on bonds. Who benefits from this feature? Why?

Q12-10. Explain what is meant by after-tax interest cost. In what way are interest payments to bondholders treated differently for income tax purposes from dividends to stockholders?

Exercises

E12-1. On January 1, 1981, the Kittrell Corporation issued $2,000,000 of 10 percent, ten-year bonds. Interest payment dates are June 30 and December 31. The effective date of the bonds was January 1, 1981, and all bonds were sold at their face amounts. Prepare the journal entries that would be made on the books of the Kittrell Corporation: (a) to record the sale of the bonds on January 1, 1981; (b) to record interest payments and interest expense each June 30 and December 31; and (c) to record the retirement of the bonds on December 31, 1990.

E12-2. The Tabb Corporation is contemplating the sale of $100,000 of 8 percent, ten-year bonds. Calculate the amount for which the bonds would be sold on their effective date if

a. the market rate is 8 percent and interest is paid annually.
b. the market rate is 6 percent and interest is paid annually.
c. the market rate is 10 percent and interest is paid annually.
d. the market rate is 10 percent and interest is paid semiannually.

E12-3. The Fait Corporation decided to raise capital by issuing bonds. The bond issue was to consist of 100 ten-year bonds each with a face value of $1,000, a bond rate of 10 percent, an effective date of January 1, 1981, and annual interest payment dates of December 31 beginning in 1981. All of the bonds were sold on January 1, 1981. Prepare the entries to record the sale of the bonds, the interest expense and interest payments for 1981 (using straight line amortization), and the retirement of the bonds on December 31, 1990, if the bonds were sold at 98. Prepare the entries to record the same events if the bonds were sold at 102.

E12-4. The Lynch Corporation sold $200,000 of 12 percent, twenty-year bonds on April 1, 1981. The effective date of the bonds was January 1, 1981, and the interest payment dates are each June 30 and December 31, beginning in 1981. The purchaser of the bonds paid face value plus accrued interest for the bonds. Prepare the journal entries that would be made on the books of the Lynch Corporation: (a) on April 1, 1981 to record the sale of the bonds; and (b) on June 30, 1981 to record the first interest payment on the bonds.

E12-5. On January 1, 1979, the Colby Corporation issued $200,000 of 10 percent, five-year convertible bonds. The conversion provision stated that the holder of each $1,000 bond could offer the bond for conversion at a stock price of $50 per share any time after December 31, 1980. Interest payment dates on the bonds were December 31 each year starting December 31, 1979. The bonds were sold on January 1, 1979, for $196,000. On January 1, 1981, the market price of the stock was $75 per share, and all of the bonds were converted. Prepare all of the journal entries that would be made on the books of the Colby Corporation with respect to the bonds from the time of their sale to the time of their conversion. (Assume the company uses the straight-line method of amortization of bond premiums and discounts.)

E12-6. Prepare a bond premium amortization table like the one shown in Figure 12-9 for the following bond issue. Round to the nearest dollar.

> Face amount of bonds, *$300,000*
> Bond rate of interest, *11 percent*
> Effective date, *December 31, 1980*
> Interest payment dates, each December 31, starting *December 31, 1981*
> Maturity Date, *December 31, 1985*
> Sold on December 31, 1980 for $311,372 to yield a 10 percent market rate

E12-7. The Olisinek Corporation issued $700,000 of 9 percent, ten-year bonds on January 1, 1981. The interest payment dates on the bonds are each December 31 beginning in 1981. The Regency Insurance Company purchased the entire bond issue on the effective date of the bonds, January 1, 1981. The market rate of interest for bonds of this type was 10 percent at the time of purchase. Calculate the selling price of the bonds and prepare the journal entries that would be made on the books of the Olisinek Corporation and on the books of the Regency Company: (a) on January 1, 1981; (b) on each December 31 from 1981 to 1990 (one example is sufficient); and (c) on December 31, 1990. Use the straight-line amortization method and round all calculations to the nearest dollar.

E12-8. The Glip Corporation needs to raise $500,000 to expand its facilities. The funds could be obtained by the issue of 25,000 shares of common stock or by the sale of bonds. The market rate for bonds of this type is 12 percent. The company already has 50,000 shares of common stock outstanding. Earnings before interest expense and income tax expense are deducted are expected to be $250,000. The corporation's tax rate is 40 percent. Calculate the approximate net income and the related earnings per share under each of the funding alternatives.

E12-9. The Rulon Corporation issued $800,000 of 12 percent, ten-year bonds. The bonds were sold on their effective date, November 1, 1980. Interest payment dates are each April 30 and October 31. The bonds were sold at a quoted price of 103. Prepare all of the journal entries that would be made on the books of the Rulon Corporation with respect to the bonds during 1980 and 1981, including adjusting entries that would be made on December 31, the end of the accounting period. Use straight-line amortization.

E12-10. On January 1, 1981, the Wather Corporation issued $100,000 of 10 percent, ten-year bonds. Interest payments are to be made annually on December 31. The bonds are callable any time after December 31, 1985, at a call price of 103. The bonds were originally sold at 98. Assuming the Wather Corporation retires the bonds on December 31, 1986, calculate the gain or loss on the early retirement of the bonds and give the journal entry that would be made on the Wather Corporation books to record the retirement. (Assume straight-line amortization of the bond discount.)

Problems

P12-1. The Hillburn Corporation issued $500,000 of 10 percent, ten-year bonds on January 1, 1981. The interest payment dates are each June 30 and December 31 beginning in 1981. The Mutual Corporation purchased the entire bond issue on the effective date of the bonds, January 1, 1981. The market rate of interest for bonds of this type was 8 percent at the time of the purchase.

Required:

1. Calculate the selling price of the bonds. Round to the nearest dollar.

2. Prepare the journal entries that would be made on the books of the Hillburn Corporation and on the books of the Mutual Company: (a) on January 1, 1981; (b) on each June 30 and December 31 (one example is sufficient); and (c) on December 31, 1990. Use the straight-line method of amortization and round calculations to the nearest dollar.

3. Show how the bonds payable would be reported on the December 31, 1983, balance sheet of the Hillburn Corporation.

4. Show how the investment in bonds would be reported on the December 31, 1983, balance sheet of the Mutual Corporation.

P12-2. On January 1, 1981, the Mead Corporation issued $800,000 of ten-year, 8 percent bonds on their effective date. Interest on the bonds is to be paid each December 31 beginning in 1981.

Required:

1. Calculate the selling price of the bonds if the market rate for bonds of this type was 6 percent on January 1, 1981. Round to the nearest dollar.

2. Prepare the journal entries on the Mead Corporation's books: (a) on January 1, 1981, to record the sale of bonds at the price calculated in Requirement 1; (b) on December 31, 1981, to record the first interest payment using straight-line amortization; and (c) on December 31, 1990, to record retirement of the debt. Round all calculations to the nearest dollar.

3. Calculate the selling price of the bonds if the market rate for bonds of this type was 10 percent on January 1, 1981. Round to the nearest dollar.

4. Prepare the journal entries to be recorded on the Mead Corporation's books: (a) on January 1, 1981, to record the sale of bonds at the price calculated in Requirement 3; (b) on December 31, 1981, to record the first interest payment using straight-line amortization; and (c) on December 31, 1990, to record retirement of the debt. Round all calculations to the nearest dollar.

P12-3. The Welsch Corporation sold $200,000 of 8 percent, five-year bonds on the effective date of the bonds, January 1, 1981. Interest payments are to be made annually on December 31 beginning in 1981. At the time the bonds were sold, the market rate for bonds of this type was 10 percent.

Required:

1. Calculate the selling price of the bonds. Round to the nearest dollar.

2. Prepare an amortization table like the one shown in Figure 12-9 for the bond.

3. Prepare all journal entries that would be made on the books of the Welsch Corporation over the life of the bond using the effective interest method of amortization.

P12-4. The Kees Corporation issued $1,500,000 of ten-year, 12 percent bonds on May 1, 1980, the effective date of the bonds. The interest payment dates of the bonds are October 31 and April 30, beginning October 31, 1980. The market rate for bonds of this type at the time the bonds were sold was 10 percent.

Required:

1. Calculate the selling price of the bonds and prepare the journal entry to be made on the books of the Kees Corporation to record the sale of the bonds. Round calculation to the nearest dollar.

2. Prepare the journal entry to be made on October 31, 1980, to record the interest payment. Amortize the bond premium on the straight-line basis. Round calculation to the nearest dollar.

3. Prepare the adjusting entry to record accrued interest expense on December 31, 1980.

4. Prepare the journal entry to record the interest payment on April 30, 1981.

P12-5. The Mequet Corporation sold 500, ten-year, 10 percent bonds on January 1, 1978, the effective date of the bonds. Each bond had a face value of $1,000. The interest payment dates of the bonds are each December 31 beginning in 1978. The bonds were sold at the quoted price of 98.

Required:

1. Assume the bonds are callable at 103 any time after December 31, 1980. If the Mequet Corporation retired all the bonds on January 1, 1982, prepare all of the journal entries that would be made on the books of the Mequet Corporation with respect to the bonds from their sale through their retirement. Amortize the discount on a straight-line basis.

2. Assume that the bonds are convertible any time after December 31, 1981, for common stock. The conversion price is $25 per share for each bond. If the market price of a share of common stock was $40 on January 1, 1982, and all bonds were exchanged for stock on that date, give all of the journal entries that would be made on the books of the Mequet Corporation with respect to the bonds from their sale to their conversion. Amortize the discount on a straight-line basis.

P12-6. The Talar Corporation sold 100 bonds to the Ralat Corporation on January 1, 1981. The face value of each bond was $1,000. The bond rate was 10 percent. The effective date of the bonds was January 1, 1981 and the maturity date was December 31, 1985. Interest payment dates are each December 31 beginning in 1981. The Ralat Corporation purchased the bonds at the quoted price of 98.

Required:

1. Prepare all journal entries that would be made on the books of the Talar Corporation with respect to the bonds from January 1, 1981, through December 31, 1985. Amortize the bond discount on the straight-line basis.

2. Prepare all journal entries that would be made on the books of the Ralat Corporation with respect to the bonds from January 1, 1981, through December 31, 1985.

3. Set up T accounts for the bonds payable and discount on bonds payable accounts for the Talar Corporation. Post to these accounts from journal entries in Requirement 1 through December 31, 1983. Show how bonds payable would be reported on the December 31, 1983, balance sheet of the Talar Corporation. Make 1984 and 1985 postings to the accounts and calculate balance in the accounts at December 31, 1985.

4. Set up a T account for investment in bonds for the Ralat Corporation. Post to this account from the journal entries in Requirement 2 through December 31, 1983. Show how investment in bonds would be reported on the December 31, 1983, balance sheet of the Ralat Corporation. Make 1984 and 1985 postings to the account and calculate the balance in the account at December 31, 1985.

P12-7. The Ross Corporation needs to raise $1,000,000 to expand its operations. The corporation is considering two alternatives for raising the capital, the sale of bonds and the sale of common stock. The bonds would be ten-year bonds with an interest rate of 12 percent. If the bonds were issued, the corporation would establish a bond sinking fund in order to have sufficient funds to retire the bonds at maturity. It is estimated that such a fund would earn 10 percent interest. Contributions to the fund would be made annually beginning on the first annual interest payment date of the bonds.

If common stock were sold to raise the capital, about 25,000 shares would have to be issued. The corporation currently has 100,000 shares of stock outstanding. Earnings before interest and income taxes are deducted are expected to average approximately $800,000 per year over the next ten years. The corporation's tax rate is 40 percent. The corporation follows a policy of paying 50 percent of net earnings out in dividends to its common stockholders.

Required:

1. Calculate the expected average net earnings per year for each of the financing alternatives.

2. Calculate the expected earnings per share under each of the financing alternatives.

3. For each of the financing alternatives, calculate the total cash to be expended each year for interest expense, income taxes, dividends, and contributions to the bond sinking fund.

P12-8. The Santor Corporation issued bonds with total face values of $200,000. The effective date of the bonds was January 1, 1981 and the maturity date was December 31, 1985. The bond rate was 12 percent. Interest payment dates are June 30 and December 31 beginning in 1981. Because of an extremely depressed bond market, the bonds were not sold until October 31, 1981. They were sold on that date at the quoted price of 98.

Required:

1. Calculate the amount received by the Santor Corporation from the sale of the bonds. Prepare the journal entry to record the sale of the bonds on October 31, 1981.

2. Record the interest payment made on December 31, 1981. Use the straight-line amortization method for the bond discount.

3. Prepare the journal entry that would be made each June 30 and December 31 from 1982 to 1985.

4. Based on the entries made in Requirements 1, 2, and 3, calculate the total interest expense that would be recorded on the bonds. Verify this amount by comparing it to the interest expense calculated by subtracting the Santor Corporation's cash receipt from the sale of the bonds from its total cash payments to bondholders.

P12-9. The Gregg Corporation issued $600,000 of five-year, 12 percent bonds on January 1, 1981, the effective date of the bonds. The annual interest payment date of the bonds is December 31, beginning in 1981. At the time the bonds were issued, the market rate for bonds of this type was 10 percent.

Required:

1. Calculate the selling price of the bonds and the premium on the bonds.

2. Prepare an amortization schedule like the one shown in Figure 12-9.

3. Prepare all of the journal entries to be made on the books of the Gregg Corporation with respect to the bonds using the effective interest method of amortization.

4. Set up T accounts for the bonds payable and the premium on bonds payable accounts. Post from the journal entries made in Requirement 3 to these accounts.

5. Calculate the total interest expense by subtracting the Gregg Corporation's cash receipts from bondholders from its total cash payments to bondholders. Compare this figure with the total interest expense recorded in Requirement 3.

P12-10. The Sahe Corporation sold 600 ten-year bonds on July 31, 1979. The face value of each bond was $1,000, and the bond interest rate was 10 percent. The effective date of the bonds was June 1, 1979, and the interest payment dates are each November 30 and May 31 beginning November 30, 1979. The bonds are callable at 102 any time after May 31, 1984. At the time the bonds were sold, the market rate for bonds of this type was 12 percent. On June 1, 1984, the Sahe Corporation retired the bonds under the terms of the call provision.

Required:

1. Calculate the cash received from the sale of the bonds and prepare the journal entry to record the sale on the Sahe Corporation books. Round calculation to the nearest dollar.

2. Prepare the journal entries that would be made on November 30, 1979, December 31, 1979, and May 31, 1980, if the discount is amortized on a straight-line basis. Round calculations to the nearest dollar.

3. Prepare the journal entry to record the retirement of the bonds on June 1, 1984.

CHAPTER 13

Corporations

Chapter Outline

13.1 *Characteristics of Corporations.* Advantages and disadvantages of the corporate form; the rights of corporate owners and the duties of the board of directors and corporate officers; structure of corporations.

13.2 *Preferred Stock and Common Stock.* Characteristics of preferred stock and common stock; advantages and disadvantages of preferred stock; the cumulative, participating, callable, and convertible features; the ideas of par, stated, and no-par value.

13.3 *Journal Entries for Preferred and Common Stock.* Discussion and illustration of the issue, conversion, repurchase, and splitting of shares of stock; the effect of these activities on stockholders' equity.

13.4 *Retained Earnings.* Discussion and illustration of extraordinary items and earnings per share, cash and stock dividends, prior period adjustments, and appropriations; the effect of these activities on stockholders' equity; book value per share of common stock.

Accounting and the Real World

As anyone who fancies a game of chance knows, the house always wins. That maxim may also be applied to the latest financial stratagem of Resorts International Inc., the pioneer of casino gambling in Atlantic City, N.J.

In effect, Resorts is trying to shrink the number of its shares and boost earnings per share by offering to exchange common shares for debt and warrants. Specifically, the company is offering to swap a new $33 principal amount, 10% subordinated debenture due in 1998, along with one warrant to purchase a share of Resorts A common at $53, for one share of either Class A or B stock. Further, Resorts says that it will accept between 500,000 and 2 million shares, but it has the right to take up to 7 million shares. (The company has the equivalent of 12.4 million shares outstanding.)

"It's a brilliant move for Resorts, and investors will benefit who keep their stock," says one source. He doubts too many shareholders will exchange their shares; however, he admits that some shareholders may want to convert their common stock, which pays no dividends, for interest-paying bonds.

In any case, trading has been heavy which is an indication that professional traders, suffering because of a paucity of mergers lately, have been actively buying the stock in hopes of profiting from the exchange. Accordingly, the profit spread between the price of Resorts stock and the value of the exchange package has narrowed.

After studying the new securities, many analysts are suggesting to their individual investors that they retain their common shares. One Wall Street broker quips that he hopes other firms will tell their customers to accept Resorts' offer while he tells his customers to keep their shares.

Worthless warrants. Using market prices of comparable Resorts' securities, analysts estimate the value of the exchange package at $33.75. For example, identical Resorts' warrants, which give the owner the option to buy Class A common at $53 until 1984, recently plunged to $9 from $13—reflecting the expectation that there will be a big increase in supply from the exchange. Thus, with Resorts selling for $32, or $19 below the warrants' exercise price, the warrants are intrinsically worthless. With increased supply, they are likely to remain depressed.

The value of the debentures can be estimated from the price of Resorts' 10% subordinated debentures due in 1999. They sell for about 75% of face value. That percentage applied to the new $33 principal-amount debentures works out to $24.75. "Yield-minded investors can get a good yield with less risk simply by buying high-quality bonds," says one analyst.

Attractive assets. Resorts' common stock has some attractive fundamentals. There is roughly $25 a share in Atlantic City real estate (approximately $30 after the exchange), according to Ellen Greenspan, who writes *Special Transactions* for the risk arbitrage department at Oppenheimer & Co. Also, while Resorts' earnings could fall this year as new competitive casinos open in Atlantic City, fewer shares outstanding should offset some of the decline. Greenspan says that this year's projected earnings of $5 a share could rise to $5.60 because of the exchange.

For the company, conditions are propitious for the exchange. Its Class A stock sells at less than five times the last 12 months earnings of $6.45 a share. When Resorts infected the market with gaming-stock fever in 1979, the same issue commanded a p/e of over 100. Although Resorts' earnings are inflated by real estate sales, the stock still sells at a modest price-earnings multiple compared with that of other gambling companies: that of Golden Nugget Inc. is 38 and that of Caesars World Inc. is 14. Moreover, interest rates have dropped sharply, and Resorts would have had to pay a lot higher coupon than 10% a few weeks ago. For now, warrants cost Resorts nothing.

The corporation is undoubtedly the dominant form of business organization in the United States and the world. The fifty or so largest U.S. corporations account for more business activity than all of the proprietorships and partnerships in the United States combined. For accounting purposes, corporations differ from the other legal forms of business organization in three areas. On the corporate income statement, income tax expense reflects the direct income tax on corporations. There is no direct income tax on proprietorships or partnerships and, consequently, no income tax expense on these income statements. Also, a corporate income statement will show a figure for earnings per share of stock outstanding. Distributions of earnings are called dividends in corporations and appear on the statement of retained earnings. These distributions are called owner withdrawals in unincorporated businesses and are shown on the statement of owners' capital. Finally, the corporate balance sheet classifies owners' equity into direct (capital stock) and indirect (retained earnings) investment, while these types of owner investment are combined and the owners' equity section is classified by owner in proprietorships and partnerships.

As corporations are examined in this chapter, each of these characteritics of corporate financial statements will be discussed in greater depth.

13.1 Characteristics of Corporations

Corporations have grown in popularity and use primarily because of the legal and business advantages inherent in the corporate form. The corporation is viewed under the law as a separate legal entity from its owners with separate rights and obligations. The corporation is a citizen in its own right, while proprietorships and partnerships are treated as extensions of the business owners under the law. Most of the advantages and disadvantages of the corporate form can be traced to the separate legal entity position of the corporation.

Advantages of the Corporate Form

The corporate form offers five unique advantages.

Limited Liability of Owners Because the corporation is a separate legal entity, corporate creditors have claims against the assets of the business but not against the personal assets of the owners. This means that, in the event of extreme business difficulty, corporate owners stand to lose only the amounts invested. Owners may choose the amount to be invested with the assurance that their other assets are not placed at risk.

Business Life Not Tied to Particular Ownership A corporation can continue to function as an entity in the face of rapid and frequent ownership changes. Because owners play a passive role in the operation of the business, ownership changes do not disrupt business activity.

Ownership Interest Easily Transferred Ownership interest in a corporation takes the form of shares of stock. That is, the ownership of a corporation may be divided into many small pieces, each of which can be bought and sold. Several organized markets (called stock exchanges) function to facilitate the transfer of shares of stock between individual corporate owners as well as between corporations and owners. Transfers of 30 to 50 million shares a day are not unusual on the New York Stock Exchange alone; and during one month in 1980, one billion shares of corporate stock were transferred on that exchange.

Accumulation of Large Amounts of Funds Because of the limited liability feature, the opportunity to purchase small amounts of ownership interest, and the ease with which this ownership can be transferred, corporations can attract large numbers of owners. This spreading of ownership interest over many large and small investors allows corporations to gather large amounts of assets. Some corporations have as many as one million owners.

Separation of Ownership, Control, and Management Functions Owners provide the assets of a corporation but (except for small, closely held corporations) do not participate in the operation of the business. Instead, control of the business is vested in a group that represents the owners (the board of directors) who, in turn, employ professional managers (the corporate officers) to operate the business. Because of this separation of functions, corporations can benefit from the services and talents of the best management group available.

Disadvantages of the Corporate Form

Some disadvantages are inherent in the corporate form. Two of the most important of these are double taxation of income and government regulation.

Double Taxation of Income As separate legal entities, corporations must pay tax on their income at a tax rate that approaches 50 percent for large businesses. Then, if a corporation pays dividends to owners, the dividend amounts are considered personal income to the owners and taxed accordingly. Because dividends are not an income statement item and are not deducted in determining corporate income subject to tax, the same income is taxed twice. This double taxation, however, applies only to amounts paid as dividends and can be avoided by retaining income in the business.

Federal and State Regulation As citizens, corporations are subject to the laws of the state in which the corporation is formed, as well as the laws of those states in which it does business. Also, corporations with public ownership have become increasingly subject to federal regulation of their activities and federal requirements for the disclosure of information.

Corporations must be formed according to the laws of a state, which is then called the state of incorporation. Typically, an application is sent to the appropriate official of the state. This application includes the **articles of incorporation,** which are the rules and guidelines by which the corporation will be run. The approved application, called the **corporate charter,** is the birth certificate of the corporation and its license to operate. Once a corporation is chartered it may sell stock to owners, elect a board of directors, and employ corporate officers.

Rights of Stock Ownership

The ownership of stock affords certain basic rights to corporate owners. The most important of these rights are as follows:

1. The right to participate in major corporate activity by a vote of shares of stock (one vote per share of stock). The most important ongoing activity for which stockholders may vote their shares is election of the board of directors. Also, stockholders may be given the right to vote on major corporate decisions, such as mergers, major new bond or stock issues, or changes in the characteristics of existing stock. These votes take place at a stockholders' meeting held once each year. In fact, stockholders' meetings are attended by very few owners, and most stockholders simply assign the right to vote their shares to the current corporate management or do not vote at all.

2. The right to participate in all dividends declared and paid by the corporation equally on a per share basis.

3. The right to participate in the distribution of corporate assets upon liquidation of the business equally on a per share basis. This distribution is subject to the prior satisfaction of the claims of corporate creditors.

4. The right to participate in new issues of stock by the corporation on a pro rata basis. This right is called the preemptive right and gives existing stockholders the right of first refusal on the same percentage of new shares as shares currently owned. The preemptive right is designed to prevent the dilution of ownership percentages by the issuing of new shares of stock to new or selected current owners. The preemptive right is the least universal of the basic rights of stock ownership and has been eliminated from many corporate shares. Most states permit the elimination of preemptive rights and disallow them unless they are explicitly provided for in the corporate charter.

Concept Summary

Characteristics of Corporations		
	Advantages	*Disadvantages*
Corporate Form	1. Limited liability of owners 2. Business life not tied to particular ownership 3. Ownership interest easily transferred 4. Accumulation of large amounts of funds is relatively easy 5. Separation of ownership, control, and management functions	1. Double taxation of income 2. Federal and state regulation
Stock Ownership	1. Participation in major corporate activity by a vote of shares of stock 2. Participation in all dividends on a per share basis 3. Participation in the distribution of corporate assets upon liquidation 4. Participation in new issues of stock on a pro rata basis (preemptive right)	1. No guaranteed amount of payments 2. No fixed time for payments

Corporate Structure

The **board of directors** holds the major decision-making authority in a corporation. Acting on behalf of the stockholders, the board sets all major policies for the business, reviews the activity of corporate management, and makes important policy decisions, such as the timing and amount of dividends and the hiring of top corporate officers.

Corporate officers usually include a president, an executive vice-president, several vice-presidents in charge of specific areas of business activity, a secretary, and a treasurer. This top management group makes all of the operating decisions of the business not specifically reserved for the board of directors.

Notice that the stockholders own the corporation but have no say in the operation of the business and only indirect influence on its major policies through the directors. The assets and income of the business belong to the corporation and become the property of stockholders only through action of the board of directors. Likewise, the debts are those of the corporation and do not accrue to the owners.

Figure 13-1 illustrates a corporate organizational structure with typical paths of authority and responsibility demonstrated.

13.2 Preferred Stock and Common Stock

The sale of stock represents a major source of assets for corporations. Stockholders supply a corporation with assets through the purchase of shares of stock, creating a claim against business assets whose satisfaction depends upon the success of the business. This direct investment of owners is called the **contributed capital** of the corporation.

Most corporations are authorized by their corporate charter to issue two types of stock and thus contributed capital comes from two classes of owners. These two types of stock, called preferred stock and common stock, result in two separate classes of ownership interest in the owners' equity section of a corporation. Common stockholders are the ultimate owners of the business, and preferred stockholders are a special ownership class with different rights and privileges.

FIGURE 13-1
Corporate
Organizational
Structure

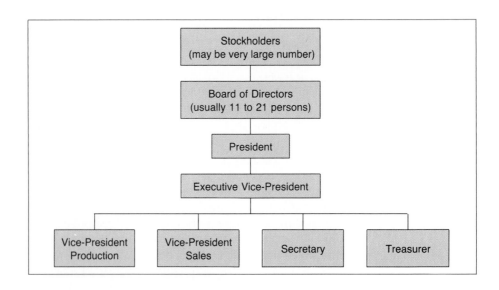

Preferred Stock

Preferred stock represents a special kind of ownership interest in a business. As an investment security, preferred stock offers some of the characteristics of bonds (debt) and some of common stock (ultimate ownership). Although preferred stockholders are owners, they occupy a position quite different from that of common stockholders.

Preferred Stock Preferences The name preferred stock derives from preferences attachable to this type of stock ownership. Preferred stock carries with it two preferences over common stock.

Holders of preferred stock have a prior claim to corporate dividends. That is, if dividends are declared by the board of directors, preferred dividends must be paid first, in full. If sufficient funds for dividends for all owners are not available, preferred stockholders have priority on whatever amounts are paid. This preference does not guarantee dividends to preferred stockholders but rather gives them first claim to any dividends paid. Only the board of directors can determine whether a dividend is appropriate and the amount of the dividend in a particular instance.

Preferred stockholders have a prior claim to the assets of the business in the event of liquidation. This prior claim is only among the corporate owners, however, because the claims of all corporate creditors are prior to those of any owners. If a corporation terminates its existence and liquidates its assets, the claims of creditors are satisfied first, then come preferred stockholders, and finally, the common stock owners receive what (if anything) remains.

Disadvantages of Preferred Stock In exchange for these preferences, preferred stock owners give up certain rights which ordinarily accrue to corporate owners. Two important prerogatives of ownership usually do *not* come with preferred stock, resulting in some disadvantages of this type of investment.

Preferred stock normally offers a fixed dividend rate and a fixed return to investors. Because of its preferences, preferred stock offers less risk to investors; thus, the fixed dividend rate is lower than the return expected by common stock owners of the same company. Ordinarily, ownership of a business allows investors to participate fully in the earnings with their return being limited only by the success of the business. Preferred stock, however, has an external limit on its return (called a *dividend rate*), which is a part of the agreement between the company and its owners. If a corporation is unsuccessful, the preferred stock owner may receive no dividend, while if the business is very successful, preferred stock owners can receive only the stipulated dividend amount.

Preferred stock shares may carry no voting power in the election of the board of directors. Because the directors are the direct representatives of stockholder interests, the voting power of corporate shares is the only input owners enjoy to the operation of the business. The lack of voting power places preferred stockholders in a less influential position in the corporate structure than that of the common stock owners.

On balance, the disadvantages of preferred stock ownership may seem more significant than the preferences. This investment form is more stable, however, and offers less risk to investors because of the dividend and liquidation preferences. As a result, there is a small but active market for the preferred shares of corporations.

Special Features of Preferred Stock

As preferred stock has matured as an investment medium, several special legal features have become associated with these shares. Four such features remain in use and are attachable to preferred stock at the option of the issuing corporation.

Cumulative Because preferred stock dividends are limited and fixed, a dividend skipped in any one year cannot be made up by the normal dividend of later years. To increase the expectation of dividend continuity, a corporation may add the cumulative feature to its preferred shares prior to issue of the stock. The cumulative feature requires that unpaid preferred stock dividends accumulate so that skipped dividends must be paid to preferred stockholders before any dividends can be paid to common stock owners.

To illustrate, assume that a corporation issues $100,000 of cumulative preferred stock which carries a fixed dividend of $10,000. If dividends are declared by the board of directors, $10,000 must be paid to preferred stockholders before any amounts can be paid to common stock. On the other hand, if no dividends are paid in 1981, the $10,000 missed dividend accumulates and $20,000 ($10,000 from 1981 and $10,000 for 1982) must be paid in 1982 before common dividends are paid. Likewise, if dividends are not paid again in 1982, $30,000 would be paid to preferred stock owners in 1983 before common dividends. Preferred stock dividends on cumulative preferred stock which have been skipped in past years are called **dividends in arrears.** The amount of dividends in arrears is disclosed by a footnote to the owners' equity section of a corporate balance sheet.

The cumulative feature is essential to the investment position of preferred stockholders and now is a part of virtually all preferred stock issues.

Participating The participating feature effectively removes the fixed dividend rate from preferred stock and allows preferred stockholders to share in all dividends paid by a corporation. When dividends are paid, the preferred stock fixed dividend is first allocated to preferred owners, then a pro rata amount is allocated to common owners. If additional dividends are to be paid, these amounts are split pro rata on the basis of regular dividends by preferred and common stockholders.

To illustrate this pro rata sharing, assume a corporation has outstanding 2,500 shares of 10 percent, $100 par value preferred stock and 100,000 shares of $15 par value common stock. If $245,000 in dividends are to be declared and there are no dividends in arrears on the preferred stock, the dividend would be split as follows:

Regular preferred stock dividend	$ 25,000
(10% × $100 = $10 per share)	
Regular common stock dividend	150,000
(10% × $15 = $1.50 per share)	
Total regular dividends	175,000
Participating preferred dividend	10,000
(25,000/175,000 × $70,000)	
Participating common dividend	60,000
150,000/175,000 × $70,000)	
Total dividends declared	$245,000
Preferred dividend per share	$14.00
($35,000 ÷ 2,500 shares)	
Common dividend per share	$ 2.10
($210,000 ÷ 100,000 shares)	

Participating preferred stock forces common owners to share large dividends with preferred owners and, thus, is not popular with common stockholders. This feature is not widely used; thus, participating preferred stock may be difficult to find.

Convertible In the same manner as bonds discussed in Chapter 12, preferred stock may carry a provision that allows these shares to be exchanged for common stock. The terms of conversion and the conversion period are fixed prior to issue of the preferred stock. The conversion feature is beneficial to preferred owners because it allows the investment form to be changed at the owner's option as investment circumstances change. Many preferred shares are convertible.

Callable Also similar to bonds, the call provision in preferred stock requires that the investor stand ready to sell the stock back to the issuing corporation for a fixed price at certain stipulated times during the life of the stock. The call price and call period are determined prior to issue of the shares. The callable provision is beneficial to corporations issuing preferred stock because it provides a mechanism for repurchasing and retiring the stock at a fixed price without going into the stock market. Most preferred shares are callable.

Common Stock

Common stockholders are the **residual owners** of a corporation. They are the ultimate risk takers of the business because all claims on business assets (including those of preferred owners) have priority over those of common stock. On the other hand, the common owners enjoy potentially unlimited returns because they may claim all assets not claimed by others.

These characteristics of common stock make it a more volatile form of investment than either preferred stock or bonds. As a corporation is successful and its income grows, the market price of common stock may rise rapidly; however, the price may also fall rapidly during difficult times

Concept Summary

Characteristics of Preferred Stock			
	Advantages	*Disadvantages*	*Beneficial Special Features*
To Issuing Corporation	1. Offers different ownership characteristics to appeal to different investors. 2. Potential return to be paid is fixed and known. 3. Does not affect control of corporation or dilute votes of common stock.	1. Second ownership class may create difficulties. 2. Market for preferred stock does not always exist or may not be active. 3. Although not guaranteed, preferred dividends often come to be viewed as a necessary fixed payment.	1. Callable—stock is easily retired if corporation desires.
To Investor	1. Offers less risk because of preferences as to dividends and assets. 2. Provides an investment that has many of the desirable characteristics of both bonds and stock.	1. Owners cannot fully participate in success of the corporation except under unusual circumstances. 2. Owners cannot express preferences for board of directors or corporate policies through voting shares. 3. Dividends are not guaranteed and may be zero.	1. Cumulative—skipped dividends must be paid before common dividends. 2. Participating—equal share in earnings is possible. 3. Convertible—stock may be exchanged for common shares if investor desires.

for a business. Figure 13-2 is a typical stock certificate of a major retailing corporation.

The articles of incorporation and corporate charter specify the maximum number for shares of preferred and common stock a corporation may issue and may assign a special value, called par value, to the shares of stock. The maximum number of shares that may be sold is called the authorized stock of the business. **Authorized shares** are sufficiently high that few corporations have actually sold all of the shares of preferred or common stock that may be sold. So long as this condition exists, the business may issue additional shares of stock anytime new funds are needed. The number of shares of stock sold to investors is called the **issued shares,** and the difference between authorized and issued shares is called **unissued shares.** Unissued stock represents a potential future source of funds for successful businesses.

Par Value

The concept of par value was conceived as a way to provide corporate creditors with a buffer against the limited liability of corporate owners. The idea was that the articles of incorporation would assign a par value per share for each class of stock. As these shares are sold to owners, the par value multiplied by the number of shares sold becomes a measure of permanent investment by corporate owners. This permanent investment is called **minimum legal capital.** In some states, shares of stock could not

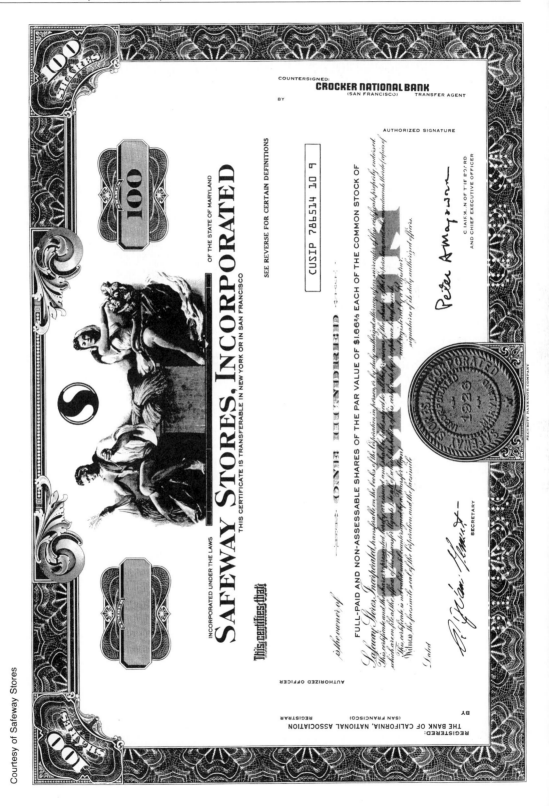

FIGURE 13-2
Stock Certificate for a
Commercial Company

Courtesy of Safeway Stores

be originally sold to investors at a price below par, while in others, if stock were sold below par value, stockholders were held liable for the difference between par and the original selling price of the stock if funds were ever needed by the corporation. Also, this permanent investment of owners could not be reduced by corporate dividends. Creditors would then be able to rely on minimum legal capital as the permanent commitment of the owners to the business.

Stated Value

After several years of use, it became clear that par values were not effective in providing protection to creditors, primarily because these values were established at unrealistically low amounts. Par value could be any amount established by the corporation. As a result, par values of $1 or $5 were not unusual on shares that sold readily at $40, $50, or more per share. Most states now allow no-par stock to be sold at the option of the issuing corporation. When no-par stock is sold, however, the board of directors usually specifies a stated value for the shares. Stated value, like par value, bears no necessary relationship to the actual market price of the stock. Par and stated value may be viewed as arbitrary values assigned to shares of stock by the articles of incorporation (par value) or the board of directors (stated value).

13.3 Journal Entries for Preferred and Common Stock

The articles of incorporation authorize a corporation to issue shares of stock. No assets are realized, however, until these shares of stock are sold to investors. The issue of stock is one of the important owners' equity activities, but a corporation may also convert, repurchase, or split its stock. Figure 13-3 outlines the types of events that typically occur with respect to preferred and common stock, and each of these events is discussed in this section. The par or stated value of the shares plays a role in the accounting treatment of each of these events.

FIGURE 13-3
Events that Affect
Preferred and
Common Stock

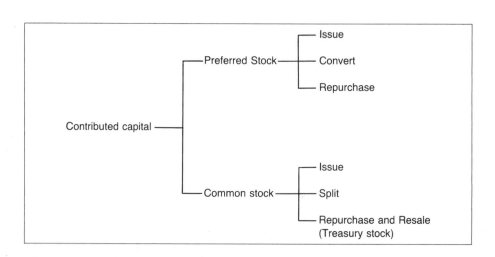

Issue

As shares of preferred or common stock are sold, corporate assets (usually cash) increase and owners' equity increases. When stock carries a par or stated value, the increase in owners' equity must be separated between the amount representing minimum legal capital and the amount in excess of legal capital.

Preferred Stock with Par Value For example, assume that on January 31, 1982, a new corporation issues 100 shares of $10 par value preferred stock. If the shares are sold for $12 each, the following entry would record the issue:

```
01/31/82  Cash .........................................  1,200
              Preferred stock ..............................         1,000
              Paid-in capital in excess of par value—preferred  ..      200
```

If the shares were sold for $9 each, the following entry would be necessary

```
01/31/82  Cash .........................................   900
          Discount on preferred stock .....................   100
              Preferred stock ..............................         1,000
```

In both instances, cash increases by the amount actually received for the shares, and the owners' equity account preferred stock increases by par value multiplied by the number of shares issued. These amounts will not be equal unless the stock is sold at par value; therefore, a third account is usually necessary. This third account will be an adjunct to preferred stock if the shares are sold at a price above par or a contra if the shares bring a price below par.

These two situations would be disclosed on a balance sheet prepared on January 31, 1982 as follows:

Sold at $12

Stockholders' Equity

```
Contributed capital
   Preferred stock, $10 par value ...................................  $ 1,000
   Paid-in capital in excess of par value—preferred  ..................      200   $ 1,200
```

Sold at $9

Stockholders' Equity

```
Contributed capital
   Preferred stock, $10 par value ...................................  $ 1,000
   Discount on preferred stock ....................................      (100)   $   900
```

Stockholders' equity always increases by the amount received for the shares, which is the amount of new assets provided to the business.

Common Stock With Par or Stated Value The same principles apply to the issue of common stock. Par or stated value is usually sufficiently low on common stock so that a sale of shares at a price below these values is unusual. Suppose 500 shares of common stock with a stated value of $5 per share are sold for $20 each on February 15, 1982. The entry to record this transaction would be

```
02/15/82 Cash .........................................   10,000
             Common stock  ..............................             2,500
             Paid in capital in excess of stated value—
                common  ...................................             7,500
```

As always, the common stock account increased by the stated value (or par value) multiplied by the number of shares sold (500 × $5). Stockholders' equity, however, increases by the amount of new assets provided because of the use of an adjunct to the common stock account to reflect the excess amount received (500 × $15).

A balance sheet prepared on February 28, 1982, would reflect both issues of stock in the following way, assuming that the preferred stock is issued at $12:

Stockholders' Equity

Contributed capital
Preferred stock, $10 par value .... $ 1,000
Common stock, $5 stated value   2,500
Paid in capital in excess of par value—preferred   200
Paid in capital in excess of stated value—common   7,500
Total contributed capital $11,200

No-Par Common Stock Occasionally, common stock will be no-par, and the board of directors will choose not to establish a stated value for the shares. In this instance, the entire amount received for the shares is credited to the common stock account, and no paid-in capital is created. If the common stock just discussed were issued without a stated value, the entry would be

```
02/15/82 Cash .........................................   10,000
             Common stock  ..............................            10,000
```

Stock Issued for Services or Property Both preferred and common stock are normally issued for cash. Sometimes, however, stock may be exchanged for noncash assets or for professional services required by the business. The essential question here is the proper dollar valuation for the asset or services acquired. If the asset or service can be objectively valued by independent appraisal, this value should be used for the transaction. If not, an objective valuation should be established for the stock given up.

Suppose, for example, on May 15, 1982, a company receives legal services from a law firm which is willing to accept 25 shares of $10 par value preferred stock in payment. If the normal fee for such services is $275, the transaction would be recorded as follows:

```
05/15/82 Legal expense  ..............................     275
           Preferred stock  ............................              250
           Paid-in capital in excess of par value—preferred ..        25
```

The acquisition of land or other asset for common stock could present a valuation problem, particularly if the asset possesses some unusual characteristics. An objective valuation for the stock given up is often easier to establish for this type of exchange. Assume 100 shares of common stock, stated value $5, are given in exchange for a parcel of land on June 1, 1982. If a block of common stock had been sold recently, that selling price could be used to establish the value of the transaction. Let us say that 200 shares had been sold within the week of the land acquisition for $5,000 ($25 per share). The land acquisition journal entry would be

```
06/01/82 Land  .........................................   2,500
           Common stock  ..............................              500
           Paid-in capital in excess of stated value—common        2,000
```

Conversion

Assume that the preferred stock described above is convertible into common stock at a rate of one preferred share for one common share and that holders of fifteen shares decide to convert their shares on May 1, 1982. The entry to record the conversion would be

```
05/01/82 Preferred stock  ............................     150
           Paid-in capital in excess of par—preferred  .........      30
           Common stock  ............................               75
           Paid-in capital in excess of stated value—
             common  ...............................              105
```

The preferred stock account is debited (decreased) for par value multiplied by the number of shares being converted (15 × $10), and paid-in capital on preferred stock is debited (decreased) for a pro rata amount of the excess over par originally paid in by these preferred stock owners (15 × $2). Common stock is increased by stated value of the new common shares issued in exchange (15 × $5), and paid-in capital on common stock is increased by an amount necessary for the entry to balance. In this way, the credit to paid-in capital on common stock is the difference between the total preferred stock equity being converted and the stated value of the common shares exchanged. Total contributed capital and total stockholders' equity do not increase as a result of the conversion of preferred to common stock; only the composition of these amounts is changed.

Repurchase

From time to time, a corporation may wish to repurchase its own shares either to retire the shares or to hold them for resale at a later time. Because most preferred stock is callable, the repurchase of preferred shares normally occurs through the call process. Preferred stock may occasionally be repurchased by the issuing company going into the stock market, however.

On the other hand, common shares are never callable and can only be reacquired by purchase from owners at an agreed-upon price. Thus, when common stock is repurchased, it is usually held to be resold to new owners, while the call of preferred shares usually indicates the intention to retire the stock.

Consider the following stockholders' equity section of a balance sheet at July 31, 1982:

Stockholders' Equity

Contributed capital	
Convertible preferred stock, $10 par value	$ 1,000
Common stock, $5 stated value	2,500
Paid-in capital in excess of par value—preferred	200
Paid-in capital in excess of stated value—common	7,500
Total contributed capital	11,200
Retained earnings	5,000
Total stockholders' equity	$16,200

This basic data will be used throughout the remainder of this section.

Retiring Preferred Stock Assume that the preferred stock is callable at $13 per share and that the issuing company decides to call one-half of the shares on August 1, 1982, and retire them. The journal entry to record this transaction would be

08/01/82 Preferred stock	500	
Paid-in capital in excess of par value—preferred	100	
Retained earnings	50	
Cash		650

As shares are repurchased, a pro rata (in this instance, one-half) amount of the preferred stock and paid-in capital amounts are retired. Because the call price is higher than the original selling price of the shares, these preferred owners are withdrawing from the business more assets than were provided when the shares were originally sold. In effect, each share retired (fifty shares) receives a $1 extra dividend (call price − original selling price) from the business as shares are repurchased. The debit to retained earnings reflects this (50 × $1). The credit to cash is for the amount actually paid to repurchase the shares.

Now suppose that on August 31, 1982, the issuing corporation repurchases twenty-five preferred shares on the open market for $11 per share and retires them. This transaction would be recorded as follows:

08/31/82 Preferred stock	250	
Paid-in capital in excess of par value—preferred	50	
Cash		275
Paid-in capital from stock transactions		25

Again, preferred stock and paid-in capital are decreased by pro rata amounts for the shares repurchased (one-fourth of the original shares issued), and cash is decreased by the amount paid for the shares (25 × $11). The primary difference between this transaction and the previous one is that here the repurchase price is less than the original selling price. This means that these preferred stockholders provided the business with more assets (25 shares × $12) than they withdrew (25 shares × $11) as their shares are repurchased. The claim on these assets shifts to the remaining owners of the corporation as this group of preferred stockholders relinquish their ownership. This new claim of remaining owners is reflected in the establishment of an additional paid-in capital account.

The owners' equity section of the balance sheet at September 1, 1982, after the two repurchases of preferred stock would appear as follows:

Stockholders' Equity

Contributed capital	
Convertible preferred stock, $10 par value, callable at $13	$ 250
Common stock, $5 stated value	2,500
Paid-in capital in excess of par value—preferred	50
Paid-in capital in excess of stated value—common	7,500
Paid-in capital from stock transactions	25
Total contributed capital	10,325
Retained earnings	4,950
Total stockholders' equity	$15,275

Notice that the total effect of the repurchases of preferred stock is a reduction in total assets (cash) by $925 and a reduction in owners' equity by the same amount as compared to stockholders' equity before the transactions on July 31, 1982.

Treasury Stock

Because common stock represents the residual ownership of the business, these shares are seldom retired as they are repurchased. Instead, the repurchased shares are held to be used in stock option plans for officers and employees, to be issued as bonds or preferred stock are converted, or to be resold at a later time. Shares of stock that have been originally sold by a corporation and then repurchased, but not retired, are called **treasury stock.** Most reacquired common stock is treasury stock.

There are three distinct measures of a corporation's capital stock: authorized shares, issued shares, and outstanding shares. An understanding of these three measures contributes to an appreciation of treasury stock.

Authorized Shares As discussed earlier, each corporation is allowed a legal maximum number of shares that may be issued. This legal maximum, called the authorized shares of the corporation, is a part of the articles of incorporation. To sell more than its authorized number of shares, a business must change its articles of incorporation.

Issued Shares The authorized shares that have been sold by the business to owners are called issued shares. Issued shares may be equal to the number of shares authorized but may not be greater. When a corporation has sold fewer than its authorized number of shares, it has unissued stock that may be sold at any time.

Outstanding Shares Outstanding shares are shares that have been sold and remain in the hands of owners. Outstanding shares may be equal to issued shares but may not be greater. The difference between issued stock and outstanding stock is those shares that have been sold to owners and then repurchased. This is treasury stock. Current ownership interest in a corporation is represented by the oustanding shares. Stock held by owners (outstanding) plus stock repurchased and held by the corporation (treasury) gives the total issued shares of the business.

    When a firm repurchases its own shares of common stock, the general result is a decrease in assets (usually cash) and a decrease in owners' equity. In effect, a portion of owners' claims are being satisfied by the repurchase of their ownership interest.

    The two generally accepted approaches to recording the purchase and resale of treasury stock are the *par method* and the *cost method.* The cost method is the most widely used technique for recording treasury stock transactions and this discussion will be limited to that technique.

Treasury Stock Illustrated

Assume the following with respect to the common stock appearing in the stockholders' equity section at September 1, 1982:

1. Authorized shares are 1,000.

2. Issued shares are 500. Original price was $20 per share.

3. On September 15, 1982, 100 shares are repurchased for $23 per share.

4. On October 1, 1982, 50 of the repurchased shares are resold to new owners for $25 per share.

5. On October 15, 1982, 25 of the repurchased shares are resold to new owners for $22 per share.

Repurchasing Treasury Shares The treasury stock repurchase would be recorded in the following manner using the cost method:

```
09/15/82  Treasury stock ...................................   2,300
          Cash  ........................................              2,300
```

As common stock is reacquired, a special contra account, called treasury stock, is established. Treasury stock is a contra account to the entire owners' equity section and is debited for the repurchase cost of the shares. Cash is credited for the same amount. The reduction in owners' equity is accomplished by deducting the treasury stock account from total owners' equity on the balance sheet. Notice that the common stock and paid-in capital accounts are not affected by the repurchase of common treasury shares, because the assumption is that these shares will be resold shortly.

Resale Above Cost If the shares are resold for an amount above repurchase price, the following entry is made:

```
10/01/82  Cash  ........................................  1,250
              Treasury stock  ..............................        1,150
              Paid-in capital from stock transactions  ..........         100
```

This entry reflects the basic ideas behind the cost method. Treasury stock has been debited for the cost of the shares as they are acquired. As treasury shares are resold, the treasury stock account is credited for the purchase price of the shares being resold (50 shares × $23). Then, if the price received for the treasury shares is higher than their purchase cost, an additional paid-in capital account is credited for the difference (50 shares × $2) between the purchase price ($23 per share) and the resale price ($25 per share). Cash is debited for the amount received from the resale (50 shares × $25).

Resale Below Cost If the shares are resold for an amount below repurchase price, the following entry is made:

```
10/15/82  Cash  .........................................      550
              Paid-in capital from stock transactions  .............       25
              Treasury stock  ..............................               575
```

The credit to treasury stock is always for the number of shares sold multiplied by the purchase price of the shares (in this instance, 25 shares × $23), and the debit to cash, for the amount received (here, 25 shares × $22).

Paid-in capital from stock transactions, which reflects the net effect on stockholders' equity of the acquisition and resale of treasury shares taken together, cannot carry a debit balance; therefore, this account can be debited for a maximum of the amount of its credit balance. If the difference between the resale price and acquisition price of the treasury shares requires a larger debit amount, retained earnings would be debited. Also, there may be no credit balance in paid-in capital from stock transactions, in which case retained earnings would be debited.

Effect on Stockholders' Equity The stockholders' equity section of the balance sheet on October 31, 1982, after the treasury stock transactions discussed above and the information on authorized and issued common shares would be

Stockholders' Equity

Contributed capital
Convertible preferred stock, $10 par value, callable at $13 .... $ 250
Common stock, $5 stated value, 1,000 shares authorized, 500 shares issued,
   25 shares held in treasury 2,500
Paid-in capital in excess of par value—preferred 50
Paid-in capital in excess of stated value—common 7,500
Paid-in capital from stock transactions 100
Total contributed capital 10,400
Retained earnings 4,950
   15,350
Treasury stock (at cost) .... (575)
   Total stockholders' equity $14,775

Total stockholders' equity is $500 less than the figure for September 1, 1982 (before treasury stock transactions). This reduction can be partly explained by the twenty-five treasury shares held by the corporation at a cost of $23 per share, a reduction in total stockholders' equity. The $575 reduction is offset by the net increase in paid-in capital from stock transactions, which resulted from the resale of fifty treasury shares at a resale price above their acquisition price and the resale of twenty-five shares below their acquisition price. Note, also, that the owners' equity descriptions for preferred and common stock reflect the characteristics of each of these types of ownership interest in their title.

Stock Split

From time to time a corporation may increase the number of its shares outstanding by a stock split. Stock splits increase by some multiple the number of shares (usually common) outstanding and reduce the par or stated value of the shares proportionately. For example, a two-for-one stock split would result in twice as many shares outstanding after the split as before, while a three-for-one split would result in three times as many shares after as before. Because the assets of a corporation are not affected by a stock split and total owners' equity does not change, the result of a split is to divide existing ownership interest into more pieces. Each owner benefits proportionately from a split, however, so the individual claim on assets and ownership interest is unchanged by a stock split.

Shares outstanding and par or stated value are the only factors affected by a stock split. Because no account balances are changed, a journal entry is not necessary to record a split. Instead, a notation (called a *memo entry*) is made in the general journal describing the split and its effect on common stock.

Assume a corporation declares a two-for-one stock split on common shares on November 1, 1982. This event would be noted as follows in the general journal

11/01/82 Stock split of two common shares for one resulting in an increase in
      shares outstanding to 1,000 shares (from 500) and a reduction in par
      value to $2.50 (from $5.00)

The most important effect of a stock split is on the market price of the stock. Most often, the market price of the shares falls in proportion to the increase in the number of shares in the hands of investors, because each share represents a smaller claim on the assets of the corporation. This reduction in the market price of the stock, which occurs without affecting the financial position or prospects of the company, is the primary reason for the use of stock splits. Such a market price reduction can result in increased investor activity in the stock, a desirable goal for many businesses.

Concept Summary

Journal Entries for Preferred and Common Stock		
	Preferred Stock	*Common Stock*

Issue	Cash
	  Preferred stock
	  Paid-in capital in excess of
	    par value—preferred
		Cash
		  Common stock
		  Paid-in capital in excess of
		    stated value—common

Conversion of Preferred to Common	Preferred stock
	Paid-in capital in excess of par value—preferred
	  Common stock
	  Paid-in capital in excess of stated value—common	

Repurchase	Preferred stock
	Paid-in capital in excess of par
	  value—preferred
	Retained earnings
	  Cash
	(if repurchase price is greater
	  than original selling price)
	
	or
	
	Preferred stock
	Paid-in capital in excess of par
	  value—preferred
	  Cash
	  Paid-in capital from stock
	    transactions
	(if repurchase price is less than
	  original selling price)
		Treasury stock
		  Cash

Resale	Does not usually occur	Cash
		  Treasury stock
		  Paid-in capital from stock
		    transactions
		(if resale price is greater than
		  acquisition price)
		
		or
		
		Cash
		Paid-in capital from stock
		  transactions (or Retained
		  earnings)
		  Treasury stock
		(if resale price is less than
		  acquisition price)

13.4   Retained Earnings

Retained earnings measures the indirect investment of owners in a corporation brought about by the retention of earned assets in the business. Hence, retained earnings is sometimes called the earned capital of the business. Earlier discussions of retained earnings focused on net income and cash dividends for a period as the reasons for a change in indirect investment. While it is true that these are the primary factors accounting for the change in retained earnings, there may be other events in the life of most businesses that affect the amount of indirect investment. Figure 13-4 illustrates the events that can affect retained earnings. Each of these events is discussed in this section.

Net Income

Corporate net income is normally the result of revenues for a period minus expenses (including income tax expense) for that period. Corporations, however, may engage in events that affect the profits of the business but are unusual in nature and occur infrequently. Unusual and infrequent events that produce gains or losses are called **extraordinary items.** To be an extraordinary item, an event must be considered both unusual and infrequent.

Extraordinary Items Unusual means that the event giving rise to the gain or loss must be clearly unrelated to ordinary and on-going activities of the business. Infrequent means that the event is not likely to occur again in the foreseeable future. The determination that a particular event and the gain or loss resulting from it is unusual and infrequent must take into account the nature of normal business activity, the history of the business, and the location and environment of the business. Some examples of events that are generally considered extraordinary and some that are not follow:

Extraordinary	*Not Extraordinary*
1. Major catastrophies, such as floods, earthquakes, and the like	1. Sale of property, plant, and equipment or intangibles
2. Seizure of assets by a foreign government	2. Sale of investment securities
	3. Change in any estimate, such as depreciation, uncollectible accounts, and the like

FIGURE 13-4
Events that Affect
Corporate Earned
Capital

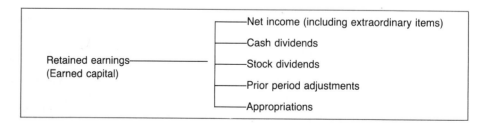

The determination of whether or not an event is extraordinary requires judgment, and different individuals may reach different conclusions about a particular event. Also, by their very definition these events are rare for all businesses. When they do occur, however, the gains or losses resulting from them may be quite large and the effect on net income, significant.

To avoid confusion about the source of a corporation's net income and the likelihood that the income will continue into future periods, accounting principles require the separation of extraordinary items from income produced by ordinary operations. In addition, the income tax effect of extraordinary items is included with the item and separated from income taxes attributable to income from normal activities.

Presentation of Extraordinary Items To illustrate these ideas, assume a business has produced revenues of $200,000 and expenses (excluding income taxes) of $100,000 for the year 1982, and that an income tax rate of 40 percent is applicable. Assume further that assets with a book value of $30,000 are seized by a foreign government and are expected never to be returned. The income statement for 1982 would reflect the year's activities in the following manner:

Sample Company
Income Statement
For the Year Ending December 31, 1982

Sales revenue	$200,000
Expenses	100,000
Income before taxes	100,000
Income tax expense	40,000
Income before extraordinary items	60,000
Loss from seizure of assets by foreign government (net of tax saving of 40% × $30,000 = $12,000)	18,000
Net income	$ 42,000

The income from ordinary profit-seeking activities (income before extraordinary items) is clearly separated from the unusual and infrequent event that affected net income. For the purpose of predicting future income levels, the effect of extraordinary items should be disregarded because they are unlikely to occur again. The tax consequences of the two types of activities are also separated. This company will actually pay income taxes of only $28,000 ($40,000 − tax saving of $12,000 on extraordinary item), although the income taxes attributable to ordinary income are clearly shown.

Earnings Per Share

Because earnings per share (EPS) is an important part of a corporate income statement, EPS figures reflect the separation of ordinary and extraordinary activity. EPS relates relevant profit-seeking activity for a period to a per share basis. When a business reports extraordinary items, there are three important measures of activity on the income statement. Thus, three EPS figures would be shown as follows:

1. $$\frac{\text{Income before extraordinary items}}{\text{Average number of common shares outstanding}}$$

2. $$\frac{\text{Extraordinary items}}{\text{Average number of common shares outstanding}}$$

3. $$\frac{\text{Net income}}{\text{Average number of common shares outstanding}}$$

Two points about these calculations should be emphasized. First, any dividends claimed by preferred stockholders (whether declared and paid or not) should be deducted from income before extraordinary items and from net income before these EPS calculations are made. Second, a computation of weighted-average number of shares outstanding is more meaningful than a simple year-end figure for shares outstanding. Because income is earned throughout the year, relating income to shares that represent ownership interest during the year equates the numerator and denominator of the calculation. Suppose a company has 8,000 shares of common stock outstanding at January 1, 1982, and issues 2,000 new shares on April 1 and 1,000 new shares on July 1. Weighted-average number of shares can be determined as follows:

8,000 shares outstanding all year =	8,000
2,000 shares outstanding ¾ year =	1,500
(2,000 × ¾)	
1,000 shares outstanding ½ year =	500
(1,000 × ½)	
Weighted-average shares outstanding for the year	10,000
Total shares outstanding at year's-end	11,000

Using the income statement data given earlier in this section, EPS presentation would be as follows:

Earnings per share of common stock

Income before extraordinary items	$ 6.00
($60,000 ÷ 10,000 shares)	
Extraordinary loss (net of tax)	(1.80)
($18,000 ÷ 10,000 shares)	
Net income	$ 4.20
($42,000 ÷ 10,000 shares)	

Dividends

Cash dividends represent a distribution of assets that have resulted from profit-seeking activities to the owners of a corporation. The result of dividend payments is a decrease in assets (cash) and a decrease in stockholders' equity (retained earnings). Preferred dividends tend to be fixed by the preferred stock contract, and common dividends are limited only by the success of the business and the decisions of the board of directors.

Cash Dividends   To pay a cash dividend, corporations must meet two criteria:

1. *Sufficient cash must be available.* Although property dividends (dividends paid in other than cash) are possible, they are very rare. Most dividends are paid in cash; therefore, enough cash must be available to pay each stockholder with the same class of stock the same amount of dividend per share. No dividend difference can be made on a per share basis for the same type of stock.

2. *The business must be in a legal dividend position.* A dividend cannot be paid that would result in total stockholders' equity being reduced below the minimum legal capital amount. In most states, a legal dividend position has been more restrictively defined to mean a credit balance in retained earnings large enough to cover the anticipated dividend. Most corporations, then, view the ceiling on dividends to be the amount of retained earnings, although few would actually distribute even this amount to owners.

When a dividend is decided upon by a corporation, three dates become important to both the company and its owners. These dates are the declaration date, the record date, and the payment date.

Declaration Date The declaration date is the date on which the intention of the business to pay a dividend is made public. Once dividends are declared, a legal liability is created for the amount of the dividend. Dividends are no longer discretionary, and the amount of dividends declared must be paid. On this date, a journal entry is made recording the dividend and the liability.

Record Date To receive the declared dividend, stockholders must own shares on this date. The length of time a share has been owned prior to the record date or the disposal of the share immediately after the record date do not affect the payment of the dividend. For this reason, the record date is always included in the dividend declaration announcement and follows the declaration date by two to four weeks. No journal entry is required on the record date; however, a good deal of activity takes place immediately after this date as corporations update their stock ownership records. This record of the identity, address, and number of shares owned by each stockholder is called the *stockholders' ledger*. Shares of stock sold after the date of record, but before the payment date, are sold "ex-dividend," which means without the right to receive the dividend.

Payment Date The payment date is the date on which the declared dividend will be paid. The payment date is also a part of the dividend declaration announcement and follows the record date by two to four weeks. A journal entry that reflects the payment of the dividend liability and reduces cash is made on this date.

Journal Entries for a Cash Dividend

Suppose on December 1, 1982, a $1 per share dividend is declared on 1,500 shares of preferred stock and a $.50 per share dividend declared on 10,000 shares of common stock. The date of record for these dividends is December 15, and the dividend will be paid on December 31. The complete cycle of journal entries for these dividends would be

```
12/01/82  Preferred dividends ............................  1,500
          Common dividends ............................  5,000
            Dividends payable ............................           6,500
12/15/82  No entry on this date
12/31/82  Dividends payable ............................  6,500
            Cash  ......................................           6,500
```

The accounts preferred dividends and common dividends would be closed to retained earnings and would appear on the statement of retained earnings. If a balance sheet were prepared between the declaration date and payment date, dividends payable would be reported among current liabilities.

Stock Dividends

In addition to or instead of a cash dividend, corporations sometimes declare and "pay" a stock dividend. Stock dividends involve no distribution of assets to owners and, therefore, cause no increase or decrease in total owners' equity. A stock dividend is a dividend payable in shares of stock of the company declaring the dividend. In a stock dividend, each owner receives new shares equal to some fixed fraction of the number of shares owned before the dividend. For example, one-for-five (20 percent), one-for-ten (10 percent), or one-for-twenty (5 percent) stock dividends would not be unusual. In each of these instances, stockholders receive additional shares of stock as a dividend in proportion to shares already owned so each owner claims the same percentage ownership after the dividend as before. Because total assets have not changed, the total claim of each owner is also unchanged. Each ownership interest is now represented by more shares of stock.

Stock Dividends versus Stock Splits Stock splits tend to increase shares outstanding by some multiple, while stock dividends increase shares by a fraction. This difference is reflected in the accounting treatment of stock dividends. Stock dividends cause no change in total assets or total owners' equity; however, a change in the composition of owners' equity does result from a stock dividend. This change in owners' equity results from the capitalization of retained earnings which accompanies a stock dividend. The capitalization of retained earnings requires journal entries to record the stock dividend.

Suppose a company had the following owners' equity section on December 31, 1981:

Stockholders' Equity

Contributed capital
  Common stock, $5 stated value, 1,000 shares authorized, 500 shares issued and
    outstanding . . . . $ 2,500
  Paid-in capital in excess of stated value—common 7,500
Total contributed capital 10,000
Retained earnings 5,000
  Total stockholders' equity $15,000

Assume that on January 15, 1982, this company declares a 10 percent stock dividend (10% × 500 shares outstanding = 50 new shares outstanding) to be distributed on January 30, 1982. If the market price of the stock on January 15, 1982, was $25 per share, the entry to record the stock dividend declaration would be

01/15/82 Retained earnings 1,250
  Stock dividend to be distributed 250
  Paid-in capital in excess of stated value—common 1,000

Notice that an amount equal to the market value of the shares in the stock dividend (50 new shares × $25) is removed from retained earnings and transferred permanently to contributed capital. This does not change total stockholders' equity but does reflect the additional shares now outstanding.

If the stock dividend was classified as "large" (meaning new shares exceeded 25 percent of the shares outstanding prior to the stock dividend), only the par or stated value of the new shares would be debited to retained earnings and credited to common stock. The accounting treatment of large stock dividends differs from that of small stock dividends only in the amount used to record the transaction.

Stock dividend to be distributed is not a liability (because it is not a claim on assets) and would appear in the stockholders' equity section if a balance sheet were prepared before the "payment" date of the stock dividend.

The entry to record the "payment" of the stock dividend would be

01/30/82 Stock dividend to be distributed 250
  Common stock 250

After the stock dividend is distributed, the common stock and paid-in capital accounts reflect the transfer of $1,250 from earned capital to contributed capital. The total stockholders' equity is unchanged and would be reported as follows on January 31, 1982:

Stockholders' Equity

Contributed capital
    Common stock, $5 stated value, 1,000 shares authorized, 550 shares issued and
        outstanding .... $ 2,750
    Paid-in capital in excess of stated value—common   8,500
Total contributed capital 11,250
Retained earnings   3,750
    Total stockholders' equity $15,000

The difference between the stockholders' equity sections at December 31, 1981, and January 31, 1982, because of the stock dividend are

1. Fifty additional shares are issued and outstanding at January 31, 1982.

2. Contributed capital is $1,250 higher and earned capital is $1,250 lower at January 31, 1982.

Reasons for Stock Dividends Corporations use stock dividends in place of or as a supplement to cash dividends for many reasons. Some of the most important of these reasons are

1. *Lack of cash.* Companies with long histories of dividend consistency may not want to give the impression of a skipped dividend even if the cash position of the business will not allow a cash dividend to be paid. Stock dividends can be substituted for cash dividends and, although they are not the same type of distribution, can keep a long dividend record going.

2. *Income tax effect.* Cash dividends are taxed as income to stockholders, while stock dividends are not considered taxable income and are not taxed until the shares received are sold. Stock dividends can be a way to pass along to owners the benefits of successful profit-seeking activities under favorable tax circumstances.

3. *Market price effect.* Because the increase in shares outstanding is usually small in a stock dividend, the market price of all shares of stock of the company distributing the dividend may not fall. If the price does not fall, or does not fall proportionate to the increase in shares, each stockholder enjoys an increase in the total market value of his investment (more shares × same market price per share). Stock dividends, then, may be a way for a corporation to convey value to its owners without distributing corporate assets.

Prior-Period Adjustments

Sometimes a business will discover that an error of a material amount was made in a prior period. Occasionally, these errors affect income for the period in which the error was made. Because income for a period affects retained earnings, the result of this type of error is an understatement or overstatement of assets with a corresponding understatement or overstatement in retained earnings.

    The correction of an error of a prior period should have no impact on income of the current period, so prior period adjustments for the correction of errors involve a direct debit or credit to retained earnings. For example, assume that in January 1981 a company truck was completely demolished in an accident. The truck had cost $5,000 and had been depreciated $1,000 per year for three years at the time of the accident. No additional depreciation was taken after the accident. Because no insurance was collected for the truck, the transaction to reflect the loss of the truck was overlooked and not recorded. If this error was discovered December 31, 1982, the following entry for a prior period adjustment would be made:

12/31/82	Retained earnings	2,000	
	Accumulated depreciation: truck	3,000	
	Truck		5,000

The debit to retained earnings decreases that account to the proper balance. This is the balance that would have been reflected in retained earnings if the $2,000 loss in 1981 had been correctly recorded. Notice that this entry does not affect income for the current period but does correct both assets and retained earnings.

Presentation of Prior-Period Adjustments Prior-period adjustments appear as adjustments to the beginning balance of retained earnings in a statement of retained earnings. Because only the correction of material errors of a prior period and certain unusual income tax adjustments qualify as prior-period adjustments, this type of event is quite rare. This is particularly true for large businesses with good accounting systems and annual audits.

Appropriations

In most states, the legal maximum a corporation may pay in dividends is the amount of the credit balance in retained earnings. From time to time, a board of directors may wish to communicate to stockholders that the effective maximum amount of dividends is actually less than this legal maximum. Retained earnings appropriations are a technique for communicating this information.

Reasons for Retained Earnings Appropriations

Retained earnings appropriations may occur because they are required by law, because they are required by contract, or because they are desired by the board of directors.

Required By Law Some states require an appropriation of retained earnings equal to the cost of treasury stock acquired with each repurchase of shares. In this way, as the number of shares outstanding decreases, so does the total maximum allowable dividend. The journal entry to record this appropriation would be

Retained earnings	XX	
Retained earnings appropriated for the purchase of treasury stock ..		XX

Required By Contract Sometimes when corporations borrow large sums of money, the creditor would like to limit potential dividend distributions to owners until the money is repaid. An effective technique for doing so is an appropriation of retained earnings, and such an appropriation may be a part of the loan contract. If so, the appropriation entry would be

Retained earnings	XX	
Retained earnings appropriated for loan contract		XX

Desired By the Board of Directors The directors may want to communicate to stockholders their intention to base dividends on an amount much lower than the legal dividend maximum. This may be true because of certain future contingencies expected by the board or because of the desire to retain large amounts of assets in the business for growth purposes. An entry to communicate this intention to owners through the appropriation of retained earnings would be

Retained earnings	XX	
Retained earnings appropriated for contingencies		XX

Appropriations of retained earnings, no matter the reason, have no effect on the assets or owners' equity of a company, and do not change retained earnings in total. These actions simply divide retained earnings into appropriated and unappropriated amounts. When the need for the appropriation is past, an entry is made to reverse the separation and return appropriated amounts to the retained earnings account.

Presentation of Retained Earnings Appropriations An illustration of the retained earnings section of a balance sheet where there have been appropriations of retained earnings appears below (amounts have been assumed).

Unappropriated retained earnings		$200,000
Retained earnings appropriated for:		
Treasury stock purchases	$75,000	
Loan contract	35,000	
Contingencies	50,000	160,000
Total retained earnings		$360,000

Book Value

The final calculation of relevance to corporate owners' equity is called **book value per share** of common stock. The idea here is to relate the total claim of the owners on the assets of the business to each share of common stock. Owners' equity measures the total claim of owners (preferred and common) and is often called the net assets (assets − liabilities) of the business. Because common stockholders are the residual owners of the business and claim everything not claimed by others, the book value calculation is made for common stock only.

Assume the following owners' equity exists for a corporation.

Stockholders' Equity

Contributed capital
  Convertible preferred stock, $10 par value, callable at $13 .... $ 1,000
  Common stock, $10 stated value
    1,000 shares authorized, 500 shares issued and outstanding 2,500
  Paid-in capital in excess of par value—preferred 200
  Paid-in capital in excess of stated value—common 7,500
Total contributed capital 11,200
Retained earnings 5,100
  Total stockholders' equity $16,300

All of the net assets (owners' equity) of the business may be claimed by the common stockholders except that claimed by preferred owners. The amount of net assets claimed by preferred stock can be measured by the call price (redemption value) of the preferred shares plus any dividends in arrears which would have to be paid upon retirement of the preferred stock. Total stockholders' equity minus the claim of preferred owners gives the amount attributable to common owners. This amount divided by the number of common shares outstanding gives book value per share of common stock as computed on the following page.

Concept Summary

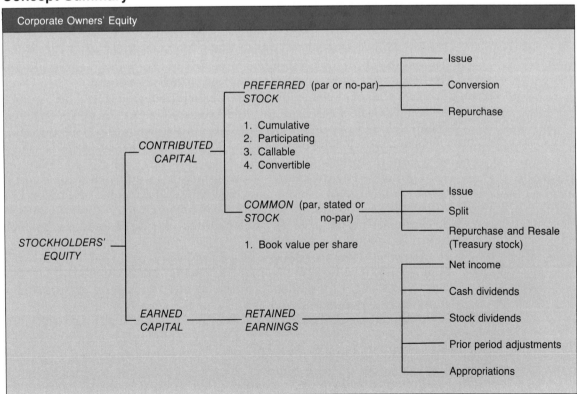

Total stockholders' equity	$16,300
− Preferred stock claims (100 shares × $13)	1,300
Net assets of common stock	$15,000
Shares of common stock outstanding	500
Book value per share of common stock ($15,000 ÷ 500)	$30

Interpreting Book Value Although book value per share is an important figure for many corporate activities such as mergers and acquisitions, two cautions about its use are in order.

There is no necessary relationship between book value and market price per share of common stock. The market price of a share of common stock is dependent upon the expected future earnings and dividends of the company, general economic conditions, and a host of other subjective factors. When used carefully, however, book value can be an indicator of the general reasonableness of the market price of common stock.

There is no necessary relationship between book value per share and the amount each share of stock would receive if the business were terminated. When a corporation goes out of business and its assets are sold, the amounts received for these assets is likely to be different (higher in some cases and lower in others) from their book values. Thus, actual net assets are likely to be different from the amount depicted on the balance sheet.

Summary

The advantages of limited liability, indefinite life, ease of ownership transfer, and the ability to accumulate large amounts of funds have resulted in the dominance of corporations as a legal form of business.

Two classes of ownership interest called preferred stock and common stock may exist in corporations. Preferred stock represents a special ownership class with certain preferences over other owners, but with no voting rights and with a fixed dividend rate. Preferred stock is no longer a widely used form of ownership interest.

Common stock represents the residual or "true" owners of a corporation. The claim of common stockholders on the income and assets of a corporation is subordinate to all other claims; however, common owners do claim all that remains after other claims are satisfied and, hence, their return is potentially unlimited.

Preferred stock may have a par value or may be no par. The life cycle of preferred stock from the issuing corporation's point of view is: (1) original issue and (2) subsequent repurchase and retirement, or subsequent conversion to common shares.

Common stock may have a par value, a stated value, or may be no par. The life cycle of common stock may include: (1) original issue, (2) stock split, (3) subsequent repurchase, and (4) resale, or issue as a stock dividend.

Preferred and common stock and their related accounts measure the direct investment of owners in a corporation. This direct investment is called the contributed capital of the corporation.

Retained earnings measures the indirect investment by the owners and is called the earned capital of the corporation. Earned capital reflects the results of net income (including the effect of extraordinary items) over the life of the business, cash and stock dividends over the life of the business, and the effect of prior period adjustments.

The book value per share of common stock reflects the claim of each common share on the assets of the corporation. Book value per share is not necessarily related to the market value (selling price) of the share or to the amount that share might receive if the business were terminated.

Part Four continues the owner/investor viewpoint of business established in this chapter. Investment by individuals and businesses in the securities of corporations is discussed in Chapter 14.

Key Terms

Articles of incorporation	**Minimum legal capital**
Authorized shares	**Outstanding shares**
Board of directors	**Paid-in capital in excess of par**
Book value per share	**(stated value)**
Callable preferred stock	**Participating preferred stock**
Cash dividend	**Par value**
Common stock	**Preferred stock**
Contributed capital	**Prior-period adjustment**
Convertible preferred stock	**Residual owner**
Corporate charter	**Retained earnings appropriation**
Cumulative preferred stock	**Stated value**
Dividends in arrears	**Stock dividend**
Double taxation	**Stock split**
Extraordinary item	**Treasury stock**
Issued shares	**Unissued shares**
Limited liability	

Comprehensive Review Problem

The stockholders' equity section of the S. Weller Corporation's balance sheet at December 31, 1981, is shown below:

Contributed capital	
Convertible preferred stock, $8 par value	$ 40,000
Common stock, $5 par, 100,000 shares authorized,	
20,000 shares issued and outstanding	100,000
Paid-in capital in excess of par—preferred	10,000
Paid-in capital in excess of par—common	200,000
Total contributed capital	350,000
Retained earnings	725,000
Total stockholders' equity	$1,075,000

The following transactions affected stockholders' equity during 1982:

March   *1* All 5,000 shares of preferred stock were converted into common stock at a rate of two shares of preferred for one share of common.

April   *1* The stockholders approved a two for one stock split voted by the board of directors. The shares are to be distributed May 1.

May 30 The company purchased 1,500 shares of its common stock on the open market for $22 per share.

September 1 The company gave 500 shares of its treasury stock in exchange for a small building. There was some question as to the value of the building so the company used the current market price of the stock, $25 per share, to determine the value of the transaction.

1 S. Weller Corporation issued 10,000 shares of previously unissued common stock at a price of $25 per share.

November 1 A 10 percent stock dividend was declared, the shares to be distributed December 1. The market price of the stock on November 1 was $24 per share.

December 1 The stock dividend was distributed.

15 A cash dividend of $2 per share was declared, payable January 15 to holders of record at December 31.

31 The net income for the year ended December 31, 1982, was $165,000 after an extraordinary loss of $49,000 (net of tax of $21,000).

Required:

1. Prepare journal entries to record the transactions described above including closing entries.

2. Prepare a statement of retained earnings for 1982 and the stockholders' equity section of the balance sheet at December 31, 1982.

3. Assume that the weighted average number of common shares outstanding during 1982 was 40,000. Calculate earnings per share for 1982.

Solution to Comprehensive Review Problem

1.

S. WELLER CO.
General Journal

Date	Transaction Accounts	Debit	Credit
1982			
Mar 1	Preferred stock	40,000	
	Paid-in capital in excess of par—preferred	10,000	
	Common stock		12,500
	Paid-in capital in excess of par—common		37,500
	To record conversion of 5,000 shares of preferred stock to 2,500 shares of common stock		
April 1	Stockholders approved a 2 for 1 stock split to be distributed May 1. The split will result in an increase of shares outstanding to 45,000 (from 22,500) and a reduction in par value to $2.50 (from $5.00)		
May 30	Treasury stock	33,000	
	Cash		33,000
	Repurchased 1,500 shares of common stock at $22 per share		
Sept 1	Building	12,500	
	Treasury stock		11,000
	Paid-in capital from stock transactions		1,500
	To record reissuance of 500 shares of treasury stock (cost: 500/1,500 × 33,000 = $11,000). The building value was based on the price of the stock ($25 × 500 = $12,500).		

	1	Cash	250,000	
		Common stock		25,000
		Paid-in capital in excess of par—common		225,000
		Issued 10,000 additional shares of common stock at $25 per share		
Nov	1	Retained earnings	129,600	
		Stock dividend to be distributed		13,500
		Paid-in capital in excess of par—common		116,100
		Declared 10% stock dividend (10% × 54,000 shares = 5,400 shares). The market value of the shares was $24 × 5,400 shares = $129,600. Par value of transaction = $2.50 × 5,400 shares = $13,500.		
Dec	1	Stock dividend to be distributed	13,500	
		Common stock		13,500
		Distribution of stock dividend		
	15	Dividends	118,800	
		Dividends payable		118,800
		To record declaration of a $2 per share dividend on common stock ($2 × 59,400 = $118,800)		
	31	Income summary	165,000	
		Retained earnings		165,000
		To close income summary account		
	31	Retained earnings	118,800	
		Dividends		118,800
		To close dividends account		

2.

S. WELLER CO.
Statement of Retained Earnings
For the Year Ended December 31, 1982

Retained earnings, December 31, 1981		$ 725,000
Net income		165,000
Dividends		
Cash dividend, $2 per share	$118,800	
10% stock dividend	129,600	(248,400)
Retained earnings, December 31, 1982		$ 641,600

S. WELLER CO.
Stockholders' Equity
December 31, 1982

Contributed capital	
Common stock, $2.50 par, 100,000 shares authorized, 60,400 issued (1,000 shares held in treasury)	$ 151,000
Paid-in capital in excess of par—common	578,600
Paid-in capital from stock transactions	1,500
Total contributed capital	731,100
Retained earnings	641,600
	1,372,700
Treasury stock (at cost)	(22,000)
Total stockholders' equity	$ 1,350,700

3.

Income before extraordinary items	$ 214,000
Extraordinary loss (net of tax savings of $21,000)	(49,000)
Net income	$ 165,000

Earnings per share
Income before extraordinary items

($214,000 ÷ 40,000)	$ 5.35
Extraordinary loss, net of tax	
($49,000 ÷ 40,000)	(1.22)
Net income ($165,000 ÷ 40,000)	$ 4.13

Questions

Q13-1. Specify the advantages and disadvantages of the corporate form of business organization.

Q13-2. Describe the four basic rights of stock ownership.

Q13-3. What are the advantages and disadvantages of preferred stock from the point of view of the issuing corporation? From the point of view of the preferred stockholder?

Q13-4. Define residual ownership. Who are the residual owners of a corporation?

Q13-5. Contrast the effect on the assets and owners' equity of a corporation of calling *versus* converting preferred stock.

Q13-6. What is treasury stock? What is the effect on owners' equity when treasury stock is resold at a price above its repurchase price? At a price below its repurchase price?

Q13-7. Distinguish the accounting treatment of stock splits from that of stock dividends. Why do corporations use stock dividends?

Q13-8. What are the similarities between extraordinary items and prior-period adjustments? What are the differences?

Q13-9. Summarize the accounting activity that occurs at the declaration, record, and payment dates for a cash dividend.

Q13-10. Describe how book value per share of common stock is calculated. What does this figure represent?

Exercises

E13-1. List the basic rights of ownership of a share of stock. How do the rights of a preferred stockholder and common stockholder differ?

E13-2. Match the following terms with their definitions.

a. corporation	*g.* par value
b. common stock	*h.* treasury stock
c. preferred stock	*i.* stock split
d. cumulative	*j.* book value
e. callable	*k.* stock dividend
f. convertible	

1. ___ The amount of net assets applicable to each share of outstanding common stock.

2. ___ Stock that carries certain preferences over the common stock, such as a prior claim on dividends.

3. ___ A feature of stock that permits the stock to be redeemed at the option of the corporation.

4. ___ The face amount of a share of capital stock.

5. ___ An increase in the number of shares of stock accompanied by a pro rata reduction in the par value per share.

6. ___ An artificial being, invisible, intangible, and existing only in contemplation of the law.

7. ___ A feature of preferred stock which provides that, if dividends are reduced or omitted in any year, the dividends missed must be paid prior to payment of dividends on the common stock.

8. ___ A distribution of additional shares of a corporation to the stockholders in proportion to their existing holdings.

9. ___ Stock of a corporation that has been legally issued, fully paid for, and subsequently reacquired by the corporation but not formally retired.

10. ___ A type of stock that possesses all of the basic rights of ownership.

E13-3. Snowden Corporation was organized January 2, 1982, with the authorization to issue 100,000 shares of $100 par value, noncumulative 6 percent preferred stock and 500,000 shares of common stock with a par value of $10 per share. 20,000 shares of the preferred stock were issued at $125 per share, and 50,000 shares of the common stock were issued at $17 per share during the first month of operations. Net earnings for the first month were $60,000. Prepare the stockholders' equity section of the balance sheet at the end of the first month.

E13-4. Hardesty Corporation received a charter from the state and was authorized to issue 10,000 shares of $100 par value 7 percent preferred stock and 100,000 shares of no-par common stock with a stated value of $5 per share. 2,000 shares of the preferred stock were sold to an underwriting firm for $230,000. 10,000 shares of the common stock were sold for cash at $12 per share, and 5,000 shares of the common stock were sold at a subsequent date for $15 per share. Prepare general journal entries to record the above transactions.

E13-5. Perino Corporation's balance sheet contained the following amounts:

Cash	$ 42,500	Current liabilities	$ 34,000
Inventory	60,000	Long-term liabilities	98,000
Long-term investments	67,500	Common stock, 10,000 shares	340,000
Plant assets	425,000	Paid-in capital—common stock	17,000
		Retained earnings	106,000

Based on the above information, answer the following questions.

1. What would be the maximum amount that could be distributed in dividends?

2. What journal entries would be made on the declaration date, date of record, and payment date assuming a $25,000 cash dividend was declared?

3. If a balance sheet was prepared between the declaration date and payment date, how would this information be reported on the balance sheet?

E13-6. Ballard Corporation issued 75,000 shares of 6 percent $100 par convertible preferred stock for $8,775,000 on January 3, 1981. A 6 percent dividend was declared and paid on the preferred stock December 31, 1981. On January 6, 1982, all of the preferred stock was converted on a three for one basis into Ballard's $25 par common stock.

Required:

1. Prepare a journal entry to record the sale of the preferred stock on January 3.

2. Record the declaration and payment of the cash dividend on the preferred stock on December 31, 1981.

3. Record the conversion of the preferred stock on January 6, 1982.

E13-7. Galatas Corporation has 30,000 shares of $5 cumulative and convertible preferred stock of $50 par and 150,000 shares of $10 par common stock. Net income totals $155,000 in year 1, $355,000 in year 2, and $400,000 in year 3. At the beginning of year 3, 5,000 shares of preferred stock were converted into common shares at a conversion ratio of two for one. If Galatos follows a policy of distributing 60 percent of net income each year, prepare a schedule indicating the amount of dividends distributable to each class of stock each year.

E13-8. Christiansen Corporation has the following items in its stockholders' equity section at December 31, 1982:

Preferred stock, 6%, par value $100	$400,000
Common stock, no par, 20,000 shares outstanding	200,000
Paid-in capital in excess of par—preferred	70,000
Retained earnings	150,000

Required:

Compute the book value per share of the preferred and common stock. The preferred stock is noncumulative and nonparticipating and is callable at $120 per share.

E13-9. Misuraca Corporation sold 10,000 shares of common stock, par $10 for $12 per share. Misuraca subsequently repurchased 2,000 shares of its own outstanding stock at a price of $14 per share, which it held as treasury stock. 500 of these treasury shares were subsequently resold at $15 per share.

Required:

Prepare journal entries to record the above transactions.

E13-10. The following information is available regarding Holtzendorff Corporation:

Common stock, par $5, authorized 100,000 shares, outstanding entire year, 50,000 shares	$350,000
5% preferred stock, par $100, nonconvertible, authorized 10,000 shares, outstanding all year, 2,000 shares	200,000
Income before extraordinary items and taxes	135,000
Extraordinary loss	(12,000)
Applicable tax rate for all items	40%

Required:
Prepare the required earnings per share presentation.

Problems

P13-1. Collier Corporation received a charter from the state authorizing 300,000 shares of common stock, par value $30 per share. During the first year, 120,000 shares were sold at $38 per share. 200 additional shares were issued in payment for legal services valued at $8,000. Net income of $50,000 was earned the first year, and cash dividends of $20,000 were declared and paid at the end of the year. Liabilities were $35,000 at year's end.

Required:
Determine the following amounts at year's end.

1. Legal capital

2. Contributed capital

3. Owners' equity

4. Total assets

5. Unissued common stock

6. Outstanding common stock

7. Treasury stock

P13-2. The stockholders' equity section of Mitzie Minkos Corporation on the balance sheet at December 31, 1981, contained the following information:

6% convertible preferred stock, $50 par value, authorized, issued and oustanding 5,000 shares (Note 1)	$ 250,000
Common stock, $3.00 par value, authorized 500,000 shares, issued and oustanding 100,000 shares	300,000
Paid-in capital in excess of par value—common	200,000
Retained earnings	500,000
Total stockholders' equity	$1,250,000

Note 1—The preferred shares are convertible at any time into common shares at a conversion ratio of three common shares for each preferred share.

The following transactions occurred during 1982:

January 9 All of the preferred shares were converted into common shares.
May 12 A 5 percent stock dividend was declared to be distributed June 13 to stockholders of record May 31.
June 30 A two for one stock split took place.
    30 Net earnings for the six months were $60,000.

The market price of Mitzie Minkos common stock was as follows:

January 9	$9
May 12	$10
May 31	$9.50
June 13	$11.00

Required:
1. Prepare journal entries to record the above transactions.

2. Prepare the stockholders' equity section at June 30, 1982, giving effect to the above transactions.

P13-3. England Corporation had the following stockholders' equity accounts at December 31, 1981:

7% preferred stock, $100 par value	$170,000
Paid-in capital in excess of par value—preferred	85,000
Common stock, $5 par value	50,000
Paid-in capital in excess of par value—common	30,000
Retained earnings	72,000

The following treasury stock transactions took place during 1982:

a. Repurchased thirty shares of the common stock at $7 per share.
b. Repurchased twenty shares of the preferred stock at $106 per share.
c. Resold twenty shares of the common stock at $6 per share.
d. Resold ten shares of the preferred stock at $110 per share.

Required:

1. Prepare journal entries for all the above treasury stock transactions assuming the cost method is used.

2. Prepare the stockholders' equity section of the balance sheet at December 31, 1982, assuming net earnings for the year were $35,000 and that cash dividends of 10,000 were declared and paid.

P13-4. The following items appeared on the adjusted trial balance of Green Corporation on December 31, 1982. Assume a flat 40 percent corporate tax rate on all items, including the casualty loss and gain on sale of fixed assets.

Sales	$456,000
Rent revenue	960
Interest revenue	360
Gain on sale of fixed assets	3,400
Selling expenses	54,400
General and administrative expenses	44,000
Interest expense	600
Major casualty loss (pre-tax)	18,000
Cost of goods sold	140,000
Prior period adjustment (net of tax)	2,400
Common stock shares (par $10)	
Outstanding January 1, 1982	20,000
Sold and issued May 1, 1982	4,000
Sold and issued November 1, 1982	6,000

Required:

Prepare a proper income statement including EPS calculations.

P13-5. Listed below are a number of transactions of Brooks Corporation during 1982. For each item, indicate how it should be reported on the financial statements by entering the correct code letter below.

a. Revenue on income statement
b. Expense on income statement
c. Gain on income statement
d. Loss on income statement
e. Extraordinary gain on income statement
f. Extraordinary loss on income statement
g. Prior period adjustment on retained earnings statement
h. Balance sheet item

1. __ Cost of goods sold

2. __ Interest collected from a customer on a note receivable

3. __ Earthquake damages

4. __ Gain on sale of fixed asset

5. __ Total amount of cash and credit sales for the period

6. __ Estimated warranties payable

7. __ Gain on disposal of long-term investment in stock

8. __ Error in calculating depreciation expense of the previous period

9. __ Rent collected in advance

10. __ Loss due to expropriation of a plant by a foreign country

11. __ Material gain on extinguishment of long-term debt

12. __ A material write down of inventory which had become obsolete

13. __ A year-end bonus paid to the manager of a branch store for superior performance during the year

14. __ A material loss sustained during the year because of a strike by employees

15. __ Loss on disposal of a segment of a business

P13-6. Farley Corporation, which operates on a calendar year, was audited for the first time early in 1982. During the course of the audit, it was discovered that, on July 1, 1979, an invoice in the amount of $10,000 for the purchase of a fixed asset was debited to an administrative expense account rather than to an asset account. The fixed asset has a useful life of five years and no salvage value. Farley Corporation uses the straight-line depreciation method for all of its fixed assets. The net income previously reported for 1979 was $45,000; for 1980, $52,000; and for 1981, $55,000. Ignore income tax effects.

Required:
1. Prepare any journal entry that is required in 1982 when the error is discovered.

2. Prepare the depreciation entry for 1982.

3. Compute the corrected income for 1979, 1980, and 1981.

P13-7. Dell Corporation has the following stock outstanding:

Preferred stock, 6%, $100 par value—5,000 shares
Common stock, $25 par value—30,000 shares

Required:
Determine the amount of dividends payable to preferred shareholders and to common shareholders under each of the following assumptions:

1. Preferred stock is noncumulative and nonparticipating. Dividends to be distributed are $60,000.

2. Preferred stock is cumulative and nonparticipating. Two years' dividends are in arrears. Dividends to be distributed are $144,000.

3. Preferred stock is noncumulative and fully participating. Dividends to be distributed are $196,000.

4. Preferred stock is cumulative and fully participating. Four years' dividends are in arrears. Dividends to be distributed are $180,000.

P13-8. Salcedo Corporation records revealed the following information at year's end:

a. Error in computing depreciation in previous year, $7,000 understatement of depreciation.

b. Appropriation during the year of retained earnings for reserve for bond sinking fund, $24,000. The appropriation balance at the end of the previous year was $82,000.

c. The balance in unappropriated retained earnings at the end of the preceding year was $140,000.

d. Dividends declared on preferred stock at the end of the current year were $15,000.

e. A 15 percent stock dividend was declared and paid on the common stock August 1 of the current year. Par value of the stock issued was $18,000. Fair market value was $25,000.

f. Treasury stock purchased during the current year and held at the end of the year cost $16,000. State law requires the appropriation of retained earnings for the cost of treasury stock. This was the first purchase of treasury stock by the corporation.

g. Net income for the year was $148,000.

Required:
Prepare a statement of retained earnings for Salcedo Corporation for the current year.

P13-9. Raspanti Corporation has the following stock outstanding:

Convertible preferred stock, noncumulative, $150 par value	$450,000
Common stock, 3,000 shares, $75 par value	225,000
Paid-in capital in excess of par—preferred	24,000
Paid-in capital in excess of par—common	9,000
Retained earnings	63,000

Required:
Give the required journal entry for each of the following independent situations:

1. The preferred shares are converted to common stock on a two-for-one basis.

2. The preferred shares are converted to common stock on a four-for-one basis.

3. The preferred shares are converted to common stock on a one-for-one basis.

4. The preferred stock is also callable, and it is called at $160 per share and retired.

FINANCIAL
ANALYSIS

CHAPTER 14

Marketable Securities and Investments

Chapter Outline

14.1 *Marketable Securities.* Discussion of marketable debt securities, which are recorded at cost and whose carrying value is not changed; discussion of marketable equity securities, which are recorded at cost, but whose market declines below cost are reflected in an allowance account and in the income statement.

14.2 *Long-term Investments.* Presentation of the lower of cost or market method for equity securities with a ready market; the cost method for equity securities without a ready market; and the equity method for investments where there is significant influence.

14.3 *Consolidations.* Discussion of basic concepts of business combinations; illustration of the consolidated balance sheet at date of acquisition; introduction to minority interests; presentation and contrast of the purchase and pooling methods, including a discussion of goodwill.

14.4 *Financial Statements Subsequent to Acquisition.* Illustration of financial statements including consolidated statements of income and retained earnings; introduction to additional complexities in consolidations.

Accounting and the Real World

The Equity of Equity Accounting

If Company A owns between 20 and 50 percent of company B, A is required to report a portion of B's earnings equal to A's percentage of ownership. Nevertheless, B continues to show 100 percent of its earnings. It's called equity accounting.

The crux of the problem lies in how you define "earnings." Most investors think of earnings as the money a company has to spend—the dollars left over after all the obligations are taken care of. But that's not how the accountants define it: "Earnings are simply not synonymous with cash or working capital," explains Michael J. Walters, a partner with Peat, Marwick, Mitchell & Company, a big-eight accounting firm. So, earnings aren't necessarily dollars you can spend.

Take a modest example. Giant Bendix Corporation ($3.8 billion revenues) has a 21 percent interest in ASARCO, a metals producer. Bendix adds on to its income statement some $25.5 million from ASARCO, driving up its earnings to $163 million. Mark this, however: When ASARCO was losing money, Bendix carefully kept its interest below 20 percent. But when it became apparent that ASARCO was going to start to make money in 1978, Bendix bought more stock and started to pick up earnings. Bendix is not doing anything shady. It is simply complying with generally accepted accounting principles (GAAP).

Before 1971, earnings were generally brought in only when a firm achieved a 51 percent interest—clear control, in a second company. Now that seems logical. You run a company, you get the earnings. But that isn't entirely true. Even at 51 percent, you can't simply take those earnings.

But companies like the idea of being able to report those earnings and wanted to carry it a step further and bring in earnings from minority investments. After all, they said, you can have control over the use of much of a firm's income with less than 51 percent of its stock. You can elect directors, and those directors mean influence over dividend policy and most other major decisions. That influence, they argued, should give them the right to show a portion of the resulting income on their own income statements. The Accounting Principles Board (APB) was compliant, and all that remained was to pick a percentage at which significant influence would be presumed.

Somewhat arbitrarily, the APB set forth 20 percent as the point at which you could presume control. Earnings could be brought in with a smaller investment if you could prove control. So now Saul Steinberg is taking in 3 percent of Reliance Group's profits, claiming that his own Leasco is run by the same group of directors and that this demonstrates control.

Forbes, March 31, 1980, page 104–105.

There are basically two types of securities: stocks and bonds. Both are only pieces of paper, but ownership of either carries with it certain rights and privileges. The primary characteristics of these securities are:

1. Stocks represent ownership of a corporation. The owner of stocks can get a financial return in two ways: receiving dividends from the company and selling the stock for a price higher than was paid for it. Stocks are often called **equity securities.**

2. Bonds represent IOUs from either corporations, the U.S. government, or others; thus, the bond is basically a note. The issuer (the corporation or the government) sells these securities while promising to pay a fixed interest on the borrowed money and then to return the principal amount at some later maturity date. Bonds are often called **debt securities.**

The basics of accounting for equity securities and debt securities are discussed in this chapter.

14.1 Marketable Securities

Corporations, themselves, often acquire stocks and bonds for a variety of reasons. It is important to understand the various business purposes for acquiring securities, because accounting for ownership of stocks and bonds depends upon the business purpose involved.

Business
Purposes

Short-Term Revenue A corporation may have excess cash which it would like to invest. The purpose here is to earn a somewhat higher rate of interest than could be earned from certificates of deposit.

Long-Term Revenue A corporation may make investments that will not be turned into cash during the next year. An example would be the purchase of stock in a company that was felt to have excellent long-range potential.

Long-Term Influence A corporation may wish to influence the decisions of another company without actually controlling it. For example, companies will buy a substantial percentage of the stock of important suppliers to ensure consistent deliveries.

Long-Term Control A corporation may wish to acquire another company so that it becomes an extension of the acquiring company. An example would be the acquisition of Taylor Wine Company by the Coca-Cola Company.

Equity securities can be purchased for any of the above four purposes, but debt securities can be purchased only for the first two. Debt securities provide revenue, but they do not provide influence or control.

Classification

As mentioned above, a corporation can buy equity securities (stocks) and debt securities (bonds) for short-term or long-term revenue purposes; however, it may not be immediately clear whether a security has a short-term or a long-term purpose. This distinction is quite important because securities with a short-term purpose are classified as current assets, while securities with a long-term purpose are classified as noncurrent assets. For example, suppose X Corporation buys 1,000 shares of IBM stock. By itself, the transaction does not indicate whether to classify these securities as short-term or long-term.

Management Intent The controlling factor in short-term versus long-term classification is the intent of management. If management purchased the security for short-term uses and intends to liquidate it (that is, sell it and turn it into cash) during the next year, then it should be classified as a current asset. Specific examples of the uses of such a security would be

1. as a contingency fund that is liquidated as the need arises.

2. as a store of cash that is temporarily idle because of the seasonality of the business.

3. as a short-term speculation that will be sold as appropriate.

For a security to serve satisfactorily for any of these uses, it is essential that the company be able to sell the security quickly and easily. To facilitate the purchase and sale of securities, there are a number of securities exchanges. The most famous of these is undoubtedly the New York Stock Exchange, which deals only in stocks; but there are many others that deal in equity securities. In addition, there are a number of exchanges for the purchase and sale of bonds. The term *market* is often used instead of exchange. Thus, in business the terms *stock market* and *bond market* refer to places where such securities are sold and purchased. The person who buys and sells in the market for the investor is called a *broker*, and his charges are called *brokerage fees*.

For a security to be classified as a current asset, (1) it must be possible to sell the security in a ready market and (2) management must intend to convert it into cash within one year (or the operating cycle, whichever is longer). Such a security is called a *marketable security*.

Marketable Debt Securities

A marketable debt security not only promises to pay interest, but also promises to pay back the face amount of the debt. Thus, the purchaser can always get back at least this face amount by holding the security to maturity. As a result, fluctuations (usually small) in the amount the debt could be sold for are generally ignored. (Chapter 12 discusses and explains the reasons for such changes.)

The accounting procedures for marketable debt securities are then (1) to record the investment at its cost and (2) to record as revenue the interest payments received or accrued. The cost of the asset will include the cost of the security plus any brokerage fees and transfer taxes that must be paid in connection with the purchase. The asset valuation will not change during the period it is held. If interest on the debt has accrued at the end of an accounting period, then an adjusting entry must be made to recognize the revenue and create a receivable.

Record Purchase Suppose that the B Corporation purchased $10,000 of bonds from the I Corporation, and the bonds paid 9½ percent interest each June 30. If the purchase was on July 1 and the brokerage fee was $25, the entry to record it would be

Marketable securities, I Corp. bonds	10,025	
Cash		10,025

Record Revenue If the end of the accounting period is December 31, the adjusting entry at that date is:

Interest receivable	475	
Interest revenue		475

To accrue one-half year's interest

$$\$475 = \tfrac{1}{2} \times (9\tfrac{1}{2}\% \times \$10,000)$$

The interest receipt on June 30 of the next year (assuming the bond was still held) would be recorded as

Cash	950	
Interest receivable		475
Interest revenue		475

Marketable Equity Securities

There is no guaranteed maturity value for stocks as there is for bonds. For this reason, stock prices fluctuate more than do bond prices. Additionally, if stock prices do decline, there is no guarantee that they will rise in the future. As a result, the FASB has ruled that marketable equity securities must be shown on the balance sheet at the lower of cost or market. Cost refers to the purchase price of the security plus any brokerage fees or taxes. Market refers to what the security could be sold for in the stock market.

Lower of Cost or Market The lower of cost or market method here applies to aggregate cost and aggregate market. The cost figure is the total cost of all marketable equity securities, while the market figure is the total market value of the same securities. Any excess of aggregate cost over aggregate market value must be shown in a contra account (called a valuation allowance), thus reducing cost to market value.

This lower of cost or market rule is very similar to the lower of cost or market rule for inventory. There is an important difference, however. For inventory, the lower of cost or market rule can be applied to *each item* of inventory or to the entire inventory. Thus, the value of 5 items out of 1,000 items could be written down to market, while the remaining 995 items were unaffected. With marketable equity securities, the lower of cost or market rule is only applied to the aggregate value of *all items*. Thus, 5 equity securities could be worth less than cost, but if the aggregate value is not less than aggregate cost, there is no write-down.

Adjusting Entry for Loss At the end of each accounting period, an adjusting entry must be made to state the contra account properly. Suppose stocks that cost $12,000 had a market value at the end of the year of $10,000. The adjusting entry (similar to depreciation) would be

Loss on valuation of securities	2,000	
Allowance for excess of cost over market		2,000

Adjusting Entry for Gain If the market value in the subsequent period increased to $11,000, then the adjusting entry would be

Allowance for excess of cost over market	1,000	
Gain on valuation of securities		1,000

Thus, if market value is recovering from prior losses, the allowance account is debited and a gain, credited; however, the securities can never be written up above cost, and the allowance account can never be reduced below zero or have a debit balance.

Contrast with Sale of Equipment The valuation account is a contra asset, as is accumulated depreciation; however, the two accounts are not used the same way when the related asset is sold.

Assume a company owns a piece of equipment with a cost of $10,000 and accumulated depreciation of $2,000. If the equipment was sold for $11,000, the entry would be

Cash	11,000	
Accumulated depreciation	2,000	
Equipment		10,000
Gain on sale of equipment		3,000

Thus, the gain is the difference between the sale price and the book value.

In the sale of a security, the related contra account is ignored because the gain on the *sale* of the security is the difference between the sale price and the cost. The valuation allowance is only used to reflect the gain or loss on the *valuation* of securities.

Assume a company owns one security with cost of $10,000 and related valuation allowance of $2,000. If the security was sold for $11,000, the entry would be

```
Cash  ...............................................  11,000
     Marketable securities  ..................................        10,000
     Gain on sale of securities  .............................         1,000
```

At the end of the year, the valuation allowance should be $0 instead of $2,000, and the adjusting entry would be

```
Allowance for excess of cost over market  ..................  2,000
     Gain on valuation of securities  .........................         2,000
```

Thus, there is again a $3,000 gain, but in this instance, the gain is broken down into both sale and valuation components.

Valuation and Sale Thus, there are two types of gains: a gain on the *valuation* of securities and a gain on the *sale* of securities. Similarly, there are losses on the valuation of securities and losses on the sale of securities. Gains and losses on the valuation of securities do not involve a transaction with another party, so these are called **unrealized gains or losses.** Gains and losses on the sale of securities do involve a transaction with another party, so they are called **realized gains or losses.**

Concept Summary

Realized versus Unrealized Gains and Losses		
Event	*Loss*	*Gain*
Valuation of security	Unrealized loss	Unrealized gain
Sale of security	Realized loss	Realized gain

Sample Company

For example, suppose the F Corporation owned the following marketable equity securities as of December 31, 1981 and December 31, 1982, but did not own any prior to 1981.

		12/31/81			12/31/82	
Security	Cost	Market	Excess	Cost	Market	Excess
Company 1	$ 5000	$ 6700	($1700)	$ 5000	$4000	$1000
Company 2	7500	3000	4500	7500	3700	3800
Company 3	2000	1600	400	1500	1000	500
	$14500	$11300	$3200	$14000	$8700	$5300

The adjusting entry for December 31, 1981, would be

Loss on valuation of securities	3,200	
Allowance for excess of cost over market		3,200

This valuation loss would be reported under other revenues and expenses in the income statement for 1981.

The balance sheet as of December 31, 1981, would show the following:

Marketable securities (cost)	$ 14,500
Less: Allowance for excess of cost over market	(3,200)
Net marketable securities	$ 11,300

During 1982, one-fourth of the stock in Company 3 was sold for $375. The cost is one-fourth of $2,000 or $500. The entry would be

Cash	375	
Loss on sale of securities	125	
Marketable securities		500

The adjusting entry for December 31, 1982, would then be

Loss on valuation of securities	2,100	
Allowance for excess of cost over market		2,100

The $2,100 is the figure needed to bring the allowance account up from $3,200 to $5,300.

14.2 Long-Term Investments

Methods of accounting for bonds as long-term investments were discussed in Chapter 12. This section will deal only with equity investments.

If a security is intended for long-term purposes, it must be classified as an investment. Investments are placed on the balance sheet between current assets and property, plant, and equipment. The company purchasing the investment is called the investor, while the company whose securities were purchased is called the investee. As stated earlier, the basic criterion for classification of securities as current or noncurrent is the intent of management. Thus, if management intends to hold the securities, they should be classified as an investment even if the securities could be sold easily in a ready market.

Lower of Cost or
Market Method

Equity securities that have a ready market can be long-term. The accounting procedures for them are similar to the procedures for marketable securities. The basic difference is that valuation gains and losses are not reflected on the income statement, but are instead debited and credited directly to shareholder's equity. Gains and losses from the *sale* of long-term securities are handled in the same way as those from short-term securities.

The aggregate cost and aggregate market value are determined for long-term equity securities just as they were for short-term securities. In addition, there will be a valuation allowance just as for short-term securities. However, the adjusting entry is different. For short-term securities the entry was

Loss on valuation of securities (income statement account) ...	2,000	
Allowance for excess of cost over market		2,000

If the very same securities were classified as long-term, the entry would be

Unrealized loss on long-term securities (stockholders' equity account)	2,000	
Allowance for excess of cost over market		2,000

The balance sheet presentation of this account would be as follows:

Stockholders' equity
Unrealized capital
Unrealized loss on long-term securities 2,000

A subsequent recovery in the market value above the cost of the long-term securities would give rise to the following entry:

Allowance for excess of cost over market	2,000	
Unrealized loss on long-term securities		2,000

Again, the allowance account cannot go below zero, and the long-term equity securities cannot be written up above cost. The account "Unrealized loss on long-term securities" is a contra-equity account and has a debit balance.

Other Long-Term Classifications

For classification purposes, management's intent sometimes cannot be completely controlling because of possible outside factors. In practice, the incentive is for management to classify securities as current because that will increase the percentage of assets that are current, thus making the balance sheet look more "liquid" and the company look like a better credit risk. The company may then find it easier to borrow money and may do so at more favorable interest rates. For these reasons, management may wish to classify securities as current when they cannot be converted to cash as quickly or as easily as a current classification would indicate because there is no market, no *active* market, or no *ready* market for the securities.

No Market The securities may not be publicly traded in a major exchange. In this instance, the stock is said to be closely held, because it is owned by relatively few people. The problem here is that it may be difficult to sell the securities quickly without a substantial loss because so few people own the stock.

No Active Market The securities may be a substantial percentage of the total outstanding securities of the issuing firm. For this reason, they may be difficult to sell, especially in large quantities.

No Ready Market The securities may not have a good market for a variety of reasons: (1) there could be a high degree of ownership concentration of the remaining securities outstanding, (2) very few shares might be traded, even on a public exchange, and (3) the market price of the security may vary so widely that it is not clear how much the securities could be sold for.

In any of these instances, the security should be classified as long-term and should be accounted for as an investment.

Cost Method

The basic method of accounting for investments that do not have a ready market is the cost method. Under this method, the investment account is debited with the full cost of the asset. The full cost includes the basic cost of the security, any brokerage fees associated with the purchase, and any transfer taxes that must be paid. Revenue is recognized as dividends are received. Even if an investee company regularly pays a dividend of a specific amount at a specific time each year, *dividends are not accrued.*

Subsequent Changes in Value The investment account is never written up, no matter how great the increase in the value of the investment; however, the investment can be written down if there is a serious and permanent decline in the investment's value. For example, if one-half of the investee company's assets are destroyed by a fire or flood without insurance, it may become necessary to write down the investment to a new value. Fluctuations in the value of the investment (including declines) are generally ignored, however.

Example Assume that the C Corporation purchased, as an investment, 1,000 shares of stock in the M Company, where the M Company stock is not traded on an exchange. In this instance, the cost method of accounting must be used because these securities do not have a ready market. If the shares cost $50 each, the entry to record the purchase would be

Investment in M Company	50,000	
Cash		50,000

Any earnings of the M Company or increase in its value are ignored. If the M Company pays a dividend of $1.25 a share, the entry to record this cash receipt by C Company would be

Cash	1,250	
Dividend revenue		1,250

Equity Method   Using the accounting methods discussed so far, income is recognized by the investor when dividends are received from the investee. However, this approach to income recognition leads to a possible abuse: when the investor has a significant influence on the dividend policy of the investee, the investor can time dividend payments so as to manipulate its net income. As an example, if the investor wanted to cover a slight down-turn in its primary business, it could simply boost dividend payments from the investee.

Another problem specific to the cost method is that the investment account balance will become increasingly unrelated to the actual worth of the investment. As result of successful operations, the underlying assets of the investee will grow, but with the cost method, this growth is not reflected in the accounts.

The accounting solution to these problems is use of the equity method when an investor has **significant influence** over the investee. An investor is presumed to have significant influence over the investee if the investor owns 20 percent or more of the investee's outstanding stock. Under the equity method, the investee's net income is reflected in the books of the investor as the income is earned by the investee: the investment account is debited and a revenue account is credited for the investor's share of the investee's net income. Dividends represent a reduction of the investee's assets and, thus, reduce the investment account: cash is debited, and the investment account is credited.

What, in effect, is happening is that the investment account measures the investment cost plus the investor's share of the undistributed earnings since the investment was made. Thus, the investment account of the investor will reflect all changes to the investee's retained earnings.

Example The following example will illustrate the procedures involved in the use of the equity method:

1. On January 1, 1981, the OR Company purchased 40 percent of the outstanding shares of the EE Company at $8 per share. The EE Company has 15,000 shares outstanding.

The entry on the books of the OR Company would be

Investment in EE Company	48,000	
Cash		48,000
To record investment (40% × 15,000 × $8)		

2. During 1981, the EE Company had net income of $10,000 and paid $5,000 in dividends. These events would require two entries:

Investment in EE Company	4,000	
Equity in earnings of EE		4,000
To record equity in earnings (40% × $10,000)		

and

Cash	2,000	
Investment in EE Company		2,000
To record receipt of dividends (40% × $5,000)		

3. During 1982, the EE Company had a net loss of $2,000 and paid no dividends. The journal entry would be

Equity in loss of EE	800	
Investment in EE Company		800
To record equity in loss (40% × $2,000)		

Equity in earnings of EE and equity in loss of EE are both income statement accounts.

Losses of the investee are also reflected in the equity method. Thus, the investment account at the end of 1982 will have a balance of $49,200 (48,000 + 4,000 − 2,000 − 800). The increase of $1,200 from the date of acquisition represents the OR Company's 40 percent share of the undistributed earnings of the EE Company. Retained earnings of the EE Company will be $3,000 (10,000 − 5,000 − 2,000) higher than the balance on January 1, 1981. Forty percent of this $3,000 is the $1,200 increase in the investment account.

Concept Summary

Accounting for Long-Term Investments			
	Lower of Cost or Market Method	*Cost Method*	*Equity Method*
Presumption of influence	Little or no influence	Little or no influence	Significant influence
Ownership	Less than 10%	Less than 20%	More than 20%
Market	Ready market	No ready market	Either
Acquisition at cost	Investment Cash	Investment Cash	Investment Cash
Market value decline	Unrealized loss Allowance	No entry	No entry
Investee reports earnings	No entry	No entry	Investment Equity in earnings
Investee pays dividends	Cash Investment revenue	Cash Investment revenue	Cash Investment

14.3 Consolidations

A common thread throughout the recent American business scene, especially since the 1960s, is the acquisition of one corporation by another. Interestingly enough, however, there were similar waves of business combinations during the late 1920s and at the beginning of the twentieth century. Acquisition of other companies offers decided advantages in terms of salary and prestige for the management of the acquiring company. (For the management of the acquired company, the prospects are not good, perhaps explaining the fight against acquisition by some managements.) Apart from benefit to management, there are two basic arguments to explain why acquisitions are good for the shareholders:

1. The steady growth of the acquisition-minded company is attractive to stock purchasers, and the stock will command a higher price.

2. The diversification afforded by acquisitions reduces the risk associated with the business and, thus, helps the stock command a higher price.

There is little evidence to support either of these arguments. Investors do not seem to pay a premium for the acquiring company's stock. Also, investors would have a lower risk of ownership if they owned stock in two separate companies, rather than in a single, combined company.

Types of Business Combinations

There are three basic types of business combinations: consolidation, merger, and acquisition. If the stockholders of two separate companies, Company X and Company Y, exchange their stock for that of a third company and X and Y cease to exist, the combination is a **consolidation.** If (1) Company X acquires all of the stock of Company Y, (2) Company X transfers Y's assets and liabilities to the books of Company X, and (3) Company Y ceases to exist as a legal entity, then the combination is a **merger.**

If Company X acquires all of the stock of Company Y, but Company Y continues to exist as a legal entity, then the combination is an **acquisition.** Company X, which owns the stock of Company Y, is called the *parent.* Company Y, which is owned by Company X, is called the *subsidiary.* Though legally separate, Company X and Company Y can be operated in concert to further the objectives of Company X, and consolidated financial statements that combine accounting information about both companies can be prepared.

Consolidated Financial Statements

In the remainder of this chapter, the basics of accounting for consolidated financial statements are discussed. The whole problem of consolidated financial statements can become extraordinarily complicated, and large sections of advanced accounting textbooks and courses are devoted to this topic. As a result, this chapter will concentrate on the fundamental concepts.

Fundamental Example To illustrate these concepts, the following fundamental example will be used. P Company has the following balance sheet at December 31, 1981:

P COMPANY
Balance Sheet
December 31, 1981

Assets		*Equities*	
Cash	$ 50,000	Liabilities	$ 20,000
Inventory	70,000	Capital stock	150,000
Other assets	130,000	Retained earnings	80,000
Total assets	$250,000	Total equities	$250,000

At the same time, S Company has the following balance sheet:

S COMPANY
Balance Sheet
December 31, 1981

Assets		*Equities*	
Cash	$ 10,000	Liabilities	$ 10,000
Inventory	50,000	Capital stock	80,000
Other assets	50,000	Retained earnings	20,000
Total assets	$110,000	Total equities	$110,000

If P Company were to buy S Company, P would get $110,000 of assets but would have to assume $10,000 of liabilities. Thus, the net assets (that is, assets − liabilities) that P would get would be $100,000. Assume, then, that on January 1, 1982, P Company issued 1,000 shares of stock (where each share was valued at $100) in exchange for all the stock of S Company. The entry to record this acquisition would be

Investment in S	100,000	
Capital stock		100,000

and the balance sheet for P Company as of January 1, 1982, would be

P COMPANY
Balance Sheet
January 1, 1982

Assets		*Equities*	
Cash	$ 50,000	Liabilities	$ 20,000
Inventory	70,000	Capital stock	250,000
Investment in S	100,000	Retained earnings	80,000
Other assets	130,000		
Total assets	$350,000	Total equities	$350,000

There is no entry on the books of S Company for this transaction because P Company acquired S Company stock from the stockholders of S Company. As a result, the balance sheet of S Company does not change.

Consolidated
Balance Sheet

Although P Company has, in essence, acquired S Company, there are two separate companies, with two separate sets of accounting records and with two separate sets of financial statements. However, because P controls S, the management of P controls the assets and liabilities of S in the same manner as it controls the assets and liabilities of P. What is needed, then, is an overall view of the combined assets and liabilities of P and S to get a correct picture of the resources under the command of P. Such an overall view is called a consolidated balance sheet.

The acquisition process thus creates a new accounting entity, called "P Company and Consolidated Subsidiary." The financial statements for

Concept Summary

Fundamental Example

P COMPANY AND SUBSIDIARY S COMPANY
Case 1: Consolidated Balance Sheet Working Paper
January 1, 1982
Date of Acquisition

	P Company	S Company	Eliminations DR	Eliminations CR	Consolidated
ASSETS					
Cash	50000	10000			60000
Inventory	70000	50000			120000
Investment in S	100000			100000	
Other assets	130000	50000			180000
	350000	110000			360000
EQUITIES					
Liabilities	20000	10000			30000
Capital stock					
P Company	250000				250000
S Company		80000	80000		
Retained earnings					
P Company	80000				80000
S Company		20000	20000		
	350000	110000	100000	100000	360000

The consolidated balance sheet is the following:

P COMPANY AND CONSOLIDATED SUBSIDIARY
Balance Sheet
January 1, 1982

Assets		Equities	
Cash	$ 60,000	Liabilities	$ 30,000
Inventory	120,000	Capital stock	250,000
Other assets	180,000	Retained earnings	80,000
Total assets	$360,000	Total equities	$360,000

this new accounting entity will be developed from the statements of P and S separately, so P and S will continue to produce financial statements for their individual companies.

Elimination Entry

To prepare the consolidated balance sheet, the process basically substitutes the net assets of the subsidiary company for the investment account of the parent company. This is most easily accomplished using a worksheet approach, as illustrated in the concept summary entitled Fundamental Example. The substitution is made by eliminating the investment account of the parent against the owners' equity accounts of the subsidiary. After this elimination has been made, the assets and liabilities of the two companies can be combined. Thus, in the Fundamental Example, the elimination entry, is

Capital stock, S Company	80,000	
Retained earnings, S Company	20,000	
Investment in S		100,000

This elimination entry is not made on the books of either company. It only appears on the working paper, which is merely a convenient aid in the preparation of consolidated financial statements.

The elimination in the Fundamental Example substitutes the net assets of S for the investment account of P. The amounts in the consolidated column on the right of the worksheet are simply the sum of the balances for each individual company. The capital stock and retained earnings for the consolidated entity are the same as those for the parent. This fact reflects the reality that the owners of the parent actually own both the companies.

Minority Interest

The Fundamental Example assumed that P Company acquired 100 percent of the stock of S Company. Suppose, however, that P Company only acquired 90 percent of S Company for $90,000 of stock rather than 100 percent for $100,000 of stock. The consolidated entity under the control of the P Company shareholders is the same size (with net assets of $330,000) as it would be with 100 percent ownership. Indeed, the assets and liabilities of both companies are unaffected by the difference in ownership. The only thing affected is owners' equity.

S Company has $100,000 of net assets. Thus, the owners of P Company own $90,000 of those net assets, while the other shareholders of S Company own $10,000. These other shareholders of S are called minority shareholders because they necessarily own a minority of the shares of S. But, by virtue of owning $10,000 of S, these minority shareholders own $10,000 of the consolidated entity. The amount of the consolidated entity owned by the minority shareholders of subsidiaries is called the minority interest. Minority interest is in the subsidiary, but this must be reflected in the consolidated statements; therefore, of the $330,000 net assets of the consolidated entity, the owners of P Company own $320,000, while the minority shareholders of S Company own $10,000.

Elimination Entry The appropriate elimination entry in this instance is illustrated in Figure 14-1. The investment account has a $90,000 balance, because that was the cost of the investment. Ninety percent of the owners' equity accounts of S Company are eliminated, because that is the per-

FIGURE 14-1
Minority Interests

P COMPANY AND SUBSIDIARY S COMPANY
Case 2: Consolidated Balance Sheet Working Paper
January 1, 1982

	P Company	S Company	Eliminations DR	CR	Consolidated
ASSETS					
Cash	50000	10000			60000
Inventory	70000	50000			120000
Investment in S	90000			90000	
Other assets	130000	50000			180000
	340000	110000			360000
EQUITIES					
Liabilities	20000	10000			30000
Capital stock					
P Company	240000				240000
S Company		80000	72000		8000 M
Retained earnings					
P Company	80000				80000
S Company		20000	18000		2000 M
	340000	110000	90000	90000	360000

P Company and Consolidated Subsidiary
Balance Sheet
January 1, 1982

Assets		Equities	
Cash	$ 60000	Liabilities	$ 30000
Inventory	120000	Minority interest	10000
Other assets	180000	Capital stock	240000
		Retained earnings	80000
Total assets	$ 360000	Total equities	$ 360000

P COMPANY AND CONSOLIDATED SUBSIDIARY
Balance Sheet
January 1, 1982

Assets		Equities	
Cash	$ 60,000	Liabilities	$ 30,000
Inventory	120,000	Minority interest	10,000
Other assets	180,000	Capital stock	240,000
		Retained earnings	80,000
Total assets	$360,000	Total equities	$360,000

centage of S owned by P. The minority interest can then be extended to the consolidated column as the remaining balance in the owners' equity accounts of the subsidiary. To identify the minority interest, the letter M is placed on the right of the amount in the consolidated column. When preparing consolidated balance sheets, it is customary to combine all minority interests into one balance and place it above the owners' equity accounts of the majority shareholders. The corresponding consolidated balance sheet is also shown in Figure 14-1. In effect, this process substitutes the total net assets of the subsidiary for the investment account, but then records the minority interest in those net assets.

Purchase Method

The acquisition of S Company by P Company was illustrated in the Fundamental Example. In that example, P issued 1,000 shares of $100 stock to buy all the stock of S, a total investment of $100,000. The book value of the net assets of S was also equal to $100,000. Thus, the elimination entry for the consolidated statements was

Capital stock, S Company	80,000	
Retained earnings, S Company	20,000	
Investment in S		100,000

Suppose the S Company shareholders refused to sell their shares in S for only 1,000 shares of P and insisted on 1,200 shares of P. Suppose further that P agreed to this arrangement. The elimination entry would be

Capital stock, S Company	80,000	
Retained earnings, S Company	20,000	
	?	
Investment in S		120,000

The investment in S account must be $120,000 (1,200 shares $\times$ $100/share), but the elimination entry does not balance in the same way it did before. What is happening is that P Company is willing to pay more than book value for S Company.

Book Value Payment of more than book value occurs in most acquisitions. One of the reasons is that accounting records assets at cost and does not revalue them upward if they increase in value. Thus, a company may own very valuable land which is "on the books" for its purchase price; the purchase could have been made twenty years before and the land now may be worth many times what was paid for it.

As discussed in Chapter 1, assets that have increased in value (such as land) are not revalued because there has been no exchange. But, when P Company acquires S Company, an exchange takes place; hence, the assets can be revalued. In the example above, P Company values S Company at $20,000 more than its book value, and it is reasonable to then increase the valuation of S Company assets by this $20,000. If the cash and inventory of S Company are fairly stated, the elimination entry would be

Capital stock, S Company 80,000
Retained earnings, S Company 20,000
Other assets 20,000
    Investment in S   120,000

Differential The elimination entry adds $20,000 to other assets. This difference between the valuation of the company and the book value of the net assets acquired is called the differential. In this instance, the assumption is that the "other assets" are undervalued and, hence, the differential ($20,000) is assigned to other assets.

This method of accounting for acquisitions is called the purchase method. The purchase method involves the allocation of the purchase cost among the assets acquired and the liabilities assumed. Each asset or liability is assigned an amount equal to its fair value at the date of acquisition. Generally, the fair value will exceed the book value of the net assets acquired, thus giving rise to a positive differential, as mentioned above. Only occasionally will the cost be less than book value.

Goodwill The earlier discussion assumed that the other assets of S Company were undervalued by the $20,000 differential. There is another possibility, however. Each of the assets may be properly valued, but S Company may be worth more as a whole than the total of all its specific assets. Thus, a good reputation, favorable location, or larger-than-normal earnings may make the purchaser willing to pay more than the value of the net assets. In this instance, the differential is assigned to an asset called goodwill.

Figure 14-2 illustrates the working paper for the consolidated balance sheet in this instance. The elimination entry is

Capital stock, S Company 80,000
Retained earnings, S Company 20,000
Goodwill 20,000
    Investment in S   120,000

The asset goodwill appears on the consolidated balance sheet, but not on the balance sheet of either P Company or S Company. Goodwill is an intangible asset or, simply, an intangible. It must be amortized over forty years or less, giving rise to amortization expense. This amortization expense must be deducted for financial statement purposes, but cannot be deducted for income tax purposes.

Pooling of Interests Method

The purchase method is used in most business combinations but another method of accounting, called the pooling of interests method, must be used in some instances. This method basically combines the assets, liabilities, and owners' equity of the two firms, using their book values. The rationale is that, in some instances, companies simply unite their ownership interests. The consolidated entity is, thus, a straightforward combination of two companies which were formerly operated separately. As a result, the assets, liabilities, and owners' equity are unchanged; they are merely com-

FIGURE 14-2
Purchase Method
Differential Assigned to Goodwill

P COMPANY AND SUBSIDIARY S COMPANY
Case 3: Consolidated Balance Sheet Working Paper
January 1, 1982

	P Company	S Company	Eliminations DR	CR	Consolidated
ASSETS					
Cash	50000	10000			60000
Inventory	70000	50000			120000
Investment in S	120000			120000	
Other assets	130000	50000			180000
Goodwill			20000		20000
Total assets	370000	110000			380000
EQUITIES					
Liabilities	20000	10000			30000
Capital stock					
P Company	270000				270000
S Company		80000	80000		
Retained earnings					
P Company	80000				80000
S Company		20000	20000		
Total equities	370000	110000	120000	120000	380000

bined. Thus, to compare future financial statements to those of the past, it is necessary to continue the past accounting methods.

Requirements Governing Use of This Method Strictly speaking, the purchase and pooling of interests methods are not alternative procedures in the sense that LIFO and FIFO are. If certain requirements are met, the pooling of interests method must be used. If all of these requirements are not met, the purchase method must be used. The circumstances that will require the use of the pooling of interests method are (generally speaking):

1. The acquisition must be a single transaction. The acquisition cannot stretch over years of small acquisitions. Additionally, the acquisition cannot depend on the occurrence of certain future events.

2. The companies must be independent. The companies cannot own part of each other. This also means that neither party company can be owned by any other company.

3. The parent must acquire at least 90 percent of the subsidiary. Anything less than 90 percent will require the use of the purchase method.

4. The parent can issue only stock for the subsidiary stock. If the parent uses cash or notes to acquire the subsidiary stock, then the combination must be accounted for as a purchase.

Application to Cases 1, 2, and 3 The first two cases of consolidated balance sheets considered earlier would be accounted for in the same way using the purchase method as they would using the pooling of interest method. The reason is that the stock issued had the same value as the book value of the net assets acquired. Thus, in both methods, the investment account neatly canceled the owners' equity accounts of the subsidiary.

In Case 3, however, the stock issued had a value of $20,000 more than the book value of the net assets acquired. This differential was then assigned to an asset account. The pooling of interests method does not allow asset revaluation, so the difference is used to reduce retained earnings, as in Figure 14-3. Thus, the assets and liabilities of both firms will be combined in the consolidated balance sheet at their book values.

Consolidated Owners' Equity Prior to the acquisition, P Company's owners' equity consisted of capital stock of $150,000 and retained earnings of $80,000 for a total of $230,000. Also, prior to the acquisition, S Company's owners' equity consisted of capital stock of $80,000 and retained earnings of $20,000, for a total of $100,000. Consolidated owners' equity using the pooling of interests method is $330,000, the sum of P's ($230,000) and S's ($100,000). This is a fundamental characteristic of the pooling of interests method.

FIGURE 14-3
Pooling of Interests Method

P COMPANY AND SUBSIDIARY S COMPANY
Case 4: Consolidated Balance Sheet Working Paper
January 1, 1982

			P Company	S Company	Eliminations DR	Eliminations CR	Consolidated
ASSETS							
Cash			50000	10000			60000
Inventory			70000	50000			120000
Investment in S			120000			120000	
Other assets			130000	50000			180000
Total assets			370000	110000			360000
EQUITIES							
Liabilities			20000	10000			30000
Capital stock							
P Company			270000				270000
S Company				80000	80000		
Retained earnings							
P Company			80000		20000		60000
S Company				20000	20000		
Total equities			370000	110000	120000	120000	360000

Elimination Entry The different elimination entries would be:

	Purchase Method		Pooling of Interests Method	
Other assets	20,000		–0–	
Capital stock, S Company	80,000		80,000	
Retained earnings, S Company	20,000		40,000	
Investment in S		120,000		120,000

14.4 Financial Statements Subsequent to Acquisition

Earlier discussions of consolidations focused on accounting for some of the various possibilities as of the date of acquisition; however, it is also necessary to look at accounting for subsequent periods of operation and the preparation of appropriate financial statements. In particular, the discussion will consider accounting for an additional year of operation, preparing an income statement and a retained earnings statement for the year and a balance sheet as of the end of the year. This will suffice because subsequent years basically will be a repetition of the first year.

The illustration will extend the Fundamental Example. That working paper gave the consolidation as of January 1, 1982, the date of acquisition. Because P owned more than 20 percent of S, the equity method was used in accounting for the investment in S. The adjusted trial balances as of December 31, 1982, for the P Company and S Company are the following:

	P Company		S Company	
Cash	$ 50,000		$ 10,000	
Inventory, 12/31	90,000		60,000	
Investment in S	120,000			
Other assets	130,000		60,000	
Liabilities		$ 35,000		$ 10,000
Capital stock		250,000		80,000
Retained earnings, 1/1		80,000		20,000
Dividends	20,000		10,000	
Sales		85,000		50,000
Equity in income of S		30,000		
Cost of goods sold	55,000		15,000	
Other expenses	15,000		5,000	
	$480,000	$480,000	$160,000	$160,000

From these adjusted trial balances, it is possible to prepare an income statement, statement of retained earnings, and balance sheet for both P Company and S Company. What is necessary now is to prepare these statements for the consolidated entity. To do so, the working paper used so far must be extended, because it is designed only for preparation of the balance sheet. This process requires a three-part working paper, one part for each of the three related statements. Such a three-part working paper is illustrated in the concept summary entitled Financial Statements Subsequent to Acquisition.

Before discussing details, it is first necessary to look at the overall picture. The top part is the income statement section, whose bottom line is net income for P Company, S Company, and the consolidated entity. Net income is then a line in the retained earnings section, whose bottom line is retained earnings as of the end of the year. Finally, retained earnings as of the end of the year becomes a line in the balance sheet section. Thus, the three parts of a working paper all connect.

Elimination Entries

Eliminate Equity in Subsidiary Net Income To avoid double counting, the equity in S Company's net income which was included in P Company's income statement must be eliminated. S Company's sales and expenses will be combined with those of P Company; thus, S Company is properly reflected in the consolidated income statement. The elimination entry would be

Equity in income of S	30,000	
Investment in S		30,000

Eliminate Subsidiary Dividends It is necessary to eliminate the dividends paid by S Company to P Company, because the dividends were not paid outside of the consolidated entity. The elimination entry would be

Investment in S	10,000	
Dividends, S Company		10,000

Eliminate Investment Account The final entry is to eliminate the investment account as was done at the beginning of the year. The effect of the first two eliminations is to restore the balance in the investment account to where it was at the beginning of the year. The elimination entry would then be

Retained earnings, S Company	20,000	
Capital stock, S Company	80,000	
Investment in S		100,000

Characteristics of the Working Paper

All three consolidated financial statements can be developed from the consolidated column of the working paper. In addition, three important characteristics of the working paper should be mentioned. They are as follows:

1. The debits and credits for the elimination entries are typically not equal in any of the three parts of the working paper; however, they are equal in total for all three parts.

2. P Company net income is the same as consolidated net income. This is not a coincidence, but rather a fundamental aspect of the equity method. The equity in income of S in effect substitutes in the P Company income

Concept Summary

Financial Statements Subsequent to Acquisition

P COMPANY AND SUBSIDIARY S COMPANY
Consolidated Statements Working Paper
December 31, 1982

	P Company	S Company	Eliminations DR	CR	Consolidated
Income statement:					
Sales	85000	50000			135000
Equity in income of S	30000		30000 A		
Total revenues	115000	50000			135000
Cost of goods sold	55000	15000			70000
Other expenses	15000	5000			20000
Total expenses	70000	20000			90000
Net income	45000	30000	30000	-0-	45000
Statement of Retained Earnings:					
Retained earnings, 1/1					
P Company	80000				80000
S Company		20000	20000 C		
Net income	45000	30000	30000	-0-	45000
	125000	50000			125000
Dividends					
P Company	20000				20000
S Company		10000		10000 B	
Retained earnings, 12/31	105000	40000	50000	10000	105000
Balance sheet:					
Cash	50000	10000			60000
Inventory	90000	60000			150000
Investment in S	120000		10000 B	30000 A	
				100000 C	
Other assets	130000	60000			190000
Total assets	390000	130000			400000
Liabilities	35000	10000			45000
Capital stock					
P Company	250000				250000
S Company		80000	80000 C		
Retained earnings	105000	40000	50000	10000	105000
Total equities	390000	130000	140000	140000	400000

Elimination entries:

A Eliminate equity in S Company net income
B Eliminate dividends from S Company to P Company
C Eliminate investment account as at date of acquisition

statement for the additional revenues and expenses of S added for the consolidated statement.

3. P Company retained earnings is the same as consolidated retained earnings. Again, this is not a coincidence, but rather another fundamental aspect of the equity method.

Acquisition During Accountin . Period When the subsidiary is acquired other than at the beginning of the year, the income statement is treated differently, depending upon whether the acquisition is treated as a purchase or as a pooling of interests. If the combination is accounted for as a purchase, the consolidated income statement will include the income statement accounts of the parent for the whole year but the income statement accounts of the subsidiary only from date of acquisition. If the combination is accounted for as a pooling of interests, the consolidated income statement will include the income statement accounts of both companies for the entire year, as if the companies had been combined or operating as one company from the beginning of the year.

Unconsolidated Subsidiaries Even though one company controls another, they do not necessarily prepare consolidated statements. If the parent and the subsidiary are in vastly different businesses, combining their assets and liabilities may not produce meaningful results. The best example is that of a manufacturing firm which owns a finance company. The purpose of the finance company is to make it easier for the customers of the manufacturing firm to buy its products. (Many major manufacturers, such as Ford Motor Company and General Motors, have such wholly owned subsidiaries.) However, the mix of assets and liabilities of the finance company is quite different from that of the parent. A consolidation with the manufacturing firm would produce a misleading picture.

Where consolidated financial statements are not prepared, the equity method is used to account for the investment. As pointed out above, this method approximates a full consolidation because both the net income and retained earnings of the parent will be the same as consolidated net income and retained earnings. Further, the investment account on the parent's balance sheet summarizes the net assets of the subsidiary.

Intercompany Receivables and Payables When developing a consolidated balance sheet, it is necessary to look at the consolidated entity as a whole. Thus, if the parent owes money to the subsidiary, or vice versa, then from a consolidated standpoint, the receivable and payable offset each other. For example, if P Company owed $10,000 to S Company, the situation would be the following:

P Company		S Company	
Payable to S	10,000	Receivable from P	10,000

Both the receivable and the payable are eliminated when a consolidated balance sheet is prepared. The elimination entry on the working paper would be:

Payable to S	10,000	
Receivable from P		10,000

This makes sense because there is no debt or receivable from outside the consolidated entity.

Cost Method May Be Used When the consolidated financial statements were developed after the date of acquisition, it was assumed that the equity method of accounting for the subsidiary was used. It is possible to use the cost method instead. The cost method makes the elimination entries different, but the resulting consolidated financial statements will be exactly the same, whether the cost method or the equity method is used.

Summary

There are two types of corporate securities. Debt securities promise a fixed return to the investor but provide the investor no opportunity to influence or control the policies of the business. Equity securities provide a return that is a function of the success of the business but offer the opportunity to influence or control company policies.

Marketable equity securities are accounted for using a lower of cost or market approach. The difference between aggregate cost and aggregate market at the end of each accounting period is reflected on the income statement unless market exceeds cost.

Long-term equity securities that are held for revenue purposes are also accounted for using a lower of cost or market approach; however, the difference between aggregate cost and aggregate market is reflected directly in owners' equity rather than on the income statement.

Long-term equity securities that are held for other than revenue purposes are accounted for by one of three approaches. When an investor owns less than 20 percent of the equity securities of an investee, little or no influence is presumed and the cost method of accounting for the investment is used. When an investor owns between 20 percent and 50 percent of the equity securities, significant influence is presumed and the equity method of accounting is used.

When more than 50 percent of the equity securities of a business are owned and the investor and investee are in similar businesses, the financial statements are consolidated. An acquisition may be treated as a purchase or a pooling of interests. The purchase method treats the acquisition as an accounting event, and acquired assets may be revalued and added to the book value of the assets of the acquiring company at their market value for the purpose of consolidated statements. The pooling method simply adds the book value of the acquired assets to the book value of the assets of the acquiring company and reports the result on consolidated statements.

The fourth and final financial statement in the package of statements produced by businesses is presented in Chapter 15, and cash and funds flows are discussed.

Key Terms

Acquisition	Merger
Consolidated financial statements	Minority interest
Consolidation	Pooling of interests method
Cost method	Purchase method
Debt security	Realized gain or loss
Elimination entry	Significant influence
Equity method	Unconsolidated subsidiary
Equity security	Unrealized gain or loss
Marketable security	

Comprehensive Review Problem

The Whale Distributing Company, Inc. has generated excess cash and engages in the following investments during 1982:

January 1 Acquired 40 percent of the 200,000 outstanding shares of Plankton Corporation, a major supplier of Whale. The purchase was designed to ensure a continued supply of products and cost Whale $10 per share.

March 1 Purchased 1,000 shares of Tuna Company, a family-held business, for $22 per share. These shares represent 5 percent of Tuna Company's shares outstanding.

June 1 Bought 500 shares of Exxon Corporation for $25,000 in anticipation of collecting several quarterly dividends before selling the shares in January of 1983.

July 1 Dividends declared were as follows:

Plankton $0.50 per share
Tuna $1.25 per share
Exxon $2.00 per share

August 1 Received dividends declared on July 1.
October 1 Exxon declared a dividend of $2.50 per share.
November 1 Received dividends from Exxon which were declared on October 1.
December 31 Tuna Company announced annual income for 1982 of $45,000. 1982 income for Plankton Corporation was $650,000. Exxon income for 1982 was $12 per share.

December 31 Dividends declared were as follows:

Plankton $0.50 per share
Tuna $1.25 per share
Exxon $2.00 per share

December 31 The year-end closing price for Exxon was $48.

Required:

1. Give all required journal entries for the investment transactions described above.

2. Show how each of these investments would be reported on the balance sheet of Whale at December 31, 1982.

Solution to Comprehensive Review Problem

1.
WHALE DISTRIBUTING COMPANY, INC.
General Journal

Date	Transaction Accounts	Debit	Credit
1982			
Jan 1	Investment in Plankton	800,000	
	Cash		800,000
	Purchased 80,000 shares (40% × 200,000) at $10 per share		
Mar 1	Investment in Tuna	22,000	
	Cash		22,000
	Purchased 1,000 shares at $22 per share		
June 1	Marketable securities—Exxon	25,000	
	Cash		25,000
	Purchased 500 shares at $50 per share		
July 1	[No entry made when dividends are declared by investee company. Dividends are not accrued.]		
Aug 1	Cash	40,000	
	Investment in Plankton		40,000
	Received dividends: $0.50 per share × 80,000 shares		
1	Cash	1,250	
	Dividend revenue		1,250
	Received dividends: $1.25 per share × 1,000 shares		
1	Cash	1,000	
	Dividend revenue		1,000
	Received dividends: $2.00 per share × 500 shares		
Oct 1	[No entry made when dividends are declared by investee company. Dividends are not accrued.]		
Nov 1	Cash	1,250	
	Dividend revenue		1,250
	Received dividends: $2.50 per share × 500 shares		
Dec 31	Investment in Plankton	260,000	
	Equity in earnings of Plankton		260,000
	Equity of 40% × $650,000 = $260,000		
	[No entry for Tuna income because the cost method is used. No entry for Exxon income because it is a marketable security. No entry made when dividends are declared by investee. Dividends are not accrued.]		
31	Loss on valuation of securities	1,000	
	Allowance for excess of cost over market		1,000
	Marketable security valuation loss: ($50 cost − $48 market) × 500 shares		

2. *Current assets*

Marketable securities—Exxon (cost)	$	25,000	
Allowance for excess of cost over market		(1,000)	$ 24,000
Investments			
Investment in Plankton		1,020,000	
Investment in Tuna		22,000	1,042,000

Questions

Q14-1. Give four reasons individuals or businesses might purchase corporate securities.

Q14-2. What conditions have to hold for a debt security to be classified as a current asset? For an equity security to be classified as a current asset?

Q14-3. Contrast lower of cost or market as it is applied to marketable securities and to long-term investments.

Q14-4. Describe the cost method of accounting for long-term investments.

Q14-5. Describe the equity method of accounting for long-term investments.

Q14-6. List two reasons mergers may be advantageous to stockholders. List two reasons they may be unfavorable.

Q14-7. What is meant by consolidated statements? How do these statements relate to the financial statements of the parent prior to consolidation?

Q14-8. What are the general requirements for an acquisition to be treated as a pooling of interests?

Q14-9. How are assets and liabilities valued under the purchase method of accounting for acquisitions? How does this differ from valuation under the pooling of interests method?

Q14-10. Explain how the excess of cost over book value may be treated under the purchase method of accounting for acquisitions.

Exercises

E14-1. On July 1, 1981, the Rader Corporation purchased Alpha Corporation bonds with total face values of $20,000. Rader paid $20,000 for the bonds and paid a brokerage fee of $50 on the transaction. The bonds pay 9 percent interest each June 30. Record on Rader's books the purchase of the bonds on July 1, 1981, the adjusting entry to be made at December 31, 1981, and the receipt of interest on June 30, 1982.

E14-2. On August 20, 1981, the Mex Company invested some idle cash in marketable equity securities which it intended to sell within the next year. The Mex Company purchased 1,000 shares of RML stock for $20 per share. At December 31, 1981, the market value of the RML stock was $18 per share. On March 1, 1982, the Mex Company sold 500 shares of the RML stock for $21 per share. Give the journal entries that would be made with respect to the RML stock on August 20, 1981, December 31, 1981, and March 1, 1982. Assume that the RML stock was the only stock held by the Mex Company.

E14-3. The Piper Corporation acquired 100 percent of the stock of the Sesna Corporation on December 31. The book value and the market value of the Sesna Corporation at that date are given below.

SESNA CORPORATION
December 31, 1982

	Book Value	Market Value
Assets		
Cash	$ 20,000	$ 20,000
Accounts receivable (net)	40,000	40,000
Inventory	100,000	100,000
Property, plant, and equipment (net)	80,000	120,000
Other assets	10,000	10,000
Total assets	$250,000	$290,000
Liabilities & Owners' Equity		
Accounts payable	$ 30,000	
Notes payable	20,000	
Common stock	50,000	
Retained earnings	150,000	
Total liabilities & owners' equity	$250,000	

1. If the Piper Corporation paid $300,000 in cash for Sesna Corporation, what would be the amount of goodwill reported on the consolidated financial statements of the Piper Corporation and Subsidiary at December 31, 1982? Show your calculation.

2. If the Piper Corporation acquired the Sesna Corporation by issuing stock worth $300,000 and used the pooling of interests method to record the acquisition, what would be the amount of goodwill reported on the consolidated financial statements at December 31, 1982? Explain.

E14-4. At December 31, 1982, the Stemper Corporation holds the following portfolio of short-term investments in marketable equity securities:

Stock	Date of Purchase	No. of Shares	Original Cost per share	Market value per share 12/31/82
RTD Corp.	06/14/82	200	$10	$14
Rider Corp.	01/15/81	500	25	19
PXZ Corp.	12/16/81	400	18	17
Boh Corp.	03/04/82	600	11	14

At what amount should marketable securities be reported on Stemper's December 31, 1982 balance sheet?

E14-5. On August 23, 1982, the Mayfry Corporation purchased 1,000 shares of Wimble Corporation stock for $25 per share. The Wimble stock is traded on several stock exchanges. Mayfry purchased the stock as a long-term investment. On October 31, the Mayfry Corporation received a cash dividend of $2 per share from the Wimble Corporation. The market value of the Wimble Corporation stock at December 31, 1982 was $23 per share. The stock purchased by Mayfry on August 23 is the only Wimble stock owned by Mayfry and is approximately 10 percent of the total outstanding voting shares of common stock of the Wimble Corporation.

1. Give the entries in the accounts of the Mayfry Corporation to record the purchase of the Wimble Corporation stock, the receipt of the cash dividend, and the adjusting entry to be made at December 31, 1982.

2. What effect do these transactions have on the reported income of the Mayfry Corporation for the year ended December 31, 1982?

E14-6. The Prejean Company owns 1,000 shares of stock of the Ingot Company. During 1982, the Ingot Company reported net income of $80,000 and paid total dividends of $15,000. Give the journal entries that would be made on the books of the Prejean Company for 1982 with respect to Ingot Company investment assuming

1. Prejean Company owns 20 percent of the stock of the Ingot Company and uses the equity method of reporting; and

2. Prejean Company owns 10 percent of the stock of the Ingot Company and uses the cost method of reporting the investment.

E14-7. On July 1, 1982, the Platt Company acquired 100 percent of the outstanding voting common stock of the Slatt Company. From January 1, 1982, to June 30, 1982, the Slatt Company earned net income of $40,000. From July 1, 1982, to December 31, 1982, the Slatt Company earned net income of $60,000. On December 31, 1982, the Slatt Company paid dividends of $5,000. The Platt Company uses the equity method of accounting for the investment.

1. Give the journal entries that would be made on the books of the Platt Company to record its share of the Slatt Company income and its receipt of dividends during 1982, assuming the acquisition was recorded using the purchase method.

2. Give the journal entries that would be made on the books of the Platt Company to record its share of the Slatt Company income and its receipt of dividends during 1982, assuming the acquisition was recorded using the pooling of interests method.

E14-8. On January 1, 1982, the Alpha Corporation purchased 90 percent of the Omega Corporation by issuing 20,000 shares of common stock. The book value of Omega's net assets at the time of purchase was $260,000. Their market value was $300,000. The transaction was recorded using the pooling of interests method. During 1982, the Omega Corporation reported net income of $30,000 and paid cash dividends of $4,000. Prepare all of the entries that would be made on the books of the Alpha Corporation during 1982 with respect to the investment in Omega Corporation, assuming the equity method of accounting is used. Calculate the value of minority interest on a consolidated balance sheet at December 31, 1982.

E14-9. On March 31, 1982, the Prather Company purchased all of the 10,000 outstanding voting shares of stock of the Smither Company. The Prather Company paid $140,000 in cash for the acquisition. Summarized balance sheet data on the two companies immediately before the acquisition is as follows:

	Prather Company	Smither Company
Assets	$600,000	$150,000
Equities		
Liabilities	$ 40,000	$ 10,000
Common stock	300,000	100,000
Retained earnings	260,000	40,000
Total equities	$600,000	$150,000

1. Give the entry in the accounts of the Prather Company to record the acquisition of this long-term investment assuming the purchase method is used.

2. Prepare a consolidation worksheet immediately after acquisition using the purchase method.

E14-10. The Larson Manufacturing Company has invested in the equity securities of several other corporations. Details of these investments are as follows:

a. 1,000 shares of the LBD Corporation were purchased on the open market as a short-term investment of idle cash.

b. 55 percent of the stock of the Micro Parts Corporation was purchased to assure Larson of an uninterrupted supply of parts essential to its manufacturing process.

c. 20 percent of the stock of Acme Distributing Corporation was purchased so that Larson might influence key policies of the company.

d. 10 percent of the stock of Alternate Power Corporation, a closed corporation whose stock is not traded on any market, was purchased as a long-term investment.

e. 90 percent of the stock of the Usry Finance Corporation was purchased so that Larson could assure major customers of financing, if necessary.

f. 5 percent of the stock of the Zeta Corporation, a publicly held corporation whose stock is traded on several markets, was purchased as a long-term investment.

For each of the investments listed above, indicate whether the Larson Manufacturing Company should report the investment using the cost method, the lower of cost or market method, the equity method, or consolidated financial statements. Justify your answers.

Problems

P14-1. In early 1981, the Krantz Company purchased some stock as a short-term investment. Prior to 1981, the Krantz Company owned no short-term marketable equity securities. At December 31, 1981, the Krantz Company held the following portfolio of short-term marketable equity securities.

Stock	No. of Shares	Cost per Share	Market Value per Share at 12/31/81
L Corp.	1,000	$20	$17
M Corp.	2,000	15	16

On June 1, 1982, 1,000 shares of M Corporation stock were sold for $17 per share. On December 31, 1982, information on the portfolio of short-term investments was as follows:

Stock	No. of Shares	Cost per Share	Market Value per Share at 12/31/82
L Corp.	1,000	$20	$20
M Corp.	1,000	15	18

Required:

1. Give the adjusting entry, if any, that would be made on the books of the Krantz Company at December 31, 1981, with respect to short-term marketable equity securities.

2. Give the journal entry that would be made on the books of the Krantz Company on June 1, 1982, to record the sale of the M Corporation stock.

3. Give the adjusting entry, if any, that would be made on the books of the Krantz Company at December 31, 1982, with respect to short-term marketable equity securities.

P14-2. During 1982, the Delp Company purchased marketable equity securities of several companies. Prior to 1982, the Delp company owned no such securities. The purchases made during 1982 were: 500 shares of L Company stock at $20 per share; 1,000 shares of M Company stock at $15 per share; and 750 shares of N Company stock at $10 per share. The Delp Company intends to hold these stocks as long-term investments. The purchases did not give the Delp Company influence or control over the L, M, or N companies. For the year ended December 31, 1982, the L Company reported net income of $100,000 and paid dividends of $.20 per share; the M Company reported net income of $270,000 and paid dividends of $.50 per share; and the N Company reported net income of $80,000 and paid no dividends. On December 31, 1982, L Company stock was selling for $21 per share; M Company stock was selling for $10 per share, and N Company stock was selling for $8 per share.

Required:

1. What method should the Delp Company use in reporting these investments?

2. Give the journal entries the Delp Company would make to record the purchase of the stock assuming cash was paid at the time of acquisition.

3. Give the journal entries the Delp Company would make to record its share of the net income and/or dividends of the L, M, and N companies.

4. Give any adjusting entry that the Delp Company would have to make at December 31, 1982, with respect to these investments. Does this entry affect the income of the Delp Company? Explain.

P14-3. On January 1, 1982, the Formidable Corporation purchased 100 percent of the outstanding common stock of the Diminutive Corporation. The Formidable Corporation purchased the Diminutive Corporation for an amount equal to the book value of Diminutive's net assets. The Formidable Corporation has decided to use the equity method of accounting for its investment in Diminutive Corporation. Comparative balance sheets of the two companies at December 31, 1981 and December 31, 1982, are presented below.

DIMINUTIVE CORPORATION
Balance Sheets

	Dec. 31, 1981	Dec. 31, 1982
Assets		
Cash	$ 50,000	$ 76,000
Accounts receivable	75,000	82,000
Inventories	115,000	136,000
Property, plant, and equipment (net of		
depreciation)	364,000	352,000
Total assets	$ 604,000	$ 646,000
Equities		
Current liabilities	$ 92,000	$ 81,000
Common stock (no par)	250,000	250,000
Retained earnings	262,000	315,000
Total equities	$ 604,000	$ 646,000

FORMIDABLE CORPORATION
Balance Sheets

	Dec. 31, 1981	Dec. 31, 1982
Assets		
Cash	$ 800,000	$ 200,000
Accounts receivable	421,000	569,000
Inventories	1,677,000	1,739,000
Investment in Diminutive Corp.	—	565,000
Property, plant, and equipment (net of		
depreciation)	3,756,000	3,942,000
Total assets	$6,654,000	$7,013,000
Equities		
Current liabilities	$ 968,000	$ 864,000
Bonds payable	1,000,000	1,000,000
Common stock (no par)	1,500,000	1,500,000
Retained earnings	3,186,000	3,649,000
Total equities	$6,654,000	$7,013,000

For the year ended December 31, 1982, the net income and dividends for the two corporations were as follows:

	Diminutive Corp.	Formidable Corp.
Net income	$ 65,000	$ 543,000
Dividends	12,000	80,000

Required:

1. How much did Formidable Corporation pay for the acquisition of the Diminutive Corporation? Prepare the journal entry to record the acquisition on Formidable's books.

2. By how much did the investment in Diminutive Corporation change during 1982 subsequent to the acquisition? Prepare the journal entries to record these changes on the books of the Formidable Corporation.

3. By how much did the total owners' equity of the Diminutive Corporation change during 1982? Explain these changes.

4. What is the amount of net income to be reported on the consolidated income statement of the Formidable Corporation and subsidiary for the year ended December 31, 1982?

P14-4. On August 15, 1982, the Vidal Corporation purchased 5,000 shares of voting common stock of the BDC Corporation for $10 per share. The Vidal Corporation intends to hold the stock as a long-term investment. For the year ended December 31, 1982, the BDC Corporation reported net income of $250,000, and paid dividends of $.50 per share on December 31, 1982. The market value of the BDC Corporation stock on December 31, 1982 was $9 per share. The BDC stock is the only stock owned by the Vidal Corporation.

Required:

Give the method that should be used by Vidal for reporting the investment and give all of the journal entries that would be made on the books of the Vidal Corporation during 1982 with respect to the BDC stock in each of the following independent situations:

1. The BDC stock is not readily marketable, and 5,000 shares are 10 percent of the total outstanding voting common stock.

2. The BDC stock is readily marketable, and 5,000 shares are 10 percent of the total outstanding voting common stock.

3. The BDC stock is readily marketable, and 5,000 shares are 20 percent of the total outstanding voting common stock.

4. The BDC stock is readily marketable, and 5,000 shares are 80 percent of the total outstanding voting common stock.

P14-5. On July 31, 1982, the Piker Corporation acquired all of the common stock of the Sique Corporation. Immediately before the acquisition, the balance sheets of the two companies were as follows:

	Piker Corp.	Sique Corp.
Assets		
Cash	$285,000	$ 10,000
Receivables (net)	65,000	54,000
Inventories	156,000	96,000
Operational assets (net)	274,000	150,000
Total assets	$780,000	$310,000
Equities		
Current liabilities	$ 60,000	$ 45,000
Long-term debt	120,000	95,000
Common stock	480,000	100,000
Retained earnings	120,000	70,000
Total equities	$780,000	$310,000

The fair value of the Sique Corporation's inventory at July 31, 1982, is $110,000. All other assets and liabilities of the Sique Corporation have a fair value equal to their balance sheet value.

Required:

1. Prepare the entry to be made on the Piker Corporation books to record the acquisition using the purchase method, assuming that it paid $184,000 in cash for the stock of the Sique Corporation.

2. Prepare the consolidation elimination entry that would appear on a worksheet to prepare a consolidated balance sheet immediately after the acquisition, assuming the facts in Requirement 1.

3. Prepare the entry to be made on the Piker Corporation books to record the acquisition using the pooling of interests method, assuming Piker issued 17,000 previously unissued shares of its $10 par value stock (market value of $12 per share) for the Sique Corporation stock.

4. Prepare the consolidation elimination entry that would appear on a worksheet to prepare a consolidated balance sheet immediately after the acquisition, assuming the facts in Requirement 3.

P14-6. On October 31, 1982, the Portsmith Corporation acquired all of the outstanding stock of the Strifer Corporation by issuing 40,000 shares of Portsmith stock with a market value of $20 per share. The individual balance sheets of the two companies immediately prior to the combination are presented below.

	Portsmith Corp.	Strifer Corp.
Assets		
Cash	$ 250,000	$ 100,000
Receivables	400,000	210,000
Inventories	740,000	520,000
Property, plant, and equipment (net)	1,960,000	820,000
Total assets	$3,350,000	$1,650,000
Equities		
Current liabilities	$ 310,000	$ 170,000
Long-term debt	890,000	680,000
Common stock	1,500,000	600,000
Retained earnings	650,000	200,000
Total equities	$3,350,000	$1,650,000

The fair values of all items on the Strifer Corporation's balance sheet are equal to their balance sheet values.

Required:

1. Prepare the entry to be made on the books of the Portsmith Corporation to record the acquisition, assuming that 100 percent of the Strifer Corporation stock was acquired and the purchase method is used.

2. Prepare a consolidated balance sheet worksheet for the Portsmith Corporation and consolidated subsidiary Strifer Corporation at November 1, 1982.

P14-7. On December 31, 1981, the Proxmire Corporation acquired 80 percent of the outstanding stock of the Shafter Corporation for $130,000 in cash. The individual balance sheets of the two corporations immediately prior to the acquisition are given below.

	Proxmire Corp.	Shafter Corp.
Assets		
Cash	$210,000	$ 30,000
Receivables (net)	80,000	50,000
Inventories	100,000	40,000
Property, plant, and equipment (net)	310,000	120,000
Total assets	$700,000	$240,000
Equities		
Payables	$ 50,000	$ 20,000
Other current liabilities	35,000	10,000
Long-term debt	155,000	60,000
Common stock	300,000	100,000
Retained earnings	160,000	50,000
Total equities	$700,000	$240,000

All assets and liabilities of the Shafter Corporation have fair values equal to their book values.

Required:

1. Prepare the journal entry to be made on the books of the Proxmire Corporation to record the acquisition.

2. Prepare a consolidated balance sheet worksheet for the Proxmire Corporation and subsidiary Shafter Corporation at January 1, 1982.

3. Prepare the consolidated balance sheet for the Proxmire Corporation and subsidiary at January 1, 1982.

P14-8. On January 1, 1982, the Plait Company acquired 100 percent of the outstanding common stock of the Sosser Company for $225,000 in cash. At the time of the acquisition, the book value of each asset and liability on the Sosser Company's books was equal to its fair value, and the Sosser Company's owners' equity was as follows:

Common stock	$200,000
Retained earnings	25,000

At December 31, 1982, the financial statements of the two companies were as follows:

	Plait Co.	Sosser Co.
Income Statements		
Sales	$350,000	$ 80,000
Equity in income of Sosser Co.	10,000	—
Total revenues	360,000	80,000
Cost of goods sold	190,000	46,000
Other expenses	110,000	24,000
Total expenses	300,000	70,000
Net income	$ 60,000	$ 10,000

Balance Sheets

Assets

Cash	$ 60,000	$ 20,000
Accounts receivable	45,000	25,000
Inventories	115,000	85,000
Investment in Sosser Co.	230,000	—
Property, plant, and equipment (net)	320,000	120,000
Total assets	$770,000	$250,000

Equities

Current liabilities	$ 75,000	$ 20,000
Long-term debt	150,000	—
Common stock	400,000	200,000
Retained earnings	145,000	30,000
Total equities	$770,000	$250,000

During 1982, the Sosser Company paid dividends of $5,000, and the Plait Company paid dividends of $10,000.

Required:

1. Prepare the journal entries that were made on the books of the Plait Company during 1982 to record the acquisition of the Sosser Company, and the Plait Company's share of Sosser's net income. The Plait company uses the equity method to record its investment in the Sosser Company.

2. Verify that these entries were made on Plait's books by: (a) setting up T accounts for the investment in Sosser Company and equity in income of Sosser Company; (b) posting entries given in Requirement 1 to these accounts; and (c) comparing the balances in these accounts with those shown in the Plait Company financial statements.

3. Prepare a worksheet to develop a consolidated income statement and a consolidated statement of retained earnings for the year ended December 31, 1982, and a consolidated balance sheet at December 31, 1982.

P14-9. At December 31, 1981, the Beta Corporation held no investments in securities. During 1982, Beta was involved in the following transactions involving investments in marketable securities:

April	*1*	Purchased $6,000 of 8 percent, ten-year bonds of the **AB** Corporation at face value. Interest payment dates are March 31 and September 30.
June	*20*	Purchased 500 of the 80,000 outstanding shares of stock of the **DE** Corporation for $10 per share.
August	*8*	Purchased 100 of the 20,000 outstanding shares of stock of the **GH** Corporation for $25 per share.
September 30		Received the semiannual interest payment on the AB Corporation bonds.
December 31		Received a cash dividend of $2 per share on the GH Corporation stock. Market value of the securities at December 31 were as follows:

Security	Market
AB Corp. bonds	100%
DE Corp. stock	$5
GH Corp. stock	$30

Required:

1. Prepare all of the entries to be made on the books of the Beta Corporation during 1982 with respect to its investments, assuming that all investments are short-term.

2. Prepare all of the entries to be made on the books of the Beta Corporation during 1982 with respect to its investments, assuming that all investments are long-term.

3. What would be the effect of these transactions on Beta Corporation's pretax income for 1982 if the securities were classified as short-term? What would be the effect if the securities were classified as long-term?

CHAPTER 15

Statement of Changes in Financial Position

Chapter Outline

15.1 *Overview of the Statement of Changes in Financial Position.* Discusses the need for a fourth basic financial statement to explain the differences between successive balance sheets; presents the structure of this new statement; illustrates the concepts with the statement of changes in financial position for General Motors.

15.2 *Sources and Uses of Funds.* Presents the basic sources of funds: (1) sale of noncurrent assets, (2) issue of debt, (3) issue of stock, (4) successful operations; presents the basic uses of funds: (1) purchase of noncurrent assets, (2) retirement of debt, (3) dividends, and (4) unsuccessful operations; explains the relationship between net income and working capital from operations.

15.3 *T Account Approach to Statement Preparation.* Develops procedure to prepare statement: (1) calculate change in working capital, (2) prepare T accounts for accounts with a change, (3) add T accounts for funds from operations and funds flow summary, (4) reproduce entries that gave rise to changes, (5) prepare statement using funds from operations and funds flow summary T accounts.

15.4 *Conversion from Working Capital Basis to Cash Basis.* Contrasts statement on a working capital basis with cash basis; explains relationship between working capital from operations and cash from operations; presents T account approach to develop statement on a cash basis from a working capital basis.

15.5 *Interpretation of the Statement of Changes in Financial Position.* Discusses implications of the statement; emphasizes the importance of the mix of sources and uses of funds; presents examples of statements reflecting expanding and contracting firms, plus successful and unsuccessful firms.

Accounting and the Real World

Who Reads What in Annual Reports?

In late 1977, the Securities and Exchange Commission released the findings of a landmark study on investor information needs, which was conducted by its Advisory Committee on Corporate Disclosure. This study, involving the participation of nearly 5,000 individual investors, has generated extensive recommendations for reform from within Congress and the SEC. Some results are given below.

Percentage of Respondents Who Read the Section of the Annual Report

Report Section	*Thoroughly*	*Casually*
Income statement	86%	14%
Balance sheet	74	26
Management's description and interpretation	73	27
Statement footnotes	52	48
Statement of changes in financial position	**52**	**48**
Auditor's report	40	60

One important question in the preparation of the statement of changes in financial position is whether a firm should use cash, working capital, or some other quantity as its concept of "funds." To determine preferences, selected financial statement users and preparers were surveyed by mail. Two financial statement user groups were selected: (1) financial analysts, who advise clients on the purchase and sale of stock, and (2) bankers, who lend money. The financial statement preparer group was defined as controllers (that is, the chief accountants) of the Fortune 500 corporations. The question and responses are summarized below.

Assuming that all important changes in financial position are disclosed within the statement of changes in financial position, which of the following do you feel should be emphasized in the statement?

	Financial Analysts	*Bankers*	*Controllers*
Working capital	35%	43%	73%
Cash	65	57	27

525

Some problems with the statement of changes in financial position should be apparent.

Financial Executive, April 1980 ("How Good Are Investor's Data Sources," by Reckers and Stagliano)

The National Public Accountant, February 1975, the official publication of the National Society of Public Accountants

All four basic financial statements were mentioned in Chapter 1, and three of these statements were discussed in Chapter 2. The fourth statement, the statement of changes in financial position, was deferred at that point because it is so complex. Now that the proper groundwork has been laid, this important statement will be discussed in detail. This final statement explains those transactions between balance sheet dates which are not explained by the income statement.

15.1 Overview of the Statement of Changes in Financial Position

Balance sheets often provide the balance in each account for two consecutive years. Thus, for example, the balance sheet might present the amount of cash the company had at the end of 1979 and at the end of 1978. This type of statement is called a **comparative balance sheet** because it compares balance sheets for two consecutive years.

The income statement provides a great deal of information concerning what happened to the company between the time of the two balance sheets; however, as was discussed in Chapter 2, the income statement is limited to only certain types of events (namely, profit-seeking events). For this reason, the income statement cannot and does not fully explain all changes from one balance sheet to the next. For example, the issue of stock and the purchase of equipment do not appear on the income statement.

Thus, the need arises for a financial statement to explain the changes between one balance sheet and the next. Such a statement exists, and it becomes the fourth and final basic financial statement. Because the balance sheet is often called the statement of financial position, this new statement is called the **statement of changes in financial position.** The statement of changes in financial position will explain why the second balance sheet is different from the first.

The statement of changes in financial position is derived from other financial statements, primarily the comparative balance sheets and the income statement, plus some additional information. The statement of changes in financial position is not derived from the adjusted trial balance in the same way that the income statement, statement of retained earnings, and balance sheet are. This new statement must be approached from another direction. Hopeless confusion is inevitable if an attempt is made to force the statement of changes in financial position into the mold of the other three statements.

Figure 15-1 is a statement of changes in financial position for General Motors. Because the corporation consolidates its financial statements with those of its subsidiaries (as discussed in Chapter 14), the title of this statement includes the word *consolidated*.

To give an introductory example of the information this statement provides, consider long-term debt. The comparative balance sheets (not presented) reveal long-term debt decreased by $98.9 million. But long-term debt could have decreased by that amount in an infinite variety of ways. Line 6 of the statement in Figure 15-1 reveals that the company issued $41.3 million in new long-term debt, and Line 15 reveals that the company retired $140.2 million in long-term debt. This issue and retirement explain the change in long-term debt, since $140.2 − $41.3 = $98.9.

Basic Financial Statements

The balance sheets are prepared at specific points in time. In the General Motors example, the times were December 31, 1978, and December 31,

FIGURE 15-1
Statement of Changes in Financial Position for a Large Corporation

General Motors Corporation
Statement of Changes in Consolidated Financial Position
For the Year Ended December 31, 1979
(Dollars in Millions)

Source of Funds

Net income	$2,892.7
Depreciation of real estate, plants and equipment	1,236.9
Amortization of special tools	1,950.4
Deferred income taxes, undistributed earnings of nonconsolidated subsidiaries and associates, etc.—net	(321.2)
Total current operations	5,758.8
Proceeds from issuance of long-term debt	41.3
Proceeds from disposals of property—net	166.9
Proceeds from sale of newly issued common stock	249.9
Other—net	125.4
Total Sources	6,342.3

Application of Funds

Dividends paid to stockholders	1,533.2
Expenditures for real estate, plants and equipment	3,371.8
Expenditures for special tools	2,015.0
Investments in nonconsolidated subsidiaries and associates	542.8
Retirements of long-term debt	140.2
Total Applications	7,603.0
Increase (Decrease) in working capital	($1,260.7)

Increase (Decrease) in Working Capital by Element

Cash, marketable securities and time deposits	($1,068.4)
Accounts and notes receivable	(608.3)
Inventories	499.6
Prepaid expenses	(265.9)
Accounts, drafts and loans payable	307.0
United States, foreign and other income taxes payable	466.2
Accrued liabilities	(590.9)
Increase (Decrease) in working capital	($1,260.7)

Courtesy of General Motors

1979. The income statement covers the time period between balance sheets, but it reflects only **operating events.** There are, however, two additional types of events: financing events and investing events. For example, **financing events** are those where the firm issues stock or debt, usually for cash. Any cash receipt other than from a profit-seeking activity is a financing event. **Investing events,** for example, are those where the firm acquires additional long-term assets, retires debt, or retires stock. Any cash disbursement other than for a profit-seeking activity is an investing event. An example of an investing event would be the payment of cash for a building, while the issue of stock for cash would be a financing event.

It is precisely these financing and investing events that the income statement does not reflect. The concern in this chapter is explaining these changes between successive balance sheets. Changes that result from profit-seeking activities are reflected on the income statement. Other changes result from financing and investing events; these are reflected on the statement of changes in financial position.

Structure of the Statement of Changes in Financial Position

The statement of changes in financial position became a required financial statement in 1971, a relatively recent development in accounting. At that time, the title of the statement was determined and the structure of the statement established.

Funds Defined The statement of changes in financial position is, in a sense, a funds flow statement. Two definitions of funds are possible: (1) funds can be defined as **cash,** and (2) funds can be defined as **working capital.** If funds are defined as cash, the statement reflects cash inflows from financing events and cash outflows for investing events.

The cash definition of funds is used only rarely in financial reporting. As in the General Motors statement in Figure 15-1, most companies define funds as working capital:

$$\text{Funds} = \text{current assets minus current liabilities}$$
$$= \text{working capital}$$

An increase in any current asset (such as cash) would represent an increase in funds, while an increase in any current liability (such as accounts payable) would represent a decrease in funds. Similarly, a decrease in any current asset represents a decrease in funds, while a decrease in any current liability represents an increase in funds.

A working capital definition of funds is intuitively appealing. Working capital represents the amount of "free" current assets, that is, the amount of current assets in excess of the amount necessary to pay off current liabilities. Thus, if working capital goes up, that is "good"; and if working capital goes down, that is "bad."

When a working capital definition of funds is used, the statement must include a schedule explaining the changes within working capital. Figure 15-1 provides such a schedule at the bottom of the statement. Cash and near-cash decreased by $1,068,400,000 during the year; thus, working capital decreased by that amount. Similarly, accounts and notes receivable decreased and, thus, working capital decreased. Inventories, on the other hand, increased, and therefore, working capital increased. Prepaid expenses, the last current asset, decreased and thereby decreased working capital.

Changes in current liabilities have the opposite effect on working capital. Accounts, drafts, and loans payable decreased by $307,000,000. This decrease in a current liability increased working capital. The decrease in income taxes payable had the same effect. On the other hand, accrued liabilities increased by $590,900,000 and, thus, decreased working capital.

Approach Defined Most financing events involve the receipt of cash, and most investing events involve the disbursement of cash; however, there are important exceptions, such as the purchase of equipment by signing a note.

Each noncash financing and investing event can be broken down into both a financing activity and investing activity. Thus, acquiring an asset while incurring a liability can be considered a two-step process: (1) receiving cash by incurring the liability, a financing event, and (2) disbursing cash to buy the asset, an investing event. This duality can be expressed in terms of debits and credits. The following transaction

Equipment	5,000	
Notes payable		5,000

can be thought of as if it occurred in the following two steps

Cash	5,000	
Notes payable		5,000

and

Equipment	5,000	
Cash		5,000

This treatment of a noncash financing and investing event as both a cash financing event and a cash investing event is called the **all financial resources approach.** The basic idea behind the all financial resources approach is to incorporate all significant financing and investing events into the statement of changes in financial position, not just the events having a cash effect. However, for every dollar added as a financing event using the all financial resources approach, a corresponding dollar is added as an investing event. Thus, for these events, sources equal uses and there is no change in funds. The all financial resources approach, however, results in the reporting of these events on the statement of changes in financial position.

Format Specified The basic format of the statement of changes in financial position is as follows:

Sources of funds for the period (financing activities)

− Uses of funds for the period (investing activities)

= Change in funds for the period

The statement for General Motors in Figure 15-1 follows this basic format except that "application of funds" is used as a title instead of "uses of funds."

If funds are defined as cash, the "bottom line" of the statement is the change in the cash figure, which need not be further explained. If funds are defined as working capital, the "bottom line" of the statement is the change in working capital. Because working capital has a number of components, a schedule explaining the change in working capital by component must be included as part of the statement, as it is in Figure 15-1.

Concept Summary

Basic Sources and Uses of Funds		
	Sources	*Uses*
Asset balances which are outside of fund	Decrease (Sale of property)	Increase (Purchase of equipment)
Liability balances which are outside of fund	Increase (Issue debt)	Decrease (Retire debt)
Owners' equity balances	Increase (Issue stock)	Decrease (Pay dividends)
Operations	Positive (Funds from operations)	Negative (Funds used in operations)

15.2 Sources and Uses of Funds

The statement of changes in financial position has three basic components: (1) sources of funds, (2) uses of funds, and (3) change in funds. As shown in Figure 15-1, both the sources of funds section and the uses of funds section will have a number of line items. No matter how many line items appear on a statement, there are four basic sources of funds and four basic uses of funds.

Assets

An asset balance decrease from one balance sheet to the next indicates a source of funds. An example would be the sale of property. In Figure 15-1, General Motors reports proceeds of $166.9 million from the disposal (sale) of property.

An asset balance increase represents a use of funds. An example would be the purchase of equipment. In Figure 15-1, General Motors reports expenditures of $3,371.8 million for real estate, plants, and equipment; expenditures of $2,015 million for special tools; and investments of $542.8 million in unconsolidated subsidiaries. All three correspond to increases in asset balances.

Liabilities

A liability balance increase represents a source of funds. An example would be the issuance of debt. General Motors reports proceeds of $41.3 million from the issuance of debt.

A liability balance decrease represents a use of funds. An example would be the retirement of debt. General Motors reports the retirement of $140.2 million of long-term debt.

Owners' Equity

An owners' equity balance increase represents a source of funds. An example would be the issuance of stock. General Motors reports proceeds of $249.9 million from newly issued common stock.

An owners' equity balance decrease represents a use of funds. Examples would include the purchase of treasury stock or the payment of dividends. General Motors reports payments of $1,533.2 million in dividends to stockholders.

Operations

Operations can be either a source or a use of funds, depending upon the success or the lack of success of operating activities. The funds generated from operations can be derived by making a series of adjustments to the net income figure.

Net income is the difference between revenues and expenses for a period, but not all revenues provide working capital and not all expenses involve the outlay of working capital. For example, depreciation is an expense (and, hence, a deduction on the income statement), but it does not involve the outlay of working capital. Thus, to get **working capital from operations,** depreciation must be added back to net income. Depreciation is not a source of funds; but because it was a deduction to get net income, it must be added back to get working capital from operations.

Thus, deriving working capital from operations involves beginning with net income and making two sets of adjustments. The first set of adjustments is to add back income statement deductions that do not affect working capital. These deductions include depreciation, amortization, depletion, deferred income taxes, amortization of bond discounts, and losses on the sale of noncurrent assets. The second set of adjustments is to subtract out income statement additions that do not affect working capital. These additions include amortization of bond premium, equity in the earnings of unconsolidated subsidiaries in excess of dividends received, and gains on the sale of noncurrent assets. General Motors reports earnings of $2,892.7 million and, after a series of adjustments, reports working capital from operations of $5,758.8 million.

Concept Summary

Schematic of Working Capital from Operations			
Net Income			$X
+ income statement deductions not affecting working capital	Depreciation	$X	
	Amortization	X	
	Depletion	X	
	Deferred income taxes	X	
	Amortization of discount on bonds payable	X	
	Losses on sale of noncurrent assets	X	
– income statement additions not affecting working capital	Amortization of premium on bonds payable	(X)	
	Equity in unconsolidated subsidiary net income	(X)	
	Gains on sale of noncurrent assets	(X)	X
Working Capital from Operations			$X

Transactions Affecting Working Capital

There are three basic types of transactions from a working capital perspective: transactions wholly within working capital, transactions partly within and partly without working capital, and transactions wholly without working capital.

Transaction Wholly Within Working Capital An example of a transaction wholly within working capital would be the collection of an account receivable. This transaction involves an increase in cash, but an equal decrease in accounts receivable. Thus, the total amount of working capital does not change, and the transaction is not reported on the statement of changes in financial position. Similarly, making a short-term bank loan is a transaction wholly within working capital. Cash increases, but a current liability also increases by the same amount. As a result, the amount of working capital does not change, and the transaction is not reported on the statement of changes in financial position. In summary, a transaction wholly within working capital is never relevant to the statement of changes in financial position, working capital basis.

Transaction Partly Within, Partly Without Working Capital An example of a transaction partly within and partly without working capital would be the selling of a building for cash. This transaction involves not only an increase in cash, but also an equal increase in working capital. There is a decrease in an asset, but it is not a current asset. Thus, the decrease does not affect working capital. Because this transaction increases working capital, it will be reported on the statement of changes in financial position.

Suppose a piece of equipment with a book value of $6,000 was sold for $10,000. This should be reported as a source of funds of $10,000, and there would be a separate line item on the statement for sale of equipment.

However, net income would include $4,000 of gain from the sale of this equipment. This gain increased net income but the funds have already been counted in the $10,000 figure. Thus, in determining funds from operations, the $4,000 gain must be subtracted from net income. Similarly, if the same equipment was sold for $5,000, there would be a source of funds of $5,000, and the $1,000 loss would be added to net income to determine funds from operations.

Another transaction of this type would be reclassification of long-term debt as short-term. This transaction occurs when a long-term bond payable becomes due in the upcoming accounting period. Such a transaction involves a decrease in working capital because current liabilities increase. As a result, it is reported on the statement of changes in financial position as a use of working capital.

In summary, a transaction partly within and partly without working capital is always relevant to the statement of changes in financial position, working capital basis.

Transactions Wholly Without Working Capital Examples of transactions wholly without working capital are the purchase of land by issuing stock and equipment by using a note. As discussed earlier, the all financial resources approach breaks these transactions into two parts, both a source and a use of cash. Using the working capital definition of funds, this type of transaction is both a source and use of working capital. Issuing the stock would be reported as a source of working capital, while the purchase of land would be reported as a use of working capital and similarly for the equipment. However, if the transaction wholly without working capital is not a major financing or investing event, it is omitted on the statement of changes in financial position. An example would be the declaration and payment of a stock dividend or a stock split. In summary, a transaction wholly without working capital is relevant to the statement of changes in financial position, working capital basis, if the transaction represents a major financing or investing event. These transactions wholly without working capital are called noncash financing and investing events, or direct exchanges. The all financial resources approach assures the disclosure of these important events on the statement of changes in financial position.

Concept Summary

Transactions that Affect Working Capital		
Type	*Example*	*Relevance*
Wholly within fund	Collecting a receivable	Never relevant
Partly within, partly without fund	Selling a building for cash	Always relevant
Wholly without fund	Acquiring land with stock	Sometimes relevant

15.3   T Account Approach to Statement Preparation

The discussion of the statement of changes in financial position in the last section did not include a systematic procedure for developing the statement. A five-step procedure for developing this statement is discussed in this section. The discussion is based on the income statement, statement of retained earnings, and comparative balance sheets for A Typical Corporation, Inc., given in Figure 15-2.

Step 1: Calculate the Change in Funds

The first step is to calculate the change in funds for the period. The change in funds can be calculated from the comparative balance sheets. It is important to understand that the statement of changes in financial position is not prepared or read to determine the change in funds. This change is

FIGURE 15-2
Sample Financial
Statements

A TYPICAL CORPORATION, INC.
Statements of Income and Retained Earnings
For the Year Ended December 31, 1982

Sales		$234,800
Expenses		
Cost of goods sold	$ 103,900	
Depreciation	6,700	
Interest expense	4,000	
Salaries expense	66,900	
Income taxes	8,500	190,000
Net income		44,800
Retained earnings, December 31, 1981		27,600
Dividends		(33,900)
Retained earnings, December 31, 1982		$ 38,500

A TYPICAL CORPORATION, INC.
Comparative Balance Sheets
December 31

	1982	*1981*
ASSETS		
Cash	$ 15,700	$ 29,300
Accounts receivable	41,000	22,500
Inventory	43,700	27,900
Plant, property, and equipment	58,200	54,500
Accumulated depreciation	(24,000)	(17,300)
Total assets	$ 134,600	$ 116,900
LIABILITIES & OWNERS' EQUITY		
Accounts payable	$ 12,700	$ 7,300
Interest payable	1,100	2,100
Notes payable (short-term)	5,900	2,700
Bank loan payable (long-term)	10,400	13,700
Capital stock	66,000	63,500
Retained earnings	38,500	27,600
Total liabilities & owners' equity	$ 134,600	$ 116,900

determined before the statement is prepared. The "bottom line" of the income statement is the focus of that statement; however, the "bottom line" of the statement of changes in financial position is just a balancing figure.

Step 2: Make a T Account for Each Nonfund Balance Sheet Account with a Change

The second step is to make a T account for each nonfund balance sheet account with a change, enter the changes for each account, mark each change with a △, and draw a line. The resulting T accounts are shown in the top portion of Figure 15-3. It is important to realize that these T accounts are merely mechanical aids. They should not be confused with general ledger accounts.

The statement of changes in financial position reconciles changes in account balances. Thus, each account must have the amount of change so there will be a figure to reconcile. The △ is placed next to the figure to indicate that it is a change in account balance rather than a transaction

FIGURE 15-3
T Accounts for
Statement Preparation,
Working Capital Basis

A TYPICAL CORPORATION, INC.

Plant, property, and equipment		Accumulated depreciation	
△ 3,700			6,700 △
C 3,700			6,700 B

Bank loan payable	Capital stock	Retained earnings
△ 3,300	2,500 △	10,900 △
E 3,300	2,500 F	D 33,900 / 44,800 A

Funds from operations

(net income) A	44,800
(depreciation) B	6,700
funds from operations	51,500

Funds flow summary

(issue of stock) F	2,500	3,700	C (purchase of equipment)
		33,900	D (declaration of dividends)
		3,300	E (repayment of bank loan)
	2,500	40,900	
	51,500		
sources	54,000	40,900	uses

amount or a balance in the account. Finally, a line is placed under the figure to distinguish between the change figure and the entries that will be made below the line to explain the change. These entries appear in Figure 15-3.

Step 3: Prepare Two New T Accounts

The third step is to prepare two new T accounts, one for funds from operations and one, a funds flow summary. These two accounts will be used to prepare the statement of changes in financial position as follows:

1. A debit in funds from operations represents an increase in funds from profit-seeking activities.

2. A credit in funds from operations represents a decrease in funds from profit-seeking activities.

3. A debit in funds flow summary represents a source of funds from a financing event.

4. A credit in funds flow summary represents a use of funds for an investing event.

These new accounts are at the bottom of Figure 15-3.

Step 4: Reproduce Entries

The fourth step is to *reproduce* the entries that gave rise to the changes in account balances. This step utilizes the two T accounts prepared in Step 3. The two rules to follow are:

Rule 1: Use *funds from operations* for every debit or credit to an income statement account.

Rule 2: Use *funds flow summary* for every debit or credit to an account within the fund (current asset or current liability).

The entries for A Typical Corporation, Inc., appear as labeled in Figure 15-3.

A. Net income is the first item on the statement of changes in financial position, so that entry is made first. Net income is recorded as a credit to retained earnings, while the corresponding debit (usually income summary) must go to funds from operations **(Rule 1).**

B. Depreciation is an expense and, therefore, reduced net income. However, depreciation is only a bookkeeping entry and does not involve the outlay or outflow of working capital. As a result, it must be added back to net income. The original entry was a debit to depreciation expense and a credit to accumulated depreciation. This entry is reproduced by debiting funds from operations **(Rule 1)** and by crediting accumulated depreciation.

C. The property, plant, and equipment account increased by $3,700. This indicates a purchase of equipment which is a use of working capital. The entry is reproduced by debiting plant, property, and equipment and crediting funds flow summary **(Rule 2)** in the place of cash.

D. As shown on the statement of retained earnings, there was a payment of $33,900 in dividends, which is a use of working capital. To reproduce the entry involves debiting retained earnings and crediting funds flow summary **(Rule 2)** in the place of cash.

E. The bank loan payable decreased by $3,300. This was a use of working capital because the loan is noncurrent. If the loan was current (like the notes payable in this same example), there would be no use of working capital because the transaction would be wholly within the fund. To reproduce the entry involves debiting bank loan payable for $3,300 and crediting funds flow summary by $3,300 **(Rule 2)** instead of cash.

F. Capital stock increased by $2,500, indicating an issue of stock. This is a source of funds. Funds flow summary is debited for $2,500 **(Rule 2)** replacing cash, and capital stock is credited for $2,500.

All changes in account balances from the comparative balance sheets are now fully explained. The balances in the two T accounts, funds from operations and funds flow summary, can now be determined. As an arithmetic check, the difference between the debits and credits in these T accounts should equal the change in working capital. For the example company, the difference is $51,500 − $38,400 = $13,100, which is the change in working capital.

Step 5: Prepare the Statement of Changes in Financial Position

The fifth step is to prepare the statement of changes in financial position from the funds from operations and funds flow summary accounts. All of the information necessary for the preparation of the statement is now available in these two T accounts. The resulting statement is given in Figure 15-4, together with a **schedule of changes in working capital.**

Concept Summary

Steps in Preparation of Statement of Changes in Financial Position
1. Calculate the change in funds for the period.
2. Make a T account for all nonfund balance sheet accounts with a change; enter the change for each account; mark the change with a △; and draw a line.
3. Prepare two new T accounts, one for funds from operations and one for funds flow summary.
4. Reproduce entries that gave rise to the change in account balances with the following substitutions: a. Use funds from operations for every debit or credit to an income statement account. b. Use funds flow summary for every debit or credit to a working capital account.
5. Prepare the statement of changes in financial position from funds from operations and funds flow summary.

FIGURE 15-4
Working Capital
Statement

A TYPICAL CORPORATION, INC.
Statement of Changes in Financial Position, Working Capital Basis
For the Year Ended December 31, 1982

Sources of funds

Operations
Net income $44,800
Depreciation 6,700
Total funds from operations $51,500
Issuance of capital stock   2,500
Total sources of funds   54,000

Uses of funds

Purchase of equipment 3,700
Declaration of dividends 33,900
Repayment of bank loan 3,300
Total uses of funds   40,900
Increase in working capital $13,100

Schedule of Changes in Working Capital
December 31

	1982	1981	Increase (Decrease)
Cash	$ 15,700	$29,300	$(13,600)
Accounts receivable	41,000	22,500	18,500
Inventory	43,700	27,900	15,800
Total current assets	100,400	79,700	
Accounts payable	12,700	7,300	(5,400)
Interest payable	1,100	2,100	1,000
Notes payable	5,900	2,700	(3,200)
Total current liabilities	19,700	12,100	
Working capital	$ 80,700	$67,600	$ 13,100

15.4   Conversion from Working Capital Basis to Cash Basis

As discussed in Section 15.1, the statement of changes in financial position can be prepared on either the working capital basis or the cash basis. Even though the working capital basis is used most often, cash basis statements are sometimes reported. The T account approach to the conversion from the working capital basis to the cash basis is described in this section.

The primary difference between the two bases is traceable to the difference between **working capital from operations** and **cash from operations.** As presented in section 15.2, transactions wholly within working capital are not reported on the statement of changes in financial position using the working capital basis. An example would be the payment of accounts payable.

When the working capital basis is being used, such transactions are not reported, but they do represent uses of cash and are reported under the cash basis. Cash from operations can be derived by adjusting the working capital from operations figure for changes in noncash current assets and liabilities that are related to operations.

Most current assets and current liabilities are related to profit-seeking operations. There are, however, two primary exceptions: marketable securities and notes payable.

1. Marketable securities are not related to normal profit-seeking activity. This current asset can be bought and sold independently of other operations with a resulting effect on cash. An increase in marketable securities is a use of cash and a decrease in marketable securities is a source of cash.

2. Notes payable are not related to operations the way accounts payable and interest payable are. Borrowing money and repaying it, even on a short-term basis, does not lead to revenue or expense. Any interest, however, does give rise to expense; hence, interest payable is related to operations. An increase in notes payable is a source of cash and a decrease in notes payable is a use of cash.

Concept Summary

Schematic of Cash from Operations		
Working Capital from Operations		$X
+ 1. Decreases in noncash current assets related to operations (all except marketable securities)	$ X	
2. Increases in current liabilities related to operations (all except notes payable)	X	
− 1. Increases in noncash current assets related to operations (all except marketable securities)	(X)	
2. Decreases in current liabilities related to operations (all except notes payable)	(X)	X
Cash From Operations		$X

There is a five-step procedure to prepare the statement of changes in financial position, cash basis, from the statement of changes in financial position, working capital basis. These steps are described below and illustrated with the example used in Section 15.3, A Typical Corporation, Inc.

Step 1: Calculate the Change in Cash

The first step is to calculate the change in cash for the period. This calculation provides the "bottom line" figure of the statement of changes in financial position, cash basis. This "bottom line" is merely a balancing figure for the statement. From the comparative balance sheets in Figure 15-2, the cash balance decreased by $13,600.

Step 2: Make a T Account for Each Noncash Working Capital Account with a Change

The second step is to make a T account for each noncash *working capital* account with a change, enter the changes for each account, mark the change with a △, and draw a line. These T accounts represent the noncash accounts not included in the preparation of the statement on a working capital basis. Figure 15-5 demonstrates these T accounts for the sample company.

Step 3: Prepare Two New T Accounts

The third step is to prepare two new T accounts, one for cash from operations and one for cash flow summary. These T accounts will begin with all of the information in the funds from operations and funds flow summary T accounts and are shown in Figure 15-3. Additional entries will be made to these T accounts.

Step 4: Reproduce Entries

The fourth step is to reproduce the entries that gave rise to the changes in the new account balances. The rules that apply here are similar to those used in the working capital case:

FIGURE 15-5
T Accounts for Statement Preparation, Cash Basis

A TYPICAL CORPORATION, INC.

Accounts receivable	Inventory	Accounts payable
△ 18,500	△ 15,800	5,400 △
G 18,500	H 15,800	5,400 I

Interest payable	Notes payable
△ 1,000	3,200 △
J 1,000	3,200 K

Cash from operations

(net income)	A 44,800	18,500 G	(increase in accounts receivable)
(depreciation)	B 6,700	15,800 H	(increase in inventory)
(increase in accounts payable)	I 5,400	1,000 J	(decrease in interest payable)
cash from operations	21,600		

Cash flow summary

(issue of stock)	F 2,500	3,700 C	(purchase of equipment)
(increase in short-term borrowings)	K 3,200	33,900 D	(declaration of dividends)
		3,300 E	(repayment of bank loan)
	5,700	40,900	
	21,600		
sources	27,300	40,900	uses

Rule 1: Use cash from operations for every debit or credit to an income statement account.

Rule 2: Use cash flow summary for every debit or credit to cash.

Entries A through F are the same as the entries for the working capital case. Additional entries include G through K.

G. Accounts receivable increased by $18,500. This indicates uncollected credit sales of this amount. Uncollected credit sales do not provide cash, but they do provide working capital because accounts receivable is included in working capital. The original entry was a debit to accounts receivable and a credit to sales revenue. This entry is reproduced by debiting accounts receivable and by crediting cash from operations **(Rule 1).**

H. Inventory increased by $15,800, and this increased working capital without providing cash. Because this increase represents purchases of inventory items which were not sold and, therefore, not a part of cost of goods sold, the entry is reproduced by debiting inventory and crediting cash from operations **(Rule 1).**

I. Accounts payable increased by $5,400, thus reducing working capital but not affecting cash. The original entry was, in essence, a debit to cost of goods sold (through purchases) and a credit to accounts payable. The entry is reproduced by debiting cash from operations **(Rule 1)** and crediting accounts payable.

J. Interest payable decreased by $1,000, thus increasing working capital without increasing cash. Interest expense is part of the entry that creates interest payable. Thus, reproducing the entry involves debiting interest payable and crediting cash from operations **(Rule 1).**

K. Notes payable increased by $3,200. This account, unlike the others, is not related to operations. To reproduce the entry involves debiting cash flow summary **(Rule 2)** and crediting notes payable.

All changes in account balances are now fully explained. The balances in the cash from operations and cash flow summary T accounts can now be determined. As an arithmetic check, the debit and credit differences in these T account balances should equal the change in cash. The amounts in Figure 15-5 give a difference of $40,900 − $27,300 = $13,600, which is the decrease in cash.

Step 5: Prepare the Statement of Changes in Financial Position

The fifth step is to prepare the statement of changes in financial position from the cash from operations and cash flow summary accounts. All of the information necessary for the preparation of the statement is now available in the two T accounts, cash from operations and cash flow summary. The resulting statement is given in Figure 15-6.

FIGURE 15-6
Cash Basis Statement

A TYPICAL CORPORATION, INC.
Statement of Changes in Financial Position, Cash Basis
For the Year Ended December 31, 1982

Sources of Cash

Operations

Net income	$ 44,800	
Depreciation	6,700	
Increase in accounts payable	5,400	
Increase in accounts receivable	(18,500)	
Increase in inventory	(15,800)	
Decrease in interest payable	(1,000)	
Total cash from operations		$21,600
Increase in short-term borrowings		3,200
Issue of capital stock		2,500
Total sources of cash		27,300

Uses of cash

Purchase of equipment	3,700	
Payment of dividends	33,900	
Repayment of bank loan	3,300	
Total uses of cash		40,900
Decrease in cash		$13,600

15.5 Interpretation of the Statement of Changes in Financial Position

The statement of changes in financial position provides valuable information if the user reads it carefully and views the statement as a whole. Even though both the income statement and the statement of changes in financial position describe activities for the accounting period, the income statement is easier to interpret because there is one summary, or "bottom line" figure, namely net income. Over the years, this net income figure has become the most important piece of financial information about a company.

The statement of changes in financial position does not have such a useful, summary, "bottom line" figure. The figure at the bottom of the statement, the change in funds for the period, could easily be calculated without the statement, directly from the comparative balance sheets. As a result, the information provided by the statement of changes in financial position is more subtle and more difficult to interpret. The interpretation of the statement of changes in financial position is discussed and illustrated in the remainder of this chapter.

Retailer, Inc.

Figure 15-7 is the statement of changes in financial position for Retailer, Inc., for two years. Casually glancing at the bottom figure of each statement ($5,000,000 and $72,000,000, respectively) might lead one to believe that the firm did not do well in 1981, but did much better in 1982. This conclusion would be in error.

1981 The statement in 1981 portrays a normal business year. The firm had net income of $38,000,000. After adding back expenses that did not involve the outlay of working capital, working capital from operations can be computed. Depreciation was $12,000,000 and reflected the allocation of past costs, not a working capital outflow. Deferred income taxes of $2,000,000, while treated as a current expense, will not be paid until the indefinite future and do not affect working capital. Thus, the firm generated $52,000,000 in working capital from operations. The firm did not borrow money or generate any other funds, so the total sources of funds were $52,000,000.

The firm paid $21,000,000 to its stockholders as dividends. Thus, dividends are 55 percent of net income and 40 percent of working capital from operations. These figures are common for a mature firm, that is, one that is no longer growing rapidly.

The firm also spent $26,000,000 to purchase new property, plant, and equipment. Depreciation is often considered a measure of the consumption of assets. As a result, it may appear that, with depreciation of $12,000,000 and new purchases of $26,000,000, the firm is greatly expanding its capacity. However, depreciation is the allocation of past acquisition costs, which were substantially lower than present costs. For this reason, it will typically take more than $12,000,000 just to replace the assets consumed in 1981. Further investigation would be necessary, but this appears to be only a modest increase in capacity. Again, this is normal for a mature firm.

The total uses of funds are, therefore, $47,000,000, and the firm shows a small increase of $5,000,000 in working capital. This additional working capital will probably be needed to finance the somewhat higher level of operations. Again, this is typical for a mature firm.

FIGURE 15-7
Retailer, Inc.

	1982	1981
RETAILER, INC. Statement of Changes in Financial Position, Working Capital Basis Year Ended December 31 Amounts in Thousands		
Sources of funds		
Operations		
Net income	$ 3,500	$ 38,000
Depreciation	13,500	12,000
Deferred income taxes	3,000	2,000
Total funds from operations	20,000	52,000
Issuance of long-term debt	100,000	–0–
Total sources of funds	120,000	52,000
Uses of funds		
Dividends	21,000	21,000
Purchase of property, plant, and equipment	27,000	26,000
Total uses of funds	48,000	47,000
Increase in working capital	$ 72,000	$ 5,000

In summary, then, 1981 appears to be a normal year for Retailer, Inc. There is a normal payout of dividends, there is a modest increase in capacity, and there is a corresponding modest increase in working capital.

1982 The statement in 1982 portrays a bad operating year made worse by bad financing and investing decisions. The firm has net income of $3,500,000, less than 10 percent of the net income of the previous year. After adding back expenses not involving the outlay of working capital, the firm has working capital generated from operations of $20,000,000. This is approximately 40 percent of the working capital from operations generated in the previous year.

Retailer, Inc., has total sources of funds in 1982 of $120,000,000, up from $52,000,000 in 1981; however, in 1982, the firm borrowed $100,000,000. As a result, more funds are available in 1982 than 1981, but this is traceable to a large financing activity.

To keep shareholders happy, most firms try to maintain a consistent dividend policy. Many shareholders count on receiving their dividend checks on a regular basis and make plans based upon the expectation of that income. They dislike an unpleasant surprise in the form of a reduced dividend. Retailer, Inc., paid $21,000,000 in dividends in 1982, the same amount as in 1981; however, for this company, maintaining the dividend payout is a major error. Dividends are larger than net income, so the firm is disbursing to owners more assets than it created. Even more striking, dividends are larger than working capital from operations. In essence, then, the firm is borrowing money to pay dividends to its owners. This is bad financial practice and may hurt the credit rating of the firm, as well as the price of its stock, and could threaten its future.

The company purchased $27,000,000 of property, plant, and equipment in 1982, approximately the same amount as in 1981. As a result, the total uses of funds for 1982 are roughly the same as in 1981. Thus, the firm increased its working capital by $72,000,000 in 1982, up from $5,000,000 in 1981. However, 1982 was an extremely poor year: the only reason working capital increased at all was because the firm borrowed $100,000,000 of long-term debt.

Wholesaler, Inc.

Figure 15-8 is the statement of changes in financial position for Wholesaler, Inc., for the year ended December 31, 1981, using both the working capital basis and the cash basis. This company is small, but rapidly expanding. In a situation like this, the cash basis statement provides important additional information for financial statement users.

Working Capital Basis The working capital basis statement shows rapid growth for the company in 1981. The firm generated $75,000 in funds from operations and borrowed $250,000 on a long-term basis. Thus, the firm had total sources of working capital of $325,000.

The firm paid $15,000 in dividends, which is 30 percent of net income and 20 percent of funds from operations. For the mature business, Retailer, Inc., dividends were 55 percent of net income and 40 percent of funds from

FIGURE 15-8
Wholesaler, Inc.

WHOLESALER, INC.
Statement of Changes in Financial Position
Year Ended December 31, 1981

	Working Capital Basis		Cash Basis	
Sources of funds				
Operations				
Net income	$ 50,000		$ 50,000	
Depreciation	25,000		25,000	
Increase in accounts payable			60,000	
Increase in accounts receivable ...			(90,000)	
Increase in inventory			(25,000)	
Total funds from operations		$ 75,000		$ 20,000
Issuance of long-term debt		250,000		250,000
Total sources of funds		325,000		270,000
Uses of funds				
Dividends	15,000		15,000	
Purchase of property, plant, and				
equipment	275,000		275,000	
Total uses of funds		290,000		290,000
Increase (decrease) in funds		$ 35,000		$(20,000)

operations. As these statements show, rapidly expanding businesses generally have lower dividend payouts than do mature businesses. The reason is that expanding firms need the cash for the purchase of additional inventory and fixed assets necessary for expansion.

The company purchased $275,000 of property, plant, and equipment. These new assets total more than the amount of new debt. Thus, the new assets were financed both by funds generated by operations and by borrowed funds.

The uses of funds total was $290,000, so there was a net increase in working capital of $35,000. Such an increase would be necessary for an expanding business to finance a higher level of operations.

Cash Basis Even though the working capital basis is used by most companies, it is sometimes useful to focus on a cash definition of funds. Cash is necessary for a business to pay its suppliers and employees. Payments to employees cannot be delayed. When a business is expanding, it often has enough working capital but not enough cash on hand to meet obligations as they arise.

Wholesaler, Inc., had a typical experience for a growing firm: (1) net income was $50,000; (2) working capital increased by $35,000; but (3) the cash balance decreased by $20,000. This cash situation is extremely serious. One way to become bankrupt is for liabilities to exceed assets; however, it is also possible to become bankrupt when the firm does not have enough cash to pay bills when they are due. The cash basis statement of changes in financial position can explain the change in cash during an accounting period and why cash decreased while net income was positive and working capital increased. Figure 15-8 provides the cash basis statement parallel to the working capital basis statement.

Concept Summary

Interpreting the Funds Statement

W. T. Grant's profitability, turnover, and liquidity ratios had trended downward over the ten years preceding bankruptcy. But the most striking characteristic of the company during that decade was that it generated no cash internally. Although working capital provided by operations remained fairly stable through 1973, this figure can be a very poor indicator of a company's ability to generate cash. Through 1973, the W. T. Grant Company's operations were a net user, rather than provider, of cash.

Grant's continuing inability to generate cash from operations should have provided investors with an early signal of problems. Yet, as recently as 1973, Grant stock was selling at nearly twenty times earnings. Investors placed a much higher value on Grant's prospects than an analysis of the company's cash flow from operations would have warranted.

W. T. Grant Company Net Income, Working Capital, and Cash Flow From Operations For Fiscal Years Ending January 31, 1966, to 1975

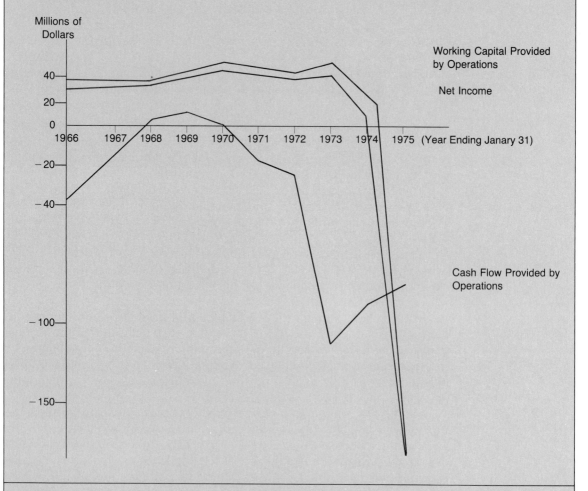

"Cash Flows, Ratio Analysis and the W. T. Grant Company Bankruptcy," by Largay and Stickney, *Financial Analysts Journal*, July/August 1980.

The only differences in this example between the working capital basis and the cash basis statements are additional adjustments to determine the funds from operations figure. This is also true in general: there can be other differences between the working capital basis and the cash basis statements, but the most important difference for most businesses is in the funds from operations figure.

The first additional adjustment in funds from operations is adding back the $60,000 increase in accounts payable. This increase in accounts payable indicates that cost of goods sold on the income statement exceeded the amount of cash paid out for goods and, thus, cash from operations is greater than net income and working capital from operations by this amount.

The second additional adjustment is subtracting the $90,000 increase in accounts receivable. This increase in accounts receivable shows credit sales by the firm which have not been collected and, thus, cash generated by operations is less than net income and working capital from operations.

The final additional adjustment is subtracting the $25,000 increase in inventory. This change shows increased investment in inventory to support a higher level of sales. Thus, the company has to finance an increase in inventory, as well as the increase property, plant, and equipment. The inventory increase represents purchases of inventory that did not become expenses in the current period; therefore, cash from operations is less than net income and working capital from operations.

After these additional adjustments are made, the result is cash from operations of $20,000 while working capital from operations is $75,000 ($55,000 more). The reasons for this difference are shown to be uncollected receivables and increased inventory, both necessary for an expanding business, offset only in part by unpaid payables. This same $55,000 is also the difference between the increase in working capital of $35,000 and the decrease in cash of $20,000. The cash needs of an expanding business make the statement of changes in financial position, cash basis particularly important for financial statement users.

Summary

Three types of events occur between balance sheet dates: operating, financing, and investing events. The income statement focuses on the operating events and reports the accrual effect of these events. The statement of changes in financial position focuses on the financing and investing events and reports the effect of these events on business funds. Together, these two statements explain all changes that occur from one balance sheet to the next.

The statement of changes in financial position is not an accrual based statement and, thus, cannot be prepared from accounting records, which are accrual based. Instead, this statement must be prepared from comparative balance sheets, and income and retained earnings statements for the period between these balance sheets. By a series of adjustments, these accrual statements provide the information necessary for a statement of changes in financial position.

The statement of changes in financial position provides information on the funds flows of a business. Funds may be defined as either cash or working capital; thus, the statement may be prepared on a cash basis or a working capital basis. In either instance, the all financial resources approach is used. This approach assures that all major financing and investing events are reported on the statement, even those not directly affecting cash or working capital.

The basic format of a statement of changes in financial position is as follows:

$$
\begin{aligned}
&\text{Sources of funds (cash or working capital)}\\
-\ &\underline{\text{Uses of funds (cash or working capital)}}\\
=\ &\text{Change in funds for the period (cash or working capital)}
\end{aligned}
$$

If the working capital basis is used, a schedule of changes in working capital must be prepared to accompany the statement of changes in financial position.

The external users of financial statements and the methods by which they can gather information about a business from its financial statements are discussed in Chapter 16.

Key Terms

All financial resources approach	**Statement of changes in financial**
Cash from operations	**position, working capital or cash**
Comparative balance sheet	**basis**
Financing event	**T account approach**
Funds from operations	**Working capital**
Investing event	**Working capital from operations**
Operating event	
Schedule of changes in working capital	

Comprehensive Review Problem

Given below are the statements of income and retained earnings for 1982 and comparative balance sheets as of the end of 1981 and 1982 for Illustration, Inc.

ILLUSTRATION, INC.
Income Statement
For the Year Ended December 31, 1982
(000s)

Revenues

Sales revenue	$1,200	
Interest revenue	15	$1,215

Expenses

Cost of goods sold	675	
Selling expenses	125	
Administrative expenses	100	
Depreciation expense	50	
Amortization expense	10	
Interest expense	25	985
Operating income		230
Gain on sale of equipment		10
Income before income taxes		240
Income taxes		105
Net income		$ 135

Statement of Retained Earnings (000s)

Retained earnings, December 31, 1981	$ 310
Net income for the year	135
Dividends	(75)
Retained earnings, December 31, 1982	$ 370

ILLUSTRATION, INC.
Comparative Balance Sheets
December 31
(000s)

	1982	1981

ASSETS

Current Assets

	1982	1981
Cash	$ 52	$ 62
Accounts receivable (net)	150	110
Inventory	195	165
Supplies	20	34
Total current assets	417	371

Noncurrent assets

	1982	1981
Equipment	380	350
Accumulated depreciation, equipment	(60)	(50)
Building	411	411
Accumulated depreciation, building	(100)	(80)
Land	62	0
Patent	30	40
Total noncurrent assets	723	671
Total assets	$1,140	$1,042

LIABILITIES & OWNERS' EQUITY

Current liabilities

	1982	1981
Accounts payable	$ 70	$ 95
Accrued liabilities	32	27
Notes payable	100	90
Total current liabilities	202	212
Bonds payable	250	250
Premium on bonds	18	20
Common stock	60	50
Paid-in capital	240	200
Retained earnings	370	310
Total liabilities & owners' equity	$1,140	$1,042

Additional information:

1. Equipment with a cost of $35,000 and accumulated depreciation of $20,000 was sold. New equipment was purchased for cash during the accounting period.

2. Land was acquired by issuing 1,000 shares of $10 par value common stock. The remaining land was purchased for cash.

Required:

1. Use the T account approach to prepare a statement of changes in financial position on a working capital basis. Include a schedule of changes in working capital.

2. Use the T account approach to prepare a statement of changes in financial position on a cash basis.

Solution to Comprehensive Review Problem

1. Working Capital Basis T Accounts
   (Change in working capital = increase of $56,000.)

	Equipment		
△	30		
G	65	35	F

Accumulated depreciation, equipment			
		10	△
F	20	30	C

Accumulated depreciation, building			
		20	△
		20	C

	Land		
△	62		
I	50		
J	12		

	Patents		
		10	△
		10	D

	Premium on bonds		
△	2		
E	2		

	Common stock		
		10	△
		10	H

	Paid-in capital		
		40	△
		40	H

	Retained earnings		
		60	△
B	75	135	A

Funds from operations

(net income)	A	135	2	E	(amortization of bond premium)
(depreciation)	C	50	10	F	(gain on sale of equipment)
(amortization)	D	10			
funds from operations		183			

Funds flow summary

(equipment sale)	F	25	75	B	(dividends)
(issue stock for land)	H	50	65	G	(equipment purchase)
			50	I	(land for stock)
			12	J	(land purchase)
		75	202		
		183			
sources		258	202		uses

ILLUSTRATION, INC.
Statement of Changes in Financial Position, Working Capital Basis
For the Year Ended December 31, 1982
(000s)

Sources of funds
Operations

Net income	$ 135	
Depreciation	50	
Amortization	10	
Bond premium amortization	(2)	
Gain on sale of equipment	(10)	
Total funds from operations		$183
Sale of equipment		25
Stock issued for land		50
Total sources of funds		258

Uses of funds

Cash dividends	75	
Purchase of equipment	65	
Purchase of land	12	
Land acquired by stock	50	
Total uses of funds		202
Increase in working capital		$ 56

Schedule of Changes in Working Capital
December 31

	1982	1981	Increase (Decrease)
Cash	$ 52	$ 62	$(10)
Accounts receivable	150	110	40
Inventory	195	165	30
Supplies	20	34	(14)
Total current assets	417	371	
Accounts payable	70	95	25
Accrued liabilities	32	27	(5)
Notes payable	100	90	(10)
Total current liabilities	202	212	
Working capital	$215	$159	$ 56

2. Cash Basis T Accounts

(Change in cash = decrease of $10,000)

Accounts receivable				Inventory	
△	40		△	30	
K	40		L	30	

Supplies				Accounts payable	
	14	△	△	25	
	14	M	N	25	

Accrued liabilities				Notes payable	
	5	△		10	△
	5	O		10	P

Cash from operations

(net income)	A	135	2	E (amortization of bond premium)
(depreciation)	C	50	10	F (gain on sale of equipment)
(amortization)	D	10	40	K (accounts receivable)
(supplies)	M	14	30	L (inventory)
(accrued liabilities)	O	5	25	N (accounts payable)
cash from operations		107		

Cash flow summary

(equipment sale)	F	25	75	B (dividends)
(issue stock for land)	H	50	65	G (equipment purchase)
(notes payable)	P	10	50	I (land for stock)
			12	J (land purchase)
		85	202	
		107		
sources		192	202	uses

ILLUSTRATION, INC.
Statement of Changes in Financial Position, Cash Basis
For the Year Ended December 31, 1982
(000s)

Sources of cash
Operations

Net income	$ 135	
Depreciation	50	
Amortization	10	
Bond premium amortization	(2)	
Gain on sale of equipment	(10)	
Supplies decrease	14	
Accrued liabilities increase	5	
Accounts receivable increase	(40)	
Inventory increase	(30)	
Accounts payable decrease	(25)	
Total cash from operations		$107
Sale of equipment		25
Stock issued for land		50
Borrowing on notes payable		10
Total sources of cash		192

Uses of cash

Cash dividends	75	
Purchase of equipment	65	
Purchase of land	12	
Land acquired by stock	50	
Total uses of cash		202
Decrease in cash		$ 10

Questions

Q15-1. List three examples of operating events. Of financing events. Of investing events.

Q15-2. What is the all financial resources approach to the statement of changes in financial position?

Q15-3. Define working capital. Describe three events that affect working capital but not cash.

Q15-4. What does working capital from operations measure? What does cash from operations measure?

Q15-5. Give the formula for the adjustment of net income to determine working capital from operations.

Q15-6. Give the formula for the adjustment of working capital from operations to determine cash from operations.

Q15-7. What is the schedule of changes in working capital? Explain the purpose of this schedule and state when its preparation would be necessary.

Q15-8. List the five steps necessary in the T account approach to the preparation of a statement of changes in financial position.

Q15-9. Why is a statement of changes in financial position prepared by adjusting figures from other financial statements? Why is it impossible to prepare this statement directly from the adjusted trial balance?

Q15-10. More than 90 percent of published financial statements use the working capital basis for the statement of changes in financial position. Why is this basis chosen so frequently?

Exercises

E15-1. For each of the following events, indicate the amount (if any) by which working capital changes and whether the change (if any) is an increase or a decrease.

  a. Sell merchandise for $800 cash.
  b. Purchase equipment costing $2,000 by paying $400 in cash and signing 120-day note for the balance.
  c. Retire bonds payable, $500,000, at a price of 105 prior to maturity date with cash.
  d. Issue a 25 percent stock dividend on capital stock with a par value of $700,000.
  e. Depreciate equipment, $4,000.
  f. Purchase land and building costing $250,000 for $50,000 cash and a $200,000, twenty-year mortgage note.
  g. Borrow $100,000 signing a three-year, 12 percent note.
  h. Collect $500 of account receivable.
  i. Purchase merchandise costing $75,000 on account.

E15-2. A company sold a piece of machinery during the year for $20,000. The journal entry made to record the transaction was as follows:

Cash	20,000	
Accumulated depreciation	50,000	
Machinery		65,000
Gain on sale of machinery		5,000

The gain on the sale of machinery was included in net income. What is the effect of the transaction on working capital? How would net income be adjusted on a statement of changes in financial position to arrive at working capital from operations? How would the sale of machinery be reported on the statement of changes in financial position?

E15-3. The Maxim Company uses accrual accounting and prepares its statement of changes in financial position using a working capital definition of funds and the all financial resources concept. Indicate how each of the following items would appear on the statement of changes in financial position for the year by classifying it as: (1) added back to net income to get working capital from operations; (2) subtracted from net income to get working capital from operations; (3) reported as a nonoperating source of working capital; (4) reported as a nonoperating use of working capital; or (5) reported as both a nonoperating source and use of working capital.

  a. Depreciation expense of $12,000.
  b. Proceeds of bank loan, $50,000.
  c. Payment of cash dividend of $8,000.
  d. Sale of operational asset for $52,000, the book value of the asset.
  e. Purchase of equipment for $20,000 cash.

f. Conversion of $100,000 of bonds payable to capital stock.

g. Amortization expense of $4,000.

h. Write-down of short-term marketable securities $1,500 to reduce to market.

i. Exchange of land for a building with no gain or loss involved.

j. Reclassification of $15,000 of long-term notes payable to short-term notes payable.

E15-4. Identify three different transactions that could cause bonds payable to decrease assuming no asset other than cash was used to retire the debt. Explain briefly how each of these transactions would be reported on a statement of changes in financial position, working capital basis. Would any of these transactions be handled differently if the statement was prepared using a cash definition of funds? If so, why?

E15-5. The Mosby Corporation reported working capital from operations for the year ended December 31, 1982, of $48,000. Calculate the company's cash from operations for the year using the following schedule of changes in working capital:

	12/31/82	12/31/81	Increase (Decrease)
Cash	$ 9,100	$12,500	$(3,400)
Accounts receivable	32,600	23,000	9,600
Inventory	56,100	49,800	6,300
Prepaid expenses	2,700	3,900	(1,200)
Total current assets	100,500	89,200	
Accounts payable	25,600	33,000	7,400
Accrued liabilities	8,400	5,200	(3,200)
Notes payable	15,000	20,000	5,000
Total current liabilities	49,000	58,200	
Working capital	$ 51,500	$31,000	$ 20,500

E15-6. The current assets and current liabilities sections of the comparative balance sheets of Bates, Inc., at December 31, 1982, and 1981 are presented below.

	1982	1981
Current assets		
Cash	$ 41,900	$ 60,200
Marketable securities at cost	12,500	11,100
Accounts receivable (net)	96,600	112,300
Inventories	278,300	234,900
Prepaid expenses	2,100	4,700
Total current assets	$431,400	$423,200
Current liabilities		
Accounts payable	$ 87,100	$102,500
Accrued liabilities	9,800	8,200
Current portion of long-term debt	10,600	12,400
Short-term notes payable	206,000	187,000
Total current liabilities	$313,500	$310,100

Prepare a schedule of changes in working capital for the year ended December 31, 1982.

E15-7. The following information is taken from the annual report of Hunt, Inc.:

	December 31	
	1982	1981
Current assets	$120,000	$ 95,000
Property, plant, and equipment	290,000	250,000
Accumulated depreciation	(96,000)	(79,000)
Current liabilities	83,000	86,000
Capital stock	100,000	80,000
Retained earnings	131,000	100,000

Net income for 1982 was $56,000. Cash dividends declared during the year amounted to $25,000. No items of property, plant, and equipment were sold during the year. The capital stock issued during the year was issued for cash. Prepare a statement of changes in financial position for the year ended December 31, 1982, for Hunt, Inc., using a working capital definition of funds.

E15-8. Below is a summary of the transactions of a company for one year.

    a. Sales, $200,000
    b. Cost of goods sold, $90,000
    c. Operating expenses involving cash or accruals, $30,000
    d. Depreciation expense, $10,000
    e. Income tax expense (no deferrals involved), $20,000
    f. Sale of equipment with book value of $10,000 for $12,000 cash
    g. Purchase of equipment for $20,000 cash
    h. Issuance of stock for $30,000 cash
    i. Cash dividends paid, $5,000

Set up a schedule in the format shown below to indicate the net amount by which each transaction affects income, working capital from operations, and/or working capital from financing and investing activities. Increases should be shown as unbracketed amounts, decreases as bracketed amounts, and no effect as a dash.

(1)	(2)	(3)	(4)
Transaction	Income	Working Capital from Operations	Working Capital from Financing and Investing

E15-9. Using the schedule called for in Exercise 15-8, foot Columns 2, 3, and 4 of the schedule to calculate income, working capital from operations, and net working capital from financing and investing activities. From this schedule, prepare a statement of changes in financial position, working capital basis.

E15-10. The following information was taken from the records of the Kadid Company for the month of June:

    a. Cash sales, $12,000
    b. Credit sales, $8,000
    c. Collection of accounts receivable, $5,000
    d. Cash purchases of merchandise, $6,000
    e. Credit purchases of merchandise, $4,000
    f. Payment of accounts payable, $2,000
    g. Cash payment of current operating expense, $1,500
    h. Payment of expenses accrued at end of May, $200
    i. Expenses accrued at end of June, $400

j. Depreciation expense, $300

k. Inventory at May 31, $20,000; inventory at June 30, $18,000

Prepare a cash basis income statement and an accrual basis income statement for the month of June based on the information provided above.

Problems

P15-1. The Hock Corporation was organized on January 1, 1982. During the year ended December 31, 1982, the corporation completed the following transactions:

    a. Sold 10,000 shares of common stock for a total of $200,000 cash.

    b. Borrowed $50,000 on a one-year, 12 percent note dated April 1.

    c. Purchased equipment costing $20,000 with cash.

    d. Sold bonds with total face value of $100,000 for cash at face amount.

    e. Declared a cash dividend of $12,000 to be paid in February 1983.

    f. Sold merchandise, $170,000 for cash, $40,000 on credit.

    g. Purchased merchandise, $115,000 for cash, $25,000 on credit. Of the total purchased, $105,000 was cost of goods sold and $35,000 was in ending inventory.

    h. Paid operating expenses of $65,000 in cash.

    i. Accrued expenses of $10,000 at December 31.

    j. Recorded depreciation of $2,000 on equipment.

Required:

Give a journal entry to record each of the above transactions (assuming accrual basis accounting), and indicate the net effect of each transaction on cash, on working capital and on income. Use the following format for your answer:

Journal Entry	Increase (Decrease) in Cash	Increase (Decrease) in Working Capital	Increase (Decrease) in Income

P15-2. The information provided below was taken from the annual report of the Duphine Corporation.

Income Statement
For the Year Ended December 31, 1982

Sales	$ 420,000
Cost of goods sold	290,000
Gross profit	130,000
Operating expenses (including depreciation)	70,000
Income before income taxes	60,000
Income taxes	15,000
Net income	$ 45,000

Statement of Retained Earnings
For the Year Ended December 31, 1982

Balance, January 1	$ 14,000
Net income for the year	45,000
Dividends	(20,000)
Balance, December 31	$ 39,000

Comparative Balance Sheets
December 31

	1982	1981
ASSETS		
Cash	$ 24,000	$ 23,000
Accounts receivable (net)	45,000	38,000
Inventory	110,000	92,000
Property, plant and equipment	88,000	62,000
Accumulated depreciation	(43,000)	(31,000)
Total assets	$ 224,000	$ 184,000
LIABILITIES & OWNERS' EQUITY		
Liabilities		
Accounts payable	$ 56,000	$ 63,000
Accrued liabilities	6,000	5,000
Income taxes payable	15,000	12,000
Notes payable	8,000	—
Total liabilities	85,000	80,000
Owners' Equity		
Capital stock, no par	100,000	90,000
Retained earnings	39,000	14,000
Total owners' equity	139,000	104,000
Total liabilities & owners' equity	$ 224,000	$ 184,000

Additional information:

a. During the year, equipment with an original cost of $8,000 and accumulated depreciation of $2,000 was sold for book value.
b. In November 1982, the company borrowed $10,000 from the bank signing a three-year note payable.
c. During the year, capital stock was sold for $10,000 cash.

Required:

Using the T account approach, prepare a statement of changes in financial position, working capital basis. Provide a schedule of changes in working capital.

P15-3. The following information was taken from the annual report of the Manx Corporation:

Comparative Balance Sheets
December 31

	1982	1981
ASSETS		
Cash	$ 9,000	$ 6,000
Accounts receivable (net)	33,000	27,000
Inventory	76,000	84,000
Property, plant and equipment	152,000	140,000
Accumulated depreciation	(83,000)	(68,000)
Total assets	$ 187,000	$ 189,000

LIABILITIES & OWNERS' EQUITY

Accounts payable	$ 26,000	$ 24,000
Notes payable (short-term)	10,000	—
Capital stock	100,000	95,000
Retained earnings	51,000	70,000
Total liabilities & owners' equity	$ 187,000	$ 189,000

Additional information:

a. The net loss for 1982 was $13,000.
b. Cash dividends of $6,000 were declared and paid during 1982.
c. No items of property, plant, or equipment were sold during 1982.
d. $10,000 was borrowed from the bank and a 120-day note signed.
e. Capital stock was sold for cash.

Required:

1. Prepare a statement of changes in financial position, working capital basis, using the T account approach. Provide a schedule of changes in working capital.

2. Prepare a statement of changes in financial position, cash basis, using the T account approach to convert from working capital basis to cash basis.

P15-4. Comparative balance sheets of the Castle Corporation at December 31, 1981 and 1982 are presented below.

Comparative Balance Sheets
December 31

	1982	1981
ASSETS		
Cash	$ 18,000	$ 26,000
Accounts receivable	42,000	37,000
Inventories	107,000	93,000
Prepaid expenses	4,000	3,000
Land	150,000	150,000
Plant and equipment	369,000	300,000
Accumulated depreciation	(137,000)	(105,000)
Patents (net of amortization)	12,000	15,000
Total assets	$ 565,000	$ 519,000

LIABILITIES & OWNERS' EQUITY		
Accounts payable	$ 56,000	$ 48,000
Accrued liabilities	8,000	10,000
Long-term debt	165,000	100,000
Capital stock, no par	300,000	300,000
Retained earnings	36,000	61,000
Total liabilities & owners' equity	$ 565,000	$ 519,000

Additional information:

a. The net loss for 1982 was $19,000.

b. Cash dividends of $6,000 were declared and paid during 1982.

c. Equipment with an original cost of $17,000 and accumulated depreciation of $6,000 was sold for $9,000. The loss was included in net income.

d. $65,000 was borrowed from the bank and a three-year note signed.

e. No patents were acquired or sold during the year.

Required:

Prepare a statement of changes in financial position for the Castle Corporation for the year ended December 31, 1982, using a working capital definition of funds. Use the T account approach to statement preparation. Provide a schedule of changes in working capital.

P15-5. Refer to the data provided for the Castle Corporation in Problem 15-4.

Required:

1. Set up T accounts for all working capital accounts in which there is a change except cash and enter changes in the accounts. Set up T accounts for cash from operations and cash flow summary.

2. Reproduce entries that give rise to changes in the working capital accounts to convert to cash basis.

3. Prepare a statement of changes in financial position, cash basis.

P15-6. Below is the statement of changes in financial position of the London Corporation for the year ended December 31, 1982.

Sources of funds
Operations

Net income	$180,000	
Depreciation expense	75,000	
Amortization expense	8,000	
Loss on sale of investments	13,000	
Total funds from operations		$276,000
Issuance of stock upon conversion of bonds		100,000
Sale of marketable securities		54,000
Sale of bonds		200,000
Total sources of funds		630,000

Uses of funds

Dividends	30,000	
Purchases of operational assets	453,000	
Conversion of bonds	100,000	
Total uses of funds		583,000
Increase in working capital		$ 47,000

Schedule of Changes in Working Capital
December 31

	1982	1981	Increase (Decrease)
Cash	$ 70,000	$ 80,000	$(10,000)
Marketable securities	—	67,000	(67,000)
Accounts receivable	125,000	120,000	5,000
Inventories	200,000	90,000	110,000
Total current assets	395,000	357,000	
Accounts payable	120,000	108,000	(12,000)
Accrued liabilities	32,000	28,000	(4,000)
Notes payable	15,000	40,000	25,000
Total current liabilities	167,000	176,000	
Working capital	$228,000	$181,000	$ 47,000

Required:
Answer the following questions about the statement and the activities of the London Company for the year ended December 31, 1982.

1. Is the statement prepared on a working capital basis or a cash basis?

2. How much working capital was provided by operations during the year?

3. How much cash was provided by operations during the year? Show calculations.

4. What is the primary reason that cash provided is less than working capital provided by operations?

5. How much working capital was provided by creditors?

6. What is the effect of the conversion of bonds on working capital? Why is it reported twice on the statement?

7. Does it appear that the acquisition of operational assets represents expansion of facilities or merely replacement of worn-out facilities?

8. What was the book value of marketable securities sold?

9. Why might the company have been willing to sell these investments at a loss?

10. How much cash was paid to creditors on notes payable, excluding interest? Why is this not reported as a use of funds on the statement of changes in financial position?

P15-7. Comparative balance sheets for the Wrent Corporation at December 31, 1981 and 1982, and the company's income statement for the year ended December 31, 1982 are as follows:

WRENT CORPORATION
Comparative Balance Sheets
December 31

	1982	1981
ASSETS		
Current assets		
Cash	$ 11,000	$ 25,000
Accounts receivable (net)	356,000	295,000
Inventories	449,000	423,000
Prepaid expenses	9,000	10,000
Total current assets	825,000	753,000
Natural resources (at cost less depletion)	421,000	361,000
Land, building, and machinery	2,657,000	2,285,000
Accumulated depreciation	(995,000)	(836,000)
Total assets	$2,908,000	$2,563,000
LIABILITIES & OWNERS' EQUITY		
Current liabilities		
Current portion of long-term debt	$ 46,000	$ 37,000
Accounts payable	158,000	144,000
Accrued liabilities	96,000	63,000
Income taxes payable	65,000	67,000
Short-term notes payable	13,000	222,000
Total current liabilities	378,000	533,000
Long-term debt, excluding current portion	732,000	443,000
Deferred income tax credit	280,000	250,000
Capital stock	1,103,000	985,000
Retained earnings	415,000	352,000
Total liabilities & owners' equity	$2,908,000	$2,563,000

WRENT CORPORATION
Income Statement
For the Year Ended December 31, 1982

Sales (net)	$3,675,000
Cost of goods sold	2,992,000
Gross profit	683,000
Operating expenses (including depreciation and depletion)	426,000
Income from operations	257,000
Gain on sale of equipment	3,000
Income before income taxes	260,000
Income taxes	109,000
Net income	$ 151,000

Additional information regarding activities during 1982:

a. Cash dividends of $88,000 were declared and paid during the year.

b. Equipment was sold during the year. The original cost of the equipment was $77,000, and accumulated depreciation on the equipment at the time of sale was $57,000.

c. Purchases of property, plant, and equipment were paid for with cash and $118,000 worth of Wrent Corporation common stock.

d. No natural resources were sold during the year. Investments in new natural resources amounted to $72,000, all cash.

e. During the year, a $100,000 short-term note was refinanced on a long-term basis, that is, a short-term note was retired by signing a long-term note. Bonds with total face value of $300,000 were sold at face during 1982.

Required:

Prepare a statement of changes in financial position, working capital basis, for the Wrent Corporation for the year ended December 31, 1982. Use the T account approach. Provide a schedule of changes in working capital.

P15-8. The information below is taken from the 1982 annual report of the Rackley Corporation.

RACKLEY CORPORATION
Comparative Balance Sheets
December 31

	1982	1981
ASSETS		
Current assets		
Cash	$ 43,100	$ 37,800
Accounts receivable	310,600	306,900
Inventories	962,400	896,300
Prepaid expenses	21,200	25,700
Total current assets	1,337,300	1,266,700
Property, plant and equipment	1,748,100	1,522,000
Accumulated depreciation	(863,300)	(716,500)
Intangible assets (net)	67,400	73,100
Total assets	$2,289,500	$2,145,300
LIABILITIES & OWNERS' EQUITY		
Current liabilities		
Accounts payable	$ 108,100	$ 96,800
Accrued liabilities	26,200	32,700
Current portion of long-term debt	200,000	300,000
Short-term notes payable	321,500	296,800
Total current liabilities	655,800	726,300
Long-term debt	808,600	714,700
Capital stock, no par	631,500	566,800
Retained earnings	193,600	137,500
Total liabilities & owners' equity	$2,289,500	$2,145,300

Additional information:

a. Net income for 1982 was $78,800.

b. Cash dividends declared and paid during 1982 were $22,700.

c. A piece of machinery was sold during 1982 for $52,000. The original cost of the machinery was $125,000, and its accumulated depreciation at the time it was sold was $78,000. No other noncurrent assets were sold during 1982.

d. Machinery and equipment costing $351,100 was purchased during the year. Of this amount, $300,000 was paid in cash and the balance of the purchase price was paid with Rackley stock. No intangible assets were acquired during the year.

e. During 1982, $300,000 of bonds were sold at face amount.

f. Capital stock other than that used for the purchase of equipment (see d above) was sold for cash.

Required:

1. Prepare a statement of changes in financial position, working capital basis, for the Rackley Corporation for the year ended December 31, 1982. Use the T account approach. Provide a schedule of changes in working capital.

2. Prepare a statement of changes in financial position, cash basis, for the Rackley Corporation for the year ended December 31, 1982. Use the T account approach for converting from working capital basis to cash basis.

CHAPTER 16

Financial Statement Analysis

Chapter Outline

16.1 *Introduction to Financial Statement Analysis.* The basic steps of financial analysis; introduction to the concept of standards of performance and historical, external, and expected standards; introduction to ratios as tools of financial analysis.

16.2 *Operating Ratios.* Common-size income statements; the calculation, meaning, and interpretation of the gross profit percentage, operating profit percentage, and net income percentage.

16.3 *Financial Condition Ratios.* Liquidity and solvency; the calculation, meaning, and interpretation of the current ratio, quick ratio, equity ratio, and times interest earned ratio; the characteristics of debt and owners' equity as sources of assets.

16.4 *Asset Use Ratios.* Asset use as an indication of management efficiency; the calculation, meaning, and interpretation of the average collection period of receivables and inventory turnover; the operating cycle of a business.

16.5 *Market Test Ratios.* The quality of earnings; the calculation, meaning, and interpretation of earnings per share, the price-earnings ratio, and dividend yield; growth and dividend companies.

16.6 *Overall Ratios.* The concept and application of financial leverage; the calculation, meaning, and interpretation of return on total assets and return on common equity.

Accounting and the Real World

Who's Where in the Stock Market

Amid dire predictions and short-term frenzies, the market keeps proving that it may very well be the place to be over the long term. That's sometimes obscured by well-known but incomplete measures of what the "market" is.

For example, if you'd bought 1,029 stocks on the last trading day of 1975 and held them all, winners and losers, until November 19, 1980—*Forbes'* measuring period—the average increase would have been 161 percent. Compare that to the Dow Jones industrial average, up only 16 percent over the same period.

You'd have made money on three out of four of the 1,029 stocks; and on well over half, you'd have kept ahead of the double-digit cost-of-living increases—an average 10½ percent a year—that prevailed during that five-

Rank 80	*Rank 79*	*Company*	*5-Year Price Change*	*1976–80 Price Range*	*Recent Price*	*Shares Outstanding (millions)*	*Total Market Value (millions)*	*Latest 12-Month Earnings Per Share*	*Price/ Earnings Ratio*	*Indicated Annual Dividend*	*Current Yield*
1	★	Resorts International	4,100.0%	69½– ⅝	26¼	11.0	$ 290	$ 4.27	6	none	0.0%
2	3	Wang Laboratories	2,780.2	45¼– 1¼	44⅛	56.0	2,469	1.08	41	$0.12	0.3
3	★	Mitchell Energy & Development	2,488.9	59¾– 2⅜	58¼	35.9	2,090	2.41	24	0.20	0.3
4	★	Caesars World	1,827.2	36⅛– ⅝	13⅜	26.2	351	1.29	10	none	0.0
5	★	National Medical Enterprises	1,784.5	37⅝– 1⅞	37⅛	19.1	711	1.98	19	0.60	1.6
6	4	Humana	1,526.7	67 – 3⅞	65¾	18.1	1,189	3.07	21	1.20	1.8
7	40	Shearson Loeb Rhoades	1,487.0	35⅞– 2¼	35¼	13.8	485	5.38	7	0.48	1.4
8	43	Tosco	1,485.7	42 – 2⅝	41⅝	20.5	855	3.80	11	none	0.0
9	13	Subaru of America	1,400.0	21¾– ½	20⅝	6.0	124	2.55	8	0.32	1.6
10	174	Texas Oil & Gas	1,379.5	83½– 5⅜	81	47.6	3,852	2.96	27	0.36	0.4
11	6	Teledyne	1,366.5	212 –14	205	13.8	2,835	20.95	10	none	0.0
12	242	Chic & North Western	1,362.9	70¼– 4¼	64	4.4	284	8.00	8	none	0.0
13	145	Kay	1,359.0	32½– 2⅛	31½	3.1	97	3.15	10	0.75	2.4
14	34	Nucor	1,344.7	74¼– 4⅞	71¼	6.8	485	7.43	10	0.44	0.6
15	17	American Medical International	1,245.0	39⅞– 2⅞	39⅛	14.6	572	2.11	19	0.64	1.6

year period. In fact, about 40 percent of the 1,029 doubled in price, one out of four tripled, and 171 stocks quadrupled or did even better.

Among the big gainers in the table above, both unranked last year, are number one Resorts International and number four Caesars World. Both proved not only that somebody made a lot of money during the gambling-stock craze of 1978–79, but also what risks it carried. Resorts International soared to 69½ at the height of the frenzy but was at 26¼ at the end of the *Forbes'* measuring period November 19; Caesars, up to 36⅛, fell to 13⅜. Among the top five, though, were three glamour stocks that showed more stability—Wang Laboratories, Mitchell Energy, and National Medical Enterprises—all selling late in 1980 near their 1976–1980 highs.

Forbes, January 5, 1981, page 279.

Financial statements are the primary output of the financial accounting process. As such, they represent the most significant information on which persons and groups outside a business assess the financial position and earnings performance of that business. These "outsiders" include stockholders and potential stockholders, creditors and potential creditors, financial analysts and brokers, governmental agencies (such as the SEC and IRS), legislators, judges, labor unions, and the general public. Together, these groups are called the external users of financial statements because they have no regular access to the internal activities and records of a business. For them, financial statements necessarily become the basis by which business activity and the performance of company management are judged.

Financial statements are an excellent barometer of a business's progress. Reading this barometer requires a fundamental understanding of what financial statements are, how they are prepared, and the "story" contained in them. Financial analysts read this barometer to determine the important relationships present in a set of financial statements and interpret the implications of these relationships for the business. Then, they use these interpretations as a basis for predicting future business earnings performance and financial position.

16.1 Introduction to Financial Statement Analysis

The basic idea of financial analysis is to capture and highlight the important relationships on a set of financial statements. An effective way to do so is by creating ratios that express these important relationships in numerical form. Because many relationships exist among numbers on the income statement and balance sheet and different external groups may want to focus on different aspects of a business's activities, many ratios may be computed; however, a relatively small group of ratios are considered most indicative of business progress.

Analysis and interpretation of these ratios requires benchmarks of what might be considered good or, at least, acceptable performance. In other words, a ratio that expresses an important relationship numerically is of little use unless some standard is available to which the ratio can be compared. Standards are a critical part of financial statement analysis.

With ratios and standards, a knowledgeable financial statement user can predict the likely course and results of future business activity. This prediction is the essence of financial analysis.

The Steps of Financial Analysis

Financial statement analysis, then, can be thought of as a three-step process. The steps are as follows:

1. Determine appropriate standards of good or acceptable performance that will serve as benchmarks to which computed ratios can be compared.

2. Compute ratios that express important relationships about the area of business activity in which the user is interested.

3. Analyze and interpret these comparisons and use the analysis to predict what is likely to occur with respect to the business in the future.

Standards of Performance

Financial analysis depends upon the existence of standards of performance in each of the areas of business activity being analyzed. Standards are yardsticks by which actual performance can be measured; however, standards are also only approximations of good performance, and the choice of standards may be quite subjective. Because no standard is perfect, the quality of financial analysis can be improved by using as many different performance benchmarks as possible in a given situation.

Three different types of standards are commonly used in external financial analysis. These are the historical standard, the external standard, and the expected standard.

Historical Standard When the historical standard is used, the standard of comparison is a company's own past performance. In effect, the company being analyzed is compared to its own previous performance on a ratio-by-ratio basis. This type of standard enables an analyst to determine trends over time and gives an objective measure of progress. Care must be taken, however, in interpreting results using historical standards for two reasons. First, the periods of past performance many not be representative of the company's normal circumstances and, thus, may be unusually good or poor. When this is true, the base of comparison is not indicative of expected performance and incorrect conclusions can be drawn. Second, even if previous financial statements and ratios depict normal circumstances, a company's situation may have changed so much as to make the past an invalid basis of comparison. For example, a company could have merged with another, started a new product line or dropped an old product, or made some other change in the basic operating structure of the business. Ratios of past years would make potentially misleading benchmarks in these instances. Nonetheless, historical standards make excellent starting points for financial analysis.

External Standard When an external standard is used, the company being analyzed is compared to other firms of its approximate size or in its same industry on a ratio-by-ratio basis. Thus, the performance of others in similar circumstances provides an objective measure of a business's level of success. It is this kind of comparison across companies that external analysts are usually most interested in making. Again, care must be taken to assure that there are enough similarities between companies to make a comparison potentially meaningful. For example, two companies could be in the same industry but one might be highly diversified while the other might sell only in that one industry. When coupled with the historical performance of each of the companies being considered, however, external comparisons can provide strong information about the performance and potential of each firm.

Expected Standard The expected standard is difficult to apply because it is usually based on some special knowledge, experience, or expertise on the part of the analyst. Basically, this standard is what the investment market or the analyst expects in the way of performance from a company or industry. This expectation may be based on a rule of thumb developed

Concept Summary

Benchmarks of Performance			
Type of Standard	*Description*	*Primary Usefulness*	*Cautions In Use*
Historical	Compares the company's present performance to its own past performance on a ratio-by-ratio basis	1. Helps to determine trends over time 2. Gives an objective measure of progress	1. Past may not be representative of normal circumstances 2. Company's situation may have changed so much that the past is an invalid basis for comparison
External	Compares the company's performance to that of other firms of the same size or in the same industry on a ratio-by-ratio basis	Provides an objective measure of the business's success	Companies must be similar enough to make comparisons meaningful
Expected	Compares the company's performance to what the investment market or the analyst expects in the way of performance—often based on a rule of thumb or hunch	1. May be tailored to particular size or industry characteristics 2. Allows user to "do his own thing" in evaluating performance	Subjective and may reflect the hidden preferences of the analyst

over many years or simply on a hunch. No matter how carefully expected standards are developed, they are subjective and may reflect the hidden preferences of the person performing the financial analysis. Because this type of standard can be extremely useful, stock and bond brokers and investment bankers have all developed within their firms industry experts who gain a "feel" for an industry and provide these expected standards.

Ratios

Ratios are simply numerical expressions of the relationship between two numbers. A ratio can be created between any two numbers, including any numbers from financial statements. For example, a ratio could be created between the amount of intangible assets and the amount of income taxes paid by a company in any given year. This ratio would be meaningless, however, because there is no necessary relationship between these numbers. The point is that ratios can express only a relationship that already exists between numbers.

Items from financial statements that are significantly related to each other must first be selected. Then, the relationship between them can be conveniently and effectively expressed in ratio form.

Ratio Groups Most ratios convey information about one aspect of a business's operating, financing, or investing activities. It is helpful in financial analysis to group ratios that focus on the same area of business activity and interpret these ratios as a group rather than individually. This lessens the possibility of being misled by one unusual or out-of-step ratio. Commonly used ratios can be thought of as falling into one of the five following groups:

1. Operating ratios

2. Financial condition ratios

3. Asset use ratios

4. Market test ratios

5. Overall ratios

Each of these groups tells a story about some important aspect of business activity. Subsequent sections of this chapter present and interpret each of these ratios.

16.2 Operating Ratios

Operating ratios have to do with the profit margins of a business and are made up of numbers from the income statement. Income statements give numbers for revenues, expenses, gains and losses, and net income. In all of these numbers, the size of the business (that is, volume of activity) is an important factor. Because of this, comparison of companies of different size can be difficult. An effective technique to facilitate the comparison of large, medium, and small companies is to remove volume from the income statement. This can be done by expressing all components of the income statement as a percentage of the net sales figure. In this way, the focus of the statement becomes profit margins, and volume differences are no longer a factor. Income statements prepared this way are called **common size** statements.

Common Size Statements

Figure 16-1 illustrates two income statements in traditional and common size form for companies of different volumes of activity. Notice that the common size statement is stated in percentages with net sales as the anchor of the statement. All figures are expressed relative to net sales, which removes from the numbers any size or volume considerations. In this way, all income statement figures have a common base.

An attempt to compare the earnings performance of the Big and Small companies using traditional income statement figures would likely meet with frustration because of the vastly different sizes of the companies. However, a quick glance at the common size statements points up some significant differences. Three of these figures are the most important operating ratios.

Gross Profit Percentage The ratio of gross profit to net sales, called the gross profit percentage, gives the amount remaining from each dollar of sales revenue after deducting the acquisition cost of the units sold. It is an important figure because it depicts the difference between selling price and cost for each unit sold. Small Company has $0.56 remaining from each sales dollar to cover other expenses and income taxes and to provide net income, while Big Company has only $0.47. This does not necessarily mean that Small Company will be more profitable than Big Company, but it does give important information about the markup between cost and selling price. This information would be particularly meaningful if these companies sold the same product or products.

FIGURE 16-1
Traditional and Common Size Income Statements

	Big Company Income Statement For 1982		Small Company Income Statement For 1982	
Sales revenue	$ 195,000,000	103%	$457,000	100.5%
Sales returns	5,000,000	3	2,000	.5
Net sales revenue	190,000,000	100	455,000	100
Cost of goods sold	100,000,000	53	200,000	44
Gross profit	90,000,000	47	255,000	56
Selling expenses	35,000,000	19	75,000	16
Administrative expenses	12,000,000	6	30,000	7
Interest expense	10,000,000	5	10,000	2
Income before income taxes	33,000,000	17	140,000	31
Income taxes	15,000,000	8	68,000	15
Operating profit	18,000,000	9	72,000	16
Extraordinary loss or gain (net of taxes)	(2,000,000)	1	10,000	2
Net income	$ 16,000,000	8%	$ 82,000	18 %

Operating Profit Percentage The ratio of operating profit to net sales, called the operating profit percentage, indicates the amount remaining from each sales dollar after all normal and recurring expenses (including income taxes) have been deducted. As such, the operating profit percentage is probably the best indicator of current earnings performance and, when studied over time, of future earnings potential. Only the normal and recurring profit-seeking activities of the business affect operating profit. The performance gap between the Small and Big companies is actually wider here with operating profit percentages of 16 percent for Small and only 9 percent for Big. This difference indicates that Small Company is more efficient in controlling the expenses it incurs than is Big Company.

Net Income Percentage The ratio of net income to net sales, called the net income percentage, gives the amount of each sales dollar that accrues to the owners of the business. This figure is often called the profit margin of the business; however, it should be used with care because it may include the effects of unusual and nonrecurring activities. These extraordinary items may increase or decrease net income but would not be expected to occur again and are not related to normal profit-seeking activities. In this instance, Small Company enjoyed an extraordinary gain while Big Com-

Concept Summary

Operating Ratios		
Ratio	*Calculation*	*Meaning*
Gross profit percentage	$\dfrac{\text{Gross profit}}{\text{Net sales}}$	Amount remaining from each sales dollar after deducting the acquisition cost of the units sold. This is the amount each sales dollar contributes to covering operating expenses and net income.
Operating profit percentage	$\dfrac{\text{Operating profit}}{\text{Net sales}}$	Amount remaining from each sales dollar after all normal and recurring expenses (including interest and income taxes) have been deducted. This is the amount each sales dollar contributes to net income after being adjusted for extraordinary items.
Net income percentage	$\dfrac{\text{Net income}}{\text{Net sales}}$	Amount remaining from each sales dollar after all activities (normal and extraordinary) of the period are considered. This is the amount of each sales dollar which accrues to owners.

pany's net income was lowered by an extraordinary loss. Of course, in the absence of extraordinary items, operating profit and net income are identical.

16.3   Financial Condition Ratios

Ratios of financial condition focus on the financial strength and debt-paying ability of a business. Because the balance sheet portrays financial position, most numbers necessary for these ratios come from that statement. The idea is to select those numbers from the balance sheet of a business that best exhibit its financial strength or lack of it.

Financial strength can be viewed from two perspectives: liquidity and solvency. **Liquidity** is a short-term view of financial strength and has to do with a business's ability to meet its current obligations as they come due. **Solvency** is a long-term concept of financial strength and is concerned with the ability of a business to handle its long-run obligations in a smooth and orderly manner. Both liquidity and solvency must be examined to determine financial strength.

The four financial condition ratios can be divided into liquidity and solvency ratios. The two liquidity ratios are the current ratio and the quick ratio. Solvency ratios are the equity (debt) ratio and the times interest earned ratio.

Sample Financial Statements

Figure 16-2 presents comparative condensed balance sheets for Small Company, whose income statement was given in Figure 16-1. Small Company's income statement and statement of retained earnings are also included for the accounting period between these balance sheets. These financial statements will be used to illustrate ratios of financial condition, as well as all of the remaining ratios throughout this chapter.

Liquidity Ratios

Liquidity ratios depict the short-term debt-paying ability of a business. As such, these ratios focus on current assets and current liabilities. Current liabilities are the obligations that must be satisfied in the upcoming accounting period or operating cycle, whichever is longer, and current assets will be used to retire these obligations.

Current Ratio The current ratio is the ratio of current assets to current liabilities. It is calculated as follows:

$$\text{Current ratio} = \frac{\text{current assets}}{\text{current liabilities}}$$

Using the financial statements from Figure 16-2, the current ratio for Small Company for 1981 and 1982 would be

1982	*1981*
$\dfrac{\$18{,}000 + \$50{,}000 + \$56{,}000}{\$27{,}000} = 4.6$	$\dfrac{\$35{,}000 + \$40{,}000 + \$48{,}000}{\$33{,}000} = 3.7$

FIGURE 16-2
Financial Statements
for Small Company

Income Statement
For 1982

Sales revenue	$457,000	100.5%
Sales returns	2,000	.5
Net sales revenue	455,000	100
Cost of goods sold	200,000	44
Gross profit	255,000	56
Selling expenses	75,000	16
Administrative expenses	30,000	7
Interest expense	10,000	2
Income before income taxes	140,000	31
Income taxes	68,000	15
Operating profit (income before extraordinary items)	72,000	16
Extraordinary gain (net of taxes)	10,000	2
Net income	$ 82,000	18%

Statement of Retained Earnings
For 1982

Retained earnings, December 31, 1981	$108,000
Net income for the year	82,000
Dividends for the year	(50,000)
Retained earnings, December 31, 1982	$140,000

Balance Sheets
December 31

	1982	1981
ASSETS		
Cash	$ 18,000	$ 35,000
Accounts receivable (net)	50,000	40,000
Inventory	56,000	48,000
Property, plant, and equipment (net)	315,000	280,000
Total assets	$439,000	$403,000
LIABILITIES & OWNERS' EQUITY		
Current liabilities	$ 27,000	33,000
Bonds payable	100,000	90,000
10% preferred stock, $100 par	50,000	50,000
Common stock, $10 par	50,000	50,000
Paid-in capital in excess of par value—common	72,000	72,000
Retained earnings	140,000	108,000
Total liabilities & owners' equity	$439,000	$403,000

These calculations show an increasing current ratio and a large margin of safety between current assets and current liabilities. In fact, the margin may be larger than necessary to provide liquidity for the business. An extensively used rule of thumb is that a current ratio of two to one should provide sufficient liquidity.

The following points should be kept in mind when interpreting the current ratio:

1. From the point of view of a short-term creditor, the higher the current ratio, the better. A high current ratio indicates a large margin of protection for the creditor.

2. From the management point of view and that of owners of the business, a current ratio can be too large. Any cushion of current assets beyond that necessary to assure short-term debt-paying ability ties up company assets and prevents the business from using these assets in a more productive manner. For example, the return on cash (bank interest) is much lower than the return on a long-term investment. Clearly, then, to the extent that a company holds assets in the form of cash, it gives up some potential return. The need for liquidity overrides this extra potential return, but current assets in excess of the amounts needed for liquidity should not be maintained.

3. Because the current ratio is calculated using year-end figures, the ratio may not be indicative of the liquidity position of the business during the accounting period. This is particularly true given that companies often take steps to improve their current ratio (such as paying off large amounts of current liabilities) immediately before the end of the accounting period.

Quick Ratio Most current liabilities will be paid in cash during the upcoming accounting period. This means that a business's liquidity will ultimately depend upon the conversion into cash of the other current assets. Some current assets, particularly inventory and prepaid expenses, are not quickly convertible into cash. Because inventory is usually the largest current asset, the current ratio may give a misleading picture of the true short-term debt-paying ability of a business. A second liquidity test, called the quick ratio or acid test, can be used to support the current ratio or to replace it. The quick ratio removes the least liquid current assets (inventory and prepaid expenses) from the calculation. The remaining current assets (cash, marketable securities, accounts receivable) can be quickly converted to cash and are called, collectively, *quick assets.*

The quick ratio is the ratio of quick assets to current liabilities and is calculated as follows:

$$\text{Quick ratio} = \frac{\text{quick assets}}{\text{current liabilities}}$$

Using the sample financial statements, the quick ratio for Small Company for 1981 and 1982 would be

1982	*1981*
$\dfrac{\$18,000 + \$50,000}{\$27,000} = 2.5$	$\dfrac{\$35,000 + \$40,000}{\$33,000} = 2.3$

The quick ratio matches the most liquid assets with the immediate obligations of the business; therefore, a quick ratio of one to one is generally considered to indicate satisfactory liquidity.

| Interpretation of Liquidity Ratios | Taken together, the current and quick ratios can give an external analyst a strong indication of a business's short-term debt-paying ability. Small Company exhibits strong liquidity, perhaps more than is necessary. |

Solvency Ratios

Solvency has to do with the ability to meet obligations in a smooth and orderly manner as they come due over the long run. Two ratios, the equity (debt) ratio and the times interest earned ratio reflect this ability.

A business can acquire assets from

1. nonowners, resulting in the creation of fixed obligations (debt), and

2. owners, resulting in the creation of owners' equity.

Debt holders enjoy a higher priority claim on the assets of the business. As a result, the cost of acquiring assets by using debt is lower than the cost of acquiring those assets from owners. In addition, interest is deductible in determining income taxes while dividends are not. The true cost of debt, then, is the after-tax interest paid on the amounts borrowed. For example, suppose two companies have identical income before interest figures but that Company B has interest expense of $1,000 and Company A has no interest expense. Income taxes and net income for these companies would be calculated as follows:

	Company A	Company B
Income before interest	$20,000	$20,000
Interest expense	–0–	1,000
Income before income taxes	20,000	19,000
Income taxes (assume 40%)	8,000	7,600
Net income	$12,000	$11,400

Even though Company B had extra interest expense of $1,000, its net income was only $600 lower than that of Company A because the tax deductibility of interest saved Company B $400 in income taxes. The true interest cost to Company B was $600 ($1,000 interest paid − $400 income taxes saved). If the $1,000 interest paid represented an interest rate of 10 percent, the after-tax interest rate would be 6 percent. The after-tax interest rate can be calculated as follows:

Effective interest rate	10%
× 1 − income tax rate	.6 (1 − .4)
= after-tax interest rate	6%

Debt is a low-cost source of assets for most businesses, and owners' equity is generally a higher-cost source over the long run.

High-Risk Characteristics of Debt There is, however, another side to debt that must be considered. The incurrence of debt requires that fixed interest payments be met at stipulated times. Interest must be paid in bad times as well as good, while dividends are paid at the discretion of the board of directors. During periods of low income and cash flow, a business may simply not pay a dividend. Interest, however, cannot be skipped without placing in jeopardy the existence of the business. This means that acquiring assets through debt carries more risk to the business than securing those assets from owners.

The two sources of assets a business may use, then, exhibit the following characteristics:

1. Debt is low cost (interest is tax deductible) but high risk (interest payments must be met).

2. Owners' equity is high cost (dividends are not tax deductible and owners must enjoy a higher return in the long run) but low risk (dividends are discretionary).

Equity Ratio A business should seek to acquire its assets in a manner that reduces both cost and risk. Because the two sources of assets exhibit different characteristics, reducing cost and risk requires a balanced use of both sources. An important factor in solvency, therefore, is the balance of debt and equity. The equity (or debt) ratio shows the percentage of a company's assets that were financed by owners' equity (or debt). It is the ratio of total owners' equity to total assets and is calculated as follows:

$$\text{Equity ratio} = \frac{\text{total owners' equity}}{\text{total assets}}$$

Using the balance sheets for Small Company from Figure 16-2, the equity ratios would be

1982

$$\frac{\$50,000 + \$50,000 + \$72,000 + \$140,000}{\$439,000} = 71\%$$

1981

$$\frac{\$50,000 + \$50,000 + \$72,000 + \$108,000}{\$403,000} = 69\%$$

The debt ratios would be 29 percent in 1982 and 31 percent in 1981 because equity plus debt must account for the total assets of the business.

Times Interest Earned Ratio Creditors of a business know that their claims on business assets are sound to the extent that a large cushion exists between annual income and the fixed interest payments that must be covered by that income. As the margin of safety between these figures shrinks, the possibility exists that legally required interest payments will not be met on schedule. Failure to make these payments would, of course, have serious implications for the financial stability and solvency of the business. For this reason, a second important solvency test is the times interest earned ratio. This ratio compares annual interest expense to the income for the period available to cover interest. It is the ratio of income before interest, taxes, and extraordinary items to annual interest expense and is calculated as follows:

Times interest earned ratio

$$= \frac{\text{income before interest, taxes, and extraordinary items}}{\text{annual interest expense}}$$

Using the financial statements of Small Company, only the ratio for 1982 can be calculated because only one income statement is given.

$$\frac{\text{operating profit (income before extraordinary items)} + \text{interest} + \text{taxes}}{\text{interest expense}}$$

$$= \frac{\$72,000 + \$10,000 + \$68,000}{\$10,000} = 15 \text{ times}$$

The movement of this ratio over time would be important, but the level of interest coverage is very high for Small Company. This ratio indicates that income could fall to a fraction of its current level and interest charges would still be covered. A times interest earned of five to seven is generally thought to represent a satisfactory cushion of safety for creditors.

Interpretation of Solvency Ratios

An interpretation of the equity and times interest earned ratios for Small Company gives some insight into the business. The company is very solvent (perhaps overly so) and, if these ratios held over time, may be too conservatively managed. The high equity ratio and very high times interest earned ratio tell exactly the same story; that is, the Small Company could benefit from the use of low-cost debt in the future acquisition of assets. The additional risk that would be incurred with this debt could easily be handled by the company.

Remember that, in the interpretation of any ratio, there is a range of good or acceptable performance within which the ratio should fall. This acceptable range is established by the use of historical, external, and expected standards by the analyst. Statements like "the higher the ratio, the better" or "the lower, the better" are generally not true for the external analyst.

Concept Summary

Financial Condition Ratios			
	Ratio	*Calculation*	*Meaning*
Liquidity	Current ratio	$\dfrac{\text{Current assets}}{\text{Current liabilities}}$	The number of times the most immediate obligations of a business are covered by current assets available to satisfy those debts.
	Quick ratio	$\dfrac{\text{Cash} + \text{marketable securities} + \text{receivables}}{\text{Current liabilities}}$	The number of times the most immediate obligations of a business are covered by its most liquid assets available to satisfy those debts.

(continued on next page)

Concept Summary *(continued)*

	Ratio	Calculation	Meaning
Solvency	Equity ratio	$$\frac{\text{Owners' equity}}{\text{Total assets}}$$	The percentage of total assets which have been financed by the owners of a business.
	Times interest earned ratio	$$\frac{\text{Income before interest, taxes, and extraordinary items}}{\text{Interest expense}}$$	The margin of safety between income available to cover the fixed interest obligations of a business and the annual amount of that interest.

16.4   Asset Use Ratios

In addition to maintaining sufficient current assets to assure liquidity, it is important that the most significant current assets be efficiently managed. The efficient management of accounts receivable and inventory can be critical to a company's profitability and financial condition. Receivables and inventory are usually the largest current assets, and both are related to important income statement figures. Sales on credit give rise to accounts receivable so there is a relationship between net sales revenue and receivables. Likewise, the acquisition cost of goods on hand becomes an expense as these units are sold, so there is a natural relationship between cost of goods sold and inventory. Asset use ratios explore these relationships to produce numbers that indicate how receivables and inventory are being handled.

Accounts Receivable

The maximum benefit from credit sales of merchandise can be realized only if the accounts receivable resulting from these sales are collected in a prompt and orderly manner.

Average Collection Period A ratio called the average collection period of receivables can be calculated to show how long on the average it takes a business to collect its receivables. The first step in calculating this ratio relates the net credit sales for an accounting period to the average amount of accounts receivable for that period as follows:

$$\text{Receivables turnover} = \frac{\text{net credit sales}}{\text{average accounts receivable}}$$

Average accounts receivable should be determined by adding the ending receivables balance for each month of the year and dividing by twelve; however, this information is seldom available to the external analyst. Instead, a simple average that adds receivables from the beginning of the period (from the previous balance sheet) and the end of the period (from the current balance sheet) and divides by two may be used.

The **receivables turnover** can then be divided into 365 days per year to determine the number of days on the average it has taken to collect accounts receivable.

$$\text{Average collection period} = \frac{365 \text{ days}}{\text{receivables turnover}}$$

Again, using the Small Company financial statements from Figure 16-2, the average collection period for 1982 would be calculated as follows (assuming that all sales revenue for the period represents credit sales):

Accounts receivable, beginning of year	$40,000	
Accounts receivable, end of year	$50,000	

$$\text{Average accounts receivable} = \frac{\$40,000 + \$50,000}{2} = \$45,000$$

$$\text{Receivables turnover} = \frac{\$455,000}{\$45,000} = 10.1$$

$$\text{Average collection period} = \frac{365}{10.1} = 36 \text{ days}$$

On the average, it has taken Small Company thirty-six days to collect the amounts owed from its credit sales. Whether this is a favorable or unfavorable sign would depend upon the normal credit terms offered by Small Company. If credit terms call for payment within thirty days, collections have been slightly slow. If credit terms call for payment within 45 or 60 days or longer, collections are very fast.

Interpretation of the Average Collection Period

As is usually true, the average collection period should fall within an acceptable range approximating the number of days indicated by credit terms. An average collection period significantly higher than the credit terms offered indicates that large amounts of cash are being tied up in receivables for long periods of time with a resulting effect on the company's ability to meet its obligations. On the other hand, a very low average collection period may indicate that the company is selling on credit only to those customers who pay very quickly. Sales could be increased in these circumstances by loosening credit somewhat and selling to some customers who may be slower in paying. This additional revenue would result in higher net income for the business. A rule of thumb commonly applied is that an average collection period of one and one-third times the days allowed by credit terms is satisfactory. Small Company's average collection period of thirty to forty days is an indication that accounts receivable are being efficiently managed.

Inventory

Cost of goods sold can be held to a minimum for a given sales level through the effective management of inventory.

Days To Sell Average Inventory A ratio can be computed that relates average inventory to the cost of goods sold for the period. This ratio, called

inventory turnover, shows how long it takes on the average to sell the typical amount of inventory held during the year and is calculated as follows:

$$\text{Inventory turnover} = \frac{\text{cost of goods sold}}{\text{average inventory}}$$

As was true of receivables turnover, a monthly average is ideal, but an average of beginning and end-of-year inventory is likely to be all that is available to the external analyst. The inventory turnover can then be divided into 365 in the same manner as was receivables turnover to determine the number of days required to sell the amount of an average inventory.

$$\text{Days to sell average inventory} = \frac{365 \text{ days}}{\text{inventory turnover}}$$

In this manner, the days to sell an average inventory for the Small Company for 1982 can be computed as follows:

Inventory, beginning of year	$ 48,000	
Inventory, end of year	$ 56,000	
Average inventory $=$	$\dfrac{\$48,000 + \$56,000}{2}$	$= \$52,000$
Inventory turnover $=$	$\dfrac{\$200,000}{\$52,000}$	$= 3.8$
Days to sell average inventory $=$	$\dfrac{365}{3.8}$	$= 96 \text{ days}$

Interpretation of the Inventory Turnover

The average amount held in inventory during the year requires ninety-six days to sell. Interpretation of this ratio would necessarily depend upon the type of inventory being sold. If perishable goods (such as grocery items or flowers) make up the inventory, ninety-six days would be completely unacceptable. On the other hand, if the inventory was furniture or jewelry, selling out a complete inventory each ninety-six days might be satisfactory. Care is necessary in the interpretation of inventory turnover, and the use of historical and external standards is required.

Inventory may turn over each two or three days in a grocery store but only once each two or three months in a furniture store. When the number of days required to sell an average inventory is high compared to a reasonable standard, it is an indication that the inventory being held is larger than it should be or that the wrong mix of goods is being purchased. In either event, large amounts of cash are tied up in inventory (affecting debt-paying ability), and extra costs of storage, handling, insurance, and inventory shrinkage are being incurred (affecting profitability).

At first glance, it might seem that the smaller the number of days required to sell an average inventory, the better. It turns out not to be so, however. Although a rapid turnover of inventory is efficient, there are some potential costs associated with it. Selling an average inventory very quickly relative to an appropriate standard indicates that the amount of inventory on hand at any time is small compared to the volume of goods being sold. The danger of such a situation is the likelihood of having insufficient inventory on hand at some point and losing sales as a result. If out-of-stock situations occur frequently, customers may be lost completely. This latter hazard, that of losing customers and all of the future sales they may generate, encourages businesses to stock sufficient inventory. Thus, the inventory turnover ratio should fall within an acceptable range.

Concept Summary

Asset Use Ratios		
Ratio	*Calculation*	*Meaning*
Receivables turnover	$\dfrac{\text{Net credit sales}}{\text{Average accounts receivable}}$	The number of times the average amount owed to the business by customers is exceeded by the net credit sales of the period.
Average collection period of receivables	$\dfrac{365 \text{ days}}{\text{Receivables turnover}}$	The number of days on the average the business requires to collect its receivables; the average time receivables are outstanding.
Inventory turnover	$\dfrac{\text{Cost of goods sold}}{\text{Average inventory}}$	The number of times the average amount of inventory on hand is sold during an accounting period
Days to sell an average inventory	$\dfrac{365 \text{ days}}{\text{Inventory turnover}}$	The number of days required to sell the average amount of inventory held during an accounting period.

Operating Cycle

One final point about asset use ratios should be made. A business's operating cycle is the time required to convert inventory into accounts receivable through sales and then to convert accounts receivable into cash through collection. The length of an operating cycle for any business can be computed as the sum of days required to sell an average inventory plus the average collection period of receivables. The operating cycle for Small Company would be

Days to sell an average inventory	96
Average collection period of receivables	36
Operating cycle	132 days

A lengthy operating cycle relative to a company's own performance in the past or to the performance of other companies engaged in the same type of activity indicates inefficient use of inventory and receivables.

16.5   Market Test Ratios

It is important for owners and potential owners to be able to get a reading on the perception of the investment market to the activities of a business. Market test ratios use information from a company's financial statements together with external information to gauge the reaction of the investment market to business profits and dividends.

The three market test ratios (1) relate the income for a business to the number of shares that exercise a claim on that income (earnings per share), (2) reflect the quality of a business's earnings (price-earnings ratio), and (3) relate dividends to the amount an owner must pay to receive those dividends in the future (dividend yield).

Earnings per Share as an Analytical Tool

The calculation of earnings per share was discussed in Chapter 13. This ratio is a required part of the presentation of a corporate income statement. The external analyst need only understand the meaning and proper use of the ratio because, in most instances, it will already be calculated. Earnings per share is a residual concept involving only the residual owners of the business (common stockholders) and the recurring income that accrues to them. The calculation determines the amount of corporate income each share of ownership interest may claim as follows:

$$\text{Earnings per share} = \frac{\text{operating profit} - \text{preferred dividend commitment}}{\text{average number of common shares outstanding}}$$

Operating profit should be used because this figure conveys the results of the normal and recurring profit-seeking activities of the business. Preferred dividends are subtracted out even if they are not paid and, in the case of cumulative preferred stock, any dividends in arrears should also be deducted. The average number of shares should take into account all changes in the number of shares outstanding during the period.

Using the data from the Small Company financial statement given in Figure 16-2, the earnings per share calculation would be

Preferred stock dividends for 1982 (10% × $50,000) = $5,000

Earnings per share (operating income) of common stock =

$$\frac{\$72,000 - \$5,000}{\$5,000} = \$13.40$$

Price-Earnings Ratio   Earnings per share can be related to the average market price of a common stock share during the year in which the earnings were produced. The price-earnings ratio indicates how many times one year's earnings per share each share of stock is currently selling for.

$$\text{Price-earnings ratio} = \frac{\text{average market price of a share of stock}}{\text{earnings per share}}$$

Because daily stock price quotations would normally be available to an external analyst, the yearly low and high price at which the stock was sold during the year can be determined. This low and high may be used to calculate an average stock price. For example, if the common stock of Small Company had been sold for prices ranging from $200 to $278 per share during 1982, the price-earnings ratio for 1982 would be

High stock price for 1982 $278
Low stock price for 1982 $200

$$\text{Average stock price for 1982} = \frac{\$278 + \$200}{2} = \$239$$

$$\text{Price-earnings ratio} \quad = \frac{\$239}{\$13.40} \quad = 17.8 \text{ times}$$

Quality of Earnings

The price at which a share of stock will sell is dependent upon the investment market's perception of

1. the quality of a company's earnings, and

2. the dividend policy of the company.

Although two companies may report identical earnings for a year, investors may believe that the earnings of one company are derived from a source that is more stable and likely to continue than that of the other. In addition, the particular accounting principles chosen by one company to report its income may be more conservative than those chosen by the other. Generally speaking, earnings that are stable or increasing and produced by normal and recurring activities are considered "quality" earnings. This is especially true if these earnings are reported without using accounting principles that result in an upward effect on income for a given set of activities.

Investors attempt to determine the quality of earnings and seek out companies whose earnings are considered to be of high quality. The market price of a share of stock reflects both the level and quality of a company's earnings. By relating market price to earnings per share, the price-earnings ratio removes earnings level as a consideration. This ratio, then, is an expression of the faith of investors in the earnings of a business. A high price-earnings ratio indicates a perception of quality earnings, while a low price-earnings ratio may indicate skepticism about earnings.

Dividend Policy

A second factor in the price-earnings ratio is the percentage of annual earnings distributed to stockholders in the form of dividends. Retention and reinvestment of earnings increases the likelihood that future earnings levels will be higher and sounder, thus improving the potential quality of future earnings. Distribution of a large percentage of earnings to owners limits the potential for future earnings growth. Companies that distribute a small percentage of annual earnings to stockholders are sometimes called *growth companies,* while companies that distribute a large percentage of earnings are called *dividend companies.* Growth companies would normally exhibit a higher price-earnings ratio than would dividend companies.

Shares of the common stock of most large companies sell at price-earnings ratios of from five to fifteen.

Dividend Yield Many investors purchase common stock with the anticipation of regular and substantial dividends. To these investors, the amount of dividends paid each year is important. The relationship of annual dividends to the average market price of common stock is important to investors interested in maximizing dividend return. This ratio, called dividend yield, is calculated as follows:

$$\text{Dividend yield} = \frac{\text{dividends per share}}{\text{average market price of a share of stock}}$$

Dividends per share can be determined from the financial statements, and the average market price is the same as that described for the price-earnings ratio.

For Small Company, the dividend yield for 1982 would be

Dividends paid for 1982	$50,000
Preferred dividends (10% × 50,000)	5,000
Common dividends for 1982	$45,000
Average number of common shares outstanding	5,000
Dividends per share	$9.00
Dividend yield $= \dfrac{\$9.00}{\$239}$	$= 3.8\%$

Concept Summary

Market Test Ratios		
Ratio	*Calculation*	*Meaning*
Earnings per share	$\dfrac{\text{Operating profit } - \text{ preferred dividend commitment}}{\text{Average number of common shares outstanding}}$	This is the amount of earnings of the current period which may be claimed by each residual share of ownership interest (common stock).
Price-earnings ratio	$\dfrac{\text{Average market price of a share of common stock}}{\text{Earnings per share}}$	This is the number of times the average price of a share of stock exceeds the current share of income claimed by it. It represents a perception by investors of the quality of a firms earnings and the appropriateness of its dividend policy.
Dividend yield	$\dfrac{\text{Dividends per share}}{\text{Average market price of a share of common stock}}$	This is the percent return to investors on common stock which takes the form of cash dividends received. To this should be added the return to investors which takes the form of stock price appreciation.

The dividend yield (return) for Small Company is quite small, particularly as compared to the yield on Small Company bonds (10 percent) and preferred stock (10 percent). This is consistent with the high price-earnings ratio calculated previously.

Remember that the total return to common stockholders is more than simply the dividend return. In successful companies, such as Small Company, the return to common owners includes any increases in the market price of the stock over the period of stock ownership. These stock price increases result in expected future earnings increases and reflect continued high quality earnings.

Dividends are taxed as ordinary income to stockholders as they are received. Increases in the market price of stock are not taxable to owners until the shares are sold, and then only at favorable capital gains tax rates. In spite of the unfavorable tax treatment accorded dividends, they remain a popular form of return on common stock to investors.

16.6 Overall Ratios

Each group of ratios already discussed focuses on a particular area of business activities. By using these ratios, the analyst hopes to get a reading on the performance of the company and its management in that area. Care should be taken in interpreting these ratios individually because a misleading picture of a company as a whole can result from the analysis of only one or two areas of activity.

To support the conclusions reached by analyzing ratios of profit margin, financial condition, asset use, and market activity, a set of ratios that summarize the results of all company activity is needed. Overall ratios, called **return on investment (ROI)**, do just this. These overall ratios are not substitutes for the detailed information gathered by using other ratios. Instead, return on investment simply gives a broad overview of company success and should be used in conjunction with other ratios. To most investors, however, the return on investment ratios are the single most important calculations to be made and interpreted.

Two return on investment ratios are most important. These are return on total assets and return on common stock equity.

Return on Total Assets

A business acquires assets from creditors or owners, then combines and uses these assets to earn as much return (income) as possible. In evaluating a business and its management, it is important to know how successfully the assets of the business were used. Assets are a limited commodity in that no business can have as many as it may desire. Return on total assets shows how management has used the assets entrusted to the business without regard to how those assets were acquired. The ratio relates the earnings of the business before deducting any return to the suppliers of assets to the average total assets available during the period and is calculated as follows:

$$\text{Return on total assets} = \frac{\text{operating profit} + \text{interest expense}}{\text{average total assets}}$$

Operating profit is used as the starting point for the calculation because it is a measure of the profits resulting from normal and recurring activities. Extraordinary items affect net income in varying degree from company to company but are extremely unlikely to occur again. As a result, an analyst can be misled by using net income when extraordinary items are present. Interest expense is added back to operating profit because this ratio is measuring the income earned by all assets, no matter what their source. A measure of income before any distributions to the suppliers of assets removes consideration of how the assets have been acquired.

From the financial statements of Small Company, the return on total assets can be calculated as follows

Total assets, December 31, 1981	$403,000
Total assets, December 31, 1982	$439,000

$$\text{Average total assets} = \frac{\$403,000 + \$439,000}{2} = \$421,000$$

$$\text{Return on total assets} = \frac{\$72,000 + \$10,000}{\$421,000} = 19\%$$

The return is quite high and, therefore, favorable; however, interpretation would require reference to the past performance of Small Company and comparison to other companies of similar circumstances.

The Components of Return on Total Assets   It is interesting to note that return on total assets is the product of two other ratios,

$$\frac{\text{net sales}}{\text{average total assets}} \times \frac{\text{operating profit} + \text{interest expense}}{\text{net sales}}$$

The net sales numerator and denominator cancel out, resulting in the formula for return on total assets. The important point here is that, by dividing return on total assets into its component parts, it becomes easier to see how a company can improve its return. The number of sales dollars generated per dollar of assets is called the asset turnover of the business. An improved return on investment can result from the generation of more sales dollars per dollar of assets (volume) or from increased efficiency at the current volume level resulting in a higher operating profit margin.

Return on Common Equity

Several groups have claims on the amount earned by total assets. The return to creditors takes the form of interest, and the return to preferred stockholders is dividends. Both interest and preferred dividends are fixed, and the amount remaining after deducting these fixed amounts accrues to the common stockholders. An important consideration for common stock investors is the return on common equity ratio and how this return compares to the return on total assets. The return on common equity ratio relates earnings available to common stockholders to the average amount of common equity during the period and is calculated as follows:

$$\text{Return on common equity} = \frac{\text{operating profit} - \text{preferred dividend commitment}}{\text{average common stock equity}}$$

Operating profit is already net of the return to creditors (interest expense), and the return to preferred stockholders (preferred dividends) is subtracted to arrive at normal and recurring income available to common stockholders.

The return on common equity for Small Company is calculated as follows

Common equity, December 31, 1981		$230,000
Common equity, December 31, 1982		$262,000

$$\text{Average common equity} = \frac{\$230,000 + \$262,000}{2} = \$246,000$$

$$\text{Return on common equity} = \frac{\$72,000 - \$5,000}{\$246,000} = 27\%$$

The return on common equity for Small Company is high and very favorable. Also, the return on common equity is higher than the return on total assets. This latter relationship is favorable to common stock owners and indicates the existence of positive financial leverage (sometimes called **trading on the equity**).

Financial Leverage

Positive financial leverage occurs whenever a business is able to earn a higher rate of return on its assets (return on total assets) than it pays to the creditors (interest expense) and preferred stockholders (preferred dividends) who have supplied the assets. The difference between the amount earned on total assets and the fixed amounts paid to these groups accrues to the common stockholder. This results in a return on common equity which is greater than the average return on total assets.

For example, consider the following circumstance for Small Company:

Return on total assets	19%
Return paid to creditors	10%
Return paid to preferred stockholders	10%

Because 19 percent was earned on all assets and only 10 percent was paid to creditors and preferred stockholders for the assets supplied by them, an extra 9 percent on those assets accrues to common stock owners. This extra 9 percent on the assets financed through debt and preferred equity drives the return on total common equity up from 19 percent to 27 percent. If a company paid more to creditors and preferred stockholders than it earned on total assets, the result would be negative financial leverage. Return on common equity would be less than return on total assets, indicating that the extra amount paid to debt and preferred stock was being subsidized by the common stockholders.

The Use of Debt Financing Positive financial leverage is most often achieved through the use of debt financing of assets. Recall that debt is a low-cost source of assets, and the expectation is that more can be earned on these assets than is paid to finance them. However, debt is also a high-risk source of assets. As debt financing is used and positive financial leverage achieved, the leveraged company also accepts more risk. Each company and external analyst must determine the best trade-off between the favorable effect of financial leverage and the negative effect of additional risk. This trade-off results in most companies using a combination of debt and equity to finance their assets.

Concept Summary

Overall Ratios (ROI)		
Ratio	*Calculation*	*Meaning*
Return on total assets	$$\frac{\text{Operating profit } + \text{ interest expense}}{\text{average total assets}}$$	This is the average percentage return (earned) on all company assets without regard for how the assets were financed. It reflects how well company management has used all of the assets entrusted to it.
Return on common equity	$$\frac{\text{Operating profit } - \text{ preferred dividend commitment}}{\text{average common stock equity}}$$	This is the percentage return (earned) on the equity of common stockholders in the business. When this ratio is higher than return on total assets, common stockholders are benefitting from the positive effects of financial leverage.

All of the relationships and ratios presented in this chapter and the external groups of analysts likely to be interested in each ratio are brought together in the final Concept Summary of the chapter.

Concept Summary

Summary of Ratios and Their Use		
Ratio	*Calculation*	*Used by*
1. Gross profit percentage	$$\frac{\text{Gross profit}}{\text{Net sales}}$$	Investors
2. Operating profit percentage	$$\frac{\text{Operating profit}}{\text{Net Sales}}$$	Investors

(continued on next page)

Concept Summary *(continued)*

Ratio	Calculation	Used by
3. Net income percentage	$$\frac{\text{Net income}}{\text{Net sales}}$$	Short-term creditors Long-term creditors Investors
4. Current ratio	$$\frac{\text{Current assets}}{\text{Current liabilities}}$$	Short-term creditors Long-term creditors
5. Quick ratio	$$\frac{\text{Cash + marketable securities + receivables}}{\text{Current liabilities}}$$	Short-term creditors
6. Equity ratio	$$\frac{\text{Owners' equity}}{\text{Total assets}}$$	Long-term creditors Investors
7. Times interest earned	$$\frac{\text{Income before interest, taxes, and extraordinary items}}{\text{Interest expense}}$$	Long-term creditors
8. Average collection period of receivables	$$\frac{365 \text{ days}}{\text{Net credit sales/Average accounts receivable}}$$	Short-term creditors Investors
9. Days to sell an average inventory	$$\frac{365 \text{ days}}{\text{Cost of goods sold/Average inventory}}$$	Short-term creditors Investors
10. Earnings per share	$$\frac{\text{Operating profit − preferred dividend commitment}}{\text{Average number of common shares outstanding}}$$	Long-term creditors Investors
11. Price-earnings ratio	$$\frac{\text{Average market price of a share of common stock}}{\text{Earnings per share}}$$	Investors
12. Dividend yield	$$\frac{\text{Dividends per share}}{\text{Average market price of a share of common stock}}$$	Investors
13. Return on total assets	$$\frac{\text{Operating profit + interest expense}}{\text{Average total assets}}$$	Long-term creditors Investors
14. Return on common equity	$$\frac{\text{Operating profit − preferred dividend commitment}}{\text{Average common stock equity}}$$	Investors

Summary

Financial statements provide external analysts with the most objective and reliable information about the earnings performance and financial position of a business. Financial statement analysis involves the following three steps:

1. Choose appropriate standards of performance.

2. Compute ratios that express relevant relationships.

3. Compare ratios to standards and interpret the results as the basis for predicting the future.

Three commonly used standards of performance are historical standards, external standards, and expected standards. Historical standards compare a company's current performance to its own past performance, while external standards compare the performance of one company to that of other companies in approximately the same circumstances. Expected standards require the application of special knowledge, experience, expertise or rules of thumb by an analyst.

Operating ratios convey information about the profit margins of a business. They come directly from income statement numbers and make possible the comparison of companies of vastly different size by removing volume of activity as a consideration.

Ratios of financial condition depict the liquidity and solvency of a business. These ratios of debt-paying ability are of particular interest to creditors.

Asset use ratios reflect how efficiently a business has managed its two most critical assets: accounts receivable and inventory. Short-term creditors are particularly interested in asset use ratios because the completion of the operating cycle is a primary source of cash for most businesses.

Market test ratios reflect investment market reaction to the perceived quality of a company's earnings. Investors (owners and prospective owners) are most interested in these ratios.

Only overall ratios portray all aspects of business activity. As such, these return on investment (ROI) ratios are the single best barometers of company performance for investors.

In Chapter 17, the basic accounting assumptions presented in Chapter 1 are discussed in more detail and alternative assumptions are considered.

Key Terms

Asset use ratios
Average collection period
Common size statement
Current ratio
Days to sell average inventory
Dividend yield
Equity ratio
Financial condition ratios
Inventory turnover
Liquidity
Market test ratios
Net income percentage
Operating profit percentage
Operating ratios

Overall ratios
Price-earnings ratio
Quick ratio (acid test)
Receivables turnover
Return on common equity
Return on investment (ROI)
Return on total assets
Solvency
Standards of performance (historical, external, and expected)
Times interest earned ratio
Trading on the equity (financial leverage)

Comprehensive Review Problem

Below is information for Bethel Bowling Ball Company, Inc.

BETHEL BOWLING BALL COMPANY, INC.
Balance Sheets

	End of	
	Year 2	Year 1
ASSETS		
Current assets		
Cash	$ 25,000	$ 35,000
Accounts receivable (net of allowance)	70,000	50,000
Inventories	45,000	35,000
Total current assets	140,000	120,000
Noncurrent assets		
Property, plant, and equipment	320,000	245,000
Accumulated depreciation	(85,000)	(60,000)
Total noncurrent assets	235,000	185,000
Total assets	$375,000	$ 305,000
LIABILITIES & STOCKHOLDERS' EQUITY		
Current liabilities		
Accounts payable	$ 50,000	$ 40,000
Long-term liabilities		
8% bonds payable	100,000	100,000
Stockholders' equity		
5% preferred stock, $10 par	15,000	15,000
Common stock, $2 par	52,000	40,000
Paid-in capital—common	78,000	60,000
Retained earnings	80,000	50,000
Total stockholders' equity	225,000	165,000
Total liabilities & stockholders' equity	$375,000	$ 305,000
Closing market price per share of common stock	$13.50	$10.50

New shares of common stock were issued on July 1, Year 2.

BETHEL BOWLING BALL COMPANY, INC.
Income Statement
For Year 2

Sales (all on credit)		$ 185,000
Cost of goods sold		102,000
Gross profit		83,000
Expenses		
Selling	$ 13,700	
Administrative	10,300	
Interest	8,000	32,000
Income before income taxes		51,000
Income taxes		12,750
Operating profit		38,250
Extraordinary loss (net of tax effect of $800)		(2,500)
Net income		$ 35,750

BETHEL BOWLING BALL COMPANY, INC.
Statement of Retained Earnings
For Year 2

Retained earnings, end of Year 1		$ 50,000
Net income		35,750
Dividends: Preferred	$ 750	
Common	5,000	(5,750)
Retained earnings, end of Year 2		$ 80,000

Required:
1. Compute the following ratios for Year 2:

    a. Operating
        (1) Gross profit percentage
        (2) Operating profit percentage
        (3) Net income percentage
    b. Financial condition
        (4) Current ratio
        (5) Quick ratio
        (6) Equity ratio
        (7) Times interest earned
    c. Asset use
        (8) Average collection period of receivables
        (9) Inventory turnover
    d. Market test
        (10) Earnings per share
        (11) Price-earnings ratio
        (12) Dividend yield
    e. Overall
        (13) Return on total assets
        (14) Return on common equity

2. How much is Bethel marking up its products on cost to get selling price?

3. What percentage of total assets was supplied by debt in Year 1? In Year 2?

4. How long is the operating cycle of the business?

5. Are the common stockholders of Bethel experiencing positive or negative leverage? How much?

Solution to Comprehensive Review Problem

    1. Ratios
       a. Operating
        (1) Gross profit percentage

$$\frac{\text{gross profit}}{\text{net sales}} = \frac{\$83,000}{\$185,000} = 45\%$$

        (2) Operating profit percentage

$$\frac{\text{operating profit}}{\text{net sales}} = \frac{\$38,250}{\$185,000} = 21\%$$

        (3) Net income percentage

$$\frac{\text{net income}}{\text{net sales}} = \frac{\$35,750}{\$185,000} = 19\%$$

b. Financial condition

   (4) Current ratio

$$\frac{\text{current assets}}{\text{current liabilities}} = \frac{\$140{,}000}{\$50{,}000} = 2.8$$

   (5) Quick ratio

$$\frac{\text{quick assets}}{\text{current liabilities}} = \frac{\$25{,}000 + \$70{,}000}{\$50{,}000} = 1.9$$

   (6) Equity ratio

$$\frac{\text{owners' equity}}{\text{total assets}} = \frac{\$225{,}000}{\$375{,}000} = 60\%$$

   (7) Times interest earned

$$\frac{\text{operating profit } + \text{ interest } + \text{ taxes}}{\text{interest expense}} =$$

$$\frac{\$38{,}250 + \$8{,}000 + \$12{,}750}{\$8{,}000} = 7.4$$

c. Asset use

   (8) Average collection period

$$\text{receivables turnover} = \frac{\text{net credit sales}}{\text{average accounts receivable}} =$$

$$\frac{\$185{,}000}{\$60{,}000} = 3.08$$

$$\text{average collection period} = \frac{365 \text{ days}}{\text{receivables turnover}} = 119 \text{ days}$$

   (9) Inventory turnover

$$\frac{\text{cost of goods sold}}{\text{average inventory}} = \frac{\$102{,}000}{\$40{,}000^*} = 2.6$$

$$^*\$40{,}000 = \frac{1}{2}\,(\$45{,}000 + \$35{,}000)$$

d. Market test

   (10) Earnings per share

$$\frac{\text{operating profit } - \text{ preferred dividends}}{\text{average number of common shares outstanding}} =$$

$$\frac{\$38{,}250 - \$750}{23{,}000^*} = \$1.63$$

$$^*23{,}000 = 20{,}000 + (\tfrac{1}{2} \times 6{,}000)$$

   (11) Price-earnings ratio

$$\frac{\text{average market price}}{\text{earnings per share}} = \frac{\$12^*}{\$1.63} = 7.4$$

$$^*\$12 = \frac{\$10.50 + \$13.50}{2}$$

(12) Dividend yield

$$\frac{\text{dividends per share}}{\text{average market price}} = \frac{\$5,000 \div 26,000}{\$12} = 1.6\%$$

e. Overall

(13) Return on total assets

$$\frac{\text{operating profit} + \text{interest expense}}{\text{average total assets}} = \frac{\$38,250 + \$8,000}{\$340,000^*} = 14\%$$

$$^*\$340,000 = \frac{\$305,000 + \$375,000}{2}$$

(14) Return on common equity

$$\frac{\text{operating profit} - \text{preferred dividends}}{\text{average common equity}} = \frac{\$38,250 - \$750}{\$195,000^*} = 19\%$$

$$^*\$195,000 = \frac{\$165,000 + \$225,000}{2}$$

2. Bethel's markup on cost is

$$\frac{\text{gross profit}}{\text{cost of goods sold}} = \frac{\$83,000}{\$102,000} = 81\%$$

3. The percentage of assets provided by debt is

Year 2	Year 1
$\dfrac{\$150,000}{\$375,000} = 40\%$	$\dfrac{\$140,000}{\$305,000} = 46\%$

4. The operating cycle is

Average collection period	119 days
+ Days to sell average inventory	140 days*
Operating cycle	259 days

$$^*140 \text{ days} = \frac{365 \text{ days}}{\text{inventory turnover}} = \frac{365 \text{ days}}{2.6}$$

5. The common stockholders are experiencing 5 percent positive leverage, calculated as follows:

Return on common equity	19%
− Return on total assets	14
Positive leverage	5%

Questions

Q16-1. Describe the three steps of financial statement analysis.

Q16-2. Give three commonly used standards of performance and cite an advantage and a disadvantage of each.

Q16-3. Explain how operating ratios remove volume as a factor in the comparison of companies.

Q16-4. Define liquidity. Give two liquidity ratios and specify which external groups might be most interested in these ratios.

Q16-5. Define solvency. Give two solvency ratios and specify which external groups might be most interested in these ratios.

Q16-6. Compare the risk and cost characteristics of debt and equity as sources of long-term funds for a business.

Q16-7. What is the operating cycle of a business? How can the length of this cycle be calculated?

Q16-8. What factors affect the price-earnings ratio? How can the common stock of two companies with identical net incomes sell at different price-earnings ratios?

Q16-9. Contrast return on total assets and return on common equity. Why are these figures likely to be different?

Q16-10. What is financial leverage? How do common stockholders benefit from financial leverage?

Exercises

E16-1. Indicate how each of the following ratios is computed and briefly explain what each ratio indicates about a business.

    a. Operating profit percentage
    b. Quick ratio
    c. Times interest earned
    d. Average collection period of receivables
    e. Price-earnings ratio
    f. Return on common equity

E16-2. Indicate whether the ratios would increase, decrease, or remain the same in each of the following cases. Consider each case to be independent of the others.

Case I: The quick ratio is 1.6 to 1. How will this ratio change if inventory is purchased for cash? If inventory is purchased on credit, what will be the effect?

Case II: The net income percentage is 24 percent. What would be the effect of an increase in sales returns?

Case III: Times interest earned is 3. What would be the effect of an increase in income tax rates?

Case IV: The average collection period of receivables is thirty-eight days. What would be the effect of the write-off of accounts receivable against the allowance account?

Case V: The return on common equity is 18 percent. What would be the effect of the issuance of 10,000 shares of common stock? Of the retirement of 5,000 shares of preferred stock?

E16-3. Net income (loss) is as shown for each of the following cases:

	1982	*1981*
a.	$ 48,000	$ 30,000
b.	$ 16,000	$ 16,000
c.	$ 20,000	$(20,000)

d.	–0–	$ 5,000
e.	$(10,000)	–0–
f.	$(45,000)	$ 15,000
g.	$(14,000)	$(14,000)
h.	$ 20,000	$ 32,000
i.	$ 40,000	–0–
j.	$(40,000)	$ 10,000

Indicate the dollar change, the percentage change, and 1982/1981 ratio for each case above.

E16-4. The income statements of Guyton Company, a retail establishment, are given below in thousands of dollars for 1982 and 1981:

GUYTON COMPANY
Comparative Income Statements
For the Year Ended December 31

	1982	1981
Sales	$ 200,000	$ 160,000
Cost of goods sold	116,000	66,000
Gross profit	84,000	94,000
Selling expenses	15,000	12,000
Administrative expenses	11,000	9,000
Interest expense	4,000	6,000
Income before income taxes	54,000	67,000
Income taxes	24,000	30,000
Operating profit	30,000	37,000
Extraordinary gain net of tax of $2,250	5,250	—
Net income	$ 35,250	$ 37,000

Prepare common size income statements for 1982 and 1981.

E16-5. The balance sheets of Guyton Company, a retail establishment, are given below in thousands of dollars for 1982 and 1981:

GUYTON COMPANY
Comparative Balance Sheets
December 31

	1982	1981
ASSETS		
Cash	$ 14,000	$ 8,000
Marketable securities	4,000	8,000
Accounts receivable (net)	26,000	18,000
Inventory	18,000	14,000
Plant assets (net)	138,000	132,000
Total assets	$ 200,000	$ 180,000
LIABILITIES & OWNERS' EQUITY		
Current liabilities	$ 28,000	$ 32,000
Bond payable, due 1990	48,000	40,000
Common stock, $20 par	60,000	60,000
Retained earnings	64,000	48,000
Total liabilities & owners' equity	$ 200,000	$ 180,000

Prepare common size balance sheets by expressing all figures as a percentage of total assets.

E16-6. Refer to the data in Exercises 16-4 and 16-5. Compute the following ratios:

    a. Average collection period of receivables, assuming that all sales are on credit for 1982.

    b. Earnings per share for 1982 and 1981.

    c. Return on total assets for 1982.

    d. Gross profit percentage for 1982 and 1981.

    e. Operating profit percentage for 1982 and 1981.

    f. Net income percentage for 1982 and 1981.

    g. Days to sell an average inventory in 1982.

    h. Return on common equity for 1982.

E16-7. Refer to the data in Exercise 16-5. Compute for 1982 and 1981 the two liquidity ratios and the two solvency ratios described in the chapter. Compare each ratio computed to the rule of thumb for that ratio and tell whether you would consider the ratio to be an indication of sufficient liquidity or solvency.

E16-8. Joanen Corporation had net credit sales for 1982 of $360,000. Accounts receivable had a balance at the beginning of the year of $53,000 and an ending balance of $61,000. The corporation's gross profit was 30 percent of net credit sales. Beginning inventory was $75,000 and ending inventory was $82,000.

Compute the number of days in Joanen Corporation's operating cycle.

E16-9. The following information relates to Rome Corporation for the current year:

Net earnings before extraordinary items	$145,000
Extraordinary loss, net of tax	$ 10,000
Net earnings	$135,000
6% preferred stock, par $100	$ 60,000
Common stock, par $5	
outstanding January 1, 20,000 shares	
Issued May 1, 5,000 shares	25,000 shares
Market price of common stock	
January 2	$20
December 31	$35
Total dividends paid during the year	$ 32,000

Compute the following ratios for Rome Corporation:

    a. Earnings per share

    b. Price-earnings ratio

    c. Dividend yield

E16-10. The three corporations described below all have assets of $100,000. Each corporation has operating income before taxes and interest of $20,000. Assume that the appropriate corporate tax rate is 40 percent.

Corporation A	8% Bonds	$ 40,000
	Common stockholders' equity	60,000
Corporation B	6% Preferred Stock	$ 40,000
	Common stockholders' equity	60,000
Corporation C	Common stockholders' equity	$100,000

Compute the earnings after taxes and the return on the common stockholders' equity for each corporation.

Problems

P16-1. Given below are a list of terms and a list of definitions. Enter on the line to the left of the term the letter of the definition that is the most appropriate.

Terms

1. ___ external users of financial statements
2. ___ common size statements
3. ___ expected standard
4. ___ ratios
5. ___ standards
6. ___ operating ratios
7. ___ historical standard
8. ___ financial statements
9. ___ external standard
10. ___ solvency

Definitions

a. numerical expressions of the relationship between two numbers
b. the primary output of the financial accounting process
c. stockholders, creditors, governmental agencies, labor unions
d. yardsticks by which actual performance can be measured
e. based on a company's own past performance
f. the ability of a business to handle its long-run obligations in a smooth and orderly manner
g. based on the performance of other firms of approximately the same size in the same industry
h. based on some special knowledge, experience, or expertise on the part of the analyst
i. ratios having to do with the profit margins of a business
j. all components of the statements are expressed as a percentage of a certain item on the statements

P16-2. The 1981 and 1982 balance sheet and income statement data for Blanc Company are presented below:

	1982	1981
Balance Sheets		
ASSETS		
Cash	$ 4,125	$ 4,500
Account receivable (net)	9,625	5,250
Inventory	13,750	15,250
Fixed assets (net)	43,750	40,000
Total assets	$71,250	$65,000
LIABILITIES & OWNERS' EQUITY		
Current liabilities	$13,750	$15,000
8% bonds	20,000	20,000
Capital stock ($1.25 par)	30,000	25,000
Retained earnings	7,500	5,000
Total liabilities & owners' equity	$71,250	$65,000

Income Statements

Revenue	$87,500	$75,000
Cost of goods sold	52,000	45,000
Gross profit	35,000	30,000
Expenses	30,000	22,500
Income before taxes	5,000	7,500
Income taxes	1,500	2,250
Net income	$ 3,500	$ 5,250
Dividends paid	$ 2,500	$ 3,000
Average market price of stock	$1.32	$2.45

Required:

Answer the following questions.

1. What is the number of times bond interest was earned in 1982? In 1981?

2. What is the earnings per share for 1982? For 1981? Assume new stock is issued January 2 each year.

3. What is the rate earned on average stockholders' equity in 1982?

4. What is the gross profit percentage in 1982 and 1981?

5. What is the average collection period of receivables in 1982 assuming credit sales were 82 percent of total revenue?

6. What is the return on total assets?

7. What is the amount of positive financial leverage in 1982?

8. What is the net income percentage for 1982 and 1981?

9. What is the price earnings ratio for 1982? For 1981?

P16-3. The following information is available for Harvey Corporation:

Sales	$900,000 (including $300,000 cash sales)
Gross profit margin	60 percent
Average inventory per month	$60,000
Average monthly balance in trade receivables	$150,000
Operating expenses	$320,000
Number of days in business year	365
Income tax rate	40 percent

Required:

Compute the following:

1. Inventory turnover

2. Days to sell an average inventory

3. Trade receivable turnover

4. Average collection period of receivables

5. Operating profit percentage

P16-4. Using the information below, complete a balance sheet in good form. Show all computations.

1. Current liabilities to stockholders' equity, 0.6 to 1.

2. Stockholders' equity, $1,000.

3. Current ratio, 2:1.

4. Inventory turnover (based on ending inventory), 50 times.

5. Shares of $5 par value capital stock outstanding, 120. Stock was issued at par.

6. Average collection period of receivables (based on year-end receivables), 14.6 days.

7. Sales for the year, $25,000 (80 percent are credit sales).

8. Gross profit percentage, 40 percent.

9. Current assets consist of cash, accounts receivable, and inventory.

10. There are no long-term liabilities.

P16-5. The comparative financial statements for the Zarah Zeringue Company for 1981 and 1982 are given below.

	1982	1981
Balance Sheets		
ASSETS		
Cash	$ 1,600	$ 2,200
Accounts receivable (net)	2,400	2,800
Inventory	6,000	5,600
Fixed assets (net)	10,000	8,600
Total assets	$20,000	$19,200
LIABILITIES & OWNERS' EQUITY		
Current liabilities	$ 3,000	$ 3,400
Long-term liabilities (8% interest)	7,000	7,000
Common stock (par $10)	8,000	8,000
Retained earnings	2,000	800
Total liabilities & owners' equity	$20,000	$19,200
Income Statements		
Sales	$30,000	$28,000
Cost of goods sold	18,000	17,000
Gross profit	12,000	11,000
Operating expenses	8,600	8,100
Pretax income	3,400	2,900
Income taxes	1,000	900
Net income	$ 2,400	$ 2,000

Additional information:
1. Two-thirds of the sales are cash sales.

2. Interest expense is included in operating expenses.

3. During 1981, $1,200 of cash dividends were declared and paid.

4. The average market price of common stock was $22 in 1982.

Required:
1. Prepare a common size income statement and balance sheet for 1982 and 1981.

2. Compute the amount of change and percent of change from 1981 to 1982 for each item in the financial statements.

P16-6. Refer to the data in Problem 16-5 to answer the following questions.

1. By what amount and what percent did working capital change?

2. What was the average income tax rate in each year?

3. What was the receivable turnover for 1982?

4. What was the average collection period of receivables in 1982?

5. What was the inventory turnover in 1982?

6. How many days did it take to sell an average inventory in 1982?

7. What was the length of the operating cycle of the business in 1982?

8. What was the return on total assets in 1982?

P16-7. Refer to the data in Problem 16-5.

Required:

1. Compute three operating ratios for 1982.

2. Compute two ratios of liquidity for 1982.

3. Compute two ratios of solvency for 1982.

4. Compute three market test ratios for 1982.

P16-8. Tanya Corporation is evaluating a new project that would require an investment of $200,000. It is estimated that the project will add revenues of $133,333 and will involve additional operating expenses of $100,000, exclusive of any financing costs. Tanya's earnings for the past several years have averaged 6 percent (after income taxes) on the total assets at the beginning of the year. It is estimated that this earnings rate will continue into the current year. Three possible financing plans are being considered by Tanya:

a. Sell $200,000 of 7 percent bonds.

b. Sell $100,000 of 6 percent bonds and sell 500 shares of 6 percent preferred stock, $100 par at $200 each.

c. Sell 2,000 shares of common stock at $100 each.

The equities of Tanya Corporation at January 1 of the current year were as follows:

Current liabilities	$ 10,000
Long-term liabilities	90,000
Common stock	50,000
Retained earnings	100,000

Required:

Compute the expected return on average common equity for each of the three plans assuming an income tax rate of 50 percent.

P16-9. The condensed financial statements of the Michael Corportion for the years 1981 and 1982 are as follows:

	1982	1981

Balance Sheets

ASSETS

	1982	1981
Cash	$ 26,000	$ 16,000
Receivables	50,000	40,000
Inventories	80,000	60,000
Plant and equipment	160,000	80,000
Accumulated depreciation	(40,000)	(20,000)
Total assets	$276,000	$176,000

LIABILITIES & OWNERS' EQUITY

	1982	1981
Accounts payable	$ 40,000	$ 16,000
Dividends payable	–0–	8,000
Bonds payable (9%), issued January 1, 1982	40,000	–0–
Common stock ($100 par)	120,000	100,000
Retained earnings	76,000	52,000
Total liabilities & owners' equity	$276,000	$176,000

Income Statements

	1982	1981
Sales (all on credit)	$300,000	$175,000
Cost of goods sold	200,000	110,000
Gross profit	100,000	65,000
Operating expenses	76,000	38,000
Net income	$ 24,000	$ 27,000

Required:

Compute the following ratios.

1. Current ratio for 1982 and 1981.

2. Quick ratio for 1982 and 1981.

3. Receivable turnover in 1982.

4. Return on total assets in 1982.

5. Inventory turnover in 1982.

6. Gross profit margin on sales in 1982 and 1981.

7. Earnings per share in 1982 and 1981. Assume $20,000 of stock was sold June 1, 1982.

8. Return on common equity in 1982.

9. Price earnings ratio at December 31, 1982. Assume the average market price for 1982 was $106.

10. Debt to total assets at December 31, 1982, and December 31, 1981.

P16-10. Financial information from the statements of Pamela Corporation for the past four years is presented below.

	1982	1981	1980	1979
Net sales	$200,000	$160,500	$156,000	$145,000
Cost of goods sold	140,000	104,325	102,960	100,050
Gross profit	60,000	56,175	53,040	44,950
Net income	14,000	6,420	7,500	8,625
Ending merchandise inventory (FIFO basis)	20,000	31,250	20,600	25,500
Accounts receivable, end of year	22,000	11,250	12,500	10,000

All sales are on credit with terms 2/10, n/30. Assume a 365-day year.

Required:

1. For each of the four years, compute the following:

   a. Gross profit as a percentage of sales.
   b. Net income as a percentage of sales.
   c. Operating expenses as a percentage of sales.
   d. Days to sell ending inventory.
   e. Collection period of ending accounts receivable.

2. Indicate whether you would consider the trend in each item (a through e) favorable, unfavorable, or neutral. Give a brief explanation of your answer.

CHAPTER 17

Accounting Principles and Changing Prices

Chapter Outline

17.1 *Accounting Principles Revisited.* A review of the basic assumptions of accounting discussed in Chapter 1; discussion of the important accounting concepts of materiality, consistency, objectivity, comparability, conservatism, cost, disclosure, and matching.

17.2 *Revenue Recognition.* Discussion of the problem of identifying those transactions that give rise to revenue, that is, those where the revenue is earned and is objectively measurable; illustration of the methods for recognizing revenue during production, at the point of sale, and as cash is collected.

17.3 *Constant-Dollar Accounting.* Presentation of the problem of inflation and the measurement of inflation by the consumer price index; illustration of constant-dollar methods using an inflation-adjusted measuring unit instead of historical cost.

17.4 *Current-Cost Accounting.* Presentation of the problem posed when asset prices change at rates different from the general price level; illustration of current-cost methods to segregate the results of operations, changes in the general price level, and changes in specific prices.

Accounting and the Real World

Deflating Those
Hefty Profits

Suppose you bought a house for $25,000 in 1955 and you rented it out in 1978 at a sum that cleared you $5,000 after expenses. What kind of a return are you getting on your investment—20 percent? Not so fast. There's another factor. That house could now be sold for $75,000, the cost to buy another one just like it. So, maybe your return is only 6.7 percent—$5,000 on $75,000.

Does it make any difference which figure you use? Maybe not with a house, where current return is relatively unimportant. But if you are running a business, it makes a very big difference whether you figure your return is 20 percent or 6.7 percent. At 20 percent you'd be delighted to invest more money. At 6.7 percent you'd be better off with the interest on a savings account.

Which brings us to the subject of inflation accounting. Inflation accounting is a lot more complicated than our house-renting example, but the house will serve by way of illustration. If you use the original cost of the house to figure your return, you are using historical-cost accounting. That's what business uses today. It values your assets at what they originally cost, no matter how much more valuable they may have become after years of inflation. If you use the cost of replacing the house to figure your return, you are using current-cost accounting.

A new report by the accounting firm of Price Waterhouse & Company details the effects of inflation on 215 businesses, including 157 industrial firms. It shows that:

- Sales growth from 1975 to 1979 averaged 76 percent, or about 15 percent a year, when calculated by historical accounting methods. But when adjusted for inflation, growth shrank to only 33 percent, or less than 8 percent a year.

- Income, when adjusted for inflation, was only 60 percent of the figure reported under traditional accounting methods.

- The corporations' tax rates, when traditionally calculated, averaged 39 percent. But when restated to account for inflation, they averaged an effective 53 percent.

- Dividends were about 33 percent of after-tax income when calculated by historical-cost accounting. They jumped to 65 percent when adjusted for inflation.

- Without accounting for inflation, stock prices rose an average of 74 percent from 1975 to 1979. Considering double-digit inflation, however, stocks rose only 24 percent in value during that five-year period, not much more per year than the return available from passbook savings accounts.

Forbes, April 2, 1979, page 96–100.

This chapter returns to the basic assumptions underlying accounting as outlined in Chapter 1. Because of the knowledge acquired and the sophistication gained from the study of earlier chapters, the discussion here can be more conceptual and more in depth.

One main focus of this discussion is revenue recognition. This process involves identifying those transactions that give rise to revenue. In most instances, revenue is recognized at the point of sale. There are, however, several important exceptions.

The second main focus of discussion is the effect of inflation on accounting numbers and the response of accounting to it. There are two basic approaches to dealing with the effect of inflation: constant-dollar accounting and current-cost accounting.

17.1   Accounting Principles Revisited

Chapter 1 presented the basic six assumptions underlying accounting. These assumptions are:

1. Each business is a separate accounting entity, distinguished from other businesses and from its owners.

2. Each business is a going concern that will continue operations indefinitely.

3. Each business will report on its activities at least once a year.

4. Each business uses the dollar as its measuring unit.

5. Each business measures events according to their value at the time they occur.

6. Each business provides information regarding its operations (income statement), financial position (balance sheet), and changes in its financial position.

Accounting
Guidelines

These assumptions have been very useful in the development of accounting in the preceding chapters; however, they are not a complete guide to dealing with accounting problems because they are sometimes ambiguous in their application. Situations often arise where more than one accounting treatment could satisfy these basic assumptions. As a result, accounting requires guidelines in choosing the most appropriate treatment.

Accounting uses eight guidelines in the application of its basic assumptions. These guidelines are materiality, consistency, comparability, objectivity, conservatism, cost, disclosure, and matching.

Materiality The materiality guideline divides all accounting items into two groups: (1) those that may influence users of the financial statements (called *material items*) and (2) those that do not (called *immaterial items*). Material items are considered significant enough that they must be treated in accordance with accepted accounting procedure. Immaterial items, on the other hand, may be treated in the easiest possible way.

An example of the application of this guideline is in accounting for uncollectible accounts. If uncollectible accounts are an insignificant factor in the company's operations (that is, uncollectible accounts are immaterial), the direct write-off method can be used because it is the easiest. If, on the other hand, uncollectible accounts are material, the allowance method must be used to measure properly the income for the period.

Another example is in accounting for bonds payable. Bond discounts and premiums can be amortized using either the effective interest method or the straight-line method. If the difference between these methods is material, the effective interest method must be used to measure income properly. If immaterial, discounts and premiums can be amortized using the straight-line method, which is easier.

Materiality is also used in the presentation of information on the financial statements. Because too much data can obscure the important points, good reporting involves the exclusion or summarization of immaterial items. An example in the Exxon balance sheet from Chapter 2 is the single figure for cash, which summarizes numerous bank accounts. Exxon and its auditors agree that listing individual accounts would be an immaterial benefit.

Consistency The consistency guideline states that a business should use the same accounting procedures each period. Thus, for example, if LIFO is used as an inventory cost flow assumption in 1981, it should have been used as the cost flow assumption in 1980. This implies that, if FIFO was used in 1980, the financial statements for 1980 should be restated assuming the use of LIFO.

The consistency guideline aids the users of financial statements. The choice of accounting procedure (such as LIFO versus FIFO) is often arbitrary; but whatever method is chosen, it should be applied consistently. If different procedures were used in different periods, it would be difficult to distinguish between the effects of changing business operations and the effects of changing accounting procedures.

Comparability The comparability guideline states that different firms should apply the same accounting procedure in a similar way so that it is possible for users of financial statements to make comparisons. For example, suppose an investor is deciding between Firm A and Firm B. If both firms use LIFO but in a different way, comparison of their financial statements is made more difficult. Differences in net income may be the result of differences in business success, or may be solely the result of differences in choice of accounting procedure.

The consistency and comparability guidelines are quite similar, but consistency applies to the same firm for different periods, while comparability applies to different firms for the same period.

Objectivity The objectivity guideline states that accounting methods should be sufficiently objective that two independent individuals would arrive at the same value or result if they both employed the same method. This does not mean that judgment and estimations are not used: they are inevitable. It means that estimates should be based on more than one person's opinion. For this reason, an estimate of uncollectible accounts based upon past collection experience is acceptable for an accounting entry. On the other hand, one person's estimate of the outcome of a lawsuit is not acceptable.

The objectivity guideline is relied upon in the difference in accounting treatment between marketable and nonmarketable securities. Because the value of marketable securities can be objectively determined from market transactions, changes in value can be reflected in the accounting records. The value of nonmarketable securities, on the other hand, cannot be determined objectively; thus, changes in value for them cannot be included.

Conservatism The conservatism guideline states that, if there is a choice of accounting method, the method that gives the lowest value for assets and revenues or the highest value for liabilities and expenses should be chosen. An example of the application of this guideline is the lower of cost or market rule in accounting for inventories and marketable securities. If a security increases in value above its cost, a revenue is not recognized and assets are not increased; however, if the same security declines in value below its cost, an expense is recognized and assets are decreased. The rationale of conservatism is that a pessimistic outlook is less likely to result in unpleasant surprises, such as an unexpected bankruptcy, than is an optimistic outlook.

Cost The cost guideline states that assets are recorded at their cost to the firm. Expenses, then, are measured by the cost to the firm of the assets consumed. Chapter 1 defined expense as a measure of the decrease in net assets caused by profit-seeking activity. Conceivably, this asset decrease could be measured by the value of the asset when it is consumed. Accounting, however, ignores subsequent movement in value.

Assume that a firm sells tires and has purchased twenty tires at $50 each. If on July 1, the manufacturer raises the price to $60, this increase in the cost to replace the tires is ignored. If the tires are sold on August 14 for $80 each, the revenue would be $20 \times \$80 = \$1,600$, and the expense would be $20 \times \$50 = \$1,000$. Thus, income is $600.

Suppose, however, that the expense on August 14 is measured at $60 per tire or $1,200 total. Income is thus $\$1,600 - \$1,200 = \$400$; but in addition, there is income traceable to when the tires rose in value on

July 1. This income is $10 per tire or $200. The total income is still $600 ($400 + $200). Thus, the cost guideline is a simplifying one: subsequent movements in value are ignored because they are washed out when the asset is consumed.

Disclosure The disclosure guideline states that the financial statements should report all material and relevant information. As discussed above, only material items should be reported, so that the user will not be presented with too much detail; but the relevant information may consist of more than can be included in the financial statements themselves. This relevant information must be reported in footnotes.

For example, there should be a footnote telling the user what inventory accounting method, such as LIFO or FIFO, was used in the preparation of the financial statements. Also, any changes in accounting method should be disclosed, as should major events, such as lawsuits or strikes, affecting the company.

Matching The matching guideline states that revenue recognition is primary. Expenses related to the production of that revenue are reported in the same period as the revenue. An example of the application of this guideline is in uncollectibles accounting. The allowance method tries to record the expense associated with uncollectibles in the period the revenue from the sale is measured.

Another example is in construction. Costs of construction are accumulated in an asset account until construction revenue is recognized. Only then are they recognized as expenses. Construction accounting is discussed in greater detail later in the chapter.

Using the matching guideline, net income measures the difference between the revenue recognized in a period and the expenses associated with the production of that revenue. Thus, expense recognition involves two steps: (1) associating the expense with a revenue and (2) recognizing the expense in the period in which the revenue is recognized.

Concept Summary

Accounting Guidelines		
Guideline	*Explanation*	*Application*
Materiality	Only items that could influence users of financial statements need be treated in accordance with GAAP.	Low cost items of equipment can be expensed rather than capitalized.
Consistency	A business should use the same accounting procedures each period.	LIFO or FIFO can be used, but the choice must be applied consistently.
Comparability	Different businesses should use the same procedure in the same way.	LIFO should be applied by different firms in the same way.

(continued on next page)

Concept Summary *(continued)*

Guideline	Explanation	Application
Objectivity	Different persons should get the same value if they use the same method.	Subjective opinions regarding such events as the outcome of a lawsuit are excluded.
Conservatism	When there is a choice, the method giving the lowest value for assets and revenues and the highest value for liabilities and expenses should be used.	Decreases in inventory value are recognized, increases are not.
Cost	Movements in asset value after acquisition should be ignored.	Expense is measured by the cost to the firm of the asset consumed.
Disclosure	All material and relevant information should be reported.	Financial statements should describe accounting methods used and disclose major events affecting the company.
Matching	Revenue recognition is primary; expenses are matched to revenues.	Costs are accumulated in an asset account until revenue is recognized.

17.2   Revenue Recognition

Because of the matching guideline, revenue recognition effectively determines income recognition. As discussed in Chapter 16, net income is a primary concern to investors and creditors; therefore, revenue recognition is critically important to their perception of the company. Unfortunately, however, it is often difficult to determine when to recognize revenue.

Conditions of Revenue Recognition

In general, accrual accounting recognizes revenue when two conditions are met:

1. *The revenue is earned.* This means that the economic process giving rise to the revenue is effectively complete. In addition, costs associated with the revenue have been incurred.

2. *The revenue is objectively measurable.* The ultimate amount of cash need not have been completely received, but it should be possible to estimate accurately the amount that will eventually be received.

It is quite possible for one condition to be met without the other; therefore, it is important to realize that both conditions must be met before accrual accounting recognizes a revenue.

The most common revenue-producing activities, cash sales and normal credit sales, meet both of these conditions. The revenue is earned because the sale is complete. In a cash sale, the revenue is objectively measurable because the cash received can be counted. In a normal credit sale, the revenue is objectively measurable because past collection experience enables credit managers or accountants to estimate accurately the amount that will ultimately be collected.

Earned, Not Measurable Suppose that there is a credit sale where collection is very uncertain and there is no past collection experience on which to base an estimate of collectibility. In this instance, the revenue is earned because the sale is complete; however, the revenue is not objectively measurable because the amount of cash to be collected cannot be estimated accurately.

Measurable, Not Earned Suppose a subscriber sends in payment for a three-year subscription to a magazine. In this instance, the revenue is objectively measurable because cash is received; however, the revenue has not been earned because the goods paid for, the magazine, have not been delivered.

Timing of Revenue Recognition	For the overwhelming majority of business firms, the two conditions for revenue recognition are met at the point of sale. In some situations, however, these conditions can be met before or after the point of sale. Basically, there are three times at which revenue can be recognized: during production, at the point of sale, or as cash is collected.

During Production The accounting method that recognizes revenue during production is called the **percentage of completion method.** The idea behind this method is that, if 50 percent of the work has been done and a fixed contract price exists, then 50 percent of the revenue should be recognized. The primary instance where revenue is recognized during production is in the construction industry.

The percentage of completion method can be effective and useful; however, there are three main difficulties in its application.

1. It is based on an estimate of costs. In all construction (and long-term construction in particular), costs can exceed expectation. Thus, it is quite possible to spend $400,000 of an estimated $800,000 and only be 25 percent complete, rather than 50 percent complete.

2. It requires separate calculations and adjusting entries for each construction project each accounting period. Making these calculations and adjusting entries can be quite time-consuming.

3. It can be abused by inflating costs, which increases period income.

There is no question that revenue is earned as construction progresses. But, because of the problem of cost estimation, the revenue may not be objectively measurable. In some instances, cost estimates can be supplemented by an engineer's or architect's estimate of percentage of completion. In many instances, though, there is so much uncertainty about eventual costs and the amount completed that the revenue cannot be considered objectively measurable. In these instances, revenue recognition must be deferred until the completion of the project. However, if costs can be accurately estimated, generally accepted accounting principles dictate that the percentage of completion method be used.

The **completed contract method** of revenue recognition waits until all costs of construction have been incurred. Given a fixed contract price, this implies revenue is objectively measurable and can then be recognized. This method does not involve the difficult estimations of the percentage completion method, but it does result in wide fluctuations in income. The entire income of a three-year project will be recognized in the third year, with no income at all in the first and second years.

Point of Sale Revenue is recognized at the point of sale by any company whose principal activity in the earnings process is selling. An example of this circumstance is a wholesaler. The earnings process for this type firm is: (1) purchase of inventory, (2) credit sale of inventory, and (3) collection of cash. In this situation, however, the earnings process is essentially complete at the time of the sale. The ultimate collection of cash can be estimated on the basis of past experience. In addition, the costs of the sale (such as the cost of the inventory and its shipment) have all been incurred and, hence, can be accurately measured. Point of sale has been the method of revenue recognition used in previous chapters.

Concept Summary

Contrast of Accounting Methods for Construction	
During Production (percentage of completion)	*Point of Sale (completed contract)*
Based upon estimate of costs, which may be incorrect.	Waits until all costs have been incurred. There are no estimation problems.
Requires additional calculations and entries each period.	Has only one revenue and one expense entry at completion.
Can be abused by inflating costs, thus increasing period income.	Is more difficult to abuse because project is complete.
Reflects the economic reality of the construction, at least approximately.	Does not reflect economic reality. Causes net income to fluctuate widely.

As Cash Is Collected When revenue is recognized as cash is collected, the method for doing so is the **installment method.** This method measures revenue only as cash is collected. It is used when

1. *financing, not selling, is the primary activity.* Two examples of such businesses are some furniture stores and retail land sales. In both instances, the businesses exist to finance the purchase.

2. *cash collections cannot be estimated.* In many instances, credit is extended very easily, losses from uncollectible accounts are very high, and the collection percentage cannot be estimated reliably.

The basic idea behind the installment method is that income from the sale of a product should be recognized each period in proportion to the cash received. Thus, if one-half of the cash is received, one-half of the income should be recognized.

In practice, the installment method is used primarily because it is useful for tax purposes. With the installment method, tax is due only as the cash from the sale is received. With the point of sale method, tax may be due even when no cash has been received from the sale. As a result, many businesses that permit extended payments and do not use the installment method must borrow money to pay their taxes each year. The installment method eases this cash flow problem.

Though the installment method can be useful for tax purposes, it is unacceptable for financial statement purposes except in unusual circumstances. The generally accepted approach is to use an appropriate estimate of allowance for uncollectible accounts and uncollectible accounts expense.

17.3 Constant-Dollar Accounting

Chapter 1 and the first part of this chapter stated that the monetary assumption of accounting is that the dollar will be used as the measuring unit. Thus, land purchased for $10,000 in December 1960 will still appear in the financial statements for December 1980 at $10,000. This historical-cost amount is not changed.

Constant-dollar and current-cost methods are often employed by financial analysts trying to comprehend the effects of changing prices on financial statements. In addition, the largest companies in retailing, manufacturing, banking, and insurance are now required by the FASB to present certain selected constant-dollar and current-cost data as supplementary information in their annual reports. These data are purely supplementary and do not affect the basic financial statements. However, to understand these disclosures and their significance, it is necessary to have an understanding of constant-dollar and current-cost.

Everyday experience indicates that the purchasing power of the dollar is constantly decreasing. Decreasing purchasing power of the dollar is called *inflation*. Because of inflation, it may be helpful to use a dollar of constant purchasing power as the measuring unit rather than a historical cost dollar. This approach is called the constant-dollar approach because amounts recorded at different times are all adjusted to units of constant purchasing power.

General Price-Level versus Specific Price-Level Changes

It is important here to distinguish between general price-level changes and specific price-level changes. General price-level changes apply to goods and services as a whole. Prices of specific goods and services, however, may change at either a faster or a slower rate than prices in general. For example, the general price level may go up 13 percent, but the cost of a specific asset may go up 5 percent or 20 percent or not at all. The focus in this section is on the effects of general price-level changes on financial statements. The effects of specific price-level changes are discussed in the next section.

Consumer Price Index

An important question is how to measure the decline in the purchasing power of a dollar over time, so that dollars at different times can be properly compared. The most widely used measure of inflation is the *consumer price index for all urban consumers (CPI-U)* developed each month by the Bureau of Labor Statistics of the United States Department of Labor. This index measures how much it costs to buy a fixed "basket" of goods each month. This basket consists of most items purchased by urban consumers, such as housing, gasoline, and food. The index of this basket in 1967 is given the value 100, and the index in every other period is the percentage of the 1967 prices that are charged in that period.

Figure 17-1 gives the CPI-U each month and the yearly average for 1951 through 1979. The yearly average for 1967 has index 100, while the yearly average for 1979 is 217.5. This means that the basket costing $100 in 1967, cost $217.50 in 1979. Thus, prices more than doubled in those twelve years.

Conversion of Historical Cost to Constant Dollar The CPI-U can be used to convert from historical cost to dollars of constant purchasing power. The basic idea is to convert from the dollars at the time of the transaction to the dollars at the time of the financial statements. Doing so presents a minor difficulty because financial statements are usually presented at the end of the month while the index is an average for the month. However, the difference will not be material if, say, the December figure is used for December 31.

Example Consider the example mentioned earlier of land purchased for $10,000 in December 1960. Referring to Figure 17-1, the index is 89.3 for December 1960 and 229.9 for December 1979. To convert those 1960 dollars to December 1979 dollars requires mutliplying by the to/from ratio:

$$\text{Asset cost} \times \frac{\text{index adjusting to}}{\text{index adjusting from}} = \text{cost in constant dollars}$$

$$\$10,000 \times \frac{229.9}{89.3} = \$25,745$$

Thus, $10,000 in December 1960 dollars is equivalent to $25,745 in December 1979 dollars. This land would have a dollar figure of $25,745 assigned to it on the December 31, 1979, balance sheet.

Price-Level-Adjusted Financial Statements

The process of restating historical costs in dollars of constant purchasing power is called **constant-dollar accounting** and can be applied systematically to arrive at a complete set of price-level-adjusted financial state-

FIGURE 17-1

Consumer Price Index for All Urban Consumers (CPI-U)

Year	Jan.	Feb.	Mar.	Apr.	May	June	July	Aug.	Sep.	Oct.	Nov.	Dec.	Avg.
1951	76.1	77.0	77.3	77.4	77.7	77.6	77.7	77.7	78.2	78.6	79.0	79.3	77.8
1952	79.3	78.8	78.8	79.1	79.2	79.4	80.0	80.1	80.0	80.1	80.1	80.0	79.5
1953	79.8	79.4	79.6	79.7	79.9	80.2	80.4	80.6	80.7	80.9	80.6	80.5	80.1
1954	80.7	80.6	80.5	80.3	80.6	80.7	80.7	80.6	80.4	80.2	80.3	80.1	80.5
1955	80.1	80.1	80.1	80.1	80.1	80.1	80.4	80.2	80.5	80.5	80.6	80.4	80.2
1956	80.3	80.3	80.4	80.5	80.9	81.4	82.0	81.9	82.0	82.5	82.5	82.7	81.4
1957	82.8	83.1	83.3	83.6	83.8	84.3	84.7	84.8	84.9	84.9	85.2	85.2	84.3
1958	85.7	85.8	86.4	86.6	86.6	86.7	86.8	86.7	86.7	86.7	86.8	86.7	86.6
1959	86.8	86.7	86.7	86.8	86.9	87.3	87.5	87.4	87.7	88.0	88.0	88.0	87.3
1960	87.9	88.0	88.0	88.5	88.5	88.7	88.7	88.7	88.8	89.2	89.3	89.3	88.7
1961	89.3	89.3	89.3	89.3	89.3	89.4	89.8	89.7	89.9	89.9	89.9	89.9	89.6
1962	89.9	90.1	90.3	90.5	90.5	90.5	90.7	90.7	91.2	91.1	91.1	91.0	90.6
1963	91.1	91.2	91.3	91.3	91.3	91.7	92.1	92.1	92.1	92.2	92.3	92.5	91.7
1964	92.6	92.5	92.6	92.7	92.7	92.9	93.1	93.0	93.2	93.3	93.5	93.6	92.9
1965	93.6	93.6	93.7	94.0	94.2	94.7	94.8	94.6	94.8	94.9	95.1	95.4	94.5
1966	95.4	96.0	96.3	96.7	96.8	97.1	97.4	97.9	98.1	98.5	98.5	98.6	97.2
1967	98.6	98.7	98.9	99.1	99.4	99.7	100.2	100.5	100.7	101.0	101.3	101.6	100.0
1968	102.0	102.3	102.8	103.1	103.4	104.0	104.5	104.8	105.1	105.7	106.1	106.4	104.2
1969	106.7	107.1	108.0	108.7	109.0	109.7	110.2	110.7	111.2	111.6	112.2	112.9	109.8
1970	113.3	113.9	114.5	115.2	115.7	116.3	116.7	116.9	117.5	118.1	118.5	119.1	116.3
1971	119.2	119.4	119.8	120.2	120.8	121.5	121.8	122.1	122.2	122.4	122.6	123.1	121.3
1972	123.2	123.8	124.0	124.3	124.7	125.0	125.5	125.7	126.2	126.6	126.9	127.3	125.3
1973	127.7	128.6	129.8	130.7	131.5	132.4	132.7	135.1	135.5	136.6	137.6	138.5	133.1
1974	139.7	141.5	143.1	143.9	145.5	146.9	148.0	149.9	151.7	153.0	154.3	155.4	147.7
1975	156.1	157.2	157.8	158.6	159.3	160.6	162.3	162.8	163.6	164.6	165.6	166.3	161.2
1976	166.7	167.1	167.5	168.2	169.2	170.1	171.1	171.9	172.6	173.3	173.8	174.3	170.5
1977	175.3	177.1	178.2	179.6	180.6	181.8	182.6	183.3	184.0	184.5	185.4	186.1	181.5
1978	187.2	188.4	189.8	191.5	193.3	195.3	196.7	197.8	199.3	200.9	202.0	202.9	195.4
1979	204.7	207.1	209.1	211.5	214.1	216.6	218.9	221.1	223.4	225.4	227.6	229.9	217.5

ments. The traditional approach in which costs remain at the dollar value recorded at the time of purchase is called **historical-cost accounting.**

Purchasing Power Gain or Loss

The purpose of price-level-adjusted financial statements is to present all balance sheet and income statement items in terms of balance-sheet-date dollars. This restatement in terms of balance-sheet-date dollars gives rise to a new income statement item called the *purchasing power gain or loss.* Assume that the firm had $10,000 in cash on December 1960 and that cash remained untouched until December 1979. The firm still had $10,000 in cash, but the purchasing power of that cash decreased. This purchasing power loss can be calculated as follows:

Cash, December 1960 converted to December 1979 dollars:

$$\$10,000 \times \frac{229.9 \ (\text{December 1979})}{89.3 \ (\text{December 1960})} = \$25,745$$

Cash, December 1979	10,000
Purchasing power loss	$15,745

Thus, by leaving this $10,000 untouched during this period, the firm suffered a $15,745 purchasing power loss.

Unpaid Liability On the other hand, an unpaid liability over time will give rise to a purchasing power gain because the liability will be repaid with dollars of lower purchasing power. For example, suppose the firm owes $1,000 on December 31, 1978, and still owes $1,000 on December 31, 1979. The purchasing power gain is calculated as follows:

Payable, December 31, 1978, converted to December 31, 1979, dollars:

$$\$1,000 \times \frac{229.9 \text{ (December 1979)}}{202.9 \text{ (December 1978)}} = \$1,133$$

Payable, December 31, 1979 $\qquad\qquad\qquad\qquad$ (1,000)
Purchasing power gain $\qquad\qquad\qquad\qquad\qquad\;$ $ 133

Monetary Items versus Nonmonetary Items To compute the purchasing power gain or loss requires a distinction between monetary and non-monetary items. Monetary items are those items that are fixed in terms of dollars, regardless of changes in the value of the dollar. Examples include cash, accounts receivable, and accounts payable. These items are not adjusted. Nonmonetary items are those items that are not monetary, such as inventory and property, plant, and equipment. The values of these items are adjusted from the time they are recorded to the balance sheet date.

Concept Summary

Monetary versus Nonmonetary Items		
	Assets	*Liabilities*
Monetary	Cash Accounts receivable Notes receivable Bonds Refundable deposits	Accounts payable Notes payable Dividends payable Bonds payable Deferred income tax
Nonmonetary	Inventory Stock Property, plant, and equipment Patents and trademarks Goodwill	(Rare, except when obligated to provide goods or services)

Note: Owners' equity items are nonmonetary.

Formula In general, the purchasing power loss is given by the following formula:

Beginning net monetary items converted to end-of-year dollars
+ Monetary item inflows converted to end-of-year dollars
− Monetary item outflows converted to end-of-year dollars
_____

Ending net monetary items as if they were nonmonetary
− Ending net monetary items (already stated at end-of-year dollars)
_____

= Purchasing power loss (or gain if negative)

The purchasing power gain or loss is, thus, caused by holding monetary items in a period of general price-level changes. A more complex illustration of the purchasing power loss is given in the comprehensive review problem at the end of this chapter.

Depreciable Assets

Earlier, an adjustment for land was illustrated. Depreciable assets are more complicated to adjust than are nondepreciable assets, such as land. For depreciable assets, not only does the asset cost have to be adjusted, but accumulated depreciation and the yearly depreciation charge have to be adjusted, also.

Assume a company showed a historical-cost balance of $650,000 in its equipment account on December 31, 1979, and that $500,000 of the equipment had been purchased in 1978 with the remainder purchased in 1979. To make the calculations easier, the equipment is assumed to have been purchased evenly over the year, so the average figures for 1978 (195.4) and 1979 (217.5) can be used. The conversion to December 31, 1979, dollars is accomplished as follows:

Year of Purchase	Historical-Cost Amount	×	Index Adjusting To	÷	Index Adjusting From	=	Constant-Dollar Amount
1978	$500,000	×	229.9	÷	195.4	=	$588,280
1979	150,000	×	229.9	÷	217.5	=	158,552
	$650,000						$746,832

The equipment account would then have a $746,832 balance on a price-level-adjusted basis.

Depreciation Further assume that this company used a 10 percent depreciation rate with a full year's depreciation taken in the first year. Conversion of 1979 depreciation to December 31, 1979, dollars would be accomplished with the following computation:

Year of Purchase	Historical-Cost Depreciation	×	Index Adjusting To	÷	Index Adjusting From	=	Constant-Dollar Amount
1978	$ 50,000	×	229.9	÷	195.4	=	$ 58,828
1979	15,000	×	229.9	÷	217.5	=	15,855
	$ 65,000						$ 74,683

Depreciation in the 1979 income statement would be $74,683. Accumulated depreciation would be calculated as follows:

Year of Purchase	Historical- Cost Accumulated Depreciation	×	Index Adjusting To	÷	Index Adjusting From	=	Constant- Dollar Accumulated Depreciation
1978	$100,000	×	229.9	÷	195.4	=	$117,656
1979	15,000	×	229.9	÷	217.5	=	15,855
	$115,000						$133,511

Accumulated depreciation would be $133,511 on the December 31, 1979, balance sheet.

Constant-Dollar Income Statement

This type of price-level adjustment can be made for every nonmonetary item; however, the price-level-adjusted assets will not equal the price-level-adjusted liabilities plus the price-level-adjusted owners' equity without an additional adjustment. This additional adjustment is the purchasing power gain or loss. The purchasing power gain or loss is included on the income statement and incorporated into retained earnings, making the balance sheet balance.

The price-level-adjusted income statement is the historical-cost income statement modified by the use of indexes *plus* a purchasing power gain or loss. To ease the calculations, income statement items like sales revenue and salary expense are converted from the average index for the year to the end-of-year index. For example, assume sales for 1979 were $50,000. The 1979 price-level-adjusted income statement would have a sales figure of

$$\text{sales} \times \frac{\text{end-of-year index}}{\text{average-for-year index}}$$

$$= \$50,000 \times \frac{229.9}{217.5}$$

$$= \$52,851.$$

Cost of Goods Sold The only complicated adjustments are depreciation (discussed above) and cost of goods sold. Cost of goods sold must be broken down into its component parts:

$$
\begin{array}{l}
\text{Beginning inventory} \\
+ \text{ Purchases} \\
\underline{- \text{ Ending inventory}} \\
= \text{ Cost of goods sold}
\end{array}
$$

Assume a company had $5,000 of inventory on January 1, 1979, purchased $10,000 of inventory during 1979, and had $6,000 of inventory on December 31, 1979. The company will not have bought the ending inventory evenly over the year, so inventory turnover figures must be considered. Assuming the inventory turns over four times a year, a reasonable assumption is that the inventory on the balance sheet is purchased evenly over the last quarter of the year. Purchases, however, will take place evenly over the year. Thus, the cost of goods sold calculation is

	Historical Cost	×	Index Adjusting To	÷	Index Adjusting From	=	Constant Dollar
Inventory, January 1, 1979	$ 5,000	×	229.9	÷	201.9*	=	$ 5,693
Purchases	10,000	×	229.9	÷	217.5	=	10,570
	15,000						16,263
Inventory, December 31, 1979	(6,000)	×	229.9	÷	227.6**	=	(6,061)
Cost of goods sold	$ 9,000						$ 10,202

*Average index for the last quarter of 1978 = (200.9 + 202 + 202.9)/3.
**Average index for the last quarter of 1979 = (225.4 + 227.6 + 229.9)/3.

The comprehensive review problem at the end of this chapter provides an example of price-level-adjusted statements. This type of accounting is still very controversial.

Concept Summary

Constant-Dollar Accounting	
Arguments For	Arguments Against
Assists users in understanding effects of inflation on the business.	Inflation effects are too complex to be clarified by mechanical adjustments.
Purchasing power gains and losses are reported separately.	Purchasing power gains cannot be distributed or reinvested.
Creditors are better informed of the cushion supporting their claims.	Businesses with huge liabilities can show gains all the way until bankruptcy.
All financial statement items are presented using the same measuring unit.	The relevant change is the change in the specific asset cost, not the general price level.
Restatement will usually indicate a higher income tax and dividend payout rate.	Users might assume that restated amounts reflect current value in some sense.

17.4 Current-Cost Accounting

So far, accounting has measured the acquisition cost of assets. Two versions of acquisition cost measurement have been presented: (1) using the unchanged dollar value at the time of acquisition (historical-cost accounting), and (2) using a dollar value in terms of constant purchasing power (constant-dollar accounting).

Components of Net Asset Increases

Any version of accounting based on acquisition cost has certain theoretical difficulties. To understand these problems requires an appreciation of the three fundamental components of net asset increases. These components are (1) results of operations, (2) results of general price-level changes, and (3) results of specific price changes. Results of operations is the component of income attributable to the operating activities of the business, such as purchasing, marketing, selling, and collecting. Results of general price-level changes is the component of asset increases attributable to inflation. Results of specific price changes is the component of asset increases attributable to owning assets whose costs change at a rate different from that of the general price level.

Historical-cost accounting does not separate these three figures. For example, suppose a company purchased one hundred faucets on January 1, 1981, for $5 each when the CPI-U was 250. On December 31, 1981, the CPI-U was 300 and the faucets would cost $7 to replace in inventory. Sixty faucets were sold on December 31 for $10 each. Historical-cost accounting would show

Sales ($10 × 60 units)	$600
Cost of goods sold ($5 × 60 units)	300
Net income	$300

Ending inventory would be $200 ($5 cost × 40 units).

Holding Gain

This accounting description is a simplification of what is occurring. Because the faucets cost $7 to replace at the end of the year, the company saved money by buying the faucets at the beginning of the year for $5. This cost savings can be calculated as follows:

Replacement cost of inventory, December 31 ($7 × 100 units)	$ 700
Historical cost of that inventory ($5 × 100 units)	(500)
Cost savings from early purchase	$ 200

This cost savings can also be viewed as a holding gain, because the value of the faucets went up while they were owned (held) by the company. The term holding gain is generally used in this context.

In addition, because the faucets cost $7 to replace, it is somewhat misleading to use $5 per unit in the calculation of cost of goods sold. Because it would cost $7 per unit to replenish the supply of faucets, cost of goods sold might more accurately be reported as $420 ($7 × 60 units).

A more complete picture of what is occurring could then be presented as follows:

Sales ($10 × 60 units)	$ 600
Cost of goods sold ($7 × 60 units)	(420)
Income from operations	180
Holding gain on inventory items	200
Net income	$ 380

Ending inventory would be $280 ($7 × 40 units). The increase in inventory valuation was $200; of that, $120 was included in cost of goods sold and $80 was included in ending inventory.

Holding Gain, Net of Inflation

Even this figure is a simplification because it does not incorporate the effects of inflation. The holding gain is, in large measure, fictional because the general price level changed during the year. Thus, the calculation above of the holding gain is somewhat misleading because it combines dollars from two different times: the beginning of the year and the end of the year. The same concepts and techniques discussed in the previous section are applicable here. The company spent $500 for inventory at the beginning of the year when the price index was 250. Converting to end-of-year dollars gives:

$$\$500, \text{ beginning } \times \frac{300 \text{ (end-of-year index)}}{250 \text{ (beginning-of-year index)}} = \$600$$

Therefore, the fictional gain or inflation component is $600 − $500 = $100. Holding gain could more accurately be calculated as follows:

Replacement cost of inventory, December 31	$ 700
Historical cost of inventory	(500)
Holding gain	200
Inflation component ($600 − $500)	(100)
Holding gain, net of inflation	$ 100

The holding gain, net of inflation, could also be calculated as:

Replacement cost of inventory, December 31	$ 700
Constant-dollar cost of inventory	(600)
Holding gain, net of inflation	$ 100

Thus, a more accurate picture of what is occurring could be presented as follows:

Sales ($10 × 60 units)	$ 600
Cost of goods sold ($7 × 60 units)	(420)
Income from operations	180
Holding gain, net of inflation	100
Net income	$ 280

Ending inventory would be $280 ($7 × 40 units). Sales and cost of goods sold do not have to be restated because they are already expressed in end-of-year dollars. Thus, current-cost accounting builds upon the constant-dollar accounting of the last section, but adds the effects of the holding gain, net of inflation.

Figure 17-2 provides a summary of the balance sheet and income statement for a company using the three different accounting models.

Effectiveness of Current-Cost Accounting

Returning to the three components of net asset increases mentioned at the beginning of this section, the current-cost approach is the only one that separates all three. Results of operations are identified as $180, the income from operations. Results of price-level changes are identified as $100, the inflation component credited directly to capital stock. Results of holding assets are identified as $100, the holding gain, net of inflation.

FIGURE 17-2
Comparison of
Different Accounting
Models

	Historical Cost	Constant Dollar	Current Cost
Balance sheet, January 1, 1981			
Inventory	$ 500	$ 600	$ 600
Capital stock	(500)	(600)	(600)
	$ 0	$ 0	$ 0
Income statement for 1981			
Sales	$ 600	$ 600	$ 600
Cost of goods sold	300	360	420
Income from operations	300	240	180
Holding gain, net of inflation			100
Net income	$ 300	$ 240	$ 280
Balance sheet, December 31, 1981			
Cash	$ 600	$ 600	$ 600
Inventory	200	240	280
Capital stock	(500)	(600)	(600)
Retained earnings	(300)	(240)	(280)
	$ 0	$ 0	$ 0

Current-Cost
Accounting—
Inventory

This example of inventory accounting is simpler than most realistic circumstances. To handle more complicated situations, the following formula should be used:

Current cost of inventory, beginning of year
+ Purchases during the year at historical costs
− Current cost of inventory, end of year
+ Holding gain for the year
―――――――――――――――――――――――
= Cost of goods sold at current cost

Checking the information in Figure 17-2 gives $500 + $0 (there were no purchases) − $280 + $200 = $420, which is the correct figure for cost of goods sold.

Five pieces of information are used in this formula. Thus, if four of them are known, the fifth can be calculated. Of the information required, the current cost of inventory at the beginning and end of the year must be determined by all companies. The purchases during the year are automatically stated at their current costs on the purchase dates. This leaves two unknowns: cost of goods sold at current cost and the holding gain. In many instances, cost of goods sold at current cost can be calculated from historical-cost records (plus some additional data). Then, the holding gain can be calculated.

Assume the following information is known for 1979:

	Quantity	Average Unit Price	Current Cost
Inventory, beginning of year	3,571	$140	$ 500,000
Purchases, during the year	12,903	155	2,000,000
Inventory, end of year	(4,571)	175	800,000
Unit sales	11,903		

The need is to determine the current cost as of the date the inventory was sold; therefore, it is necessary to determine the average cost per unit. One method is to take the average of the beginning and ending unit prices.

$$\text{Average cost/unit} = \frac{1}{2}\,(\text{cost/unit, beginning} + \text{cost/unit, ending})$$

$$= \frac{1}{2}\,(\$140 + 175)$$

$$= \$157.50$$

Cost of goods sold at current cost would then be calculated as follows:

$$\text{Cost of goods sold, current cost} = \text{average cost/unit} \times \text{unit sales}$$
$$= \$157.50 \times 11,903$$
$$= \$1,874,723$$

This method will produce an accurate result if (1) any increase or decrease in quantities occurs evenly during the year and (2) any change in current cost occurs evenly during the year. If the changes in quantities or current cost do not occur evenly, then the year must be broken down into smaller segments (such as quarters or months) for analysis. The approach used above can then be applied to the shorter time periods and the results summed to get the totals for the year.

By rearranging the formula given earlier, the holding gain for the year can be calculated as follows:

Holding gain = Cost of goods sold, current cost =	$1,874,723
− Inventory, beginning	− 500,000
− Purchases	− 2,000,000
+ Inventory, ending	+ 800,000
=	$ 174,723

Holding Gain, Net of Inflation— Inventory

To calculate the holding gain, net of inflation, requires a more comprehensive procedure. For this example, the calculation is as follows:

	Current Cost, Unadjusted	×	Index To	÷	Index From	=	Current Cost, End-of-Year Dollars
Inventory, beginning of year	$ 800,000						$ 800,000
Purchases	500,000	× 229.9	÷	202.9	=		566,535
	2,000,000	× 229.9	÷	217.5	=		2,114,023
							2,680,558
Cost of goods sold	1,874,723	× 229.9	÷	217.5	=		(1,981,604)
							698,954
Holding gain, net of inflation							$ 101,046

Current Cost— Property, Plant, and Equipment

The general concepts of current cost that are applicable to inventories are also applicable to property, plant, and equipment. Thus, owning these assets will also give rise to a holding gain. The calculation of a holding gain for property, plant, and equipment is both more and less complicated than the similar calculation for inventories. The calculation is more complicated because depreciation must be considered, but is less complicated because there are fewer transactions. The holding gain associated with property, plant, and equipment is derived from the following formula:

> Current cost, beginning of year, net of accumulated depreciation
> + Additions at historical cost (which is the current cost at that time)
> − Depreciation at current cost
> − Disposals at the net amount realized
> + Holding gain
> _____
> = Current cost, end of year, net of accumulated depreciation

This formula involves six pieces of information. If five of them are known, the sixth can be calculated. Assume the following current-cost information has been determined for 1979:

Current cost, January 1 (net)	$5,500,000
Current cost, December 31 (net)	6,800,000
Additions	600,000
Depreciation	400,000
Disposals (net realized)	100,000

The holding gain can then be calculated as follows:

$$
\begin{aligned}
\text{Holding gain} = \ &\text{Current cost, December 31 (net)} = \$6,800,000 \\
&+ \text{Depreciation} \qquad\qquad\quad + \quad 400,000 \\
&+ \text{Disposals} \qquad\qquad\qquad\ + \quad 100,000 \\
&- \text{Current cost, January 1 (net)} \ - \ 5,500,000 \\
&- \text{Additions} \qquad\qquad\qquad\ - \quad \underline{600,000} \\
&\qquad\qquad\qquad\qquad\qquad\quad = \$1,200,000
\end{aligned}
$$

Estimate of Current Cost Of the information required, the current cost at the beginning and end of the year will need to be determined by all companies. Additions during the year are automatically stated at their current cost when they are purchased. Depreciation is calculated based on the average current cost during the year.

Assume equipment was purchased on January 1 for $100,000. The equipment is depreciated using the straight-line method over ten years, so it is depreciated 10 percent per year. The current cost of the equipment new on December 31 is $110,000. The average current cost is

$$\frac{1}{2}(\$100,000 + \$110,000) = \$105,000$$

The current cost depreciation would then be

$$10\% \times \$105,000 = \$10,500$$

Accumulated depreciation in current-cost accounting is always the same percentage of the gross current cost as in historical-cost accounting. In the above example, after one year under historical-cost accounting, the accumulated depreciation is $10,000, or 10 percent of the asset cost. In the current-cost case, accumulated depreciation would be

$$10\% \times \$110,000 = \$11,000$$

The situation is summarized in the following chart:

	Cost	Depreciation	Accumulated Depreciation Percent	Accumulated Depreciation Amount
Historical cost	$100,000	$10,000	10	$10,000
Current cost	110,000	10,500	10	11,000

Under current-cost accounting, accumulated depreciation is not the total of the depreciation amounts on the various income statements. Even in this example, depreciation is $10,500 and accumulated depreciation is $11,000. The difference (in this instance, $500) is called "backlog depreciation" and is included in the calculation of the holding gain. The reason for this difference is the use of average current cost for determining depreciation, while the current cost at the end of the year is used for the balance sheet.

Holding Gain, Net of Inflation— Property, Plant, and Equipment

Property, plant, and equipment must also be restated on a current-cost basis. The calculation of the holding gain, net of inflation, is very similar to the calculation for inventory and is as follows.

	Current Cost, Unadjusted	×	Index To	÷	Index From	=	Current Cost, End-of-Year Dollars
Property, plant, and equipment (net), end of year	$6,800,000						$6,800,000
Property, plant, and equipment (net), beginning of year	5,500,000	×	229.9	÷	202.9	=	6,231,888
Additions	600,000	×	229.9	÷	217.5	=	634,207
Disposals	100,000	×	229.9	÷	217.5	=	(105,701)
Depreciation	400,000	×	229.9	÷	217.5	=	(422,805)
							6,337,589
Holding gain, net of inflation							$ 462,411

It may seem, then, that current-cost accounting is clearly superior to historical-cost accounting, and in these textbook examples, it might be so. However, for real companies, there are many difficulties involved in the use of current-cost accounting.

Concept Summary

Current-Cost Accounting	
Arguments For	*Arguments Against*
Matches current costs with current revenues to separate effects of price changes.	Estimated current costs are too subjective.
	(continued on next page)

Concept Summary

(Continued)

Arguments For	Arguments Against
Holding gains are reported in the period in which they occur, making manipulation of income more difficult.	Holding gains are not verified by an exchange transaction.
Current costs give a better indication of the worth of the business than do historical costs.	Current costs do not disclose what a firm is "worth."
Financial statements of different firms would be more comparable; the LIFO versus FIFO problem would disappear.	Financial statements would still not be comparable because current costs can be determined in different ways.
If market prices are available, current costs can be as verifiable as historical costs.	Historical costs record what actually happened. Users can make their own adjustments.

Summary

The basic assumptions underlying accounting presented in Chapter 1 always apply; however, in complex situations, more than one accounting alternative may be consistent with these assumptions. Financial accounting practice is based upon eight guidelines that help to determine the proper treatment of business events and how they should be reported. The guidelines are materiality, consistency, objectivity, comparability, conservatism, cost, disclosure, and matching.

Because of the matching guideline, revenue recognition, in essence, determines income recognition. Accrual accounting recognizes revenue when the revenue is earned and can be objectively measured. Applying these recognition criteria may result in revenue being recognized at one of three possible points. The point applicable to most businesses is the point of sale. Revenue recognition during production occurs most often in long-term construction contracts where costs are known or can be reasonably estimated and a fixed contract price exists. In some instances, revenue can only be objectively measured as cash is collected because of high uncollectible accounts experiences and, thus, revenue is recognized after the point of sale.

One of the most important assumptions behind financial accounting is the monetary assumption. The amount of dollars used to value a transaction and its effect on financial statements may be historical cost as presented throughout this book, constant dollar (historical cost adjusted for general price level changes), or current cost (constant dollar adjusted for the current replacement cost of certain assets).

Purchasing power gains or losses may result when either constant-dollar or current-cost valuation is used. Holding gains or losses may result only when current-cost valuation is used.

Key Terms

Comparability
Completed contract method
Consistency
Constant dollar
Consumer price index
Current cost
Disclosure
General price level
Holding gain (loss)
Installment method
Matching

Monetary item
Nonmonetary item
Objectivity
Percentage of completion method
Purchasing power gain or loss
Revenue recognition
Specific price level

Comprehensive Review Problem

Below are the historical-cost statements of income and retained earnings for Adjusted Company, Inc., for 1979 and the historical-cost balance sheet as of December 31, 1979.

ADJUSTED COMPANY, INC.
Statement of Income and Retained Earnings
Year Ended December 31, 1979

Sales		$60,000
Expenses		
Cost of goods sold	$40,000	
Operating expenses	8,000	
Depreciation	2,000	
Total expenses		50,000
Income before income taxes		10,000
Income taxes		5,000
Net income ($5.00 per share)		5,000
Retained earnings, December 31, 1978		2,500
Retained earnings, December 31, 1979		$ 7,500

ADJUSTED COMPANY, INC.
Balance Sheet
December 31, 1979

ASSETS

Current assets		
Cash	$ 5,500	
Accounts receivable	8,000	
Inventory	12,000	
Total current assets		$25,500
Noncurrent assets		
Equipment, net of accumulated depreciation		5,000
Total assets		$30,500

LIABILITIES & STOCKHOLDERS' EQUITY

Current liabilities
Accounts payable . . . . $ 6,500

Stockholders' equity
Capital stock (1,000 shares issued and outstanding) $16,500
Retained earnings   7,500
  Total stockholders' equity   24,000
  Total liabilities & stockholders' equity $30,500

The following facts are known about Adjusted Company:

a. Inventory turns over four times a year.

b. The equipment was purchased in 1977 for $10,000. It is depreciated over five years on a straight-line basis. One-half of a year's depreciation was taken in 1977.

c. The capital stock was issued in 1977.

d. The current cost of inventory on December 31, 1979, was $12,500.

e. The current cost of inventory on December 31, 1978, was $9,000.

f. Purchases were $44,000 in 1979.

g. The weighted average current cost of the units sold in 1979 was $1.05. 40,000 units were sold.

h. The current cost of equipment on December 31, 1979, was $15,000 gross and $7,500 net of accumulated depreciation.

i. The current cost of equipment on December 31, 1978, was $13,000 gross and $9,100 net of accumulated depreciation.

j. There were no additions to or disposals of equipment during 1979.

k. Constant-dollar retained earnings as of December 31, 1978, measured in end-of-year 1979 dollars, was $1,607.

l. Current-cost retained earnings as of December 31, 1978, measured in end-of-year 1979 dollars, was $4,140.

m. On December 31, 1978 total monetary assets were $10,000 and total monetary liabilities were $6,000.

Required:

1. Prepare the income statement, statement of retained earnings, and balance sheet for Adjusted Company, Inc., using constant-dollar accounting.

2. Prepare the income statement, statement of retained earnings, and balance sheet for Adjusted Company, Inc., using current-cost accounting.

Solution to Comprehensive Review Problem

1. *Purchasing Power Gain or Loss* Purchasing power gain or loss can be calculated directly as follows:

	Historical Cost	×	Index To	÷	Index From	=	Constant Dollar
Total monetary assets, December 31, 1978	$10,000	×	229.9*	÷	202.9**	=	$11,330
Total monetary liabilities, December 31, 1978	(6,000)	×	229.9	÷	202.9	=	(6,798)
Net monetary assets, December 31, 1978	4,000	×	229.9	÷	202.9	=	4,532

Additions:						
Sales	60,000	× 229.9	÷ 217.5***	=	63,421
	64,000				67,953
Deductions:						
Purchases	44,000	× 229.9	÷ 217.5	=	46,509
Operating expenses	8,000	× 229.9	÷ 217.5	=	8,456
Federal income taxes	5,000	× 229.9	÷ 217.5	=	5,285
	57,000				60,250
	7,000				7,703

Total monetary assets, December 31, 1979	13,500		13,500
Total monetary liabilities, December 31, 1979	6,500		6,500
Net monetary assets, December 31, 1979	$ 7,000		7,000
Purchasing power loss			$ 703

*Index = end of year, 1979.
**Index = end of year, 1978.
***Index = average for year, 1979.

The first set of adjustments on the worksheet are labeled *A1* through *I1*. These adjustments result in the constant-dollar adjusted trial balance as of December 31, 1979.

A1, Inventory. The inventory entry is a nonmonetary item and must be adjusted. Because inventory turns over four times a year, ending inventory was purchased over the last quarter of 1979. The index adjusting from should then be 227.6, the average for the last quarter of 1979.

$$\$12,000 \times 229.9 \div 227.6 = \$12,121$$

ADJUSTED COMPANY, INC.
Adjusted Trial Balance
December 31, 1979

	Historical Cost	Adjustments DR	Adjustments CR	Constant-Dollar (End of Year, 1979)	Adjustments DR	Adjustments CR	Current Cost (End of Year, 1979)
Cash	5,500			5,500			5,500
Accounts receivable	8,000			8,000			8,000
Inventory	12,000	121*A1*		12,121	379*A2*		12,500
Equipment, net of accumulated depreciation	5,000	1,333*B1*		6,333	1,167*B2*		7,500
Accounts payable	(6,500)			(6,500)			(6,500)
Capital stock	(16,500)		4,400*C1*	(20,900)			(20,900)
Retained earnings	(2,500)	893*D1*		(1,607)		2,533*C2*	(4,140)
Sales	(60,000)		3,421*E1*	(63,421)			(63,421)
Cost of goods sold	40,000	3,497*F1*		43,497	897*D2*		44,394
Operating expenses	8,000	456*G1*		8,456			8,456
Depreciation	2,000	533*H1*		2,533	427*E2*		2,960
Federal income taxes	5,000	285*I1*		5,285			5,285
		7,118	7,821				
Purchasing power loss		703		703			703
	–0–	7,821	7,821	–0–	2,870	2,533	
Holding gain, net of inflation						337	(337)
					2,870	2,870	–0–

B1, Equipment. Equipment is a nonmonetary item. To avoid concern about the month of purchase, the average index for 1977 will be used.

$$\$5,000 \times 229.9 \div 181.5 = \$6,333$$

C1, Capital stock. Capital stock is a nonmonetary item, and, hence, must be adjusted. The stock was issued in 1977, so the constant-dollar amount is calculated using the average for that year.

$$\$16,500 \times 229.9 \div 181.5 = \$20,900$$

D1, Retained earnings. Retained earnings is a nonmonetary item; however, the constant-dollar retained earnings figure as of December 31, 1978, is known to be $1,607.

E1, Sales. The sales entry must be adjusted from average 1979 dollars to end-of-year dollars. The assumption is that sales were relatively constant over the year.

$$\$60,000 \times 229.9 \div 217.5 = \$63,421$$

F1, Cost of goods sold. The cost of goods sold item must be adjusted by breaking it down into its component parts:

	Historical Cost	×	Index To	÷	Index From	=	Constant Dollar
Inventory, January 1, 1979	$ 8,000	×	229.9	÷	201.9*	=	$ 9,109
Purchases	44,000	×	229.9	÷	217.5	=	46,509
	52,000						55,618
Inventory, December 31, 1979	(12,000)	×	229.9	÷	227.6**	=	(12,121)
Cost of goods sold	$ 40,000						$ 43,497

*Average last quarter, 1978.
**Average last quarter, 1979.

G1, Operating expenses. The operating expenses item must be adjusted from average dollars to end-of-year dollars. The assumption is that expenses were relatively constant over the year.

$$\$8,000 \times 229.9 \div 217.5 = \$8,456$$

H1, Depreciation. The depreciation entry must be adjusted to be the same percentage of the constant-dollar equipment as it was of historical-cost.

$$\frac{\$2,000}{\$5,000} = 40\%$$

$$40\% \times \$6,333 = \$2,533$$

I1, Federal income taxes. The federal income taxes entry should be adjusted from average-year dollars to end-of-year dollars.

$$\$5,000 \times 229.9 \div 217.5 = \$5,285$$

2. Direct Calculation of the Holding Gain, Net of Inflation

	Current Cost, Unadjusted	×	Index To	÷	Index From	=	Current Cost, End of Year, 1979
Inventory, December 31, 1979	$12,500						$ 12,500

Inventory, January 1, 1979	9,000 × 229.9 ÷ 202.9* =	10,198
Purchases	44,000 × 229.9 ÷ 217.5** =	46,509
		56,707
Cost of goods sold	42,000 × 229.9 ÷ 217.5** =	(44,394)
		12,313
Holding gain, net of inflation		$ 187

	Current Cost, Unadjusted ×	Index To ÷	Index From =	Current Cost, End of Year, 1979
Equipment (net), December 31, 1979	$ 7,500			$ 7,500
Equipment (net), January 1, 1979	9,100 ×	229.9 ÷	202.9* =	10,310
Additions	—0—			—0—
Disposals	—0—			—0—
Depreciation	2,800 ×	229.9 ÷	217.5** =	(2,960)
				7,350
Holding gain, net of inflation				$ 150

*Index-end of year, 1978.
**Index-average for year, 1979.

The second set of adjustments are labeled *A2* through *E2*. These adjustments result in the current-cost-adjusted trial balance as of December 31, 1979.

A2, Inventory. Write up to current cost of $12,500 on December 31, 1979.

B2, Equipment. Write up to current cost of $7,500 on December 31, 1979.

C2, Retained earnings. Make adjustment for previously recognized holding gains included in December 31, 1978, retained earnings by adjusting up to $4,140.

D2, Cost of goods sold

Number of items sold 40,000
Weighted average current cost per unit in 1979 .... $ 1.05
Current cost of goods sold $42,000
Restatement to end-of-year dollars:

$$\$42,000 \times \frac{229.9 \text{ (end of year, 1979)}}{217.5 \text{ (average for year, 1979)}} = \$44,394$$

E2, Depreciation
Current cost, December 31, 1979 .... $15,000
Current cost, December 31, 1978 .... $13,000
Average current-cost (½ ($15,000 + $13,000)) $14,000
Depreciable life .... 5 years
Depreciation as stated at average unadjusted current cost ($14,000 × 20%) .... $ 2,800
Restatement to end-of-year dollars:

$$\$2,800 \times \frac{229.9 \text{ (end of year, 1979)}}{217.5 \text{ (average for year, 1979)}} = \$2,960$$

ADJUSTED COMPANY, INC.
Statements of Income and Retained Earnings
Year Ended December 31, 1979

	Historical Cost	Constant Dollar	Current Cost
Sales	$60,000	$63,421	$63,421
Expenses			
Cost of goods sold	40,000	43,497	44,394
Operating expenses	8,000	8,456	8,456
Depreciation	2,000	2,533	2,960
Total expenses	50,000	54,486	55,810
Income before income taxes	10,000	8,935	7,611
Income taxes	5,000	5,285	5,285
Income from operations	5,000	3,650	2,326
Purchasing power loss		(703)	(703)
Holding gain, net of inflation			337
Net income	5,000	2,947	1,960
Retained earnings, December 31, 1978	2,500	1,607	4,140
Retained earnings, December 31, 1979	$ 7,500	$ 4,554	$ 6,100

ADJUSTED COMPANY, INC.
Balance Sheet
December 31, 1979

	Historical Cost	Constant Dollar	Current Cost
ASSETS			
Current assets			
Cash	$ 5,500	$ 5,500	$ 5,500
Accounts receivable	8,000	8,000	8,000
Inventory	12,000	12,121	12,500
Total current assets	25,500	25,621	26,000
Noncurrent assets			
Equipment, net of accumulated depreciation	5,000	6,333	7,500
Total assets	$30,500	$31,954	$33,500
LIABILITIES & STOCKHOLDERS' EQUITY			
Current liabilities			
Accounts payable	$ 6,500	$ 6,500	$ 6,500
Stockholders' equity			
Capital stock (1,000 shares issued and outstanding)	16,500	20,900	20,900
Retained earnings	7,500	4,554	6,100
Total stockholders' equity	24,000	25,454	27,000
Total liabilities & stockholders' equity	$30,500	$31,954	$33,500

Questions

Q17-1. List the basic assumptions underlying financial accounting. Are these assumptions any different from those presented in Chapter 1?

Q17-2. Give the eight guidelines for accounting practice and reporting.

Q17-3. What criteria must be met for revenue, and consequently income, to be recognized? Explain.

Q17-4. Distinguish three points at which revenue could be recognized and give an example of each.

Q17-5. Contrast the percentage of completion and the completed contract methods of revenue recognition.

Q17-6. What is the installment method of revenue recognition? Give an example of a business that might use this method.

Q17-7. Define constant dollar as it applies to financial statements. What is the relationship of constant dollar to historical cost?

Q17-8. Explain purchasing power gains or losses. How are they derived?

Q17-9. Define current cost as it applies to financial statements. What is the relationship of current cost to constant dollar?

Q17-10. Explain holding gains or losses. How are they derived?

Exercises

E17-1. Identify each of the following items as monetary or nonmonetary. **(Note:** Income statement items are considered monetary if they measure changes in monetary assets and liabilities; they are considered nonmonetary if they measure changes in nonmonetary assets.)

a. Cash
b. Accounts receivable
c. Inventories
d. Investments in stock of another company
e. Property, plant, and equipment
f. Accounts payable
g. Common stock
h. Sales
i. Cost of goods sold
j. Salary expense
k. Depreciation
l. Rent expense

E17-2. In 1981, the Dole Construction Company entered into a long-term contract to construct a factory. The contract price was $1,500,000, and the estimated costs of construction were $1,000,000. Construction was begun on February 1, 1981, and completed November 15, 1982. At December 31, 1981, Dole had incurred $700,000 of the total costs. In 1982, total costs of construction were $300,000. How much income before taxes would the Dole Construction Company recognize in 1981 and 1982, respectively, if: (1) the completed contract method was used and (2) the percentage of completion method was used?

E17-3. The market price of the common stock of the Cal Corporation at December 31 was as follows:

1975—$40
1976—$48
1977—$56
1978—$47
1979—$42

Restate these market prices to December 31, 1979, constant dollars.

E17-4. The EZ Furniture Company sold several items of furniture to a customer on July 31, 1981. The furniture cost EZ $300. The customer signed an installment sales contract whereby he agreed to pay $60 per month for twelve months. The payments were due on the last day of each month beginning August 31, 1981. The customer made all payments on time. If the EZ Furniture Company uses the installment sales method of accounting for the sale, how much income before taxes would they recognize in 1981 and how much would they recognize in 1982? How much of the total income recognized in the two years is actually interest revenue, if the customer could have bought the furniture for $600 at the time of the purchase?

E17-5. In January, 1977, the Omega Corporation purchased a computer for $200,000. The computer was depreciated using the straight-line method with an estimated life of five years and no salvage value. The replacement cost (new) of the computer at December 31, 1979, was $150,000. Calculate the net value of the computer that would be reported on a December 31, 1979 (a) historical-cost balance sheet, (b) constant-dollar balance sheet, and (c) current-cost balance sheet. What is the total holding gain or loss, net of inflation, on the computer for the three years ended December 31, 1979?

E17-6. In July 1975, Larry Houk and Keith Kittrell set up a corporation. Each man bought one-half of the stock for $100,000. The corporation immediately put $50,000 of the money into a savings account and purchased a piece of land costing $150,000 with the remainder of the cash. The land was leased, and this was the only profit-directed activity of the corporation. Each year the interest revenue and lease revenue were collected, taxes and other expenses were paid, and the net income was distributed to the two stockholders. The balance sheet of the corporation at December 31, 1979, was as follows:

ASSETS
Funds	$ 50,000
Land	150,000
Total assets	$200,000

EQUITIES
Common stock	$200,000
Total equities	$200,000

   a. Restate the $50,000 put into the savings account in terms of December 31, 1979, constant dollars. How much purchasing power has this $50,000 lost between July 1975 and December 31, 1979?

   b. Restate the historical cost of the land and the historical proceeds of the common stock in terms of December 31, 1979, constant dollars.

   c. Prepare a constant-dollar balance sheet at December 31, 1979. Treat the purchasing power loss as a deficit.

E17-7. The Sante Company reported the following cost of goods sold on its income statement for the year ended December 31, 1979:

Cost of goods sold

Beginning inventory	$ 130,000	
Purchases	580,000	
Cost of goods available for sale	710,000	
Ending inventory	(150,000)	$560,000

The company uses the FIFO cost flow assumption in accounting for inventories. Inventory turns over approximately four times a year so that inventory at any time generally consists of items purchased in the previous three months. Purchases are made evenly throughout the year. Calculate the constant-dollar value of inventory at December 31, 1979, and the constant-dollar cost of goods sold for 1979.

E17-8. In October 1977, the Empire Corporation was formed with capital contributions of $175,000. The corporation immediately sold $50,000 of 8 percent, ten-year bonds. Of the total $225,000 in corporate assets, $20,000 was put into a savings account and $205,000 was used to purchase land. The only profit-directed activity of the corporation was the leasing of the land. The only income of the corporation was interest revenue and rent revenue on the land. The expenses of the corporation were met from the rent revenue, and the net income each year was distributed to the stockholders. The historical-cost balance sheet of the corporation at December 31, 1979, was as follows:

ASSETS

Funds	$ 20,000
Land	105,000
Total assets	$225,000

EQUITIES

Bonds payable	$ 50,000
Common stock	175,000
Total equities	$225,000

a. Calculate the purchasing power loss on the funds in the savings account from October 1977 to December 31, 1979. Calculate the purchasing power gain on the bonds payable from October 1977 to December 31, 1979. What is the net purchasing power gain or loss on the net monetary assets of the corporation from October 1977 to December 31, 1979?

b. Prepare the general price-level-adjusted (that is, constant-dollar) balance sheet for the corporation at December 31, 1979.

E17-9. Below is a summary of the net changes in monetary items of the GDX Corporation during 1979. It may be assumed that all changes in monetary items occurred evenly throughout the year.

	Balance 12/31/78 Debit (Credit)	Debit	Credit	Balance 12/31/79 Debit (Credit)
Cash	25,000		14,000	11,000
Accounts receivable	295,000	61,000		356,000
Accounts payable	(330,000)		40,000	(370,000)
Long-term debt	(500,000)		200,000	(700,000)

Calculate the purchasing power gain or loss for the year 1979 by completing the following steps:

1. Restate each account to December 31, 1979, constant-dollars by restating the beginning balance from December 31, 1978, dollars to December 31, 1979, dollars and restating the net change in the account from average 1979 dollars to December 31, 1979, dollars. The restated balance in each account will be the combination of the restated beginning balance and the restated net change.

2. Calculate the purchasing power loss as a result of holding each monetary asset and the purchasing power gain as a result of holding each liability. The gain or loss for each item will be the difference between the actual December 31, 1979, balance in the account and the restated balance calculated in Step 1.

3. Combine all purchasing power gains and losses to arrive at the total purchasing power gain or loss on net monetary assets.

Problems

P17-1. The Delta Construction Company contracted to build a plant for $750,000. Construction was started in January 1980 and was completed in March 1982. Data relating to the contract are summarized below.

	1980	1981	1982
Cost incurred during the year	$300,000	$250,000	$50,000
Estimated cost to complete	360,000	55,000	

Required:

1. Assume the company used the completed contract method of recognizing income on the contract. How much income would be recognized in 1980, in 1981, and in 1982? Under this method, what would be the balance in the construction in process account at the end of 1980, at the end of 1981, and upon completion of the contract?

2. Assume the company used the percentage of completion method of accounting for the contract. How much income would be recognized in 1980, in 1981, and in 1982? Under this method, what would be the balance in the construction in process account at the end of 1980, at the end of 1981 and upon completion of the contract?

P17-2. The Voltz Corporation accounts for its retail sales of land on the installment basis because the collection of contracts is not reasonably assured. The sales and cost of sales for the three years of the corporation's existence are as follows:

	1980	1981	1982
Sales	$500,000	$600,000	$800,000
Cost of sales	400,000	450,000	560,000

To use the installment basis for recognition of revenue, the corporation maintains a separate installment contracts receivable account for each year. Receivables on contracts signed in separate years are kept in separate accounts. The balances in the 1980, 1981, and 1982 accounts for installment contracts receivable at the beginning and end of 1982 were as follows:

	January 1, 1982	December 31, 1982
Installment contracts receivable, 1980	$ 60,000	$ 3,000
Installment contracts receivable, 1981	340,000	100,000
Installment contracts receivable, 1982		400,000

The company uses the direct write-off method of accounting for uncollectible accounts expense, and no accounts were written off during 1982.

Required:
Calculate the income to be recognized in 1982 by the Voltz Corporation on its retail land sales using the installment basis of revenue recognition.

P17-3. The Maher Corporation purchased all of the machinery and equipment it currently owns in January 1979 for $400,000. The assets are being depreciated on a straight-line basis with an estimated life of ten years and no salvage value. Current costs of the machinery and equipment, net of accumulated depreciation, were $378,000 at December 31, 1978, and $360,000 at December 31, 1979. No machinery or equipment was purchased or sold between January 1979 and December 31, 1979.

Required:
1. Calculate the net value of machinery and equipment and the related depreciation expense that would be reported on historical-cost financial statements at December 31, 1979.

2. Calculate the net value of machinery and equipment and the related depreciation expense that would be reported on constant-dollar financial statements at December 31, 1979.

3. Calculate the net value of machinery and equipment and the related depreciation expense and holding gain or loss, net of inflation, that would be reported on current-cost financial statements at December 31, 1979.

P17-4. The Randall Corporation, a merchandising concern, reported the following cost of goods sold for the year 1979:

Inventory, January 1, 1979	$ 42,000
Purchases	280,000
Cost of goods available for sale	322,000
Inventory, December 31, 1979	47,000
Cost of goods sold	$275,000

Additional information:
  a. The corporation uses FIFO costing methods in valuing inventories, and it can be assumed that inventory at January 1, 1979, consisted of items purchased during the last quarter of 1978 and that inventory at December 31, 1979, consisted of items purchased during the last quarter of 1979.
  b. Purchases are made evenly throughout each year.
  c. The current cost of inventories held at December 31, 1979, was $50,000. The current cost of inventories held at January 1, 1979, was $43,000.

Required:
1. Calculate the cost of goods sold and value of ending inventory on a constant-dollar basis.

2. Calculate the cost of goods sold and the value of ending inventory on a current-cost basis. What is the holding gain, net of inflation, for the year?

P17-5. The monetary items on the balance sheet of the Pilaw Corporation at December 31, 1978, and December 31, 1979, are presented below:

	December 31	
	1979	1978
Cash	$ 40,000	$ 80,000
Accounts receivable	185,000	160,000
Accounts payable	(150,000)	(130,000)
Notes payable	(75,000)	(50,000)
Net monetary assets	$ 70,000	$ 60,000

Additional information:

a. Sales of $600,000 were made evenly throughout 1979.
b. Purchases of $450,000 were made evenly throughout 1979.
c. Operating expenses (excluding depreciation) of $75,000 were incurred evenly throughout 1979.
d. Equipment was purchased in March 1979 for $80,000.
e. $25,000 was borrowed from the bank in October 1979.
f. Dividends of $20,000 were paid on December 31, 1979.

Required:
Calculate the purchasing power gain or loss of the Pilaw Corporation for the year ended December 31, 1979.

P17-6. The Canade Corporation purchased equipment costing $200,000 in June 1977. The equipment was depreciated on a straight-line basis with an estimated life of ten years and no salvage value. In June 1979, a piece of equipment that had cost $40,000 was sold for $45,000. Also in June 1979, a new piece of equipment was purchased for $60,000. The new equipment was to be depreciated on the same basis as all other equipment. Current costs for the equipment were $240,000 at December 31, 1978, and $260,000 at December 31, 1979. Current cost depreciation for 1979 was $25,000.

Required:
1. Calculate the value of the equipment, net of accumulated depreciation, at December 31, 1979, and the depreciation expense for the year ended December 31, 1979, using each of the following approaches:

a. Historical cost
b. Constant dollar
c. Current cost

2. Calculate the holding gain or loss, net of inflation, for 1979 on the equipment.

P17-7. The historical-cost balance sheet of the Sialle Corporation at December 31, 1978, is presented below.

SIALLE CORPORATION
Balance Sheet
December 31, 1978

ASSETS

Current assets

Cash		$ 32,500
Accounts receivable		41,000
Inventories		65,800
Total current assets		139,300

Property, plant, and equipment

Land		42,000
Plant and equipment	$ 97,000	
Less: Accumulated depreciation	(9,100)	87,900
Total property, plant, and equipment		129,900
Total assets		$269,200

LIABILITIES & OWNERS' EQUITY

Current liabilities

Accounts payable	$ 46,700
Notes payable	28,000
Total current liabilities	74,700
Long-term debt	50,000
Total liabilities	124,700

Owners' Equity

Capital stock	120,000
Retained earnings	24,500
Total owners' equity	144,500
Total liabilities & owners' equity	$269,200

Additional information:

a. The corporation issued all capital stock currently outstanding in April 1976.

b. The land was purchased in May 1976.

c. Of the total $97,000 of plant and equipment, $85,000 was acquired in January 1977 and the remaining $12,000 was acquired in January 1979. The company is depreciating all items of plant and equipment on a straight-line basis using an estimated life of twenty years and no salvage value.

d. The company uses the FIFO cost flow assumption for inventories. Inventories at December 31, 1978, consisted of purchases made evenly during the last quarter of 1978.

Required:

Restate the December 31, 1978, balance sheet to a constant-dollar balance sheet at December 31, 1978.

Appendix A: User Dictionary of Key Terms

accelerated depreciation (10) methods of depreciation that recognize larger-than-proportionate amounts of depreciation during the early years of an asset's life and smaller-than-proportionate amounts in the later years.

account (3) a symbol standing for a specific asset, liability, owners' equity, revenue, or expense which is used to accumulate the effects of transactions.

accounting controls (7) internal controls aimed at protecting assets from being lost or stolen and ensuring that accounting records are accurate and complete.

accounting cycle (3) the process a business goes through to record, classify, summarize, and communicate financial information.

accounting period (1) the intermediate time period in the life of a business which is the basis for reporting on the activities of the business.

accounts payable (5) amounts owed by the business to its suppliers of goods and services which are to be paid in the upcoming accounting period.

accounts receivable (5) amounts owed to the business by its customers for credit sales of merchandise or services which are expected to be collected in the upcoming accounting period.

accrual accounting (2) a system of accounting in which revenues are recognized when earned and expenses are recognized without regard for the receipt or payment of cash.

accrued expense (4) expense that has been incurred in the current accounting period but will not be paid until the next accounting period. Accrued expenses are recorded by adjusting entries.

accrued interest (12) bond interest that accumulates from the effective date of bonds or last interest payment to the date the bonds are sold. Because bond purchasers receive full interest checks, accrued interest is added to the selling price of bonds sold between interest dates.

accrued revenue (4) revenue that has been earned in the current accounting period but will not be collected until the next accounting period. Accrued revenues are recorded by adjusting entries.

accumulated depreciation (4) a contra-asset account that appears on the balance sheet as a deduction from the acquisition cost of a property, plant, and equipment asset. The balance in the accumulated depreciation account reflects the total depreciation taken on the asset since acquisition.

acquisition (10) purchase or construction of a noncurrent productive asset.

acquisition (14) a business combination in which one company acquires all of the stock of another company, but both companies continue to exist and operate as separate legal entities. The companies are called the parent (for acquiring company) and the subsidiary (for acquired company), and may prepare consolidated financial statements for the combined entity.

acquisition cost (2) the sum of all expenditures that are necessary and reasonable to purchase, transport, and ready a noncurrent productive asset for its intended use in business operations, except for interest charges incurred to purchase the asset.

additions and betterments (10) subsequent expenditures that significantly alter an asset. An **addition** is a significant component added to an asset, and a **betterment** improves the asset's capacity to perform in its intended function. These alterations benefit future periods and are capitalized.

adjunct account (6) a valuation account whose balance increases the balance in a general ledger account to which it pertains. Purchases is an adjunct account to inventory.

adjusted trial balance (4) the trial balance prepared after all adjusting entries have been made and posted. It summarizes the effects of both internal and external transactions on the accounts of a business.

adjusting entries (4) entries made at the end of an accounting period to record the cumulative effects of internal events. These entries bring the books of a business up-to-date.

administrative controls (7) internal controls designed (1) to promote efficient operations by reducing waste and duplication of effort and (2) to encourage compliance with company policies and procedures.

after-tax interest cost (12) the net cost of acquiring funds through debt; the amount of interest paid on the debt minus the taxes saved by deducting the interest paid in the determination of taxable income.

aging accounts receivable (8) a method of estimating uncollectible accounts by applying different percentage estimations of uncollectible accounts to different ages of accounts receivable. The longer the account receivable has remained uncollected, the higher the probability it will become uncollectible.

all financial resources approach (15) the treatment of a noncash financing and investing event as both a cash fi-

643

nancing and a cash investing event. The all financial resources approach incorporates all significant financing and investing events into the statement of changes in financial position.

allowance for uncollectible accounts (8) a contra account used to reduce the balance in accounts receivable to an amount the company estimates it will collect.

allowance method (8) method of accruing uncollectible accounts at the end of an accounting period by estimating either the percentage of credit sales that will not be collected or the percentage of ending accounts receivable that will not be collected.

American Institute of Certified Public Accountants (AICPA) (1) the national professional association of certified public accountants.

amortization (10) process of allocating the cost of intangible assets to expense over the periods that benefit from the use of the assets.

annuity (11) a series of equally spaced payments of the same amount.

articles of incorporation (13) rules and guidelines by which a corporation agrees to conduct its activities. These articles must be submitted to the appropriate state official when application is made to form a corporation.

asset (1) a financial and productive resource which is controlled by a business, results from a specific transaction, and is expected to possess future value for the business.

asset use ratios (16) ratios that depict the efficiency of use by company management of two important assets. Asset use ratios are the average collection period of receivables and the number of days needed to sell an average inventory.

audit (7) systematic examination of accounting records. An audit may be conducted internally by company personnel or externally by an independent certified public accountant.

audit trail (7) references in accounting records that make it possible to check journal sources of all debits and credits, find source documents supporting journal entries, and trace source documents through the ledger to their appearance on financial statements.

authorization (7) approval of a transaction by a responsible official.

authorized shares (13) the maximum number of shares of common and preferred stock that a corporation may sell to owners. Authorized shares are specified in the corporate charter and articles of incorporation.

average collection period (16) ratio calculated to show how long on the average it takes a business to collect its receivables.

balance sheet (1) one of the two primary financial statements, which depicts the financial position of a business as of a point in time by listing its assets, liabilities, and owners' equity.

balance sheet approach (8) the method of estimating uncollectible accounts expense as a percentage of the ending balance in accounts receivable. Emphasis is on the statement of accounts receivable at its net realizable value.

bank reconciliation (8) process of explaining any differences between the cash balance per the company

records and the cash balance per the monthly bank statement.

bank statement (8) monthly statement from a bank to its customer which provides the bank's records of the deposit and check-paying activities of the month. Information shown includes the beginning balance, the date and amount of each deposit, the date and amount of each check paid by the bank, miscellaneous bank charges, and the ending cash balance.

basic accounting equation (1) Assets = Liabilities + Owners' Equity.

basic inventory formula (6) formula used to calculate cost of goods sold in a periodic inventory system: Inventory on hand at beginning of the period plus purchases minus purchase discounts (if the gross method is used) plus freight in minus purchase returns equals cost of goods available for sale minus inventory on hand at the end of the period equals cost of goods sold.

basic inventory system (6) the approach used to record and account for the purchases and sales of inventory items. Two basic inventory systems are widely used: the periodic approach and the perpetual approach.

bearer bond (12) a bond for which the investor is *not* identified on the bond certificate. Also called a **coupon bond.**

beginning inventory (9) the dollar amount of inventory on hand at the beginning of an accounting period.

board of directors (13) major decision-making body of a corporation. Acting on behalf of the stockholders, the board of directors makes all major decisions for the business, establishes policies, and reviews the activity of corporate management.

bonds payable (5) formal IOUs that a company sells to investors who are willing to lend the company money. Bonds payable represents a long-term liability that will be satisfied over several accounting periods.

bond rate of interest (coupon rate, stated rate) (12) the interest rate a bond issuer agrees to pay investors on each interest payment date.

book value (10) the acquisition cost of an asset minus the total depreciation taken on the asset as shown by the accumulated depreciation account.

book value per share (13) the claim of each share of common stock on the residual assets of the business.

borrower (12) the seller or issuer of bonds. The borrower may be a corporation or other business, government agency, or nonprofit organization.

callable bond (12) a bond that may be repurchased by the issuer from investors at a predetermined price during stipulated periods of time in the bond's life.

callable preferred stock (13) preferred stock that may be repurchased by the corporation from owners at a predetermined price during stipulated periods of time.

capital expenditure (10) an expenditure that is debited to an asset and becomes a part of an asset's cost. These expenditures are expected to benefit future accounting periods.

capital stock (2) the portion of owners' equity that results when owners directly and voluntarily invest assets in a corporation.

cash basis accounting (2) a system of accounting in which revenues and expenses are recognized only when cash is received or paid.

cash disbursements journal (7) special journal designed to record all outflows (disbursements) of cash.

cash dividend (13) cash distributed by a corporation to its stockholders that represents a percentage of the amounts earned by the corporation.

cash equivalent cost (6) invoice cost of a purchase of products minus the purchase discount allowed. Also called **net invoice cost.**

cash from operations (15) cash-basis income. Cash from operations measures the amount by which cash increased as a result of successful operations.

cash receipts journal (7) a special journal used to record all receipts of cash.

Certified Public Accountant (CPA) (1) an independent professional accountant, licensed by a state, who offers a variety of accounting services to the public on a fee basis.

chart of accounts (3) a listing of all accounts in the general ledger in numerical order indicating their sequence in the ledger. It could also contain a description of each account and guidance on when each should be used.

closing entries (4) journal entries made at the end of an accounting period (1) to reduce the balance in all temporary accounts to zero, (2) to transfer the difference between revenue and expense to owners' equity, and (3) to transfer the effect of dividends or withdrawals to owners' equity.

common size statement (16) a financial statement made in percentages, rather than dollar amounts, such as an income statement in which all figures are expressed as a percentage of net sales.

common stock (13) stock representing the class of owners who have residual claims on the assets of a corporation after all debt and preferred stockholders' claims have been met; a part of corporate owners' equity.

comparability (17) the accounting guideline which states that different firms should apply the same accounting procedure in a similar way so that it is possible for users of financial statements to make meaningful comparisons.

comparative balance sheet (15) a balance sheet presenting information about the same company for more than one year.

completed contract method (17) a method of revenue recognition used in the construction industry in which revenue and expense for a job are recognized only when the job is completed, even if work on the job spans more than one accounting period.

compound interest (11) interest calculated on the principal amount plus previously accumulated interest.

conservatism (9) an accounting guideline which implies that all valuations used in financial accounting should guard against the overstatement of assets and income.

consistency (17) an accounting guideline which states that a business should use the same accounting procedures each period so that financial statements will be comparable from year to year.

consolidated financial statements (14) financial statements that combine the accounting information for a parent company and subsidiary which exist and operate as separate legal entities. Two methods of preparing consolidated financial statements are widely used: the purchase method and the pooling method.

consolidation (14) a business combination in which the stockholders of two companies exchange their stock for shares of a third company and the original two companies cease to exist. Only one entity, the consolidated one, remains.

constant-dollar (17) an accounting system based on an inflation-adjusted monetary unit.

consumer price index (17) index developed each month by the Bureau of Labor Statistics of the United States Department of Labor which measures how much it costs to buy a fixed basket of goods. This amount is expressed as a percentage of the cost of the same goods in one base year, currently 1967.

consumption (10) the use of services represented by non-current productive assets. Consumption is recorded by allocating the cost of these assets over the periods that benefit from their use.

contingent liability (8) a potential liability; if an uncertain event were to occur, a liability would be recognized. Contingent liabilities are generally disclosed in a footnote to the financial statements.

contra-asset account (4) an asset account (such as accumulated depreciation) that has a credit balance and is used to reduce the value of another asset account indirectly, while retaining the original cost of the asset.

contributed capital (13) the total direct investment of owners in a corporation through the purchase of shares of stock; one of two major categories of corporate owners' equity.

control account (7) a general ledger account for which detailed subsidiary ledgers are maintained. Accounts payable and accounts receivable are always control accounts.

convertible bond (12) a bond that the bondholder may exchange for common stock at a predetermined price over a stipulated time period specified in the bond agreement.

convertible preferred stock (13) preferred stock that can be exchanged for common stock on terms and at a time fixed prior to issue of the preferred stock.

corporate charter (13) a state license granted a corporation to operate. It is the approved application of incorporation.

corporate income tax payable (5) a liability created to reflect the federal income tax on the earnings of a corporation.

corporation (1) a business incorporated under the laws of one of the states. It may have any number of owners and exists as a legal entity that is separate from them.

cost flow assumption (9) a method of determining dollar amounts for ending inventory and cost of goods sold by making some assumption about how purchase costs are transferred to the income statement. The three most commonly used assumptions are weighted average; first-in, first-out (FIFO); and last-in, first-out (LIFO).

cost method (14) a basic method of accounting for investments, where the investment account is debited with the full cost of the security. The investment account is never written up, although it may be written down if there is a serious and permanent decline in the investment's value.

cost of goods sold (6) an expense representing the purchase cost of products sold to customers by a merchandising business.

cost-to-selling-price percentage (9) the relationship of cost of goods sold to net sales for an accounting period; used in estimating inventory by the retail method.

credit (3) the right side of any account.

credit balance (3) an account balance in which the sum of the credit entries exceeds the sum of the debit entries.

credit entry (3) a number written on the right side of any account.

cumulative preferred stock (13) preferred stock on which unpaid preferred stock dividends accumulate so that missed dividends must be paid to preferred stockholders before any dividends can be paid to common stockholders.

current assets (5) assets that are expected to be converted to cash or used up within one accounting period or operating cycle (whichever is longer) from the balance sheet date.

current-cost (17) an accounting system based on the current replacement cost of an asset rather than on its historical cost.

current liabilities (5) the obligations or debts of a business that are expected to be satisfied within the upcoming accounting period or operating cycle (whichever is longer) by the use of current assets. Examples are accounts payable and short-term notes payable.

current ratio (16) a liquidity ratio that demonstrates the relationship of current assets to current liabilities.

customer statements (7) billing statements sent to credit customers.

days to sell average inventory (16) a ratio used to determine the average number of days required to sell an average amount of inventory.

debit (3) the left side of any account.

debit balance (3) an account balance in which the sum of the debit entries is greater than the sum of the credit entries.

debit entry (3) a number written on the left side of any account.

debt security (14) bonds and other amounts owed to the company from either corporations or the U.S. government. They provide revenue to the investor, but no influence or control.

defalcation (7) fraudulent appropriation of assets. Defalcation is the term commonly used in accounting for **embezzlement.**

deferred charges (5) a noncurrent asset representing long-term prepayments.

deferred income taxes (11) the difference between income tax expense for an accounting period (based on income before taxes from the income statement) and income tax actually paid or payable (based on taxable income from the income tax return). Deferred income taxes is usually a liability representing income taxes to be paid in later years.

deferred revenue (unearned revenue) (4) a liability reflecting the obligation to render services or deliver goods in the future for which payment has already been received.

depletion (10) the process of allocating the cost of natural resources to the periods that benefit from their use.

deposits in transit (8) deposits that have been received and recorded by the company, but have not yet been received and processed by the bank when the bank statement is prepared.

depreciation (4) the process of allocating the cost of tangible operating assets to the periods that benefit from the use of these assets.

depreciation base (10) the dollar amount to be allocated to expense over the life of a property, plant, and equipment asset. It is calculated as acquisition cost minus salvage value.

depreciation method (10) the calculation technique used to spread the depreciation base over the useful life of a property, plant, and equipment asset.

direct investment (2) the amount of the assets of a business that the owners have contributed by a direct and voluntary investment of funds in the business. It is reported as a part of the owners' capital account in an unincorporated business and as capital stock in a corporation.

direct write-off method (8) method of accounting for uncollectible accounts in which expense is recognized when an individual account is determined to be uncollectible.

disclosure (17) the accounting guideline which states that all material and relevant facts should be revealed to investors and creditors in the financial statements.

discount (12) the sum by which the face amount of a bond exceeds its selling price. The discount represents an extra amount of interest the investor will receive from the issuer over the life of the bond.

discount amortization (12) the accounting technique for systematically writing off a portion of a bond discount to recognize the proper amount of interest expense by the issuer.

discount a note (8) sell a note receivable to a bank.

discount on notes payable (11) contra-liability account that represents the difference between the face amount of a note and the cash proceeds. The balance will be transferred to interest expense over the life of the note.

dishonor a note (8) fail to pay the amount owed when the note is due.

disposal (10) the discarding of a property, plant, and equipment asset by scrapping the asset, selling the asset, or trading it in on a new asset.

dividends (2) assets disbursed to the owners of a corporation.

dividends in arrears (13) the amount of regular dividends on cumulative preferred stock that have not been paid in previous accounting periods and have accumulated. These amounts are not liabilities, but they must be paid before dividends can be paid to common stockholders.

dividend yield (16) a market ratio measuring the percent return to owners of common stock which takes the form of cash dividends received.

double-declining-balance (10) an accelerated method of depreciation calculated by multiplying a constant depreciation rate (equal to twice the straight-line rate) by the book value of the asset.

double-entry bookkeeping (3) a technique for the orderly recording and classification of business transactions in which the dollar amount of debits equals the dollar amount of credits for each transaction.

double taxation (13) corporate earnings distributed as dividends are taxed first as corporate income and second as personal income of the owners of the corporation.

duality (3) the principle that, for every transaction, there is a debit effect and a credit effect on the accounts, which must be equal to maintain the balance of the basic accounting equation.

earnings per share (2) the amount of a corporation's current period income each share of common stock may claim.

effective date (12) the first date on which bonds may be sold and the date on which bonds begin to accrue interest.

effective interest amortization (12) a method of amortizing bond discount or premium which causes bond interest expense to be a constant percentage of the carrying value of the bond, and, thus, to be different each period.

elimination entry (14) working paper entry used in the preparation of consolidated financial statements to eliminate the investment account of the parent company against the owners' equity account of the subsidiary. Elimination entries are not made on the books of either the parent or the subsidiary.

embezzlement (7) fraudulent appropriation of assets; also called **defalcation.**

ending inventory (9) the dollar amount of inventory on hand at the end of an accounting period.

entity (1) an accounting assumption which states that all businesses are separate units (entities) from other businesses and from the personal activities of their owners.

equity method (14) a method of accounting for investment in securities when the investor has significant influence over the investee. The investment account measures the investment cost plus the investor's share of undistributed earnings, thus reflecting all changes to the investee's retained earnings.

equity ratio (16) a solvency ratio showing the percentage of a company's assets financed by owners' equity.

equity security (14) stock that represents ownership of a corporation and can provide revenue, influence, and control.

expense (2) decrease in assets or increase in liabilities caused by the profit-seeking activities of a business during an accounting period.

explicit interest (11) the interest rate stated on the face of a note.

external events (4) events that take place between a business and persons or other businesses. They occur at discrete points in time when a business interacts with its environment.

extraordinary item (13) an unusual and infrequent event that gives rise to a gain or loss reported on the income statement. To be an extraordinary item, the event must be clearly unrelated to ordinary and ongoing activities of the business and not likely to occur again in the forseeable future.

extraordinary repairs (10) unusual and non-recurring repair expenditures which usually extend the useful life of a property, plant, and equipment asset. Extraordinary repairs are considered capital expenditures because they create a future benefit.

face amount (8) the amount stated as owed on the face of a note.

factor (11) number from tables used in computing present and future values of lump sums and annuities.

federal income taxes withheld (11) liability representing amounts withheld from employees' wages for federal income tax. The amount must be remitted to the federal government.

Federal Insurance Contributions Act (FICA) (11) the act that authorized social security taxes, a payroll tax paid in part with money withheld from employees' wages and in part with contributions made by employers.

federal unemployment tax (11) a payroll tax on employees' wages which employers are required to remit to the federal government.

financial accounting (1) accounting activities concerned with supplying financial information about an organization to individuals and groups outside the organization.

Financial Accounting Standards Board (FASB) (1) an independent group consisting of accountants, business and investment professionals, and a representative of the academic community which establishes accounting principles, rules, and procedures.

financial condition ratios (16) a group of four ratios that focus on the financial strength and debt-paying ability of a business. The group consists of the current ratio, equity (debt) ratio, quick (acid test) ratio, and times interest earned ratio.

financial statements (1) financial reports that convey information about the financial position of a business at a point in time (balance sheet) and summarize the profit-seeking activities of the business (income statement) and the financing and investing events of the business (statement of changes in financial position) over a period of time.

financing event (15) a cash receipt not from a profit-seeking activity, such as the receipt of cash from the issuance of stock or from a bank loan.

first-in, first-out (FIFO) (9) an inventory cost flow assumption by which the first purchase costs of inventory are the first costs transferred to the income statement and attached to goods sold.

f.o.b. (6) free on board, the phrase used to indicate when the transfer of legal title takes place between the seller and the buyer of a product. F.o.b. shipping point indicates that the title passes to the buyer when the goods are shipped, and f.o.b. destination indicates that the goods are the property of the seller until they are received by the buyer.

freight (transportation) (6) the cost of transporting goods from the seller to the buyer. This cost is included in the purchase cost of goods only if paid by the buyer.

fringe benefits (11) amounts accruing to employees or others in excess of the salaries or wages earned by them that result in the total cost of a labor force being more than the salaries or wages earned. Examples include employer's matching social security, unemployment tax, and contributions to pension plans.

funds from operations (15) the amount of total revenues that produce funds minus expenses that require funds, presented as net income plus and minus certain adjustments.

future value (11) the value at a future date of an amount paid or received today and invested at a given interest rate.

gain or loss (10) net increases (**gain**) or decreases (**loss**) in assets which result from events that are not related to the normal profit-seeking activities of a business.

general price level (17) changes in the prices of goods and services as a whole, measured in accounting by the consumer price index.

generally accepted accounting principles (GAAP) (1) accounting guidelines used to produce and report financial information about an organization to external users. Their application assures outsiders that the information they receive is objective and consistently presented.

going concern (1) an accounting assumption which states that each business entity has an indefinite life and that there is no expectation that the business will terminate its activities in the foreseeable future.

gross method (6) the recording of inventory purchases at the invoice cost of the goods.

gross profit (6) the difference between net sales revenue and cost of goods sold for a merchandising firm; also called **gross margin.**

gross profit method (9) an inventory estimation technique which uses the historical gross profit percentage of a business to determine the dollar value of inventory.

gross profit percentage (9) the percentage relationship of gross profit to net sales revenue.

historical cost (2) the original acquisition cost of an asset and the basis for the accounting valuation of assets.

holding gain or loss (17) difference between the current cost of an asset at the end of a period and the current cost of that asset at the beginning of the period.

implicit interest (11) interest that is not stated on the face of the note but is charged, in effect, by not giving the maker the face value of the note.

imprest petty cash system (8) petty cash system by which a constant balance is maintained in the petty cash account. Cash is withdrawn using vouchers, and the total of the vouchers plus the cash on hand is always equal to the constant balance.

income statement (1) a statement that reports the results of operations of a business for a period of time by matching its revenues and expenses to determine net income for the period. It is one of the two primary financial statements.

income statement approach (8) a method of estimating uncollectible accounts expense as a percentage of credit sales of the period. With this approach, the emphasis is on the proper statement of income for the period.

income summary (4) an account created to hold income statement information temporarily until the balance is transferred to owner's capital or retained earnings.

income tax expense (5) federal tax on a corporation's earnings.

indirect investment (2) the amount of the assets of a business that the owners have contributed by not withdrawing those created assets to which they have a claim. It is measured as net income minus dividends (or withdrawals) summed over the life of the business, and is reported as a part of the owners' capital account in an unincorporated business and as retained earnings in a corporation.

installment method (17) a method of revenue recognition where revenue is recognized as cash is received, not at the point of sale.

intangibles (5) productive, noncurrent assets that are not characterized by tangible existence. Examples are patents, copyrights, trademarks and trade names, and goodwill.

interest payment date (12) the date on which promised interest payments are made to bondholders. Interest payment dates are usually semiannual.

internal control (7) organizational plan and other measures designed to safeguard assets, check the accuracy and reliability of accounting data, promote operational efficiency, and encourage adherence to managerial policies.

internal events (4) transactions that take place wholly within the firm without the direct involvement of other persons or businesses. These events tend to be continuous in nature.

internal revenue service (IRS) (1) a federal agency empowered to administer the Internal Revenue Code and collect the appropriate amounts of income taxes from individuals and businesses. The IRS may determine what is acceptable accounting treatment of events with income tax consequences.

interpolation (11) estimation of a value between two known values or two values given in a table.

inventory (5) a current asset representing the acquisition cost of products held for resale to customers.

inventory costing method (9) a technique used to assign costs to ending inventory on the balance sheet and to cost of goods sold on the income statement.

inventory errors (9) errors in processing or recording inventory transactions, such as incorrect counting of inventory on hand or mistakes in the recording of purchases, freight, and returns. Such errors affect cost of goods sold, net income, and the balance sheet.

inventory estimating technique (9) a technique used to estimate inventory on hand in a periodic inventory system when a firm wishes to avoid taking a physical inventory count. Two widely used estimating techniques are the gross profit method and the retail method.

inventory turnover (16) an asset use ratio which shows how long it takes on the average to sell a typical amount of inventory held during the year.

investing event (15) a cash disbursement not made for a profit-seeking activity, such as the payment of cash for a building.

investments (5) noncurrent assets, such as the stocks and bonds of another business, held as long-term investments rather than as a temporary use of cash.

invoice cost (6) the gross amount charged the buyer by the seller for products purchased.

issued shares (13) the number of shares of stock sold to investors. The number of issued shares may be equal to but not greater than the number of authorized shares.

journal (3) a chronological record of transactions showing the debit and credit amounts to be entered in the ledger accounts.

journalize (3) to record transactions in a journal.

land improvements (10) an asset account for the cost of improvements to land that have a limited life and are subject to depreciation, such as fences, parking lots, and driveways.

lapping (7) theft of cash collections on accounts receivable. The theft from the first customer is concealed by using cash received from a second customer, the theft from the second customer is covered by cash received from a third customer, and so on.

last-in, first-out (LIFO) (9) an inventory cost flow assumption by which the costs of the last purchase of inventory will be the first costs transferred to the income statement and attached to cost of goods sold.

ledger (3) a collection of the individual accounts of a business used to classify transactions and determine their cumulative effect on the accounts.

lender (12) the payee or purchaser of bonds, usually called the **investor.**

leverage (12) the use of low-cost borrowed funds (debt) to improve the rate of return to owners; also called **trading on the equity.**

liability (1) a debt or legal obligation of a business which results from the acquisition of assets from a person or group other than the owners of the business.

limited liability (13) the legal protection given corporations whereby the liability of corporate owners in the event of extreme business difficulty is limited to the amount they have invested in the corporation. Corporate creditors have claims against the assets of a business, but not against the personal assets of the owners.

liquidity (16) the ability of a company to meet its current obligations as they come due. It is a measure of short-term debt-paying ability.

long-term liabilities (5) the obligations or debts of a business that are not expected to be satisfied within the upcoming accounting period or operating cycle (whichever is longer), but are expected to be outstanding for several accounting periods into the future. Examples are bonds payable and long-term notes payable.

lower of cost or market (9) a rule that requires a write-down of inventory to its replacement cost when the goods can be replaced at less than their original cost and recognizes a special loss for the period in which the decline occurred.

lump sum (11) a single amount invested or received as opposed to a series of payments (annuity).

lump sum purchase (10) the purchase of several different assets, such as land and a building, for a single purchase price requiring allocation of the purchase cost.

maker (8) the individual or firm that borrows money and evidences the debt with a note.

managerial accounting (1) accounting activities concerned with supplying the information needs of the decision-making and control group in an organization.

manufacturing business (6) a business that purchases raw materials, transforms those materials into a finished product, and sells the finished product to customers.

market test ratios (16) a group of ratios that relate the income of a business to the number of shares that exercise a claim on that income (earnings per share), reflect the quality of business earnings (price-earnings ratio), and relate dividends to the amount an owner must pay in order to receive those dividends in the future (dividend yield).

marketable securities (5) short-term, temporary investments that can and will be quickly converted to cash.

marketable security (14) a security that can be quickly and easily purchased or sold in a market. These securities may be stocks or bonds and are held as current assets.

market rate of interest (effective rate) (12) the rate of return desired by bond investors. It is a function of the perceived risk of the bond and is used to find the present equivalent of future amounts promised by the bond.

markup (6) the percentage relationship of gross profit to cost of goods sold; the percent added to cost to determine selling price.

matching (17) the concept of reporting expenses related to the production of revenue in the same period in which the revenue is recognized.

materiality (5) accounting guideline which states that only accounting items that could influence users of the financial statements (material items) must be treated in accordance with GAAP.

maturity date (8) the date at which an obligation, such as a note or bond, is due.

maturity value (8) the total amount (principle plus interest) of an obligation at its maturity date.

merchandising business (6) a business that purchases an inventory product from suppliers and, in turn, sells that product to customers.

merger (14) a business combination in which one company acquires all of the stock of another and transfers all of the assets and liabilities of the acquired company to the books of the acquiring company. The acquired company ceases to exist after the merger.

minimum legal capital (13) the permanent investment of corporate owners in a corporation. Minimum legal capital is equal to the par or stated value of a share of stock multiplied by the number of shares issued.

minority interest (14) the amount of a consolidated entity owned by the minority shareholders of the subsidiary.

monetary item (17) an item that is fixed in terms of dollars, regardless of changes in the value of the dollar (e.g., cash, accounts receivable, and accounts payable). Monetary items are not adjusted in constant-dollar or current-cost statements.

moving average (9) the method of applying a weighted average cost flow assumption in a perpetual inventory system which requires a new average cost each time a purchase of inventory is made.

natural resources (10) tangible, property-related assets with long but limited lives, such as oil wells, gas wells, gold mines, and coal mines.

net bond liability (12) the face amount of bonds issued, minus any unamortized discount, or plus any unamortized premium. This amount represents the approximate present equivalent of expected payments to satisfy the liability.

net income (2) the amount by which assets have increased as a result of successful profit-seeking activities. Income is equal to the difference between revenues and expenses for a given accounting period.

net income percentage (16) an operating ratio that indicates the amount of each sale dollar accruing to the owners of the business for an accounting period.

net method (6) the recording of inventory purchases at the cash equivalent cost (invoice cost minus purchase discounts).

net purchases (6) the cost of inventory items purchased during an accounting period after adding and deducting all appropriate inventory transactions except sales of goods. It is calculated as purchases plus freight or transportation minus purchase returns (and minus purchase discounts if the gross method of recording purchases is used).

noncurrent assets (5) those assets whose future benefit is expected to extend beyond the next accounting period.

nonmonetary item (17) an item that is *not* fixed in terms of dollars regardless of changes in the value of the dollar. Nonmonetary items, such as inventory and property, plant, and equipment, are adjusted for changes in the price level from their acquisition date in constant-dollar and current-cost financial statements.

notes payable (5) a short- or long-term liability evidenced by a formal, legal document promising to pay a specified amount on a specific future date.

notes receivable (5) an amount owed to the business by customers or others which is evidenced by a formal, legal document.

objectivity (17) accounting guideline which states that accounting methods should be sufficiently objective that two independant individuals would arrive at the same value if they used the same method.

operating cycle (5) the time span between the purchase of goods for resale (inventory) and the receipt of cash from the sale of those goods to customers.

operating event (15) an accounting event resulting from profit-seeking activities.

operating profit percentage (16) an operating ratio that indicates the amount remaining from each sale dollar after all normal and recurring expenses (including income taxes) have been deducted.

operating ratios (16) a group of ratios that have to do with the profit margins of a business and include the gross profit percentage, operating profit percentage, and net income percentage.

outstanding checks (8) checks that have been written and recorded in the company records but which have not yet been paid by the bank and subtracted from the bank balance.

outstanding shares (13) shares that have been sold and remain in the hands of corporate owners. The number of outstanding shares may be equal to but cannot be greater than the number of issued shares.

overall ratios (16) return-on-investment ratios that summarize the result of all company activity for an accounting period. The two most important overall ratios are return on total assets and return on common stock equity.

owners' equity (1) owners' claims against the assets of a business resulting from owners' investments in the business. It is a residual claim on all assets not specifically claimed by outsiders.

padding (7) a means of issuing checks to others and then appropriating them by either (1) issuing checks to employees who have quit or been fired or (2) adding fake employees to the payroll.

paid-in capital in excess of par (stated) value (13) adjunct account to a common or preferred stock account which represents the difference between par or stated value and the original selling price of the stock.

participating (13) a feature of preferred stock that allows preferred stockholders to share on a pro rata basis in all dividends paid by a corporation. It effectively removes the fixed dividend rate from preferred stock.

partnership (1) an unincorporated business formed by the investment of two or more persons who control the activities of the business. Legally, the partners and the business are inseparable.

par value (13) an arbitrary value assigned to a share of stock by the articles of incorporation and the corporate charter. It provides a measure of the minimum legal capital of the corporation.

payee (8) the firm or individual that is to receive payment at a note's maturity date.

payroll register (11) organized method of developing each employee's gross salary (or wages) and then taking the proper deductions to arrive at net pay.

percentage of completion method (17) a method of revenue recognition used in the construction industry in which revenue for a job is recognized in proportion (1) to the costs incurred or (2) to the portion of the job completed.

periodic inventory system (6) a system of accounting for inventories in which a continuous record of inventory activity is not maintained during the period, and the cost of sales is recorded as an adjusting entry at the end of the period.

permanent accounts (4) balance sheet accounts (e.g., assets, liabilities, and owners' equity). Unlike revenue, expense, dividend, and withdrawal accounts, permanent accounts are not closed at the end of the accounting period.

perpetual inventory system (6) a system of accounting for inventories in which a continuous record of all inventory activity during an accounting period is maintained.

petty cash (8) cash kept on hand to pay for small expenses, such as postage due, which cannot be handled conveniently by check.

physical flow (9) the actual physical movement of specific inventory items through a business.

physical inventory (7) an actual count of inventory items on hand as of some point in time.

point of sale (6) the recognition of revenue at the time a sale is made with allowance made for amounts not expected to be collected. This method is used by any company where selling is the principal activity in the earnings process.

pooling of interests method (14) a method of accounting for acquisitions in which the assets, liabilities, and owners' equity of the two firms are combined using their book value. Pooling of interest is an acceptable method only under certain conditions.

post (3) to transfer debit and credit amounts and audit trail information from the journal to individual accounts in the ledger.

post-closing trial balance (4) trial balance taken after closing entries have been made and posted.

posting reference (3) in a journal, the account number which indicates that the transaction has been posted to the ledger. In a ledger, the journal and page from which the amount has been posted.

preferred stock (13) a type of stock ownership that carries preferences as to dividends and assets in the event of liquidation over common stockholders. In return, preferred stock owners give up certain rights normally accruing to corporate owners.

premium (12) the amount by which the selling price of a bond exceeds its face amount. The premium represents a reduction in the amount of interest the investor will receive from the issuer over the life of the bond.

premium amortization (12) the accounting technique for systematically writing off a portion of a bond premium to recognize the proper amount of interest expense by the issuer.

prepaid items (5) services for which a business has paid in advance but not received as of the balance sheet date. Generally, the services are classified as current assets even though the service may not be received for several years.

present value (11) value today of an amount to be paid or received later, discounted at an interest rate.

price-earnings ratio (16) a market ratio used to relate earnings per share to the average market price of a common stock share during the period in which the earnings were produced.

prior-period adjustment (13) the correction of an error made in a prior accounting period by a direct debit or credit to retained earnings in the current period. Prior-period adjustments appear as an adjustment to the beginning balance of retained earnings in the statement of retained earnings.

property, plant, and equipment (5) tangible, productive, long-lived assets used to operate a business, such as buildings, machines, tools, and land.

purchase discount (6) a reduction in the purchase price of goods to be taken by the buyer for early payment of the bill.

purchase method (14) method of accounting for the acquisition of a subsidiary which involves the allocation of the purchase cost among the assets acquired and liabilities assumed so they are stated at their fair value at the time of acquisition.

purchase return (6) damaged or unsatisfactory goods returned to suppliers.

purchases (6) an adjunct account used to record the acquisition cost of merchandise purchased during an accounting period for resale to customers. The purchases account is used only in a periodic inventory system.

purchases journal (7) special journal used to record all credit purchases of assets.

purchasing power gain or loss (17) gain or loss caused by holding monetary items in a period of general price level changes.

quick ratio (acid test) (16) a liquidity ratio that matches the most liquid assets of a business with its most immediate financial obligations.

rate of return (12) the actual rate earned by an investor on his investments.

realized gain or loss (14) gain or loss on the sale of securities.

receivables turnover (16) an asset use ratio that relates the net credit sales for an accounting period to the average amount of accounts receivable for that period.

registered bond (12) a bond that bears the name of the investor on the bond certificate. The issuer must maintain a current list that identifies uniquely each bond and its owner.

replacement cost (9) the cost of replacing an item already in inventory; also called **market** as in lower of cost or market.

residual owner (13) common stockholders are called residual owners because they claim all assets and income not specifically claimed by debt holders and preferred stockholders.

retail method (9) an inventory estimation technique in which inventory is valued at retail selling price and converted to cost for financial statement purposes by using the current period cost to selling price percentage.

retained earnings (2) the portion of owners' equity which measures assets created by the successful operation of a business and retained in the business rather than distributed to owners.

retained earnings appropriation (13) an account established to communicate that certain amounts of retained earnings are not available for dividends. These appropriations may be required by law or by contract, or may be desired by the board of directors.

return on common equity (16) an overall ratio that depicts the percentage return on the equity of the common stockholders in the business. Financial leverage is a factor in this ratio.

return on investment (ROI) (16) a category of ratios that compares the income derived from an investment for a period to the investment for that period. They are rate of return calculations that measure the success of an investment. Two ROI ratios are widely used: return on total assets and return on common equity.

return on total assets (16) an overall ratio that depicts the average percentage return on all company assets without regard for how the assets were financed.

revenue (2) increases in assets resulting from the profit-seeking activities of a business during an accounting period.

revenue expenditure (10) an expenditure that contains no future benefit beyond the accounting period in which it is incurred. Revenue expenditures become expenses as they are incurred in the current accounting period.

revenue recognition (17) the recording of revenue when it is earned and is objectively measurable. The economic process giving rise to the revenue must be effectively complete and the costs associated with the revenue must have been incurred.

risk rating (12) the amount of risk associated with a particular bond issue as determined by an independent financial service. The rating assigned is related to factors such as the financial strength and profitability of the issuer, the issuer's past history with bonds, and the current amount of debt carried by the issuer.

sales discount (6) a reduction in the selling price of goods because customers pay early.

sales journal (7) special journal used to record the *credit* sales of goods to customers.

sales return (6) a contra-revenue account used to record the selling price of goods returned by customers.

salvage (residual) value (10) an estimate of what a property, plant, and equipment asset is likely to be sold for at the end of its useful life.

schedule of accounts payable (7) a list of individual supplier accounts payable balances which details the total amount owed by the business.

schedule of accounts receivable (7) a list of individual customer accounts receivable balances which details the total amount owed to the business.

schedule of changes in working capital (15) listing of working capital accounts for two consecutive years and their changes to explain the composition of change in working capital for a period. It is included with the statement of changes in financial position prepared on a working capital basis.

Securities and Exchange Commission (SEC) (1) a federal agency created in 1934 to administer all federal securities laws governing the trading of investment securities and defining acceptable practice in the selling of securities to the general public. The SEC is legally empowered to determine the proper accounting treatment of certain events.

service business (6) a business that sells a service, such as a particular talent or knowledge, rather than a tangible, physical product.

significant influence (14) the condition that results from an investor's owning 20 percent or more of the outstanding stock of a corporation. An investor must use the equity method of accounting for an investment if it has significant influence over the investee.

sinking fund (12) an independent fund established by a bond issuer by payments over the life of a bond to a trustee of the fund. The periodic payments plus the earnings on the fund are designed to accumulate to an amount sufficient to retire the bonds at maturity.

sole proprietorship (1) an unincorporated business owned and completely controlled by one individual. Legally, the business and the owner are inseparable.

solvency (16) the ability of a business to meet long-run obligations in a smooth and orderly fashion.

special journal (7) a supplementary journal used to record repetitive transactions in a manner that facilitates classification and internal control.

specific identification (9) a method of assigning a dollar value to ending inventory and cost of goods sold by differentiating products and recording each product's individual cost so that costs of specific products can be recognized as they remain on hand or are sold.

specific price level (17) changes in prices of specific goods and services, which may occur at a faster or slower rate than changes of prices in general.

standard of performance (historical, external, and expected) (16) measures of performance against which the financial ratios of a specific business may be evaluated. The basis for comparison may be a company's past performance (historical), the activities of similar businesses (external), or the expectations of the investment market or a financial analyst (expected).

state income taxes withheld (11) liability to the state government for income taxes withheld from employees' wages.

state unemployment tax (11) a payroll tax on employees' wages that employers are required to remit to a state unemployment fund.

stated value (13) an arbitrary value that may be assigned to shares of stock without a par value by the board of directors.

statement of changes in financial position (working capital or cash basis) (15) a statement that explains the differences between two consecutive balance sheets.

stock dividend (13) a dividend paid in shares of stock of the company declaring the dividend. Each owner receives new shares equal to some fixed fraction of the number of shares held before the dividend. The total claim of each owner remains unchanged, but each ownership interest is represented by more shares of stock.

stock split (13) an increase in the number of stock shares outstanding by some multiple together with a proportional reduction in the par or stated value of each share. The effect of the split is to divide ownership interest into more shares without affecting assets or total ownership interest.

straight-line (*10*) a depreciation or amortization technique that results in an equal amount of an asset's cost being allocated to each year of the asset's life.

straight-line amortization (*12*) the amortization of a bond discount or premium so that an equal amount is written off each year and the borrower incurs a uniform interest expense.

subsequent expenditure (*10*) an expenditure that occurs after a property, plant, and equipment asset is in use and functioning. Subsequent expenditures may be treated as revenue or capital expenditures.

subsidiary ledger (*7*) a ledger that provides a detailed breakdown of summary information appearing in a general ledger account. Subsidiary ledgers are most commonly used for payables and receivables.

sum-of-the-years'-digits (*10*) an accelerated method of depreciation calculated by multiplying the depreciation base of an asset by a decreasing depreciation rate. The depreciation rate is calculated as the years of useful life of the asset remaining at the beginning of each year divided by the sum of years of useful life.

supplies (*5*) current assets, such as cleaning materials, paper, and pens, which are purchased to be used up in the normal course of business operations.

T account (*3*) a simplified form of an account which looks like a large letter **T**. The title of the account is written on the horizontal line. Then, debits are entered on the left of the vertical line and credits are entered on the right.

T account approach (*15*) procedure used to develop the statement of changes in financial position from comparative balance sheets, the income statement, and statement of retained earnings.

temporary accounts (*4*) accounts that are closed out at the end of an accounting period. Non-balance-sheet accounts, such as revenue, expense, dividends, and withdrawals, are temporary accounts.

time value of money (*11*) the concept that a dollar can be invested to earn interest. For this reason, a dollar received *now* is preferable to a dollar received in the future.

times interest earned ratio (*16*) a financial condition ratio used to measure a company's solvency by comparing the annual interest expense to the income for the period available to cover the interest.

timing differences (*8*) differences in the cash balance per the bank statement and the cash balance per the company books caused by outstanding checks and deposits in transit. No journal entries are necessary to correct timing differences.

trading on the equity (financial leverage) (*16*) positive financial leverage that occurs whenever a business is able to earn a higher rate of return on its assets than it pays to its creditors and preferred stockholders. It results in a return on common equity which is higher than the return on total assets.

transaction (*1*) a business event that affects one or more of the components of the basic accounting equation ($A = L + OE$).

transaction analysis (*3*) the process of determining the debit and credit effects of an accounting event.

treasury stock (*13*) shares of stock originally issued by a corporation and then repurchased, but not retired. Treasury stock may be resold at any time by a corporation.

trial balance (*3*) a summary listing of the debit or credit balances of all accounts in the ledger. This listing provides an overview of the accounts and ensures the equality of debits and credits.

uncollectible accounts expense (*8*) the amount of accounts receivable that will not be collected. This may be the actual amount of uncollectible accounts if the direct write-off method is used, or an estimated amount if the allowance method is used.

unconsolidated subsidiary (*14*) a firm in which a parent company owns more than 50 percent of the stock but which is not consolidated because it is in a business unrelated to that of the parent.

underwriter (*12*) a financial middleman who purchases bonds or stock directly from the issuing company in large or medium lots and then sells these securities to investors who wish to purchase smaller quantities.

unissued shares (*13*) shares of corporate stock that are authorized but have never been sold to stockholders. They are measured as the amount of authorized shares minus the amount of issued shares.

units-of-output (*10*) a depreciation or depletion technique in which the depreciation base is divided by the estimated total units of output expected from the asset to determine the depreciation per unit of activity. Annual depreciation expense is calculated as the depreciation per unit of activity multiplied by the actual units of activity for the period.

unrealized gain or loss (*14*) gain or loss on the valuation of securities resulting from the application of the lower of aggregate cost or market rule.

useful life (*10*) the time period of expected benefit to a business from the use of a property, plant, and equipment asset.

voucher system (*7*) a method of controlling cash in which vouchers are used to authorize cash disbursements. Under this system, the voucher register and check register replace the purchases journal, cash disbursements journal, and accounts payable subsidiary ledger.

weighted average (*9*) a method of assigning a dollar value to inventory and cost of goods sold in which each unit of ending inventory and each unit sold carries a cost equal to the average cost of all units of inventory.

withdrawals (*2*) assets disbursed to the owners of a proprietorship or partnership; the equivalent in unincorporated businesses to corporate cash dividends.

withholdings (*11*) amounts retained by an employer from the salaries or wages earned by employees that are to be paid to others on behalf of the employee. As a result of withholdings, the amounts actually received by employees are less than the amounts earned by them. Examples include federal and state income tax withheld, social security withheld, and various insurance plans contracted by the employee.

working capital (*15*) current assets minus current liabilities. Working capital represents the amount of current assets held in excess of those needed to pay current liabilities.

working capital from operations (*15*) the amount of working capital that results from profit-seeking activities.

worksheet (*5*) an informal document prepared by an accountant for his or her own use in developing financial statements.

write-off (*8*) removal of a specific customer account from accounts receivable when the company determines the money will *not* be collected from the customer.

Appendix B:
IBM Financial
Statements for 1980

Report of Management

Report of Independent Accountants

Responsibility for the integrity and objectivity of the financial information presented in this Annual Report rests with IBM management. The accompanying financial statements have been prepared in conformity with generally accepted accounting principles, applying certain estimates and judgments as required.

IBM maintains an effective system of internal accounting control. It consists, in part, of organizational arrangements with clearly defined lines of responsibility and delegation of authority. We believe this system provides reasonable assurance that transactions are executed in accordance with management authorization, and that they are appropriately recorded, in order to permit preparation of financial statements in conformity with generally accepted accounting principles and to adequately safeguard, verify and maintain accountability of assets. An important element of the system is an on-going internal audit program.

To assure the effective administration of internal control, we carefully select and train our employees, develop and disseminate written policies and procedures, provide appropriate communication channels, and foster an environment conducive to the effective functioning of controls. We continue to believe that it is essential for the company to conduct its business affairs in accordance with the highest ethical standards, as set forth in the IBM Business Conduct Guidelines. These guidelines, translated into numerous languages, are distributed to employees throughout the world, and reemphasized through internal programs to assure that they are understood and followed.

Price Waterhouse & Co., independent accountants, are retained to examine IBM's financial statements. Their accompanying report is based on an examination conducted in accordance with generally accepted auditing standards, including a review of internal accounting controls and tests of accounting procedures and records.

The Audit Committee of the Board of Directors is composed solely of outside directors, and is responsible for recommending to the Board the independent accounting firm to be retained for the coming year, subject to stockholder approval. The Audit Committee meets periodically and privately with the independent accountants, with our internal auditors, as well as with IBM management, to review accounting, auditing, internal accounting controls and financial reporting matters.

John R. Opel
John R. Opel
President and Chief Executive Officer

Dean P. Phypers
Dean P. Phypers
Senior Vice President, Finance & Planning

To the Stockholders
and Board of Directors of International
Business Machines Corporation

In our opinion, the accompanying consolidated financial statements, appearing on pages 21 through 31, present fairly the financial position of International Business Machines Corporation and its subsidiary companies at December 31, 1980 and 1979, and the results of their operations and changes in financial position for the years 1980, 1979 and 1978, in conformity with generally accepted accounting principles consistently applied. Also, in our opinion, the Five-Year Comparison of Selected Financial Data for 1976 through 1980 presents fairly the financial information included therein. Our examinations of these statements were made in accordance with generally accepted auditing standards and accordingly included such tests of the accounting records and such other auditing procedures as we considered necessary in the circumstances.

Price Waterhouse & Co.

January 27, 1981
New York, N.Y.

Price Waterhouse & Co.

International Business Machines Corporation
and Subsidiary Companies

Consolidated Statement of Earnings
for the year ended December 31:

	1980		1979		1978
	(Dollars in millions except per share amounts)				
Gross Income:					
Sales..	$ 10,919		$ 9,473		$ 8,755
Rentals..	10,869		10,069		9,781
Services.......................................	4,425		3,321		2,540
		$ 26,213		$ 22,863	$ 21,076
Cost of sales	4,197		3,267		2,838
Cost of rentals	3,771		3,491		3,251
Cost of services...........................	2,181		1,655		1,395
Selling, development and engineering, and general and administrative expenses	10,324		9,205		8,151
Interest expense............................	273		141		55
		20,746		17,759	15,690
		5,467		5,104	5,386
Other income, principally interest		430		449	412
Earnings before income taxes		5,897		5,553	5,798
Provision for U.S. Federal and non-U.S. income taxes		2,335		2,542	2,687
Net Earnings..		$ 3,562		$ 3,011	$ 3,111
Per share...................................		$ 6.10		$ 5.16	$ 5.32

Average number of shares outstanding:
1980–583,516,764
1979–583,373,269
1978–584,428,584

International Business Machines Corporation and Subsidiary Companies

Consolidated Statement of Financial Position at December 31:

	1980		1979	
	(Dollars in millions)			
Assets				
Current Assets:				
Cash	$ 281		$ 298	
Marketable securities, at lower of cost or market	1,831		3,473	
Notes and accounts receivable—trade, less allowance:				
1980, $195; 1979, $188	4,562		4,299	
Other accounts receivable	315		372	
Inventories, at lower of average cost or market	2,293		1,842	
Prepaid expenses	643	$ 9,925	567	$ 10,851
Rental Machines and Parts	15,352		13,742	
Less: Accumulated depreciation	6,969	8,383	6,815	6,927
Plant and Other Property	11,018		9,002	
Less: Accumulated depreciation	4,384	6,634	3,736	5,266
Deferred Charges and Other Assets		1,761		1,486
		$ 26,703		$ 24,530
Liabilities and Stockholders' Equity				
Current Liabilities:				
Taxes	$ 2,369		$ 2,365	
Loans payable	591		933	
Accounts payable	721		682	
Compensation and benefits	1,404		1,217	
Deferred income	305		233	
Other accrued expenses and liabilities	1,136	$ 6,526	1,015	$ 6,445
Deferred Investment Tax Credits		182		140
Reserves for Employees' Indemnities and Retirement Plans		1,443		1,395
Long-Term Debt		2,099		1,589
Stockholders' Equity:				
Capital stock, par value $1.25 per share	3,992		3,974	
Shares authorized, 650,000,000				
Issued: 1980 – 584,262,074; 1979 – 583,973,258				
Retained earnings	12,491		11,012	
	16,483		14,986	
Less: Treasury stock, at cost	30		25	
Shares: 1980 – 455,242; 1979 – 378,715		16,453		14,961
		$ 26,703		$ 24,530

International Business Machines Corporation
and Subsidiary Companies

Consolidated Statement of Changes in Financial
Position for the year ended December 31:

	1980	1979	1978
	(Dollars in millions)		
Source of Working Capital:			
Net earnings	$ 3,562	$ 3,011	$ 3,111
Items not requiring the current use of working capital:			
Depreciation....................	2,362	1,970	1,824
Net book value of rental machines and other property retired or sold	1,009	779	562
Other....................	90	353	287
Total from operations:....................	7,023	6,113	5,784
Proceeds from stock sold or issued under employee plans	422	416	341
Long-term borrowings	604	1,450	74
	8,049	7,979	6,199
Application of Working Capital:			
Investment in rental machines....................	4,334	4,212	2,724
Investment in plant and other property	2,258	1,779	1,322
	6,592	5,991	4,046
Less: Depreciation of manufacturing facilities capitalized in rental machines....................	397	351	247
	6,195	5,640	3,799
Increase in deferred charges and other assets....................	275	338	132
Cash dividends paid or payable....................	2,008	1,506	1,763
Reduction of long-term debt	94	146	45
Treasury stock purchased for employee plan	484	454	373
Capital stock purchased and canceled	—	—	440
	9,056	8,084	6,552
Decrease in Working Capital	$(1,007)	$ (105)	$ (353)
Changes in Working Capital:			
Cash and marketable securities....................	$(1,659)	$ (259)	$(1,376)
Notes and accounts receivable....................	206	537	1,030
Inventories and prepaid expenses....................	527	252	594
Taxes....................	(4)	(261)	(82)
Loans payable	342	(691)	(69)
Accounts payable and accruals	(419)	(185)	(372)
Dividend payable	—	502	(78)
Decrease in working capital	(1,007)	(105)	(353)
Working Capital at beginning of year....................	4,406	4,511	4,864
Working Capital at end of year....................	$ 3,399	$ 4,406	$ 4,511

International Business Machines Corporation
and Subsidiary Companies

Consolidated Statement of Stockholders' Equity
for the year ended December 31:

	Capital Stock	Retained Earnings	Treasury Stock	Total
		(Dollars in millions)		
1978				
Balance, January 1, 1978	$ 3,961	$ 8,678	$ (21)	$ 12,618
Net earnings		3,111		3,111
Cash dividends declared ($502 payable March 10, 1979)		(1,763)		(1,763)
Capital stock issued under employee plans (303,903 shares)	17			17
Purchases (5,571,100 shares) and sales (5,541,948 shares) of treasury stock under employee plan–net		(56)	(3)	(59)
Capital stock purchased and canceled (6,916,800 shares)	(46)	(394)		(440)
Tax reductions applicable to stock related to employee plans..............................	10			10
Balance, December 31, 1978	3,942	9,576	(24)	13,494
1979				
Net earnings		3,011		3,011
Cash dividends declared		(1,506)		(1,506)
Capital stock issued under employee plans (391,300 shares)...............................	24			24
Purchases (6,357,500 shares) and sales (6,319,289 shares) of treasury stock under employee plan–net		(69)	(1)	(70)
Tax reductions applicable to stock related to employee plans.............................	8			8
Balance, December 31, 1979	3,974	11,012	(25)	14,961
1980				
Net earnings		3,562		3,562
Cash dividends declared		(2,008)		(2,008)
Capital stock issued under employee plans (288,816 shares).............................	16			16
Purchases (7,674,300 shares) and sales (7,597,773 shares) of treasury stock under employee plan–net		(75)	(5)	(80)
Tax reductions applicable to stock related to employee plans..............................	2			2
Balance, December 31, 1980.......................	$ 3,992	$ 12,491	$ (30)	$ 16,453

International Business Machines Corporation and Subsidiary Companies

Notes to Consolidated Financial Statements:

Significant Accounting Policies

Principles of Consolidation: The consolidated financial statements include the accounts of International Business Machines Corporation and its U.S. and non-U.S. subsidiary companies. The equity method is used to account for investments in joint ventures and affiliated companies in which IBM has 50% or less ownership.

Translation of Non-U.S. Currency Amounts: Assets and liabilities denominated in currencies other than U.S. dollars, are translated to U.S. dollars at year-end exchange rates, except that inventories and plant, rental machines and other property are translated at approximate rates prevailing when acquired. Income and expense items are translated at average rates of exchange prevailing during the year, except that inventories charged to cost of sales and depreciation are

translated at historical rates. Exchange gains and losses are included in earnings currently.

Gross Income: Gross income is recognized from sales when the product is shipped or in certain cases upon customer acceptance, from rentals in the month in which they accrue, and from services over the contractual period or as the services are performed. Rental plans include maintenance service and contain discontinuance and purchase option provisions. Rental terms are predominantly monthly or for a two-year period, with some covering periods up to five years.

Depreciation: Rental machines, plant and other property are carried at cost and depreciated over their estimated useful lives. Depreciation of rental machines is computed using the sum-of-the-years digits method. Depreciation of plant

and other property is computed using either accelerated methods or the straight-line method.

Retirement Plans: Current service costs are accrued currently. Prior service costs resulting from improvements in the plans are amortized generally over 10 years.

Selling Expenses: Selling expenses are charged against income as they are incurred.

Income Taxes: Income tax expense is based on reported earnings before income taxes. It thus includes the effects of timing differences between reported and taxable earnings that arise because certain transactions are included in taxable earnings in other years. Investment tax credits are deferred and amortized as a reduction of income tax expense over the average useful life of the applicable classes of property.

Non-U.S. Operations

		1980	1979	1978
		(Dollars in millions)		
At end of year:	Net assets employed			
	Current assets	$ 5,547	$ 5,826	$ 5,690
	Current liabilities	3,911	3,608	3,345
	Working capital	1,636	2,218	2,345
	Plant, rental machines and other property, net	6,823	5,477	4,424
	Deferred charges and other assets	971	839	738
		9,430	8,534	7,507
	Reserves for employees' indemnities and retirement plans	1,443	1,395	1,072
	Long-term debt	437	294	206
		1,880	1,689	1,278
	Net assets employed	$ 7,550	$ 6,845	$ 6,229
	Number of employees	146,973	146,800	144,593
For the year:	Gross income from sales, rentals and services	$ 13,787	$ 12,244	$ 11,040
	Earnings before income taxes	$ 2,946	$ 2,731	$ 2,881
	Provision for U.S. Federal and non-U.S. income taxes	1,044†	1,304	1,321
	Net earnings	$ 1,902	$ 1,427	$ 1,560
	Capital expenditures	$ 3,367	$ 2,800	$ 2,162

† See Taxes on page 26.

Undistributed earnings of non-U.S. subsidiaries included in consolidated retained earnings amounted to $6,108 million at December 31, 1980, $5,529 million at December 31, 1979, and $5,002 million at December 31, 1978. These earnings are indefinitely reinvested in non-U.S. operations. Accordingly, no provision has been made for taxes that might be payable upon remittance of such earnings.

Research and Development

Research and development expenses amounted to $1,520 million in 1980, $1,360 million in 1979 and $1,255 million in 1978.

Retirement Plans

The company and its U.S. subsidiaries have trusteed, non-contributory retirement plans, covering substantially all regular and part-time employees, for which accrued costs are funded. At December 31, 1980, there were 12,460 individuals receiving benefits under the plans. Most subsidiaries outside the United States have retirement plans under which funds are deposited with trustees, reserves are provided, or annuities are purchased under group contracts. The cost of all plans for 1980, 1979 and 1978 was $1,109 million, $971 million and $877 million respectively. Unfunded or unaccrued prior service costs under all plans amounted to $821 million at

December 31, 1980, and $788 million at December 31, 1979.

In accordance with Statement of Financial Accounting Standards Nos. 35 and 36, a comparison of estimated benefits and net assets for U.S. retirement plans is provided as follows:

At December 31	1980	1979
	(Dollars in millions)	
Actuarial present value of accumulated benefits:		
Vested	$ 5,166	$ 4,163
Nonvested	168	143
	$ 5,334	$ 4,306
Net assets available for benefits	$ 5,712	$ 4,268

The assumed rate of return used in determining the actuarial present value of accumulated

benefits was 4¾ percent for both 1980 and 1979.

Since no required method of calculation is prescribed for non-U.S. plans, data for such plans is computed in the normal actuarial manner. At December 31, 1980 and at December 31, 1979 the market value of fund assets and reserves of non-U.S. plans exceeded or approximated the actuarially computed value of vested benefits.

Notes and Accounts Receivable–Trade

At December 31, 1980, notes and accounts receivable—trade included $608 million of installment receivables maturing after one year, net of unearned interest. Of this amount, 56% matures in 1982 and the balance in decreasing amounts through 1985. Annual interest rates on installment receivables generally range from 6% to 21%.

Taxes

	1980	1979	1978
	(Dollars in millions)		
Earnings before U.S. Federal and non-U.S. income taxes:			
U.S. operations	$ 2,951	$ 2,822	$ 2,917
Non-U.S. operations	2,946	2,731	2,881
	$ 5,897	$ 5,553	$ 5,798
Provision for U.S. Federal and non-U.S. income taxes:			
U.S. operations	$ 1,291	$ 1,238	$ 1,366
Non-U.S. operations	1,044	1,304	1,321
	2,335	2,542	2,687
Real estate, personal property, state and local franchise (including state income taxes of $138 million in 1980, $127 million in 1979, and $165 million in 1978), social security and other taxes	1,480	1,315	1,185
Total	$ 3,815	$ 3,857	$ 3,872
The components of the provision for U.S. Federal and non-U.S. income taxes are as follows:			
U.S. Federal income taxes:			
Estimated currently payable	$ 776	$ 914	$ 1,121
Net tax effects of timing differences	(34)	86	41
Net deferred investment tax credits.	42	30	22
	784	1,030	1,184
Non-U.S. income taxes:			
Estimated currently payable	1,546	1,575	1,561
Net tax effects of timing differences	5	(63)	(58)
	1,551	1,512	1,503
Total provision.	$ 2,335	$ 2,542	$ 2,687

The consolidated effective U.S. Federal and non-U.S. income tax rate was 39.6% in 1980 compared with a U.S. statutory rate of 46.0%. The lower effective tax rate on earnings of non-U.S. operations accounts for 5.3 percentage points of the difference in the rates. The consolidated tax provision for 1980 includes the effect of a reduction of prior periods income tax liabilities of $224 million (38¢ per share), resulting from changes in tax laws and other adjustments of prior years income tax expenses. Of this amount, $207 million relates to non-U.S. operations.

Marketable Securities

	December 31, 1980	December 31, 1979
	(Dollars in millions)	
U.S. Government securities.	$ 494	$ 1,295
Time deposits and other bank obligations.	1,070	1,668
Corporate bonds, notes and other fixed-term obligations.	267	510
Total	$ 1,831	$ 3,473
Market value	$ 1,831	$ 3,475

Inventories

	December 31, 1980	December 31, 1979
	(Dollars in millions)	
Finished goods...	$ 524	$ 452
Work in process..	1,518	1,158
Raw materials and operating supplies...	251	232
Total	$ 2,293	$ 1,842

Rental Machines and Parts

Rental machines and parts are comprised of capitalized machines, rental machine work in process and field service parts. Rental machines include machines installed with IBM in the amount of $1,886 million and $1,509 million at December 31, 1980 and 1979, respectively, with accumulated depreciation of $1,396 million and $1,180 million. Rental machine work in process and field service parts, carried at the lower of average cost or market, totaled $3,595 million and $3,344 million at December 31, 1980 and 1979.

Plant and Other Property

	December 31, 1980	December 31, 1979
	(Dollars in millions)	
Land and land improvements..	$ 623	$ 569
Buildings	4,351	3,536
Factory, laboratory and office equipment	6,044	4,897
	11,018	9,002
Less: Accumulated depreciation	4,384	3,736
Total	$ 6,634	$ 5,266

Rental Expense and Lease Commitments

Rental expense amounted to $375 million in 1980, $319 million in 1979 and $278 million in 1978. Minimum rental commitments, in millions of dollars, under noncancellable leases for 1981 and thereafter are as follows: 1981, $344; 1982, $263;1983, $199; 1984, $144; 1985, $108; and after 1985, $447. These leases are principally for the rental of office premises. Many of the leases contain renewal options and many provide for the payment of a proportionate share of maintenance, insurance and taxes in addition to the minimum annual rentals. The above amounts exclude minor amounts of sublease income.

Interest Cost

During 1980, interest on borrowings amounted to $325 million. Of this amount, $52 million was capitalized in the cost of buildings under construction, resulting in a net earnings increase of $31 million. Prior to 1980, all interest was charged against income as incurred.

Exchange Gains and Losses

Net earnings in 1980 include exchange gains of $24 million, resulting from fluctuations in the value of the U.S. dollar in relation to other currencies. This consists principally of unrealized gains from the translation of foreign currency assets and liabilities, and compares with exchange losses of $52 million in the year 1979 and gains of $113 million in 1978.

Litigation

In January, 1969, the Department of Justice filed a civil antitrust complaint against IBM under Section 2 of the Sherman Antitrust Act, charging the company with monopolizing commerce in general purpose digital computers in the United States. Trial of the case began in May, 1975, and is currently in progress.

The government continues to seek divestiture relief, requesting that IBM be reorganized into several independent and competing organizations and that IBM be enjoined from continuing its alleged monopolistic practices.

Five private plaintiffs, for themselves and certain subsidiaries, instituted lawsuits against IBM in 1973 and 1974 alleging Federal antitrust law violations. These actions remain in progress. They seek damages, trebled in accordance with the antitrust laws, and in some cases, injunctive relief.

The three trials which have thus far taken place have resulted in the dismissal of the antitrust claims against IBM.

In litigation brought by Memorex Corporation and certain of its subsidiaries, a District Court order directing a verdict in favor of IBM and dismissing the action was affirmed by the United States Court of Appeals for the Ninth Circuit. Certain foreign claims remain pending in the District Court. The decision of the District Court covered a major portion of the claims, which totaled $3,150 million after trebling. Memorex has indicated it will appeal further.

In a lawsuit by Forro Precision, $36 million in damages, after trebling, were sought. After trial, the antitrust charges against IBM were dismissed, and non-antitrust damage verdicts of $2.7 million for Forro and $.3 million for IBM were entered. Both parties are appealing.

Damages sought in an action brought by Transamerica Computer Company total $390 million after trebling. After the jury was unable to reach a verdict, the District Court decided the case in IBM's favor. Transamerica is appealing.

Two other lawsuits, in which the plaintiffs seek damages aggregating $276 million after trebling, remain in the pretrial discovery stage.

In December, 1980, the Commission of the European Communities filed a "statement of objections" seeking modification of certain IBM business practices in the Common Market area. The Commission may also seek to impose fines. Most of the practices to which the Commission has objected have been successfully defended by IBM in the United States.

IBM has denied the charges in all of these proceedings and is vigorously defending each.

Long-Term Debt	December 31, 1980	December 31, 1979
	(Dollars in millions)	
U.S. Operations:		
9½% notes due 1986	$ 500	$ 500
9⅜% debentures due 2004 (with sinking fund		
payments 1985 to 2003)	500	500
10.80% notes due 1983 to 1986	300	300
Other (average interest rate at December 31, 1980,		
in parentheses) payable in:		
German marks, due 1985 to 1988 (10.1%)	254	—
Swiss francs, due 1986 (6.2%)	112	—
	1,666	1,300
Non-U.S. Operations:		
Various obligations (average interest rate		
at December 31, 1980, in parentheses) payable in:		
French francs, due 1982-1991 (10.7%)	178	131
U.S. dollars, due 1982-1992 (15.0%).	150	78
Other currencies, due 1982-2010 (13.0%)	109	85
	437	294
	2,103	1,594
Less: Unamortized discount, related to the		
9½% notes and 9⅜% debentures.	4	5
Total	$ 2,099	$ 1,589

Annual maturity and sinking fund requirements in millions of dollars
on long-term debt outstanding at December 31, 1980, are as follows:
1982, $51; 1983, $122; 1984, $212; 1985, $212; 1986, $931; 1987
and beyond, $575.

Lines of Credit

At December 31, 1980, the company had
unused lines of credit available with a number of
U.S. banks. These lines of credit permit the company to borrow, from time to time, up to an aggregate of $2,000 million outstanding at any time,
at interest rates not to exceed the banks' prime rate.
In addition, a number of non-U.S. subsidiaries had
available unused lines of credit of approximately
$875 million. Interest rates on borrowings would
vary from country to country depending on local
market conditions. About $100 million of such
unused lines require the payment of commitment
fees, which generally range from ¼% to ½%.

Stock Purchase Plan

The 1976 Employees Stock Purchase Plan
enables employees who are not participants in a
stock option plan to purchase IBM's capital stock
through payroll deductions of up to 10% of their
compensation. The price an employee pays for
a share of stock is 85% of the average market price
on the date the employee has accumulated
enough money to buy a share. During 1980,
7,597,773 treasury shares were sold to employees
for $404 million. At December 31, 1980,
7,442,342 reserved unissued shares remain available for purchase under the Plan. Beginning
in 1981, the company will discontinue its current
practice of purchasing shares for the Plan in
the market. Authorized but unissued shares will
be used for the Plan.

Stock Option Plans

The stock option plans provide for granting
officers and other key employees options
to purchase IBM's capital stock at 100% of the
market price on the day of grant. Options have a
maximum duration of 10 years and may be
exercised in four annual installments, commenc-
ing one year from date of grant.

The following table summarizes stock option
transactions during 1980:

	Number of Shares	
	Under Option	Available for Option
Balance at		
January 1, 1980	11,835,115	3,728,775
Options granted	1,465,844	(1,465,844)
Options terminated	(165,013)	64,164
Options exercised	(193,463)	—
Balance at		
December 31, 1980	12,942,483	2,327,095
Exercisable at		
December 31, 1980	8,951,546	

IBM received $10.8 million for the 193,463 shares
purchased during 1980. The 12,942,483 shares
under option at December 31, 1980, are at option
prices ranging from $41.60 to $85.40 per share.

Geographic Area and
Industry Segment Information

For purposes of segment reporting, financial information by geographic area and industry segment for the years 1980, 1979, and 1978 is summarized below.

It should be recognized in connection with the geographic area and industry segment information, that there exist material interdependencies and overlaps among IBM's operating units. The reported information follows IBM's administrative profit centers, and does not take into account significant intercenter dependencies and overlaps with respect to engineering, manufacturing, components, technologies and know-how, business expertise, products and customers, to the extent such activities are not reasonably quantifiable or measurable. In addition, the allocations made of indirect and common costs, and jointly used assets, involved the extensive use of estimation techniques. Accordingly, the information is provided for purposes of achieving an understanding of IBM's operations, but may not be indicative of the financial results of, or investments in, the reported areas and segments were they independent organizations, nor useful for comparisons with operations of other companies.

Geographic Areas

	1980	1979	1978
	(Dollars in millions)		
United States			
Gross income—Customers	$ 12,426	$ 10,619	$ 10,036
Interarea transfers	1,615	1,101	830
Total	$ 14,041	$ 11,720	$ 10,866
Net earnings	1,725	1,612	1,560
Assets at December 31	13,737	12,631	10,097
Europe/Middle East/Africa			
Gross income—Customers	$ 9,932	$ 8,837	$ 7,778
Interarea transfers	491	531	392
Total	$ 10,423	$ 9,368	$ 8,170
Net earnings	1,511	1,082	1,124
Assets at December 31	9,573	8,987	7,876
Americas/Far East			
Gross income—Customers	$ 3,855	$ 3,407	$ 3,262
Interarea transfers	450	410	304
Total	$ 4,305	$ 3,817	$ 3,566
Net earnings	398	355	460
Assets at December 31	3,975	3,358	3,145
Eliminations			
Gross income	$ (2,556)	$ (2,042)	$ (1,526)
Net earnings	(72)	(38)	(33)
Assets	(582)	(446)	(347)
Consolidated			
Gross income	$ 26,213	$ 22,863	$ 21,076
Net earnings	$ 3,562	$ 3,011	$ 3,111
Assets at December 31	$ 26,703	$ 24,530	$ 20,771

In the Europe/Middle East/Africa area, European operations accounted for approximately 95% of gross income in 1980, 1979, and 1978.

Net earnings in 1980 include the effect of a reduction of prior periods tax liabilities of $17 million in the United States, $187 million in Europe/Middle East/Africa, and $20 million in Americas/Far East.

Interarea transfers, consisting principally of completed machines, sub-assemblies and parts, are priced at cost plus an appropriate service charge, applied consistently throughout the world. The cost and service charges that relate to asset transfers are capitalized and depreciated or amortized by the importing area. Interarea accounts receivable, the unamortized portion of service charges, and the net change during the year in unamortized service charges, have been eliminated in consolidation.

Industry Segments	1980	1979	1978
	(Dollars in millions)		
Information-Handling Business:			
Data Processing			
Gross income — Customers	$ 21,367	$ 18,338	$ 17,074
Operating income	5,330	4,737	5,113
Assets at December 31	21,088	17,373	13,598
Depreciation expense	2,061	1,683	1,552
Capital expenditures	6,027	5,359	3,438
Office Products	4,135	3,849	3,390
Gross income — Customers	479	566	381
Operating income	3,377	3,316	3,061
Assets at December 31	287	275	260
Depreciation expense	537	608	591
Capital expenditures			
Federal Systems	647	612	549
Gross income — Customers	37	35	32
Operating income	371	329	316
Assets at December 31	13	11	11
Depreciation expense	27	23	16
Capital expenditures			
Other Business	64	64	63
Gross income — Customers	3	6	4
Operating income	36	39	39
Assets at December 31	1	1	1
Depreciation expense	1	1	1
Capital expenditures			
Consolidated	$ 26,213	$ 22,863	$ 21,076
Gross income — Customers	$ 5,849	$ 5,344	$ 5,530
Operating income	(382)	(240)	(144)
General corporate and interest expense	430	449	412
Other income, principally interest	$ 5,897	$ 5,553	$ 5,798
Earnings before income taxes	$ 24,872	$ 21,057	$ 17,014
Assets identified to segments	1,831	3,473	3,757
Marketable securities	$ 26,703	$ 24,530	$ 20,771
Total assets at December 31	$ 2,362	$ 1,970	$ 1,824
Depreciation expense	$ 6,592	$ 5,991	$ 4,046
Capital expenditures			

IBM's operations, with very minor exceptions, are in the field of information-handling systems, equipment and services. However, for purposes of segment reporting, IBM's information-handling business has been reported as three segments:

Data Processing — consists of information-handling products and services such as data processing machines and systems, computer programming, systems engineering, education and related services and supplies for commercial and government customers.

Office Products — consists of information-handling products, systems and services such as electric and electronic typewriters, magnetic media typewriters and systems, information processors, document printers, copiers, and related supplies and services for commercial and government customers.

Federal Systems — consists of specialized information-handling products and services for United States space, defense and other agencies and, in some instances, other customers.

Other Business consists of educational, training and testing materials and services for school, home and industrial use.

Intersegment transfers of products and services similar to those offered to unaffiliated customers are not material.

Gross Income by Segment††

	1980	1979	1978
	(Dollars in millions)		
Data Processing segment:			
Equipment			
Sales	$ 7,622	$ 6,332	$ 5,944
Rentals	9,557	8,816	8,568
	17,179	15,148	14,512
Maintenance contracts, program products, parts and supplies			
Sales	416	388	422
Rentals	59	54	51
Services	3,713	2,748	2,089
	4,188	3,190	2,562
	21,367	18,338	17,074
Office Products segment			
Sales	2,183	2,084	1,784
Rentals	1,253	1,199	1,162
Services	699	566	444
	4,135	3,849	3,390
All other segments			
Sales	698	669	605
Services	13	7	7
	711	676	612
Total	$ 26,213	$ 22,863	$ 21,076

†† This information should be read in conjunction with the Industry Segments notes on pages 29 and 30. Gross income from rentals includes maintenance service on rented equipment. Gross income from services consists of maintenance service on sold equipment, program products and other services.

Five-Year Comparison of Selected Financial Data

		1980	1979	1978	1977	1976
		(Dollars in millions except per share amounts)				
For the year:	Gross income from sales, rentals and services	$ 26,213	$ 22,863	$ 21,076	$ 18,133	$ 16,304
	Net earnings	3,562	3,011	3,111	2,719	2,398
	Per share†	6.10	5.16	5.32	4.58	3.99
	Cash dividends paid	2,008	2,008	1,685	1,488	1,204
	Per share†	3.44	3.44	2.88	2.50	2.00
	Investment in plant, rental machines and other property	6,592	5,991	4,046	3,395	2,518
At end of year:	Total assets	$ 26,703	$ 24,530	$ 20,771	$ 18,978	$ 17,723
	Net investment in plant, rental machines and other property	15,017	12,193	9,302	7,889	6,963
	Working capital	3,399	4,406	4,511	4,864	5,838
	Long-term debt	2,099	1,589	285	256	275
	Stockholders' equity	16,453	14,961	13,494	12,618	12,749

† Adjusted for 1979 stock split.

Management's Discussion of Financial Condition
and Results of Operations

Financial Condition

IBM's financial statements present a consolidation of the many business units and subsidiaries that comprise IBM's operations. Although the financial statements are expressed in U.S. dollars, IBM's business activities are conducted throughout the world in many currencies and in differing economic and social environments. The presentation of the financial results is intended to assist the reader in assessing the company's recent performance, as well as to provide some insight into IBM's future prospects.

During the past two years, the company's operations were characterized by heavy demand for its products and services, and by significant investment in plants, equipment and personnel to meet that demand. These trends are expected to continue for the foreseeable future. Management believes that new and improved technology will continue to lead the way toward expanded growth and opportunity in the information processing industry. In inflationary times, customer interest in improving productivity creates added demand.

The company intends to compete in this expanding market across the entire spectrum of information products and services. IBM's objective is to expand the business commensurate with appropriate returns to our stockholders. To achieve this objective in our highly competitive industry, the company will continue to invest heavily in research and development in order to provide new and improved products for the marketplace; to continue as a leader in quality, reliability and service to the customer; and to utilize the technology, productive capacity and techniques that assure low-cost production.

For the past decade, funds for IBM's expansion have been generated principally from the profits from operations. More recently, substantial investments in lease inventory and in plant and equipment to expand the business have made it necessary to seek other sources of capital. Despite recent borrowings, the company has a relatively low debt-to-equity ratio and continues to retain an excellent credit rating.

The rate of growth of customer purchase, as opposed to rental of IBM products, has fluctuated widely. This volatility affects the availability of internal funds required for operational needs, as well as for investment in rental machines. Given the company's practice of offering both lease and purchase plans for virtually all products, cash requirements to fund rental machines are likely to remain substantial.

It can be expected that the investments required to enable the business to grow, particularly if aggravated with double-digit inflation and the current high cost of borrowing, will continue to bring pressure on profit margins. Technological advances, continuing emphasis on productivity improvements and cost control, and selective price adjustments can be expected to mitigate some of the effects of inflation. However, the company intends to continue to seek adequate financial returns commensurate with the risk and with the need to fund the growth of the business.

There is always inherent risk in major expansion of physical elements of the business, and it should be recognized that economic, social and competitive conditions may change, thus affecting the growth plans of the company. International operations often pose added competitive risks in terms of economic protectionism and nationally supported industries. In addition, high inflation will bring continuing pressure on all costs and expenses. However, management has carefully evaluated these risks and has concluded that the present business strategy is the proper one for the company, its stockholders and employees.

Indicative of the company's physical growth, IBM's 1980 capital expenditures amounted to $6,592 million, following expenditures of $5,991 million in 1979. Gross fixed assets were $26,370 million at year-end 1980, an increase of $3,626 million, or 15.9%, over 1979. Plant, machinery and equipment and other property increased by $2,016 million, following an increase in 1979 of $1,567 million over 1978. During 1980, 4 million square feet of new space was added to IBM's worldwide manufacturing and development facilities, with a total of more than 8 million square feet under construction at the end of the year.

Rental machines and parts at year-end 1980 were $15,352 million, an increase of $1,610 million over 1979, after increasing by $2,002 million in 1979 over 1978. This growth represents a 31% increase over the two-year period. The investments result from the heavy demand for IBM's products.

These heavy investments were a major factor contributing to decreases in working capital of $1,007 million in 1980, $105 million in 1979, and $353 million in 1978. Although working capital provided from operations during this period has been substantial, the company entered into long-term borrowings of $2,054 million during the past two years. The company also engaged in some short-term borrowing, principally for operating needs. At the end of 1980, $2,875 million of unused lines of credit were also available. The company's requirement for significant capital investment is expected to continue for the next several years.

The company's funding strategy is based upon a conservative capital structure. Relatively low debt ratios and a strong balance sheet position enable management to consider a full range of financing options, both in the U.S. and abroad, for future capital needs. The choices will ultimately depend upon prevailing money market and economic conditions.

Results of Operations

A number of major factors contributed to 1980 gross income and earnings results. Among the positive factors were a resurgence of purchases of data processing equipment, continued heavy shipments of rental machines, price adjustments that were implemented in late 1979 and during 1980, the rapid growth of customer services, lower tax obligations and to some extent, the effects of currency fluctuations. The company also continues to direct and monitor a program of strict cost and expense controls.

In the data processing segment, purchases of equipment were $7,622 million, an increase over 1979 of $1,290 million, or 20.4%. Gross income from rentals and services grew 14.7% to $13,329 million, compared to the 8.5% growth in 1979 over 1978. Within this total, gross income from equipment rentals increased by 8.4% in 1980, compared to a 2.9% increase in 1979. Services gross income from maintenance, program products and other services continued to show the highest growth rates, exceeding the prior year by 35.1%, although at somewhat lower profit margins than for equipment. The concurrent gross income growth in all three areas of the data processing segment attests to the sustained demand for IBM's products and services.

However, there were substantial related cost pressures prevalent worldwide, principally higher product costs associated with initial shipments of new products, changes in the mix of products shipped, the buildup of manufacturing capacity, and the effects of inflation on all costs and expenses.

Also affecting consolidated results were the reduced earnings of the office products segment, which was affected by the tight economy pervading much of the world in 1980. Although gross income grew by $286 million, an increase of 7.4% over 1979, it was not sufficient to offset the increased costs and expenses. The mix of products shipped, expenses associated with new products, and the effects of inflation were contributing factors.

Overall, consolidated net earnings before income taxes increased 6.2% over 1979, as compared to a decrease of 4.2% in 1979 from 1978.

A major factor contributing to 1980 net earnings was a reduction in income tax provisions. U.S. Federal and non-U.S. income taxes were 39.6% of earnings before such taxes in 1980, compared to 45.8% in 1979 and 46.3% in 1978. The 1980 rate reduction was primarily in non-U.S. operations and resulted principally from adjustments of certain prior-period tax liabilities, including the effect of U.S. legislation that affected the tax treatment of pension costs relating to certain non-U.S. operations.

Net earnings in 1980 increased by 18.3% over 1979, following a decline in earnings of 3.2% in 1979 as compared to 1978.

Management believes that the growth prospects for IBM's business will remain strong. In spite of the tight economy, incoming orders and shipments exceeded the high levels established in 1979, increasing the year-end backlog over that of last year. With sustained demand, large backlogs of unfilled orders and the expansion of production capacity, it is expected that heavy shipments of products, as well as substantial services activity, will continue. However, the purchase portion of the shipments, which more immediately affects income and cash receipts than do rental shipments, cannot be accurately predicted. Technology will continue to act as a force driving down the costs of production and therefore the costs of computing. However, high inflation is likely to persist, impacting all costs and expenses and exerting continued pressures on profitability. Volume and technology-driven investments in productive capacity and in rental machines are likely to continue to generate external funding requirements that result in greater interest expense.

Inflation and Changing Prices

In view of the high inflation rates in recent years, traditional financial reports based upon historical costs are being supplemented by new and untested measures for reflecting economic reality. The company, as measured in inflated dollars, has trebled its gross and net income over the past decade. Real growth, although difficult to measure with any precision, was substantially lower. IBM's results for 1979 and 1980 have been restated using the Current Cost and Constant Dollar methods prescribed by the Financial Accounting Standards Board. Although still experimental, and providing only approximations, the methods used are an attempt to deal with the effects of inflation on earnings. The restated information is provided on pages 34 to 36 of this report.

Capital Expenditures

During 1980, IBM's growing business, together with the company's need to replace obsolete equipment, required a worldwide investment of $6,592 million, including $4,334 million for rental machines.

Retirements, covering obsolete and dismantled equipment, as well as rental machines sold that previously were under lease to customers, amounted to $2,966 million in 1980, including $2,724 million of rental machines. These retirements were charged against amounts provided out of prior and current years' earnings, or against cost of sales.

The major IBM facilities that were completed or under construction throughout the world during the year are listed below.

United States	Purpose	Sq. Ft. (in thousands)
* Tucson, Arizona	Mfg. & Dev.	1,695
Charlotte, North Carolina	Mfg. & Dev.	1,464
† Austin, Texas	Mfg. & Dev.	1,296
New York, New York	Mktg.	1,031
† San Jose, California	Mfg. & Dev.	1,010
† Raleigh, North Carolina	Mfg. & Dev.	984
† Burlington, Vermont	Mfg. & Dev.	761
† Rochester, Minnesota	Mfg. & Dev.	699
† Manassas, Virginia	Mfg. & Dev.	672
Houston, Texas	Mktg.	408
† Boca Raton, Florida	Mfg. & Dev.	348
† Endicott, New York	Mfg.	340
St. Louis, Missouri	Mktg.	308
*† East Fishkill, New York	Dev.	190
*† Yorktown, New York	Adm. & Dev.	175
*† Lexington, Kentucky	Dev.	154

Non-U.S. Countries		
Toronto, Canada	Adm. & Mktg.	678
† Boeblingen, West Germany	Mfg.	447
Kawasaki, Japan	Mktg.	440
Milan, Italy	Distr. Center	424
† Portsmouth, England	Adm.	365
Buenos Aires, Argentina	Mktg.	347
† Vimercate, Italy	Mfg.	342
London, England	Mktg.	300
Santa Palomba, Italy	Mfg.	290
† Toronto, Canada	Mfg.	277
Stuttgart, West Germany	Adm. & Mktg.	276
† Greenock, Scotland	Mfg.	266
† Mainz, West Germany	Mfg.	232
Herrenberg, West Germany	Mktg.	225
† Jarfalla, Sweden	Mfg.	219
† Essonnes, France	Mfg.	167
† Hannover, West Germany	Mfg.	153
† Yasu, Japan	Mfg.	150

* Completed in 1980.
† Additions to existing facilities.

Information on Effects of Changing Prices

Statement of Financial Accounting Standards No. 33, Financial Reporting and Changing Prices, prescribes procedures to adjust certain financial information for the estimated effects of inflation, for both the Current Cost method and the Constant Dollar method. The information is provided as an additional measurement of financial activity, inasmuch as it is generally recognized that financial statements prepared under the traditional historical cost basis do not adequately reflect the impact of inflation. It should be recognized that these measurements represent only approximations, and that the techniques and measurement bases may undergo changes over time.

Current Cost

The Current Cost method is intended to indicate the estimated effects of inflation on earnings, as measured by substituting the estimated current cost of acquiring certain assets in place of the actual acquisition costs. Current costs were based on external price indices, latest production costs, current price quotations, or land appraisal values. The results of these adjustments are reflected in the restatements of assets and earnings.

The restated items are inventories, plant and other property, rental machines, cost of sales, rentals and services and depreciation expense. Gross income, and expenses other than depreciation, are not adjusted as they are presumed to have occurred proportionately over the year. For purposes of comparability to 1980 current cost information, 1979 current cost data is converted to 1980 dollars of purchasing power, as measured by movement of the Consumer Price Index for all Urban Consumers (CPI-U).

Because purchasing power declines during periods of inflation, a gain or loss results from holding monetary assets and liabilities. These include cash and claims to cash, and amounts owed, which are fixed in terms of number of dollars to be received or paid.

The Current Cost method gives recognition to technological advances, productivity gains, and improved manufacturing processes. Because most of IBM's assets are high-technology items subject to such improvements, the company believes the Current Cost method is more reflective of the impact of inflation on IBM than the Constant Dollar method. However, neither method is intended to precisely measure the effects of inflation.

Comparison of Selected Financial Data Adjusted for Changes in Specific Prices (Current Cost)

	As Reported in Financial Statements	Restated in 1980 Dollars	
	1980	1980	1979
	(Dollars in millions except per share amounts)		
Gross income from sales, rentals and services	$ 26,213	$ 26,213	$ 25,955
Cost of sales, rentals and services	10,149	10,373	9,710
Expenses and other income	10,167	10,308	10,209
Provision for U.S. Federal and non-U.S. income taxes	2,335	2,335	2,886
Net earnings	$ 3,562	$ 3,197	$ 3,150
Earnings per share	$ 6.10	$ 5.48	$ 5.40
Stockholders' equity (net assets)	$ 16,453	$ 18,295	$ 18,870
Loss from decline in purchasing power of net monetary assets		$ 273	$ 517
Increase in general price level of inventories and plant, rental machines and other property		$ 2,129	$ 2,086
Increase in specific prices		457	761
Excess of increase in general price level over increase in specific prices		$ 1,672	$ 1,325

The company's 1980 financial results, when adjusted for changing prices under the prescribed procedures, reflect a decline of $365 million from reported earnings. This erosion is attributable to the upward restatement of asset values, arising from estimated increases in expenditures to acquire such assets at present prices. The portion of depreciation expense charged to earnings which is related to this revaluation of assets is reflected in earnings in its entirety, because the increased depreciation is not deductible for income taxes.

The net book value of plant, other property and rental machines of $15,017 million, as reported in the Statement of Financial Position, when restated at current cost, increases to $16,873 million. However, the net book value of rental machines and parts of $8,383 million, included therein, when restated at current cost decreases to $7,929 million, principally as a result of technological advances and productivity improvements.

The restatement of assets resulted in increasing depreciation expense charged to earnings by $277 million, bringing the total to $2,639 million. Inventories decreased from $2,293 million to a current cost of $2,240 million.

The 1979 reported earnings of $3,011 million, when adjusted for changing prices in 1979 purchasing power dollars, declined to $2,775 million, a decrease of $236 million. These restated earnings, when converted to 1980 purchasing power dollars, increased to $3,150 million. Thus, the increase in 1980 reported earnings of $551 million over 1979 becomes an increase of only $47 million when current cost earnings for both years are expressed in dollars of equivalent purchasing power.

The losses from declines in purchasing power reflect the company's net monetary asset position. The reduction in 1980 losses when compared to 1979, reflects increased debt and the conversion of monetary assets into production capacity and rental machines.

IBM and other high technology companies achieve substantial benefits from technology and technology-related activities in countering some of the effects of inflation. Nevertheless, inflation continues to erode industries' ability to fund the expansion and replacement of their

existing productive capacity. The inflation adjusted information serves to emphasize the need to reconsider national tax policies to further recognize the debilitating effects of inflation.

Constant Dollar

The Constant Dollar method is intended to indicate the estimated effects of inflation on company earnings as measured by changes in the purchasing power of the dollar, utilizing the movement of the U.S. Consumer Price Index for all Urban Consumers (CPI-U) as the sole indicator of changing prices on all assets to be adjusted.

The restated items are inventory, plant and other property, rental machines, cost of sales, rentals and services, and depreciation expense. The reported amounts for these items have been converted into the equivalent purchasing power of average 1980 dollars, by applying to the original cost of the applicable assets, the increase in the CPI-U for the elapsed period from acquisition to 1980. The adjusted assets and the related adjustments of depreciation expense are substituted for

the actual acquisition costs and depreciation expense. Gross income, and expenses other than depreciation, are not adjusted as they are presumed to have occurred proportionately over the year. For purposes of comparability to 1980 constant dollar information, 1979 data is converted to 1980 dollars of purchasing power, as measured by movement of the CPI-U.

Comparison of Selected Financial Data Adjusted for General Inflation (Constant Dollar)	As Reported in Financial Statements 1980	Restated in 1980 Dollars 1980	Restated in 1980 Dollars 1979
	(Dollars in millions except per share amounts)		
Gross income from sales, rentals and services	$ 26,213	$ 26,213	$ 25,955
Cost of sales, rentals and services....................................	10,149	11,064	10,311
Expenses and other income...	10,167	10,335	10,207
Provision for U.S. Federal and non-U.S. income taxes	2,335	2,335	2,886
Net earnings...	$ 3,562	$ 2,479	$ 2,551
Earnings per share	$ 6.10	$ 4.25	$ 4.37
Stockholders' equity (net assets)	$ 16,453	$ 19,176	$ 18,872

Restated net earnings under the Constant Dollar method inappropriately imply that costs, although heavily impacted by inflation, have not benefited from countervailing effects of productivity gains, technological advances and improved manufacturing processes. Furthermore, the prescribed price

index, the U.S. CPI-U, which is used for both U.S. and non-U.S. operations, may not be indicative of the rate of inflation the company has experienced in either the U.S. or its non-U.S. subsidiaries.

The loss from decline in purchasing power is the same under both methods. Therefore, the

information and comments provided in the Current Cost section are applicable.

The restatement of assets resulted in an increase in depreciation expense charged to earnings, from the reported amount of $2,362 million, to $3,041 million.

Five-Year Comparison of Selected Financial Data Adjusted for General Inflation (Constant Dollar)

The amounts shown below have been converted into the equivalent purchasing power of 1980 dollars by applying to the amounts reported for the years 1976 to 1979, the rate of changes in the average CPI-U from that year to year 1980.

	1980	1979	1978	1977	1976
			(Dollars in millions except per share amounts)		
Gross income from sales, rentals and services................................	$ 26,213	$ 25,955	$ 26,620	$ 24,657	$ 23,600
Cash dividends paid per share†	$ 3.44	$ 3.91	$ 3.64	$ 3.40	$ 2.90
Market price per share† (at December 31) ...	$ 67.88	$ 73.09	$ 94.26	$ 92.98	$ 101.01
Average Consumer Price Index for all Urban Consumers (1967 = 100.0)	246.8	217.4	195.4	181.5	170.5

The actual market price of IBM stock on the New York Stock Exchange composite tape at December 31, for years 1976 to 1980 (adjusted for stock split) was $69.78, $68.38, $74.63, $64.38 and $67.88 respectively.

† Adjusted for 1979 stock split.

Selected Quarterly Data

1980	Gross Income	Gross Profit	Net Earnings	Per Share Earnings	Per Share Dividends	Stock Prices High	Stock Prices Low
				(Dollars in millions except per share and stock prices)			
First Quarter.........	$ 5,748	$ 3,611	$ 681	$ 1.17	$ .86	$ 72.00	$ 51.38
Second Quarter.......	6,181	3,813	764	1.31	.86	60.38	50.38
Third Quarter........	6,479	3,981	884†	1.51†	.86	69.13	58.38
Fourth Quarter.......	7,805	4,659	1,233†	2.11†	.86	72.75	63.25
Total.............	$ 26,213	$ 16,064	$ 3,562	$ 6.10	$ 3.44		

† Includes the effect, $70 million (12¢ per share), and $154 million (26¢ per share) in the third and fourth quarters respectively, of reductions in income tax expense applicable to prior years.

1979	Gross Income	Gross Profit	Net Earnings	Per Share Earnings	Per Share Dividends	Stock Prices High	Stock Prices Low
First Quarter.........	$ 5,295	$ 3,434	$ 667	$ 1.14	$ .86	$ 80.19	$ 73.63
Second Quarter.......	5,355	3,374	667	1.15	.86	80.50	72.13
Third Quarter........	5,384	3,396	669	1.14	.86	76.75	65.75
Fourth Quarter.......	6,829	4,246	1,008	1.73	.86	69.50	61.13
Total.............	$ 22,863	$ 14,450	$ 3,011	$ 5.16	$ 3.44		

There were 737,230 stockholders of record at December 31, 1980. During 1980, stockholders received $2,008 million in cash dividends. The regular quarterly cash dividend payable March 10, 1981, will be at the rate of $.86 per share. This dividend will be IBM's 264th consecutive quarterly cash dividend.

The stock prices reflect the high and low prices for IBM's capital stock on the New York Stock Exchange composite tape for the last two years, adjusted for the 1979 stock split.

Index

†